Archaeologies of the Roman Mediterranean

B—S—R

BRITISH SCHOOL
AT ROME
ARCHAEOLOGY

Archaeologies of the Roman Mediterranean

Papers Presented in Honour of Professor Simon Keay

Edited by
Kristian Strutt, Anna Collar, Paul S. Johnson
and Katherine Crawford

ARCHAEOPRESS ARCHAEOLOGY

ARCHAEOPRESS PUBLISHING LTD
13-14 Market Square
Bicester
Oxfordshire OX26 6AD
United Kingdom
www.archaeopress.com

ISBN 978-1-80583-178-5
ISBN 978-1-80583-179-2 (e-Pdf)

© the individual authors and Archaeopress 2026

Front Cover: Depiction of the Severan Magazines in charcoal, ink, wax crayon and watercolour (Artwork: Rose Ferraby)

Back Cover: Portus Archaeological Park in charcoal, ink, wax crayon and watercolour (Artwork: Rose Ferraby)

Part One: Stairs in the Portus Archaeological Park in charcoal, ink, wax crayon and watercolour (Artwork: Rose Ferraby)

Part Two: Representation of Portus and the Trajanic Harbour in charcoal, ink, wax crayon and watercolour (Artwork: Rose Ferraby)

Part Three: Columns in the Portico of Claudius in charcoal, ink, wax crayon and watercolour (Artwork: Rose Ferraby)

This volume has been produced with the aid of funding from the University of Southampton and the British School at Rome

This book is available direct from Archaeopress or from our website www.archaeopress.com

Professor Simon Keay FBA (1954-2021)

(Photo © Sophie Hay)

B—S—R
BRITISH SCHOOL
AT ROME
ARCHAEOLOGY

Archaeological Monographs of the British School at Rome Series builds on the prestigious and long-standing Monographs series of the British School at Rome. It showcases archaeological research from across Italy in the form of excavation monographs, thematic essay collections, and conference proceedings.

Series Editor: Stephen Kay

Chair of Archaeology: Ian Haynes

Director of the British School at Rome: Abigail Brundin

Contents

Part 1: Mediterranean Port and River Systems

Part 2: Mediterranean Trade and Connectivity

Part 3: Roman Landscapes and Urban Centres

Introduction by the Editors

This volume was initially conceived by colleagues of Simon shortly after his retirement in 2021, following a long career in the Department of Archaeology at the University of Southampton. In that initial guise, it was intended to create a Festschrift that would reflect the influence that Simon and his work had upon the archaeological community, and provide a space for those of us who knew him and his work to acknowledge and pay tribute to that influence. Sadly, Simon passed away before work on the volume had even really begun. We are now bringing the same intention to bear not as something that Simon himself can appreciate, but in his memory instead.

The editors of this volume all have their own memories of Simon, whether as a colleague, a mentor, a supervisor, a teacher, or a line manager (or even all of the above). It is therefore a privilege to have been asked to be involved in the production of this volume, and to be given the opportunity to write this introduction. While Simon's untimely passing has left a huge gap in our scholarly community, in the lives of his friends (many of whom have contributed to this volume), and his family, the process of reading and collating the papers contained herein has also brought back numerous fond (and in some cases amusing) memories of the years where Simon was an energetic and vibrant presence within our lives.

Simon's Career

As other contributions within this volume will make clear, Simon's career in some ways is a classic three-act play. His early career was spent working in Spain, followed by fieldwork in Italy with Martin Millett where his long and close connection with the British School at Rome underpinned his work in the Tiber Valley and at Portus, which in turn formed the centrepiece of the latter stages of his career, as the whole of the Mediterranean was drawn within the orbit of his research through the Portuslimen project.

The volume fittingly opens with a contribution from Martin Millett who, as one of Simon's oldest friends and colleagues in archaeology, was present at so many pivotal moments over the last 50 years. The long connection with, and important contribution to, the British School at Rome is then discussed from the perspective of its former Director Andrew Wallace-Hadrill, whose tenure at the BSR began at the same time as Simon and Martin were beginning to realise their plans for research on the Roman towns of the middle and lower Tiber Valley.

The Volume

The contributions in this volume have been made by Simon's friends, colleagues, and former students. Contributions therefore range from those written by people close to Simon from the early years of his work in Spain, through to more recent students pushing the boundaries of archaeological research with new techniques and approaches. The structure of the volume is defined by three broad interrelated themes, interspersed with more-personal reflections on Simon's life and work. These core themes encapsulate the enduring questions within the work Simon carried out in the Mediterranean, from discussions of port and river systems, to trade and connectivity more generally, and touch on the enduring concern for the relationships between landscapes and urban centres.

The volume opens with a section on Mediterranean port and river systems. Contributions by Alessandra Bousquet, Roberta Cascino, Fabrizio Felici, Barbara Lepri, and Sabrina Zampini; Carlo Pavolini; Javier Bermejo Meléndez, Juan Campos Carrasco, and Renato Sebastini, and Cristian D'Ammassa and Gian Luca Gregori focus on the imperial harbours at Portus, while Emilia Mataix Ferrandiz, Peter Campbell, Christer Bruun, and Letizia Ceccarelli broaden the focus to issues surrounding the port system at the mouth of the Tiber, the roles of individual functionaries within that system, and the movement of goods upriver beyond the ports themselves. This first section is rounded off by papers from Nicolas Carayon and Corrine Sanchez and Ada Lasheras González, who deal with the ports of Narbonne and Tarragona respectively.

The second section of the volume broadens the focus to trade and connectivity in the Mediterranean, with the first contribution by Alessia Contino addressing the presence of African amphorae at Ostia and Rome. Pascal Arnaud then writes about liquid foodstuffs and their relationship to social organisation. César Carreras and Joan Mayoral explore the relationship between Catalonia and North Africa through rescue excavations. The contribution from Michele Bonifay presents a reappraisal of the amphora typology developed by Simon during his doctoral research in Catalonia, offering a gentle critique, and an important update on the origins and contents of the material to which

Simon gave his name. We then have two papers which continue the theme of amphora studies, by Tom Brughmans, Jordi Pérez González, and Juan Remesal Rodríguez, and Juan Moros Diaz through studies of epigraphic marks and stamps respectively. Papers by Naseem Raad, Francesc Rodríguez Martorell, and Dario Bernal-Casasola, Miguel Ángel Cau Ontiveros, José Luis Portillo Sotelo, José Alberto Retamosa Gámez, Leandro Fantuzzi, Sebastià Munar i Llabrés, Carlos de Juan, Jaume Cardell Perelló, Alessandra Pecci, Alejandro Valenzuela, Enrique García Riaza, and Piero Berni Millet, use amphorae from urban contexts in Beirut and Tarragona, and from Mallorca to explore questions about economic connectivity in the Mediterranean. Dragana Mladenović and Maria Carmen Moreno Escobar look at the connections inland from the Tiber ports of Portus, Ostia, and Rome. Patricia Terrado broadens the study to the occupations of residents at these port complexes, while Emanuela Spagnoli reflects on a coin of Trajan found on Simon's excavations at Portus in 2009, as a starting point for discussing coin circulation at Ostia and Portus.

The final section of the volume focuses on the relationships between landscape and urbanism in the Roman world. Sophie Hay and Stephen Kay offer a personal reflection on working for and with Simon on surveys of Roman towns from the Tiber Valley, to north Africa and across the Mediterranean. Fernando Amores and Álvaro Jiminéz-Sancho reflect on the significance of the Roman walls of Seville. Jose Manuel Rodríguez Hidalgo and Pilar Leon draw us back to the site of Italica where the ideas which would drive the Roman Towns in the Middle and Lower Tiber Valley project had their genesis in the work undertaken by Simon and others in the 1990s. This focus on the Guadalquivir is continued by Pablo Garrido González who approaches the hinterland of Italica from the perspective of resource extraction, while José Beltrán Fortes and María Luisa Loza Azuaga return us to Peñaflor, the other urban centre in the valley at which Simon developed the approaches that would be used to such great effect later in the Tiber Valley. The contribution of Mariarosaria Barbera discusses the relationship between Simon and the administration of the archaeological park of Ostia and Portus, before Elena Pomar of the BSR discusses work at Matrice which can be seen as a direct successor to the projects conducted under Simon's auspices during his time as Assistant Director at the BSR. Frank Vermeulen and Devi Taelman then present the results of their own work at Setempeda on the Adriatic coast of Italy, and Isabel Rodá, Miguel Loza, Javier Niso, and Anna Gutiérrez Garcia-Moreno discuss commercial aspects of marble trade at Álava/Araba. The final contribution by Kristian Strutt concludes the volume recounting the impact of Simon's work in the Tiber Delta.

An incredible amount of help was received in the compiling, editing, and publication of this volume. Open access publication was made possible through a University of Southampton Faculty of Humanities research grant together with funds from the Department of Archaeology. In addition to Simon's friends and colleagues who have contributed with papers for the volume, the editors would like to thank Letizia Ceccarelli, Pablo Garrido Gonzalez, and Ferreol Salomon for making checks on papers in Italian, Spanish, and French respectively. We would also like to thank Rose Ferraby for contributing artwork for the volume. The editors would also like to thank Mike Schurer and the editorial team at Archaeopress for their continued support and advice throughout the process of publication. Finally we would like to extend our gratitude to Stephen Kay at the British School at Rome for his support and input throughout the production of this work. Without his support none of this would have been possible.

The editors hope that this volume reflects the impact that Simon had on research and learning in the Mediterranean. With these contributions, the authors highlight the diverse nature of the themes within the discipline that Simon influenced, and the range of individuals demonstrates Simon and his nurture of collaborations and his support of those entering into studies of Roman archaeology. We would also hope that, while these papers reflect the academic contribution of Simon, it will bring back fond memories of Simon's character and good humour. He is sorely missed.

Simon Keay and the Archaeology of the Mediterranean[1]

Martin Millett

Simon and I first met in the queue to register as undergraduate students at the Institute of Archaeology in October 1974. He was just back from a year abroad in Australia where his work had included time on an uncle's sheep station where he picked up some vocabulary that stayed with him. How many times at the end of a day's fieldwork did you hear that Simon was 'dry as a dead dingo's donger'? (Other phrases are not to be printed...)

The intake in our year numbered only about 16 undergraduate students, and four of us (me, Simon, Jeremy Evans, and Lawrence Wright) with an interest in Roman archaeology had tutorials with Richard Reece who encouraged us to think 'outside the box'. Generally, the undergraduate course at the Institute (at that time an independent unit within the University of London and not yet part of UCL) was informal. There were lectures to attend, a library in which to read, and a common room where everyone mixed and long discussions took place. The common room encouraged interactions between students at all levels and staff as well as visiting academics. Other student contemporaries who were to remain active in Roman archaeology included Paul Arthur, Simon James, Rick Jones, and Tony King, with Amanda Claridge, Tom Blagg, and John Lloyd amongst the research staff with whom we mixed. Memorably, Keith Hopkins was also around for one year whilst he was on sabbatical leave, and this led to a series of coffee-time discussions that had a strong impact on us.

There were surprisingly few demands on undergraduates to write essays and assessment was based on end-of-year examinations. This left those keen on the subject enormous scope to read and explore things as their interests allowed. Alongside this, there was a substantial requirement to undertake fieldwork with a minimum of 12 weeks required for graduation. Simon used this opportunity to explore aspects of the subject that appealed to him, with an especial emphasis on the courses on Late Antiquity, coins, and pottery (offered by Richard Reece) and epigraphy (taught by John Wilkes). His undergraduate dissertation was on the coins from Kathleen Kenyon's excavation of the theatre at Verulamium, but Simon's passion was already focused on Mediterranean archaeology with a particular interest in the later Roman period and the economy. I well remember him enthusing about Ottelo Testaguzza's *Portus* volume (1970), with him showing me the plans of the site in the Institute library. He was equally assiduous in reading the old Soprintendenza guides to the sites of Rome, impressing the rest of us with his depth of knowledge.

The requirement for us to do fieldwork was important, and Simon grasped the opportunity to work in Italy where he dug first at Rice University's excavation of a villa on the *via Gabina* (where he met David Mattingly), and later on Andrea Carandini's excavation of the Roman villa at Settefinestre (usually referred to as 7F). These also offered the opportunity for Simon to become familiar with other sites in Italy, and importantly to network with a generation of diggers who were later to become significant figures in Italian archaeology. Amongst the Institute contingent at 7F, Simon formed a strong friendship with Paul Arthur, travelling and digging with him on a number of sites.[2] It was at this time that Simon also had his first links with the British School at Rome I think via Molly Cotton whose support to young archaeologists in Italy was so important.

I was already well embedded in British archaeology, and Simon was happy to work on the excavations that I was running on the Roman site at Neatham in the Easter and summer of 1976. His voluntary labour here (and later at Cowdery's Down at Easter 1978) brought my reciprocal contribution to his own excavation at Vilauba in Catalunya (see below). Digging together was enormous fun, and through our undergraduate year we grew to be good friends socialising together, digging together, and debating archaeology, often ending up at the flat that he shared with his brothers at 73 Onslow Square, South Kensington. He was away digging at 7F when our degree results came out in June 1977, and following an agreed arrangement, I telephoned him from the Post Office in Trafalgar Square to a

---

[1] This contribution is a personal reflection. It complements the obituaries that I wrote for the *Guardian* (9 May 2021 <https://www.theguardian.com/science/2021/may/09/simon-keay-obituary> and the *Papers of the British School at Rome* (89 (2021): 1-8) <https://doi.org/10.1017/S0068246221000064>. For a fuller appreciation of his academic contribution see I. Rodà de Llanza 'In honorem et memorian Simon J. Keay, Adlectus Inter Hispanos (1954–2021)', *Madrider Mitteilungen* 62 (2021) <https://doi.org/10.34780/0x61-xn18> and M. Millett 'Keay, Simon 1954–2001', *Biographical Memoirs of Fellows of the British Academy* 21 (2023): 1-13 <https://www.thebritishacademy.ac.uk/publishing/memoirs/21/keay-simon-1954-2021/>.
[2] For an excellent photograph of Simon – with big hair – see Arthur 1991, pl. VIII.

phone box in Orbetello to tell him his result. This was followed by us meeting at 7F and then travelling to visit Rome in August 1977. By that stage, we had both been awarded British Academy grants to do our doctorates (masters degrees not being expected at that time). Whilst I moved to Oxford for my doctoral studies, Simon stayed at the Institute where he was supervised by John Wilkes. Rather to my surprise, he decided to work not on Italy, but on Spain. Simon had family connections in Alella, near Barcelona and in the French part of Catalunya and following the death of Franco in 1975, Spain offered immense opportunities. The closed academic system of the Fascist era was coming to an end and there was an awakening of interest in archaeology amongst a new generation who were reasserting Catalan national identity through the exploration of its past.

Simon's research picked up on his interest in ceramics, Late Antiquity, and trade. The archaeology of the late Roman period in Iberia had been largely neglected until then, as had the considerable number of amphorae that lay unstudied in museums and excavation archives. These provided an opportunity and a challenge for Simon. He soon travelled to Barcelona where he patiently and gradually gained permission to study these collections, often being kept sitting round for days in museum offices waiting to gain permission for access from museum directors. I am very sorry that I have lost the postcards he sent at this time vividly describing these experiences, the cockroach-infested rooms that he rented and the interminable delays in getting to see the collections. His academic drive, sense of humour, and sense of the absurd not only carried him through but also gained him the respect of other young archaeologists in Catalunya who became his firm friends. Simon had a flair for languages and he was keen to converse in both Castilian and Catalan, the latter being immensely significant given its suppression by Franco and its increasing cultural importance in the late 1970s. Simon excavated with the team led by Enrico San Martí at Empúries, and there and elsewhere, he developed strong lifelong friendships with a group of archaeologists that included Javier Aquilué, Xavier Dupré I Raventos, Ricardo Mar, Josep-Maria Nolla and Isabel Rodà de Llanza. The outcome of Simon's doctoral research was a substantial new study of late Roman amphorae of the western Mediterranean which included a new typology. Once published this became a major work of reference, and the Keay typology remains the principal work of reference for the whole of the Roman Empire (Keay 1984).

Simon's first year's work in Catalunya led to an invitation to lead a new excavation on the Roman villa at Vilauba (Camós) in the province of Girona jointly with the local museum curator Josep Tarrús i Galter, and with Josep-Maria Nolla. The first season was somewhat hand-to-mouth and Simon asked me (and other friends including Tom Blagg) to join the team. The local town Banyoles – nowadays a sophisticated resort – was then as described by Simon 'a one horse town where someone had shot the horse'! The presence of foreign archaeologists came as something of a shock to the residents too, including the local twitchy Guardia Civil officer who was reputed to have shot someone for jumping a red traffic light! The team was based at a local campsite and ate at a nearby restaurant where cockroaches again put in an appearance, but the experience was enormous fun. The archaeology was also impressive and as the project developed over the period of Simon's involvement (1978-83) it produced excellent results, with the identification of an olive press of Visigothic date and a long developmental sequence (Roure *et al.* 1988). The excavation was also a success socially, not only bringing young Catalan and UK archaeologists together and introducing new methods and ideas to Catalan archaeology, but also socially. In the final two years of Simon's role in the project, as a newly appointed lecturer at Durham University, I brought students to work on the site. Amongst them was Nina Inzani whom Simon went on to marry.

Amongst the innovations at the Vilauba project, was some emphasis on the site within its local landscape, and his developing interest in this led to the next stage of Simon's career in Spain which began shortly after his appointment to a lectureship at Southampton in 1985. He and I had visited Tarragona in 1983 and talked to Xavier Dupré, then the provincial archaeologist there, about the prospect of starting a regional survey in the hinterland of the Roman city. This project came to fruition at the same time that Dupré was leading new excavations in the town itself with the creation of the Taller-Escola d'Arqueologia. We were joined in running the survey by Josep-Maria Carreté, and starting from a modest exploratory season in 1985, we worked through a series of month-long seasons until 1990, collecting surface finds in the mornings, washing and quantifying the finds in the afternoons. It was intensive, hot work, but in the tradition of Simon's projects also greatly enjoyable. In addition to masses of Roman finds which transformed understanding of the Roman landscape, the countryside was also full of unexpected things and odd people – appealing to Simon's sense of the absurd and allowing his sense of humour full reign. We also settled to having lunch each day at a tiny but excellent restaurant in Tarragona (Bar Maximo), where after a long morning in the field, wine flowed and practical jokes flourished. The result of the project was not only a new study of the rural landscape – the first such systematic rural survey in Roman Spain – but also a series of methodological advances in survey interpretation (Carreté *et al.* 1995).

Alongside his fieldwork, Simon also wrote a major synthesis of Roman Spain (Keay 1988) the first such volume in English for 30 years. By this stage, Simon was well known and respected across the Iberian Peninsula and also fulfilled an important role in communicating the results of research in the region to the English-speaking world. He did this through promoting conference sessions and ensuring that these were published and also by facilitating visits by Spanish students and scholars to Southampton. The latter having a substantial long-term impact on the careers of many.

The late 1980s also marked the expansion of Simon's active research horizon beyond Catalunya and a shift towards an interest in urban sites. This was first exemplified through his fieldwork and excavation at Celti (Peñaflor) in Andalucía (1987-92). Working with José Remesal Rodríguez and John Creighton and with students from Southampton, he undertook large-scale survey and a stratigraphic excavation at this site which was a key centre for olive oil production and its trade to Rome (Keay et al. 2000a). As well as contributing significantly to understanding of this key region, this project was also methodologically innovative, using geophysics and survey alongside excavation (it was also a major logistical challenge, given the fierce climate!).

The methods developed at Peñaflor were also applied to great effect at the totemic site of Italica where the team used large-scale electrical resistance survey and magnetometry, providing impressive new evidence for the Hadrianic planned town, discovering a new suite of monumental baths as well as the late antique defensive wall (Creighton et al. 1999). In southern Spain, Simon subsequently went on to work with Southampton colleagues on regional urban systems, using GIS and methods of network analysis to investigate urban systems, again pushing the boundaries of research and methodology and thus contributing to urban studies more generally (see for instance Keay and Earl 2006).

In the mid-1990s Simon's research focus moved from Spain to Italy, although it initially remained focused on urban sites. Following the appointment of Andrew Wallace-Hadrill as Director of the British School at Rome, Simon and I talked about developing the work that he had pioneered in Spain, using geophysics to map Roman urban sites. This was to form part of the broader Tiber Valley Project in which Simon also took a leading role (Keay et al. 2020). For the towns work, we first planned exploratory work at Falerii Novi and Ocriculum in 1997, but in the event, it was not possible to do much at the latter site in that initial season. However, the small area covered at Falerii provided spectacular results, and this provided the springboard for our Roman Towns of the Tiber Valley Project (Keay et al. 2000b; Keay and Millett 2016). These surveys were each undertaken by a small team which created an excellent and creative atmosphere in which new ideas were discussed and promoted, whilst everyone had enjoyed the conviviality of working in rural Italy.

This work also proved a catalyst that led to the wider adoption of magnetic survey within Italian archaeology, and also led Simon actively to promote the use of geophysical survey at Southampton and in the BSR. When the results from Falerii were seen by Lidia Paroli she recognised their potential for helping the Soprintendenza to manage the site of Portus. As a result, we were invited to undertake a survey of the grounds surrounding the hexagonal harbour there at the end of 1998, and this led to the complete survey of the port complex published in 2005 (Keay et al. 2005). This proved a key moment in Simon's career, as he went on the lead major excavations on the site (2007-16) as well as further survey of its hinterland, truly transforming understanding of the site and its place within the Roman Mediterranean. This work also put Simon at the centre of archaeology in Italy, establishing him as a key figure in Classical Archaeology. The sheer scale of the excavation, its innovative planning and execution, and its mission to involve a truly international group of students and professional archaeologists served as a beacon on European collaboration.

In keeping with the ethos that had characterised his work throughout his career, the Portus project generated a steady stream of papers and books. In these, as well as presenting the remarkable fieldwork results, Simon placed the findings in a broader historical and archaeological context, developing in particular ideas about the systems used in the port and its broader networking. These stimulating ideas put Portus at the centre of debates about the Roman economy, and also provided the springboard for his final project, the ERC funded *Portuslimen* Project.[3] In this Simon extended his thinking to a canvas that covered the whole Mediterranean, drawing on evidence and new fieldwork from 30 sites to explore their character and interconnections in order to understand their role in integration under the Roman Empire. This bold and imaginative project drew on a wide variety of different types of evidence and brought together a wide range of people. It demonstrates Simon's mastery of the subject at the height of his intellectual powers, and as such also illustrates the scale of his loss.

---

[3] For the research design, see his introduction in chapter 1 of Arnaud and Keay 2020.

Bibliography

Arnaud, P. and S.J. Keay (eds) 2020. *Roman Port Societies*. Cambridge: Cambridge University Press.

Arthur, P. 1991. *The Romans in Northern Campania* (Archaeological Monographs of the British School at Rome 1). London: British School at Rome.

Carreté, J.M., S.J. Keay and M. Millett 1995. *A Roman Provincial Capital and its Hinterland: The Survey of the Territory of Tarragona, Spain, 1985-1990* (Journal of Roman Archaeology Supplementary Series 15). Ann Arbor: Journal of Roman Archaeology.

Creighton, J., D. Jordan, S.J. Keay, I. Rodà de Llanza and J.M. Rodríguez Hidalgo 1999. La Itálica de Adriano. Resultados de las prospecciones arqueológicas de 1991 y 1992. *Archivo Español de Arqueología* 72 (num. 179-180) (1999): 73-97. <https://doi.org/10.3989/aespa.1999.v72.297>.

Keay, S.J. 1984. *Late Roman Amphorae in the Western Mediterranean: A Typology and Economic Study; The Catalan Evidence* (BAR International Series 196). Oxford: BAR (2 vols) – revised edition issued in 2011.

Keay, S.J. 1988. *Roman Spain*. London: British Museum Press – translated as S. Keay *Hispania Romana*. Barcelona: Ausa Editorial, 1992.

Keay, S.J., J. Creighton and J. Remesal Rodriguez 2000a. *Celti (Peñaflor): The Archaeology of a Hispano-Roman Town in Baetica*. Oxford: Oxbow – translated as S. Keay, J. Creighton and J. Remesal Rodriguez 2001. *Celti (Peñaflor): la arqueología de una ciudad hispanorromana en la Baetica; prospecciones y excavaciones 1987-1992*. Seville: Empresa Pública de Gestión de Programas Culturales.

Keay, S.J., M. Millett, S. Poppy, J. Robinson, J. Taylor, and N. Terrenato 2000b. Falerii Novi: a new survey of the walled area. *Papers of the British School at Rome* 68: 1-93.

Keay, S.J. and G. Earl 2006. Structuring of the provincial landscape: the towns of central and western Baetica in their geographical context, in G. Cruz Andreotti, P. Le Roux and P. Moret (eds) *La invención de una geografía de la Península Ibérica*, II: *La época imperial*: 305-58. Madrid: Casa de Velázquez.

Keay, S.J., M. Millett, L. Paroli and K.D. Strutt 2005. *Portus: An Archaeological Survey of the Port of Imperial Rome* (British School at Rome Archaeological Monograph 15). London: British School at Rome.

Keay, S.J. and M. Millett 2016. Republican and early Imperial Towns in the Tiber Valley, in A.E. Cooley (ed.) *A Companion to Roman Italy*: 357-77. Oxford: Blackwell.

Keay, S.J., M. Millett and C. Smith 2020. The Tiber Valley Project: an introduction, in H. Patterson, R. Witcher and H. Di Giuseppe *The Changing Landscape of Rome's Northern Hinterland: The British School at Rome's Tiber Valley Project*: 1-8. Oxford: Archaeopress.

Roure i Bonaventura, A., P. Castanyer, J.-M. Nolla, S.J. Keay and J. Tarrús 1988. *La vil.la romana de Vilauba (Comós)*. Girona: Generalitat de Catalunya & La Diputació de Girona.

Simon Keay and the British School at Rome

Andrew Wallace-Hadrill

I first met Simon in 1994 at an auction of artworks in London to raise funds for the British School at Rome (BSR). He was introduced to me by Tim Potter, who asserted in his confident way that Simon would be my successor as Director of the BSR. He would indeed have made a brilliant Director, but though he was never prepared to move his family to Rome, he made an extraordinary contribution to the School through his archaeological projects. On my arrival in Rome we launched, aided and abetted by Tim Potter, a new policy for archaeology, diverting funds from a plethora of small grants to a new position of Assistant Director for Archaeology, held with conspicuous success by Helen Patterson. Her Tiber Valley Project aimed not only to revisit the Ward-Perkins South Etruria Survey, but to collaborate with colleagues from British and Italian universities in new projects in the area. In an atmosphere of great excitement, as many as a dozen teams gradually came together, with a kaleidoscope of projects, from epigraphy to analysis of basalt road-paving. Conspicuous among them was the project of Simon and Martin Millett on Roman Towns in the Tiber Valley.

Simon and Martin brought their experience of geophysical prospection from Spain to the site of Falerii Novi (beloved, by no coincidence, by Tim Potter). The survey delivered spectacular results and led to surveys of a range of other sites, including Otricoli and Teano. Not only did they demonstrate the potential of geophysics for generating new insights into Roman towns, but in those early days of the archaeological application of geophysical survey, they showed the potential of such research to generate its own funding. Simon set up the Archaeological Prospection Service of Southampton (APSS) based on his own university, employing Kris Strutt and Sophie Hay; the collaboration with BSR meant that APSS raised its own funding, while BSR added Stephen Kay to the team and invested in geophysical equipment for use in the increasing number of projects in Italy. As the reputation of the service spread in Italy, it attracted more and more interest, culminating in the invitation to work in Portus Traiani. Simon's skill at promptly publishing his results (scarcely the norm in archaeology) also ensured that each project was its own publicity.

The Portus Project saw the BSR act as a trusted third party in a tense standoff between the Ostia Soprintendenza Archeologica, under Anna Gallina Zevi, and the landowners of the Portus estate, the Sforza Cesarini family, under the Duke, Ascanio, and his son Don Muzio. The project was an archaeological success, transforming our understanding of the Roman port. But it was also a diplomatic success, thanks to the personal charm of Simon. Anna and Fausto Zevi were firm friends of the BSR, and got on famously with Simon. But he got on equally well with the Sforza Cesarini family. Not the least of his skills was his linguistic fluency (his excellent Italian long had a Spanish inflection) which enabled him to establish good relationships with the many Italians who had little or no English. I have happy memories of magnificent lunches in the Sforza Cesarini villa on the shore of the hexagonal basin of the Roman port. It was the fruit of such diplomatic success that both parties, Soprintendenza and Sforza Cesarini family, were equally pleased with the results, the Soprintendenza because they demonstrated that there were indeed Roman remains beneath the land, the family because they showed that these were in a limited area. That led the project to grow and grow, until it became the principal focus of Simon's works, and surveying was reinforced by major excavations, and Portus became the starting point for a much larger project on Roman ports.

In 2006 he took on the new position of Research Professor in Archaeology at the BSR. This enabled him not only to expand the activities of the geophysics prospection team, but to intensify his study of the imperial port complex of Portus, supported by a generous AHRC grant. Excavation revealed not only an imperial palace and shipsheds (as one might predict), but a small amphitheatre. So unexpected was this that when he presented the first traces of this oval structure at the BSR, he was uncertain how to interpret it. I pointed out that the Romans used oval structures for one type of building above all, just like the one he had already discovered at Teano. All these discoveries changed our image of the greatest of Roman artificial ports for ever. A series of conferences on Roman ports made an enormous impact and sealed the status of the BSR as a centre for archaeology.

All Simon's projects relied on teamwork, made possible by Simon's natural talents as a team leader (in tandem, needless to say, with the complementary skills of Martin). Technically, his command of the ancient sources and his command of Italian won him the deep respect of Italian colleagues, but it was his kindness, generosity of spirit, and sense of fun that made him a joy to work with. The young scholars he brought into the project have developed flourishing careers, Kris Strutt as an outstanding geophysicist, Stephen Kay as Archaeological Manager of the BSR, and Sophie Hay as part of the team in the Parco Archeologico di Pompei, as well as the many others who worked on the Tiber Valley Project, like Paul Johnson, now Honorary Fellow at Nottingham, and Graeme Earl, now Professor of Archaeology at SOAS. The good that men do lives after them.

A note on the artwork

Rose Ferraby

The visual work in this volume was made in Portus in 2008. Simon encouraged those of us working on the excavations to experiment, galvanising a strong sense of creative collaboration and innovation amongst the team. He gave us the space to try and create different kinds of records of the site. And so, these artworks were made as part of a small, limited-edition book that I made about the site. Some of the images were used on a set of Portus T-shirts that still linger in many of our wardrobes; a faded cotton memory of very happy times. The artwork was inspired by the many years I spent at Portus. I was particularly interested in the way that the umbrella pines had become so much a part of the archaeological landscape, their towering, slim shapes a contrast to the hefty endurance of the architecture. Ancient engineering and present-day ecologies intersect to create a place unlike any other. For me, the images are full of deep memories of happy years spent in Italy working on sites with Simon; times of learning and laughter.

Ancient warehouses and trees in the Portus Archaeological Park, drawn with charcoal, ink, wax crayon and watercolour (artwork: Rose Ferraby)

List of Contributors

Fernando Amores, Senior Lecturer, University of Seville. Email: famores@us.es

Prof. Miguel Ángel Cau Ontiveros, Catedrático de Arqueología. ICREA Research Professor. ICREA/ERAAUB, IAUB, Universitat de Barcelona, Passeig Lluís Companys, 23, 08010 Barcelona. Email: macau@ub.edu

Pascal Arnaud, Professeur émérite Université Lumière-Lyon 2, HISOMA, UMR n° 5189, 5/7 rue Raulin, F-69007 LYON. Email: arnaudp2003@yahoo.fr

Mariarosaria Barbera, già dirigente Ministero Beni e Attività Culturali, già direttrice del Parco Archeologico di Ostia antica. Email: mar.barbera@gmail.com

Prof. Dr José Beltrán Fortes, Catedrático de Arqueología. Departamento de Prehistoria y Arqueología de la Universidad de Sevilla. c/ María de Padilla, 1, 41004 – Sevilla (España). Email: jbeltran@us.es

Javier Bermejo-Meléndez, Universidad de Huelva. Javier.bermejo@dhis1.uhu.es

Prof. Darío Bernal-Casasola, Catedrático de Arqueología. Universidad de Cádiz. Facultad de Filosofía y Letras, Avda. Dr Gómez Ulla s/n, 11003 Cádiz. Email: dario.bernal@uca.es

Dr Piero Berni Millet, Investigador asociado. Institut Català d'Arqueologia Classica (ICAC). Plaça d'en Rovellat, s/n, 43003 Tarragona Email: pbernim@gmail.com

Michel Bonifay, Directeur de Recherche émérite au CNRS, MMSH – Centre Camille Jullian, 5 rue du Château de l'Horloge CS 90412, 13097 Aix-en-Provence, France. Email: michel.bonifay@univ-amu.fr

Tom Brughmans, Associate Professor, Social Resilience Lab, Aarhus University, Building 1483-523, Jens Chr. Skous Vej 4, 8000 Aarhus, Denmark. Email: t.b@cas.au.dk

Christer Bruun, Professor, Department of Classics, University of Toronto, 125, Queen's Park, Toronto, Ontario, M5S 2C7, Canada. Email: christer.bruun@utoronto.ca

Juan M. Campos Carrasco, Universidad de Huelva. Email: campos@uhu.es

Dr Peter B. Campbell, Director, Heritage Crime Investigations, Inc., The Lion Brewery, Oxford, UK, OX1 1JE. Email: peterbcampbell@gmail.com

Claudio Capelli, Università degli Studi di Genova, Italy; Research Fellow of the Centre Camille Jullian (Aix Marseille Univ, CNRS, CCJ, Aix-en-Provence, France). Email: capelli.archeo@gmail.com

Dr Nicolas Carayon, Chargé d'étude et de recherche, Ipso Facto, 12 Impasse Delpech, F-13003 Marseille. Email: nicolas.carayon@ipsofacto.coop

César Carreras, Senior Lecturer, Dept. of Antiquity Sciences, Faculty of Arts, Autonoma University of Barcelona, Edifici B (Campus UAB), 08193 Bellaterra (Spain). Email: cesar.carreras@uab.cat

Dr Roberta Cascino, Research Fellow, the British School at Rome, Via Gramsci 61, 00197 Rome. Email: casinor@libero.it

Mr Jaume Cardell Perelló. Jefe de Servicio de Arqueología. Consell de Mallorca, Plaça Hospital 4, 07012, Palma de Mallorca. Email: jacardell@conselldemallorca.net

Julien Cavero, Ingénieur d'étude, CNRS FR 3747 Maison de l'Orient et de la Méditerranée, 7 rue Raulin, F-69007 Lyon. Email: julien.cavero@cnrs.fr

Dr Letizia Ceccarelli, Department of Chemistry, Materials and Chemical Engineering 'Giulio Natta', Politecnico di Milano, Piazza Leonardo da Vinci 32, 20133 Milano, Italy. Email: letizia.ceccarelli@polimi.it

Dr Anna Collar, Associate Professor, Department of Archaeology, University of Southampton, Highfield, Southampton, SO17 1BF, UK. Email: A.Collar@soton.ac.uk

Alessia Contino, Funzionario Archeologo, Ministero della Cultura-Segretariato regionale per il Lazio, UCCR Lazio, Via di San Michele 22, 00153 Roma. Email: alessaia.contino@cultura.gov.it

Dr Katherine Crawford, Senior GIS Specialist, Chronicle Heritage. Email: kathacrawford@gmail.com

Dott. Cristian D'Ammassa, Escuela de Doctorado in Investigación histórica y patrimonial, Universidad de Huelva. Email: cristian.dammassa@alu.uhu.es

Dr Carlos de Juan Fuertes, Investigador Senior, Universidad de Valencia. Facultad de Geografía e Historia. Av. de Blasco Ibáñez, 28, El Pla del Real, 46010 Valencia. Email: carlos.juan-fuertes@uv.es

Dr Leandro Fantuzzi. Profesor de Arqueología. ERAAUB, IAUB, Universitat de Barcelona, Passeig Lluís Companys, 23, 08010 Barcelona. Email: lfantuzzi@ub.edu

Fabrizio Felici, Parsifal Cooperativa di Archeologia, Via Macedonia 77, 00179 Roma. Email: fa.felici@gmail.com

Dr Rose Ferraby, Independent archaeologist and artist, and Honorary Research Fellow at University of Exeter. Email: R.ferraby2@exeter.ac.uk

Prof. Enrique García Riaza. Catedrático de Historia Antigua. Universitat de les Illes Balears. Edif. Ramon Llull, Ctra. Valldemossa Km. 7,5. 07122 Palma. Email: garcia.riaza@uib.es

Pablo Garrido González, Jefe de Servicio de Conjuntos Arqueológicos y Monumentales, Consejería de Cultura y Deporte, Junta de Andalucía, Levíes 17, 2ª pl. 41004 Sevilla. Email: pablo.garrido.gonzalez@juntadeandalucia.es

Prof. Gian Luca Gregori, Dipartimento di Scienze dell'Antichità, Sapienza Università di Roma. Email: gianluca.gregori@uniroma1.it

Dr Sophie Hay, Press Office, Archaeological Park of Pompeii, Via Plinio, 26, Pompeii 80045 (NA). Email: sophie.hay@cultura.gov.it

Alvaro Jiménez Sancho PhD, Independent Archaeologist. Email: arqueolator@gmail.com

Dr Paul S. Johnson, Director at Magnitude Surveys and Honorary Research Fellow in Roman Archaeology, Department of Classics and Archaeology, University of Nottingham, University Park, Nottingham, NG7 2RD. Email: Paul.Johnson@nottingham.ac.uk

Dr Stephen Kay, Archaeology Manager, The British School at Rome, Via Gramsci 61, 00197 Rome. Email: s.kay@bsrome.it

Dr Ada Lasheras González, Membre scientifique, École des hautes études hispaniques et ibériques – Casa de Velázquez, C/ Paul Guinard, 3 – Ciudad Universitaria 28040 Madrid. Email: ada.lasheras@casadevelazquez.org

Pilar León-Castro Alonso, Catedrática emérita de Arqueología de la Universidad de Sevilla. Email: mpleon@us.es

Barbara Lepri, Independent Researcher. Email: barbaralepri@gmail.com

Dra. María Luisa Loza Azuaga, Conservadora de Patrimonio de la Junta de Andalucía. Instituto Andaluz del Patrimonio Histórico. Avda. de los Descubrimientos, s/n, 41092 – Sevilla (España). Email: marial.loza@juntadeandalucia.es

Emilia Mataix Ferrándiz, Ramón y Cajal Fellow, Law faculty, International University of Catalonia, C/Inmaculada 22, 08017 Barcelona, Spain. Email: emataix@uic.es

Joan Mayoral, Archaeologist at CASC (Centre d'Arqueologia Subaquàtica de Catalunya), Pedret, 95, 17007 Girona (Spain). Email: joanmayoral@gencat.cat

Martin Millett FBA, MAE, Emeritus Laurence Professor of Classical Archaeology, Senior Fellow, McDonald Institute for Archaeological Research, Life Fellow, Fitzwilliam College, University of Cambridge, Faculty of Classics, Sidgwick Avenue, Cambridge, CB3 9DA. Email: mjm62@cam.ac.uk

Dr Dragana Mladenović, LEIZA, Leibniz-Zentrum für Archäologie, Ludwig-Lindenschmit-Forum 1, 55116 Mainz, Germany. Email: dragana.mladenovic@leiza.de

Dr Maria del Carmen Moreno Escobar, Lux Building, Helgonavägen 3, Lund, Sweden. Email: maria.moreno_escobar@klass.lu.se

Juan Moros Diaz, Doctor en Arqueología por la Universidad de Barcelona, Pertenezco al grupo: CEIPAC, Universidad de Barcelona. Email: juanmorosdiaz@gmail.com

Mr Sebastià Munar i Llabrés, Arqueólogo subacuático. Email: munarillabres@gmail.com

Prof. Carlo Pavolini, Università della Tuscia. Email: carlo.pavolini48@gmail.com

Dr Alessandra Pecci, Profesora de Arqueología. ERAAUB, IAUB, Universitat de Barcelona, Passeig Lluís Companys, 23, 08010 Barcelona. Email: alepecci@gmail.com

Jordi Pérez González, Prof. Ayudante Doctor de Historia Antigua, Historia y Filosofía, Historia Antigua, Edificio Filosofía y Letras, C/Colegios, 2. Email: jordi.perezg@uah.es

Elena Pomar, Geophysics and archaeology researcher, British School at Rome, Via Antonio Gramsci 61. Email: e.pomar@bsrome.it

Dr José Luis Portillo Sotelo, Investigador postdoctoral. Universidad de Cádiz. Facultad de Filosofía y Letras, Avda. Dr Gómez Ulla s/n, 11003 Cádiz. Email: joseluis.portillo@uca.es

Naseem Raad, PhD, Program Coordinator, Marine Sciences and Culture, American University of Beirut, P.O. Box 11-0236 / Department of History and Archaeology, Riad El-Solh / Beirut 1107 2020, Lebanon. Email: nr46@aub.edu.lb

Dr José Alberto Retamosa Gámez, Investigador postdoctoral. Universidad de Granada. Departamento de Prehistoria y Arqueología, Campus Universitario de Cartuja s/n 18071 Granada. Email: jose.retamosa@ugr.es

José Manuel Rodríguez Hidalgo, Arqueólogo jubilado de la Consejería de Cultura de la Junta de Andalucía. Dirección del domicilio particular: Calle Manuel Casana número 11, 2ª A. 41005 Sevilla (España). Email: rhitalica@gmail.com

Dr Francesc Rodríguez Martorell, Institut Català d'Arqueologia Clàssica – Pl. d'en Rovellat s/n, 43003,Tarragona (Spain). Email: frodriguez@icac.cat

Dr Corinne Sanchez, Directrice de recherche, CNRS UMR 5140 – Archéologie des sociétés méditerranéennes, Université Paul Valéry, route de Mende, F-34199 Montpellier. Email: corinne.sanchez@cnrs.fr

Renato Sebastiani, Soprintendenza Speciale Archeologia Belle Arti e Paesaggio di Roma. Email: Renato.sebastiani18@gmail.com

Emanuela Spagnoli, Professore associato di Numismatica, Università degli Studi di Napoli Federico II – Dipartimento di Studi Umanistici studio 810 – via Nuova Marina 33 – 80133 NAPOLI (Italia). Email: emanuela.spagnoli@unina.it

Dr Kristian Strutt, Principal Teaching Fellow, Department of Archaeology, University of Southampton, Highfield, Southampton, SO17 1BF, UK. Email: kds@soton.ac.uk

Dr Devi Taelman, Vrije Universiteit Brussel, Department of History, Archaeology, Arts, Philosophy and Ethics, Pleinlaan 2, 1050 Brussels, Belgium & Ghent University, Department of Archaeology, Sint-Pietersnieuwstraat 35, B- 9000 Gent, Belgium. Email: Devi.Taelman@VUB.be

Patricia Terrado Ortuño, Lecturer at Universitat Rovira i Virgili, Facultat de Lletres. Departament d'Història i Història de l'Art. Avinguda Catalunya, 35, 43002 Tarragona (Spain). Email: patricia.terrado@urv.cat

Dr Alejandro Valenzuela, Investigador postdoctoral. ARQUEOUIB, Universitat de les Illes Balears, Ctra. Valldemossa Km. 7.5, 07122, Palma de Mallorca. Email: avalenol@gmail.com

Prof. dr. Em. Frank Vermeulen, Ghent University, Department of Archaeology, Sint-Pietersnieuwstraat 35, B- 9000 Gent, Belgium. Email: frank.vermeulen@ugent.be

Prof. Andrew Wallace-Hadrill, Faculty of Classics, University of Cambridge, Sidgwick Avenue, Cambridge CB3 9DA. Email: Aw479@cam.ac.uk

Sabrina Zampini, Independent Researcher. Email: sabrinazampini@yahoo.it

Part 1:
Mediterranean Port
and River Systems

1. Con Simon alla scoperta di Portus: I contesti ceramici Traianei del Palazzo Imperiale e dei *Navalia* rinvenuti nelle campagne di scavo 2007-11

Alessandra Bousquet, Roberta Cascino, Fabrizio Felici, Barbara Lepri, Sabrina Zampini

Introduzione

L'iniziativa di pubblicare questo volume, ci ha messo uno di fronte all'altro a parlare di Simon e a riflettere su quale fosse l'aspetto in cui ciascuno di noi si sentisse verso di lui più debitore. Ne è scaturito questo lavoro, che vuole testimoniare quanto Simon abbia contribuito alla nostra crescita professionale e personale. Nel 2007 con l'inizio delle ricerche archeologiche presso il Palazzo Imperiale siamo approdati anche noi a Porto e con noi una moltitudine di persone provenienti da diverse parti del mondo: è stato come risvegliare la vitalità dell'antico porto imperiale con il via vai di studiosi, appassionati e specialisti, tutti motivati, indaffarati a fare, cercare, produrre, scambiare, capire, confrontare, organizzare ecc. Un vero porto di mare! Ognuno portava con sé la sua specializzazione, il suo bagaglio culturale e il suo carattere. Tutto questo è stato sempre molto interessante e stimolante, così come, ovviamente, non sempre altrettanto facile! Se oggi abbiamo maturato la consapevolezza che questa esperienza (ancora in corso!) è stata fin qui non solo bella, ma anche altamente formativa e se ancora adesso tutti noi possiamo beneficiare dell'ottima riuscita del Portus Project, lo dobbiamo innanzitutto a Simon: alla sua grande capacità di coordinare e gestire un gruppo così eterogeneo di persone, sapendo toccare le corde giuste per far sentire ognuno partecipe e motivato verso lo scopo comune. Lui ha saputo armonizzare il contributo di molti, in uno scambio continuo di idee con uno sviluppo quasi seminariale, estremamente formativo sia per gli specialisti che per gli studenti che vi hanno preso parte. Se oggi il sito di Portus è sempre più aperto al pubblico lo dobbiamo anche alla sua visione che ha fortemente contribuito a realizzare un sogno, quello di Lidia Paroli, anche lei prematuramente scomparsa. Noi, chiamati da Simon a far parte dello staff del Portus Project, vogliamo continuare lungo la strada da lui tracciata. È nostra intenzione evitare che si disperdano le energie, le passioni e i risultati del lavoro di Simon e per questo, insieme a tutti gli altri colleghi del Portus Project, stiamo portando avanti gli studi e le pubblicazioni da lui già avviati. Il contributo che abbiamo scelto di presentare in questo volume è un esempio dell'impegno che abbiamo assunto in questo senso. Si tratta di un lavoro che abbiamo presentato in occasione del convegno su Traiano, organizzato da Simon e tenutosi alla British School at Rome il 22 gennaio del 2011, i cui atti non sono stati ancora pubblicati. Abbiamo scelto di riprendere tale contributo, debitamente aggiornato, vista la rilevanza dei risultati scientifici raggiunti (seppur in via preliminare) e soprattutto vista la stretta connessione alle tematiche e agli interessi cari a Simon.

Lo Scavo

Le ricerche presso il cosiddetto Palazzo Imperiale a *Portus*, condotte nelle campagne di scavo realizzate tra il 2007 e il 2015 (Keay *et al.* 2011; 2012), hanno permesso di individuare una complessa sequenza stratigrafica costituita da circa 1800 unità stratigrafiche e articolata in 10 periodi (1, 2, 3, 4, 5, 6A, 6B, 6C, 7, 8), che documenta l'occupazione del sito dall'età di Claudio (Periodo 1), quando in questo settore l'unica attività superstite è la realizzazione della banchina, all'età moderna (Periodo 8) (Tabella 1.1) (Figg. 1.1-1.2).

Complessivamente sono stati identificati 8 edifici la maggior parte dei quali faceva parte del Palazzo Imperiale (Edifici 1, 2, 3, 4, 6, 8). Un altro edificio (Edificio 5) formava il complesso dei "*Navalia*". Un ulteriore edificio di incerta funzione, il numero 7, è stato individuato nel corso del Portus Project, immediatamente ad E dei *Navalia* e da questi ben distinto, oltre la recinzione nella tenuta del Duca Sforza Cesarini (Tabella 1.2).

Le diverse campagne di scavo hanno permesso di ritrovare una notevole quantità di materiale ceramico, per un totale di 66.539 frammenti. I materiali rinvenuti non sono distribuiti cronologicamente in modo omogeneo (Grafico 1.1) e si concentrano particolarmente nel III secolo e alla fine del V secolo d.C. in corrispondenza di due eventi critici: la realizzazione del cosiddetto anfiteatro nel Palazzo Imperiale (Periodo 4) e la costruzione delle mura tardo antiche (Periodo 6A). I depositi di questi periodi servirono a consolidare il terreno prima della costruzione dell'anfiteatro o a colmare e ricreare nuove superfici dopo le demolizioni.

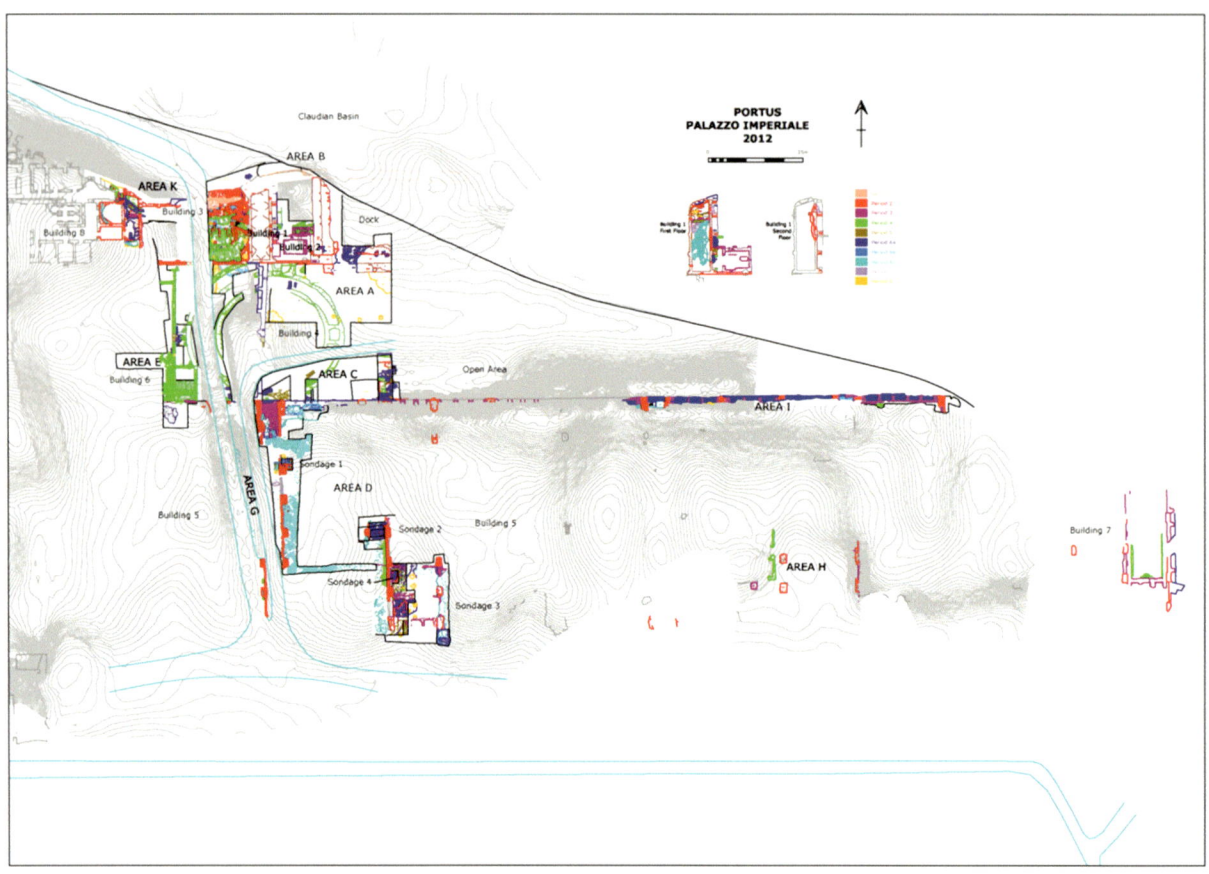

Figura 1.1: Pianta con indicazione delle aree di scavo.

Figura 1.2: Veduta aerea dello scavo.

Tabella 1.1: La periodizzazione.

Periodo	Cronologia	Interventi principali
1	Metà-tardo I secolo d.C.	Molo.
2	115-120 d.C. circa	Moli, Edifici 1, 3, 5, 8.
3	134-140 d.C. circa	Edificio 2, ristrutturazione dell'Edificio 5.
4	200-225 d.C. circa	Edificio 4, interventi negli Edifici 1, 2, 5 e 8.
5	375-400 d.C. circa	Demolizione dell'Edificio 4, costruzione dell'Edificio 6, interventi negli Edifici 1, 2, 5 e 8.
6A	Post 450 d.C.	Spoglio degli Edifici 5, 6, 8; costruzione delle Mura tardoantiche; sepolture.
6B	Post 530 d.C.	Chiusura della Porta delle Mura tardoantiche.
6C	Post 530-550 d.C.	Demolizione degli Edifici 5, 3, 6 e 8 per la realizzazione di un aggere alle spalle delle Mura tardoantiche e di nuovi livelli di calpestio.
7	Prima metà del XV secolo d.C.	Riuso degli Edifici 1 e 5.
8	XIX-inizi XX secolo	Taglio del sentiero attraverso gli Edifici 3-6; piantumazione della tenuta; trincee archeologiche.

Tabella 1.2: Edifici che costituiscono il Palazzo Imperiale e i "Navalia".

Edificio	Interpretazione	Periodo
1	Castellum Aquae	2
2	Cisterna	3
3	"Peristilium Industriale"	2
4	"Anfiteatro"	4
5	"Navalia"	2-5
6	Nuova Fronte del Palazzo Imperiale	5
8	"Peristilium Residenziale"	2

Figura 1.3: Ceramica a Pareti Sottili, Atlante II 1/117.

Al loro interno sono presenti, oltre a detriti edilizi, impressionanti quantitativi ceramici composti essenzialmente da anfore.

I contesti Traianei

In questa sede abbiamo scelto di presentare i materiali[1] associati alla costruzione dei moli, degli edifici 1, 3, 8 (cosiddetto Palazzo Imperiale) e dell'edificio 5 (interpretato come Navalia), rinvenuti negli anni 2007-11. I depositi in questione sono essenzialmente composti da sabbia utilizzata per colmare l'area tra i moli prima della realizzazione degli edifici e successivamente per rialzare i piani di calpestio degli edifici stessi fino ai pavimenti. Qui i materiali costituiscono una percentuale minima degli interri e possono essere utilizzati essenzialmente come indicatori cronologici. La classe

più attestata[2] è quella delle anfore (181 frammenti), seguita dalla ceramica comune (149 frammenti), dalle ceramiche fini (61 frammenti) e da più ridotte quantità di vetri (17), marmi (12) e lucerne (1) (Grafico 1.2).

I dati cronologici più utili ai fini dell'interpretazione dei contesti provengono dalle ceramiche fini, nell'ambito delle quali la classe più attestata è la ceramica a pareti sottili, seguita da scarse quantità di sigillata africana A, italica e tardoitalica decorata a matrice. La ceramica a pareti sottili è rappresentata da numerosi esemplari di boccalini tipo Atlante II 1/109 (A. Ricci in Atlante II: 266), prodotto a partire dall'età augustea, e tipo Atlante II 1/117 (A. Ricci in Atlante II: 271) (Figura 1.3), attestato nei contesti ostiensi a partire dall'età flavia, rispettivamente con decorazione sabbiata e a

---

[1] L'equipe per lo studio dei reperti è costituita da Alessandra Bousquet (anfore non africane), Roberta Cascino (africana da cucina, ceramiche comuni da fuoco), Fabrizio Felici (ceramiche fini), Pina Franco (anfore africane), Eleonora Gasparini (marmi), Barbara Lepri (vetri), Davide Mancini (lucerne, ceramiche medievali) e Sabrina Zampini (anfore non africane, ceramiche comuni da mensa/dispensa).

[2] I materiali qui citati verranno presentati in dettaglio nella pubblicazione finale degli scavi, che è in avanzato stato di preparazione.

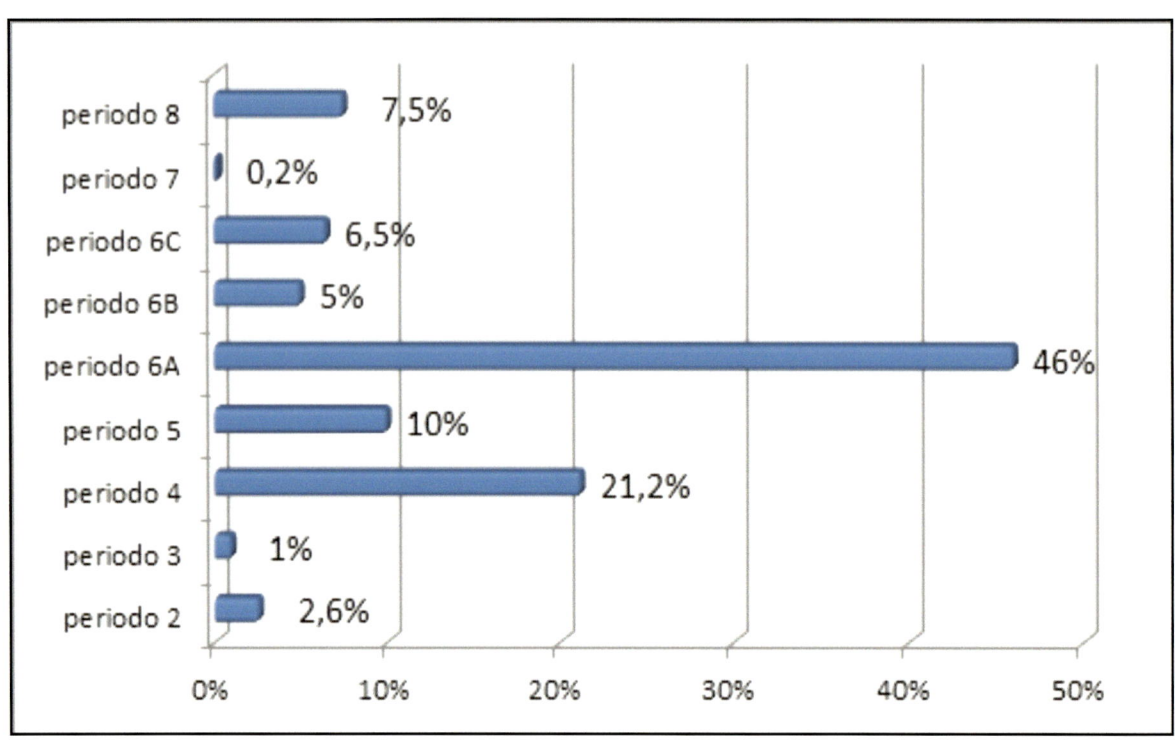

Grafico 1.1. Scavi 2007-15, la ceramica per periodo.

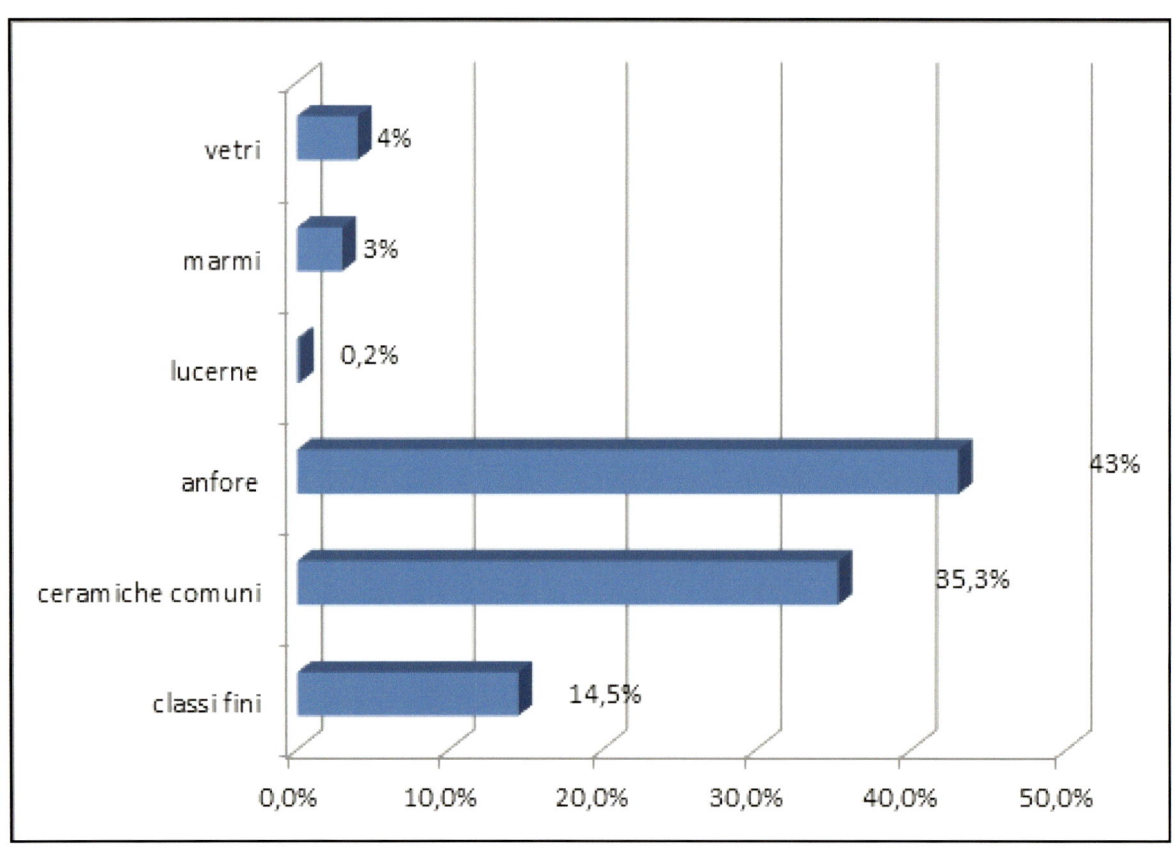

Grafico 1.2. I materiali dei contesti Traianei scavati tra il 2007 e il 2011.

Figura 1.4: Sigillata Africana A, Hayes 8A.

Figura 1.5: Sigillata Tardoitalica decorata a matrice, Dragendorff 29.

scaglie di pigna. Alcuni frammenti sono attribuibili ad un esemplare di boccalino "a collarino" Atlante II 1/122 (A. Ricci in Atlante II: 267), attestato anch'esso nelle stratigrafie ostiensi a partire dall'età flavia. Un frammento documenta, inoltre, la produzione Betica delle coppe a guscio d'uovo (Atlante II 2/417), presenti nelle stratigrafie ostiensi tra l'età di Claudio e l'età adrianea (A. Ricci in Atlante II: 293). La sigillata africana è rappresentata da pochi frammenti, tutti riconducibili alla produzione A¹, ben attestata dalla prima età flavia, tra i quali sono presenti alcuni esemplari della coppa Hayes 8A (Hayes 1972: 33-35, fig. 4; Atlante I: 26-27) (Figura 1.4). Per la sigillata italica sono invece rappresentati i piatti tipo Conspectus 20.4 (Conspectus p. 86, tav. 18; Rizzo 2003), tra i più diffusi nella seconda metà del I secolo d.C., e tipo Conspectus 3, il più comune nell'ultima produzione liscia (Conspectus p. 56, tav. 3; Rizzo 2003). Un esemplare di coppa tipo Dragendorff 29 (Dragendorff 1895; Rizzo 2003) (Figura 1.5) documenta la presenza della sigillata tardoitalica decorata a matrice, la cui diffusione iniziò a partire dagli anni 80 del I secolo d.C.

I frammenti di ceramiche comuni presenti negli strati traianei sono solo poco più di un centinaio: troppo pochi per trarre conclusioni di carattere generale, ma comunque utili a confermare la datazione fornita dalle ceramiche fini. Inoltre, la ceramica comune da mensa e dispensa è leggermente più numerosa di quella da cucina, come si vede nel grafico (Grafico 1.3).

Sebbene le ceramiche comuni rappresentino nel complesso un campione piuttosto esiguo, sono attestati diversi frammenti di produzione non locale, tra questi:

un tegame di ceramica a vernice rossa interna tipo Goudineau 1970 n. 28; alcuni frammenti di ceramica africana da cucina tra cui coperchi, riconducibili ai tipi editi in Atlante I, tavola CIV 1 e 3 (S. Tortorella in Atlante I: 212), e una casseruola, confrontabile con il tipo presente in Atlante I, tavola CVIII 3 (S. Tortorella in Atlante I: 220); infine alcuni frammenti di ceramica proveniente probabilmente dall'Egeo. In merito a questi ultimi sono presenti, nella ceramica da cucina, gli orli di una casseruola e di una olla, identificabile con i tipi editi in Pavolini 1996, rispettivamente fig. 10 n. 2 e 6, e fig. 10, n. 4, mentre nella ceramica da mensa e dispensa compare il frammento di una brocca trilobata riconducibile al tipo edito in Pavolini 1996, fig. 6, n. 1. Nei contesti traianei sono completamente assenti i frammenti di ceramica comune da mensa e dispensa di produzione africana, che diventeranno invece molto numerosi a partire dall'età severiana.

Per quanto riguarda le anfore, dagli strati traianei in esame provengono 181 frammenti, dei quali solo 21 sono relativi a parti significative: una quantità decisamente esigua rispetto alle anfore presenti nei contesti portuensi più tardi[3]. Le anfore identificate sono riconducili a tipi databili nei primi secoli dell'impero, in fase quindi negli strati che stiamo presentando.

Si tratta soprattutto di anfore spagnole, in particolare le olearie betiche Dressel 20 (H. Dressel, CIL XV, 2, I, tav. 2), l'anfora per il *defrutum* Haltern 70 e anfore da *garum*, betiche o lusitane. Diversi i contenitori vinari:

---

[3] In totale, nei periodi successivi, sono stati recuperati più di 50.000 frammenti anforici

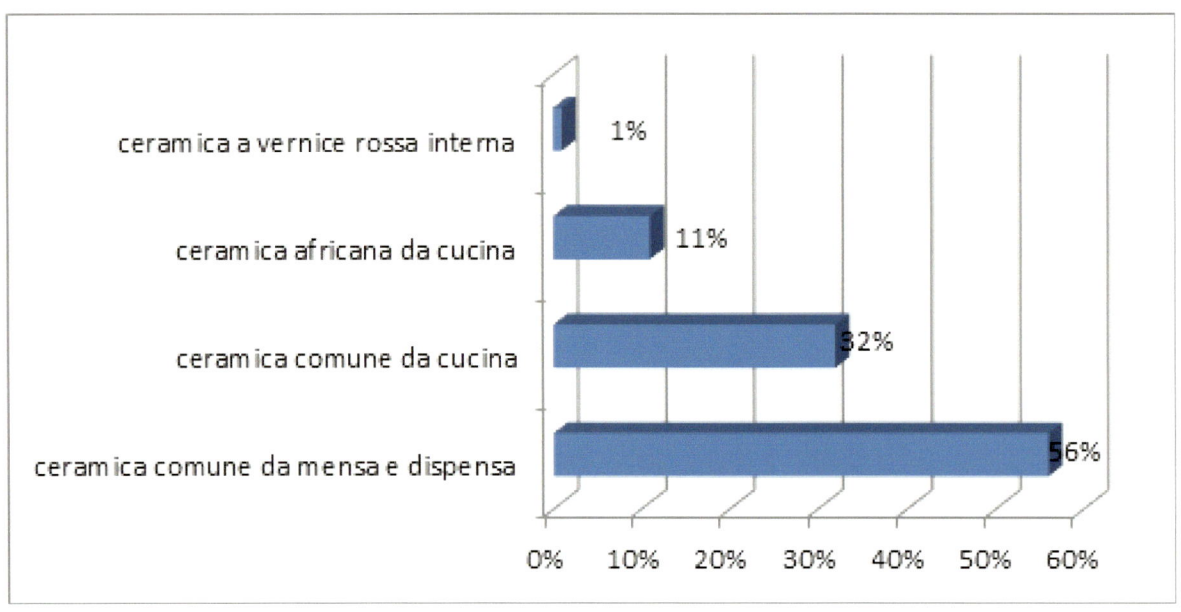

Grafico 1.3. Le ceramiche comuni dai contesti Traianei (2007-11).

Figura 1.6: Vetri, Isings 34.

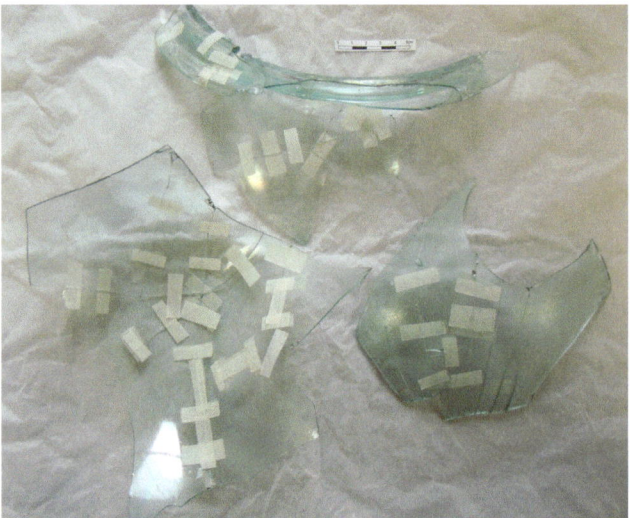

Figura 1.7: Vetri, Isings 67a.

è attestata la Dressel 2-4, presente con impasti gallici, tarraconesi e africani, mentre dal Mediterraneo orientale provengono la Dressel 5 e la Camolodunum 184 (Hawkes e Hull 1947); tra i contenitori vinari a fondo piatto si registra invece la presenza dell'anfora (Ostia II, 523) con "ansa a fiorellino" e dell'anfora Gallica 4 (Laubenheimer 1985).

Dalle stratigrafie riferibili ad interventi di età traiana individuati nelle Aree A, C, e D provengono in totale 17 frammenti di vetro, tutti riferibili a produzioni soffiate a canna libera e realizzate in vetro verde-azzurro,

verde chiaro e incolore, in alcuni casi bianco latteo per deterioramento. Tra questi, solo una minima parte è identificabile e attribuibile, in particolare, a forme frequentemente attestate tra la seconda metà del I e il II secolo d.C., anche in area romano-ostiense (Lepri et Saguì 2018: fig. 4.): un esemplare di bicchiere Isings 1957 34 (Figura 1.6) e un'olla Isings 1957 67a (Figura 1.7), entrambi rinvenuti nell'area C (US 3130). Sono presenti, inoltre, alcune intrusioni dalle stratigrafie successive. Si tratta di un bicchiere AR 103 (Fünfschilling 2015: 379) e di una parete con decorazione a "filamenti serpentiformi" (US 2330), entrambe produzioni in vetro incolore di età antonina-severiana (Lepri 2021: 66 e 69, fig. 31.1.13; 102-11, figg. 56-60)[4] e dunque coevi all'attività della fornace da vetro rinvenuta nel cortile dell'area B[5]. Pertinenti allo stesso periodo, e più in generale alla media età imperiale, sono i due frammenti di lastre da finestra in vetro soffiato verde chiaro rinvenute nell'area C (US 3059)[6].

Infine, dallo stesso deposito sabbioso dell'area C appena citato (US 3130) provengono gli unici reperti marmorei rinvenuti nei depositi traianei: tessere musive, e frammenti di lastre di marmo bigio venato e di ardesia.

Nel loro complesso i materiali considerati, pur nella loro scarsità, costituiscono un insieme abbastanza omogeneo, fatta eccezione per infiltrazioni più tarde nei vetri, ben inquadrabile agli inizi del II secolo d.C., che, unito ai numerosi bolli laterizi rinvenuti (cf. infra), contribuisce alla datazione delle strutture del periodo 2.

Bibliografia

Atlante I – AA.VV., *Atlante delle forme ceramiche*, I: *Ceramica fine romana nel bacino mediterraneo (medio e tardo impero)*. Roma: Istituto della Enciclopedia italiana, 1981.

Atlante II – AA.VV., *Atlante delle forme ceramiche*, II: *Ceramica fine romana nel bacino mediterraneo (tardo ellenismo e primo impero)*. Roma: Istituto della Enciclopedia italiana, 1985.

Conspectus – AA.VV., *Conspectus formarum Terrae Sigillatae Italico modo confectae*. Bonn: Habelt, 1990.

Dragendorff, H. 1895. Terra sigillata. Ein Beitrag zur Geschichte der griechischen und römischen Keramik. *Bonner Jahrbücher* 96: 18-155.

Foy, D. e S. Fontaine 2008. Diversité et evolution du vitrage de l'Antiuquité et du haut Moyen Âge. Un état de la question. *Gallia* 65: 405-59.

Fünfschilling, S. 2015. *Die römischen Gläser aus Augst und Kaiseraugst: Kommentierter Formenkatalog und ausgewählte Neufunde 1981-2010 aus Augusta Raurica*, 2 vol. (Forschungen in Augst 51). Augst: Raurica.

Goudineau, C. 1970. Note sur la céramique à engobe interne rouge-pompéien ("Pompejanish-Roten Platten"). *Mélanges de l'école française de Rome* 82: 159-86.

Haltern – S. Loeschcke, Keramische Funde in Haltern. Ein Beitrag zur Geschichte der augusteischen Kultur in Deutschland. *Mitteeilungen der Altertums-Kommission für Westfalen* 5 (1909): 101-322

Hayes, J.W. 1972. *Late Roman Pottery*. London: British School at Rome.

Hawkes, C.F.C. e M.R. Hull 1947. *Camulodunum: First Report on the Excavation at Colchester 1930-1939*. Oxford: Oxford University Press.

Keay, S., G. Earl e F. Felici 2011. Excavation and survey at the Palazzo Imperiale 2007-2009, in S. Keay e L. Paroli (eds) *Portus and its Hinterlands*: 67-88. London: British School at Rome.

Keay, S., G. Earl, F. Felici, P. Copeland, R. Cascino, S. Kay e C. Triantafillou. 2012. Interim report on an enigmatic new Trajanic building at Portus. *Journal of Roman Archaeology* 25: 486-512.

Isings, C. 1957. *Roman Glass from Dated Finds*. Groningen: Wolters.

Laubenheimer, F. 1985. *La production des amphores en Gaule Narbonnaise*. Paris: Les Belles Lettres.

Lepri, B. 2013. Il vetro della media età imperiale nelle stratigrafie delle "Terme di Elagabalo", in C. Panella e L. Saguì (eds), *Valle del Colosseo e pendici nord-orientali del Palatino: Materiali e contesti*, II: 139-60. Roma: Scienze e lettere.

Lepri, B. 2021. *Il vetro tra II e III secolo d.C.: produzione e distribuzione in area romano-ostiense (Fecit te 15)*. Roma: Scienze e lettere.

Lepri, B. e L. Saguì 2018. Vetri e indicatori di produzione vetraria a Ostia e a Porto, *Mélanges de l'école française de Rome* 130.2: 399-409.

Marangou Lerat, A. 1985. *Le vin et les amphores de Crète de l'époque classique à l'époque impériale* (Études crétoise, 30). Atene: École française d'Athènes.

Mattiuzzo, V. 2014. Vetri, in S. Falzone e A. Pellegrino (eds), *Scavi di Ostia, XV: Insula delle Ierodule (c.d. casa di Lucceia Primitiva: III,IX,6)*: 320-24. Roma: Il cigno GG edizioni.

Ostia II – AAVV, *Ostia, II: Le Terme del Nuotatore: Scavo dell'ambiente I* (Studi miscellanei 16). Roma: De Luca, 1970

Pavolini, C. 1996. Ceramica comune da Ostia. Il commercio delle forme chiuse in ceramica comune, in AA.VV., *Les cèramiques communes de Campanie et de Narbonnaise (Ier s. av. J.-C. –I[e] ap. J.-C.): la vaisselle de cuisine et de table, actes des journées d'étude (Naples, 1994)* (Coll. CJB, 14). Napoli: Publications du Centre Jean Bérard.

Rizzo, G. 2003. *Instrumenta Urbis, I: Ceramiche fini da mensa, lucerne ed anfore a Roma nei primi due secoli dell'Impero*. Roma: Ecole française de Rome.

---

[4] Si tratta di forme e decorazioni caratteristiche di questi secoli in area romano-ostiense.

[5] La testimonianza portuense è ad oggi l'unica attestazione di forno da vetro di età imperiale dell'intera area romano ostiense, dalla quale tuttavia emergono sempre più numerosi indicatori di produzione vitrea databili tra il II e il III secolo d.C. (Lepri 2021: 26-27).

[6] I dati cronologici ad oggi disponibili sulle lastre da finestra soffiate non risultano anteriori alla fine del II secolo d.C. (Foy e Fontaine 2008: 430), come mostrano anche le attestazioni dell'area romano-ostiense. Si vedano, ad esempio, il contesto dell'area delle cd "Terme di Elagabalo" a Roma (Lepri 2013: 141) e quello dell'Insula delle Ierodule a Ostia (Mattiuzzo 2014: 321).

2. Le relazioni fra Ostia e Porto nella tarda antichità dopo le prospezioni dirette da Simon Keay sull'Isola Sacra

Carlo Pavolini

L'archeologia di *Portus* e dell'Isola Sacra ci si presenta oggi con un volto totalmente nuovo (Figura 2.1), dopo le ricerche eseguite con metodologie geofisiche (ma anche con i tradizionali sistemi della prospezione topografica e dello scavo stratigrafico) nel quadro del *Portus Project,* di cui Simon Keay è stato l'animatore e il promotore, oltre che il direttore scientifico. La nostra conoscenza di questo territorio ha compiuto così, in pochi anni, un balzo in avanti che ha compensato due secoli di difficoltà e di aporie delle moderne indagini sui bacini imperiali a Nord della foce tiberina (Meiggs 1973: 151-53), intralciate anche da ostacoli burocratici, quali l'esproprio di una sola parte del comprensorio dei porti (Gialdroni, in corso di stampa), che perdurano a tutt'oggi. In tale contesto il *Portus Project* - che è stato portato avanti da un'alleanza ampia e articolata di istituzioni scientifiche: le università di Southampton e di Cambridge, la British School at Rome e la Soprintendenza (poi Parco) di Ostia Antica, con la collaborazione di altri Enti e studiosi di varia nazionalità e specializzazione - ha prima coinvolto, nel 1998-2004, la zona dei porti propriamente detta, il che ha dato luogo a una serie di rilevanti pubblicazioni collettive, che qui non posso elencare (ma vedi Keay e Paroli 2011); poi, nel 2008-12, ha investito l'Isola Sacra. L'archeologia di quest'ultima era anch'essa nota in precedenza solo in modo approssimativo, se si escludono i settori finora riportati alla luce della celebre necropoli (che non era, peraltro, l'unica area cimiteriale dell'isola). Vedi Calza 1940; Baldassare *et al.* 2019; Keay *et al.* 2020, d'ora in avanti *Survey*: 157-59).

Il frutto di questa seconda fase del *Portus Project,* svolta essenzialmente con lo strumento della magnetometria, consiste in un volume di straordinario interesse scientifico e storico, il Survey, appunto, del quale Simon, facendomi un grande onore, mi chiese di scrivere la premessa. Naturalmente lo feci con piacere (cf. Pavolini in *Survey*: XI-XIX), non immaginando mai di dover riprendere oggi l'argomento per rendere omaggio alla memoria del caro amico scomparso, col quale tante volte (e per me sempre con grande profitto) avevamo discusso di questi temi.

Non dirò quindi niente di particolarmente nuovo rispetto ai contenuti del libro e della mia prefazione, ma mi sembra utile provare a sintetizzarne uno specifico aspetto, quello dell'evoluzione storica del territorio in esame nel periodo tardo antico.

Per arrivarvi, però, è necessario prima parlare di una delle acquisizioni più inattese e straordinarie del *survey* di "archeologia senza scavo" eseguito dall'*équipe* di Simon sull'Isola Sacra (tale da destare sensazione già all'atto della sua prima presentazione alla stampa, quindi ancora in forme divulgative e sintetiche, nell'aprile 2014). Fra questa prima "uscita pubblica" della notizia e la comparsa del *Survey* vi sono state alcune messe a punto preliminari (in sede scientifica si possono citare Germoni *et al.* 2019; Pavolini 2019): vi è stata, in particolare, l'individuazione di un'intensa urbanizzazione - costituita da una serie di magazzini e di altri edifici - che occupa il settore meridionale dell'isola, lungo la riva destra del Tevere (Figura 2.2). Si tratta di quattro complessi quasi certamente adibiti a stoccaggio (*Survey*: 167, Buildings 1-4: cf. *Survey*: fig. 6.6), di cui tre assimilabili alla tipologia dell'*horreum* a cortile centrale. Le scoperte in questione sono state, per ora, frutto della sola magnetometria (sulle tecniche non distruttive utilizzate per l'indagine v. *Survey*:25-31). Gli spazi nei quali insistevano i depositi e le altre strutture in questione corrispondono alle Aree 32 e 33 dei settori dell'Isola Sacra nei quali è stata suddivisa l'area da indagare (cfr. *Survey*: 101-14 e fig. 4.2). Si tratta degli spazi corrispondenti alla terraferma antica, oggi scarsamente edificati perché risparmiati quasi per intero, grazie ai vincoli archeologici e urbanistici, dall'abusivismo, che ha purtroppo devastato gran parte della rimanente Isola Sacra e del Comune di Fiumicino.

Un quinto fabbricato (Building 5) ha una differente configurazione: è un'ampia area quadrangolare recintata e suddivisa internamente da filari di pilastri, che potrebbe essere interpretata, ipoteticamente, come uno spazio adibito alla prima sistemazione delle mercanzie, dopo lo sbarco dall'attigua banchina fluviale e prima dell'immagazzinamento. Va detto che piccole porzioni degli Edifici 1 e 5 erano già state viste nel corso di alcuni sondaggi di limitata estensione, praticati da Fausto Zevi nel 1968 e descritti in relazioni di Zevi e di altri, edite negli anni immediatamente successivi (*Survey*: appendice, siti G41 e G44). Le tecniche edilizie riscontrate in tali saggi (muri in *opus reticulatum* e rocchi di colonne tufacee) sembrano compatibili con

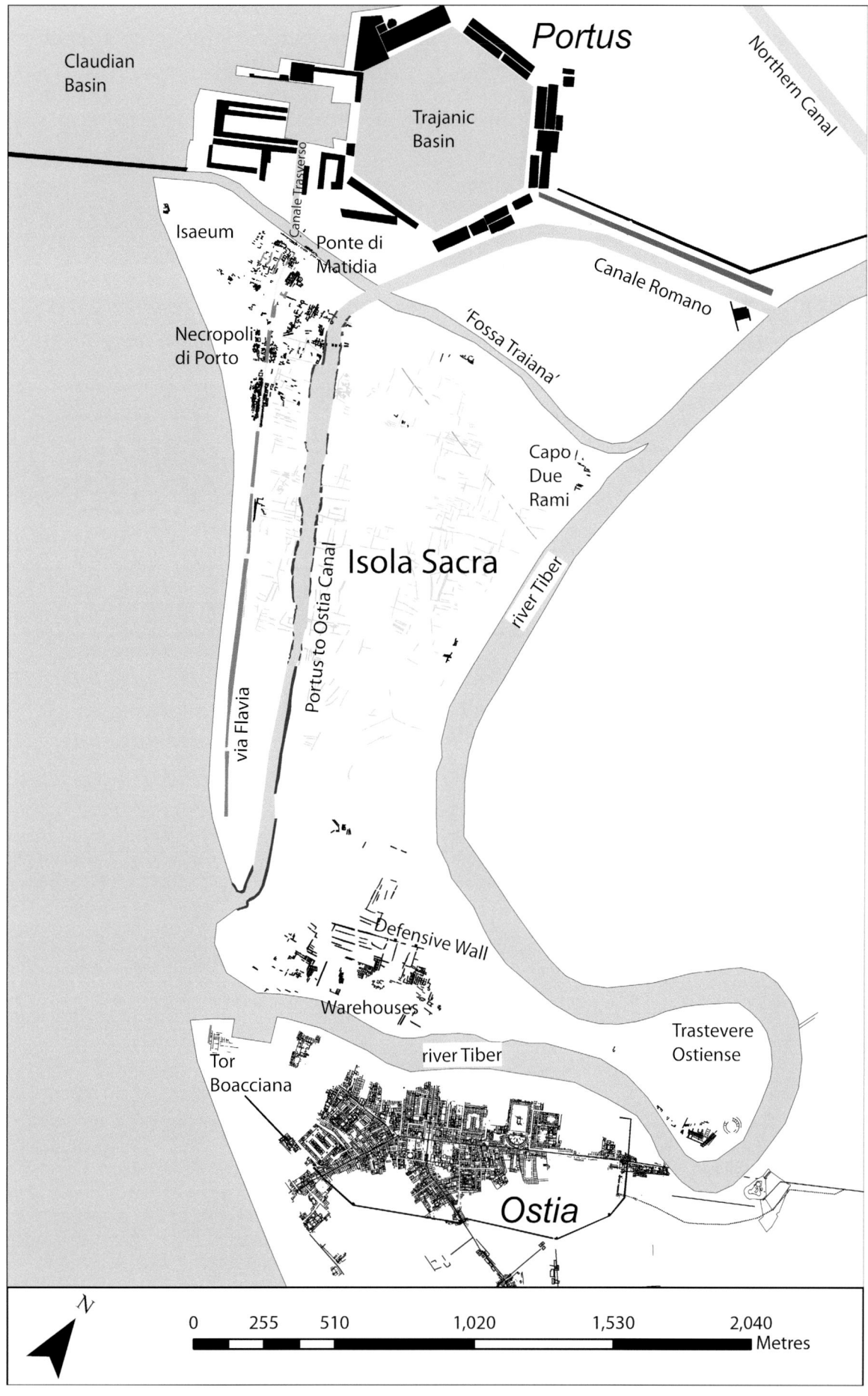

Figura 2.1. Pianta delle foci del Tevere, di *Portus*, dell'Isola Sacra e di Ostia (da *Survey*)

Figura 2.2. Pianta dei magazzini e degli altri edifici sulla sponda meridionale dell'Isola Sacra, nel "Trastevere ostiense"
(da *Survey*)

una datazione nell'ambito del I secolo d.C. Non è escluso (cf. Pavolini in *Survey*: XIX nota 21) che all'Edificio 5 appartengano anche i mosaici e i muri, ugualmente in opera reticolata, visti in scavi ancora precedenti (1959-60) effettuati a est dei limiti dell'attuale *survey* (*Survey*: appendice, siti G45-46)

Gli aspetti cronologici riguardanti questo distretto di *horrea* sono stati presi in esame, nei passi citati del *Survey*, anche sulla base di una serie di confronti con alcuni dei magazzini di maggiori dimensioni – soprattutto granari, e probabilmente pubblici e annonari – noti a Ostia, i quali peraltro presentano, in certi casi, più fasi edilizie scaglionate nel tempo. Si suppone comunque, in sintesi, che la costruzione dei depositi di quello che ormai possiamo chiamare a buon diritto il "Trastevere ostiense" sia cominciata nel corso del I secolo d.C.: ciò non esclude che l'occupazione edilizia della sponda meridionale dell'Isola Sacra abbia potuto svilupparsi in modo graduale, a partire dai fabbricati situati più a sud, appunto, cioè a diretto contatto col fiume, per poi estendersi verso nord - quindi verso l'interno dell'isola - in un periodo leggermente successivo.

Anche queste ultime sono semplici congetture, naturalmente, e ben si comprende come i curatori della prospezione - in assenza, per ora, di un consistente scavo

stratigrafico - difficilmente sarebbero potuti giungere a conclusioni più precise (*Survey*: 162). Tuttavia, a conforto delle ipotesi cronologiche che ho riportato militano anche alcune notizie precedenti, derivanti non solo dai citati saggi degli anni '50-'60, ma anche da altre e più estese indagini. Più a est, infatti, al di là della strozzatura dell'antico Fiume Morto, cioè in quella che in linguaggio corrente si può definire la "fiasca" del meandro poi interrato (su quel che segue cf. Pavolini 2019: 61-64, con descrizioni più dettagliate e con tutta la bibliografia relativa, peraltro accuratamente citata e discussa anche in *Survey*: 162-63), sono state scoperte negli anni 1990 una serie di strutture attribuibili a funzioni diverse (anche di stoccaggio). Ho cercato di riassumere tali notizie nel mio contributo del 2019 (v. in Pavolini 2019, la fig. 7 = Figura 2.3 del presente articolo): si tratta, nel loro insieme, di quelle realtà che avevano già motivato gli archeologi a parlare di un "Trastevere ostiense", come ho accennato. Gli scopritori avevano datato gli edifici rinvenuti nella "fiasca" generalmente nell'arco del I-II secolo d.C.

C'è, peraltro, anche la necessità di tenere conto del più ampio contesto storico nel quale questi dati di scavo (vecchi e nuovi) si inseriscono, e da tale punto di vista – almeno a mio avviso – la cosa più verosimile è che il grosso dell'urbanizzazione in esame sia da porre in

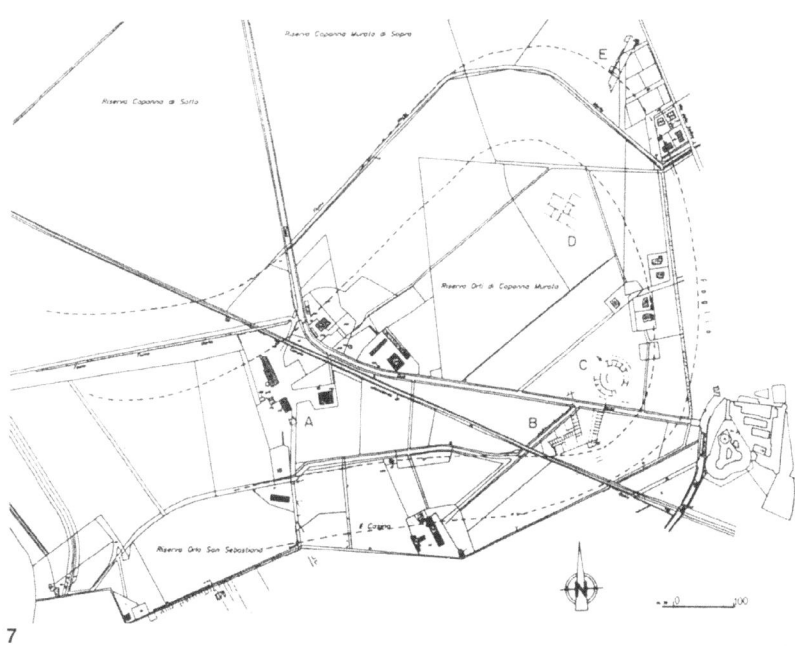

Figura 2.3. Pianta dei rinvenimenti archeologici all'interno del meandro del Tevere o Fiume Morto, nel "Trastevere ostiense" (da Pavolini 2019)

rapporto con la creazione del primo porto imperiale a nord della foce del Tevere, cioè del bacino di Claudio. Le iniziative edilizie di maggior peso individuate nel settore sud dell'Isola Sacra sarebbero state attuate dunque, in via d'ipotesi, all'incirca a partire dagli anni 50 del I secolo, o forse solo negli ultimi decenni di questo (senza essere precedute, si badi bene, da nessuna attività costruttiva di qualche rilievo che possa essere datata prima del tardo I secolo d.C., almeno allo stato dei fatti: è questo un punto molto importante, sul quale si trovano in *Survey* affermazioni chiare e motivate. Tale urbanizzazione si sarebbe poi sviluppata con maggiore ampiezza, esarebbe stata completata, nell'arco del II secolo. In altre parole – ed è anche la banale logica a suggerirlo – l'aumento della capacità di stoccaggio derivante dall'esistenza dei nuovi *horrea* sarebbe una diretta conseguenza delle opere promosse da Claudio e, ciò nonostante, le difficoltà e i difetti che, come si vide quasi subito, limitavano l'efficienza dello scalo da lui voluto. Anche a 'Ostia città', del resto, si ebbero analoghe e immediate ricadute della creazione del primo porto, ma sono tutte cose ben note e sulle quali, quindi, non mette conto di soffermarsi in questa sede.

Non mi sembra probabile, invece (ma è una perplessità che potrebbe tranquillamente essere smentita da futuri interventi di scavo, con le connesse - e più precise - datazioni su base ceramologica), che l'inizio della costruzione dei depositi "transtiberini" possa risalire già al 25-50 d.C. circa. È questa un'ipotesi - alternativa, in qualche modo, alle argomentazioni di cui sopra - che viene avanzata in *Survey* (cf. *Survey*: 162-63), ma in forma dubitativa e sulla base di considerazioni esterne, che non considerei dirimenti: da un lato la possibile datazione al 25-50 d.C. dei presunti *navalia* individuati a Ovest del 'Palazzo Imperiale' di Ostia (Heinzelmann e Martin 2002), dall'altro le analogie tipologiche (alle quali ho già accennato) che accomunano i nostri *horrea* ad alcuni complessi ostiensi, in particolare ai Grandi Horrea, la cui fase d'impianto è stata ora attribuita al primo quarto del I secolo d.C. (Boetto *et al.* 2016).

Comunque sia, è evidente che i risultati del *Survey* dell'Isola Sacra impongono già oggi (e ancor più imporranno in futuro, se verificati e integrati da dati di scavo) di cambiare il nostro modo di vedere Ostia. Bisognerà, cioè, immaginare la colonia non più come un insediamento ampio, sì, ma sostanzialmente racchiuso quasi per intero entro la cerchia delle mura tardo-repubblicane (come finora si credeva), bensì come una conurbazione estesa di qua e di là dal fiume, le cui sponde dobbiamo pensare occupate da una serie forse continua di banchine, di *docks* e di strutture d'immagazzinamento, in gran parte asportate sulla riva sinistra a causa del cambiamento moderno del corso del Tevere, come tutti sappiamo. Ed è altrettanto chiaro che questo ci costringerà a rivedere radicalmente le "idee ricevute" - e finora giustificate dalle informazioni che avevamo a disposizione - non solo circa la consistenza demografica della colonia, ma anche circa le sue relazioni con Porto e con Roma stessa (alcuni cenni nello stesso senso, e con lo stesso carattere di considerazioni del tutto preliminari e congetturali, si trovano in Pavolini 2022: 49-50).

Tutto questo però, come ho accennato all'inizio, non è altro che una sorta di antefatto. In realtà, lo scopo del presente contributo era – fin dal titolo – un altro, cioè il tentativo di mettere in luce come gli esiti delle prospezioni magnetometriche nel settore meridionale dell'Isola Sacra comportino alcune conseguenze per la nostra comprensione della storia di Ostia (e di Portus) non solo nella prima e media età imperiale, di cui finora s'è detto, ma anche nella tarda antichità.

Bisogna partire da un altro dato eclatante, rivelato sempre dall'indagine geofisica: è l'esistenza (v. Figura 3.1, "defensive wall") di un poderoso muro con andamento est-ovest (Survey: 160-65 e passim; Pavolini in Survey: XVI-XVII), che, benché visto in misura solo parziale, a buon diritto si ritiene sia stato costruito per difendere il quartiere dei depositi sopra descritto, ai cui orientamenti murari sembra uniformarsi.

Non sappiamo se - come apparirebbe logico dal punto di vista "militare" - la fortificazione si chiudesse ad est in corrispondenza della strozzatura del meandro, mentre è certo che alla terminazione ovest essa svoltava verso sud, in direzione della parete settentrionale del magazzino definito Building 1 (supra). Pur con tutte le cautele del caso, gli autori del Survey propendono per un rapporto di posteriorità del muro di difesa rispetto a quello dell'horreum (ma solo uno scavo potrà darci la soluzione del problema), e in tal caso il secondo sarebbe stato incorporato nel circuito difensivo, aumentandone l'efficienza.

Le caratteristiche fisiche della cinta assumono, in questo quadro, un'importanza fondamentale. Nel Survey (si esclude in modo deciso che essa possa costituire una prosecuzione, oltre il Tevere, della fortificazione tardo-repubblicana di Ostia, ora datata da Fausto Zevi - com'è noto - all'epoca del consolato di Cicerone. Sono infatti molto diversi, nelle due opere, i dati dimensionali e quelli riguardanti le torri: le restituzioni magnetometriche indicano, per la struttura dell'Isola Sacra, una larghezza di c. 3-5m. e la presenza di torri esterne quadrangolari, con lati dic. 6 × 8m., mentre la cinta muraria di Ostia - pur scarsamente conservata - ha uno spessore di c. 2,5m, e le sue torri (in numero minore rispetto a quelle dell'Isola Sacra) sono circolari e costruite in corrispondenza degli angoli interni.

Tali elementi strutturali sembrano segnalare piuttosto, per il muro che cinge il quartiere dei depositi del "Trastevere", forti somiglianze con un settore delle

tarde o tardissime opere di difesa della città di Portus. Si tratta (Survey: 163-65) della cd. Contromura Interna, che presenta torri quadrangolari rivolte all'esterno e misuranti c. 7 × 8m. per lato: quindi, una tipologia e delle dimensioni pressoché identiche a quelle rilevate nella ricognizione dell'Isola Sacra. A loro volta, la Contromura fa parte del più ampio circuito difensivo di Porto, il quale, sulla base dei dati stratigrafici oggi disponibili, andrebbe datato in un'epoca molto più recente rispetto alle cronologie adottate in precedenza: un tempo, infatti, queste mura erano dette "costantiniane", mentre risalirebbero invece al 470-80 circa e potrebbero essere attribuite, in via d'ipotesi, all'iniziativa di un prefetto urbano di Odoacre (Paroli e Ricci in Keay e Paroli 2011: 143-44 e passim).

In tale quadro, si può pensare che il distretto dei magazzini sul lato destro del Tevere - che in quel periodo non poteva sicuramente più essere di grande utilità per una Ostia in pieno declino - sia stato fortificato come una sorta di annesso commerciale della città di Porto, nella quale i traffici erano invece ancora fiorenti e da cui l'Isola Sacra, com'è probabile, dipendeva ormai a pieno titolo anche dal punto di vista amministrativo (così come, nei fatti, a Portus era sempre stata strettamente legata sul piano produttivo, e anche per ciò che riguarda la topografia funeraria). Non è un caso che, al contrario, Ostia non sia stata più fortificata dopo la tarda Repubblica, a parte qualche limitato restauro alle vecchie mura: né certo venne presa in considerazione - a questo fine - da Aureliano, e tanto meno dai regnanti che gli succedettero.

Sono discorsi che hanno implicazioni storiche di rilievo, com'è evidente, e tali da non poter essere riprese e sviluppate qui. Mi fa piacere, tuttavia, che Simon e gli altri curatori delle prospezioni abbiano trovato interessanti (Survey: 165) le considerazioni che a tale proposito avevo svolto in un altro contributo recente e già menzionato (Pavolini 2019, v. in particolare 64-71).

Bibliografia

Baldassarre, I., I. Bragantini, A.M. Dolciotti, C. Morselli e F. Taglietti 2019. Necropoli dell'Isola Sacra. Le ricerche 1968-1989. Ripercorrendo un'esperienza, in M. Cébeillac-Gervasoni, N. Laubry e F. Zevi (eds) Ricerche su Ostia e il suo territorio: 53-66. Roma: École française de Rome.

Boetto, G., É. Bukowiecki, N. Monteix e C. Rousse 2016. Les Grandi Horrea d'Ostie, in B. Marin e C. Virlouvet (eds) Entrepôts et trafics annonaires en Méditerranée: 177-226. Roma: École française de Rome.

Calza, G. 1940. La necropoli del Porto di Roma nell'Isola Sacra. Roma: Libreria dello stato.

Germoni, P., S. Keay, M. Millett e K. Strutt 2019. Ostia beyond the Tiber. Recent archaeological discoveries in the Isola Sacra, in M. Cébeillac-Gervasoni, *N. Laubry e F. Zevi. Segue (eds) Ricerche su Ostia e il suo territorio*: 149-68. Roma: École française de Rome.

Gialdroni, S. In corso di stampa. *L'esproprio del bacino esagonale del Porto di Traiano: proprietà privata, utilità pubblica e lo strano caso dello zoo safari.*

Heinzelmann, M. e A. Martin 2002. River port, navalia and harbour temple at Ostia: new results of the DAI-AAR project. *Journal of Roman Archaeology* 15: 5-19.

Keay, S. e L. Paroli 2011. *Portus and its Hinterland: Recent Archaeological Research.* London: The British School at Rome.

Meiggs, R. 1973. *Roman Ostia*, 2nd ed. Oxford: Clarendon Press.

Pavolini, C. 2019. Per un'archeologia del meandro ostiense o Fiume Morto, in P.O. Rossi e O. Carpenzano (eds) *Roma tra il fiume il bosco e il mare*: 58-75. Macerata: Quodlibet.

Pavolini, C. 2022. *Ostia Antica*. Roma: Carocci Editore.

Survey = Keay, S., M. Millet, K. Strutt e P. Germoni (eds) 2020. *The Isola Sacra Survey: Ostia, Portus and the Port System of Imperial Rome*. Cambridge: MacDonald Institute.

3. Investigaciones en el muelle este-oeste de *Portus*, resultados e interpretaciones

Javier Bermejo Meléndez, Juan M. Campos Carrasco, Renato Sebastiani

1. El proyecto sobre el muelle este-oeste

Desde el año 2017 hasta la actualidad, la Universidad de Huelva conjuntamente con el Parco archeologico di Ostia Antica, viene desarrollando un proyecto de investigación en el muelle este-oeste de *Portus* (Figura 3.1). A lo largo de estos últimos años, con distintas campañas de estudio, se ha podido establecer una primera aproximación arqueoarquitectónica y diacronía de la última parte del muelle incluida su cabeza o puntal; el establecimiento de un proceso evolutivo con los diferentes episodios constructivos que acontecieron en esta infraestructura desde su momento fundacional, hasta su definitivo abandono y amortización (Bermejo *et al.* 2021 a b y c; 2023 a, b y c a y b; Muñiz *et al.* 2021; Marín *et al.* 2021).

Figura 3.1. Ubicación del muelle este-oeste en Portus.

Precisamente, los datos geoarqueológicos resultantes, algunos de ellos aún en proceso de estudio, nos hablan de una infraestructura portuaria extremadamente dinámica en su configuración, con diversas fases que se sucedieron desde la primera mitad del siglo III d. C. hasta inicios del VI d. C. al menos en sus últimos 30 m de desarrollo.

A lo largo de las sucesivas campañas arqueológicas efectuadas en el muelle este-oeste, se han desarrollado diversos sondeos en su lado norte, oeste, sur y zona superior de la cabeza del muelle. Así pues, entre el otoño de 2017 y el verano de 2018, se intervinieron los sectores norte y oeste del citado muelle, en dos campañas de intervención que se centraron en la limpieza, desbroce y excavación de los niveles deposicionales inmediatos al cantil de la cabeza de la estructura mediante dos sondeos. Los restos arqueológicos y datos obtenidos se vieron complementados significativamente con las campañas realizadas en 2019, 2020 y 2021. Estas campañas, caracterizadas por la excavación de la zona superior de la cabeza y la limpieza del área sur del muelle, estuvieron planteadas desde un principio no sólo con el análisis estructural del muelle mediante fotogrametría laser combinada, sino con la realización de diversos sondeos arqueológicos, prospección geofísica y la realización de sondeos rotatorios en diversos puntos del muelle y de su área más inmediata (Figura 3.2).

La síntesis de los trabajos desarrollados a lo largo de estos años queda recogida de la siguiente forma (Figura 3.3):

Sondeo I

Este sector de excavación quedó ubicado al norte de la cabeza del muelle, con una superficie de 24 m², sus resultados han permitido establecer interesantes secuencias relativas a los últimos momentos de vida de la estructura (Figura 3.3). Desde un punto de vista estratigráfico, la aportación más destacada que aportó este sondeo viene representada por la documentación de un nivel generalizado de colmatación de la antigua línea mareal. En este nivel comenzaron a aparecer numerosos fragmentos de materiales arquitectónicos-decorativos, fundamentalmente columnas con distintas medidas, fracturas y en diversos tipos de mármol. Estos restos han sido interpretados como pertenecientes a las construcciones que se ubicaron en la parte superior, esto es, en la superficie de la cabeza del muelle. Dichos derrumbes y materiales arquitectónicos habían caído directamente sobre un nivel marino en regresión, un periodo que geomorfológicamente viene representado por una progresiva colmatación de las dársenas y canales del puerto que empezó en época tardía (Gorian *et al.* 2010). Bajo este nivel de colmatación que cubría toda el área, se constató otro en el que apoyaban todos los derrumbes y columnas anteriormente mencionados. En el ángulo oriental del sondeo, una de las áreas más interesantes desde el punto de vista arqueológico, se pudo recuperar un significativo conjunto de materiales cerámicos. Este repertorio venía representado por ánforas LRA1 (ML18/SI/1015, 3, 5, 12 y 14), LRA2 (ML18/SI/1015, 4) (Peacock y Williams 1986; Bonifay y Villedieu 1989; Bonifay y Piéri 1995) aunque también se han constatado otras como un ejemplar de Keay 36-A (ML18/SI/1015,11), Almagro 51c (ML18/SI/1015,8, 9, 10) (Keay 1984), así como producciones de ARSW D en las formas 61B, 78, 94b, 101 de Hayes (ML18/SI/1015/13), fechando estos niveles de amortización y abandono en una fecha posterior al 430/440 d.C. (Figura 3.4).

Sondeo II

Por cuanto respecta al sondeo II, ubicado en la parte occidental de la cabeza (Figura 3.3) su principal aportación para comprender la estructura en particular

Figura 3.1. Ubicación del muelle este-oeste en Portus.

y de *Portus* en general, vino de la mano de los datos de carácter geoarqueológico.

Tras la retirada de los primeros niveles superficiales, con materiales cerámicos de época romana, plásticos y vidrios del periodo contemporáneo, comenzó a documentarse un nivel por toda el área en el que se constataron los primeros derrumbes de las paredes de la cabeza del muelle, así como, de las estructuras de la parte superior de éste. Este nivel es similar al aparecido en el sondeo I y se correspondería con los últimos momentos de vida de la estructura. Debido al surgimiento del nivel freático, a una cota de - 1 m.s.n.m., no se pudo profundizar en la cimentación de ésta. Al sur del sondeo se identificó una unidad que ha resultado de especial interés para la investigación del área. Ésta se corresponde con los restos de *caementa* de uno de los vertidos que conformaron los últimos niveles de la cimentación del muelle. Este vertido presentaba un ribete o saliente que permitió sellar los sedimentos sobre los que se asentó la construcción de la estructura. Estos niveles venían representados por una importante y numerosa presencia de fauna marina, principalmente *cerastoderma* y crustáceos decápodos; una importante colonia encontrada en posición de vida,

tal y como atestiguan sus restos. Ello resulta de especial interés ya que nos transmite un momento y ambiente determinados para la construcción de este muelle, definidos como un espacio de marisma o laguna de escasa profundidad. En este sentido la especie *cerastoderma* es típica de ambientes lacustres y de marismas (lagoons eurihalinos e euritermales), y desarrolla su ciclo vital en ámbitos poco profundos, en substratos fangosos y zonas intermareales dado que soporta condiciones aéreas y subaéreas, esto es intermareales. Si aplicamos estos datos al paleoambiente, podemos considerar que el muelle fue construido en un ambiente palustre, de marismas, de escasa profundidad.

Sondeo III

Conjuntamente con los anteriores, se desarrolló un amplio sondeo a los pies del muelle, en su vertiente norte, con la intención de profundizar en el registro y obtener datos sobre su sistema de cimentación, profundidad de éste, etc. (Figura 3.3). Dicho sondeo alcanzó una profundidad de -3,00 m sobre la rasante actual y permitió poner al descubierto algunos de los elementos que formaban parte del sistema constructivo del muelle.

Frontal Oeste *(testata)*

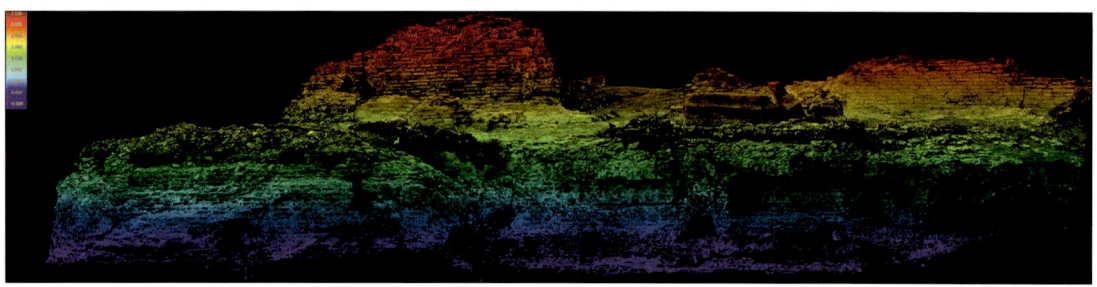

Frontal Norte *(testata)*

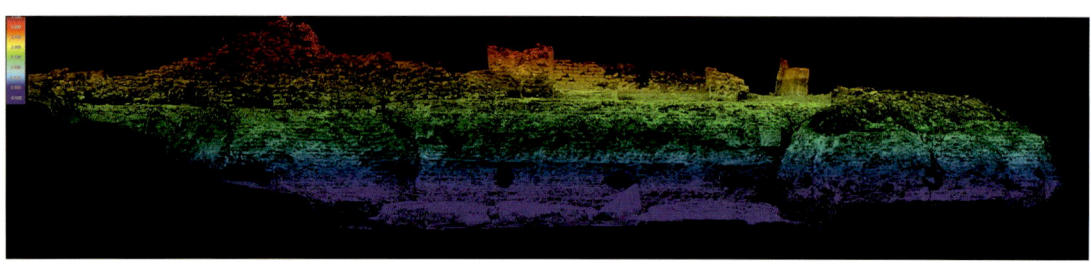

Frontal Norte

Figura 3.2. Fotogrametría de la cabeza del muelle.

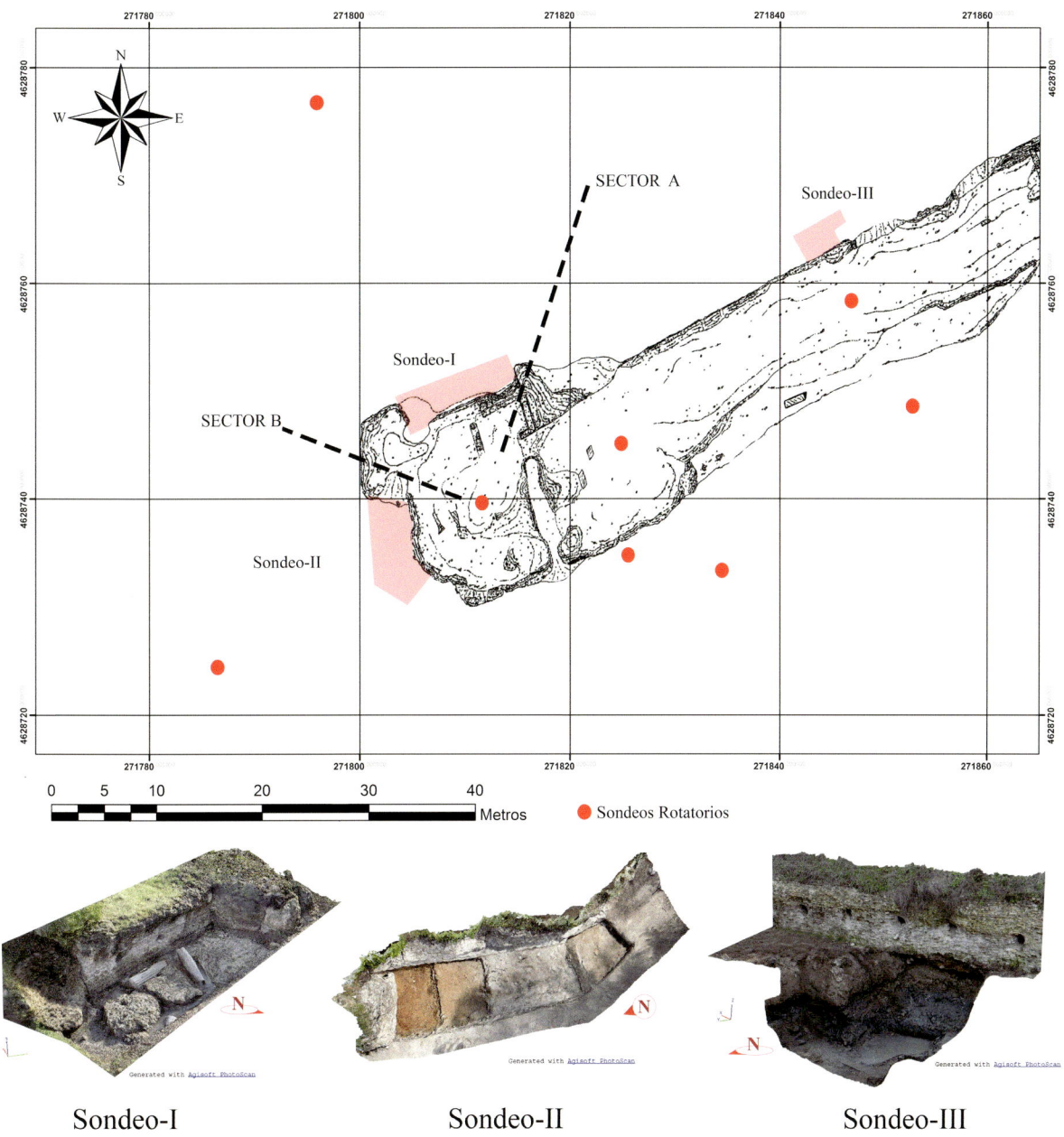

Figura 3.3. Indicación de los sectores de excavación y sondeos rotatorios realizadas en el muelle este-oeste.

A una profundidad de un metro se documentó una potente estructura horizontalizada de manera general por toda el área, adosada a los pies del muelle; dicha estructura se disponía a modo de plataforma conformada por piedras de tufo de tamaño heterométrico, la cual presentaba la característica carbonización realizada durante el proceso de construcción para facilitar su compactación. Bajo esta plataforma de piedras se documentó un potente nivel de material cerámico, conformado en su mayor parte por restos de elementos de transporte, paredes, cuellos y bordes, con una funcionalidad de drenaje. Este depósito actuaba a modo de vertido, y se

disponía conjuntamente con un importante sistema de cimentación a base de pilotes de madera hincados en el sustrato turboso del antiguo lecho. Desde el punto de vista constructivo, los pilotes presentaban una longitud de en torno a los 3 m, trabajado en uno de sus extremos en punta y combustionada para dotarla de mayor resistencia en el proceso de hincado. Los análisis de las numerosas muestras de madera obtenidas de estos pilotes revelan su adscripción a especies de tipo coníferas (*pinus*) y frondosas (*quercus*), con una edad de en torno a los cincuenta años. Este nivel de depósito cerámico se hallaba rellenando un potente encofrado de

Figura 3.4. Material cerámico recuperado en el sondeo I.

madera, esto es, el sistema de tablas que conformaron el armazón para la construcción de la cimentación del muelle.

Sondeos en la superficie del muelle

Del mismo modo se intervino sobre la superficie del propio muelle. Con esta idea se establecieron varios sondeos con un mismo objetivo, el de obtener información relativa al proceso de construcción de la cabeza del muelle, así como un primer acercamiento a las estructuras ubicadas en la zona superior y su posible articulación interna. Los resultados que dichos sondeos ofrecieron permiten establecer importantes consideraciones de manera preliminar. En resumen, descubrieron una sucesión de estructuras de diversa consideración, asociadas a las distintas etapas y fases de vida del muelle y especialmente, de la cabeza de éste (Figura 3.5).

De tal forma, los datos de excavación llevan a considerar que, en un primer momento de vida y uso de la estructura, la cabeza del muelle estuvo definida por un programa arquitectónico monumental, como testimonia la existencia de un muro perimetral que circunda toda la cabeza del muelle, del cual solo se conserva su cimentación. La aparición de un elevado

número de teselas bícromas asociadas a diversas unidades correspondientes a esta fase, permiten plantear la existencia de algún tipo de pavimentación musivaria, totalmente amortizada y perdida. Muy posiblemente el conjunto de derrumbes con columnas marmóreas documentadas a los pies de la cabeza en su lado norte, formasen parte de dicho programa arquitectónico monumental de esta fase.

Tras aquella fase, se documenta otro momento definido por la construcción de un ambiente de almacenamiento sobre la cabeza, amortizando las construcciones de la fase precedente. Ahora el espacio queda definido por un edificio de 78m² dividido en dos crujías, cuyos paramentos presentan un núcleo interior de argamasa encintado en sus caras externas mediante ladrillos fracturados en sentido horizontal. No sabemos cómo se arbitró su cierre septentrional, pues ninguna estructura se conserva por este extremo, lo que nos lleva a pensar que o bien fue un espacio diáfano abierto, o una infraestructura cerrada por una puerta corredera. Esta reforma parece desarrollarse en momentos de la primera mitad o mediados del s. V d.C., como revelan los restos monumentales caídos al lecho de la dársena a los pies de la cabeza y que se correspondían con la construcción de la primera fase. Posteriormente, este espacio parece sufrir una nueva

Figura 3.5. Vista área de las estructuras sobre la superficie del muelle.

reforma, compartimentación y recrecimiento del nivel de uso, fechados en algún momento de mediados del V y la segunda mitad del siglo VI d.C. por el material documentado en la cimentación de los pilares de las compartimentaciones, representado por cerámicas ARSW en sus Forma 61A, B y 103B (Figura 3.5-I). A este momento parece corresponderse la dotación de una segunda planta para dicho edificio, como se aprecia por los restos de escaleras documentadas.

El estudio de las relaciones estratigráficas y constructivas reveló un nuevo episodio de reformas posterior a la compartimentación del espacio anteriormente descrito. Este episodio, identificado como una nueva fase, supuso una transformación considerable de la morfología de la cabeza del muelle. Desconocemos su momento de construcción, aunque parece ser posterior a la construcción de la infraestructura anterior, pues la primera solución arquitectónica que hubo que tomar, ante la falta de espacio sobre la cabeza del muelle, fue arbitrar una nueva plataforma, adosada a la construcción inicial de éste para sustentar las nuevas infraestructuras. Se trata de un edificio de gran consistencia, pues la anchura de sus muros alcanza 1,20m, con al menos 13m² (Figura 3.5-II, III). Un programa constructivo bastante homogéneo, donde se empleó un *opus testaceum* bastante regularizado trabado con argamasa. No descartamos, dada su magnitud, que fuera una infraestructura elevada en altura con el fin de resaltar sobre las demás, ideada como faro o baliza tras la ruina de la primera infraestructura de señalización.

Desde el punto de vista cronológico, la falta de evidencias materiales impide que podamos datar las diversas reformas que experimentó esta infraestructura, aunque el análisis de su edilicia permite determinar que fueron al menos dos. La primera de ellas supuso una reducción considerable de su perímetro inicial, al verse constreñida por sus extremos oriental y meridional. La edilicia desplegada en este segundo programa se caracteriza por el empleo de un núcleo en el que además de material latericio y argamasa, morfológicamente diferente a la primera, se emplearon diversos materiales reutilizados. Igualmente, estas segundas construcciones aparecen adosadas a las anteriores, y no trabadas como sería lo normal. La segunda reforma la representan las estructuras murarias de muy pobre construcción, con las cuales se llevó a cabo una reestructuración interior de su planta, de la que nada más podemos inferir.

Finalmente, un último momento parece venir de la mano de una nueva ampliación, una segunda plataforma adosada a la anterior, sobre la que se construyó una nueva infraestructura portuaria (Figura 3.5-V, VI). De ella sólo se conserva parte de su perímetro occidental y meridional, pues el resto de la edificación, así como el añadido, se encontraba prácticamente arruinada en el momento de su intervención. Su factura es bastante irregular debido al empleo de materiales reutilizados, de hecho, entre los restos constatados se documentan ladrillos, piedras, restos de tufo y mármol.

Prospecciones geofísicas

Juntamente con la excavación del muelle se han desarrollado diversas actividades de prospección geofísica en las inmediaciones de éste con la intención de evaluar la potencialidad arqueológica del área circundante, así como corroborar la existencia de estructuras de cimentación en sus márgenes. Desde este punto de vista se han plantado varios sectores de prospección mediante georradar (GPR) y tomografía eléctrica vertical que han revelado la existencia de diversos restos soterrados. Lo más significativo viene de la mano de la documentación de diversas anomalías que flanquean el sector norte del muelle asociadas probablemente a los armazones y relleno de los encofrados detectados igualmente mediante la excavación. Junto con estas anomalías se detectó un conjunto de alineaciones correspondientes al vallado que rodeaba el muelle durante el uso del área arqueológica como zoo-safari en la década de 1970 y 1980, de lo que se documentó los últimos niveles de uso contemporáneo.

Sondeos rotatorios

Con la intención de implementar los datos obtenidos en el proceso de excavación se planteó la necesidad de realizar diversos sondeos rotatorios, un total de ocho, en las inmediaciones del muelle y sobre éste. El objetivo principal de esta actividad de sondeo pasaba por obtener un conjunto de datos a escala microespacial que permitiera obtener información añadida específica sobre la estructura y su espacio más inmediato. Los resultados preliminares de los datos obtenidos en los distintos testigos permiten una nueva visión del denominado muelle de la linterna, así pues, tres de los sondeos se realizaron sobre su superficie con el objetivo de comprobar la profundidad de la estructura y su cimentación. De la lectura de las tres columnas obtenidas en estos sondeos, estratégicamente ubicados uno en la cabeza y otros dos en el cuerpo del muelle, se ha podido comprobar la utilización de diversos tipos de *caementa*, vertidos con particularidades diferenciadas que permiten entrever diversos procesos constructivos. Asimismo, la profundidad de cada uno reveló, por primera vez en el conocimiento de los muelles de *Portus*, una densidad distinta para la estructura, siendo

de en torno a unos 5,50 m en la parte de la cabeza y de unos 6,50 m y 9 m en la zona del cuerpo[1]. La diferencia en la distinta profundidad alcanzada en la cimentación, permite plantear una hipótesis de trabajo que pasa por considerar distintas fases constructivas en la configuración del muelle, al menos referida para la parte del cuerpo y su cabeza o puntal.

2. El muelle, fases y datación

Con los datos obtenidos a través de las actuaciones anteriormente enumeradas, se ha podido establecer una serie de fases edilicias que permiten reconstruir la vida del muelle al menos en sus últimos metros de desarrollo.

En este sentido, la primera de todas estas fases se corresponde con el momento de construcción del propio muelle, al menos para los últimos 30 metros, gracias a las excavaciones realizadas en su cimentación y los sondeos rotatorios realizados en su superficie los cuales han permitido conocer la potencia constructiva del mismo.

Los resultados obtenidos nos han llevado a plantear un interesante debate cronológico que sólo futuras campañas podrán dilucidar. Por un lado, se plantea la posibilidad de que nos encontremos ante un muelle de cronología plenamente tardía; o en su defecto, lo que nos parece más factible, que se trate de una dársena donde el paulatino proceso de colmatación obligara a tener que ir planificando periódicas ampliaciones del muelle a medida que se producía la colmatación de la rada portuaria.

Desde el punto de vista constructivo, se puede establecer el empleo de un sistema arquitectónico plenamente conocido gracias a las descripciones que ya en su momento hizo el propio Vitruvio (V, 13). Para la construcción, se preparó una amplia zanja con una profundidad variable desde sus márgenes hacia el centro hasta alcanzar los 7 m aproximadamente de profundidad, cota conocida gracias a los testigos rotatorios extraídos desde la superficie del muelle. Esta imponente zanja serviría para preparar la cimentación del muelle. Así pues, los márgenes de esta se prepararon con un doble encofrado de madera. Éstos servirían para asentar la construcción desde afuera hacía adentro al configurarse como plataformas en la propia obra desde la que verter los distintos niveles de *caementa* que conformaron la cimentación. El espacio interior de los encofrados pasó a apuntalarse mediante pilotes de madera hincados en el sustrato de turba del antiguo lecho, con una longitud aproximada de 3 m y la punta endurecida mediante su combustión. Seguidamente,

---

[1] En estas medidas se incluye la parte aérea del muelle, unos dos metros de potencia que quedaban en la parte supramareal.

este armazón sería rellenado por un potente vertido de material cerámico de desecho, con una importante presencia de materiales de transporte, así como fino de mesa que otorgó una clara funcionalidad drenante a la cimentación del encofrado. Finalmente, sobre éste se dispuso otro vertido conformado a base de material pétreo heterométrico que sellaba toda el área y ofrecía una plataforma regularizada (Figura 3.6).

El material cerámico recuperado conforma un elenco de numerosos envases de transporte representados por los tipos Keay VI, VII.3, LII, XXIV, así como vajilla fina africana tipos C y D en las formas 27, 50, 182 de Hayes, y cerámica común de cocina en sus formas 196A y 197 de Hayes; en síntesis, un elenco que nos remite a una cronología de la primera mitad del s III d.C. en adelante (Figura 3.7). Debemos indicar que el repertorio cerámico recuperado se encontró en niveles sellados bajo la plataforma lo que permite ofrecer una construcción – al menos para la última parte o sector del muelle este –oeste de portus-, de momentos severianos o inmediatamente posteriores, una importante novedad en la configuración de las estructuras de *Portus*. Conjuntamente, el estudio paleobotánico de las muestras de maderas extraídas del encofrado confirma el empleo de especies como *pinus* y *quercus* con edades que oscilan en torno a los cincuenta años. Las dataciones de C14 de cuatro muestras de madera obtenidas de distintas partes del encofrado han ofrecido una datación absoluta calibrada que oscilan entre el 213-361, el 76-232, el 116-239 y 118-244, compartiendo todas las muestras el rango correspondiente al periodo de entre el 213-244, dentro de la primera mitad del s. III d.C. Una vez afianzado este nivel de encofrado con sus vertidos se pudo usar su firme a modo de plataforma de servicio desde la que poder iniciar la construcción propiamente dicha de la cimentación del muelle. Desde ésta, se verterían los distintos niveles de *caementa,* hasta alcanzar la cota rasante con esta plataforma y a partir de ahí configurar la parte vista o línea supramareal.

El sistema constructivo seguido para la parte superior del muelle sería a base de sistemas de encofrados, cuyas improntas quedan aún visibles en las negativas del sistema de *catenae*. Finalmente, una vez retirado el encofrado se procedió a su revestimiento en *opus testaceum* combinando el *opus reticulatum* en diversos puntos o ángulos de la cabeza del muelle.

Tras el proceso de construcción de este último cuerpo del muelle, la secuencia evolutiva de éste ha podido documentarse en las distintas reformas documentadas en su parte superior y más concretamente en la zona de su cabeza. Las diferentes intervenciones arqueológicas desarrolladas hasta la fecha (Bermejo *et al.* 2021 a y b) han permitido corroborar que en el aparejo empleado en su construcción existen diferencias con respecto al cuerpo del muelle que, junto con varias particularidades en la unión de ambas partes, llevan a pensar en la posibilidad de distintos momentos constructivos. Esta idea se sustenta en varios aspectos. En primer lugar, la potencia constructiva del muelle en su cabeza es sensiblemente inferior que, en su cuerpo, siendo 5,50 m en la primera frente a los 9 m del segundo. En efecto, los sondeos rotatorios realizados sobre su superficie en distintos puntos de la estructura revelan cimentaciones ha distinta profundidad. Este detalle resulta muy significativo, ya que de haberse realizado en un único momento no se entendería esta diferencia en su potencia constructiva, y más aún cuando se supone que sobre la cabeza se desarrolló un programa arquitectónico de cierto tamaño. Este dato, unido a una disposición y tamaños totalmente diferente para los troncos que conformaron las *catenae* del encofrado, revelan particularidades constructivas que bien podrían deberse a momentos constructivos sucesivos. Finalmente, en el desarrollo final del cuerpo del muelle se aprecia la unión entre éste y la cabeza, esto es, una relación constructiva que revela un adosamiento o añadido posterior. Como vemos, existen una serie de datos constructivos que apuntan la posibilidad de un muelle al cual en un momento posterior se le añade una cabeza o puntal con mayor anchura.

Estos detalles permiten individualizar, por tanto, una segunda fase constructiva representada por el adosamiento o construcción inmediata al final del cuerpo del muelle de una cabeza o puntal poligonal con una superficie de 290 m² aproximadamente. Quizás, el elemento arquitectónico más destacado de ésta fue el arbitrado en la solución de esquina, en el ángulo de unión entre ésta y el muelle, pues se optó por plantear un sistema de arcos de descarga en ladrillo. Probablemente, este sistema bien pudo concebirse con el fin de repartir las presiones y empujes de las estructuras que se desarrollaron en altura sobre la cabeza de este muelle. En efecto su superficie fue acondicionada para erigir una importante construcción cuyos restos se encontraban, casi en su totalidad totalmente arrasados bajo construcciones de fases posteriores. Pese a ello, los restos de su cimentación, que aún eran visibles en el momento de la excavación, permiten teorizar sobre la existencia de una construcción de enorme tamaño, con muros de sustentación en *opus testaceum* de 0,90 m de ancho, muy posiblemente ornamentadas mediante columnas de mármol. Este dato viene precisado por los restos caídos a los pies de la cabeza en su lado septentrional, pertenecientes a columnas marmóreas, así como restos de *opera musivaria,* que cayeron a plomo en el lecho de la dársena junto con parte de los muros y revestimientos del muelle.

En lo que concierne a la cronología de esta fase, nada sabemos sobre su momento de construcción, aunque obviamente se erigió en un momento posterior al desarrollo de la última parte del muelle, con una cronología por tanto posterior a mediados del s. III d.C. Sin embargo, mejor datado se encuentra el momento de ruina de ésta, ya que los restos de columnas y paredes pertenecientes a esa estructura cayeron a un lecho marino en regresión; un nivel en el que se recuperaron diversos materiales de transporte que ofrecen una fecha *post quem* de la primera mitad del s. V d.C. (Figura 3.4).

En cuanto a su funcionalidad, y pese al escaso material conservado, creemos que la monumentalidad de los restos bien puede avalar la hipótesis de que se erigiera sobre la cabeza una estructura turriforme de gran porte, muy posiblemente un elemento de señalización que, a modo de *lanterna* o faro interior, articularía el tránsito y la navegabilidad desde la dársena exterior o de Claudio y el *canale di collegamento*. Esta hipótesis ya fue apuntada en la década de 1930, al identificarse en su superficie los restos de construcciones asociadas a esta posible torre (Lugli y Filibeck 1935: 81-82).

Seguidamente, la excavación del área ha permitido identificar un nuevo episodio constructivo sobre la cabeza del muelle, una tercera fase edilicia que amortizaría la potente edificación precedente. Durante este periodo la cabeza de la *testata* vio cómo su tablero superior sufría una importante reestructuración espacial y funcional. Donde antes se podía apreciar una estructura de gran porte, ahora se construye un nuevo edificio de *opus testaceum* de 78m² (Figura 3.5-I). Desde el punto de vista funcional, el registro material se compone de elementos de transporte en su gran mayoría, así como cerámica común que lleva a plantear, tanto por este registro como por la posición de la construcción, en un ambiente de almacenamiento. Muy posiblemente, en estos momentos el muelle había modificado su funcionalidad inicial, al pasar de un elemento de articulación con señalización en su punta, a acoger funciones de atraque, descarga, y almacenaje.

La construcción de este ambiente y, por tanto, el cambio de funcionalidad de la cabeza del muelle se produce tras la ruina y amortización de la fase anterior. Es por tanto que su construcción debió producirse en momentos posteriores a mediados del s. V d.C., fecha en la que se produjo la ruina de la torre.

Con posterioridad se documentará nuevamente un cambio importante en la configuración no solo ya de la cabeza sino de la parte final del muelle. Este proceso parece deberse a una nueva fase constructiva que llevará pareja la ampliación de la superficie útil del mismo, así como la construcción de nuevos ambientes. Desde el punto de vista cronológico la falta de cultura material asociada a éstos y sus cimentaciones, hace que tengamos que teorizar acerca de su fecha de construcción, aunque debió producirse en momentos de la segunda mitad del s. V o comienzos del VI d.C. Del enorme programa de reformas que se acometerían con este nuevo episodio, quizás la más llamativa sea la construcción de dos plataformas adosadas al muelle y su cabeza en el lado norte, con la intención de dotar de más superficie a éste. Estas plataformas o pantalanes, con fábrica a base de vertidos de *caementa* supusieron la ampliación del espacio en 4,20m de longitud por 5,60m de anchura y 1,50m de altura. Sobre ella se proyectó la construcción de un nuevo edificio de planta turriforme de al menos 13m² (Figura 3.5-II, III), con muros de 1,20m de anchura. No existen evidencias materiales que avalen su funcionalidad, pero el ambiente bélico que se respira en *Portus* en esta fecha, con construcciones que nos hablan de una tendencia a la fortificación de éste (Keay y Paroli 2011: 7-10), apuntan a que debió tratarse de una nueva torre, en este caso concebida con una clara funcionalidad defensiva y de control. En efecto, la dinámica constructiva en los siglos tardo antiguos se muestra efervescente en otros ambientes de *Portus*, de manera que durante los siglos V-VI se asiste a una fortificación del puerto (Paroli 2004: 257-58) en donde el muelle este-oeste muestra precisamente ese proceso, al constatarse construcciones sucesivas que dotan de mayor solidez a éste.

En una última fase sucesiva, o probablemente en relación con este mismo episodio o impulso constructivo, pero en un momento inmediatamente posterior, el muelle sufriría nuevas ampliaciones con el adosamiento de nuevas plataformas, concretamente una en su lado sur y otra en el margen nororiental, en este caso adosada a la de la fase anterior (Figura 3.5-IV, V, VI). De todas ellas, la única analizada es la última, la cual presenta unas dimensiones conservadas de 9,70m por 4,80m. Aunque está zona ha sido poco intervenida, se ha podido precisar que inmediatamente después de la articulación de dicha cimentación, fue alzada sobre ella una estructura rectangular. Su factura es bastante irregular debido al empleo de materiales reutilizados. Su funcionalidad parece estar en relación con dotar de más espacio útil al muelle; su cronología resulta del todo desconocida, aunque si bien es cierto su construcción se produjo en momentos posteriores al aditamento de las plataformas anteriores, quizás en los inicios o primera mitad del s. VI d.C., dentro de ese ambiente bélico greco gótico.

Dentro de este episodio debemos encuadrar también diversas reformas que se llevaron a cabo en el resto de infraestructuras del muelle. Entre ellas se encuentran la reestructuración interna y la creación de un cuerpo de escaleras en el ambiente portuario descrito en la segunda fase; así como la remodelación interna de la segunda estructura turriforme. Todas estas nuevas construcciones se caracterizan por la pobreza y mala factura de sus muros, indicio del momentode crisis por el que estaba atravesando *Portus* en este periodo.

Este sería el último impulso constructivo acontecido sobre la cabeza del muelle, pues entre sus últimas evidencias de uso sólo se constatan varios episodios deposicionales y de derrumbe que colmatan toda el área.

Consideraciones finales

Las diversas campañas arqueológicas expuestas en esta contribución han supuesto un avance significativo en el conocimiento que se tenía sobre la estructura en cuestión. Como hemos argumentado anteriormente, las investigaciones precedentes sobre el muelle habían sido escasas, de lo que tan solo se contaban con las intervenciones en el área de la terma (Canina 1830; Panziere *et al.* 2017), así como aquellas que pusieron de relieve en la década de 1930 la importancia de un posible faro a *lanterna* en su puntal (Lugli y Filibeck 1935: 81). En este contexto de investigación es donde se encuadran las investigaciones que, desde el año 2017, la Universidad de Huelva en colaboración con el *Parco Archeologico di Ostia Antica* vienen desarrollando conjuntamente.

El resultado de las investigaciones ha puesto de relieve numerosos aspectos relativos a su fábrica, sistemas constructivos, funcionalidad de espacios y diacronía que pueden sintetizarse en un conjunto de fases:

Fase I. Esta fase viene representada por la construcción del muelle mediante una importante operación de excavación en zanja, con encofrados de madera rellenados de material cerámico con una función drenante y la hinca de pilotes. Estas cimentaciones tuvieron una doble funcionalidad, por un lado, dotar de una mayor solidez la construcción del muelle en sus flancos y, por otra, favorecer a modo de plataformas de trabajo, los vertidos de *caementa* que conformaron la cimentación del muelle y la erección de la parte vista del mismo, la cual fue revestida de una capa latericia.

Desde un punto de vista cronológico, la datación de esta primera fase correspondiente a la construcción del muelle ha sido posible gracias a la combinación de varios datos. Por un lado, de las dataciones de C14 de varias muestras de madera del encofrado, que aportan una cronología coincidente para todas ellas de la primera mitad del s. III d.C. Aquí reside una de las principales aportaciones de nuestro trabajo, dado que a la propuesta tradicional que pasaba por considerar este muelle bien del plan original del diseño del puerto de Claudio, o inmediatamente posterior o bien de época de Trajano, se comprueba que su diseño y construcción corresponde a una obra propia de época de los Antoninos. Llegados a este punto debemos ser cautos, dado que la excavación ha estado centrada en los últimos 30 m de muelle, por lo que los resultados relativos a su cronología no deben ser extrapolados a toda la totalidad de éste. Es decir, no debemos descartar la posibilidad de un muelle que se fue alargando progresivamente a medida que se produjo la colmatación de la antigua dársena de Claudio, siendo la última la detectada en nuestras investigaciones. La idea de una progradación del muelle de manera diacrónica podría guardar relación con las investigaciones realizadas en la zona del casale próximo al hexágono, donde la excavación de un tramo de unos 60 m de muelle se fechó entre Trajano y los Antoninos. Sin embargo, cierto la excavación no aportó ningún tipo de material que permita una datación del contexto excavado, y no se profundizó en su cimentación (Verduchi 2004: 239).

Fase II. La siguiente fase constructiva parece guardar relación con el adosamiento de una imponente cabeza o puntal al extremo del muelle. Sobre ésta parece proyectarse la construcción de una estructura de cierto porte, como revelan los restos de su cimentación, así como los materiales arquitectónico-decorativos caídos a los pies de la estructura, en el antiguo lecho mareal. Esta cabeza, con una forma poligonal, presenta una serie de características constructivas y de fábrica que la diferencian del cuerpo del muelle. En primer lugar, la diferencia en la profundidad de su cimentación revela una planificación constructiva distinta, esto es, no fue planteada en el mismo momento que el propio cuerpo del muelle. En segundo lugar, su fábrica muestra elementos distintos, empleo de tégulas para nivelar los vertidos de *caementa*, así como el uso de *catenae* de mayor diámetro, revelan el empleo de módulos en sus encofrados desiguales. Finalmente, existe una relación de adosamiento entre el cuerpo del muelle y su cabeza, una unión en su fábrica claramente visible en su el lado norte. Todos estos detalles permiten posicionarnos con relación a una fase distinta, a falta de una excavación que profundice en la cimentación de la cabeza y permita obtener otros datos y dataciones,. Por cuanto respecta a la cronología de la misma, poco podemos precisar de su construcción, aunque obviamente se produjo como pronto a partir de mediados del s. III d.C.

Fase III. La tercera fase viene definida por la amortización de la construcción de la anterior, datada probablemente a mediados del s. V d.C., cuando se produjo la ruina de ésta y sus restos cayeron en el lecho de la dársena a los pies del muelle. En estos momentos la cabeza ve el arrasamiento de las estructuras precedentes y la instalación de un nuevo edificio, posiblemente destinado al almacenamiento.

Fase IV. Como continuación de la anterior, toda la parte final del muelle incluida su cabeza, verá la ampliación de superficie útil al adosarse a éste distintas plataformas que a modo de pantalanes permitieron la erección de nuevas construcciones. De entre éstas destaca una caracterizada por una potente anchura en sus muros, lo que dotaba a sus alzados de un espesor y solidez significativos. La funcionalidad parece la misma que en el resto del muelle, aunque esta hipótesis no resulta nada clara, debido a la ausencia de cultura material asociada. La estructura parece responder a la construcción de un cuerpo turriforme, quizás una nueva *lanterna* o baliza. Conjuntamente, el almacén de la fase anterior parece compartimentarse y dotarse de un segundo cuerpo en altura.

Fase V. La última fase constructiva detectada en la zona más occidental del muelle viene de la mano del adosamiento de una nueva plataforma y la construcción de nuevos ambientes. El estado de ruina que actualmente presenta la misma dificulta cualquier intento de aproximación funcional, no obstante, parece responder a nuevas necesidades de ampliación de la superficie útil del muelle, en un momento de efervescencia constructiva común a otros sectores de *Portus* en la tarda antigüedad (D'Ammassa 2021; D'Ammasa *et al.* 2018). Muy probablemente, las sucesivas ampliaciones que sufre en los últimos momentos no debieron de estar distanciadas en el tiempo.

Las investigaciones realizadas a lo largo de los últimos años sobre el muelle este-oeste permiten poner de relieve la importancia que desde momentos de los Antoninos y sus sucesores, adquiere la estructura, ya que al menos su última parte parece deberse a un impulso constructivo de aquellos. Tras la construcción de su última parte o puntal, el muelle verá a lo largo de los s.s. V-VI d.C. una sucesión de fases constructivas de importancia significativa, de lo que parece estar en consonancia con otras áreas de *Portus* durante la antiguedda tardía.

Bibliografía

Bermejo, J., J.M. Campos y R. Sebastiani (2023 a), El muelle este-oeste de *Portus*, novedades geoarqueológicas en el contexto de los puertos imperiales, en *Actas del Congreso Internacional Entre Mares, emplazamiento, infraestructuras y organización de los puertos romanos, Irún, Noviembre 2021*, 39-50.

Bermejo, J., J.M. Campos y R. Sebastiani (Eds) (2023 b), Portus, investigaciones geoarqueológicas en el muelle este-oeste. Archaeopress Roman Archaeology 105.

Bermejo, J., J.M. Campos, R. Sebastiani, A. Bermejo, L. Fernández, F. Marfil, C. D'Ammassa (2023 c), El muelle este-oeste de *Portus* y sus ambientes, primeros datos sobre su configuración arquitectónica, en *Atti del VI seminario ostiense, 10, 11 di marzo 2019, Roma*, 337-352.

Bermejo, J., J.M. Campos, R. Sebastiani, C. D'Ammassa, L. Fernández, A. Bermejo y F. Marfil 2021a. Il molo est-ovest a *Portus*. Un'analisi preliminare dalla archeologia della architettura, en *Atti del V seminario Ostiense, 21-22 febbraio 2018*: 201-09. Rome: Publications de l'École française de Rome.

Bermejo, J., J.M. Campos, R. Sebastiani, L. Fernández, F. Marfil, A. Bermejo, C. D'Ammassa 2021b. El denominado muelle de la linterna en Portus. Primeras investigaciones y resultados, en *Actes du 12ème Colloque Historique de Fréjus 16 et 17 novembre 2018 – Fréjus, Les ports dans l'espace méditerranéen antique Fréjus et les ports maritimes*: 303-16. Aix-en-Provence: Presses universitaires de Provence.

Bermejo, J., J.M. Campos, R. Sebastiani, L. Fernández, A. Bermejo, F. Marfil, C. D'Ammassa, E. Baena, E. Domínguez, N.E. Rodríguez y L.J. Sánchez 2021 c, Los puertos imperiales de Roma: investigaciones geoarqueológicas en el muelle este-oeste de Portus, en J.M. Campos y J. Bermejo (eds) *Del Atántico al Tirreno, puertos hispanos e itálicos*: 583-610. Roma: L'Erma di Bretschneider.

Bonifay, M. y D. Piéri 1995. Amphores du Ve au VIIe s. à Marseille: nouvelles données sur la typologie et le contenu. *Journal of Roman Archaeology* 8: 94-120.

Bonifay, M. y F. Villedieu 1989. Importations d'amphores orientales en Gaule (Ve-VIIe siècle). *Recherches sur la céramique Byzantine. Bulletin de correspondance hellénique*, Suppl. 18: 17-46.

Canina, L. 1830. *Indicazione delle rovine di Ostia e di Porto e della supposizione dell'intero loro stato delineata in quattro tavole.* Roma

D'Ammasa, C. 2021. *Portus Romae*, fortuna e declino. Brevi note storiche, archeologiche e topografiche, en J.M. Campos y J. Bermejo (eds) *Del Atántico al Tirreno, puertos hispanos e itálicos*: 655-80. Roma: L'Erma di Bretschneider.

D'Ammasa, C., A. Manna y R. Sebastiani 2018. Indagini archeologiche tra il Canale Trasverso e l'Episcopio. Osservazioni preliminari sulle fasi post-classiche di Porto. *Mélanges de l'École française de Rome: Antiquité*, 130.2: 321-24.

Goiran, J.-P., H. Tronchère, F. Salomon, P. Carbonel, H. Djerbi y C. Ognard 2010. Palaeoenvironmental reconstruction of the ancient harbors of Rome: Claudius and Trajan's marine harbors on the Tiber delta. *Quaternary International* 216: 3-13.

Keay, S. 1984. *Late Roman Amphorae in the Western Mediterranean, a Typology and Economic Study: The Catalan Evidence* (British Archaeological Reports, 196). Oxford: Archaeopress.

Keay, S. y L. Paroli 2011. *Portus and its Hinterland: Recent Archaeological Research* (Archaeological Monographs of the British School at Rome 18). London: British School at Rome.

Lugli, G. y G. Filibeck 1935. *Il Porto di Roma Imperiale e l'agro portuense.* Roma: Instituto italianno d'arti grafiche.

Panziere, C., G. Ricci, R. Sebastiani y R. Fiorentino 2016. Le terme della lanterna. *Forma Urbis, Portus, Archeologia alle porte di Roma* 21.12: 41-43.

Paroli, L. 2004. Il porto di Roma nella tarda antichitá, en A. Gallina Zevi y R Turchetti (eds) *Le strutture dei porti e degli approdi antichi: II Seminario; Roma-Ostia Antica*: 247-66. Soveria Mannelli: Rubbettino.

Peacock, D.P.S. y D.F. Williams 1986. *Amphorae and the Roman Economy*. London: Longman.

Verduchi, P.A. 2004. Notizie e riflessioni sul porto di Roma, en A. Gallina Zevi y R Turchetti (eds) *Le strutture dei porti e degli approdi antichi: II Seminario; Roma-Ostia Antica*: 233-46. Soveria Mannelli: Rubbettino.

4. Un frammento epigrafico ostiense dai pressi della Fossa Traiana

Cristian D'Ammassa and Gian Luca Gregori

Introduzione

Nel corso di recenti indagini archeologiche condotte a Porto, presso un'area ricompresa tra la moderna via Portuense, il Canale Trasverso, la Fossa Traiana e l'Episcopio, sono state messe in luce alcune porzioni di magazzini ed un probabile impianto produttivo, aventi una fase di vita che dalla media età imperiale arriva fino all'alto medioevo. A parte i numerosi *spolia* architettonici, l'attenzione si è focalizzata su di un frammento iscritto riguardante un pontefice del culto di Vulcano, verosimilmente ammesso anche a far parte dei decurioni della colonia ostiense. Considerando che l'importanza di tale culto di Vulcano, ma non a Porto, è probabile che il frammento sia giunto qui a seguito di attività di spoliazione intraprese a partire dall'età tardoantica e sia così finito nell'area dei "depositi marmorari" prospicienti alla *Statio marmorum* portuense.

Modalità insediative a porto tra l'età tardoantica e l'alto medioevo

Presso un lotto ubicato lungo la via Portuense, nelle immediate vicinanze del palazzo episcopale, sono state di recente eseguite delle indagini archeologiche, condotte da chi scrive e sotto la direzione scientifica del Parco Archeologico di Ostia Antica[1] (Figura 4.1). Il palinsesto archeologico rinvenuto si rivela di notevole interesse per le modalità d'uso, abbandono e successiva rioccupazione dei magazzini annonari, situati nelle adiacenze della riva destra della Fossa Traiana in un periodo ricompreso tra la media età imperiale e l'alto medioevo. In quest'area già a partire dalla seconda metà del IV secolo AD (Lanciani 1868: 189; Paroli 2004: 254-57), probabilmente su impulso delle attività energetiche promosse da Costantino e dai suoi

successori (Bevelacqua 2016: 2163), sorse un nucleo abitativo munito di lì a poco di mura difensive (Paroli 2004: 262; Paroli e Ricci 2011: 127) e collegato per mezzo del Ponte di Matidia con il quartiere suburbano di Isola Sacra, presso la sponda sinistra della Fossa Traiana (Germoni 2001: 384; 2020: 173; Germoni *et al.* 2011: 239; Lauro 1993: 167; Paroli 2004: 264; Pavolini 2015: 32; Veloccia Rinaldi 1975: 13; Gatti 1911; Germoni 2020: 173-175; Germoni e Genovese 2023: 381-383.).

A seguito di una parziale riduzione dei traffici commerciali, registrata a partire dai primi decenni del VI secolo AD a causa delle incursioni germaniche (Coccia 1993: 181; *De bello Gothico* 1.26; Mannucci e Verduchi 1992: 17; Lugli e Filibeck 1935: 150-52; Testaguzza 1970: 30), ma anche della limitata agibilità del bacino esagonale, soggetto a fenomeni di insabbiamento (Coccia 1993: 190-91; 2001: 15), intere porzioni di strutture fino ad allora destinate allo stoccaggio furono dismesse e vi si installarono delle sepolture (Coccia 1996: 298-300; Coltorti *et al.* 1993: 160; Paroli 2004: 262).

Molte delle attività portuali, fino a questo momento dislocate altrove, vengono ora concentrate presso questo settore periferico, favorito dalla sua felice posizione in uno spazio compreso tra il Canale Trasverso e la Fossa Traiana, la quale sembrerebbe essere ancora mantenuta in stato di efficienza (Coccia 1993: 182, 192; 2001: 15; Nuzzo 2009: 294; Paroli 2004: 254, 257, 260, 263). Oltre alla realizzazione della Basilica, il rinnovato assetto urbano è caratterizzato dalla presenza di edifici a carattere residenziale, funzionale e artigianale (Coccia 1993: 177; 1996: 294; Coccia e Paroli 1993: 175; Lugli e Filibeck 1935: 105; Paroli 2013a: 3; Testaguzza 1970: 204; Texier 1857: 305), ricavati da preesistenti strutture di età imperiale e utilizzati a vari scopi fino all'alto medioevo, così come nei casi di una *domus solarata* e di una *domus terrinea* localizzate nelle vicinanze del complesso basilicale (Coccia 1993: 182, 193; 2001: 23; Paroli 2001: 625-26; 2004: 263; 2013b, 372; Paroli 1996: 411).

Il contesto di scavo

Nel corso delle più recenti indagini effettuate nell'area è stata messa in luce una serie di ambienti, i quali, in considerazione della loro ubicazione, assetto planimetrico originario e tecniche costruttive, trovano stretti parallelismi con i magazzini di stoccaggio ubicati

[1] Indagini archeologiche eseguite tra il 2015 e il 2018 nell'ambito delle attività di tutela territoriale e sotto la direzione scientifica di Renato Sebastiani, al quale va il ringraziamento degli Autori. Oltre a chi scrive le indagini sul campo sono state condotte e documentate con la preziosa collaborazione dei colleghi Antonio Manna (Promotionstudium, Institut fürvor- und frühgeschichtliche Archäologie und Provinzialrömische Archäologie der Ludwig-Maximilians Universität München) e Paolo Rosati (Dipartimento di Storia Antropologia Religioni Arte Spettacolo, Sapienza Università di Roma). Un ringraziamento particolare dobbiamo agli amministratori della società FM S.r.l., Moira e Flavio Scurtarelli, che con intelligenza e liberalità hanno finanziato questa ricerca. Per una disamina del contesto di scavo si vedano D'Ammassa *et al.* 2018 e D'Ammassa *et al.* 2023.

Figura 4.1. Localizzazione dell'area d'indagine su stralcio della 'Nuova Cartografia del Distretto Portuense' (Parco Archeologico di Ostia Antica; elaborazione grafica C. D'Ammassa)

all'interno dell'area demaniale degli scavi di Porto (Figura 4.2). Anche in questo caso il corpo originario, costituito da setti portanti in opera reticolata con ammorsature e ricorsi in laterizio (Boetto *et al.* 2010; Bukowiecki *et al.* 2011; Bukowiecki e Panzieri 2013; Verduchi 1996; 2005), è databile fra il II e il III secolo AD e rientra nell'ambito di un più ampio programma di manutenzione e ammodernamento delle infrastrutture portuali (Bevelacqua 2016: 2161; Lanciani 1868: 156; Lugli e Filibeck 1935: 68, 134; Mannucci e Verduchi 1992: 16; Testaguzza 1970: 28).

Esso fu oggetto di un intervento di consolidamento e sopraelevazione mediante la realizzazione di imponenti murature in mattoni dotate di archi di scarico.[2] Tra la fine del III e l'inizio del IV AD secolo, in appoggio al magazzino, venne realizzata una struttura produttiva con annesso un sistema di vasche di decantazione, che non verrà tenuta in funzione oltre la prima metà dei VI secolo AD, probabilmente a causa dell'insorgere dei primi scontri della guerra greco-gotica.

Ad eccezione di alcuni ambienti riutilizzati solamente a partire dall'età altomedievale come deposito di *spolia* architettonici, la restante area d'indagine fu interessata da processi di *obliterazione* e dinamiche di abbandono ancora da puntualizzare. Così come testimoniano le tracce di incendio e gli strati di crollo individuati presso il Saggio 1 (Figure 4.3-4.4), dove un lacerto murario di difficile lettura si presentava collassato verso

l'interno di un modesto ambiente di cui, considerando anche l'esiguità della superficie indagata, rimangono solamente i resti di un muro rasato associato ad un battuto e la risega di un pilastro.

Le consistenti tracce di materiale combusto, fra cui frammenti di travi di legno carbonizzate, sono probabilmente da mettere in relazione con un incendio che provocò il cedimento del solaio seguito dal crollo degli alzati; tale strato venne successivamente rimaneggiato e spianato. Le strutture affioranti furono poi oggetto di una spoliazione volta al recupero di materiale edilizio fino ad almeno la metà VI secolo AD, come emerge dai materiali diagnostici recuperati nello strato di cesura di tali attività[3]. Una seconda fase di occupazione di questo ambiente risulta ben espressa da azioni di livellamento dell'area e innalzamento del piano di calpestio[4], sul quale sono stati recuperati numerosi frammenti architettonici di varia tipologia, nonché due frustoli iscritti.

La provenienza di questi rinvenimenti è da ricercarsi molto probabilmente nelle attività di spoliazione intraprese in area ostiense a partire già dall'età tardoantica (Pensabene 2006: 567-68) per essere successivamente depositati in un'area nella quale, sulla scorta delle fonti antiquarie e delle moderne

---

[2] In merito a tale soluzione costruttiva nell'area di Porto, seppur con materiali diversi, si veda Verduchi 1996: 58.

[3] Come ad esempio materiale anforico del tipo Keay XIX A, Keay XXV, Keay LIV, Keay LIV B.
[4] Risistemazioni simili degli spazi si riscontrano anche presso un magazzino tardoantico, anch'esso ubicato in prossimità della Fossa Traiana all'altezza dell'Antemurale, a tale proposito si veda Paroli 2004: 250-51.

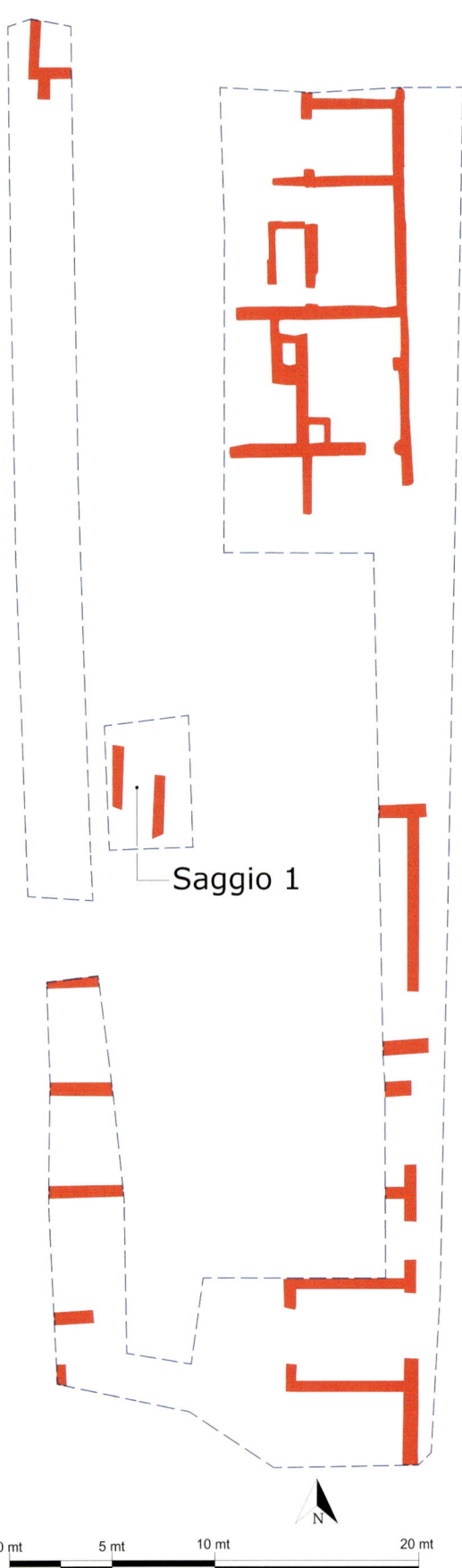

Saggio 1

Figura 4.2. Planimetria generale del contesto di scavo (rilievo ed elaborazione grafica C. D'Ammassa)

Figura 4.3. Saggio 1, panoramica sud dell'area di scavo (foto C. D'Ammassa).

cartografie dell'area portuense,[5] si era proposto di collocare i magazzini marmorari (Lanciani 1868: 180; Lugli e Filibeck 1935: 105-06; Maischberger 1997: 33; Testaguzza 1970: 189), ubicati tra un ipotetico tempio di Apollo, più recentemente attribuito a Serapide (Van Haeperen 2019) e l'Episcopio, nonché nelle vicinanze della Statio marmorum portuense (Pavolini 1986: 124; Pensabene 1994: 12-13; 2017: 484). Questa collocazione è ad oggi ulteriormente avvalorata dal palinsesto archeologico messo alla luce presso questo settore del versante meridionale del *Portus Traiani*, le cui funzioni portuali verranno mantenute in esercizio, senza soluzione di continuità, fino agli ultimi anni del IX secolo AD (Coccia 1996: 296; Paroli 2004: 254; 2013a: 372).

[C. D'A.]

Un nuovo *praetor sacris volkani* ostiense

Tra i materiali di riuso recuperati nel corso dello scavo vi è anche un frustulo epigrafico di lastra (Figura 4.5), mancante da tutti i lati (130 × 130 × 50mm), che conserva lettere appartenenti a quattro righe di testo (altezza 30-20mm); il retro è sbozzato (autopsia 5.9.2018). Già segnalato in altra sede, nell'ambito di un dettagliato resoconto sulle varie fasi di vita restituite dallo scavo (D'Ammassa *et al.* 2023), per il suo interesse merita di essere qui ripreso e approfondito:

---

[5] Al riguardo si veda la pianta di Porto realizzata nel 1933 da Italo Gismondi e allegata al volume di Giuseppe Lugli e Goffredo Filibeck (Carta N. III). Tale collocazione è desunta sulla base degli scritti di Flavio Biondo (Biondo 1558: 78-79) e di Giuseppe Rocco Volpi (Volpi 1734: 158). Numeroso materiale proveniente da Porto venne trasportato a Roma e impiegato per la realizzazione delle fontane di Piazza Colonna e Navona (Bignamini 2003: 41; Fea 1830: 139; Lugli e Filibeck 1935: 105-06; Melchiorri 1856: 1033; Testaguzza 1970: 189; Testini 1975: 62-63).

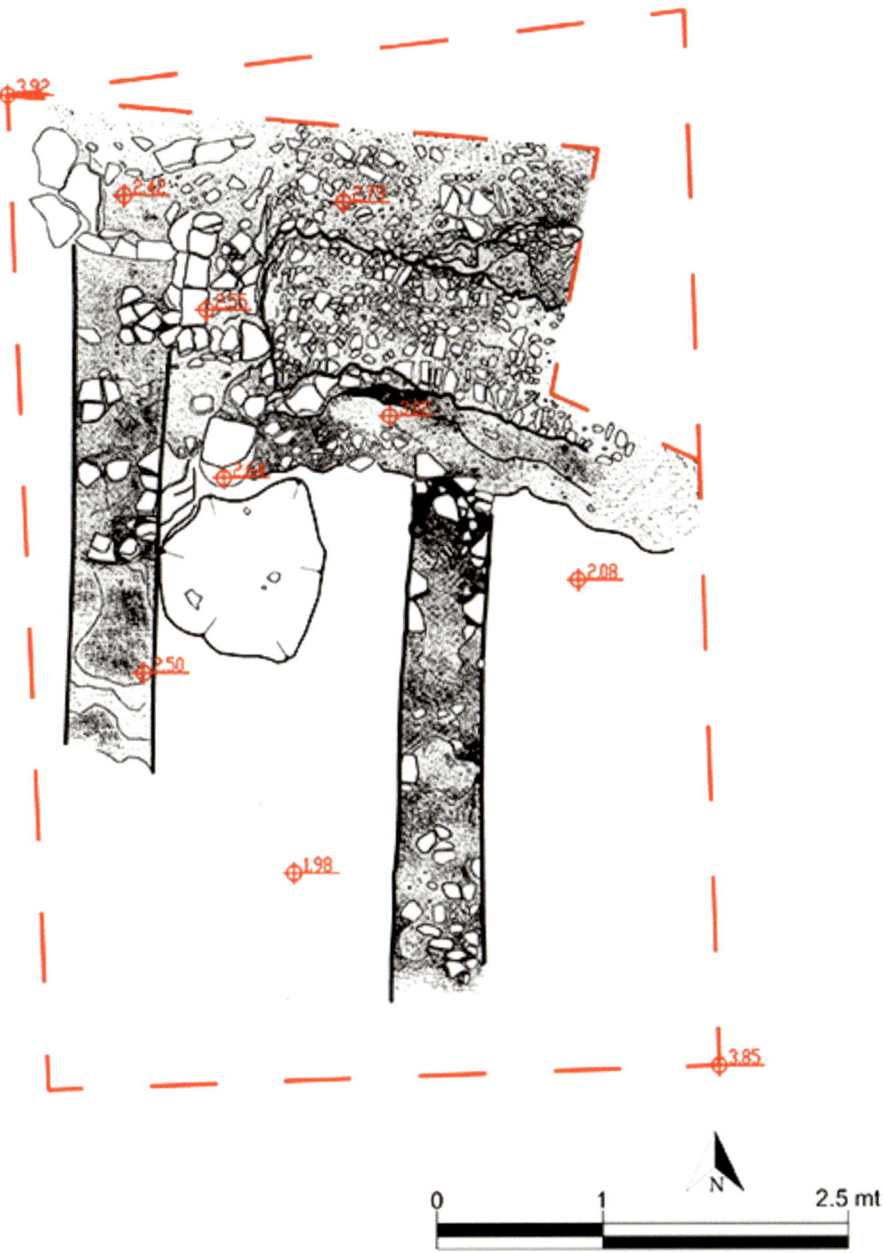

Figura 4.4. Planimetria di dettaglio delle strutture evidenziate nel Saggio 1 (rilievo ed elaborazione grafica C. D'Ammassa).

[---]+*re*+[---]
[---? *praet*]*ori sac*[---]
[---]*m decu*[---]
[---]*ECT* +[---]

Anche se non siamo in grado di calcolare il numero di righe mancanti in alto e in basso e sussistono ampi margini di incertezza sulle integrazioni delle righe conservate, è possibile formulare qualche ipotesi di

lavoro, sulla base dei confronti forniti dal ricco *corpus* epigrafico ostiense.

Se le lettere di L. 1 appartenevano alla formula onomastica del personaggio destinatario della dedica (di carattere funerario o onorario), potrebbe trovare posto qui il cognome *Iren*[*aeo*], un grecanico documentato a Ostia, come altrove, in genere tra i liberti, ma anche tra i figli di liberti[6].

---

[6] Eclatante il caso di *AE* 2013, 216 (*Formiae*), dove in età adrianea è attestato un *T. Flavius Iraeneus*, duoviro della colonia, figlio di un

29

Figura 4.5. Frustolo iscritto recuperato nel Saggio 1 (foto C. D'Ammassa).

o *decreto decurionum decurioni adlecto*,[9] cooptazione avvenuta in assenza o comunque prima che l'individuo rivestisse una qualche magistratura cittadina, che sola poteva permettere, una volta cessate le funzioni, di entrare nel consiglio dei decurioni della colonia.[10]

Non sappiamo quali altri mansioni il destinatario di questa iscrizione avesse ricoperto a Ostia e se l'ultima lettera che si conserva alla L. 4, forse una F o una T, appartenga o meno all'onomastica del dedicante.

Sul piano paleografico il frammento non sembrerebbe più tardo del II secolo AD, stando almeno alle larghe grazie alle estremità dei tratti e all'andamento ondulato solo di alcuni tratti (L. 4); grazie al nuovo ritrovamento si arricchisce la lista dei *praetores Volcani* fin qui noti, i quali, come s'è detto, proprio nel corso di quel secolo subirono una trasformazione di *status*, passando tale l'incarico da notabili locali a esponenti dell'ordine equestre (Caldelli 2014: 106-13).

[G.L.G.]

Riferimenti Bibliografici

Abbreviazioni

AE = L'Année épigraphique
CIL = *Corpus inscriptionum latinarum*. Berlin: Reimer/De Gruyter, 1863-.
EDR = Epigraphic Database Roma

Fonti antiche

Procopio = Comparetti, D. 1895-98. De Bello Gothico: *La guerra gotica di Procopio di Cesarea; testo greco emendato sui manoscritti con traduzione italiana*. Roma: Forzani.

Fonti moderne

Bevelacqua, G.S. 2016. L'ascesa della civitas Flavia Constantiniana Portuensis tra liberalitas principis e munificentia privata. L'apporto delle fonti epigrafiche, in O. Brandt e V. Fiocchi Nicolai (eds) *Acta XVI Congressus internationalis archaeologiae Christianae (Romae, 22-28.9.2013)*: 2155-70. Città del Vaticano: Pontificio Istituto di Archeologia Cristiana.
Bignamini, I. 2003. Ostia, Porto e Isola Sacra: scoperte e scavi dal Medioevo al 1801. *Rivista dell'Istituto nazionale d'archeologia e storia dell'arte*, s. 3, 58: 39-77.

Alla L. 2 la presenza di numerosi casi analoghi nell'epigrafia ostiense permette di dire che siamo di fronte a un nuovo *praetorsacris Volcani faciundis*, una istituzione di carattere religioso, attestata finora e in forma variamente abbreviata nella sola Ostia,[7] circostanza che ci assicura che il frammento sia stato recuperato a Porto in giacitura secondaria.

Di solito quest'incarico si trova subito dopo il nome, come primo di una carriera pubblica più o meno lunga. In ordine gerarchico venivano prima i *pontifices Volcani*, attestati in vari frammenti dei *Fasti Ostienses*, dove invece sono assenti gli *aediles* e i *praetores Volcani*, di rango inferiore e di cui ignoriamo le esatte mansioni. Questi ultimi sono noti finora sia da frammenti appartenenti a liste con i loro nomi, verosimilmente esposte in origine presso il tempio stesso di Vulcano,[8] sia da iscrizioni, nella maggioranza dei casi funerarie.

Sulla base dei dati in nostro possesso possiamo dire che almeno fino alla metà del II secolo AD. questi personaggi paiono appartenere all'élite locale: talora si tratta di figli di liberti, che ricevevano tale carica, evidentemente di carattere solo onorifico, addirittura prima dell'assunzione della toga virile.

In più di un caso, come parrebbe anche essere il nostro (L. 4), l'iscrizione menzionerebbe anche l'*adlectio* di tali *praetores* nell'ordine dei decurioni, con la formula variamente abbreviata *in ordinem decurionum adlecto*

---

liberto imperiale. Per Roma: Solin 2003: 463-65 (una ottantina di casi).
[7] Lo studio più recente ed esaustivo si deve a Caldelli 2014.
[8] Sulla sua discussa localizzazione: Zevi 2012: 559-63.

[9] Si vedano rispettivamente *CIL*, XIV 5=EDR147039; *CIL*, XIV 303=EDR072620, *CIL*, XIV 362=EDR143868, *CIL*, XIV 390=EDR164912, *CIL*, XIV 391=EDR164913, *CIL*, XIV 411=EDR164997, *CIL*, XIV 415= EDR165000.
[10] In generale sulle procedure dell'*adlectio* si veda ora Russo 2018: 489-97; cf. Russo 2019: 108-09.

Biondo, F. 1558. *Roma ristaurata et Italia illustrata: traduzione in buona lingua volgare per Lucio Fauno.* Venetia: Tramezino.

Boetto, G., E. Bukowiecki, N. Monteix e C. Rousse 2010. Les entrepôts d'Ostie et de Portus : les magasins de Trajan. *Mélanges de l'École française de Rome: Antiquité* 122.1:301-08.

Bukowiecki, E., C. Panzieri e S. Zugmeyer 2011. Portus. Les entrepôts de Trajan. *Mélanges de l'École française de Rome: Antiquité* 123.1: 349-57.

Caldelli, M.L. 2014. Fasti dei sacerdoti del culto di Vulcano a Ostia. *Mélanges de l'École française de Rome: Antiquité* 126.1: 95-115.

Coccia, S. 1993. Il "Portus Romae" fra tarda antichità ed alto medioevo, in L. Paroli e P. Delogu (eds) *La Storia economica di Roma nell'alto Medioevo alla luce dei recenti scavi archeologici (Atti del Seminario Roma 2-3 Aprile 1992)*: 177-200. Firenze: All'Insegna del Giglio.

Coccia, S. 1996. Il Portus Romae alla fine dell'antichità nel quadro del sistema di approvvigionamento della città di Roma, in A. Gallina Zevi e A. Claridge (eds) *'Roman Ostia' Revisited: Archaeological and Historical Papers in Memory of Russell Meiggs*: 293-307. London: British School at Rome.

Coccia, S. 2001. Il recinto fortificato dell'episcopio di Porto come epilogo di una crisi urbana, in S. Cancellieri (ed.) *L'Episcopio di Porto presso Fiumicino: metodo e prassi nel restauro architettonico*: 15-34. Roma: Gangemi Editore.

Coccia, S. e L. Paroli 1993. Indagini preliminari sui depositi archeologici della città di Porto. *Archeologia Laziale* 11: 175-80.

Coltorti, P., M.C. Gagliardo e P. Vori 1993. Il Porto imperiale di Roma: primi interventi di scavo. *Archeologia Laziale* 11: 164-66.

D'Ammassa, C., A. Manna e R. Sebastiani 2018. Indagini archeologiche tra il Canale Trasverso e l'Episcopio. Osservazioni preliminari sulle fasi post-classiche di Porto. *Mélanges de l'École française de Rome: Antiquité* 130.2: 321-24.

D'Ammassa, C., P.A. Manna e P. Rosati 2023. Portus: lo scavo di un isolato presso la fossa Traiana. Continuità, cesura e occupazione sporadica tra età imperiale, tardoantica e altomedioevale (II-VIII secolo d.C.), in M.L. Caldelli, N. Laubry e F. Zevi (eds) *Ostia e Portus dalla Repubblica alla tarda Antichità: atti del Sesto Seminario Ostiense, Ostia Antica-Roma, 10-11 Aprile 2019* (Collection de l'École française de Rome 612): 353-78. Rome: École française de Rome.

Fea, C. 1830. Intorno varj monumenti di romani acquedotti. *Bullettino dell'Istituto di corrispondenza archeologica*: 137-39.

Gatti, E. (1911), "Fiumicino. Avanzi di antiche fabbriche scoperte nell'Isola Sacra, presso S. Ippolito", Notizie degli Scavi di Antichità, 410-416.

Germoni, P. 2001. L'area delle terme dette di Matidia, in F. Filippi (ed.) *Archeologia e Giubileo: gli interventi a Roma e nel Lazio nel Piano per il Grande Giubileo del 2000*: 384-89. Napoli: Electa.

Germoni, P. 2020. Gazetteer of sites, in S. Keay, M. Millett, K. Strutt e P. Germoni (eds) *The Isola Sacra Survey: Ostia, Portus and the Port System of Imperial Rome* (McDonald Institute Monographs): 173-85. Cambridge: McDonald Institute for Archaeological Research.

Germoni, P., M. Millett, S. Keay, J. Reynolds e K. Strutt 2011. The Isola Sacra: reconstructing the Roman landscape, in S. Keay e L. Paroli (eds) *Portus and its hinterland* (Archaeological Monographs of the British School at Rome 18): 231-60. London: The British Academy.

Germoni, P., Genovese, C. (2023), "Persistenze e trasformazioni : il complesso monumentale di Sant'Ippolito all'Isola Sacra", in Caldelli, M.L., Laubry, N., Zevi, F. (a cura di), Ostia e Portus dalla Repubblica alla Tarda Antichità : studi di archeologia e di storia urbana sui porti di Roma, (Collection de l'École Française de Rome, 612), 379-392.

Lanciani, R. 1868. Ricerche topografiche sulla città di Porto. *Annali dell' Istituto di corrispondenza archeologica*: 144-95.

Lauro, M.G. 1993. Prospettive di ricerca e problematiche di tutela all'Isola Sacra. *Archeologia Laziale* 11: 164-74.

Lugli, G. e G. Filibeck 1935. *Il Porto di Roma imperiale e l'Agro Portuense.* Bergamo: Officine dell'Istituto italiano di arti grafiche.

Maischberger, M. 1997. *Marmor in Rom: Anlieferung, Lager-und Werkplätze in der Kaiserzeit.* Wiesbaden: Reichert.

Mannucci, V. e P.A. Verduchi 1996. Il porto imperiale di Roma: le vicende storiche, in V. Mannucci (ed.) *Il parco archeologico naturalistico del porto di Traiano: metodo e progetto*: 15-28. Roma: Gangemi Editore.

Melchiorri, G. 1856. *Guida metodica di Roma e suoi contorni.* Roma: Tipografia Puccinelli.

Nuzzo, D. 2009. Le iscrizioni cristiane della basilica urbana di Porto (scavi 1991-2007 e indagini dell'Ottocento) e la produzione epigrafica di imitazione filocaliana. *Vetera Christianorum* 46: 293-314.

Paroli, L. (1996), "Scavi recenti a Porto : nuovi dati sulle fasi tardo antiche e alto-medievali", Rivista di Archeologia Cristiana, 72, 410-414.

Paroli, L. 2001. Portus, in M.S. Arena, P. Delogu, L. Paroli, M. Ricci, L. Saguì e L. Vendittelli (eds) *Roma dall'antichità al medioevo: archeologia e storia del Museo Nazionale Romano - Crypta Balbi*, I: 623-26. Milano: Electa.

Paroli, L. 2004. Il porto di Roma nella tarda antichità, in A. Gallina Zevi e R. Turchetti (eds) *Le strutture dei porti e degli approdi antichi (ANSER II)*: 247-65. Soveria Mannelli: Rubbettino Editore.

Paroli, L. 2013a. Ricerche e studi sulla Basilica Portuense, in M. Maiorano e L. Paroli (eds) *La Basilica Portuense: scavi 1991-2007*: 1-7. Firenze: All'Insegna del Giglio.

Paroli, L. 2013b. Microstoria di un comparto urbano di Porto, in M. Maiorano e L. Paroli (eds) *La Basilica Portuense: scavi 1991-2007*: 365-75. Firenze: All'Insegna del Giglio.

Paroli, L. e G. Ricci 2011. Scavi presso l'Antenurale di Porto, in S. Keay e L. Paroli (eds) *Portus and its Hinterland* (Archaeological Monographs of the British School at Rome 18): 127-46. London: The British Academy.

Pavolini, C. 1986. *La vita quotidiana a Ostia*. Bari: Editori Laterza.

Pavolini, C. 2015. Il territorio di Ostia e Portus. Continuità antiche e discontinuità moderne, in A. Bruschi (ed.) *Portus, Ostia Antica, via Severiana*: 31-35. Roma: Universita di Roma La Sapienza.

Pensabene, P. 1994. *Le vie del marmo: i blocchi di cava di Roma e di Ostia; il fenomeno del marmo nella Roma Antica* (Itinerari Ostiensi 7). Roma: Ministero per i beni culturali e ambientali.

Pensabene, P. 2006. Depositi e magazzini di marmi a Porto e Ostia in epoca tardo-antica, in R. Harreither, P. Pergola, R. Pillinger e A. Pülz (eds) *Acta XIV Congressus internationalis archaeologiae Christianae (Vindobonae, 19-26.9.199)*: 561-88. Città del Vaticano: Pontificio Istituto di Archeologia Cristiana.

Pensabene, P. 2017. Porti marittimi a Porto e Ostia, fluviali a Roma e trasporto dei marmi per i cantieri dei fori imperiali, in J.M. Campos Carrasco e J. Bermejo Meléndez (eds) *Los Puertos Atlánticos Béticos y Lusitanos y su relación comercial con el Mediterráneo*: 477-502. Roma: L'Erma di Bretschneider.

Russo, F. 2018. Sullo ius adipiscendae civitatis Romanae per magistratum nella Lex Irnitana. *Gerión* 36: 481-505.

Russo, F. 2019. *Suffragium: Magistrati, popolo e decurioni nei meccanismi elettorali della Baetica romana*. Milano: Ledizioni.

Solin, H. 2003. *Die griechischen Personennamen in Rom: Ein Namenbuch*. Berlin: De Gruyter.

Testaguzza, O. 1970. *Portus: illustrazione dei Porti di Claudio e Traiano e della città di Porto a Fiumicino*. Roma: Julia Editrice.

Testini, P. 1975. La basilica di S. Ippolito, in M.L. Veloccia Rinaldi e P. Testini (eds) *Ricerche archeologiche nell'Isola Sacra* (Monografie 2): 41-143. Roma: Istituto nazionale d'archeologia e storia dell'arte.

Texier, C. 1857. Mémoires sur les ports antiques situés à l'embochure du Tibre. *Revue générale de l'architecture et des travaux publics* 15: 262-70, 300-34.

Van Haeperen, F. (2019), Fana, templa, delubra. Corpus dei luoghi di culto dell'Italia antica (FTD), Regio I. Ostie, Porto, Roma.

Veloccia Rinaldi, M.L. 1975. Il pons Matidiae e gli edifici adiacenti, in M.L. Veloccia Rinaldi e P. Testini (eds) *Ricerche archeologiche nell'Isola Sacra* (Monografie 2): 13-39. Roma: Istituto nazionale d'archeologia e storia dell'arte.

Verduchi, P.A. 1996. Il patrimonio archeologico monumentale di Porto: osservazioni preliminari sulle strutture architettoniche, in V. Mannucci (ed.) *Il parco archeologico naturalistico del porto di Traiano: metodo e progetto*: 55-60. Roma: Gangemi Editore.

Verduchi, P.A. 2005. Some thoughts on the infrastructure of the port of Rome, in S. Keay, M. Millet, L. Paroli e K. Strutt (eds) *Portus: An Archaeological Survey of the Port of Imperial Rome* (Archaeological Monographs of the British School at Rome 15): 248-57. London: The British Academy.

Volpi, G.R. 1734. *Vetus Latium Profanum*, VI. Roma: Josephus Cominus.

Zevi, F. 2012. *Culti ed edifici templari di Ostia repubblicana*. *Ostraka* (vol. spec.): 537-63.

5. The Roman Port System in the Eyes of Imperial Jurists

Emilia Mataix Ferrándiz

Introduction[1]

A port system is a set of interdependent parts forming an integrated whole. This concept was introduced by S.J. Keay, who in his well-known paper from 2012 said: 'It is becoming increasingly clear that ports cannot be viewed in isolation, or simply in relation to the sea. They occupy liminal positions between land and sea that can be appreciated only by looking at their relationships to surrounding hinterlands and to other ports' (2012: 33). Thus, one central concept to bear in mind when studying harbours is that of the connectivity between their different structures, as well as with other ports or trading areas (Horden and Purcell 2000). This means that the different structures and locations involved in the dispatch, sale, or storage of goods were an integral part of the processing of the cargo, and therefore constitute one step in a cycle of distribution. Excavations of different ancient ports (e.g. Portus, Marseille) have confirmed the accuracy and necessity of this view for the study of these ancient structures, which has been especially underlined in the different publications of Portus and the Portus Limen project (e.g. Keay *et al.* 2005; 2011; Keay and Arnaud 2020). By following that approach, it is possible to understand the different elements forming a port in their overall context and evaluate the impact of port activities on the hinterland, as well as on many other features of the societies involved in port-related operations. Once we consider human factors in relation to Roman ports it becomes necessary to look at the legal framework governing these areas, since it is through these legal dispositions that a port was defined as a place for commerce and provided a secure venue for exchanges, following customary practices while controlling the processing of merchandise (Moatti 2000).

Therefore, the main aim of this paper is to look at selected legal texts in relation to the concept of 'port system', to determine whether the way that the jurists understood ports coincides with this perception of the archaeological evidence. In addition, the study of these legal excerpts will provide new approaches to understanding port systems that could not be appreciated unless we consider the legal frameworks surrounding the human interactions that took place therein. Every legal fragment should be considered within its social context, taking into account the social context when it was written, the work it belongs to, and the underlying agenda of the author of the text. In this paper I will deal with four texts (and their related fragments), corresponding to jurists who worked during the early Severan period (second half of the second to the first half of the third centuries AD), Ulpian and Marcian.

Most texts from Justinian's compilation belong to that specific period because the compilers of the code took many texts from the archives of the imperial chancellery, and it was during this era when it reached its peak of development (Coriat 1997; Honoré 1994; 2010). Therefore, the texts presented in this paper belong to bureaucrats who worked at the imperial chancellery and wrote their books at the apex of imperial jurisprudence. The latter indicates that, even if their books were devoted to different aims, their perceptions belonged to individuals who lived and worked in an empire with settled legal and political institutions, and who in turn were part of the imperial bureaucratic machinery, which could have influenced their perceptions of a port's material and legal infrastructure. In addition, one needs to bear in mind that the Roman jurists' approach to law was quite pragmatic, resulting in the creation of an instrument that could be used in very different settings (Babusiaux 2016; Cairns and Plessis 2007; Pölonen 2016). Thus, in the texts addressed in this paper we might not find exact definitions or specific categories that apply to the spaces targeted, but instead, opinions on different matters that are aimed at providing abstract solutions to a wide range of problems. The study of various literary sources has highlighted the challenge of understanding ancient ports through the lens of a single culture (e.g. Phoenician or Greek). It emphasises that the most effective approach to studying ports is to view them as interfaces between land and sea, each with its own unique characteristics.

The Evidence of Legal Literature and its Biases

The first text corresponds to the Severan jurist Ulpian, who was a leading intellectual from Tyre, a member of

[1] This publication was made possible by a fellowship of the Käte Hamburger Kolleg 'Legal Unity and Pluralism' at the University of Münster, funded by the Federal Ministry of Education and Research (BMBF). I would like to thank the editors for all their work and also Katherine Crawford for her work editing the chapter. All the remaining errors are, of course, my own responsibility.

the imperial chancellery during the Severan dynasty, and one of the most influential writers of his time (Crifò 1976; Honoré 2002; 2004: 129-31; Liebs 1994, 863-68; Marotta 2000). The excerpt is part of Ulpian's book number 68 on the praetorian edict and says:

> **D. 50.16.59pr.** *Ulp. 68 ad Ed.* *'Portus' appellatus est conclusus locus, quo importantur merces et inde exportantur: eaque nihilo minus statio est conclusa atque munita. Inde 'angiportum' dictum est.*
>
> (A 'harbour' is the name of an enclosed space where goods are imported and transported; and in the same way a *statio* constitutes an enclosed and walled space. Whence one talks about *angiportum*.) (Transl. Watson)

The fragment belongs to one of the books commenting on the praetorian edict. In classical Rome (first century BC-second century AD), the praetor was the magistrate charged with the administration of justice, who at the beginning of his year in office published an eponymous edict, that set out the legal remedies that he would grant together with the *formulae* for those remedies (Brennan 2000). During the Principate, the praetor's edict was slowly standardised and was then set into its final form by the jurist Salvius Julianus, commonly known as Julian, under orders from the emperor Hadrian. This final composition was called the *edictum perpetuum*, or the Perpetual Edict, and is usually dated to the AD 130s. The latter means that Ulpian was commenting on a disposition that was enacted prior to Hadrian's compilation (Johnston 1999: 4; Mayer-Maly 1999: 22; Robinson 1997: 16), while his book 68 on the edict was written during the reign of Macrinus (Honoré 2002: 172). Therefore, his comment was written almost a century after the edict's enactment (AD 217-18) and reflected the views of an imperial bureaucrat living during a period characterised by its political turbulence.

A major difficulty in using the Digest is that it consists entirely of excerpts from jurists' works, which are organised by books and titles but do not indicate the context from which they were extracted. For example, in our text, the Digest fragment references Ulpian's book but does not specify which praetorian edict is being commented on. This fragment is included in the Digest's title *De verborum significatione* (On the Meaning of Words). This means that some caution is needed in the use of this evidence since what appears now to have been under one heading in the Digest may originally have been said by a jurist in connection with something quite different. Thus, to establish which edict the fragment corresponded to, it is necessary to check the reconstruction from O. Lenel (German legal historian from the late 19th century and beginning of the 20th century) labelled the *palingenesia iuris civilis*.

His work reconstructs the texts of the classical jurists from the fragments contained in the Digest and thus makes it possible to consider them in their original context. According to Lenel's reconstruction (1889[2]: 811 §1514), this fragment was part of a comment on the edict concerning the protection of public rivers to prevent some actions (e.g. constructing a port on the shore) from hampering navigation (*Ne quid in flumine publico ripave eius fiat, quo peius navigetur*, 'You are not to do anything in a public river or on its bank, which makes navigation worse'). Consequently, this fragment provides a description of ports located in riverine spaces and from my point of view, it also included sea-river spaces, since it was quite common to have rivers as points of access from an inland city to the sea (e.g. Rome, Arles). Bearing in mind that the jurist could have been referring to something as common in antiquity as a fluvio-maritime port (Arnaud 2014: 155), one needs to consider Ulpian's mention in the text of ports as enclosed spaces, as well as of the safety of the ships moored in them. These elements could give the impression that the author was referring to physical infrastructure, such as piers or docks. However, the idea that a port must necessarily be closed and protected is a mere assumption.

A ship is safer the more able it is to set sail, because the ability to set sail regularly is a strong indicator of its overall health, readiness, and safety. Regular sailing ensures that the ship is maintained, the crew is experienced and prepared, and the vessel can respond flexibly to any challenges, all of which contribute to its overall safety. If we look at the second part of the fragment, while Ulpian refers to the port as *conclusum*, he describes the *statio* as *conclusa atque munita* ('protected and fortified'). Therefore, I think that the important element to bear in mind here when talking about a port is that the ship should be protected, whether it was in an enclosed space in the port or not.

Taking as an example the case of the imperial port of Rome presented by S. Keay in his paper, it is a well-known fact that one of the major achievements of ancient Rome (as well as other cities such as *Hispalis* or Athens) was that, despite its distance from the sea, it succeeded in overcoming considerable natural constraints and developed a port infrastructure that enabled its population to be supplied from across the Mediterranean (Keay 2012: 34). Part of this success was due to Rome's connection to the sea via the Tiber River, even though the river's topography made navigation challenging. These challenges required ships to be propelled by ropes in certain areas of the river where the water flow was weaker, and the riverbanks were curved (Aguilera Martín 2012). This demanding context implied that knowledge of local navigation, and control of the river traffic (Keay *et al.* 2021) was necessary in order to navigate it successfully, as well as the existence of diverse visible structures that enabled the placement of the ships and the movement of goods. The latter can be appreciated in the diverse constructions that existed in the Tiberine canals connecting Rome with Portus and Ostia (Keay 2012: 48-49).

Impallomeni (1996a: 594-95; 1996b: 372-75) appeals to the diversity of the functions performed in a port: the ship is forced to enter it, but when it has entered and is already safe, the subsequent use of the basin was only concerned with the ease and comfort of the mooring. From my point of view, this conception of dividing the port according to the use of its structures makes no sense at all. A port needs to be understood as a whole, composed of diverse elements that allow both protection and transit. One clear example of the incongruence of Impallomeni's assertion is precisely the imperial port of Rome, which combined both the Claudian and the Trajanic basins, which were built differently and intended to meet different aims. On the one hand, the Claudian basin would have offered protection from the waves, but little safety from wind (Tac., *Ann.* 15.18), while the Trajanic basin offered a stable microclimate in which to moor, repair, and perform other activities (Keay *et al.* 2021: 390-91). However, the Trajanic basin was only one step inside the cycle of distribution of goods towards Rome and the rest of the Mediterranean. Bearing in mind that several texts in which Ulpian uses the verbs *importare* and *exportare* entail movement (D. 39.2.9.1 (Ulp. 53 *ad Ed.*); D. 12.1.4.2 (Ulp. 34 *ad Ed.*); D. 33.7.1.2 (Ulp. 20 *ad Ed.*)), it can be understood that the jurist could be indirectly referring to the whole cycle of distribution, and to the related spaces needed to allow the flow of merchandise. In that sense, Ulpian's definition would be cohesive with the notion of a port system as described by S. Keay.

The other notion included by Ulpian in his definition is that of *statio*, which he defines in the same book *ad edictum*, indicating that the word *statio* derives from *a stando: is igitur locus demonstratur, ubicumque naves tuto stare possunt* ('to stay, and therefore, that place is indicated where ships can stay in safety'; D. 43.12.1.13 (Ulp. 68 *ad Ed.*)). According to Fiorentini (2003: 170-72), there are differences between Ulpian's texts, indicating that the excerpt analysed here refers to a *statio* associated with seaports containing artificial installations such as piers and docks. Instead, in his opinion, the *statio* from D. 43.12.1.17 (see the text in the following paragraph) should refer to river ports that enabled ships to stop there. The latter seems to coincide with the opinion of Luzzatto (1965: 174) who indicated that the *stationes* were structures associated with navigation, and not with port procedures. From our point of view, both authors need to expand their conceptions. The generic nature of Ulpian's definition, induces one to recognise in the *statio* not only the fixed

river port with anchorage and storage facilities, but also any other place where a vessel could stop in safety. That polysemy is not only noticeable in legal sources, but also in the archaeological evidence, which displays the polyfunctionality of *stationes*, as well as the diversity of the features that characterised the ports with which they were associated (France and Nélis Clément 2014). In addition, the authors are creating a strong division between sea and river ports, when fluvio-maritime ports are attested not only in the material evidence (some inscriptions witness the placement of these *stationes* in sea-river areas, e.g.: *AE* 2007, 01228; *ZPE*-86-131), but also in literary texts (Arnaud 2014: 3, 12-15) and, as I argue, in Ulpian's legal fragment.

Statio designates the physical location of the different administrative offices (Coarelli 2019: 11-20). However, in this context, *stationes* would be fixed spots that would have been associated with a port where goods were processed and where ships could stay in safety. The latter implies that in these locations the cargoes were controlled, and taxes collected. Both archaeological and textual evidence (e.g. D.19.2.60.8 (Lab. 5 *Post. a Iav. Epit.*); D.43.12.1pr. (Ulp. 68 *ad Ed.*); D.43.12.1.17 (Ulp. 68 *ad Ed.*)) demonstrate that *stationes* were places of transition that ships needed to pass through when travelling into and out of a port. For example, one could mention Ephesos (*Mon. Eph.* II 26-28, §10; 42-45, §17); Gaul (Matz 2015; Long 2016); Egypt (Rossi 2015), and finally, Portus (Keay 2012: 36, 38). Another function would have been to act as centres for the policing or surveying of the surrounding areas where they were located (Fuhrmann 2012: 201-05). Thus, *stationes* could be helpful in delimiting the space occupied by a port and in the mastering of this space by the Roman emperor (France 2015).

Considering that the edict commented on by Ulpian dealt with the protection of public rivers, it is difficult to avoid the conclusion that the jurist was indirectly referring to the limitations implied by his definition regarding the creation of ports, as these needed to ensure safe navigation in public waters. Another excerpt from Ulpian's book 68 on the edict (and concisely mentioned previously), indicates:

D. 43.12.1.17. Ulp. 68 *ad Ed.* *Si in mari aliquid fiat, Labeo competere tale interdictum: 'ne quid in mari inve litore' quo portus, statio iterve navigio deterius fiat.*

(If anything is done in the sea, Labeo says that this kind of interdict will apply: 'to prevent anything being done in the sea or on the shore' by which the port, the *statio* and/or the passage of a boat is made worse.)

The first thing that one needs to consider when reading this text, is that this fragment precedes in the Digest's order the one analysed previously from Ulpian's book

68 on the edict. Therefore, the author first indicated that nothing should be done in the indicated spaces that makes navigation worse, and then he defines what constitutes a port (Lenel 1889²: 811 §1514).

Individually, ports and the elements forming their systems were protected by means of orders called prohibiting interdicts (e.g. *ne quid in loco publico* or not to be done in a public space (D. 43.12.1pr. (Ulp. 68 *ad Ed.*)). This was a 'fast track' procedure under which the praetor would adjudicate on the question of damage caused to someone's property (Labruna 1971: 61). The interdicts protected the seashores and riverbanks from harmful dumping and/or constructions, including ports and therefore, the different elements that formed their system and enabled the distribution of goods. These interdicts, issued by a praetor or other authorised official (proconsul in the provinces) at the request of a claimant and addressed to another person, were used to prevent someone from constructing anything that would affect the previous quality of the harbour facilities for sailing, mooring, and other port-related activities. That protection can be perceived in several other fragments from the same book number 68 of Ulpian, in which the author established private measures for the protection of places such as rivers, shores, and ports from being less accessible for ships or useful for fishing (D. 43.8.2.1; D. 43.12.1pr.; D. 43.12.1.19-21; D. 43.8.2.9; D. 43.8.2.11 (Ulp. 68 ad Ed.)). In that sense, other excerpts corroborate and complement that view, as it concerns the prevention of uncontrolled building on seashores and/or riverbanks (D. 43.12.1.16 (Ulp. 68 *ad Ed.*); D. 43.13.1.7 (Ulp. 68 *ad Ed.*) and prohibited any modifications that would endanger the use of the shore. Likewise, a text from Pomponius (second century AD) indicates the need to obtain a decree from the praetor to build anything on the seashore (D. 41.1.50 (Pomp. 6 ex Plaut.)). However, the *interdictum* was a provisory remedy with the purpose of protecting existing situations through a quick decision by the official, and thus it is difficult to assess how efficient this remedy was when the work had already been completed. In that case, there was the possibility of using an *actio iniuriarum* (D. 43.8.2.9 (Ulp. 68 *ad Ed.*)), but this opened the way to compensation for the harm done, not to restoration to the previous status (Arnaud 2012: 174).

Thus, what does this mean in relation to the notion of a 'port system' as described by S. Keay? It indicates that if we conceive of the port as a system encompassing all the different elements that enable the distribution and exchange of goods, then the space protected by these interdicts is broader than one would think if *port* is understood only as a location where ships moor and goods are unloaded. It means that all the elements composing the port system were susceptible to protection, and therefore the people using them for trade could apply to the authorities to safeguard their activities. However, this does not mean that individuals were not able to interfere with and alter these spaces in some ways. Therefore, a port system, more than the port itself, had areas that were subject to public rights, such as navigating, fishing, or individual rights such as owning property on the shore, that coincided with the collective use of these spaces. If we follow A. Russell's conclusions on space, what makes a space public is not collective ownership, but the absence of individual control (Russell 2016: 32-41; also, De Marco 2004: 83-85). The latter introduces the topic of the diverse layers of individual vs. public rights overlapping the spaces occupied by port systems. These are not simple questions, and therefore I will only be able to note some issues here to give an idea of the problems involved in the interaction of the public and private spheres in the context of any ancient port system.

Other Port Features Referenced in Legal Texts

The idea that the sea was not considered something that could belong to the Roman state emerges from Polybius (4.17.2), who gives a list (that includes ports) of the categories that, in Republican Rome, were considered res *publicae in patrimonio* – that is to say, the property of the Roman people – and that could be leased out by the censors (Marzano 2013: 249). During the age of Augustus, Vitruvius considered that harbours were by their nature public structures, and for that reason, they belonged to all and were of public use (Vitr. 1.3; Arnaud 2012: 172-74). However, Vitruvius was an engineer and not a jurist, and in that sense, Ulpian provides further nuances to his assertion by saying:

> **D. 50.16.17.pr.-1. Ulp. 10 *ad Ed.*** *Inter 'publica' habemus non sacra nec religiosa nec quae publicis usibus destinata sunt: sed si qua sunt civitatium velut bona. Sed peculia servorum civitatium procul dubio publica habentur. 1. 'Publica' vectigalia intellegere debemus, ex quibus vectigal fiscus capit: quale est vectigal portus vel venalium rerum, item salinarum et metallorum et picariarum.*

> (We do not regard as being 'public' those things which are sacred or hallowed or designed for public use but those things which are, the property of the citizens […] **1.** We must also regard as 'public' those taxes from which the imperial treasury derives revenue, such as a harbour tax or a tax on saltworks, mines, and pitch factories) (transl. Watson).

The fragment belongs to the commentary on the edict *de cognitoribus et procuratoribus*, so referencing magistrates in charge of court proceedings (Lenel 1889²: 455). According to this text, things are public because they belong to the citizens, an idea that is further clarified in another related fragment of Ulpian that refers to 'the Roman people' (see also: D. 50.16.17 (Ulp. 10 *ad Ed.*)).

According to this view, the *vectigal* (state tax income) gathered in ports for the use of harbours and their facilities fit in this category. This text underlines how multilayered port spaces and their associated activities interacted, since in imperial times cities could gather their own taxes after they had received this right from an emperor (Edelmann-Singer 2012: 165-69; Kritzinger 2015: 37). The number of cities that could collect taxes is still unclear; but it is probable that such was the commonest case, and that these taxes constituted a significant part of the cities' revenues (France 1999: 108; Arnaud 2016: 126). However, can one think that because these ports and/or their taxes were managed by their associated cities, they were less public than Portus, which was managed by Roman authorities? The tax concession itself was an imperial decision and constituted an extension of the emperor's power by way of his *imperium*; the situation was perhaps akin to other situations where revenues were applied to the people of Rome directly.

Thus, *imperium* was not conceptualised as a territorial power *per se*, but rather as the influence (power) that it carried (Richardson 1991: 2-9; 2010, 22-23; Ando 2020: 108). The span of the Empire was based on the power of Rome (and its corresponding emperor), rather than any defined physical limit. The latter was well exemplified in the administrative topography of the Empire, with the custom house serving as a key symbol of control over land and sea through an activity that has been described as 'taxing the sea' (Purcell 2017: 329-33). Thus, what I meant to illustrate with these lines is that, regarding the conception of ports as systems, we need to add the layer of these spaces as belonging to an empire that was also connected and constituted a system. And as the empire grew, Romanity and Roman rule ceased to be limited to Romans and their provinces and began to be replaced by ideas of a universal empire, led by an all-powerful emperor (Tuori 2016, 133-34; 216-17; 2018, 204; Mataix Ferrándiz 2022). Therefore, bearing in mind the extension of imperial power through different concessions, the space of politics was suddenly enlarged, so that every port, even if indirectly, was under the umbrella of power of the emperor (see also Ando 2019: 175-76; 187-88).

Finally, one last fragment which finalises our discussion about Roman ports. It was written by Marcian, a mysterious figure of whom we only know that he worked during the Severan period and that he probably had a role as magistrate (D. 1.6.2 (Ulp. 8 *de Off. Proc.*)) 'Aelius Marcianus, *proconsul Baeticae*', and I. 1.8.2. Buckland 1936: 275-78; Honoré 1962: 212-17; Liebs 1997: 201-02; Andrés 2004: 131-33).

D. 1.8.4.pr-1 (Marc. 3 *Inst.*). *Nemo igitur ad litus maris accedere prohibetur piscandi causa, dum tamen ullius et aedificiis et monumentis abstineatur, quia non sunt iuris gentium sicut et mare: idque et divus pius piscatoribus formianis et capenatis rescripsit.* **1.** *Sed flumina paene omnia et portus publica sunt.*

(No one, therefore, is prohibited from going on to the seashore to fish, provided they keep clear of houses, buildings, or monuments, since these are not, as the sea certainly is, subject to the *ius gentium*. So, it was laid down by the deified Pius in a rescript to the fishermen of Formiae and Capena. But almost all rivers and ports are public property.)

This fragment belongs to Marcian's third book of *institutiones*, textbooks written partly for law students and partly as commentaries on current law (Kruger 1888: 251). There has been much discussion about the aims and purpose of Marcian's work. Some believe that it was intended to serve as preparatory reading material and instructions for imperial officials (Pernice 1900: 3-7), or the staff of the chancellery or the provinces; others (Ferrini 1929: 87) think that it could have served as an introductory book to Roman law for the eastern inhabitants of the Empire, incorporated into citizenship after the *constitutio Antoniniana* (AD 212), although in such a case it may look strange that the book was not written in Greek. From either perspective, it seems that Marcian's book probably did not intend to establish rigid classifications, but rather to comment on and explain the law of his time, providing some examples and categories.

The fragment above belongs to a book under the heading *de rerum divisione*, or on the classification of things, which was important in terms of establishing whether some things or spaces are susceptible to individual ownership. For example, the sea, the seashore, the air, and running water belong to all humankind, and therefore these could not be acquired privatively by individual subjects (D. 1.8.2.1 (Marc 3 *Inst.*)). Public land had a peculiar status within the Roman system of property, in that individuals could not own it, but they could establish possession over it, a right that would closely resemble that of ownership. Buildings located on the seashores could be classified as private property (D. 43.8.2.3 (Ulp. 68 *ad Ed.*)) if there was a specific concession (Fiorentini 2003: 451, 499-50). Therefore, when Marcian indicates that most ports and rivers were public, the jurist meant that no individual could use these exclusively and that these spaces were meant to be used by all. However, similarly to the case with seashores, whether private properties were labelled as public did not entail that they would be considered part of a port, especially if one bears in mind the concept of a port system. Using Portus as a first example, excavations in the late antique Basilica *portuense* (fourth-fifth centuries AD) have revealed that prior to the construction of the temple, the area was occupied by several buildings possibly devoted to retail activities, and which underwent a continual process of development from the first to the third centuries AD (Maiorano and Paroli 2013: 11, 22, 40, 368, 372, 484). The *dolia* warehouse located in the ancient Roman port of Marseille constitutes another example of a port area that was used on a private basis; in this case, this is evidenced by the names inscribed in the *dolia* stored in the facility: the Pirani family (Hesnard 1999; Sciallano and Liou 1985; Sciallano and Marlier 2008; Carré and Cibecchini 2020: 159-62; Cheung 2024: 87-96).

One final element to take from Marcian's fragment is that the jurist indicates that, by virtue of the *ius gentium*, the seashore, as well as the sea, were accessible to all men if they respected private properties (Aubert 2020: 109-10). Concerning the *ius gentium*, its existence was a response to the fact that in most ancient empires the basic legal tenet was that the law applied to people based on the personality principle (in other words, the community to which one belonged), rather than the area principle, as is common in modern states (for example, laws applied to those living in Judea or in Egypt). In the Roman world, the law worked in a layered way, applying the personal legal principle (citizen vs. non-citizen) to a legally bounded or defined space, such as the land of the Romans, or the land of the Egyptians (Ando 2011: 2-4; Tuori 2018: 201-18; Mataix Ferrándiz 2022). In this context, the *ius gentium* was the law governing the relations of Rome with peoples other than Romans, and to the relations of the foreigners among them in Roman lands (Winkel 2013: 3553). By indicating that ports were public, Marcian was indirectly indicating that these areas were under the umbrella of the *iure gentium*, as rivers were, along with their associated activities (D. 1.8.5pr.-1 (Gaius 2 *Rer.Cott.Siv.Aur.*)). This should not surprise us since both ports and rivers were places of encounter between people from different legal backgrounds (e.g. Tyrian in Puteoli, Jews in Neapolis). In addition, recalling the first text analysed in this paper, Ulpian described a port as a place where the import and export of merchandise took place, which self-evidently involved citizens and non-citizens. Marcian's fragment responds to the context in which the jurist wrote his works (third century AD), responding to the exigencies of the exploitation of the seas, as well as to the traffic of subjects from different legal backgrounds along their shores (Dell'Oro 1963: 288-89). Bearing in mind S. Keay's concept, and the different structures and locations needed to enable these two activities, the extension of the rule of the *iure gentium* goes beyond the areas where goods were exchanged and extends over the whole of the structures forming the port system. The latter characterises Roman ports as effectively, interfaces between land and sea, where individuals from different legal backgrounds and statuses could interact and exchange goods.

Conclusion

The different fragments studied in this paper have complemented the notions underlined in S. Keay's 2012 paper. From Ulpian's definition, one can see that the jurist was not necessarily indicating that ports needed to be large, complex hubs with a highly developed infrastructure, but were rather simply protected spaces where imports and exports could take place. In that sense, ports were not only places with a specific physical layout but also encompassed their related human activities. This constitutes an expansive concept that allows one to include several kinds of ports, whether artificial and natural, and whether they were located on the seashore or along riverbanks. When we look at the archaeological evidence with the focus provided by S. Keay's paper, we can see how the whole ensemble operated. In that sense, one of the texts established the remedies (interdicts) that could be used by individuals to protect themselves when port activities affected their use of public water spaces. Embedded in that provision was a sense of mobility and flow, which would only make sense if we understood ports in relation to the different elements and structures that enabled their functioning. When we look at the jurists' legal texts, it does not seem that this vision was foreign to them, but was rather familiar, and in addition they assumed that they were dealing with the multilayered universe of human relations established in these port systems. It is then that we start to see how the rights of the community interacted with private ownership, and how different activities were organised and accommodated in relation to the spaces and their legal characterisations.

Another element that one needs to bear in mind is how the concept of Roman rule and Romanity changed over time, affecting both the legal realm and the politics applicable to these port spaces. While during the Republican period, one may have referred to ports as *res publicae in patrimonio*, as Polybius liked to tell, as the Empire grew the authority of the emperor (as extended by his magistrates and other institutional tools) was increasingly exerted over these spaces. In that way, the *stationes* and port-related taxes reminded the seafarer of the authority and extent of the power of the emperor, who sometimes allowed the provinces to manage these duties at his discretion. However, despite the ever-present imperial authority throughout the port systems, these spaces were partly governed by the *iure gentium*, which characterised these areas as places where people of different backgrounds could interact, even when operating in the land of the Romans.

In sum, I would say that a port system could indeed be defined as 'a set of interdependent component parts forming an integrated whole' (Keay 2012), to which we need to add 'wherein the rights of the individuals and the community interacted and converged'. It is in this way that we can pass beyond the material evidence and be able to see within it a world of human relationships.

Bibliography

Aguilera Martín, A. 2012. La sirga en el Tiber en época romana, in S. Keay (ed.) *Rome, Portus and the Mediterranean*: 105-23. Rome: British School at Rome.

Ando, C. 2011. *Law, Language, and Empire in the Roman Tradition*. Philadelphia: University of Pennsylvania Press.

Ando, C. 2019. The space and time of politics in civil war, in C. Rosillo-López (ed.) *Communicating Public Opinion in the Roman Republic*: 175-88. Stuttgart: Steiner.

Ando, C. 2020. Public Law and Republican Empire in Rome, 200-27 BCE, in E. Cavanagh (ed.) *Empire and Legal Thought: Ideas and Institutions from Antiquity to Modernity*: 105-24. Leiden: Brill.

Andrés, F.J. 2004. Aelio Marciano, in R. Domingo (ed.) *Juristas Universales. 1. Juristas Antiguos*: 131-33. Barcelona: Marcial Pons.

Arnaud, P. 2012. Maritime Infrastructure. Between Public and Private Initiative, in A. Kolb (ed.) *Infrastruktur und Herrschaftsorganisationim Imperium Romanum*: 161-79. Berlin: De Gruyter.

Arnaud, P. 2014. Entre mer et rivière : les ports fluvio-maritimes de Méditerranée ancienne. Modèles et solutions, in C. Sanchez and M.-P. Jézégou (eds) *Les ports dans l'espace méditerranéen antique. Narbonne et les systèmes portuaires fluvio-lagunaires. Colloque à l'espace Capdeville, Montpellier 22/23 mai 2014*: 139-55. Montpellier: Éditions de l'Association de la Revue archéologique de Narbonnaise.

Arnaud, P. 2016. Cities and maritime trade under the Roman Empire, in C. Schafer (ed.) *Connecting the Ancient World: Mediterranean Shipping, Maritime Networks and their Impact*: 117-76. Rahden: Leidorf.

Babusiaux, U. 2016. Legal writing and legal reasoning, in C. Ando, P.J. Du Plessis and K. Tuori (eds) *The Oxford Handbook on Roman Law and Society*: 176-87. Oxford: Oxford University Press.

Brennan, C. 2000. *The Praetorship in the Roman Republic*, 2 vols. Oxford: Oxford University Press.

Buckland, W.W. 1936. Marcian, in *Studi in onore di S. Riccobono*, I: 273-83. Palermo: Castiglia.

Cairns, J. and P.J. Plessis 2007. *Beyond Dogmatics: Law and Society in the Roman World*. Edinburgh: Edinburgh University Press.

Carré, M.B. and F. Cibecchini 2020. *Tableau de synthèse des timbres sur dolia maritimes*, in C. Carrato and F. Cibecchini, *Nouvelles recherches sur les dolia: l'exemple de la Méditerranée nord-occidentale à l'époque romaine (Ier s. av. J.-C.–IIIe s. ap. J.-C.)* (Revue archéologique de la narbonnaise. Supplément 50): 159-62. Montpellier: Revue archéologique de la narbonnaise.

Cheung, C. 2024. *Dolia: The Containers that Made Rome an Empire of Wine*. Princeton: Princeton University Press.

Coarelli, F. 2019. *Statio: i luoghi dell'amministrazione nell'antica Roma*. Rome: Quasar.

Coriat, J-P. 1997. *Le prince législateur*. Rome: École française de Rome.

Crifò, G. 1976. Ulpiano. Esperienze e responsabilità del giurista, in H. Temporini (ed.) *Aufstieg und Niedergang der römischen Welt*, II.15: 708-86. Berlin: De Gruyter.

Dell'Oro, A. 1963. Le 'Res communes omnium' dell'elenco di Marciano e il problema del loro fondamento giuridico. *Studi Urbinati* 31: 237-90.

De Marco, N. 2004. *I 'loci publici' dal I al III secolo: le identifcazioni dottrinali, il ruolo dell' usus, gli strumenti di tutela*. Naples: Satura.

Edelmann-Singer, B. 2012. Die Finanzielle und Wirtschaftliche Dimension der Provinziallandtage in der Römischen Kaiserzeit, in S. Günther (ed.) *Ordnungsrahmen antiker Ökonomien: Ordnungskonzepte und Steuerungsmechanismen antiker Wirtschaftssysteme im Vergleich*: 165-79. Wiesbaden: Harrassowitz.

Ferrini, C. 1929. Intorno alle Istituzioni di Marciano, in *Opere di Contardo Ferrini*, II: 85-90. Milan: Hoepli.

Fiorentini, M. 2003. *Fiumi e mari nell'esperienza giuridica romana: profili di tutela processuale e di inquadramento sistematico*. Milan: Giuffrè.

France, J. 1999. Un dispensator [(F(isci) K(astrensis)?] des trois Augustes dans le port romain de Toulon (Telo Martius). *Zeitschrift für Papyrologie und Epigraphik* 125: 272-76.

France, J. 2015. L'empereur romain et le contrôle de l'espace, in *Il princeps romano: autocrate o magistrato? Fattori giuridici e fattori sociali del potere imperiale da Augusto a Commodo*: 731-76. Pavia: Iuss Press.

France, J. and J. Nélis-Clement 2014. *La statio: archéologie d'un lieu de pouvoir dans l'empire Romain*. Bordeaux: Ausonius.

Fuhrmann, C. 2012. *Policing the Roman Empire*. Oxford: Oxford University Press.

Hesnard, A. 1999. Le port de Marseille romaine : d'Auguste à la fin du IVe de notre ère, in *Marseille: 10 ans d'archéologie, 2600 ans d'histoire, Musée d'histoire de Marseille*: 45-47. Saint-Rémy-de-Provence: Edisud.

Honoré, T. 1962. The Severian lawyers: a preliminary survey. *Studia et documenta historiae et iuris* 28: 162-232.

Honoré, T. 1994. *Emperors and Lawyers: With a Palingenesia of Third-Century Imperial Rescripts 193-305 AD*. Oxford: Oxford University Press.

Honoré, T. 2002. *Ulpian*. Oxford: Oxford University Press.

Honoré, T. 2010. *Justinian's Digest: Character and Compilation*. Oxford: Oxford University Press.

Horden, P. and N. Purcell 2000. *The Corrupting Sea: A Study of Mediterranean History*. Oxford: Blackwell.

Impallomeni, G. 1996a. La ammissibilità della proprietà privata sulle darsene interne, in *Scritti di diritto romano e tradizione romanistica*: 583-610. Padua: Cedam.

Impallomeni, G. 1996b. Le rade, i porti, le darsene e le opere a terra, in *Scritti di diritto romano e tradizione romanistica*. 367-90: Padua: Cedam.

Johnston, D. 1999. *Roman Law in Context*. Cambridge: Cambridge University Press.

Keay, S.J. 2012. The Port System of Imperial Rome, in S. Keay (ed.) *Rome, Portus and the Mediterranean*: 33-65. Rome: British School at Rome.

Keay, S.J. and P. Arnaud (eds) 2020. *Roman Port Societies: The Evidence of Inscriptions*. Cambridge: Cambridge University Press.

Keay, S.J., M. Millett, L. Paroli and K. Strutt 2005. *Portus: An Archaeological Survey of the Portus of Imperial Rome*. Rome: British School at Rome.

Keay, S.J. and L. Paroli 2011. *Portus and its Hinterland: Recent Archaeological Research*. Rome: British School at Rome.

Keay, S. *et al.* 2021. Space, accessibility and movement through the Portus Romae, in F. Vermeulen and A. Zuiderhoek (eds) *Space, Movement and the Economy in Roman Cities in Italy and Beyond*: 375-417. London: Routledge.

Kritzinger, P. 2015. Das römische Zollsystem bis in das 3. Jh. n.Chr., in P. Kritzinger, F. Schleicher and T. Stickler (eds) *Studien zum römischen Zollwesen*: 11-55. Duisburg: Reihe Geschichte.

Labruna, L. 1971. *Vim fieri veto: alle radici di una ideologia*. Naples: Jovene.

Lenel, O. 1889. *Palingenesia iuris civilis*, 2 vols. Leipzig: Tauchnitz.

Liebs, D. 1994. Domitius Ulpianus, in *Handbuch der lateinischen Literatur der Antike*, IV: 863-68. Munich: Beck.

Liebs, D. 1997. Aelius Marcianus, in *Handbuch der lateinischen Literatur der Antike*, IV: 201-05. Munich: Beck.

Long, L. 2016. Navigation et commerce dans le delta du Rhône durant l'antiquité, in C. Sanchez and M.-P. Jézégou (eds) *Les ports dans l'espace méditerranéen antique: Narbonne et les systèmes portuaires fluvio-lagunaires; Colloque à l'espace Capdeville, Montpellier 22/23 mai 2014*: 199-217. Montpellier-Lattes: Éditions de l'Association de la Revue archéologique de Narbonnaise.

Luzzatto, G.I. 1965. *Il Problema d'origine del processo extra ordinem*. Milan: Giufrè.

Maiorano, M. and L. Paroli 2013. *La Basilica Portuense: scavi 1991-2007*. Rome: All'insegna del giglio.

Marotta, V. 2000. *Ulpiano e l'Impero*. Naples: Loffredo.

Marzano, A. 2013. *Harvesting the Sea: The Exploitation of Marine Resources in the Roman Mediterranean*. Oxford: Oxford University Press.

Mataix Ferrándiz, E. 2022. *Gone under Sea: Shipwrecks, Legal Landscapes and Mediterranean Paradigms*. Leiden: Brill.

Matz, S. 2015. Die stationes des gallischen Zollbezirkes aus archäologischer Sicht in Westen nichts Neues? — Eine kurze Bestandsaufnahme, in P. Kritzinger, F. Schleicher and T. Stickler (eds) *Studien zum römischen Zollwesen*: 245-51. Duisburg: Wellem.

Mayer-Maly, T. 1999. *Römishes Recht*. Vienna: Springer.

Moatti, C. 2000. Le contrôle de la mobilité des personnes dans l'empire romain. *Mélanges de l'École française de Rome, Antiquité* 112: 925-58.

Pernice, A. 1900. Über die sogenannten res communes omnium, in *Festgabe der Gießener Juristenfakultät für Heinrich Dernburg zum 4. April 1900*: 3-28. Berlin: De Gruyter.

Pölönen, J. 2016. Framing 'law and society' in the Roman world, in C. Ando, P.J. Du Plessis and K. Tuori (eds) *The Oxford Handbook on Roman Law and Society*: 8-21. Oxford: Oxford University Press.

Purcell, N. 2017. Taxing the sea, in P. De Souza, C. Buchet and P. Arnaud (eds) *The Sea in History: The Ancient World*: 319-34. Woodbridge: Boydell & Brewer.

Richardson, J. 1991. *Imperium Romanum*: Empire and the language of power. *The Journal of Roman Studies* 81: 1-9.

Richardson, J. 2010. The meaning of *imperium* in the last century BC and the first AD, in B. Kingsbury and B. Straumann (eds) *The Roman Foundations of the Law of Nations: Alberico Gentili and the Justice of Empire*: 21-29. Oxford: Oxford University Press.

Robinson, O.F. 1997. *The Sources of Roman Law*. London: Routledge.

Rossi, L. 2015. Les temps de transport du blé égyptien : de la chôra vers Alexandrie... et vers les ports de Méditerranée. *Pallas: Revue d'études antiques* 99: 193-208.

Russell, A. 2016. *The Politics of Public Space in Republican Rome*. Cambridge: Cambridge University Press.

Sciallano, M. and B. Liou 1985. Les épaves de Tarraconaise a chargement d'amphores Dressel 2-4. *Archaeonautica* 5: 5-178.

Sciallano, M. and E. Marlier 2008. L'épave à dolia de l'île de la Giraglia (Haute-Corse). *Archaeonautica* 15: 115-54.

Tuori, K. 2016. *The Emperor of Law: The Emergence of Roman Imperial Adjudication*. Oxford: Oxford University Press.

Tuori, T. 2018. The savage sea and the civilizing law: the Roman law tradition and the rule of the sea, in H. Kopp and C. Wendt (eds) *Thalassokratographie: Rezeption und Transformation Antiker Seeherrschaft*: 201-18. Berlin: De Gruyter.

Watson, A. (ed.) 1985. *The Digest of Justinian*, 4 vols. Philadelphia: University of Philadelphia Press.

Winkel, L.C. 2013. Ius gentium, in R.S. Bagnall *et al.* (eds) *The Encyclopedia of Ancient History*: 3553-54. Malden: Wiley-Blackwell.

6. The Peutinger Map, Portus, and the Temple of Peace

Peter B. Campbell

Introduction

The Peutinger Map, also known as the Tabula Peutingeriana, is the most famous surviving Roman map. Currently housed in the Austrian National Library, it first came to light as part of the 16th-century collection of Konrad Peutinger in Augsburg, Germany (Talbert 2010: 2). It has been the subject of significant study ever since, with its origins proving enigmatic and source of an energetic discourse. The parchment dates to the 13th century (all dates AD unless otherwise noted), consisting of eleven connected segments measuring approximately 672 cm by 33 cm (22 ft by 1 ft) in total (Talbert 2010: 73-75). It depicts the world as known to the Romans, from the Atlantic Ocean in the west to Asia in the east. However, the western extreme of the map, which depicted the Atlantic coast including Britain and Iberia, is evidently missing (Talbert 2010: 91). As the outermost section of the map when rolled, the Atlantic portion was the most exposed and seemingly suffered for it.

While the parchment dates to the 13th century, it appears to be a copy of an earlier Roman map since it includes Pompeii, Herculaneum, and Oplontis which were destroyed in the AD 79 Vesuvian eruption. The map is 'not temporally coherent', as Andrew Riggsby states, containing not only the destroyed Campanian cities but also place names dating to later centuries (2019: 194). Richard Talbert argues that certain place names demonstrate original elements from the 1st century, but other information dates to the 2nd-4th centuries, such as the territory of Dacia conquered in the early 2nd century, which was subsequently lost by 270 (Talbert 2010: 134). Talbert argues for the map being 'a decorative scheme for a specific public space inside some imperial palace of the Tetrarchic period', dating to around 300 (Talbert 2010: 7). Dilke likewise argues for a 4th-century date, drawing on a 1st-century map (Dilke 1987a: 234). The current consensus is that the Peutinger Map resulted from a map created and amended during the 1st-4th centuries and then subject to a 'line of successive copies' until the 13th century (Talbert 2010: 123). The discourse about the Peutinger Map from the 16th century through today is presented in Talbert's seminal work *Rome's World: The Peutinger Map Reconsidered* (2010).

The source of the 1st-century information has been the subject of extensive debate. Historical sources refer to Roman maps beginning in the 2nd century BC (Dilke 1987b: 204-05), though physical evidence of these maps have not survived. These appear to be primarily cadastral maps indicating land ownership, but ancient sources indicate a Republican-era map of Italy painted on the Temple of Tellus (Dilke 1987b: 205; Varro, *De re rustica* 1.2.1). There are more sources for Augustan-era maps. This includes a world map, or *mappamundi*, created by Agrippa in the 1st century BC and placed on display in the Porticus Vipsania after his death (Dilke 1987b: 208). Augustus and Agrippa may have used geographical data collected during their census to create the *mappamundi*. It has been argued that the marble plan of *via Anicia* was an Augustan Forma Urbis Romae, or map of Rome, dating to the 1st century (Coarelli 2020); however, this remains the subject of intense debate and this chapter focuses on *mappamundi*. There appears to be an Augustan tradition of map-making (Rodríguez-Almeida 2002: 37), stemming from the cadastral maps but covering large geographical regions. The general consensus holds that it is evident through historical and archaeological sources that the Romans were creating representations of geographical spaces by the 1st century (Riggsby 2019: 198).

This chapter seeks to contribute to the discourse on the Peutinger Map with information from the Portus Project. Drawing on survey and excavation, evidence is presented for a visually accurate depiction of 1st-century Portus. This suggests that the original map was a physical one in Rome dating to the third quarter of the 1st century. While Talbert and Dilke present compelling arguments for a 4th-century original that drew on earlier material, the author uses the Portus evidence to propose an alternate hypothesis. In this approach, the temporal incoherence is the result of a 1st-century original map in a monumental setting that existed as a 'living document' that was updated until the 4th century. At this point, it was copied to commence the line of successive copies leading to the 13th-century Peutinger Map.

The Portus Project and the Imperial Harbour

Recent research by the Portus Project has provided a new interpretation of the imperial harbour, which contributes to our understanding of the 1st-century elements on the map. Portus is an entirely artificial harbour created in the alluvium of the Tiber north of Ostia. It was built at the direction of Claudius and later

Figure 6.1. Rome and Portus on the Peutinger Map (Austrian National Library, Cod. 324, Segm. IV).

expanded by Trajan. On the Peutinger Map, Portus is located below Rome and across the Tiber from Ostia (Figure 6.1). It is unusual that Portus is prominently illustrated with architectural features, as it is the only harbour depicted, and major cities, which are personified, do not possess this level of architectural detail.

Julius Caesar investigated the possibility of constructing a harbour prior to his assassination, as Ostia was unsuitable for large grain ships and the river mouth had issues with siltation. It was not until Claudius that the construction of Portus began. The expenditure was so enormous that the architects tried to dissuade Claudius, and though the sum is unknown, it would

have been comparable to the greatest public works project in Rome (Cassius Dio 60.11.3). Commenced in 46, the construction was completed after Claudius's death. Nero minted a sestertius depicting Portus in 64 (Figure 6.4), perhaps to mark the harbour's completion (Weiss 2013). The coin depicts two harbour moles or breakwaters, circular in shape, lined with porticos, temples, and buildings. Between the two moles is an island bearing a statue. A number of ships are anchored within the harbour and two vessels are shown entering and exiting. At the bottom is a reclining male deity, representing either the Tiber, Oceanus, or the harbour.

Despite the scale of the Claudian basin at Portus, or rather due to it, the large grain ships could not offload

Figure 6.2. Testaguzza's interpretation of the design of Portus following the excavations in the 1950s; the illustration is oriented with east on the right side (Testaguzza 1970: 154-55).

in the harbour due to windage affecting vessels with significant freeboard (Keay *et al.* 2021: 390). In fact, a storm in 62 sank 200 ships in the Claudian basin (Tacitus 15.18). Therefore, the crucial Alexandrian grain ships continued to offload at Pozzuoli in the Bay of Naples rather than Portus. It was not until Trajan expanded the harbour in 103, constructing the distinctive hexagonal inner basin which protected vessels from both wind and sea-state, that the grain ships were able to travel to the banks of the Tiber to offload.

Its distinct hexagonal shape came to represent the image of Portus in subsequent periods. Every known depiction of Portus after the 2nd century AD, from contemporary coins (Figure 6.4), gems, and poems to medieval and early modern maps, prominently features the distinctive hexagonal basin (Juvenal, *Satires* 12.75-82; Testaguzza 1970: 32-49; Bertolami Fine Art 2019: 488-89). The most visible element of Portus today remains the Trajanic basin.

Portus has been the subject of research for centuries due to interest from antiquarians. Testaguzza compiled all known depictions and reconstructions of the harbour in his volume, providing a useful resource (1970: 32-49; Fig. 6.2). A 1582 depiction of the harbour ruins and, incredibly, a reconstruction created by Ignazio and Antonio Danti is located in the Vatican's Gallerie delle Carte Geografiche. The reconstruction has the general shape of the harbour correct, but it

inaccurately reconstructs the Darsena in favour of prominently displaying the hexagonal Trajanic basin. This is to be expected, as following the construction of the Trajanic basin, the hexagonal basin is typically the sole feature that artists illustrate to depict Portus, with the hexagonal form being so recognisable, and entirely omitting the Claudian basin (Testaguzza 1970: 32-49; Keay and Woytek 2022). Modern research at Portus commenced with the 1950s archaeological programme directed by Ortello Testaguzza (1970), who excavated Portus during the construction of Leonardo da Vinci International Airport at Fiumicino. While the Trajanic basin has remained visible as a private lake, the Claudian basin is obscured by sedimentation and progradation of the coastline. Through the excavations, Testaguzza uncovered a number of harbour features, including moles, and offered the first modern reconstruction of Portus (Figure 6.3). However, he incorrectly oriented the harbour to the north and hypothesised that the internal harbour works, namely the Darsena, was one of the basin's external arms (Testaguzza 1970: 154-55).

Over a decade, the Portus Project investigated the site through survey and excavation under the direction of Simon Keay, the Parco Archeologico di Ostia Antica, and a consortium of collaborative partners (Keay and Paroli 2011; Keay 2012; Germoni *et al.* 2018). Geophysics, coring, and excavation revealed the design and construction of the Claudian harbour. The result is a reconstruction that differs fundamentally from

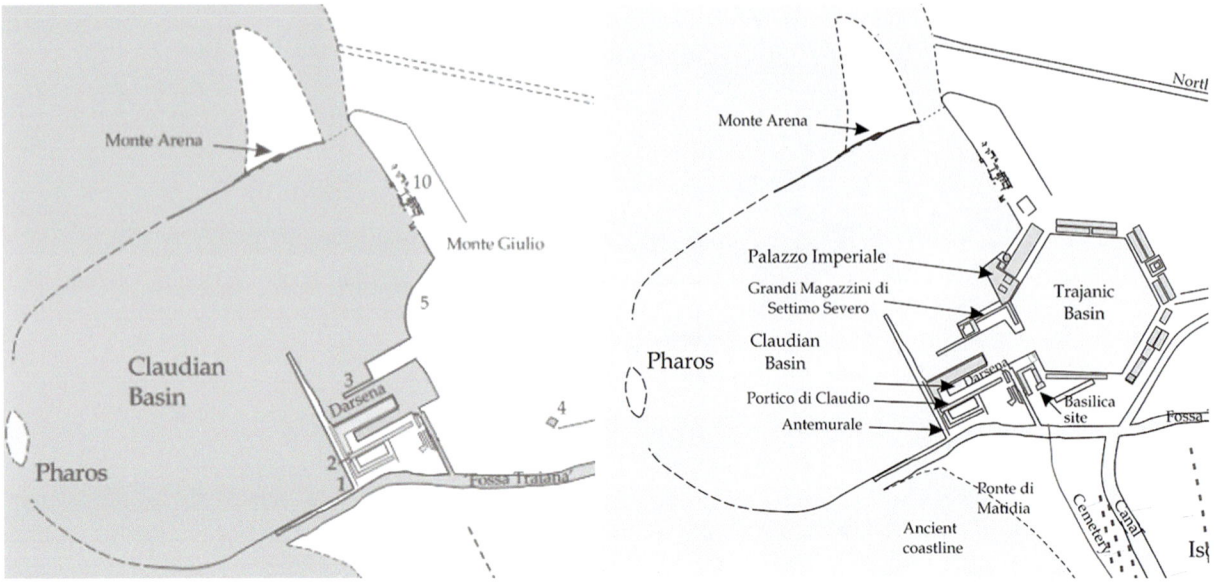

Figure 6.3. Left, the Claudian harbour at Portus (AD 46-103) and, right, the Trajanic harbour at Portus (Portus Project).

Testaguzza. The Portus Project reconstruction shows two large curving harbour moles, creating an ovoid basin oriented WSW, better suiting the depiction on Nero's sestertius than Testaguzza's interpretation. It is distinctly cross-cut inside by the Darsena, a structure formed of a monumental façade and internal harbourwork, facilitating the unloading and storage of cargo in warehouses (Keay and Paroli 2011). This internal structure cross-cut the ovoid harbour and was the most visible monumental feature for those arriving by ship. At the mouth of the harbour was an artificial island with a large lighthouse, while a series of smaller lighthouses or signal towers were located within the harbour at the ends of the internal quay such as the Darsena. The Claudian phase existed between 64-103, though perhaps used from 46 before its official completion. A great deal of the Claudian construction is only accessible today through geophysics and coring. The shape of Portus is unusual and reflects the harbour being entirely artificial and built in alluvium. Other Mediterranean harbours are part natural harbour and part built environment, leading to the irregular shapes of Alexandria, Carthage, Piraeus, Caesarea, and, nearer to Rome, Centumcellae. The exterior moles and the interior spaces of these harbours reflect the contours of the natural anchorage that existed before the built features. Only Portus has the clean distinctive lines of the ovoid breakwaters and cross-cutting Darsena, which are made possible due to the entirely artificial construction. Therefore, it was not until the geophysics and coring of the Portus Project in the 2010s that the orientation and shape were identified, which corresponds to the shape that is depicted on the Peutinger Map.

Figure 6.4. Nero's sestertius issued in 64 showing the Claudian basin of Portus (© The Trustees of the British Museum).

The illustration of Portus as it existed between 46-103 has implications, which the remainder of this chapter explores. However, more immediately, it means that there was a physical map dating to the second half of the 1st century and this depiction of Portus was copied until the 13th century. The Claudian and Trajanic phases therefore provide a *terminus ante quem* and *terminus post quem* for the original 1st-century map. The presence of Portus indicates that the map must date to after the start of construction in 46 and perhaps even after its completion in 64. Significantly, the hexagonal Trajanic basin was the most recognisable feature of Portus's second phase. Had the basin existed at the time of the original map, then one would expect to see it illustrated as it is prominently featured in depictions of the harbour from the 2nd century through the modern era. Its absence provides a *terminus post quem* of 103. The creation of the original map must date to 46-103 and, when combined with the cities destroyed by the Vesuvian eruption, perhaps even as narrow as the 15-year period of 64-79 from the completion of the harbour to the eruption.

A Physical 1st-Century AD Map

The Peutinger Map contains so much information that interpretations often reflect the scholar examining it. Carolingian and medieval scholars see a Carolingian and medieval map (Albu 2014), while Roman scholars, the author included, see a Roman map. However, a consensus has formed around a Roman date for the original due to several features. Italy composes a third of the overall map and the city of Rome is situated in the centre (Talbert 2010: 91). It features Roman roads and, as previously mentioned, Roman cities destroyed by the Vesuvian eruption. Significantly, the map is not oriented around Christian sites or symbols, with the Holy Land minimally represented, and large Christian centres like Constantinople and Antioch are seemingly added at a later date (Talbert 2010: 124, 135). This led Talbert to propose a 4th-century date for the original map, arguing that it was a propaganda piece displayed in a palace under the Tetrarchy (Talbert 2010: 7).

Every hypothesis about the Peutinger Map is an effort to explain its temporal incoherence. Talbert does this by hypothesising an organic (e.g. parchment, papyrus, etc.) map dating to *c.* 300, which draws on earlier data and receives updates in subsequent centuries. The map and its shape would have been copied until the 13th century. The author seeks to explain the incoherence as a 1st-century map made of inorganic material (e.g. marble, mosaic, etc.), which served as a 'living document' that was updated over several centuries. The Peutinger Map's elongated shape would have come after the 4th century through the process of translating the marble map into a more portable, organic, medium. In this hypothesis, the Campanian cities provide a *terminus ante quem* for the commissioning of the original map, but as a living document Constantinople, Antioch, and the Dacian toponyms were added on top of the existing map throughout its use-life.

However, there is a healthy discourse about whether the Romans had cartographic maps and whether the Peutinger Map could be a copy of one, or if the map

was based on the rich tradition of itineraries. Many of the map's illustrations are non-distinct and both the orientation of the map and the distances listed along the roads have led some to argue that the map could be created from an itinerary, or a table of place names and distances, perhaps even in the medieval period (Brodersen 2003). A parallel exists with the geographer Ptolemy's list of distances and place names, which later map-makers used to construct visual representations of a world map. In fact, an argument has been put forward that Agrippa's *mappamundi* was not cartographic, but a table of distances and place names, going so far as to argue that the Romans lacked physical maps (Arnaud 1989; Brodersen 2003). There is a strong tradition of itineraries in the Mediterranean, which includes *periploi*, that compiles geographical knowledge through the linear perspective of the traveller (Dilke 1987a). Scholars such as Nicolet view the Peutinger Map's road networks as part of this linear tradition (2015: 70). This hypothesis is not unwarranted, and the oddly-shaped Peutinger Map could have been drawn by a Roman or medieval scribe from a list of place names and measurements, a list which could have included the destroyed Campanian cities.

Scholars such as Dilke, Talbert, and Riggsby come down on the other side, arguing persuasively that cartographic maps did exist in the Roman world. Dilke and Talbert review historical maps and archaeological remains around the Roman provinces. For example, there is an account of a rhetorical school in Augustodunum in the 290s that states, 'there are pictured in that spot [...] the sites of all locations with their names, their extent, and the distance between them' (*Panegyrici latini* 9(4).20.2-21.3; Talbert 2010: 137), which implies a cartographic map. Theodosius II commissioned a map in Constantinople in 435 that does not survive today, but whose inscription implies that it was cartographic rather than distance measurements (Talbert 2010: 138-39). As for the Peutinger Map, Riggsby argues that it 'is too complex to have arisen from the formless data of itineraries and still come as close to "reality" as it actually does' (Riggsby 2019: 194). The temporal discrepancies and lack of utility for planning travel routes indicate a design meant to display, probably for conveying Rome's power, rather than an itinerary (Riggsby 2019: 194). Talbert similarly lands on a visually decorative piece since the map would not be useful for actual travel (2010: 7).

Significantly, the Peutinger Map was not the only Roman *mappamundi* to seemingly survive into the medieval period. A similar map was in the possession of the bishop of Padua in 1495, which had been acquired from the Council of Basle in the 1430s (Talbert 2010: 11). An account from the Dominican house of Colmar who wrote 'In the year 1265 I drew a map of the world onto twelve skins of parchment' (Talbert 2010: 164). Judith Herrin argues that the anonymous cosmographer of Ravenna, writing in the 7th century, had consulted a similar copy of the original map akin to the Peutinger Map, but in Latin and Greek, marking another copy of an original (2020: 281-82), also discussed by Talbert (2010: 164). There is evidence of each being separate from the Peutinger Map and from each other, suggesting that multiple *mappaemundi* were in circulation. Were these all copies of one original, or was knowledge of geography widespread? It is unknown, as the Peutinger Map is the only one to survive to the present day.

The visual depiction of Portus, correctly illustrating the design of the harbour's Claudian phase and its location relative to the Tiber and Ostia, challenges these hypotheses by providing evidence of a Roman map depicting spatial information. In particular, it demonstrates that there was a physical 1st-century AD map that provided a visual representation of the Roman Empire, rather than a medieval map drawn from a Roman itinerary. By depicting a version of Portus that only existed in the second half of the 1st century, the original map's creation can be dated to within this window. The Portus evidence thus provides new information about the map's date through visual information.

The Commissioning of the Map

The presence of the Campanian cities and the illustration of Claudian Portus limits the Italian section of the map to a 33- (46-79) or 15- (64-79) year window. Who could have commissioned the original map? One should carefully consider private commissioning by a wealthy patron or school; however, there are several reasons to think this was a public map rather than private. The fact that the map draws on geographic information from the 1st-4th centuries or was revised over the centuries suggests it was durable and accessible, and the updates reflect political power. This implies a physical, immobile plan, created in marble or mosaic, on display for several centuries, rather than a parchment or marble map in a private collection. Its lengthy use-life suggests the original map may have been a public installation in Rome, given the city's prominence and inclusion of its harbour. This may indicate commissioning by an emperor. The inclusion of state infrastructure (e.g. roads and harbours) and administrative cities (e.g. Rome, Antioch, Constantinople) could indicate state involvement. Imperial commissioning between 46-79 would limit the original map to the reigns of Claudius, Nero, Otho, Galba, Vitellius, Vespasian, or Titus.

It is improbable that the map was commissioned and constructed during the short reigns of Otho (three months), Galba (seven months), and Vitellius (eight months), all of whom died during the struggle of the Year of the Four Emperors. There is no monument constructed by any of these emperors which might have housed a map for four centuries. A similar argument can be made against Titus, as he became emperor in June AD 79 with the Vesuvian eruption following in late summer or fall. Therefore, if the map had been commissioned by Titus, one would not expect to find the destroyed cities on the completed map. This leaves Claudius, Nero, and Vespasian as the emperors who may have commissioned the original.

Claudius, who ruled from 41-54, is an intriguing candidate given his conquest of Britain in 47, which was once present on the Peutinger Map, and the inclusion of Portus, which was perhaps his most prominent project. He led other public works programmes such as aqueducts, canals, and roads, the latter of which feature on the map. Where would such a map have been located? Portus is an option as the imperial harbour that connected Rome to the locations depicted on the map; however, roads are illustrated more prominently than waterways. Perhaps the most suitable site would be the Temple of the Deified Claudius on the Caelian Hill, which Agrippina commissioned the construction of in 54. However, construction ceased when Nero murdered Agrippina in 59 and the platform was used as a nymphaeum in the area of the emperor's palace, the Domus Aurea. Following Nero's death, the temple was reconstructed by Vespasian. This date fits the Italian section of the map and the temple survived through the 4th century, after which it fell into disrepair. Portus and the temple are the best options for a Claudian building from the 1st-4th centuries that could have housed a map.

The second candidate is Nero, who ruled from 54-68 and celebrated Portus with the minting of a sestertius. Given Nero's proclivity for construction and ostentatious display, the Domus Aurea would be a fitting location to showcase a map. Nero gathered great works of art in the palace for his private viewing (Pliny, *NH* 34.84). Perhaps the map served as a personal visual depiction of the Empire. However, there is reason to discard this hypothesis, since the Domus Aurea was destroyed following Nero's death in 68, which would discount the map being a 'living document' that was updated until the 4th century. Notably, the Temple of Tellus which featured a painted map of Italy, was destroyed in the Great Fire of 64. It was rebuilt and stood into the 4th century (Platner and Ashby 1929: 511). If the map was repainted following the fire, then it may have included the new imperial harbour.

The final candidate is Vespasian, who ruled from 69-79. A former general, Vespasian sought to distance Rome from the chaos of Nero, uprisings around the empire,

Figure 6.5. An artistic reconstruction of the Forma Urbis in a hall of the Temple of Peace; Cozza proposes that there was a map of the Roman Empire on the wall opposite the Forma Urbis (Meneghini *et al.* 2009: fig. 2).

and the Year of the Four Emperors. He directed an effective propaganda campaign centred on a message of peace, which included issuing coinage depicting Peace and promoting public works and events. The most famous is the Flavian Amphitheatre, known today as the Colosseum. Suetonius writes that Vespasian 'undertook new works, the temple of Peace by the Forum and one to the Deified Claudius on the Caelian mount, which was begun by Agrippina, but almost utterly destroyed by Nero; also an amphitheatre in the heart of the city' (*Vespasian* 9.1). Having already examined the Temple of Deified Claudius, the Colosseum is hardly a suitable context for a map and no ancient author mentions one being displayed there. This leaves the centrepiece of Vespasian's campaign, the Temple of Peace (Figure

6.5), which was located among the imperial fora. The temple, constructed between 71-75 (Tucci 2017: 6), served as an effective contrast to Nero and furthered Vespasian's message of a new peaceful era.

The temple was widely lauded by ancient authors. Josephus praised the complex, writing, 'Vespasian made up his mind to build a temple of Peace. This was completed with remarkable speed and surpassed all human imagination. Not only did he have unlimited wealth at his disposal; he also adorned it with paintings and statues by the greatest of the old masters. In fact, in that temple were collected and deposited all those works that men had hitherto travelled over the whole world to see, longing to set eyes on them even when scattered in different lands' (Josephus, *Bellum Iudaicum* 7.5.7). Herodian considered the temple to be 'the largest and most beautiful of all the buildings in the city' (1.14.2). Suetonius described the masterpieces in its collections, including those that had been housed in Nero's Domus Aurea and were now visible to the public (*Vespasian* 18).

The temple contained a series of halls which housed intellectuals and physicians. Galen states that the temple was, 'the general meeting-place for all those engaged in learned pursuits' (*De libris propriis* 2). One hall likely contained the Library of Peace or archive (*tabularium*) (Taub 1993; Tucci 2017: 123). By the Severan period, the offices of the *mensorii*, property officials relating to the Praefectus Urbi, and cadastral map-makers who measured private and state properties may have been located in the north-eastern hall (Gatti 1960: 216; Meneghini and Santangeli Valenzani 2007: 66), though Tucci argues against this (2017: 142). Displayed in this hall was the famous marble plan of Rome, the Forma Urbis Romae. Created under Vespasian, it was restored following the Fire of Commodus in 192 by the Severans in *c.* 203 (Tucci 2017: 127). The Severan plan is marble, but the earlier Flavian plan might have been painted marble or plaster (Taub 1993: 12). The Forma Urbis is thought to have served as part of Vespasian's peace and public works campaign, allowing the public to see the city and its features spatially in an aerial perspective (Tucci 2017: 128). Its creation corresponds with his census of 73-75, which included public and private property, the records of which were likely kept in one of the libraries built in the area (Taub 1993: 12). The purpose of the Forma Urbis is unclear, but as Tucci argues it was likely multilayered. He states, 'both in the Flavian and Severan version, the Forma Urbis might have been a tool for propaganda, or might have had a religious meaning. In other words, the marble plan, certainly deriving from actual cadastral plans, must have had a different purpose (propagandistic, symbolic, religious, triumphal)' (Tucci 2017: 128). The Severan restoration of the marble plan demonstrates that the temple was maintained, and even updated, for centuries. The temple had a prominent position within Rome and was frequently visited by foreign dignitaries, such as Byzantine emperor Constantius II in 357. The temple was maintained until 410, but after Alaric sacked Rome it fell into disrepair. The presence of the Forma Urbis in the temple demonstrates Vespasian's interest in maps and their existence in Roman public spaces from the 1st to 5th centuries.

Significantly, there is evidence that a second map existed in the same hall as the Forma Urbis. Excavations in 1955-56 revealed red and green painted marble fragments that appeared to be part of a map (Lugli 1956; Cozza 1960: 194 n. 49; Tucci 2017: 131 n. 61). Tucci translates the findings from Cozza's notes in the British School at Rome archive, writing, 'at the foot of the wall opposite that of the Forma Urbis several marble fragments were discovered, very similar to those of the Severan plan, with red and green colours that, according to Cozza [...] might have represented the provinces of the Roman Empire' (Tucci 2017: 131; BSR, Cozza Collection, Scatola 10, Folder 31, Pianta Marmorea). Cozza referred to this map as the Forma Imperii Romae and these findings have led scholars to propose that a map of the Roman Empire was located opposite the Forma Urbis (Dudley 1967: 131-32; Coarelli 1992). In fact, as early as 1903 Rodolfo Lanciani argued that there was painted marble depicting a map in the temple (Tucci 2017: 131 n. 61). If the map painted on the Temple of Tellus, which was located in Regio IV near the Temple of Peace, was restored in 64, then it could have served as a basis for the Italian section of the map and included the imperial harbour. Cozza intended to study the marble pieces further but was sadly unable to do so before his death in 2011. Research examining these fragments with modern analytical techniques may reveal whether the wall bore a painted map.

The existence of a Forma Imperii Romae in the Temple of Peace is consistent with Vespasian's peace campaign. Taub argues that the Forma Urbis was practical, decorative, and symbolic, and inspired 'in viewers further admiration of the achievements of Vespasian' (Taub 1993: 17), and the same would have been true for the purported Forma Imperii Romae. The census under Augustus collected precise distance measurements of the provinces, resulting in Agrippa's creation of a *mappamundi* (Pliny, *NH* 3.1.16); Vespasian's census collected similar information and he may have emulated Augustus and Agrippa in creating a Forma Imperii Romae. Talbert notes the significant authority required to collect or access the data needed to create such a map (Talbert 2010: 139), an argument which offers support for a census as the source. As the last known imperial census, Vespasian's census should be considered as the source of this geographical information. This census may have led to the creation of two maps on display in the Temple of Peace: Forma Urbis Romae and Forma Imperii Romae. Rather than the elongated shape of the Peutinger Map, the map of the provinces likely had similar dimensions to the Forma Urbis. If the map in the temple is the origin of the medieval Peutinger Map, then the shape of the latter would have come from the process of translating the monumental map to a portable papyrus or parchment scroll.

Discussion

Here, then, is the possible presence of a physical map of the Roman Empire dating to the third quarter of the 1st century AD, which would have included the destroyed Campanian cities and the Claudian phase of Portus. Since the temple was actively used until the 5th century, the map could have been updated over several centuries, including by the Severans as with the Forma Urbis. The east wall of the hall bearing the Forma Urbis was completely destroyed in the fire of 193 and had to be entirely rebuilt (Tucci 2017: 246), but other sections of the temple were not so damaged. Perhaps this includes the west wall which housed the hypothesised Forma Imperii Romae. Cozza's Forma Imperii Romae would then fit the criteria of the original map, which a succession of copies led to the Peutinger Map.

To review, the proposed hypothesis states that the original map dates to the 1st century and the updates to the map are evidence of it being a living document as a painted marble map of the Roman Empire in the Temple of Peace from *c.* 75-410. It was designed as part of Vespasian's peace campaign, drawing geographic data from his census in 73-75. Much like the Forma Urbis, Res Gestae, Ara Pacis Augustae, and other monuments (Taub 1993: 16), a Forma Imperii Romae in the Temple of Peace would have delivered a political statement. While the map went out of date in 79 with the Vesuvian eruption, other elements were updated with an emphasis on political and religious influence. Talbert and Riggsby's arguments for the original map as a display piece fit with Tucci and Taub's interpretation of the Forma Urbis as a propaganda piece in its context of the Temple of Peace. The possible presence of both maps in Vespasian's peace campaign would confirm Talbert's hypothesis behind the design of the map but with a Flavian date rather than the Tetrarchy. Located in a temple frequented by visitors and foreign dignitaries to view the museum-like displays of art as well as its library and archive, the map was well positioned in Rome's intellectual centre. It would have been widely viewed and, if Gatti and Meneghini's interpretations are correct, a host of cadastral map-makers were on hand if copies were needed.

The copyists, in creating portable copies, would have produced their versions on more easily transferable media. Transfer to papyrus or parchment would allow copies to be sent around the empire for further dissemination through governors, generals, and local allies. Perhaps they copied the rectangular wall map to a proportion common to the date, that of papyri scrolls to facilitate portability (Johnson 2004: 141-43; Talbert 2010: 143 n. 53 and 54). Rectangular parchment plans are known from the medieval period, such as the 9th-century plan of the St. Gall Monastery (Stiftsbibliothek Sankt Gallen, *Codex Sangallensis* 1092), so shape was not a limitation for parchment. Papyrus was, however, another story and Talbert provides a significant discussion about papyrus in a series of notes (Talbert 2010: 143, nn. 53-56). The shape of the Peutinger Map recalls that of papyri scrolls, matching the standard height of Roman scrolls found at Oxyrhynchus (25-33cm) (Johnson 2004: 141-43; Talbert 2010: 143 n. 53).

Further, the 1:20 proportion of the Peutinger Map was not problematic, as length was not an issue with scrolls and many were longer than the map (Johnson 2004: 143-52). One can then propose that there existed a monumental map of the Roman provinces in the Temple of Peace which was copied to a papyri scroll. Subsequent copies over the centuries continued with this elongated form with at least the final copy in the 13th century being made in parchment.

If one advances the hypothesis of a monumental Forma Imperii Romae transferred to papyrus or parchment, then interesting possibilities come to light. In translating a rectangular wall (like the Forma Urbis) to parchment, the copyist constrained the perspective, skewing it longitudinally, to make the map portable. Guckelsberger determined that the Peutinger Map is largely accurate in its representation of longitude, but narrowed in latitude (2015). Pazarli's study of the islands on the map found that the relative sizes of islands are accurate, but are constrained vertically (2009: 13). Talbert notes that the Black Sea is horizontal (2010: 92), further indicating the vertical constraint of the map's features. Given the relative accuracy of the horizontal distances, the copyist may have constrained the vertical axis to fit a scroll of 1:20 proportion.

The Forma Urbis is estimated to be 13 × 18m (Tucci 2017: 128). This 1:1.4 ratio likely suited a map of Rome, but a Forma Imperii Romae might have been longer, to fit within the space of the opposing wall, or it may have covered both the opposing wall and the one between them, in which case it would have been 13 × 44m. This would mean the copyist translated a 1:1.4 or 1:3.4 map to 1:20. If one undertakes the exercise of to re-scaling the Peutinger Map from 1:20 to 1:3.4 – stretching it vertically by 5.8 times – then one has interesting results. Sicily regains its triangular shape and Cyprus, Corsica, and Sardinia regain their proportions. The vertically scaled geographic features do not resemble a modern cartographic map, but it does reinforce Guckelsberger's argument and supports a hypothesis of a copyist translating a more regularly scaled map to an elongated scroll. If, indeed, this is the case, then the copyist sacrificed the space at sea to prioritise the land. Guckelsberger and Pazarli's work on the accuracy of the latitude and size, along with the re-scaling of the Peutinger Map to the proportion of the Forma Urbis and wall-space in the hall, suggesting that the 4th-century copyist might have translated a marble Forma Imperii Romae to a more portable scroll. The discourse on Roman maps has been significantly shaped by the Peutinger Map and if it is a papyri or parchment copy of a monumental map then its skewed perspective might not be representative of Roman map-making.

This hypothesis cannot be proven or disproven until the marble fragments from the Temple of Peace are examined. The Flavian *mappamundi*, updated in the 2nd or 3rd century, perhaps by the Severans and the Byzantine emperors such as Constantius II, would have been publicly visible in the Temple of Peace to be copied until Alaric's sack of the city, at which point the temple was left to ruin and Procopius records cattle wandering the enclosure in the 6th century (*Gothic War* 8.21.11). The map would have been copied and it is likely that there were multiple circulating copies, such as in 7th-century Ravenna, Liébana in 776, Reichenau in 821/22, Colmar in 1265, and Padua, via Basle, in 1495 (Talbert 2010: 163-72). Each copy may have differences, as the Ravenna map was written in both Latin and Greek. One such copy, perhaps initially on a papyrus scroll, was copied several times until the 13th century, when this copy made it into the library of Konrad Peutinger.

Conclusion

There is much that cannot be known about the Peutinger Map; however, this chapter has sought to demonstrate that archaeological research can raise new questions about existing datasets such as the map. The fieldwork examining the imperial harbour by the Portus Project revealed the Claudian phase construction which corresponds to Portus as depicted on the map, which then linked to Cozza's previous excavation in the Temple of Peace and his papers in the BSR archive.

As with all hypotheses about the Peutinger Map, this one includes speculation and a number of assumptions. However, unlike previous hypotheses, examination of the marble fragments excavated by Cozza in the Temple of Peace may prove or disprove the hypothesis. If a Forma Imperii Romae indeed existed, the features on the map may link to the Peutinger Map, most notably if parts of the Italian section survive among the fragments.

Nevertheless, an accurate illustration of Portus during its Claudian phase offers one advancement in our understanding of Roman maps. It demonstrates that the Romans did, in fact, create spatial maps of geographic regions, not only tables of distances, itineraries, or cadastral property plans. While the Romans certainly used these forms of data, the Peutinger Map may reflect a physical map that depicted the Roman provinces from the 1st century.

Acknowledgements

This chapter is written in memory of Simon Keay, who served as my PhD advisor and later mentor while working at the British School at Rome on the Portus Project and as the Assistant Director for Archaeology and Archaeological Science. The author would like to thank Claire Burridge for archival research and discussions that led to this publication, as well as feedback from Andrew Riggsby, Richard Talbert, and Robert Coates-Stephens. All errors are my own. No new data were created or analysed in this study. Data sharing is not applicable to this article. For the purposes of open access, the author has applied a Creative Commons Attribution (CC BY) licence to any Accepted Author Manuscript version arising from this submission.

Bibliography

Arnaud, P. 1989. Pouvoir des mots et limites de la cartographie dans la géographie grecque et romaine. *Dialogues d'histoire ancienne* 15: 9-29.

Bertolami Fine Art 2019. A rare Roman agate intaglio: harbour with ships. *Glyptics: Ancient Jewelry, Auction 66, Part II*, July.

Brodersen, K. 2003. *Terra Cognita: Studien zur romischen Raumerfassung*. Hildesheim: Olms.

Coarelli, F. 1992. Le plan de via Anicia: un nouveau fragment de la Forma Marmorea de Rome, in F. Hinard and M. Royo (eds) *Rome: l'espace urbain et ses représentations*: 65-81. Paris: Presses de l'Université de Paris-Sorbonne.

Coarelli, F. 2020. *Il Foro Romano*, III. Rome: Quasar.

Cozza, L. 1960. L'aula e la parete, in G. Carettoni (ed.) *La Pianta marmorea di Roma antica: forma urbis Romae*: 177-95. Rome: Comune di Roma.

Dilke, O.A.W. 1987a. Itineraries and geographical maps in the Early and Late Roman Empires, in J.B. Harley and D. Woodward (eds) *The History of Cartography*, I: 234-57. Chicago: University of Chicago Press.

Dilke, O.A.W. 1987b. Maps in the service of the state: Roman cartography to the end of the Augustan era, in J.B. Harley and D. Woodward (eds) *The History of Cartography*, I: 201-11. Chicago: University of Chicago Press.

Dudley, D.R. 1967. *Urbs Roma*. Aberdeen: Phaidon.

Gatti, G. 1960. Data, scopo e precedenti della pianta, in G. Carettoni (ed.) *La Pianta marmorea di Roma antica: forma urbis Romae*: 211-18. Rome: Comune di Roma.

Germoni, P., S. Keay, M. Millett and K. Strutt 2018. Ostia beyond the Tiber: recent archaeological discoveries in the Isola Sacra, in M. Cébeillac-Gervasoni, N. Laubry and F. Zevi (eds) *Ricerche su Ostia e il suo territorio: atti del Terzo Seminario Ostiense*. Rome: Publications de l'École française de Rome, <https://doi.org/doi:10.4000/books.efr.3734>.

Guckelsberger, K. 2015. Mathematisch-kartographische Überlegungen zur Tabula Peutingeriana. Unpublished paper, <https://www.academia.edu/27475885/Mathematisch_kartographische_%C3%9Cberlegungen_zur_Tabula_Peutingeriana>, viewed 1 May 2025.

Herrin, J. 2020. *Ravenna: Capital of Empire, Crucible of Europe*. London: Allen Lane.

Johnson, W.A. 2004. *Bookrolls and Scribes in Oxyrhynchus*. Toronto: University of Toronto Press.

Keay, S. 2012. *Rome, Portus and the Mediterranean*. London: British School at Rome.

Keay, S. and L. Paroli 2011. *Portus and its Hinterland*. London: British School at Rome.

Keay, S., P. Campbell, K. Crawford and M. del C.M. Escobar 2021. Space, accessibility and movement through the Portus Romae, in F. Vermeulen and A. Zuiderhoek (eds) *Space, Movement and the Economy in Roman Cities in Italy and Beyond*: 375-418. New York: Routledge.

Keay, S. and B. Woytek 2022. Portvm Traiani: An interdisciplinary approach to the imagery of Trajan's harbour at Portus. *Papers of the British School at Rome* 90: 63-107.

Lugli, G. 1956. *Roma antica: Il centro monumentale*. Rome: Bardi.

Meneghini, R. and R. Santangeli Valenzani 2007. *I Fori Imperiali: Gli scavi del Comune di Roma (1991-2007)*. Rome: Viviani.

Meneghini, R., A. Corsaro and B. Pinna Caboni 2009. Il Templum Pacis alla luce dei recenti scavi, in F. Coarelli (ed.) *Divus Vespasianus: Il Bimillenario dei Flavi*: 190-201. Milan: Electa.

Nicolet, C. 2015. *Space, Geography, and Politics in the Early Roman Empire*. Ann Arbor: University of Michigan Press.

Pazarli, M. 2009. Mediterranean islands in Tabula Peutingeriana. *e-Perimetron* 4: 101-16, <http://www.e-perimetron.org/Vol_4_2/Pazarli.pdf>, viewed 1 May 2025.

Platner, S.B. and T. Ashby 1929. *A Topographical Dictionary of Ancient Rome*. Oxford: Oxford University Press.

Riggsby, A.M. 2019. *Mosaics of Knowledge: Representing Knowledge in the Roman World*. Oxford: Oxford University Press.

Rodríguez-Almeida, E. 2002. *Formae Urbis Antiquae*. Rome: Publications de l'École française de Rome, <https://doi.org/10.4000/books.efr.1886>.

Talbert, R.J.A. 2010. *Rome's World: The Peutinger Map Reconsidered*. Cambridge: Cambridge University Press.

Taub, L. 1993. The historical function of the 'Forma Urbis Romae'. *Imago mundi* 45: 9-19.

Testaguzza, O. 1970. *Portus: Illustrazione dei Porti di Claudio e Traiano e della Città di Porto a Fiumicino*. Rome: Julia Editrice.

Tucci, P.L. 2017. *The Temple of Peace in Rome*. Cambridge: Cambridge University Press.

Weiss, N.A. 2013. The visual language of Nero's Harbor Sesterii. *Memoirs of the American Academy in Rome* 58: 65-81.

7. The Ragonii of Ostia:
Was the *praefectus annonae* and *patronus coloniae* Ragonius Vincentius Celsus an Ostian?

Christer Bruun

The *praefectus annonae*, in charge of supplying Rome, was the imperial official whose actions and authority mattered the most to Ostia and the Ostians.[1] Decrees and regulations enacted by the prefect had a major impact on the economy of the harbour town and on that of its guilds and its inhabitants. Somewhat over 70 *praefecti annonae* are known to modern scholarship from the first four centuries AD.[2] Among these, the official who is most frequently encountered in the Ostian epigraphic evidence is the senator (*vir clarissimus*) Ragonius Vincentius Celsus, who held the office in the late 380s AD (see *PLRE* I, under Celsus 9). Ragonius Celsus, as I will call him in the following, is known from eight inscriptions, six of which were found at Ostia including in the harbour zone Portus, and from a passage in a letter by Symmachus.[3] The epigraphic evidence gives the impression that Ostia was of particular interest to him. Was Ragonius Celsus in fact an Ostian by birth? This contribution will investigate whether he was of local origin, a possibility thus far never entertained.

Considerable attention has been devoted by Roman social historians to the geographical origin of senators. Establishing the regional representation in the Roman senate at any given moment provides important information about empire-wide trends regarding social mobility and the distribution of wealth, besides providing an obvious indication of where political influence and power were located.[4] Therefore, it is no wonder that several scholarly contributions have been dedicated to the investigation of which senators had their origin in Rome's harbour town (Licordari 1982: 35-38; Salomies 1996: 70-76; Caldelli 2014).

In none of the studies attempting to attribute the origin of members of the Roman imperial elite to particular Italian towns has the family name *Ragonius*

been connected to Ostia.[5] One may hold that the fact that Ragonius Celsus is mentioned in six different inscriptions in the harbour town is not sufficient grounds for proposing that he had Ostian roots. The administrative authority of the *praef. annonae* may explain his being in charge of public work projects in the harbour town and could also explain why any holder of this office was honoured by various parties in Ostia.

However, there is an additional reason for suspecting that Ragonius Celsus was an Ostian: the distribution of Publii Ragonii in the epigraphic evidence from Italy. As we shall see, the *praenomen* + *gentilicium* combination 'P. Ragonius' is by far most often encountered at Ostia, and this necessitates a revision of the current view which attributes the Ragonii to the north-eastern part of the Italian Peninsula. A certain impetus for the present inquiry was provided by the publication in 2018 of a host of Ostian funerary inscriptions, which revealed seven previously unknown Ragonii at Ostia (see Zevi *et al.* 2018: nos 846-50).

The Lucii Ragonii from the North-East of Italy – a Separate Family

The presence in the Roman senate, beginning in the second half of the 2nd century AD, of senators named L. Ragonius has thus far conditioned the discussion of the provenance of those Ragonii who belonged to the imperial elite. The first known senator who bore that family name was L. Ragonius Urinatius Larcius Quintianus, who according to his entry in the *Prosopographia Imperii Romani* (*PIR*[2] R 17, published in 1999) was consul in an undetermined year during the reign of Commodus (AD 180-92). His senatorial career is well known from several inscriptions, some of which are honorific, and there is no doubt that he originated from Opitergium (modern Oderzo) in the

---

[1] * For inscriptions, *EpOst* refers to the number in Zevi *et al.* 2018, *ScO* XI refers to the number in Marinucci 1992.

[2] See the updated list in Caldelli 2020: 121-24 containing 52 office holders (until the end of Constantine I's reign); *PLRE* I (1971) 1057 for a list, no longer quite up-to-date, of 31 *praefecti annonae* from *c.* AD 270 to *c.* 400.

[3] See Symm. *Rel.* 23.3 (from AD 384/85), on which more below.

[4] Fundamental in this regard is the vast two-volume publication *Epigrafia e ordine senatorio*, Rome 1982; updates in Gregori and Caldelli 2014.

[5] I prefer not to use the term '*gens Ragonia*' in a general sense. During the Principate, when literally millions of Roman citizens inhabited the Roman world and the same family name could occur all over the Mediterranean without any family relationships tying individuals together, it is rarely meaningful to use the concept of *gens*. That term makes better sense when referring to aristocratic families and their retainers during the Roman Republic.

Augustan region of *Venetia et Histria*.[6] Both he and his son belonged to the voting tribe Papiria (*CIL* VI 1502-04 = *ILS* 1124-25, etc.), which was the tribe of Opitergium. The son, L. Ragonius Urinatius Tuscenius Quintianus, likewise reached the consulship, again in a year which cannot currently be determined (*PIR*[2] R 18). As his *PIR* entry shows, he too was honoured at Opitergium and he is mentioned in other inscriptions from the north-east as well. Ragonius was married to Flavia Venusta (*PIR*[2] F 445), which makes it a certainty that the *consul ordinarius* of AD 240, Ragonius Venustus (*PIR*[2] R 16), was their son.[7] A fourth generation reached the consulship in the person of L. Ragonius Quintianus, *cos. ord.* AD 289 (*PIR*[2] R 15; *PLRE* I Quintianus 3; cf. p. 43 'Stemma 6: Ragonii Opitergini'), while L. Ragonius Venustus, who received the *taurobolium* and the *criobolium* in May 390, may be another descendant, several generations later (*PLRE* I, Venustus 3; *CIL* VI 505 = *ILS* 4151).

This evidence allows us to state that during at least four generations and probably much longer, the senatorial Lucii Ragonii, who traced their origin to Opitergium and for at least a few generations preserved ties to that region, while obviously also owning real estate in the capital, constituted one of the wealthiest families in Italy. One would expect to see this fact reflected also in the epigraphic evidence. More specifically – since *Lucius* is the only *praenomen* known to have been used in this senatorial family – one would expect to find a good number of Lucii Ragonii in and around Opitergium and Rome. The rationale for this assumption is simple: the father's *praenomen* was regularly bestowed on at least one of his sons, and eventually on all of them, so that by the end of the 2nd century AD the Roman *praenomen* had become practically hereditary. All the sons of someone called Lucius were then most likely given that same *praenomen* (Salomies 1987: 378-89). More importantly, all male slaves freed by a L. Ragonius became L. Ragonii, and so did the freeborn sons of these freedmen, and the slaves that they in their turn manumitted, and so on. A senatorial family, which due to its wealth owned large numbers of slaves, through the Roman institution of manumission set in motion a powerful process that multiplied the family name and the *praenomen* of the *pater familias*.

The demographic realities of the ancient Mediterranean obviously interfered with a boundless spread of individuals called L. Ragonius. Because of the high child mortality in the ancient world many families may have had no offspring which survived into adulthood so as to be able to continue the family line. However, as far as finding traces of Lucii Ragonii, the latter

factor is not very relevant, since the Romans were keen to commemorate the passing of infants by erecting tombstones for them. Even if the population did not increase because so many children died young, also an epitaph for a one-year-old child named Ragonius/Ragonia, who was never able to make an impact on Roman society, is a valuable source when we attempt to establish which localities were inhabited by Ragonii.

The Ragonii Are Most Commonly Found at Ostia

A search for persons bearing the family name *Ragonius* in the Epigraphic Database Clauss Slaby (the most complete of the databases containing Latin inscriptions) provides a mixed result. If we leave aside the senatorial Lucii Ragonii mentioned above, in total some 70 Ragonii and Ragoniae appear among the known Latin inscriptions.[8] Chronologically they belong to the period from the last century BC to the 5th century AD,[9] and they are concentrated in three geographical areas: the north-east corner of the peninsula, Rome, and Ostia.

No more than five Ragonii/Ragoniae appear in a total of three inscriptions from the north-east region *Venetia et Histria*, which today includes Italian Veneto and the Pola Peninsula of Croatia. This is a somewhat disappointing result, considering that the senatorial Lucii Ragonii for several generations counted this region as their place of origin and clearly preserved ties to it. Not only did they likely continue to own property there, tended by their slaves and freedmen and -women, but before they acquired senatorial rank there must have been Ragonii living in the region for generations. This is another example of how lacunose the surviving epigraphic evidence is; a well-known fact.

The likely earliest of these inscriptions, which comes from the north-western part of the Pola Peninsula in territory belonging to Tergeste, names three individuals. One Q(uintus) Ragonius L(ucii) f(ilius) refers to his brother L(ucius) Ragonius L(ucii) f(ilius) and to what appears to be his nephew L(ucius) Ragonius L(ucii) f(ilius) (*CIL* V 479 = *Inscr.It.* X.3, 42). The two brothers both belonged to the Romilia tribe, and therefore there is as yet no connection to Opitergium, where eventually the senatorial Lucii Ragonii were established. These early Ragonii may have come from Ateste (modern Este) in Emilia Romagna, since in no other town north of the Apennines is the Romilia tribe encountered.[10] The inscription from the Pola Peninsula

---

[6] See Luciani and Pistellato 2010: 258, 261 with reference to other recent studies of the Lucii Ragonii.

[7] Assuming a consulship *c.* AD 185 for the grandfather, and one for his father *c.* 215, such a family tree is quite plausible.

[8] It does not appear that Ragonii can be found in Greek inscriptions or papyri (except for Ragonius Celer in *IGR* I 1057), but even if I have missed some rare instances, they would not have an impact on the current investigation.

[9] The earliest may be *CIL* I2 689 = X 3784 from Capua, and *CIL* I2 1145 = VI 8341 and *CIL* VI 7456 (cf. *AE* 2001, 169) from Rome.

[10] For the *tribus* of Ateste, and the frequent evidence for references to the *Romilia* in the town, see Boscolo 2010: 266, 273-77.

illustrates how at the beginning of the Principate the *praenomen* was still used for diversification purposes. The sons of Lucius were called Quintus and Lucius, the latter's son again Lucius.

Elsewhere in Italy, during the late Republic, some Ragonii used the *praenomen* Marcus, but apart from that, when other and later Ragonii are found using a *praenomen*, with one exception that name is always Publius.[11] Besides the locations already mentioned, an isolated case from North Africa (*CIL* VIII 14868), and an imperial administrator in Egypt (*IGR* I 1057; see further below), Ragonii only appear in Rome and at Ostia. The evidence from the capital consists of 31 individuals, which includes five persons encountered in late antique Christian epitaphs.[12] Some of the latter may even postdate Ragonius our *praef. annonae*, and in any case they contribute little to explaining the reason for the presence of Ragonii in the area.

At Ostia and Portus, in total 30 Ragonii are mentioned in the epigraphic evidence. Considering the total number of individuals known from Rome and Ostia, their presence is far more conspicuous in the harbour town than in the capital, since one would expect six times as many instances in Rome as in Ostia.[13] None of these two populations show any ties to the Lucii Ragonii from Opitergium, since the *praenomen* Lucius is never encountered. However, in Rome, most Ragonii use no *praenomen*; there are only six references to Publii Ragonii (the *praenomen* is used either by an individual or for his/her *patronus*). At Ostia the material is more overwhelming: in 16 cases Publius is used as a *praenomen* or appears as the *praenomen* of the father or the *patronus*. If at Rome we might think that the general absence of references to *praenomina* allows for the possibility that some connections to the senatorial Lucii Ragonii existed (who obviously had a residence in or near the capital), at Ostia there is such a massive presence of Publii Ragonii that it seems warranted to exclude ties to the senatorial family, which exclusively used Lucius as *praenomen*.

When did persons named P. Ragonius settle in Ostia and where did they come from? As seen above, the earliest known Ragonii are found at Casilinum, Rome, and near

Tergeste (where they may have arrived from Ateste), while possibly the earliest reference to a P. Ragonius appears in a text from Tarvisium in north-east Italy which cites one Ragonia P(ubli) l(iberta) Tertulla and is datable to the 1st century AD (*CIL* V 2133).[14] That Ostia should have welcomed newcomers from elsewhere in Italy is not difficult to imagine. After the construction of the harbour at Portus in the 40s and early 50s AD, and especially after Trajan's interior harbour was finished by the end of his reign, Ostia was a magnet for immigration.[15]

An early high-ranking Ragonius needs to be mentioned, namely Ragonius Celer who appears as an *epistrategos* (of an unknown district) in an inscription from Egypt dated to AD 39/40 (*PIR*[2] R 12). He was a civilian government official who had equestrian rank and had been appointed by the central government in Rome. It would undoubtedly be far too adventurous to suggest that he used his position in Egypt to set up a lucrative trading enterprise between Ostia and Egypt, as a result of which his family name, through freedmen and perhaps some family members, gained a foothold in the Ostian population. There is currently no evidence for any trading activity by Ragonius the *epistrategos*, and we do not even know if his *praenomen* was Publius.

Publii Ragonii Involved in Ostian Commerce and Industry

To postulate that the arrival of Ragonii at Ostia had to do with economic factors is, however, surely the best bet. The epigraphic evidence gives some indications of what they were engaged in. In AD 198, one Ragonius Chrysanthus heads the first *decuria* of the *fabri tignuarii*, the builders of Ostia, a position which presumably was an honour, although he was alone among his kinsmen in that context. Among the over 300 other members of the *fabri*, no other Ragonius is found; some other family names occur repeatedly in the membership list (*CIL* XIV 4569). In other sectors of the Ostian economy, P. Ragonius Erotianus is called a *collega* of painters (*pingentes*) in his epitaph (*CIL* XIV 4699), while in two instances Ragonii appear in fragmentary lists of members of Ostia's famous professional guilds (*collegia* or *corpora*), without it being possible to establish what their profession was (*CIL* XIV 264: P. Ragonius [---]; 5371 = *ScO* XI C 58: P. Ragonius Charito). Furthermore, the epitaph of one Ragonia Philete, who died at the age of 27, is decorated with a series of images of amphorae and flasks. She must have been commercially active,

---

[11] See M. Ragonius M. f. from Casilinum (modern Capua), dated to the early 1st century BC (*CIL* I2 689 = X 3784), and *CIL* VI 7456 from Rome, in which three Marci Ragonii, freedmen of a Marcus, are mentioned. Much later, *CIL* VI 25358 registers a M. Ragonius from Rome. One N(umerius) Ragonius Priscus was a member of the *vigiles* at Rome in AD 210 (*CIL* VI 1057 = VI 31234 = *ILS* 2157). The letter N, which stands for a rare *praenomen*, is possibly an error for M(arcus).

[12] See *ICUR* I 3116, VIII 23261, VIII 23262, IX 24137.

[13] The numbers used by Salomies 2002: 136 were 54,000 individuals with a *gentilicium* from Rome and 6900 from Ostia. After the publication of some 1800 previously unedited epitaphs from Ostia by Zevi *et al.* 2018, we can safely assume that the number of known individuals with a family name is still less than 9000 in the harbour town, or a sixth of the Roman total.

[14] The early dating is supported by the absence of the *D(is) M(anibus)* formula.

[15] See Salomies 2002: 152, who stated that at Ostia the family names *Galgestius*, *Laevonicus*, and *Palaus* indicate immigration from the north-east of the Italian Peninsula. *Ragonius* was not mentioned in that study.

perhaps as the owner of a tavern (See Zevi *at al.* 2018: 339 = *EpOst* 848).

While these indications of the professional activities of some Ostian Ragonii prove nothing about when or from where the first Ragonii arrived in the harbour town, they show that bearers of this family name were integrated in the local economic structures. For comparison, the only Ragonius in Rome who provides any information about his livelihood is one P. Ragonius Daphnus, *vinariarius in castris praetoriis* (*CIL* VI 9992).

The Ostian inscriptions in which Ragonii are mentioned do not contain any chronological or other information that would allow a precise dating, besides the earlier mentioned inscription of the *fabri* dated to AD 198. Almost all the texts are epitaphs, three of which lack the formula *D(is) M(anibus)*, which is an indication that they likely belong to the 1st century AD. If this criterion is reliable, the funerary plaque which lists a P. Ragonius [---], a Ragonia [---], and a Ragonia who is *P(ubli)* [*filia* or *liberta*], is the earliest evidence for Publii Ragonii at Ostia and dates to before *c.* AD 100.[16]

The evidence we have, consisting of many individual epitaphs, gives the impression of a stable presence of Publii Ragonii in the town. This is unlike some cases where a very few inscriptions contain long lists of individuals bearing the same *gentilicium*, but otherwise the name can hardly be found, as if a business enterprise had suddenly taken off but soon enough collapsed, after which the family disappeared back into obscurity.[17] Against this background, it is not a stretch to imagine that over time, some particularly successful individual among the Publii Ragonii of Ostia would have advanced to become a member of the local elite, taking a seat in the local *curia* and holding magistracies. The first generation would have been followed by other Ragonii, either direct descendants or close kin. Eventually, presumably in the 3rd century or only in the 4th, the family would have reached senatorial rank, and one day in the 380s AD Ragonius Vincentius Celsus was appointed *praefectus annonae*.

Such an epic family history would in no way be exceptional during the Roman Principate or in Late Antiquity. The natural objection – that we have no evidence whatsoever for any Ragonius belonging to the political elite of Ostia or Portus – is easily countered by pointing out that our information about the socio-political leadership of the town is extremely limited for most of the 3rd and all of the 4th century AD. We know

only about a score of the two annual *duoviri* during all of the 3rd century, and the sources for the 4th century are completely silent on the fate of the town's chief magistracy.[18] There is ample space for any number of Ragonii to have played a significant local role during a period of some two centuries. Absence of evidence is truly not evidence of absence in this case.

Actions by Ragonius Vincentius Celsus concerning Ostia and Portus

The epigraphic evidence allows us to identify several actions which involved Ragonius Celsus and were of consequence for the Ostians. We find him engaged in a rebuilding project concerning the central Terme del Foro, as revealed by an architrave bearing the text *curavit Ragonius Vincentius Celsus v. c. praefectus annonae urbis Romae et civitas fecit me[morata de propri]o* (*ScO* XI, C 1 = *CIL* XIV 4718).[19] The restoration of the inscription is inspired by the identical text found on two statue bases, one discovered in the Forum of Ostia (*CIL* XIV 4717 = *ScO* XI, C 1b), i.e., in the immediate neighbourhood of the Forum Baths, and the other from an unspecified location but probably from the same context (*CIL* XIV 139 = *ScO* XI, C 1a). The word *memorata* should be translated as 'much talked of, famous, notable',[20] and the inscriptions likely all refer to rebuilding work overseen by Ragonius Celsus and apparently paid for by the town (*civitas*), as the common formula *proprio (sumptu)* lets us understand.

Based on new research by Axel Gering and his team, it would appear that the architrave was situated above the entrance to a late antique nymphaeum on the west side of the Baths, opening towards the Forum opposite the Temple of Rome and Augustus. The rebuilding effort furthered by Ragonius Celsus may have been limited to this venue, which in Gering's recent monograph is called 'Der "Nymphäumsraum" des Ragonius Vincentius Celsus'.[21]

Not too far from the nymphaeum a *domus* was established in the 5th century, in an abandoned part of the Baths' *palaestra*, and remains of a statue gallery were discovered there in the excavations of 1938-41. Here came to light a Togatus statue which Giovanni Becatti once identified as Ragonius Celsus; recent research has rejected this identification because the footwear is that of a man of equestrian rank; Ragonius was a senator.[22]

[16] See *EpOst* 847 (no date is suggested for the inscription by the editor). The other epitaphs which are reasonably complete and lack the *D. M.* formula are *CIL* XIV 1537 and *EpOst* 849.
[17] This is the case with, for instance, individuals named Gesatius (see *ScO* XI, C 46, incorporating *CIL* XIV 5356 and 5373), or the Sexti Sextilii in *CIL* XIV 251 (for which see Bruun 2020).
[18] See Meiggs 1973: 512-14, now partly outdated; a discussion of all known magistrates will appear in Bruun, forthcoming.
[19] See Marinucci 1992: 165-66 no. C 1 for a restoration and discussion of this text; *CIL* XIV 4718 is less complete.
[20] Thus already Bruun 2015: 618. For this meaning, see *OLD*, s.v.
[21] Gering 2018: 280-1 with Fig. 223.
[22] Romeo 2019: 115-19; for the archaeological context Gering 2018: 284-86.

A third statue base from near the theatre appears to have supported a statue of Dea Roma. Ragonius Celsus's name again stands in the nominative, identifying him as the initiator, while it seems that the town paid for the statue (*CIL* XIV 4716 = *ILS* 9355).[23] The context of this find has given previous scholars and most recently Axel Gering reason to postulate that Ragonius played an important role in the late antique restoration of the theatre and the surrounding area (Gering 2018: 76-79). A further text, from Portus and quite fragmentary, likewise contains the name of Ragonius Celsus in the nominative and likely concerned the ruling emperors, judging from the word *principum* (*CIL* XIV 138 = *IPO* B 326).

Two texts have a particularly rich content. One, from Rome, was erected by the grain measurers from the harbour zone, the *mensores Portuenses*. It praises the *praef. ann.* Ragonius Celsus, their *patronus*, for his wisdom in settling their long-lasting conflict with the *caudicarii*, the bargemen who transported the imported grain from Portus up to Rome. He did this, so the *mensores* claim, in a way which satisfied both parties (*CIL* VI 1759 = *ILS* 1272; dedicated on 25 August 389, the *terminus ante quem* for his prefecture).

The other inscription, now lost, comes from Ostia or Portus and is likewise an honorific one, written in complicated and flowery late antique Latin. It lists the official career of the honorand, beginning with the appointment as barrister (*orator fori*) in the office of the urban prefect, and continuing with quaestor, triumphal praetor, consul, and *praefectus annonae*. Next, the text states that Ragonius Celsus (already) in his first years (in public office) demanded of himself all markers of virtue. Not blinded by the nobility of his family, he thoroughly demonstrated, by the richness of excellent deeds as his age advanced, how much hope of virtues he embodies. Hence, the text continues, finally our order (i.e. the town council) with the agreement of the whole town had the pleasure of choosing him as our permanent patron (*CIL* XIV 173 = VI 1760 = VI 31924).[24]

More complicated, and not just from a linguistic point of view, is a reference to Ragonius Celsus in an official report sent by the *praefectus Urbi* of Rome, Q. Aurelius Symmachus Eusebius, to the emperors in 384/85. Symmachus gives voice to deep displeasure with Celsus,

at the time a barrister within his own administration.[25] The text may be worth a closer look on another occasion; for the issue of Ragonius Celsus's origin, it may be relevant that his mother was entangled in a judicial process which somehow concerned the *praef. Urbi*, as Symmachus writes, since the prefect had jurisdiction within a radius of 100 miles around Rome. Therefore, his mother may have been a resident of Ostia, but that is all one can say.

Ragonius Celsus is one among only some 25 known *patroni* of Rome's port; in reality the number during the first four centuries AD must have been very much higher. While the existing evidence shows a preference for choosing men of Ostian origin as patrons,[26] the inscription which announces his election as patron in no way refers to Ragonius Celsus's background, except for mentioning the high status (*nobilitas*) of his ancestry.

In isolation, the position of *patronus* of Ostia-Portus is not enough to prove that Ragonius Celsus was of Ostian origin. Two other *praefecti annonae*, in office some 80 years earlier, enjoyed that same distinction, and there is nothing to show that they were Ostians.[27] Similarly, the fact that Ragonius Celsus engaged in public works at Ostia and Portus does not prove his local roots; there is epigraphic evidence for the involvement of many other late antique *praefecti annonae* in the harbour region.[28] But when these features are combined with the fact that a population of Ragonii, clearly distinct from the Lucii Ragonii from *Venetia et Histria*, had thrived at Ostia for generations and indeed for centuries, the likelihood that Ragonius Vincentius Celsus had an Ostian background increases considerably.

By Late Antiquity, Ostia had come to be characterised by the presence of numerous luxurious *domus*.[29] We have practically no information about the inhabitants of these residences; Ostia is a town of 'ghosts' in this regard. A very few inscribed lead pipes give us the names of some late antique Ostian owners of real estate, who all were members of the imperial elite.[30] Ragonius Vincentius Celsus and his closest ancestors would fit well in their company, and to judge from the available source material, at some point before the late

---

[23] The grammar of the text is somewhat puzzling, see van der Meer 2012: 29-30 (with Fig. 11) and Bruun 2015: 618.

[24] The section on offices and qualities reads: *oratori fori urban[ae] pr[a]efectur[a]e qu[a]estori pr[a]etori triu[m]phali consuli praefecto annon[a]e qui in primis annis a se petens omnia ornamenta virtutum nihil sibi de generis sui nobilitate blanditus quantum virtutum spei promittat procedentis [a]etatis excellentium factorum ubertate perdocuit hinc denique factum est ut ordo noster consensu totius c[ivi]tatis ut mer[u]it p[at]ronum sibi perpetuum libenter optaret.*

[25] See the Latin text with an English translation in Barrow 1973: 126-7 (= Symm. *Rel.* 23.3).

[26] For a list of the *patroni*, see Bruun, forthcoming.

[27] See *CIL* XIV 4403 and 4455 for the other cases (Bruun 2025: Appendix 1).

[28] Keay *et al.* 2005: 316-17 provided evidence for actions by two *praefecti annonae* during the 4th century and three during the 5th. van der Meer 2012: 59-60 pointed to a Greek inscription which may be evidence that another *praef. ann.* carried out repairs on the Forum Baths sometime after *c.* AD 330. This is not the place for a full review of the evidence.

[29] See recently Pavolini 2011, Danner 2017, and Gering 2018: passim.

[30] See Bruun 1991: 287-9, to which must be added the late-antique lead pipe inscription *AE* 2001, 629. Paucity of names in general: Pavolini 2018: 791.

4th century AD the Publi Ragonii had indeed become Ostian residents.

Abbreviations

CIL = Corpus Inscriptionum Latinarum. Berlin, 1863-.

EOS = Epigrafia e ordine senatorio, 2 vols. Rome: Edizioni di storia e letteratura, 1982.

IPO = Thylander, H. 1952. *Inscriptions du port d'Ostie* (Acta Instituti Romani Regni Sueciae 8°, no. 4). Lund: Gleerup.

PIR = Prosopographia Imperii Romani.

PLRE = A.H.M. Jones, J.R. Martindale and J. Morris (eds) 1971-92. *The Prosopography of the Later Roman Empire*, 3 vols. Cambridge: Cambridge University Press.

ScO = Scavi di Ostia.

Bibliography

Barrow, R.H. 1973. *Prefect and Emperor: The Relationes of Symmachus A.D. 384*. Oxford: Clarendon Press.

Boscolo, F. 2010. I tribules di *Atria, Ateste* e *Patavium*, in M. Silvestrini (ed.) *Le tribù romane* (Atti della XVIᵉ Rencontre sur l'épigraphie): 265-80. Bari: Edipuglia.

Bruun, C. 1991. *The Water Supply of Ancient Rome. A Study of Roman Imperial Administration* (Commentationes humanarum litterarum 93). Helsinki: Societas scientiarum fennica.

Bruun, C. 2015. Ostian Inscriptions *in situ*. *Journal of Roman Archaeology* 28: 615-20 (= review of van der Meer 2012).

Bruun, C. 2020. Transfer of property in an Ostian professional *corpus*: Sexti Sextilii and Lucii Iulii among the *lenuncularii* in *CIL* XIV 251, and a possible effect of the 'Antonine Plague'. *Arctos: Acta philologica Fennica* 54: 9-32.

Bruun, C. 2025. *Ostia-by-the-Sea. Society, Population, and Identities in Rome's Port*. New York and Oxford: Oxford University Press.

Caldelli, M.L. 2014. Senatori oriundi di Ostia: un aggiornamento, in Caldelli and Gregori 2014: 585-97.

Caldelli, M.L. and G.L. Gregori (eds) 2014. *Epigrafia e ordine senatorio, 30 anni dopo* (Tituli 10), 2 vols. Rome: Edizioni Quasar.

Danner, M. 2017. *Wohnkultur im spätantiken Ostia* (Kölner Schriften zur Archäologie 1). Wiesbaden: Reichert.

Gering, A. 2018. *Ostias vergessene Spätantike: Eine urbanistische Deutung zur Bewältigung von Verfall* (Palilia 31). Wiesbaden: Reichert.

Keay, S. *et al.* 2005. *Portus: An Archaeological Survey of the Port of Imperial Rome* (Archaeological Monographs of the British School at Rome 15). London: British School at Rome.

Licordari, A. 1982. Ascesa al senato e rapporti con i territori d'origine. Italia. Regio I (*Latium*), in *EOS* II: 9-57. Rome: Edizioni di Storia e Letteratura.

Luciani, F. and A. Pistellato 2010. Regio X (*Venetia et Histria*) – parte centro-settentrionale. *Iulia Concordia, Opitergium, Bellunum, Feltria, Acelum, Tarvisium, Altinum*, in M. Silvestrini (ed.) *Le tribù romane* (Atti della XVIᵉ Rencontre sur l'épigraphie): 253-64. Bari: Edipuglia.

Marinucci, A. 1992. Iscrizioni, in P. Cicerchia and A. Marinucci, *Le Terme del Foro o di Gavio Massimo* (Scavi di Ostia 11): 163-228. Rome: Istituto poligrafico e zecca dello stato. Libreria dello stato.

Meiggs, R. 1973. *Roman Ostia*, 2nd ed. Oxford: Oxford University Press (1st ed. 1960).

Pavolini, C. 2011. Un gruppo di ricche case ostiensi del tardo impero. Trasformazioni architettoniche e cambiamenti sociali, in O. Brandt and P. Pergola (eds) *In marmoribus vestita: Studi in onore di Federico Guidobaldi*: 1025-48. Vatican City: Pontificio Istituto di Archeologia Cristiana.

Pavolini, C. 2018. The late-antique *domus* of Ostia. *Journal of Roman Archaeology* 31: 786-93 (= review of Danner 2017).

Romeo, I. 2019. *I ritratti III. I ritratti romani dal 250 circa al VI secolo d.C.* (Scavi di Ostia 17). Sesto Fiorentino: All'Insegna del Giglio.

Salomies, O. 1987. *Die römischen Vornamen. Studien zur römischen Namengebung* (Commentationes humanarum litterarum 82). Helsinki: Societas Scientiarum Fennica.

Salomies, O. 1996. Senatori oriundi del Lazio, in H. Solin (ed.) *Studi storico-epigrafici sul Lazio antico* (Acta Instituti Romani Finlandiae 15): 23-127. Rome: Institutum Romanum Finlandiae.

Salomies, O. 2002. People in Ostia: some onomastic observations and comparisons with Rome, in C. Bruun and A. Gallina Zevi (eds) *Ostia e Portus nelle loro relazioni con Roma* (Acta Instituti Romani Finlandiae 27): 135-59. Rome: Institutum Romanum Finlandiae.

van der Meer, L.B. 2012. *Ostia Speaks: Inscriptions, Buildings and Spaces in Rome's Main Port*. Leuven: Peeters.

Zevi, F. *et al.* 2018. *Epigrafia ostiense dopo il CIL: 2000 iscrizioni funerarie*. Venice: Edizioni Ca' Foscari.

8. River Trade of Mediterranean Imports in the Mid and Upper Tiber Valley from the Imperial Period to Late Antiquity

Letizia Ceccarelli

Introduction

This paper discusses the importance of the River Tiber for the trade of Mediterranean products in Regio VI Umbria, where river connectivity and the main road network of the *via Flaminia* and *via Amerina* were crucial for the economic growth of the upper and middle Tiber Valley, from the early Imperial period to Late Antiquity. Fundamental to the understanding of settlement development along these roads and the role played by the River Tiber in trade is the work carried out by Simon Keay and Martin Millett in the Roman Towns Project, especially at Falerii Novi, conducted within the framework of the British School at Rome's Tiber Valley Project (Keay *et al.* 2004, Johnson *et al.* 2004) (Figure 8.1).

The impact of production and the corresponding effect on participating in a wide commercial network, as argued in this contribution, can shed new light on the economy of the upper Tiber Valley. However, the documentation in Umbria is scattered due to the fragmented archaeological record and the lack of systematic publications. Therefore, central to the discussion is new archaeological data, in particular for the left bank of the River Tiber where excavations and field surveys have provided evidence of production and trade along the river.

The Tiber constituted the preferred distribution network for agricultural products of Umbria which mostly focused on the market of Rome. Not only wine and building materials[1] but also vegetables and livestock (Nicoletta 2011: 236 with earlier references and discussion of the historical sources) were traded from Umbria, as the cost of transport by river was significantly lower than by roads. According to Dionysius (3.44.1) the Tiber was navigable upstream to the springs by small boats but Pliny the Elder reports that the river in spring and summer often had a low water level, so it was navigable by means of sluices.[2]

Imports used the same route north: the evidence is offered by the numerous amphorae from Spain and Africa, as well as other imported products discovered in the upper Tiber Valley.[3]

Along the stretch of the Tiber between *Ocriculum* and Todi traces of docks are well documented, some of which were still in use in modern times (for a summary see Bergamini 2008: 304 n. 68) (Figure 8.2). Otricoli, with a river port, had a strategic position both controlling the Tiber, at the confluence with the Nera, and the *via Flaminia*. Partially excavated, it was then surveyed by Simon Keay and Martin Millett in the framework of the Tiber Valley Project (Hay *et al.* 2013: 10. See also Witcher 2020: 148). North of Otricoli, on the left bank of the Tiber, the river port of Seripola near Orte was discovered in 1962-63, during the construction of a bridge across the river for the A1 Autostrada.[4] A series of structures, including baths, arranged along a road parallel to the river were in use between the mid-1st to the 5th centuries AD and possibly later (Johnson *et al.* 2004: 87-88. De Lucia Brolli and Suaria 2006: 136-49). Around 30km to the north, at the confluence of the River Paglia was the important river port at Paliano, where five docks, a quay, and numerous buildings were excavated in the 19th century.[5] The complex served Volsinii and the important manufacturing and later consumption site at Scoppieto, near Baschi.[6] The river harbour of Pian di Porto near Todi was destroyed by flooding of the Tiber in the 12th century (Bergamini 2001: 167-68). Further north at Perugia, the main port has been identified at the confluence of the Tiber and Chiascio Rivers, near Pontenuovo di Torgiano (Bergamini 2008: 294-95; Speranza 2011: 286). The river was navigable as far away as the villa of Pliny at San Giustino where the

---

[1] The upper and middle Tiber Valley was important to Rome for wood and the production of bricks and tiles, see Diosono 2008 and Witcher 2020: 188.

[2] Pliny, *epist.* 5.6.12. The waters were collected for nine days and then discharged, coinciding with the *nundinae*, as pointed out by Zuddas 2014: 137. Traces of medieval sluice boxes were identified in the piers of the Ponte Vecchio bridge at Ponte San Giovanni, near Perugia (see Cenciaioli 2009: 388).

[3] River barges, such as *lintrae*, and boats (*caudicariae*) were used to ship goods along the Tiber, as recorded in a cippus from *Urvinum Hortense* where a slave Priamus was a *magister navium*, Zuddas 2014: 141-43. Towing must have been necessary upstream.

[4] The construction of the motorway compromised the docks along the Tiber, which today are no longer visible. Systematics excavations were carried out in the mid-70s but they are mostly unpublished, De Lucia Bolli and Suaria 2006: 135.

[5] The structures, dating between the late Republican period and the beginning of the 5th century AD, were identified both along the Paglia and the Tiber, which was then diverted in 1952-62 with the construction of the Corbara dam, Bruschetti 2008. See also Diosono 2012: 200.

[6] Bergamini 2007: 87-88. The ceramic workshop was producing between the Augustan and Trajanic period.

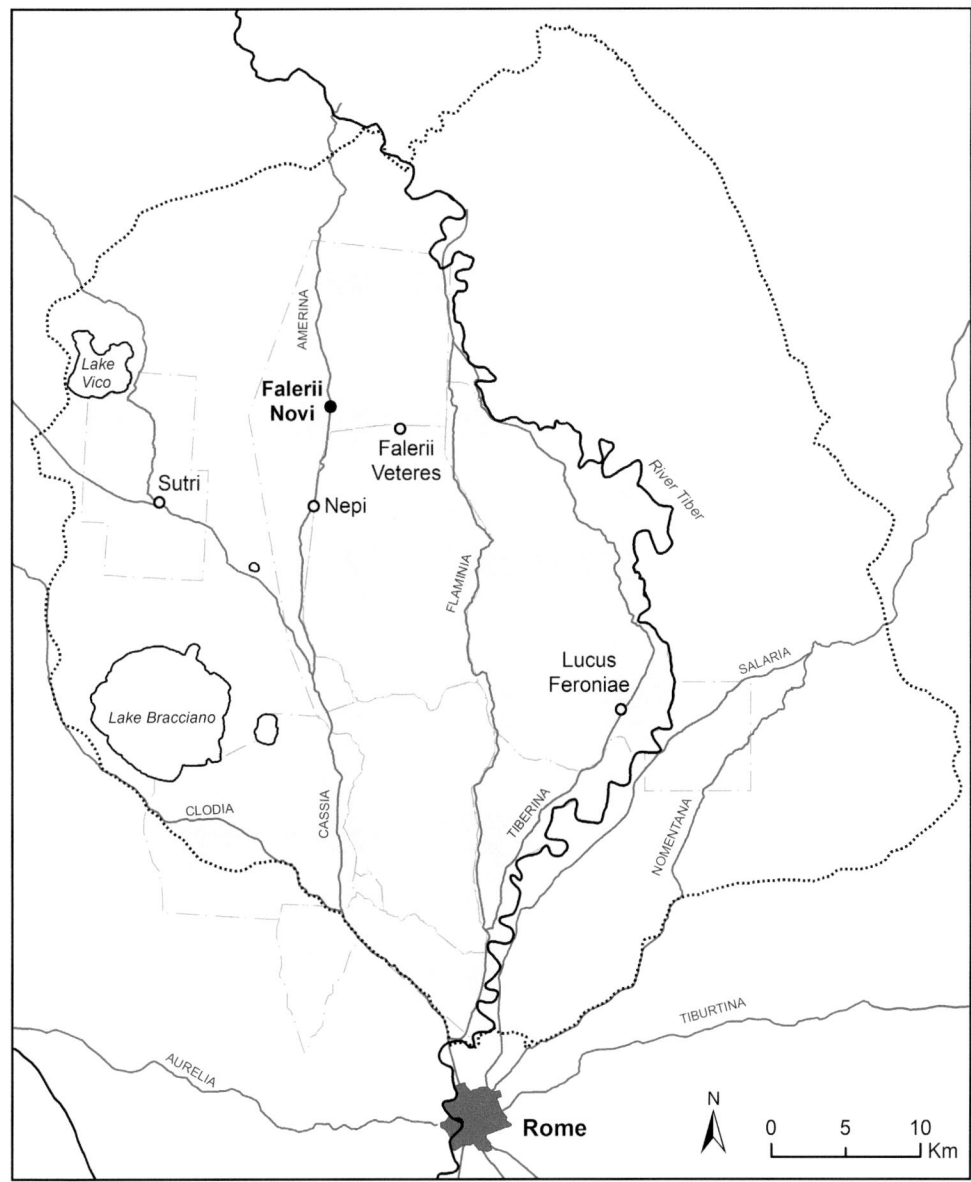

Figure 8.1. From Andrews *et al.* 2023. The Tiber and the major ancient roads in relation to Rome. The grey dotted line shows the Tiber Valley Project study area.

presence of a river trading port has been suggested (see Molina Vidal 2008: 232-33) (Figure 8.2).

The Economic System and Trade in Umbria

Generally, in the upper Tiber Valley the agricultural production, mostly wine, and trade along the river were controlled by a system of villas and farms established in the 1st century AD, abandoned between the late 2nd and mid-3rd century AD, with a revitalisation in the 4th century AD with the creation of large *fundi*.[7]

The economy of the region in the 1st to 3rd centuries AD is documented by the distribution of flat-based wine amphorae which were produced in several sites in Umbria. Despite the identification of production wasters at Spello, the only certain workshop can be placed at Montelabate (Perugia). The site is located on the left bank of the Tiber 7km to the north of *Arna* and 5.5km from the river, separated by a series of gentle hills. A series of excavation campaigns (2012-18), led to the discovery of seven Roman kilns[8] (Figure 8.3). The

---

[7] This trend was also identified in the mid-Tiber Valley, see Patterson 2020: 219-21.

[8] Kilns 1 (first phase), 3, 4, and 6 were in use in the early to mid-Imperial period, producing amphorae, thin-walled ware, and cooking ware. The earliest kiln (number 7) cannot be precisely dated, but was destroyed by the construction of a room beside kiln 6. For a detailed

Figure 8.2. Map of Umbria with the road system and location of major sites
mentioned in the text.

kilns were mainly producing flat-bottomed amphorae known as Spello type, Ostia III, 369-70 / II, 521 or Altotiberine.[9] Specialised manpower was necessary to work at the kilns which were producing a surplus of amphorae, giving the scale of the manufacture, which were acquired by other wine producers, creating a vibrant economic system also for a local and regional market.[10] The limited number of systematic excavations

of *villae* in the middle and upper Tiber Valley means there is scattered evidence for wine production. However, a wine-pressing basin, as well as a *cella vinaria* were excavated at Pliny's villa located near S. Giustino (Braconi 2007: 97-98). Other imperial villas furnished with wine-production installations have been recorded at Todi (at La Valle and Manconi *et al.* 1981: 399, site 134) and Sigillo (Villa Scirca and Bonomi Ponzi 1997: 161), whilst in others only the *cella vinaria* have been identified (see Di Giuseppantonio *et al.* 2003: 1397-1415, Deruta, Perugia Vecchia, site 42, Perugia, Valcaprara site 36, Spoleto, Villa Redenta site 122).

Conversely, the higher percentage of imported oil in amphorae suggests that Umbria was not producing

---

description and phasing of the Montelabate kilns, see Ceccarelli 2021a and Ceccarelli 2023.

[9] These were generally produced from the Tiberian–Claudian period to the early 3rd century AD; for the production at Montelabate see Ceccarelli 2017 and Ceccarelli 2021a, where earlier amphorae production is also discussed, including Dressel 2-4.

[10] See Diosono (2019: 129-30) for the wine production models in the upper Tiber Valley both for Rome and the local markets.

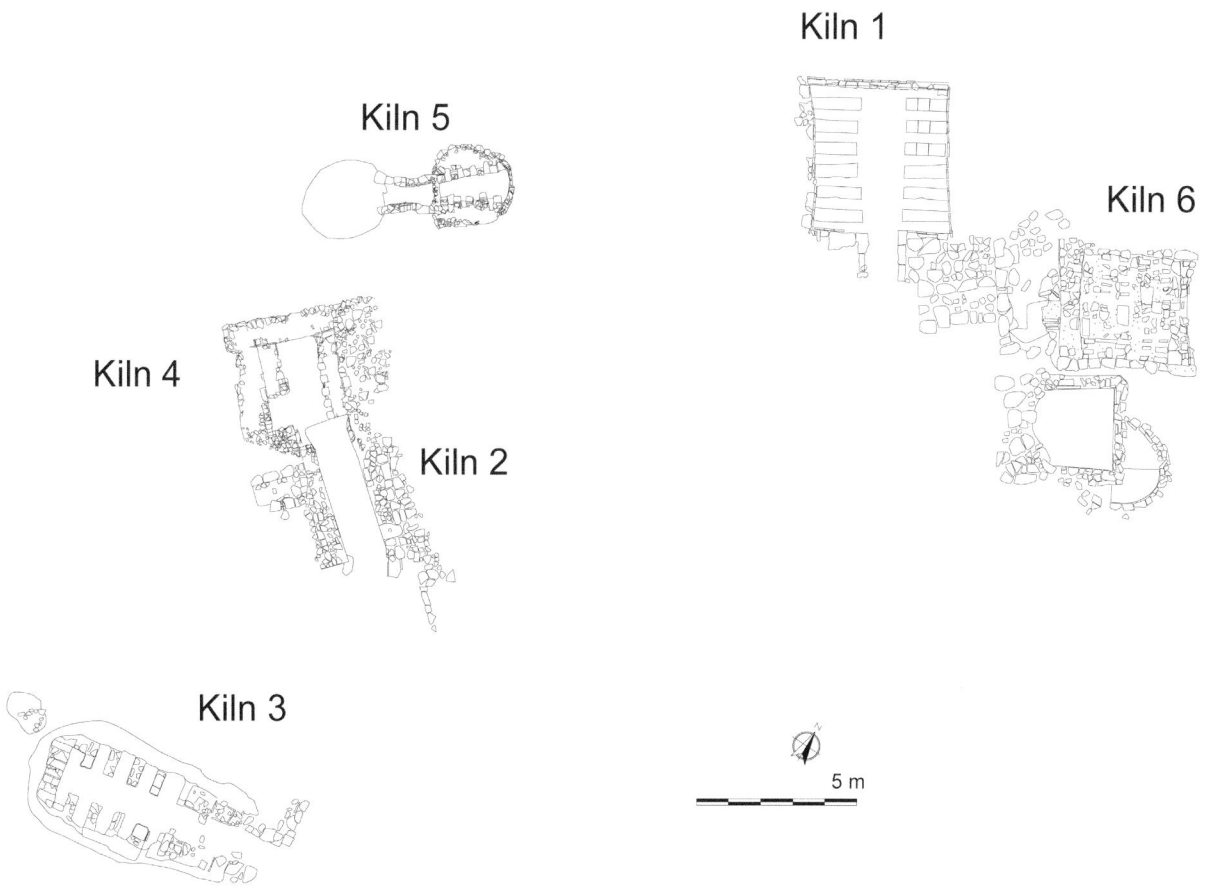

Figure 8.3. Plan of the Montelabate ceramic workshop.

enough to supply even the internal market (see also Diosono 2015: 353). After oil, fish products also played an important role in imports. The supply patterns recorded by the survey at Otricoli, between the 1st to 3rd centuries AD, with imports mostly from Betica[11] and Africa[12] are representative of the rest of the region. At the villa at Poggio Gramignano, near Lugnano in Teverina, located at 2.5km from the Tiber, wine was imported from the upper Tiber, given the high number of the Spello type amphorae discovered; whilst Spain and North Africa were the main suppliers for oil, *garum*, and fish products in the middle and later Imperial period (Martin 1999: 341-45 (Spanish amphorae: Dr 7-11, Beltran IIB, Dressel 14, Dressel 20, and Dressel 14similis); 346-56 (African: Africana I and II, Tripolitana I)). Scoppieto was part of the Mediterranean supply network for wine, where it was imported from the 1st

century AD, as well as oil and fish sauce.[13] The results from the upper Tiber Valley appear to corroborate this import pattern, as the *garum* Dressel 14 and the oil Dressel 20 amphorae are nearly ubiquitous both along the Tiber and inland, such as San Giustino, Colle Plinio,[14] *Arna* (Donnini and Rosi Bonci 2008: 72-78, site 10 and 96, site 29), Montelabate,[15] *Urvinum Hortense*,[16] Assisi,[17] and Todi.[18]

As already noted, the oil supply between the 2nd to the mid-3rd centuries AD was mostly from Africa and the containers are widespread not only in villas and settlements. Two field-walking survey campaigns, in 2010 and 2018, systematically investigated the area connecting the kilns at Montelabate to the Tiber,

---

[11] Haltern 70 (50 BC-AD 50), olive oil Dressel 20 (1st to 3rd centuries AD), and *garum* Dressel 14 amphorae (1st- to 2nd centuries), followed by the Lusitanian *garum* amphorae Dressel 14 *similis* (Zampini 2013: 109, tab. 4.13).
[12] From the second half of the 2nd century AD are attested Africana IA and later variant B and Africana IIA, which production ended in the second quarter of the 3rd century AD, see Zampini 2013: 109-10.

[13] Wine from Tarracona in Dressel 2-4 amphorae, from Betica both oil and *garum* (Dressel 20, Dressel 7-11, and Dressel 14), from Africa oil and wine (Tripolitana II, Africana IA, and Africana IIA, Africana IB), Speranza 2011: 287-92.
[14] Molina Vidal 1999: 105-06, figs 11-13 and 17. The most documented are the Dressel 7-11, followed by Dressel 14 constituting the 35% of the imports, as well as Dressel 20 amphorae.
[15] Two Dressel 14 and a Dressel 20 amphorae.
[16] A stamped Dressel 20, Donnini 2006: 90-91.
[17] Matteini Chiari 2002: 98-99, nn. 125-27.
[18] Bergamini 2007: 89.

revealing a dense occupation pattern between the 2nd to the mid-3rd centuries AD, with imported goods (Africana IA and the later variant B amphorae, including ARS and African cooking ware).

Late Antique Imports

In the upper Tiber Valley, the economic system of production and landscape management changed in the late antique period, as many villas were abandoned with a shift towards tenant-based agriculture in large estates, where the *coloni* cultivated the land and paid their tax obligations (see Ceccarelli 2021b: 323 and n. 4).

By the 4th century the taxation system changed to land-based taxes, centred on production surplus shares, evidenced by the renovation or reuse of mid-Imperial period villas in the 4th and 5th centuries AD.[19] From the 4th century AD the *canon vinarius* provided Rome with a wine supply at controlled prices,[20] which was shipped down the Tiber from Umbria in wooden barrels.[21] However, together with the *vina fiscalia*, the portion of distributed wine, was a substantial quantity of wine shipped to Rome for the free market, which provided an income for the owners of the large production estates. However, in AD 364-65 this taxation system changed, and wine was only sold at controlled prices, probably partially affecting the economy of the region (see Ceccarelli 2021b: 325 and n. 25). River trade of building material towards Rome was also part of fiscal obligations in the 4th century AD.[22]

The local wine trade using amphorae in Umbria continued in the late antique period, as suggested by small flat-based ovoid containers characterised by a short neck similar to the Spello type amphorae which were produced at Montelabate (Ceccarelli 2021b) (Figure 8.4) and Spoleto,[23] still documented in 5th-century contexts at the villa at Lugnano in Teverina,[24]

Falerii Novi[25] (Figure 8.1) and in a deposit of the late 6th century AD at *Forum Novum* (Patterson *et al.* 2005: 372-73).

Therefore, evidence of a still lively economy related to agricultural production along the Tiber is proved by its participation to a wide-ranging commercial network in the 4th and 5th centuries, continuing even in the first half of the 6th century. At Otricoli there is good evidence of not only fine ware imports[26] but also oil, *garum*, and other fish products supplied in African and eastern Mediterranean amphorae.[27] These general trends also correspond to the imports in Rome.[28] At Seripola, imported goods are documented until the mid-6th century AD.[29] At Poggio Gramignano the villa was still participating in the commercial network of wine, oil, and *garum* from Spain, Africa, and the eastern Mediterranean in the late 4th and the mid-5th centuries AD.[30] Similar imports have also been noted at Scoppieto.[31] The key role played by the river harbours as well as the road system in the distribution of amphorae in the upper Tiber Valley is also documented by the discovery of Iberian and African imports at San Giustino between the 4th and the 5th centuries AD.[32]

The economic vitality of villas and *fundi* is evidenced by the continuing imports even inland, such as at the kilns at Montelabate, where amphorae and lamps from Africa, dating to the first half of the 5th century AD, were discovered during the recent excavations, in particular *spatheia*, that would have contained either preserved olives, wine, or fish sauce (Figure 8.4).[33]

---

[19] Vera 2012: 108-12. The trend towards the reoccupation of villas in the 4th century was also identified in the mid-Tiber Valley, see Patterson 2020: 219-21. For discussion of the creation of large *fundi*, see also Diosono 2019: 129-30.

[20] Peña 1999: 18-19. For the discussion of the *canon* as tax system, see Lo Cascio 1999. According to Panella 1999: 204 the *vina fiscalia*, the portion of the distributed wine, was less than the quantity of product shipped to Rome for the free market but it was sold at controlled prices, as also argued by Vera 2005: 257.

[21] The use of wooden barrels would have allowed a larger quantity of wine to be shipped, as the city's daily wine consumption in the 4th century AD has been calculated by Peña 1999: 11 as the equivalent of 15,000 to 24,000 amphorae with a capacity of 17.5 l.

[22] By the 4th century the brick and tiles *figlinae* were privately owned and their products shipped to Rome, as noted by Patterson 2020: 244. Evidence for timber trade is supported by the discovery of a marble weight for wood dated to the end of the 4th century AD at the river port of *Ocriculum*, see Diosono 2012: 206 and Patterson 2020: 245 with earlier references.

[23] Costamagna 2015: 377-78, fig. 1.4-5. Although no kiln has been identified there are production wasters.

[24] Due to the high percentage of small amphorae of the Spello type, these containers were contemporary to the deposit rather than

residual (Martin 1999: 334). One amphora of this type was used in a mid-5th-century AD child burial (Montagnetti *et al.* 2020: 286, table 1), therefore they were still circulating.

[25] The amphorae, discovered during the 2023-24 excavation campaigns of the Falerii Novi Project are still unpublished. For the project see Andrews *et al.* 2023.

[26] African Red Slip D bowl Hayes 80a, the flanged bowl Hayes 91 A-B and dishes 61A-B, Hayes 76 and 87a produced between mid-4th to the end of the 5th centuries AD (Zampini 2013: 97 and table 4.5).

[27] Africana IIB to D, produced until the end of the 4th century, Keay 25 (mid-4th to mid-5th centuries), *spatheia* (mid-5th to mid-6th century), and LR1, produced from the 5th to the 7th centuries AD (Zampini 2013: 109-10 and table 4.13).

[28] See Patterson 2020: 247 and fig. 5.14 on the imported amphorae recovered in the South Etruria Survey.

[29] Colelli and Lupi 2006: 212-17: Almagro 5 and *spatheia*. In particular, the ARS form Hayes 104B was produced between the middle and the second half of the 6th century AD (Bonifay 2004: 181-83).

[30] From Iberia (Dressel 23 and Almagro 51A\B), North Africa (*spatheia*, Keay 39, Keay 50, Keay 59), and the eastern Mediterranean area (Late Roman 1, 3, and 5), Martin 1999: 360-61.

[31] From Iberia oil and *garum* (Dressel 23, Almagro 51C), from North Africa wine and oil (Africana IIIA, IIIC, Bonifay type 37 = Keay LIX), Speranza 2011.

[32] Almagro 51 and Africana IIC, Molina Vidal 2008: 232-33, fig. 2.

[33] Fragments of two African Red Slip lamps type *Atlante* VIII A, dated from the mid-4th to the first half of the 5th centuries AD (type 41, Bonifay 2004: 359, fig. 203), as well as two rims of *spatheia*, type Keay 26, type 31 variant 1A of Bonifay 2004: 125, fig. 67. See also Ceccarelli 2023: 290-93. According to Patterson 2020: 247 these amphorae most likely contained wine.

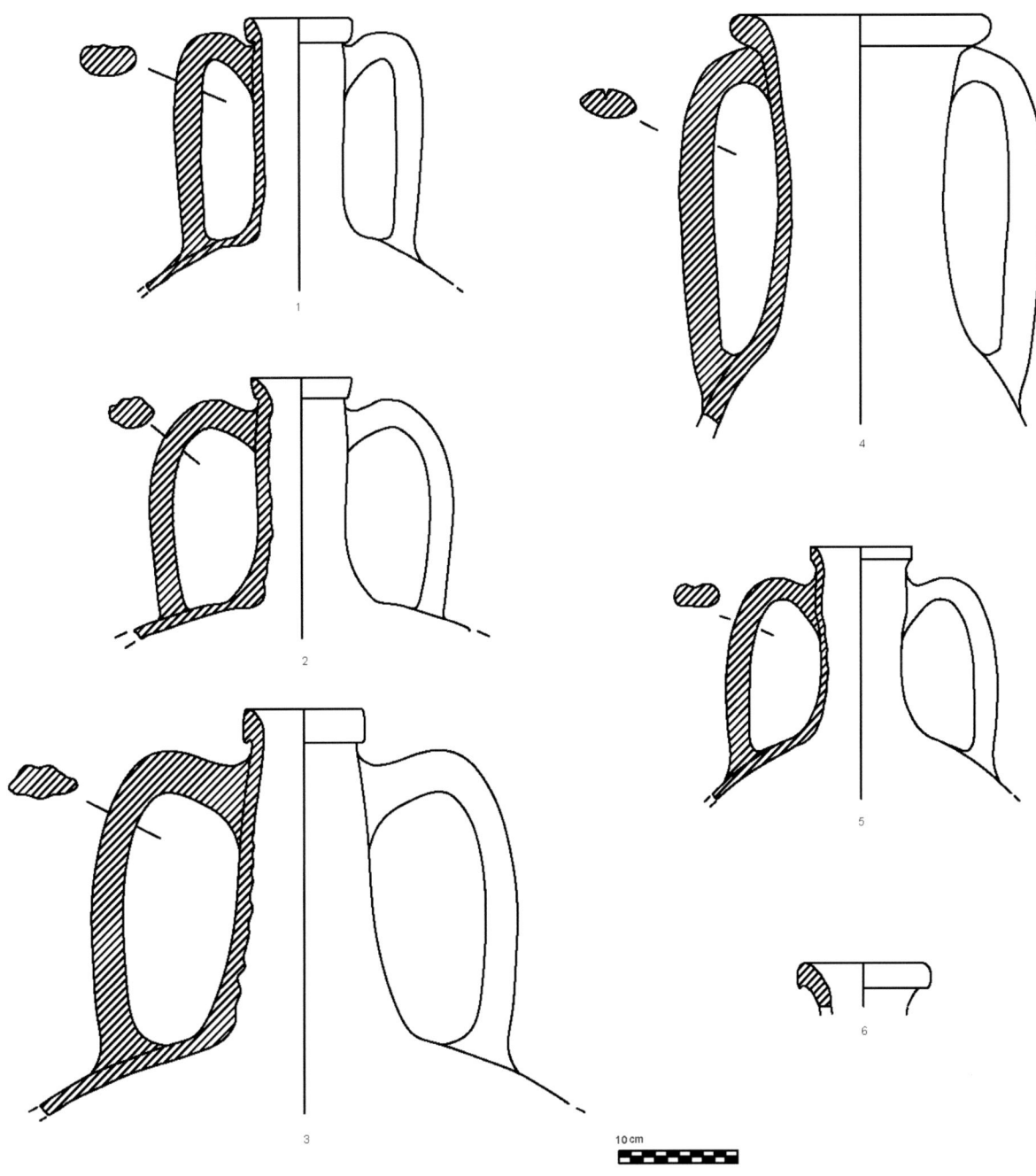

Figure 8.4. Montelabate. Amphorae production (1-3 and 5) and imports (4-6).

Conclusion

A substantial transformation of the villas and settlements in Umbria took place, starting from the mid-5th century AD, as the taxation system could have created an economic crisis with reduction of surplus for trade, generating a decrease in the demand for expensive imported goods.[34] The limited accessibility of Umbria to the ARS supply by the mid-5th century AD created a market for the imitation of forms.[35]

For instance, at Montelabate in the central decades of the 5th century AD coarse ware casseroles were produced imitating the ARS Hayes 61A/B2 forms

---

[34] As argued by Vera 2010: 12 on the change to a money-based taxation system.

[35] According to Wickham 2005: 730, the ARS distribution problems were caused by the disruptions of the end of *Annona* in AD 439. As argued by Vera 2010: 12, the late antique taxation system was no longer in kind but money based. The increase in prices, and a competitive local market, offering imitation goods, must have significantly limited the availability of ARS.

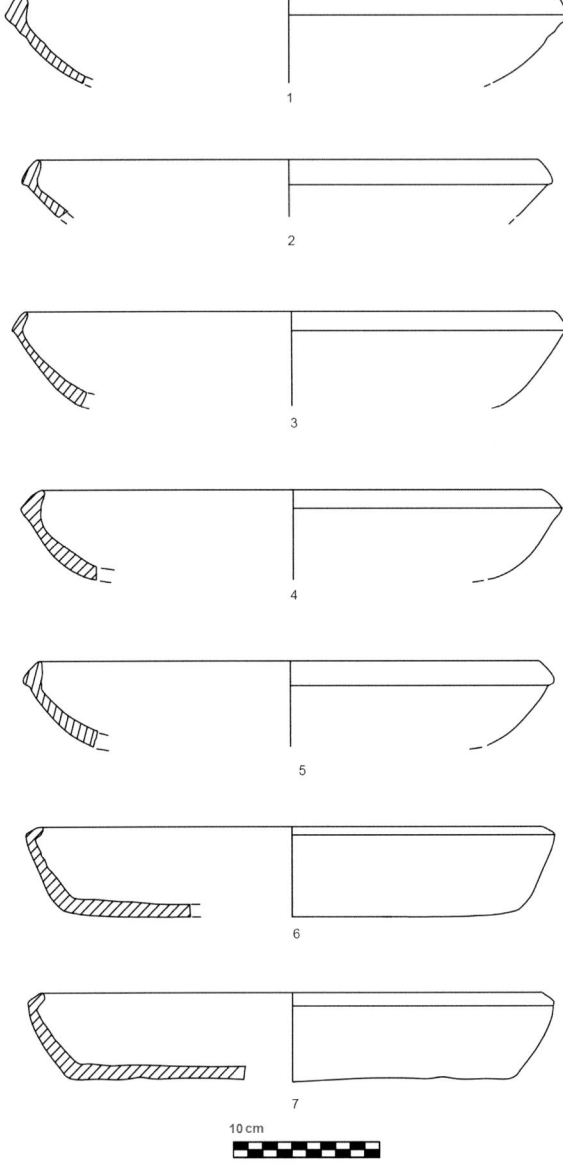

Figure 8.5. Montelabate. Casseroles imitating the ARS Hayes 61A/B2 forms.

were converted for agricultural and manufacturing activities[38] located along the Tiber and the roads were still part of the distribution network of transport amphorae, such as Otricoli and Seripola. Moreover, imports of African Red Slip produced between the mid-5th to the mid-6th centuries AD are documented at Baschi, Scoppieto, Amelia, and Orvieto, suggesting participation in commercial trade.[39] In the early 6th century AD, during the reign of Theodoric, an attempt was made to restore navigation along the Tiber as well as to maintain the road system and some buildings, as documented by the brick stamps recovered in southern Umbria.[40] However, the remaining villa system and the rural landscape occupation in Umbria was devastated by the nearly twenty years of the Greek-Gothic war (AD 535-554), as the war often took place along the via Flaminia and Amerina, with pillaging and destruction causing the subsequent demographic decline.[41]

Bibliography

Andrews, M., S. Bernard, E. Dodd, B. Fochetti, S. Kay, P. Liverani, M. Millett, F. Vermeulen 2023. The Falerii Novi Project. *Papers of the British School at Rome* 91: 9-34.

Bergamini, M. 2001. *Todi antica città degli Umbri*. Assisi: TAU.

Bergamini, M. 2007. Il rapporto col Tevere, in M. Bergamini (ed.) *Scoppieto, I: Il territorio e i materiali (Lucerne, Opus doliare, Metalli)*. Florence: Edizioni all'Insegna del Giglio: 79-96.

Bergamini, M. 2008. Scoppieto e i commerci sul Tevere, in Coarelli and Patterson 2008: 285-321.

Bonifay, M. 2004. *Études sur la céramique romaine tardive d'Afrique*. Oxford: Archaeopress.

Bonomi Ponzi, L. 1997. Il territorio nocerino in età tardo-antica e altomedievale, in M.S. Arena and L. Paroli (eds), *Umbria longobarda: La necropoli di Nocera Umbra nel centenario della scoperta; Roma, Museo dell'Alto Medioevo, 19 aprile - 26 ottobre 1997, Roma*: 161-66. Rome: De Luca.

(Ceccarelli 2017; 2021b) (Figure 8.5). The imitation was very successful and is attested in contexts of the 5th to mid-6th centuries AD, both in Umbria and the inland Tuscia. The demographic reduction in Rome[36] which limited demand for wine and other goods, could have also affected the economy of the region. Whilst several of the villas in Umbria were abandoned or showed signs of degradation of the structures including the presence of burials, such as the villa at Poggio Gramignano[37] others

[36] The crisis of the population in Rome took place between the end of the 5th and the beginning of the 6th century AD.

[37] Parts of the villa were abandoned and reused for the 59 infant and child burials, most likely being the result of a malaria epidemic, see the latest contribution by Montagnetti *et al.* 2020. Other villas showing the presence of burials are at Gubbio Via Settestrade, at Spoleto Villa Redenta (6th-7th centuries), similarly as at Sigillo Villa

Scirca and at Penna in Teverina the villa of Pennavecchia, Castrorao Barba 2020: 204-05.

[38] See Patterson 2020: 224-29 on the different categories of villas in the lower and middle Tiber Valley. For the economy of the late antique villas in Umbria see Diosono 2012: 207-08 and Di Miceli 2012: 230-33.

[39] In table 1 of Nicoletta 2011, see note above, are listed at Baschi the flanged bowl Hayes 91C produced in the central decades of the 6th century (Bonifay 2004: 179), at Amelia the form Hayes 91B produced in the central decades of the 5th century, at Orvieto form 91A produced in the mid-5th century as well as the bowl Hayes 99A dated to the end of the 5th century to the mid-6th century AD (Bonifay 2004: 181). At Scoppieto are reported the flanged bowls form Hayes 91A and 91B, Nicoletta 2011: 250-53, tables 5-7.

[40] At Spoleto, Baschi, Attigliano, and Orvieto, see Guerrini 2011: 162, fig. 21 and n. 200.

[41] Zanini and Celani 2020: 19-21 suggest that the battles concentrated around roads and main cities that fiscally controlled a territory able to supply the Byzantine army, whilst the Ostrogoths had their supply network already in place.

Braconi P. 2007. La Villa di Plinio a San Giustino, in R. Ciardiello (ed.), *La villa romana* (Archeologia 8): 83-104. Naples: L'orientale.

Bravi 2012 = *Aurea Umbria: Una regione dell'Impero nell'era di Costantino*, A. Bravi (ed.), *Bollettino per i beni culturali dell'Umbria* 10, 2012.

Bruschetti, P. 2008. Il porto romano di Pagliano presso Orvieto, in Coarelli and Patterson 2008: 323-43.

Castrorao Barba, A. 2020. *La fine delle ville romane in Italia tra Tarda Antichità e Alto Medioevo: (III-VIII secolo).* Bari: Edipuglia.

Ceccarelli, L. 2017. *Production and Trade in Central Italy in the Roman Period: The Amphora Workshop of Montelabate in Umbria. Papers of the British School at Rome* 85: 109-41.

Ceccarelli, L. 2021a. Nuovi dati di scavo sulla produzione di anfore in Umbria tra Tevere e Chiascio nel I e II secolo d.C. *FOLD&R Italy Series* 508: 2-19, <http://www.fastionline.org/docs/FOLDER-it-2021-508.pdf>, viewed 1 May 2025.

Ceccarelli, L. 2021b. Ceramic production in the late antique and early medieval territory of Perugia. *Archeologia medievale* 48: 323-24.

Ceccarelli, L. 2023. La produzione di ceramiche comuni tardoantiche nelle fornaci di Montelabate (PG). *Bollettino di Archeologia Online* 14, 2023 Supplemento 1: 287-302. <https://bollettinodiarcheologiaonline.beniculturali.it/wp-content/uploads/2023/12/2023_Suppl_1_CECCARELLI.pdf >, viewed 1 May 2025.

Cenciaioli, L. 2008. Le necropoli perugine in prossimità del Tevere, in Coarelli and Patterson 2008: 387-400.

Cirelli et al. 2015 = Cirelli E., F. Diosono and H. Patterson 2015. *Le forme della crisi: Produzioni ceramiche e commerci nell'Italia centrale tra Romani e Longobardi (III-VIII sec. d.C.); atti del convegno, Spoleto-Campello sul Clitunno, 5-7 ottobre 2012.* Bologna: Ante quem.

Coarelli and Patterson 2008 = Coarelli, F. and H. Patterson (eds) *Mercator placidissimus: The Tiber Valley in Antiquity; New Research in the Upper and Middle River Valley* (Atti del Convegno, Rome, 27-28 February 2004). Rome: Quasar.

Colelli, C. and A. Lupi 2006. VI.2 La ceramica, in P. Aureli, M.A. De Lucia Brolli and S. Del Lungo (eds) *Orte (Viterbo) e il suo territorio: scavi e ricerche in Etruria Meridionale tra Antichità e Medioevo* (British Archaeological Reports, International Series 1545): 207-28. Oxford: Archaeopress.

Costamagna, L. 2015. Note preliminari sulla ceramica di Spoleto tra V e VII secolo, in Cirelli et al. 2015: 377-86.

De Lucia Brolli, M.A. and L. Suaria 2006. Il territorio: il porto fluviale in località Seripola, in P. Aureli, M.A. De Lucia Brolli and S. Del Lungo (eds) *Orte (Viterbo) e il suo territorio: scavi e ricerche in Etruria Meridionale fra antichità e medioevo* (British Archaeological Reports, International Series 1545): 135-70. Oxford: Archaeopress.

Diosono, F. 2008. Il commercio del legname sul fiume Tevere, in Coarelli and Patterson 2008: 251-83.

Diosono, F. 2012. Paesaggio rurale, produzioni e commerci nella valle del Tevere in età tardoantica, in Bravi 2012: 199-208.

Diosono, F. 2015. Prove tecniche di ricostruzione del quadro dei materiali ceramici in Umbria tra IV e VII secolo, in Cirelli et al. 2015: 351-60.

Diosono, F. 2019. Il contesto economico e produttivo della Villa dei Mosaici di Spello, in G. Sabatini (ed.), *La Villa dei Mosaici di Spello: dallo scavo alla valorizzazione*: 128-33. Perugia: Soprintendenza Archeologia, Belle arti e Paesaggio dell'Umbria.

Di Giuseppantonio et al. 2003 = P. Di Giuseppantonio, P. Guerrini and S. Orazi, Trasformazione dell'insediamento rurale nel territorio dell'Umbria: il caso delle villae. Alcune considerazioni, in *I Longobardi dei Ducati di Spoleto e Benevento: atti del XVI congresso internazionale di studi sull'Alto Medioevo*: 1377-1419. Spoleto: Centro italiano di studi sull'alto medioevo.

Di Miceli, A. 2012. Popolamento tra città e campagna nell'Umbria tardoantica. Una nuova analisi, in Bravi 2012: 225-48.

Donnini, L. 2006. Nuovi frammenti di anfora recanti bolli, graffiti e tituli picti dagli scavi di Urvinum Hortense, in S. Menchelli and M. Pasquinucci (eds) *Territorio e produzioni ceramiche: Paesaggi, economia e società in età romana; atti del convegno internazionale, Pisa 20-22 ottobre 2005 = Territory and Pottery: Landscapes, Economy and Society in Roman Times; Proceedings of the International Meeting*: 87-92. Pisa: Pisa University Press.

Donnini, L. and L. Rosi Bonci 2008. *Civitella d'Arna (Perugia, Italia) e il suo territorio: Carta archeologica.* Oxford: Archaeopress.

Guerrini, P. 2011. Theodericus Rex nelle testimonianze epigrafiche. *Temporis Signa: Archeologia della tarda antichità e del medioevo* 6: 133-74.

Hay et al. 2013 = Hay, S., S.J. Keay and M. Millett 2013. *Ocriculum (Otricoli, Umbria): An Archaeological Survey of the Roman Town.* London: British School at Rome.

Johnson et al. 2004 = Johnson, P., S.J. Keay and M. Millett 2004. Lesser urban sites in the Tiber Valley: Baccanae, Forum Cassii and Castellum Amerinum. *Papers of the British School at Rome* 72: 69-100.

Keay et al. 2004 = Keay, S.J., M. Millett, S. Poppy, J. Robinson, J. Taylor and N. Terrenato 2004. New approaches to Roman urbanism in the Tiber Valley, in H. Patterson (ed.) *Bridging the Tiber: Approaches to Regional Archaeology in the Middle Tiber Valley* (Archaeological Monographs of the British School at Rome 13): 223-36. London: British School at Rome.

Lo Cascio, E. 1999. Canon frumentarius, suarius, vinarius: stato e privati nell'approvvigionamento dell'Urbs, in W.V. Harris (ed.) *The Transformations of Urbs Roma in Late Antiquity* (Journal of Roman

Archaeology, Suppl. 33): 163-82. Portsmouth (RI): Journal of Roman Archaeology.

Manconi *et al.* 1981 = Manconi, D., M.A. Tomei and M. Verzar 1981. La situazione in Umbria dal III sec. a. C. alla tarda antichità, in A. Giardina and A. Schiavone (eds) *Società romana e produzione schiavistica: l'Italia: insediamenti e forme economiche*, I: 371-406. Rome: Laterza.

Martin, A. 1999. Amphorae, in D. Soren and N. Soren (eds) *A Roman Villa and a Late Roman Infant Cemetery*: 329-62. Rome: L'Erma di Bretschneider.

Matteini Chiari, M. 2002. *Raccolte comunali di Assisi: materiali archeologici, cultura materiale, antichità egizie*. Milan: Electa.

Menchelli, S. 2017. Late Roman coarse wares, cooking wares and amphorae. A survey of current research in Italy, in D. Dixneuf (ed.) *LRCW 5: Late Roman Coarse Wares, Cooking Wares and Amphorae in the Mediterranean, Archaeology and Archaeometry = LRCW 5: la céramique commune, la céramique culinaire et les amphores de l'Antiquité tardive en Méditerranée, archéologie et archéométrie*: 203-21. Alexandria: Centre d'études alexandrines.

Millett, M. 2013. Introduction, in Hay *et al.* 2013: 1-12.

Molina Vidal, J. 1999. Anfore e relazioni commerciali, in P. Braconi and J. Uroz Sàez (eds) *La villa di Plinio il Giovane a S. Giustino: primi risultati di una ricerca in corso*: 103-13. Ponte San Giovanni: Quattroemme.

Molina Vidal, J. 2008. Mercantile trade in the Upper Tiber Valley: the villa of Pliny the Younger 'in Tuscis', in Coarelli and Patterson 2008: 215-49.

Montagnetti *et al.* 2020 = Montagnetti, R., D. Pickel, J. Wilson, F. Rizzo and D. Soren 2020. New research in the Roman villa and late Roman infant and child cemetery at Poggio Gramignano (Lugnano in Teverina, Umbria, Italy). *European Journal of Post-Classical Archaeologies* 10: 279-302.

Nicoletta, N. 2011. Ceramica di importazione africana, in M. Bergamini (ed.) *Scoppieto, II: I materiali (Monete, Ceramica a vernice nera, Ceramica a pareti sottili, Ceramica di importazione africana, Anfore, Manufatti e strumenti funzionali alla lavorazione dell'argilla e alla cottura, Pesi da telaio, Vetro, Osso lavorato, Metalli, Sculture, Materiale epigrafico)*: 235-82. Florence: Edizioni all'Insegna del Giglio.

Panella, C. 1999. Rifornimenti urbani e cultura materiale tra Aureliano e Alarico, in W.V. Harris (ed.) *The Transformations of Urbs Roma in Late Antiquity* (Journal of Roman Archaeology, Suppl. 33): 183-215. Portsmouth (RI): Journal of Roman Archaeology.

Patterson, H. 2020. The late antique landscapes of the middle Tiber Valley: the mid-third to mid-sixth centuries AD, in H. Patterson, R.E Witcher and H. Di Giuseppe (eds), *The Changing Landscapes of Rome's Northern Hinterland: The British School at Rome's Tiber Valley Project*: 208-50. Oxford: Archaeopress.

Patterson *et al.* 2005 = Patterson, H., A. Bousquet, S. Fontana, R. Witcher and S. Zampini 2005. Late Roman common wares and amphorae in the middle Tiber Valley, the preliminary results of the Tiber Valley Project, in J.M. Gurt i Esparraguera, J. Buxeda i Garrigós and M.A. Cau Ontiveros (eds), *LRCWI: Late Roman Coarse Wares, Cooking Wares and Amphorae in the Mediterranean; Archaeology and Archaeometry*: 369-84. Oxford: Archaeopress.

Peña, J.T. 1999. *The Urban Economy during the Early Dominate: Pottery Evidence from the Palatine Hill*. Oxford: Archaeopress.

Speranza, S. 2011. Anfore, in M. Bergamini (ed.) *Scoppieto, II: I materiali (Monete, Ceramica a vernice nera, Ceramica a pareti sottili, Ceramica di importazione africana, Anfore, Manufatti e strumenti funzionali alla lavorazione dell'argilla e alla cottura, Pesi da telaio, Vetro, Osso lavorato, Metalli, Sculture, Materiale epigrafico)*: 283-342. Florence: Edizioni all'Insegna del Giglio.

Vera, D. 2010. Fisco, Annona e commercio nel Mediterraneo tardoantico: destini incrociati o vite parallele?, in S. Menchelli, S. Santoro, M. Pasquinucci and G. Guiducci (eds), *LRCW 3: Late Roman Coarse Wares, Cooking Wares and Amphorae in the Mediterranean; Archaeology and Archaeometry, Comparison between Western and Eastern Mediterranean*: 1-18. Oxford: Archaeopress.

Vera, D. 2012. Questioni di storia agraria tardoromana: schiavi, coloni, villae. *Antiquité Tardive: Revue internationale d'histoire et d'archéologie (IVᵉ-VIIᵉ siècle)* 20: 115-22.

Wickham, C. 2005. *Framing the Early Middle Ages: Europe and the Mediterranean, 400-800*. Oxford: Oxford University Press.

Witcher, R. 2020. The early and mid-imperial landscapes of the middle Tiber Valley (c. 50 BC–AD 250), in H. Patterson, R.E Witcher and H. Di Giuseppe (eds), *The Changing Landscapes of Rome's Northern Hinterland: The British School at Rome's Tiber Valley Project*: 117-207. Oxford: Archaeopress.

Zampini, S. 2013. The pottery, in Hay *et al.* 2013: 92-111.

Zanini, E. and J. Celani. 2020. Archeologia della guerra greco-gotica: prolegomeni a una ricerca in corso, in A.R.L. Lacomba and J.M. Macias Solé (eds) *Recintos fortificados en época visigoda: historia, arquitectura y técnica constructiva*: 11-24. Tarragona: Institut català d'arqueologia clàssica.

Zuddas, E. 2014. L'Umbria dei porti, in C. Zaccaria (ed.) *L'epigrafia dei porti: atti della XVIIᵉ rencontre sur l'épigraphie du monde romain* (Aquileia, 14-16 ottobre 2010): 137-50. Trieste: Editreg.

9. Narbo Martius (Narbonne, France): "l'emporium de la Celtique toute entière"

Nicolas Carayon, Corinne Sanchez, Julien Cavero

Le port de la Celtique toute entière

Quelques décennies avant la fin du Ier siècle av. n. è., Diodore de Sicile évoque Narbonne comme le plus grand *emporion* de la région du fait de sa position (*Bibliothèque historique* 5.38) et Strabon, au Ier s. de n. è., va même jusqu'à dire qu'on peut la considérer comme «le port de la Celtique toute entière tant il surpasse les autres par le nombre des entreprises auxquelles il sert de place de commerce» (*Géographie* 4.1.12). Fondée en 118 av. n. è., la ville se trouvait en effet au carrefour des voies Domitienne et d'Aquitaine ainsi qu'au débouché de la vallée de l'Aude qui mettait en relation l'Atlantique avec la mer Méditerranée. Strabon situe la ville en arrière de l'embouchure de l'*Atax* (le fleuve Aude) et du *Narbonitis* (les étangs de Bages et de Sigean au sud de la ville). Au Ier siècle, Pline l'Ancien mentionne le lac *Rubrensis* traversé par l'*Atax* (*Histoire Naturelle* 3.32) et Pomponius Mela écrit que l'*Atax* «sauf au point où il atteint Narbo, n'est nulle part navigable» et qu'il se jette dans un vaste lac appelé *Rubraesus* qui communique avec la mer par une étroite ouverture (*Chorographie* 2.5.81). Au IVe siècle, alors que dans son poème consacré à la ville Ausone atteste encore des liens commerciaux de celle-ci avec le reste de la Méditerranée (*Classement des villes célèbres*, 16), le poète Aviénus dépeint la topographie des lieux, tantôt sous la forme d'une plaine salée dans laquelle se jette l'*Attagus*, tantôt sous la forme d'un golfe maritime. Des termes qui désignent couramment pour cet auteur une zone lagunaire dans laquelle se jette un fleuve (Ropiot 2007).

S'ils insistent sur le rôle portuaire majeur de la ville et sur sa situation privilégiée, au carrefour d'axes de circulation terrestres et maritimes, les témoignages des auteurs antiques soulignent tout autant l'importance des principales composantes du paysage narbonnais que sont le fleuve et la lagune (Strabon utilise le terme grec λιμνη qui signifie lac). Aujourd'hui à une douzaine de kilomètres de la Méditerranée et à 4 km au nord des étangs, la ville de Narbonne n'a pas d'accès direct à la mer qui se trouvait, selon Strabon, à 12 milles (18 km). Le trafic maritime mis en évidence par les épaves – en particulier celles retrouvées sur la plage de Gruissan (Solier *et al.* 1981) qui ont livré une chronologie allant du IIIe siècle av. n. è. au début du Ve. siècle – confirme l'importance du rôle joué par Narbonne dans le commerce durant toute l'Antiquité. Mais depuis des décennies, le lieu d'arrivée de ces bateaux fait l'objet de discussions. Au début du XXe siècle, Henri Rouzaud propose la théorie des avant-ports (Rouzaud 1914 ; 1917) dont le principe reste encore aujourd'hui d'actualité. Pour cet archéologue, les bateaux de haute mer ne peuvent pas remonter le fleuve dont l'embouchure se trouvait dans les étangs. Il fallait donc transborder les marchandises des navires de haute mer vers des bateaux de moindre tirant d'eau adaptés à la navigation fluvio-lagunaire et remonter le fleuve jusqu'à la ville.

Pour mieux définir ces espaces de transbordements et appréhender l'organisation du système portuaire dans sa globalité, il est nécessaire de restituer la relation topographique, largement modifiée durant ces deux derniers millénaires, entre la mer, le fleuve et la lagune : où passait le fleuve, quelle était l'extension des étangs, comment se présentait le cordon littoral et les graus qui permettaient d'y accéder ? Depuis 2010, dans le cadre d'un partenariat financé par la Région Occitanie, le CNRS, le ministère de la Culture (DRAC et DRASSM) et les villes de Narbonne et Gruissan, une étroite collaboration entre géographes, archéologues, historiens et géophysiciens a été engagée afin d'apporter des réponses à ces interrogations et restituer le paysage antique de la *Colonia Narbo Martius* (Sanchez et Jézégou 2016).

Paléogéographie de la rade narbonnaise

L'Aude joue un rôle majeur dans la mise en place de la géographie des basses plaines de l'Aude (Figure 9.1). Leur conformation actuelle est le résultat d'un processus engagé dès 5000 ans av. n. è. alors qu'une vaste baie marine occupe l'emplacement des étangs. La transgression marine holocène ralentit et la charge sédimentaire des fleuves colmate alors les basses plaines : c'est le début de la construction deltaïque (Salel *et al.* 2019). Quelques 16 millénaires auparavant, soit 21000 ans av. n. è., au maximum de la dernière période glaciaire, l'Aude s'écoule dans un étroit chenal, qui contourne par l'est le promontoire de Narbonne et longe le versant ouest de La Clape (Ambert 2000 ; 2011). Là, le fleuve bute contre une terrasse du Quaternaire supérieur (la terrasse de Coutelle) qui le dévie vers le sud et sépare en deux le complexe lagunaire holocène

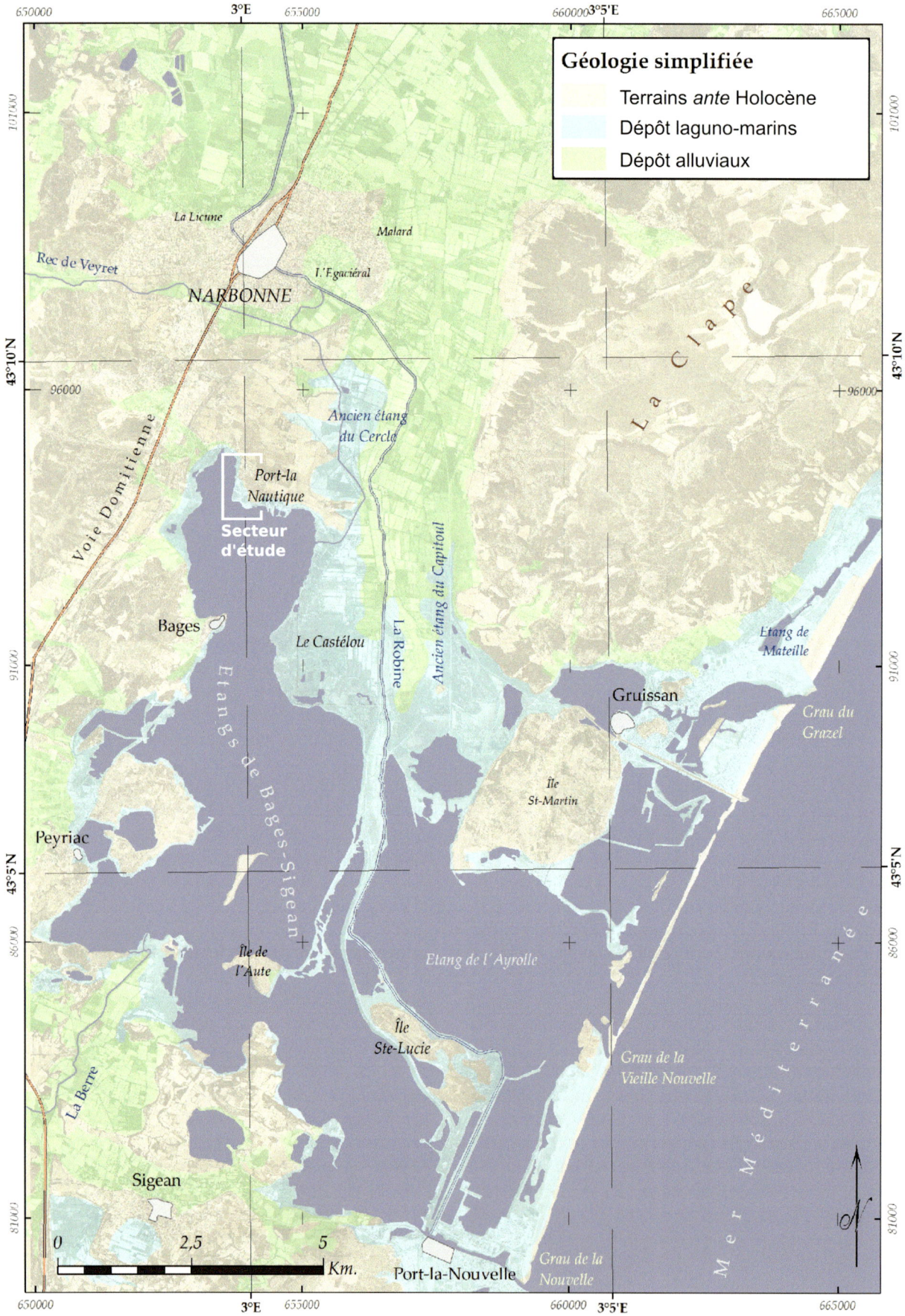

Figure 9.1. Carte géologique simplifiée superposée sur une image satellite de la région de Narbonne mettant en évidence le bassin des étangs narbonnais holocènes, partiellement déconnectés de la mer Méditerranée par un cordon sableux (J. Cavero, PCR Narbonne).

de la basse vallée de l'Aude : Narbonne-Bages-Sigean au sud, un chapelet d'étang entre Capestang, Fleury et jusqu'à Vendres au nord (Verdeil 1967 ; Ambert 2000 ; 2011). Au sud, l'étude des séquences sédimentaires au domaine du Castélou laisse supposer que l'embouchure de l'Aude se fixe au sud de Montfort vers 2000 ans av. n. è. (Dolez *et al.* 2015). Le système d'embouchure progresse ensuite vers le sud jusqu'au changement d'ère (Salel *et al.* 2019). Au nord, du côté de Vendres, l'étude de plusieurs séquences sédimentaires a mis en évidence le comblement progressif d'une ria vers 3000 av. n. è., d'abord par une sédimentation d'origine marine, puis par la construction d'un prodelta (Mulot 2014). Des données géochimiques complémentaires témoignent en effet d'une nette augmentation des apports détritiques terrigènes associée à une hausse des taux de sédimentation apparents à partir du changement d'ère (Salel *et al.* 2019). Ces informations tendraient à indiquer un possible franchissement par l'Aude du seuil de la terrasse de Coutelle, et donc la possibilité de deux bras actifs, dès l'Antiquité. L'ensemble des séquences montrent qu'à partir de l'âge du Fer, il y a environ 2500 ans, la formation de longs cordons sableux commence à isoler plusieurs bassins lagunaires qui vont être en partie colmatés par les apports sédimentaires marins et fluviaux.

Le bras méridional, dont la Robine est l'héritière, et le bras septentrional ont toujours été au centre des contributions qui ont cherché à dresser la topographie antique du narbonnais. Pour certains la branche sud serait le résultat de la construction par les romains d'une digue à Sallèles et le cours nord de la rupture de cette digue lors de la grande crue de 1316 (Reboul 1837 ; Port 1854). Pour d'autres, le cours méridional est le cours naturel du fleuve (Cons 1882) et l'antiquité de la digue de Sallèles doit être remise en question (Jourdanne 1892 ; Gayraud 1981). Il est certain en revanche qu'au moins une des embouchures de la branche sud est stabilisée par endiguement dans l'étang dès la fin du Ier siècle au niveau du site du Mandirac/Castélou. Ces aménagements seront entretenus et prolongés vers le sud jusqu'au Ve siècle, faisant de ce site une pièce maitresse du système portuaire narbonnais antique. Malgré ces découvertes et celle d'une une voie nord/sud au sortir de la ville de Narbonne sur le site des berges de la Robine, la question du cours du fleuve entre la ville et les aménagements du Mandirac/Castélou reste pour le moment en grande partie supposée. Des prospections géophysiques de grande ampleur ont permis une acquisition importante de profils tomographiques qui mettent en évidence des systèmes complexes de paléochenaux dont la succession chronologique reste difficile à établir (Sanchez *et al.* 2016). L'étude sédimentologique, associée à l'un de ces profils, a permis de décrire des séquences typiques d'un environnement estuarien et un corps sédimentaire avançant dans la lagune au gré des divagations du fleuve. L'ampleur de ces divagations restent difficile à préciser et même à contraindre latéralement en l'absence de tout indice d'occupation ancienne dans ce secteur déprimé.

Dans le courant du Ve siècle, lorsque le site portuaire du Mandirac/Castélou est abandonné, l'embouchure de l'Aude se trouve donc au bout des jetées romaines qui avaient déjà été rallongées de plusieurs centaines de mètres au IVe siècle. Pour les siècles suivants, les sources écrites sont rares. Le géographe arabe Al-'Udrī décrit au IXe siècle, une ville traversée par le "plus grand fleuve du pays des Francs" enjambé par un pont à l'aval duquel les navires de mer arrivent. Les sources ultérieures, des XIIIe et XIVe siècles, mentionnent les grandes crues qu'a connu la ville : 1232, 1306 et surtout 1316 dont la Chronique de Saint-Paul rapporte trois cents maisons détruites et cinquante personnes décédées (Larguier *et al.* 2020). L'inondation de 1316 fut un événement majeur qui vit l'Aude abandonner son lit dans Narbonne pour son cours actuel au nord. La ville se retrouve alors privée d'accès à la mer et exposée aux exhalaisons pestilentielles (Larguier *et al.* 2020). L'ensemble du réseau hydrographique est désorganisé. Le rapport de la commission des experts qui se rend sur place constate que le fleuve ne se jette plus dans l'étang de Gruissan et que cette nouvelle embouchure est "mieux placée" car il y a là plus de fond (Mouynès 1877).

De cette date, les aménagements n'auront qu'un seul objectif : ramener l'eau dans la ville. Il faut pour cela édifier un barrage en amont de Narbonne. C'est la paissière de Moussoulens qui sera construite au début du XVe siècle (Larguier *et al.* 2020). Jusqu'au XVIe siècle, les mentions de dégâts occasionnés par les crues et de travaux à entreprendre pour y remédier abondent. Par exemple les lettres du roi Louis XI du 15 octobre 1469 qui garantit les sommes employées aux réparations de la rivière d'Aude épandue dans les marais (Archives municipales de Narbonne, parchemin, AA 103, f° 106 v°). Ces aménagements successifs pour contenir le cours du fleuve repoussent son embouchure toujours plus vers le sud. En 1570, le vaste étang qui accueillait au début de notre ère les navires romains est scindé en deux. L'étude des cartes anciennes depuis le début du XVIIIe siècle atteste du rétrécissement des étangs et d'une côte nettement plus découpée, il y a ne serait-ce que quelques siècles (Cavero 2010). La sédimentation s'amplifie dès les années 1850 et les étangs se fragmentent encore plus. L'analyse paléogéographique de cet espace illustre clairement la rapidité des changements qui interviennent dans ces zones estuariennes. Les contraintes de ce milieu en perpétuelle évolution ont conditionné et conditionnent encore, pour une large part, l'installation et l'entretien d'importantes infrastructures nécessaires au maintien d'une activité portuaire.

Les éléments du système portuaire narbonnais antique

De nombreux sites antiques entourent les étangs narbonnais (Carayon *et al.* 2018) mais leur fonction portuaire reste pour la plupart à déterminer. Plusieurs secteurs comme l'île Saint-Martin à Gruissan, Mateille, Mandirac/Castélou et Port-la-Nautique ont été proposés comme des éléments importants du système portuaire (Rouzaud 1914 et 1917 ; Guy 1955 ; Solier 1981). Les sites de Saint-Martin et de la Nautique continuent à être explorés et viennent de faire l'objet d'une publication sur leur rôle respectif (Sanchez et Duperron 2021). L'un est situé à l'entrée de la lagune narbonnaise, l'autre en fond d'étang et proche de l'ancienne embouchure de l'Aude.

L'établissement de Saint-Martin, adossé au versant sud de l'île du même nom, occupe une position remarquable à proximité du grau de Vieille-Nouvelle qui assure la communication de la lagune avec la mer et immédiatement en contrebas d'une importante source pérenne d'eau douce. De grandes citernes pouvaient assurer un approvisionnement en eau douce aux navires. Des pièces de stockage, des boutiques ou bureaux disposées dès le Ier siècle autour de la cour centrale d'un bâtiment également équipé de deux balnéaires semblent particulièrement adaptées à la réalisation de transactions commerciales et à un certain nombre d'activités de service. Premier établissement rencontré par les navires venant de la mer, il est possible que le site de Saint-Martin ait joué un rôle dans le contrôle des trafics commerciaux vers et depuis Narbonne. Des opérations de rupture de charge devaient également y être assurées.

Le site de la Nautique, sur la rive nord des étangs au fond de la lagune, présente l'association d'une zone résidentielle, d'espaces de production et de stockage, et d'un bassin portuaire. La concentration de céramiques sigillées a été le premier indice archéologique d'une activité portuaire liée à l'exportation de cette vaisselle. Dès les années 1960, les découvertes subaquatiques ne laissent plus de doute sur la vocation du site : le dépotoir portuaire qui s'étend sur deux hectares a livré de grandes quantités d'amphores qui proviennent en grande majorité de la côte catalane. Les fouilles de l'Association Narbonnaise de Travaux et d'Études Archéologiques Subaquatiques à la fin des années 1990 ont permis de renouveler les connaissances sur ce site et de révéler un quai muni d'un édifice qui aurait pu servir de phare ou d'amer (ANTEAS 2012). Les recherches récentes ont révélé des fours de potiers adossés à des entrepôts au plus près du rivage et la présence d'un immense vivier de 3 500 mètres carrés (Carayon et Flaux 2016). Cette découverte a relancé l'intérêt pour la villa située en haut du plateau. Surplombant la Nautique, le site offre une vue panoramique sur les étangs et présente une riche décoration révélée par la découverte d'une statue d'Hercule en marbre, d'une mosaïque et de nombreuses terres cuites décoratives. Le premier plan d'ensemble a été dressé en janvier 2018 grâce à des prospections géophysiques, livrant une emprise de 150 m sur 15 m pour la seule aile nord. Ce site constitue donc un secteur original dans le système portuaire, au sens où la villa associée pourrait être qualifiée de *maritima*, voire d'impériale (Lafon 2001). La Nautique apparaît ainsi comme un port intermédiaire, dépendant d'une villa, fonctionnant du Ier siècle av. n. è au Ier siècle. Comme en témoigne une série de carottages récents (Flaux *et al.* 2020), une accélération de l'envasement, peut être provoquée par les aménagements littoraux, semble avoir mis fin à la fréquentation portuaire du site dans les années 60-70 apr. J.-C.

Les données archéologiques concernant le port fluvial reposent sur les découvertes urbaines en amont et sur l'embouchure canalisée de Mandirac/Castélou 6 km en aval. Les recherches pluridisciplinaires menées à l'embouchure ont mis en évidence des travaux monumentaux pour canaliser le cours d'eau et développer des espaces de déchargements (Faïsse *et al.* 2017). Les fouilles ont confirmé la présence de deux jetées parallèles construites en milieu humide qui encadrent le fleuve large d'une cinquantaine de mètres et lui assure une profondeur d'environ 3,5 à 4 m (Sanchez *et al.* 2016). D'une emprise de 15 à 25 m., les jetées sont aménagées en chaussée dès la fin du Ier siècle par l'apport de plusieurs mètres cubes de matériaux et de milliers de pieux en bois venant renforcer les berges. Ces ouvrages publics soulignent la volonté de maitriser un milieu fluctuant afin d'assurer une stabilité et une pérennité relative des lieux d'échanges. Le fonctionnement et les réparations des infrastructures sont illustrés par l'utilisation d'une épave de l'Antiquité tardive recouverte de fragments de monuments urbains démantelés (Sanchez *et al.* 2016).

La question du passage du fleuve en ville est au cœur du sujet du port urbain. Les études géomorphologiques plus anciennes avaient conclu que l'Aude ne traversait pas Narbonne et que le cours de la Robine avait été creusé dans la terrasse au moment de l'installation romaine (Verdeil 1967 ; Ambert 2000 ; Rescanières 2002). Cette hypothèse a plus récemment été revue grâce à des observations stratigraphiques réalisées au bord de la Robine, au quai d'Alsace, en amont de la ville, lors de fouilles préventives (Ginouvez *et al.* 2016 ; Ollivier 2016). Ces opérations ont mis en évidence le lit du fleuve dans son état du IIIe s. av. n. è. et son déplacement vers l'ouest au Ier s. de n. è. (Ginouvez *et al.* 2016). Ainsi, une "paléo-Robine" passait bien par Narbonne dans l'Antiquité mais a fait l'objet de modifications dès l'époque romaine. Des aménagements de berges et la présence d'entrepôts en bord de fleuve (Ginouvez *et al.* 1992) confirment la présence d'un port fluvial et la navigabilité du fleuve jusqu'à la ville.

Les études les plus récentes livrent l'image d'un système complexe et évolutif avec des sites nombreux qui ne sont pas tous contemporains et d'importants aménagements dans la lagune (Carayon *et al.* 2018). Les ports de Narbonne sont donc multiples, l'arrivée ou le départ des marchandises jusqu'à ou depuis la ville ayant nécessité un véritable système portuaire composé d'un port fluvial urbain et d'un grand nombre de sites portuaires secondaires. S'étendant de la ville aux graus, c'est ce système qui constitue le port antique de Narbonne pendant plusieurs siècles.

Les rives et les îles de cette "rade narbonnaise" a connu plusieurs sites d'occupation dont l'activité portuaire ne fait aucun doute. Ces sites portuaires ne sont pas tous contemporains et on peut restituer une succession chronologique des avant-ports au gré des aménagements nécessaires pour s'adapter tant à la mobilité des réseaux fluviaux qu'aux évolutions du commerce méditerranéen antique. Les ports entrepôts (Nieto 1988), dont font partie des villes comme Cadix, Narbonne, Ostie, Pouzzoles, Carthage et Aquilée, sont en effet des lieux de regroupement de marchandises échangées à longue distance mais également à l'échelle régionale. Loin d'être uniquement un grand port d'importation et d'exportation, Narbonne a pris également une place importante dans les échanges interprovinciaux et régionaux.

Connectivité

Les relations qu'entretenaient le port de Narbonne avec le reste du monde romain, sa connectivité donc (Horden et Purcell 2000), peut être ainsi appréhendée à deux échelles. A l'échelle macrorégionale tout d'abord, Narbonne doit être considéré, si l'on suit le modèle proposé par Nieto (1988), comme un port de redistribution. La position de Narbonne au croisement de la Via Domitia, qui reprend le tracé général de la voie Héracléenne de communication littorale qui relie l'Espagne à l'Italie, et de la Via Aquitania, entre Méditerranée et Océan Atlantique, est éminemment favorable. Le matériel archéologique découvert sur les différents sites qui composent le système portuaire montre, entre autres, des relations privilégiées avec la péninsule italique à la fin de la période républicaine et avec la Tarraconaise et la Bétique au Haut-Empire. Les productions de ces régions se retrouvent à Narbonne avant d'être soit utilisées sur place, soit redistribuées. A Port-la-Nautique, la présence d'un dépotoir de sigillées de la Graufesenque indiquent que ce site a été utilisé comme port d'exportation de ce type de céramique produite à Millau, dans le Sud du Massif Central, par voie maritime.

A l'échelle microrégionale ensuite, il apparait clairement que si Narbonne doit être considérée comme un port entrepôt, il est nécessaire d'apporter une nuance importante au modèle développé par Nieto (1988). En effet, le port principal, qui s'oppose aux ports secondaires, est, à Narbonne, composé de plusieurs sites portuaires qui peuvent être publics ou privés. Les flux considérables de marchandise n'étaient pas centralisés autour du port urbain de Narbonne mais répartis entre les différents sites composant le système portuaire. Cette organisation spatiale du système portuaire soulève la question de l'existence de circuits commerciaux privilégiés au sein même du système portuaire. Une encore hypothétique spécialisation des avant-ports de Narbonne permettrait de faciliter la gestion des flux de marchandises considérables en transit par "l'emporion de la Celtique toute entière" (Strabon, *Géographie* 4.1.12).

Conclusion

Les recherches encore en cours sur le système portuaire de Narbonne, les méthodes mises en œuvre et les résultats obtenus, illustrent les axes de recherche chers à Simon Keay. L'approche transdisciplinaire a montré toute son importance dans le cadre des travaux menés à Portus et sur le système portuaire de Rome ainsi qu'à Narbonne. Les interactions entre un milieu naturel particulièrement mouvant et les activités portuaires nécessaires à la compréhension du système portuaire narbonnais sont au cœur de la réflexion du projet ERC Portus Limen. La question de la connectivité est particulièrement importante et les recherches sur le mobilier archéologique apporteront sans doute des éléments fondamentaux concernant l'intégration de Narbonne et de son système portuaire dans les réseaux commerciaux à l'échelle macrorégionale mais aussi microrégionale. La relation qu'entretenait un système portuaire avec son hinterland immédiat est également une problématique chère à Simon et c'est en s'appuyant sur l'exemple narbonnais, ainsi que celui de Tarragone, que Simon en donne une illustration (Carayon et Keay 2021).

Références

Sources antiques

Ausone : *Œuvres en vers et en prose*, édit. M. Jasinski. Paris : Garnier, 1934-35.

Aviénus : *Ora Maritima, v. 548-611*, édit. S.J. Murphy, *Rufus Festus Avienus : Ora Maritima or Description of the Seacoast (from Brittany round to Massilia)*, Chicago : Ares, 1977, dans A. Berthelot, *Festus Avienus : Ora Maritima*. Paris : Champion, 1934.

Diodore de Sicile : *Bibliothèque historique*, V, édit. C.H. Oldfather (Loeb Classical Library), 12 vol. Londres : Heinemann, 1933-57.

Pline l'Ancien : *Histoire naturelle*, III, édit. H. Zehnacker. Paris : Les Belles Lettres, 1998.

Pomponius Méla : *Chorographie*, II, édit. M.A. Silberma. Paris : Les Belles Lettres, 1988.

Strabon : *Géographie*, III-IV, édit. G. Aujac et F. Lasserre. Paris : Les Belles Lettres, 1966.

Bibliographie

Ambert, P. 2000. Narbonne antique et ses ports, géomorphologie et archéologie, certitudes et hypothèses. *Revue archéologique de Narbonnaise* 33 : 295-307.

Ambert, P. 2011. Potentiel et contraintes du cadre géologique de Narbonne pour l'aménagement de Narbonne Antique, dans C. Sanchez C. et M.-P. Jézégou (éd.) *Zones portuaires et espaces littoraux de Narbonne et sa région dans l'Antiquité* (Collection monographies d'archéologie méditerranéenne 28) : 13-20. Lattes : Éd. De l'Association pour le développement de l'archéologie en Languedoc-Roussillon.

ANTEAS 2012. Association narbonnaise de travaux et d'études d'archéologie subaquatique en narbonnais 1987-2012, 25 ans d'archéologie subaquatique en Narbonnais, Live Book ed., 408 p.

Carayon, N. et C. Flaux 2016. Le vivier augustéen du Lac de Capelles à Port-la-Nautique, dans Sanchez et Jézégou (éd.) 2016 : 87-97.

Carayon, N., S.J. Keay, P. Arnaud et C. Sanchez 2018. The harbour system of Narbo Martius (Narbonne / F) and its facilities during antiquity, dans C. von Carnap-Bornheim, F. Daim, P. Ettel, U. Warnke (éd.), *Harbours as Objects of Interdisciplinary Research : Archaeology + History + Geosciences, International Conference* : Mainz : 151-63. Verlag des Römisch-Germanischen Zentralmuseums.

Carayon, N. et S.J. Keay 2021. Micro-regions, connectivity and "port systems". Ongoing research by the ERC Portus Limen Project, dans U. Mania (éd.) *Hafen, Stadt, Mikroregion* : 53-57. Wiesbaden : Harrassowitz.

Cavero, J. 2010. Paléogéographie des étangs narbonnais d'après les sources cartographiques anciennes. *Géocarrefour* 85.1 : 29-40.

Cons, H. 1882. L'Aude, ses alluvions et le port de Narbonne. *Bulletin de la société languedocienne de géographie* 5 : 161-234.

Dolez, L., T. Salel, H. Bruneton, G. Colpo, B. Devillers, D. Lefèvre, S.D. Muller et C. Sanchez 2015. Holocene palaeoenvironnements of Narbonne lagoons (France). *Geobios* 48 : 297-308.

Faïsse, C., V. Mathé, G. Bruniaux, J. Labussière, J. Cavero, M.P. Jézégou, D. Lefèvre et C. Sanchez 2017. Paleoenvironmental and archaeological records for the ancient landscape reconstruction of the Roman harbour of Narbonne (Aude, France). *Quaternary International* 463 : 124-39.

Flaux, C., N. Carayon, C. Faïsse, M. Guy, T. Salel et C. Sanchez 2020. Géoarchéologie de Port-la-Nautique (étangs narbonnais). Méditerranée. *Revue géographique des pays méditerranéens* 131 : 22 p.

Gayraud, M., 1981. *Narbonne antique, des origines à la fin du IIIe s.* (Revue archéologique de Narbonnaise suppl. 8). Paris : De Boccard.

Ginouvez, O., C. Jorda et S. Martin 2016. La question du port urbain et de la Robine antique : l'apport de la fouille du 14 quai d'Alsace à Narbonne, dans Sanchez et Jézégou (éd.) 2016 : 123-36.

Ginouvez, O., C. Labarussiat et H. Pomarèdes 1992. Saint-Loup : un paysage fluvial aux portes de Narbonne (étude d'impact archéologique). *Archéologie en Languedoc* 16 : 95-103.

Guy, M. 1955. Les ports antiques de Narbonne. *Revue d'études ligures* 21.3-4 : 213-40.

Horden, P. et N. Purcell 2000. *The Corrupting Sea : A Study of Mediterranean History*. Oxford : Blackwell.

Jourdanne, G. 1892. Les variations du littoral narbonnais examinées du point de vue de la concordance des données géologiques avec les descriptions des géographes de l'Antiquité. *Bulletin de la société d'études scientifiques de l'Aude* 3 : 181-201.

Lafon, X. 2001. *Villa Maritima : Recherches sur les villas littorales de l'Italie romaine, IIIe s. av. J.-C. – IIIe s. apr. J.-C.* Paris : Bibliothèque des Ecoles françaises d'Athènes et de Rome.

Larguier, G., A. Charetteur et C. Sanchez 2020. *Le Canal de la Robine*. Sigean : Les Carnets du Parc, Parc naturel régional de la Narbonnaise en Méditerranée.

Mouynès, G. 1877. *Inventaire des archives communales de Narbonne antérieures à 1790, série AA*. Narbonne : Caillard imprimeur libraire.

Mulot, M. 2014. Reconstitution morphosédimentaire de l'évolution holocène de l'étang de Vendres (Aude, France). Mémoire présenté pour l'obtention du double diplôme ingénieur ENGEES et Master 2 en Géographie Environnementale, Université de Strasbourg.

Nieto, X. 1988. Cargamento principal y cargamento secundario, dans *Navires et commerces de la Méditerranée antique : hommage à Jean Rougé* (Cahiers d'histoire 33) : 379-93. Lyon : Cahiers d'histoire.

Ollivier, J. 2016. Artisanat et commerce en bordure du canal de la Robine : 19-20 quai d'Alsace à Narbonne, dans Sanchez et Jézégou (éd.) 2016 : 109-22.

Port, C. 1854. *Essai sur l'histoire du commerce maritime de Narbonne*. Paris : Durand, Dumoulin.

Reboul, H. 1837. De l'ancien lac Rubresus et des atterrissements de l'Aude. *Bulletin de la société archéologique de Béziers* 2 : 227-34.

Rescanières, S. 2002. Essai sur le cadre géographique antique du Narbonnais, dans E. Dellong (dir.) *Narbonne et le Narbonnais* (Carte archéologique de la Gaule 11.1) : 44-51. Paris : Académie des Inscriptions et Belles-Lettres.

Ropiot, V. 2007. Peuplement et circulation dans les bassins fluviaux du Languedoc occidental, du Roussillon et de l'Ampourdan du IXe s. au début du IIe s. av. n. è. Sciences de l'Homme et Société. Université de Franche-Comté.

Rouzaud, H. 1914 Note sur les ports antiques de Narbonne. *Bulletin de la Commission archéologique de Narbonne* 13 : 279-99.

Rouzaud, H. 1917 Note sur les ports antiques de Narbonne (suite). *Bulletin de la Commission Archéologique de Narbonne* 14 : 167-94.

Salel, T., H. Bruneton, J.-P. Degeai, M. Mulot et D. Lefèvre 2019. Nouvelles données sur la dynamique des environnements fluvio-lagunaires de la basse vallée de l'Aude (France) au cours des sept derniers millénaires. *Quaternaire* 30.4 : 351-68.

Sanchez, C. et M.P. Jézégou (éd.) 2016. *Les ports dans l'espace Méditerranéen antique : Narbonne et les systèmes portuaires fluvio-lagunaires : actes du colloque international tenu à Montpellier du 22 au 24 mai 2014.* Montpellier : Lattes.

Sanchez, C. et G. Duperron 2021. À propos des "avant-ports" de Narbonne. Réflexions autour des sites de Saint-Martin et de Port-la-Nautique, dans *Actes du colloque les ports dans l'espace méditerranée antique. Fréjus et les ports maritimes, 16 et 17 novembre 2018, Fréjus, Théâtre le Forum, BIAMA* : 291-308. Aix-en-Provence : Presses Universitaires de Provence.

Sanchez, C., J. Labussière, M.P. Jézégou, V. Mathé, V. Mathieu et J. Cavero 2016, L'embouchure du fleuve antique dans les étangs narbonnais, dans Sanchez et Jézégou (éd.) 2016 : 59-70.

Solier, Y., M. Guy, G.F. Lavagne, C. Morrisson, Y. Chevalier, M. Sabrié, R. Sabrié, A. Bouscaras, G. Depeyrot et R. Marichal 1981. Les épaves de Gruissan. *Archaeonautica* 3 : 7-264.

Verdeil, P. 1967. Essai de paléo-hydrographie de l'Aude. *Bulletin de la Société d'études scientifiques de l'Aude* 47 : 61-104.

10. Los almacenes del puerto romano de *Tarraco*

Ada Lasheras González

To Simon.
Thank you for your unforgettable
kindness and generous support.

Introducción

Los estudios sobre los edificios de almacenaje de época romana cuentan con una larga y prolija tradición científica[1] a la que sin duda contribuyeron enormemente las investigaciones de Simon Keay sobre *Portus* y el sistema portuario de Roma. De hecho, todavía en una de sus últimas publicaciones, que recoge los resultados de las prospecciones realizadas en *Isola Sacra*, aportó datos de gran interés para esta línea de estudio gracias a la identificación de al menos tres nuevos almacenes en el margen septentrional del Tíber, que suponen un incremento notable de la capacidad de almacenamiento conocida hasta la fecha para Ostia (Keay *et al.* 2020: 160-62 y 167-68).

Con el deseo de continuar celebrando las grandes aportaciones de Simon Keay al ámbito de la arqueología portuaria romana, el presente artículo se centra en *Tarraco,* ciudad para la cual sus trabajos fueron igualmente de suma importancia y marcaron el desarrollo de líneas de investigación de largo recorrido. Su estrecha relación científica con esta ciudad nos imposibilita recoger aquí sus numerosas contribuciones, pero dentro de la temática portuaria y de redes de intercambio marítimas cabe destacar su estudio fundamental sobre las ánforas tardoantiguas (Keay 1984), y por supuesto, su gran proyecto europeo *PortusLimen* (2014-19). La fortuna quiso que éste último corriera en paralelo a la realización de dos tesis doctorales sobre el área portuaria de esta ciudad (Lasheras 2018; Terrado 2019), las cuales contaron con

el sincero interés del propio Simon y que, junto a los resultados de dicho proyecto sobre la rada portuaria, han permitido definir con mayor detalle la evolución del puerto tarraconense desde época tardorrepublicana hasta finales de la Antigüedad tardía[2].

Tarraco era la puerta de entrada de Roma a la península Ibérica y la capital de la extensa provincia tarraconense, por lo que desarrolló a lo largo de los siglos una amplia área portuaria que llegó a alcanzar unas 8-10 ha (Macias *et al.* 2007: 8). Las investigaciones sobre esta zona se remontan al siglo XVI, si bien sólo ha podido ser analizada en su totalidad en décadas más recientes gracias a la realización de numerosas excavaciones arqueológicas en el área meridional de la ciudad[3]. Así, a pesar de que, con mayor o menor detalle, algunos de los edificios de almacenaje del puerto tarraconense han sido publicados (Adserias *et al.* 2000: 140-41; Pociña y Remolà 2001: 90-92; Macias 2004: 31-42 y 63-66), éste es un aspecto escasamente trabajado por la arqueología de la ciudad, como ya puso de relieve Josep Maria Macias (2011: 185) en una aproximación preliminar a esta temática. El objetivo de este artículo es, por tanto, presentar un primer análisis de los principales almacenes del área portuaria de *Tarraco* en época romana (siglos I a V d.C.),[4] con especial interés en su morfología arquitectónica, técnicas constructivas, materiales asociados, ubicación y cronología.

---

[1] Resulta imposible, por su abundancia, recoger aquí todas las publicaciones sobre los almacenes de época romana. Entre las más relevantes se encuentra sin duda la obra ya clásica, pero igualmente fundamental, de Rickman 1971. Más recientes son los destacados estudios de Bukowiecki y Rousse 2007, Bukowiecki, Panzieri y Zugmeyer 2011 y Bukowiecki *et al.* 2018 sobre los almacenes de Roma y sus puertos, así como los de Chankowski 2011 y 2018 sobre los sistemas de almacenaje del período romano. En este sentido, debemos citar la publicación de dos monografías, editadas por Arce y Goffaux 2011 y Chankowski, Lafon y Virlouvet 2018, que aúnan las últimas investigaciones sobre esta materia de todo el arco mediterráneo. Finalmente, para el caso específico del almacenamiento y abastecimiento de grano debemos mencionar los exhaustivos trabajos de Salido 2013, 2015 y 2017, centrados especialmente en *Hispania* y en el Mediterráneo occidental.

[2] Los resultados del estudio del área portuaria tarraconense del proyecto *PortusLimen* y de las tesis citadas se recogen en un artículo conjunto actualmente en preparación. No obstante, en los últimos años se han publicado varios trabajos sobre esta materia, entre los que cabe destacar los de Adserias *et al.* 2000; Lasheras 2017; Lasheras y Terrado 2018 y 2022; Macias y Remolà 2005 y 2010; Terrado 2019.
[3] Un breve repaso a los estudios realizados sobre el puerto tarraconense puede encontrarse en Lasheras 2018: 24-27. Para un análisis exhaustivo de su historiografía y cartografía histórica, véase Terrado 2019: 89-164.
[4] Hemos seleccionado aquellos ejemplos mejor conservados y que permiten un análisis más detallado de las evidencias. Así pues, excluimos deliberadamente otros edificios conocidos pero que por circunstancias propias de la arqueología urbana se documentaron de manera muy parcial y no proporcionaron datos suficientes. Sin embargo, puede encontrarse una descripción de éstos en Macias *et al.* 2007: ficha 502 (edificio entre las calles de Sant Josep y Nou de Sant Oleguer) y en Lasheras 2018: 514-17 (edificio P2-10-UA6) y 532-36 (edificio P2-10-UA9).

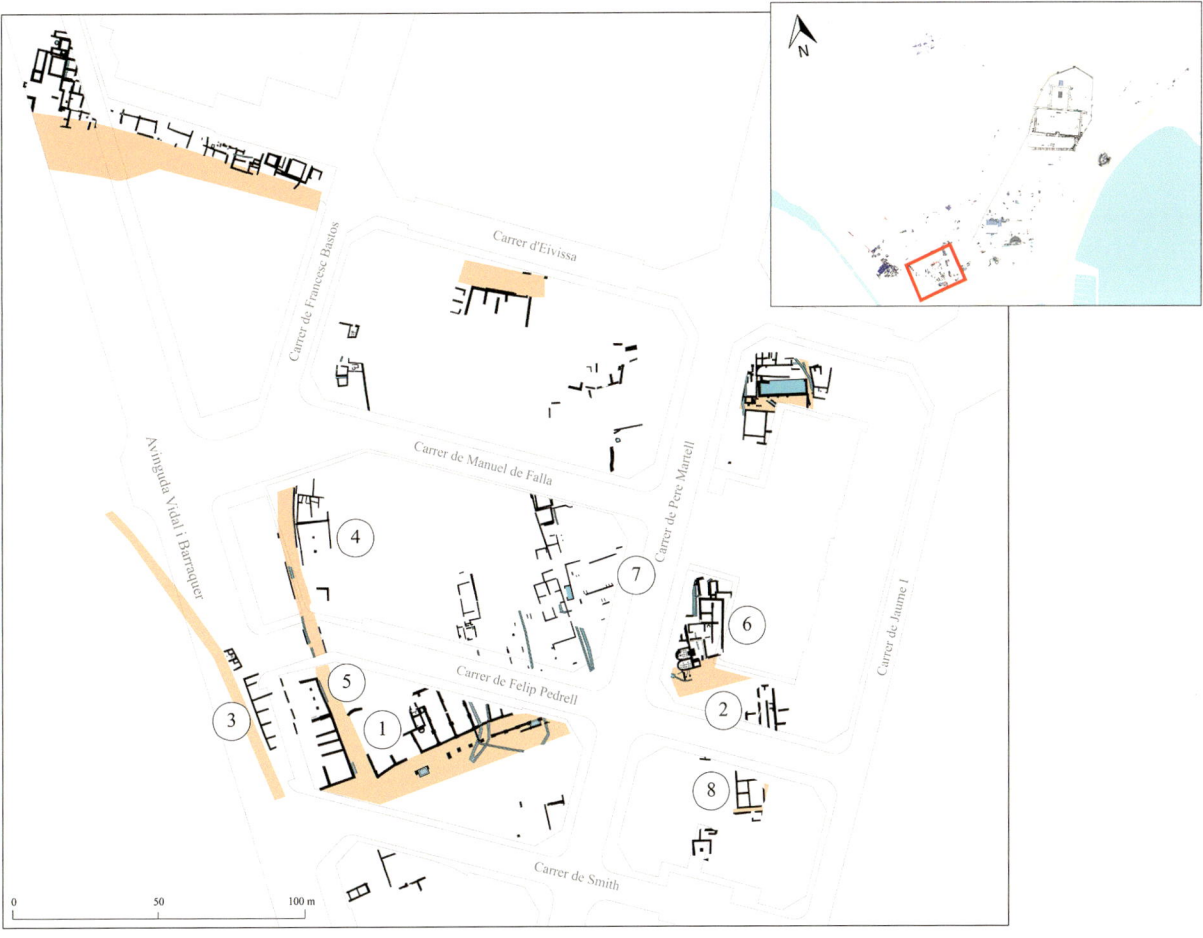

Figura 10.1. Planta arqueológica del suburbio portuario de *Tarraco*, con indicación de los almacenes mencionados en el texto (elaboración a partir de Lasheras 2018 y Macias *et al.* 2007).

Almacenes con ámbitos en batería

Uno de los edificios de almacenaje mejor conocidos del puerto tarraconense es sin duda el localizado entre las calles de Felip Pedrell, 10-12 y Vidal i Barraquer, 44-46 (Adserias *et al.* 2000: 140; Pociña y Remolà 2001: 90-92; Macias y Remolà 2010: 133; Salido 2013: 140-41; Lasheras 2018: 332-37) (Figuras 10.1.1, 10.2.1 y 3; Tabla 10.1.1). Su construcción data de finales del siglo I o inicios del siglo II y estuvo en uso probablemente hasta mediados del siglo IV o ya el siglo V, momento en que se fechan los estratos de amortización (Lasheras 2018: 335-36). Se ubicaba junto la vía marítima, una de las principales calles que vertebraba el sector occidental del área portuaria —conocido como suburbio portuario— y que *grosso modo* corría paralela a la línea de costa situada a escasos metros al sur en el periodo altoimperial (Lasheras 2018: 654; Remolà y Lasheras 2019: 76-78).

El edificio estaba formado por cinco naves de medidas similares en el lado occidental (18,40 m de largo por 6 m de ancho aproximadamente) y de al menos dos en el oriental, que alcanzarían una superficie mínima de 626,26 m². Estas dos zonas estaban separadas por un pasillo del que se conservaba el umbral y que albergaba dos canalizaciones que desaguaban al sur de la vía. A nivel constructivo, los muros estaban realizados en *opus caementicium* y contaban con un sistema regular de pilares, que pudieron servir como elementos de refuerzo o de sustentación del tejado. El pavimento se documentó parcialmente en algunas naves y estaba realizado con arcilla compactada, si bien en una fase posterior, fechada entre mediados del siglo II y el siglo III, se colocó un pavimento de *opus tessellatum* en la nave central del lado oeste. No obstante, la mayoría de los ámbitos conservaban un nivel de guijarros que debió funcionar como una capa preparatoria y aislante de la humedad, una técnica muy común en esta zona cercana al mar y al río Francolí, constatada en edificios con funciones muy diversas[5]. En el interior de las naves no se localizó ningún

---

[5]   Capas preparatorias de idénticas características se han documentado bajo el pavimento de *opus sectile* de la *domus* de la calle Pere Martell (Lasheras 2018: 490-510); bajo el de *opus signinum* de la

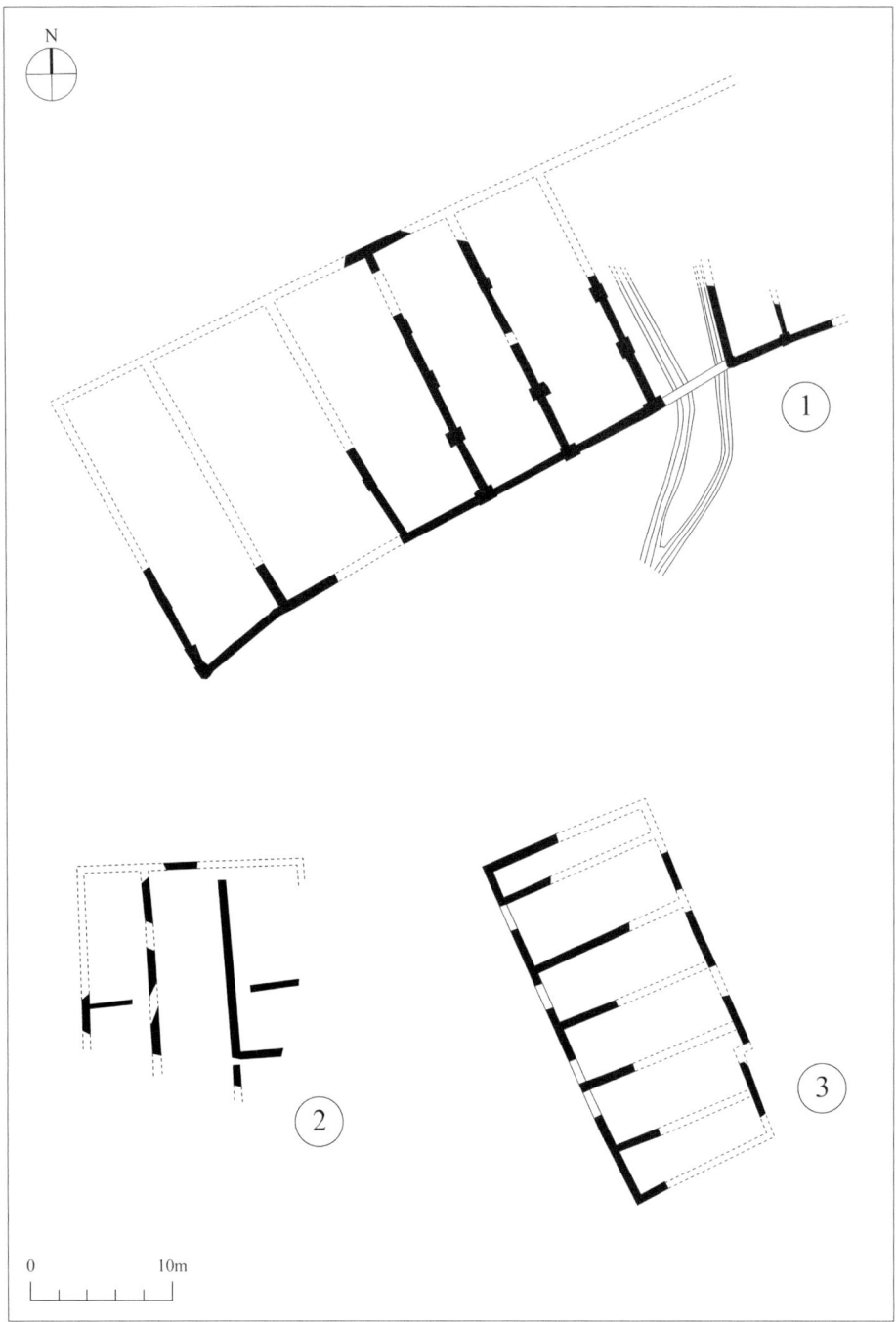

Figura 10.2. Plantas de los almacenes de ámbitos en batería localizados en el suburbio portuario.

elemento significativo relacionado con su uso, pero su ubicación dentro del entramado urbano y su morfología arquitectónica, similar a los llamados almacenes de

Septimio Severo en *Portus* o a los del muelle este de *Leptis Magna* (Rickman 1971: 128-30 y 132-36, figs. 27a y 29), son claros indicativos de su funcionalidad como almacén.

domus situada entre las calles Pere Martell y Felip Pedrell (Lasheras y Fortuny 2021: 438-40); o bien en el edificio multifuncional de finales del siglo VII localizado entre las calles Vidal i Barraquer y Smith (Lasheras y Rodríguez en prensa). Estas evidencias y la conservación de pavimentos de arcilla en algunas naves nos llevan a revisar la propuesta de Javier Salido (2013: 140), que sugería la presencia de un suelo de madera sobreelevado.

Figura 10.3. Fotografía del almacén hallado entre las calles Felip Pedrell, 10-12 y Vidal i Barraquer, 44-46 (archivo CODEX – Arqueologia i Patrimoni).

Un segundo edificio que puede incluirse dentro de este grupo es el localizado en la calle Felip Pedrell, 3-5 (Lasheras 2018: 536-42; Pociña y Remolà 2001: 90, fig. 7) (Figuras 10.1.2, 10.2.2 y 4; Tabla 10.1.2). La datación propuesta para su construcción es posterior, entre el último cuarto del siglo II y el primero del siglo III. Esta cronología se muestra acorde a su ubicación al sur de la vía marítima, indicando el progresivo avance de la línea de costa mediante la aportación de vertidos antrópicos para acondicionar esta zona de humedales (Lasheras 2018: 654; Remolà y Lasheras 2019: 76).

El estado de conservación de este edificio, mucho más fragmentario, hace que sólo conozcamos parcialmente tres naves, de planta igualmente rectangular y alargada, con un mínimo de 187,13 m². Los ámbitos este y oeste estaban compartimentados, mientras que la nave central se dividió simétricamente en un momento posterior mediante la construcción de una pared transversal. Los muros presentaban cimentaciones de *opus caementicium* y los pavimentos estaban realizados en adobe sobre una capa de guijarros, si bien este nivel preparatorio sólo se documentó en la nave central. Además, es destacable el hallazgo de un *dolium defossum* en el interior del ámbito oriental, elemento que, junto

a la morfología arquitectónica y ubicación del edificio, refuerza su interpretación como almacén.

El último ejemplo que presenta una morfología similar a los dos anteriores es el localizado en la calle Vidal i Barraquer, 44-46 (Lasheras 2018: 372-77) (Figuras 10.1.3 y 10.2.3; Tabla 10.1.3). Si bien no disponemos de una cronología precisa para su construcción, la estratigrafía confirma que estuvo en uso al menos hasta el siglo VI. En este sentido, la ubicación de este edificio junto a una vía norte-sur presumiblemente establecida en época tardoantigua (Remolà y Lasheras 2019: 79-80) parece indicar que su construcción también se llevó a cabo en este periodo.

El edificio estaba compuesto por seis naves de medidas similares —a excepción de las dos más septentrionales— que en total sumarían 231,45 m² de superficie interna. A diferencia de los ejemplos anteriores, los ámbitos estaban orientados en sentido suroeste-noreste ya que los accesos se situaban al oeste, conectando con la calle mencionada. Constructivamente estaba definido por muros de *opus caementicium* reforzados con sillares y el pavimento, de arcilla compactada, se conservó únicamente en el ámbito septentrional. También en

Figura 10.4. Fotografía del almacén hallado en la calle Felip Pedrell, 3-5 (archivo CODEX – Arqueologia i Patrimoni).

este caso se constataron elementos relevantes que apuntan a su uso como almacén, concretamente un conjunto de ánforas en la penúltima nave[6]. A ello cabe sumar su situación que, si bien no es tan cercana a la línea de costa como en los casos anteriores, se ubicaba junto a la calle norte-sur que permitiría una rápida conexión con la red viaria que atravesaba la ciudad (Remolà y Lasheras 2019: 76).

Almacenes de ámbito único

Otra tipología común entre los almacenes del puerto tarraconense es la que denominamos de ámbito único; es decir, edificios formados por un solo espacio que, por lo general, se muestra diáfano y sin compartimentación interna. Uno de los ejemplos que se adscribe a este grupo es el localizado entre las calles Manuel de Falla, 10 y Vidal i Barraquer, 40-42 (Lasheras 2018: 221-30) (Figuras 10.1.4 y 10.5.4; Tabla 10.1.4). La construcción de este edificio se data, *grosso modo*, en el siglo I y se ubicaba junto a una calle secundaria, conectada perpendicularmente con la vía marítima ya mencionada.

El edificio estaba formado por un único ámbito, para el que calculamos una superficie interna de 157,5 m[2]. Los muros estaban construidos en *opus caementicium* y presentaban sillares de refuerzo en las esquinas y junto al umbral. Dicho acceso se abría en el lado oeste y presentaba una anchura notable, de unos 3 m. El pavimento era de arcilla en la zona más septentrional, mientras que en el sureste se aprovechó el afloramiento del sustrato geológico, que fue rebajado hasta crear una superficie horizontal. Asimismo, cabe señalar la presencia de dos pilares situados en el centro de la estancia y que posiblemente funcionaran como elementos de sustentación del tejado. Por otra parte, el descubrimiento de un par de ánforas[7] junto al muro septentrional es uno de los argumentos que llevan a proponer una función de almacenamiento para este edificio, a lo que cabe añadir la amplitud del espacio interno y la gran puerta de entrada.

De morfología arquitectónica muy similar al ejemplo justo descrito es el edificio localizado en la calle Vidal i Barraquer, 44-46 (Lasheras 2018: 337-42) (Figuras 10.1.5 y 10.5.5; Tabla 10.1.5). Se ubicaba junto a la misma vía norte-sur, a unos 70 m hacia el sur del almacén

---

[6] Dentro de este conjunto cerámico se pudieron identificar un ánfora surhispana posible Keay 13A y otra lusitana posible Keay 68/91 (Lasheras 2018: 375).

[7] Se trata probablemente de ánforas surhispanas, si bien no pudo definirse el tipo específico (Lasheras 2018: 224).

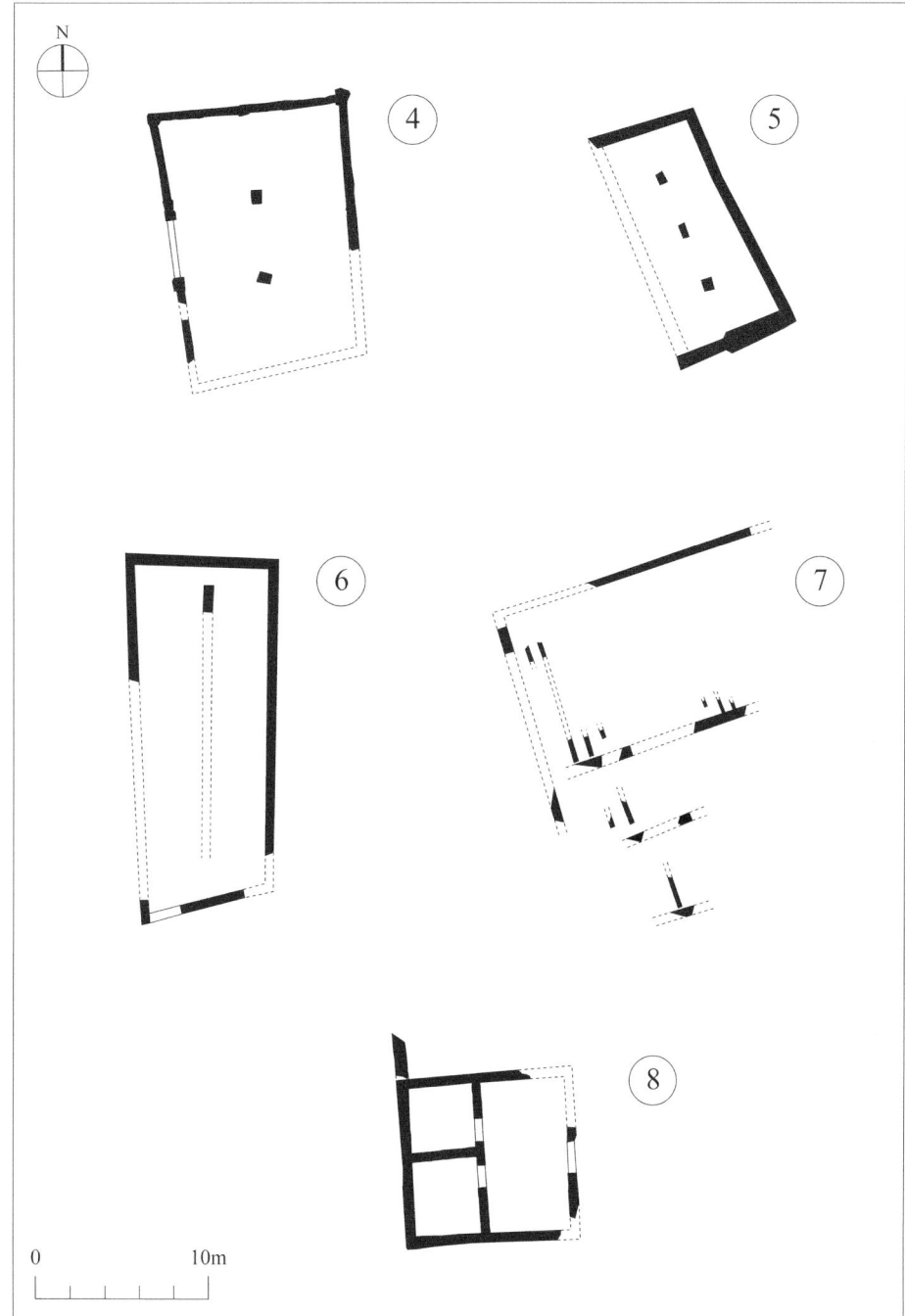

Figura 10.5. Plantas de los almacenes de ámbito único y con otras morfologías localizados en el suburbio portuario.

que acabamos de describir, aunque su construcción posiblemente tuviera lugar más tarde, ya en el siglo II.

De nuevo nos encontramos con un edificio formado por un único ámbito, pero con una superficie interna claramente menor, de 65,42 m². El estado de conservación de las estructuras hizo imposible identificar la puerta de acceso, aunque muy probablemente estuviera en la pared este, abierta a la vía mencionada. Del mismo

modo, tampoco se conservaba la pavimentación y de los muros perimetrales sólo se preservaron los cimientos, realizados en *opus caementicium*. En su interior se hallaron también tres sillares de piedra del Mèdol, alineados en sentido norte-sur en el centro de la estancia y que, como en el caso anterior, funcionarían como base para unos pilares. Sin embargo, la escasez de los datos disponibles hace que la adscripción funcional de este edificio resulte más compleja. La ubicación y morfología arquitectónica parecen apuntar a un posible uso como almacén, si bien no podemos descartar que albergara otras actividades de tipo portuario y/o mercantil.

En último lugar dentro de esta agrupación morfológica cabe mencionar el edificio excavado en el solar entre las calles Pere Martell, 50 y Felip Pedrell, 3-5 (Lasheras 2018: 524-32) (Figuras 10.1.6 y 10.5.6; Tabla 10.1.6). Su ubicación estaba más cercana a la línea de costa ya que se situaba junto a la vía marítima, a unos 70 m al este del primer almacén de ámbitos en batería analizado. La datación de su construcción es ligeramente anterior a la de dicho almacén, ya que se propone situarla entre el primer y el tercer cuarto del siglo I. Además, se constataron evidencias de uso hasta finales del siglo II o inicios del siglo III.

El edificio se definía por un único ambiente[8], de planta igualmente rectangular y con una superficie interna de 141,46 m². El acceso se localizó en el tramo más occidental del muro de cierre sur; es decir, que conectaba directamente con la vía marítima. Como es habitual, los muros perimetrales estaban realizados en *opus caementicium*, mientras que el pavimento era de adobe y se constataron múltiples reformas de éste. En el interior se documentó parcialmente un muro con la misma técnica constructiva, en sentido norte-sur y que no llegaba a adosarse a las paredes perimetrales, pero que pudo compartimentar el espacio en dos áreas de medidas similares (de 3,66 y 3,30 m de ancho por 18,30 m de largo). Tampoco en este caso se recuperaron elementos relevantes para su definición funcional, pero la ubicación y las medidas de la nave, con una longitud prácticamente idéntica a la del almacén de ámbitos en batería núm. 1, son aspectos que consideramos significativos para identificarlo como un edificio de almacenaje.

Otros ejemplos

Finalmente recogemos en esta sección aquellos ejemplos que no pueden adscribirse a ninguno de los grupos anteriores y que, además, presentan morfologías arquitectónicas distintas entre sí. Se trata por tanto de un conjunto variopinto, tanto a nivel formal como cronológico, y en el que se incluyen los únicos edificios procedentes del sector oriental del área portuaria.

Uno de los edificios de mayor interés en cuanto a la planta de las estructuras conservadas es el localizado entre las calles Pere Martell, 45-47 y Felip Pedrell, 7-9 (Lasheras 2018: 254-65) (Figuras 10.1.7 y 10.5.7; Tabla 10.1.7). Sin embargo, es también uno de los que

presenta una mayor complejidad estratigráfica, debido a que únicamente pudo ser excavado mediante sondeos. Dentro del entramado urbano del suburbio portuario, se ubicaba al norte de la vía marítima —si bien no se constató conexión directa con ninguna calle— y fue construido posiblemente en el siglo II.

De este edificio sólo se llegaron a identificar los muros de cierre norte y oeste —cuya longitud conocida es de 18,82 m y 16,91 m, respectivamente—, los cuales sugieren una planta rectangular con una superficie mínima de 318,25 m². En el interior se constataron igualmente tres muros paralelos en sentido noreste-suroeste, cuya técnica constructiva tampoco se llegó a detallar pero que parecían definir tres naves de unos 4,5 m de ancho. En relación con estos y dispuestos perpendicularmente, se encontraron otros muros con una anchura claramente menor (0,3 m) y colocados regularmente a una distancia de unos 0,7 m. No se conservan evidencias en cuanto al pavimento, pero la documentación de esta serie de muretes invita a pensar en un suelo elevado, colocado sobre estas estructuras[9]. De ser así, cabría identificar este edificio como un almacén destinado a albergar productos con unas necesidades de conservación específicas, propuesta respaldada por su cercanía a una de las vías principales del suburbio portuario.

En el sector oriental del área portuaria, concretamente en las calles Castaños, 1 y Sant Miquel, 33, se localizaron dos edificios que por sus características arquitectónicas se han relacionado con espacios de almacenaje (Figura 10.6; Tabla 10.1.9 y 10.1.10).[10] Ambos parecen corresponder a un mismo proyecto constructivo, presumiblemente de promoción pública dada su envergadura, y que urbanizó el acantilado suroeste de la ciudad a finales del tercer cuarto del siglo I (Macias 2004: 31-42, 66-73 y 166-71; 2011: 195-97).

La extensa superposición estratigráfica de la zona, donde con posterioridad se erigieron unas destacadas termas públicas, hace que las evidencias asociadas a estos dos edificios sean más bien fragmentarias. Así, del edificio occidental (Figura 10.6.1) se conservó un imponente muro con cimentaciones en *opus caementicium* de más 3 m de altura y que destaca por incluir un conjunto de contrafuertes dispuestos a una distancia regular,

---

[8] No obstante, debe señalarse que al oeste de este edificio, separado por un pasillo semejante al del almacén de ámbitos en batería núm. 1, se documentó la esquina sureste de otro edificio de características similares, planta presumiblemente rectangular y orientado en sentido norte-sur (Lasheras 2018: 514-17).

[9] Sistemas de sustentación del pavimento similares se han constatado en múltiples almacenes y graneros de *Hispania*, así como de *Portus* y Roma (Salido 2015 y 2017; Bukowiecki *et al.* 2018).

[10] En este mismo sector del área portuaria, bajo el teatro romano, se han localizado dos edificios construidos a mediados del siglo I a.C. que podrían vincularse a actividades mercantiles o de almacenaje. La fragmentación de las evidencias conservadas dificulta su clara adscripción funcional, pero cabe destacar su ubicación junto a una vía; su morfología arquitectónica, con ámbitos rectangulares dispuestos en batería; así como el uso del *opus quadratum* como técnica constructiva en aquel situado al norte (Remolà y Sánchez 2020: 391-92; cf. Mar *et al.* 1993: 14-16).

Tabla 10.1. Relación de los principales edificios de almacenaje del área portuaria de *Tarraco*. El asterisco (*) indica que el edificio no se conserva en su totalidad, por lo que las medidas indicadas son aproximadas.

Número	Localización	Cronología	Superficie interna	Planta	Orientación
1	Calle Felip Pedrell, 10-12 / Vidal i Barraquer, 44-46	Construcción a finales del siglo I d.C. o inicios del siglo II. En uso hasta mediados del siglo IV o siglo V.	626,26 m² (*)	Ámbitos en batería	Noroeste-sureste
2	Calle Felip Pedrell, 3-5	Construcción entre el último cuarto del siglo II y el primero del siglo III.	187,13 m² (*)	Ámbitos en batería	Norte-sur
3	Calle de Vidal i Barraquer (pequeña plaza frente a los números 44-46)	En uso al menos hasta el siglo VI.	231,45 m² (*)	Ámbitos en batería	Suroeste-noreste
4	Calle Vidal i Barraquer, 40-42 / Manuel de Falla, 10	Construcción en el siglo I d.C.	157,5 m²	Ámbito único	Norte-sur
5	Calle Vidal i Barraquer, 44-46	Construcción en el siglo II.	65,42 m²	Ámbito único	Noroeste-sureste
6	Calle Pere Martell, 50 / Felip Pedrell, 3-5	Construcción a mediados del siglo I d.C. En uso hasta finales del siglo II o inicios del siglo III.	141,46 m²	Ámbito único	Norte-sur
7	Calle Pere Martell, 45-47 / Felip Pedrell, 7-9	Construcción posiblemente en el siglo II.	318, 25 m² (*)	Indeterminada	Norte-sur
8	Calle Felip Pedrell, 4	Construcción en la primera mitad del siglo V.	80,37 m² (*)	Edificio con patio lateral	Norte-sur
9	Calle Castaños, 1	Construcción a finales del tercer cuarto del siglo I d.C.	-	Edificio con contrafuertes	Noreste-suroeste
10	Calle Sant Miquel, 33	Construcción a finales del tercer cuarto del siglo I d.C.	53,35 m² (*)	Edificio con patio interior	Noreste-suroeste

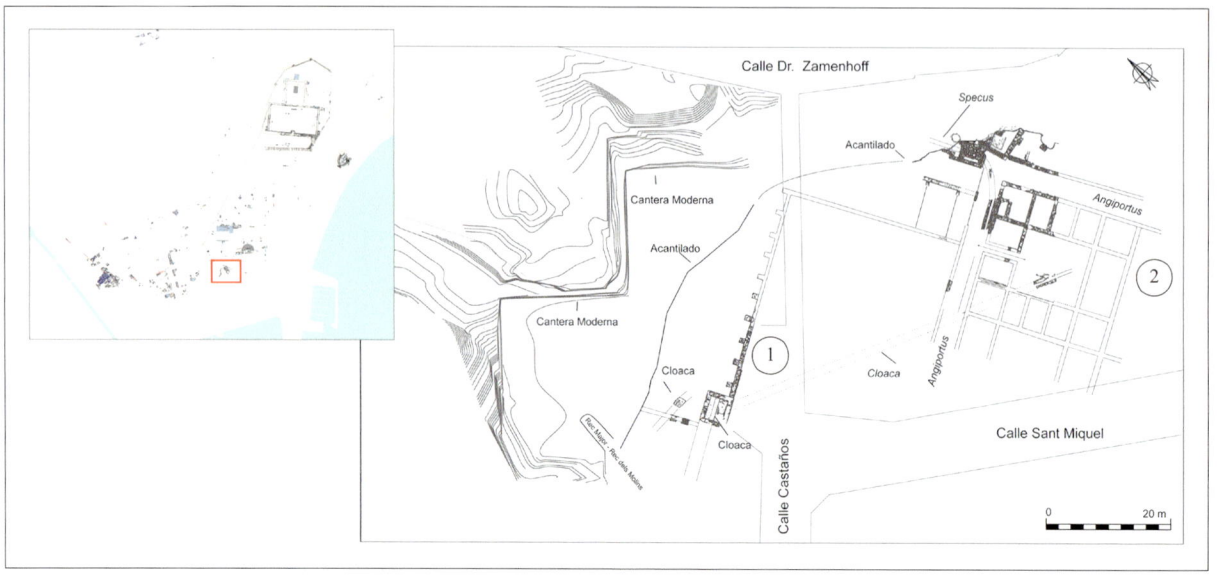

Figura 10.6. Plantas de los edificios localizados en las calles Castaños, 1 y sant Miquel, 33 (elaboración a partir de Macias 2011, fig. 6 y Macias *et al.* 2007).

Figura 10.7. Fotografía del almacén del siglo V hallado en la calle Felip Pedrell, 4 (archivo CODEX – Arqueologia i Patrimoni).

característica que se ha relacionado con los muros perimetrales de los *granaria* militares. Junto a este, separado por un pequeño pasillo o *angiportus*, se ubicaba el segundo edificio (Figura 10.6.2), formado por un conjunto de estancias rectangulares, que sumaban una superficie interna de 53,35m² y que se abrían a un patio central de dimensiones desconocidas. En este caso, la morfología arquitectónica se ha vinculado con los almacenes de patio interior especialmente bien conocidos en Ostia (Macias 2004: 166; 2011: 196).

Por último, volvemos al suburbio portuario para examinar el edificio más tardío del período romano, localizado en la calle Felip Pedrell, 4 (Lasheras 2018: 621-28) (Figuras 10.1.8, 10.5.8 y 7; Tabla 1.8). Su ubicación, a unos 30 m al sur de la vía marítima, se explica precisamente por su cronología, de primera mitad del siglo V, momento en que la línea de costa había avanzado notablemente, hasta unos 50 m con respecto a época altoimperial (Lasheras 2018: 654; Remolà y Lasheras 2019: 76).

El edificio estaba formado por al menos cuatro ámbitos, de los cuales conocemos la planta completa de tres, con una extensión total de 80,37 m². El acceso principal se abría en el muro oriental del ámbito de mayor tamaño, interpretado como un espacio descubierto o patio que conectaba con las otras dos habitaciones más pequeñas, situadas al oeste. En este sentido, destaca la composición de los distintos pavimentos, que varían según las estancias: en los ámbitos cuadrangulares estaba realizado con mortero de cal, mientras que en el ámbito oriental era de tierra batida, reforzando la hipótesis de un espacio a cielo abierto. Los muros, por su parte, fueron construidos en *opus caementicium* sobre una cimentación de guijarros, tal y como pudo constatarse en el tramo meridional del muro oeste. En cuanto a la funcionalidad, en este caso tampoco se hallaron elementos claros que nos indiquen su uso como almacén, a parte de su proximidad a la línea de costa. Además, en el ámbito rectangular se constató una pequeña zona ligeramente elevada y con evidencias de rubefacción, que podría indicar el desarrollo de actividades productivas. Sin embargo, esta polivalencia funcional no debe resultar sorprendente ya que es habitual en muchos de los edificios tardoantiguos del suburbio portuario y es también una realidad documentada en almacenes tardoantiguos de otros puntos del Mediterráneo, como en el puerto de Classe o el de Nápoles (Augenti y Cirelli 2012: 207-08 y fig. 10.2; Roncella 2010: 63-64). Del mismo modo estos ejemplos muestran la incorporación de espacios al aire libre en este tipo de edificios y, de hecho, esta morfología arquitectónica concreta tendrá continuidad en el mismo suburbio tarraconense durante el período visigodo (Lasheras y Rodríguez en prensa).

Consideraciones finales

Mucho queda aún por hacer en relación con el estudio de los almacenes de *Tarraco,* y esta primera sistematización de los ejemplos localizados en el área portuaria pretende simplemente sentar una base para futuras investigaciones. Cierto es que un análisis centrado únicamente en la morfología arquitectónica tiene evidentes limitaciones (Virlouvet 2011) y es por ello por lo que, en la medida de lo posible, hemos aportado todos los datos disponibles sobre la ubicación dentro del entramado urbano y la red viaria, la cronología y los hallazgos materiales asociados. Aun así, consideramos relevante señalar la multiplicidad de soluciones arquitectónicas constatada y, a la vez, la continuidad temporal de ciertas morfologías, siendo especialmente longevo el grupo de ámbitos en batería. Esta diversidad no sólo parece indicar una diferencia en cuanto a las necesidades de almacenamiento, sino que también se muestra acorde a las diferentes formas y funciones que adquieren los almacenes de otros enclaves del Mediterráneo, desde época altoimperial hasta el período tardoantiguo.

Sin embargo, dentro de la variedad de edificios de almacenaje tarraconense resulta interesante observar que la mayoría fueron construidos a finales del siglo I o ya en el siglo II; es decir, en el momento de mayor crecimiento y monumentalización de la ciudad. Su ubicación también sugiere una ordenación funcional del área portuaria y refuerza la idea de un sector oriental de carácter más representativo y lúdico, mientras que en el sector occidental se concentrarían los espacios de almacenamiento y mercantiles. Sin ignorar la problemática de la escasez de datos arqueológicos en el sector oriental, nos resulta igualmente sugerente advertir que gran parte de los edificios examinados se situaban alrededor de la vía marítima, la cual presumiblemente conectaría con el muelle ubicado al otro lado de la bahía portuaria, y que también enlazaría con las principales vías que confluían en la ciudad, la *via Augusta* hacia el sur y la *via De Italia in Hispanias* hacia el interior peninsular. Quedan pendientes de futuros estudios cuestiones más amplias como la relación de estos almacenes urbanos con otras estructuras de almacenamiento en el territorio adyacente, o con los puertos secundarios dentro del sistema portuario tarraconense (Lasheras y Terrado 2022; Terrado 2020). Se trata de problemáticas aun por explorar, pero de gran interés para comprender con mayor detalle el papel de *Tarraco* en la gestión, abastecimiento y distribución de productos tanto dentro de la redes de intercambio regionales como del ancho del Mediterráneo.

Bibliografía

Adserias, M., C.A. Pociña y J.A. Remolà 2000. L'hàbitat suburbà portuari de l'antiga Tàrraco. Excavacions al sector afectat pel PERI 2 (Jaume I – Tabacalera), en J. Ruiz de Arbulo (ed.) *Tàrraco 99: Arqueologia d'una capital provincial romana (Tarragona 15, 16 i 17 d'abril de 1999)*: 137-54. Tarragona: El Mèdol.

Arce, J. y B. Goffaux (eds) 2011. *Horrea d'Hispanie et de la Méditerranée romaine*. Madrid: Casa de Velázquez.

Augenti, A. y E. Cirelli 2012. From suburb to port: the rise (and fall) of Classe as a centre of trade and redistribution, en S. Keay (ed.) *Rome, Portus and the Mediterranean*: 205-21. London: British School at Rome.

Bukowiecki, É., M. Mimmo, C. Panzieri y R. Sebastiani 2018. Le système des sols surélevés dans les entrepôts d'Ostie, de Portus et de Rome : nouvelles découvertes en cours, en V. Chankowski, X. Lafon y C. Virlouvet (eds) *Entrepôts et circuits de distribution en Méditerranée antique*: 231-68. Athens: École française d'Athènes.

Bukowiecki, É., C. Panzieri y S. Zugmeyer 2011. Portus. Les entrepôts de Trajan. *Mélanges de l'École française de Rome: Antiquité* 123: 351-59.

Bukowiecki, E. y C. Rousse 2007. Ostia antica: entrepôts d'Ostie et de Portus. Les grandi horrea à Ostie. *Mélanges de l'École française de Rome: Antiquité* 119: 283-86.

Chankowski, V. 2011. Les entrepôts dans le monde romain antique, fores et fonctions. Premières pistes pour un essai de typologie, en J. Arce y B. Goffaux (eds) *Horrea d'Hispanie et de la méditerranée romaine*: 7-21. Madrid: Casa de Velázquez.

Chankowski, V. 2018. Bâtiments de stockage et circuits économiques du monde romain, en V. Chankowski, X. Lafon y C. Virlouvet (eds) *Entrepôts et circuits de distribution en Méditerranée antique*: 43-59. Athens: École française d'Athènes.

Chankowski, V., X. Lafon y C. Virlouvet (eds) 2018. *Entrepôts et circuits de distribution en Méditerranée antique*. Athens: École française d'Athènes.

Keay, S. 1984. *Late Roman Amphorae in the Western Mediterranean: A Typology and Economic Study; The Catalan Evidence*. Oxford: British Archaeological Reports.

Keay, S., M. Millett, K. Strutt y P. Germoni (eds) 2020. *The Isola Sacra Survey: Ostia, Portus and the Port System of Imperial Rome*. Cambridge: McDonald Institute for Archaeological Research.

Lasheras, A. 2017. El suburbio portuario de *Tarraco* en la Antigüedad tardía: modelos de ocupación y evolución urbana entre los siglos III y VIII, en S. Panzram (ed.) *Oppidum - civitas - urbs: Städteforschung auf der Iberischen Halbinsel zwischen Rom und al-Andalus*: 787-810. Münster: LIT.

Lasheras, A. 2018. *El suburbi portuari de Tarraco a l'Antiguitat tardana (segles III-VIII)*. Unpublished PhD dissertation, Universitat Rovira i Virgili, <http://hdl.handle.net/10803/664701>.

Lasheras, A. y K. Fortuny 2021. Domestic architecture of harbour areas: the late antique houses of the Port Suburb of Tarraco, en I. Baldini y C. Sfameni (eds) *Abitare nel Mediterraneo tardoantico: atti del III convegno internazionale del Centro interuniversitario di studi sull'Edilizia abitativa tardoantica nel Mediterraneo (Bologna 28-31 ottobre 2019)*: 435-45. Bari: Edipuglia.

Lasheras, A. y F. Rodríguez in press. Tarragona in the 8th century: new issues for discussion, en S. Esders, F. Krueger, S. Polla, T.S. Richter y C. Wickham (eds) *The 8th Century: Patterns of Transition in Economy and Trade throughout the Late Antique, Early Medieval and Islamicate Mediterranean in Multidisciplinary Perspectives*. Berlin: De Gruyter.

Lasheras, A. y P. Terrado 2022. El sistema portuario de *Tarraco* (siglos II a.C. – V d.C.), en A. Lasheras, J. Ruiz de Arbulo y P. Terrado (eds) *Tarraco Biennal: actes. 5è Congrés Internacional d'Arqueologia i Món Antic. Ports romans. Arqueologia dels Sistemes Portuaris (Tarragona, 24, 25, 26 i 27 de novembre de 2021)*: 93-108. Tarragona: Institut català d'arqueologia clàssica.

Lasheras, A. y P. Terrado 2018. New approaches to the study of the harbour of Tarraco: archaeological and literary research (3rd century BC – 8th century AD), en C. von Carnap-Bornheim, F. Daim, P. Ettel y U. Warnke (eds) *Harbours as Objects of Interdisciplinary Eesearch - Archaeology + History + Geosciences*: 165-81. Mainz: Römisch-Germanisches Zentralmuseum.

Macias, J.M. (ed.) 2004. *Les termes públiques de l'àrea portuària de Tarràco: carrer de Sant Miquel de Tarragona*. Tarragona: Institut català d'arqueologia clàssica.

Macias, J.M., I. Fiz, L. Piñol, M.T. Miró y J. Guitart 2007. *Planimetria arqueològica de Tàrraco*. Tarragona: Institut català d'arqueologia clàssica.

Macias, J.M. 2011. *Horrea* y estructuras de almacenamiento en la ciudad y territorio de *Tarraco*, en J. Arce y B. Goffaux (eds) *Horrea d'Hispanie et de la Méditerranée romaine*: 185-99. Madrid: Casa de Velázquez.

Macias, J.M. y J.A. Remolà 2005. El port de *Tarraco* a l'Antiguitat tardana, en J.M. Gurt Esparraguera y A. Ribera (eds) *VI Reunió d'Arqueologia Cristiana Hispànica (València, 8, 9 i 10 de maig de 2003)*: 175-87. Barcelona: Institut d'estudis catalans.

Macias Solé, J.M. y J.A. Remolà 2010. Portus Tarraconensis (Hispania Citerior), *Bollettino di Archeologia on line* Volume speciale: 129-40.

Mar, R., M. Roca y J. Ruiz de Arbulo 1993. El teatro romano de Tarragona: un problema pendiente. *Cuadernos de arquitectura romana* 2: 11-23.

Pociña, C.A. y J.A. Remolà 2001. Nuevas aportaciones al conocimiento del puerto de *Tarraco (Hispania Tarraconensis)*. *SAGVNTUM* 33: 85-96.

Remolà, J.A. y A. Lasheras 2019. *Ad suburbanum Tarraconis*. Del área portuaria al conjunto eclesiástico del Francolí, en J. López (ed.) *Actes del*

4t Congrés internacional d'arqueologia i Món Antic: VII Reunió d'arqueologia cristiana hispànica; el cristianisme a l'Antiguitat Tardana; noves perspectives: 75-82. Tarragona: Universitat Rovira i Virgili.

Remolà, J.A. y J. Sánchez 2020. El teatre romà, noves dades sobre el procés d'urbanització de l'àrea portuària de Tàrraco. *Tribuna d'Arqueologia* 2017-18: 385-406.

Rickman, G. 1971. *Roman Granaries and Store Buildings.* Ann Arbor: University Microfilms International.

Roncella, B. 2010. I magazzini, en D. Giampaola (ed.) *Napoli, la città e il mare. Piazza Bovio: tra romani e bizantini. Museo Archeologico Nazionale, 21 maggio - 20 settembre 2010*: 63-68. Napoli: Electa.

Salido, J. 2013. El abastecimiento de grano a las ciudades hispanorromanas. Producción, almacenaje y gestión. *Archivo español de arqueología* 86: 131-48.

Salido, J. 2015. Los graneros sobreelevados rurales en la Hispania romana: materiales y técnicas constructivas. *Arqueología de la arquitectura* 12: 1-16.

Salido, J. 2017. *Arquitectura rural romana: graneros y almacenes en el Occidente del Imperio.* Autun: Éditions Mergoil.

Terrado, P. 2019. *El puerto de Tarraco en época Romana (siglos II aC - III dC): fuentes, historiografía y arqueología.* Tarragona: Autoritat Portuària de Tarragona.

Terrado, P. 2020. *Els Ports antics de Tarraco: embarcadors, ports i platges del litoral tarraconense en època romana (S. II aC - III dC).* Tarragona: Arola.

Virlouvet, C. 2011. Les entrepôts dans le monde romain antique, formes et fonctions. Premières pistes pour un essai de typologie, en J. Arce y B. Goffaux (eds) *Horrea d'Hispanie et de la méditerranée romaine*: 7-22. Madrid: Casa de Velázquez.

Part 2:
Mediterranean Trade
and Connectivity

11. Anfore africane precoci a Roma e Ostia: alcune considerazioni sulle importazioni africane a Roma tra la tarda repubblica e la prima età imperiale

Alessia Contino

Introduzione[1]

Le anfore africane precoci sono state oggetto in anni recenti di una revisione, di dati editi e di alcuni contesti inediti, volta a definirne meglio tipologia, origine e cronologia. A questa categoria appartengono anfore prodotte tra la metà del II sec. a.C. e il II sec. d.C.: Africana Antica (ex Tripolitana Antica), Dressel 26, Ostia LIX e tipi affini (Contino 2013a; 2013b; Capelli e Contino 2013; Contino et al. 2016; Contino e Capelli 2016; 2019; Bonifay et al. 2023). Esse rappresentano le prime anfore "romanizzate" prodotte sul continente africano, con anse impostate sul collo e sulla spalla (Figura 11.1).

Il rinnovato interesse per lo studio di queste categorie di contenitori si deve in buona parte ai dati provenienti dallo scavo del Nuovo Mercato Testaccio (NMT) a Roma, che ha restituito un numero quantitativamente rilevante di questi tipi (507 FRR; NMI 233). A questa categoria si associa un consistente numero di ritrovamenti di anfore del tipo Tripolitana I (571 frr: NMI 183) in contesti di età giulio-claudia, flavia e traianea.

Il Nuovo Mercato Testaccio: contesti di provenienza

Lo scavo, effettuato tra il 2005 e il 2009 nell'area oggi occupata dal Nuovo Mercato Testaccio, ha messo in luce una stratigrafia continua dall'età tiberiana all'età contemporanea. Le indagini hanno restituito per l'età medio imperiale i resti di un *horreum* in muratura organizzato intorno ad una vasta corte di forma trapezoidale. Nei livelli sottostanti del settore orientale, in particolare nella fase compresa tra l'età tiberiana e l'età traianea, è stata individuata un'area, caratterizzata dall'impiego esclusivo di anfore vuote per la realizzazione di recinti e ambienti, interpretata come discarica e deposito di materiali per il reimpiego edilizio e costituita per la quasi totalità da frammenti di anfore rappresentative delle diverse aree produttive dell'impero, i cui contesti sono stati oggetto del presente studio.

L'area presenta una prima fase costruttiva che vede la realizzazione di diversi recinti realizzati con anfore Dressel 6 infisse nel terreno e affiancate le une alle altre.

Una seconda fase costruttiva prevede il rialzamento dei livelli dei recinti ormai pieni di materiale di reimpiego, la realizzazione di una viabilità di servizio interna e di tre ambienti coperti, la delimitazione degli spazi attraverso la realizzazione di un muro in opera reticolata a Nord, oltre cui viene realizzato un nuovo deposito di anfore Dressel 20. Le ultime fasi di vita sono costituite da scarichi indiscriminati che coprono diversi recinti (Sebastiani e Serlorenzi 2011; Contino et al. 2022) (Tabelle 11.1-11.2, Figura 11.2).

Anfore africane precoci e tripolitane

Africana Antica

Il sito di NMT ha restituito 77 frammenti di orlo attribuibili alla forma Africana Antica, di cui 71 pertinenti ai contesti in esame, alcuni di essi conservano anche il collo e/o le anse.

L'anfora presenta un corpo ovoide, un collo troncoconico e generalmente corto, un orlo leggermente svasato a sezione per lo più triangolare o sub-rettangolare. Le anse, impostate sotto l'orlo e sulla spalla, sono a sezione ellittica, con profilo semicircolare spesso irregolare, sovente segnate da nervature e da una digitatura esterna, alla base o nella parte superiore. Il fondo è conico, vuoto, a volte terminante in un bottone. Le misure medie dell'anfora sono: h. 82-94 cm; diam. max 42-47 cm; diam. orlo 12-15 cm. La capacità dell'anfora è di ca. 45 litri (Contino e Capelli 2019: 48 con bibliografia precedente) (Tavola 11.1.1-3).

L'anfora, mediamente standardizzata nella forma ma non nella metrologia e nella tecnologia, è caratterizzata da una discreta variabilità del profilo dell'orlo, da difetti di cottura e di fattura.

Presso La Longarina e presso Enserune, in Francia, si conservano esemplari di piccolo modulo[2].

Lo studio tipo-petrografico[3] mostra un'estrema variabilità degli impasti ma ha permesso di definire

[1] 'articolo consegnato nel 2021

[2] Ringrazio Albert Ribera per la notizia dell'anfora presso il museo di Enserune.
[3] Studio dei frammenti del NMT, comparato con esemplari da Pompei, Longarina, Olbia (Hyéres), Cap Camarat 2, Valencia e El-Mnihla (Ben

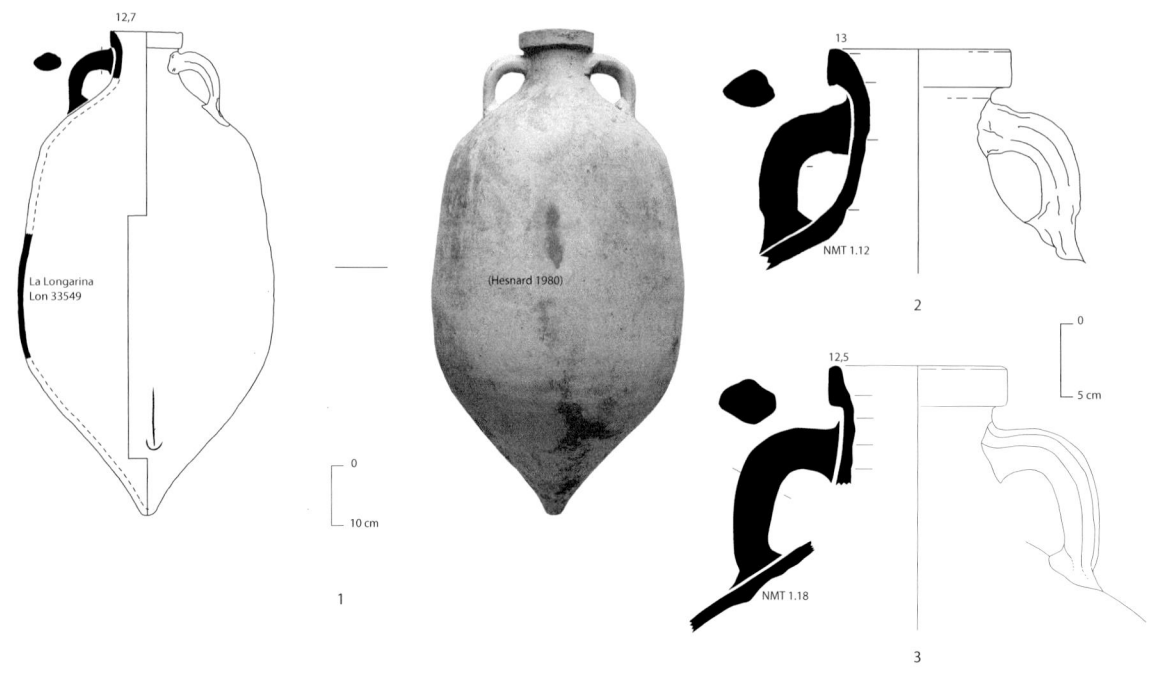

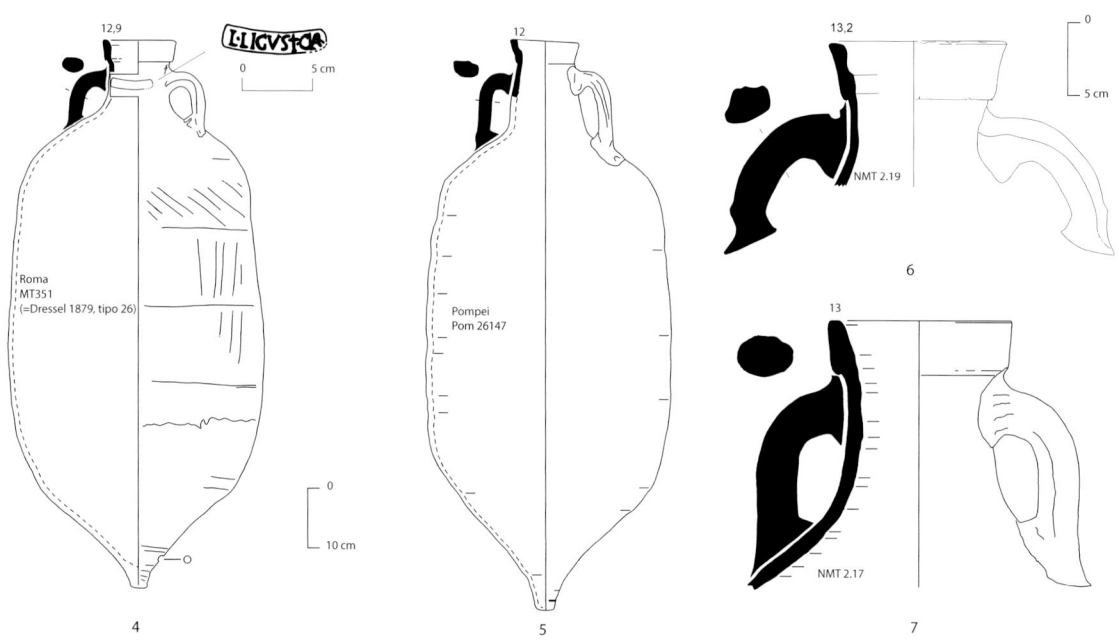

Figura 11.1. Anfore Africane Precoci. Tipi. 1. Africana Antica. 2. Dressel 26. 3. Ostia LIX. 4. Panella 1977, fig. 33. (disegni A. Contino)

3 macrofamiglie ed in particolare di individuare due produzioni, probabilmente riconducibili una all'areale cartaginese e una in generale alla Tunisia nord-occidentale (Contino e Capelli 2019: 48-57) (Figura 11.3).

Sono noti due siti con indicatori di produzione: il deposito con scarti di atelier da El-Mnihla (Tunisi), (Capelli e Contino 2013: 205-06; Ben Jerbania 2013; Capelli e Piazza 2013) e un atelier presso l'antica Utica (Ben Jerbania 2018).

Jerbania 2013; Contino e Capelli 2019), Narbonne, Toulouse e Utica (Lemaître *et al.* 2018; Benquet e Capelli 2018; Ben Jerbania 2018)

Tabella 11.1. Anfore africane precoci. 1-4 Africane Antiche. 5-8. Dressel 26. (disegni A. Contino)

CONTESTO	SETTORE	DESCRIZIONE	CRONOLOGIA
Contesto 1	Settore orientale	Prima fase di vita della discarica	Età tiberiano-neroniana
Contesto 2	Settore orientale	Seconda fase di vita della discarica	Età neroniana-flavia
Contesto 3	Settore orientale	Materiale proveniente dagli scarichi effettuati a Nord del muro in reticolato e coevi alla seconda fase della discarica.	Età neroniana-flavia
Contesto 4	Settore orientale	Ultime fasi di vita della discarica e abbandono	Età traianea.
Contesto 5	Settore orientale	Deposito di anfore Dressel 20 a nord del muro in reticolato:	Età flavio-adrianea

Tabella 11.2. NMT. Attestazioni anfore africane e tripolitane.

Anfore	tipo NMT	Contesto 1					Contesto 2-3					Contesto 4-5				
		OAF	o	a	f	NMI	OAF	o	a	f	NMI	OAF	o	a	f	NMI
Anfore Africane Precoci																
Africana Antica	AP1	53	53			53	8	8			8	10	10			10
Dressel 26	AP2	12	12			12	7	7			7	8	8			8
AP3-5	AP3-5	22	22			22	4	4			4	2	2			2
Ostia LIX	AP6	4	4			4	4	4			4	4	4			4
Ostia XXIII	AP7					0	1	1			1	1	1			1
Africane Precoci indeterminate		198		148	50	74	98		76	22	14	71		59	12	5
TOTALE		289				165	122				38	96				30
Anfore Tripolitane																
Tripolitana I	TR1	235	61	96	17	61	126	43	75	8	43	205	75	98	32	75
TripolItana II	TR2	2		2		1	1		1		1	2	1	1		2
TOTALE		2				62	127				44	207				77
Anfore Africane d'Imitazione																
Schoene Mau XXXV	IM1	12	2	9	1	5	24	10	14		10	95	25	64	6	32
Dressel 2-4	IM2					0	1			1	1	1	1			0
TOTALE		12				5	25				11	96				32
Anfore Africane Indeterminate	IND	25	25			25	6	6			6	7	7			7
TOTALE		25				25	6				6	7				7
		OAF				NMI	OAF				NMI	OAF				NMI
TOTALE CONTESTI		328				183	280				99	406				146

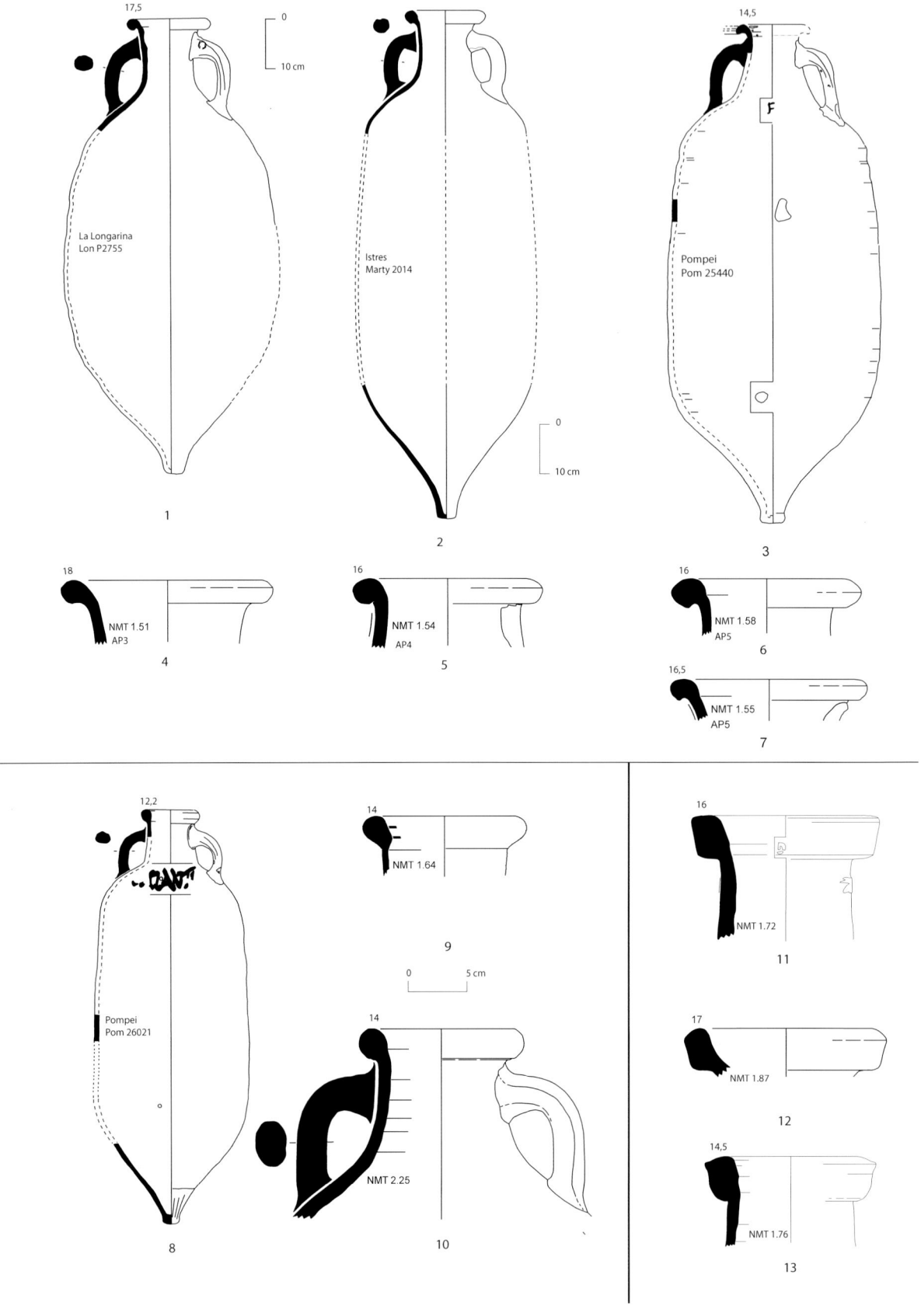

Figura 11.2. Roma. Nuovo Mercato Testaccio. A) Planimetria dell'area di scavo. (elaborazione grafica G. Verde) B) Settore orientale. Discarica/deposito per materiale edilizio. Vista d'insieme da Nord. (foto D. Putortì)

La datazione dell'anfora si colloca tra la metà del II sec. a.C. e la fine del I a.C.- inizio I d.C. (Contino e Capelli 2019: 57; Contino 2020: 100).

Dressel 26

Presso il NMT sono presenti 35 frammenti di orlo, di cui 27 pertinenti ai contesti in esame.

Il contenitore ha un corpo cilindrico di grandi dimensioni, un lungo collo generalmente dritto o leggermente troncoconico, un orlo a fascia più o meno svasato, che può presentare una caratteristica gola interna. Le anse a fascia più o meno massicce, sono impostate sul collo e sulla spalla, a volte con nervature. Il fondo è cavo di forma conica o "a bicchierino" di grandi dimensioni. Le misure medie dell'anfora sono: h. 98- 101 cm; diam. max 41-44 cm; diam. orlo 12-13,5 cm. (Tavola 11.1.4-7)

Anche in questo caso, dal punto di vista petrografico, si segnala la estrema variabilità degli impasti che permette di definire solo macrofamiglie attribuibili alla Tunisia nord occidentale mentre si esclude la provenienza dalla Sicilia orientale, come precedentemente proposto (Peña 2007). È stato possibile correlare alcuni campioni al gruppo di anfore Africane Antiche provenienti dall'areale cartaginese, suggerendo un fil rouge di continuità tra le prime anfore ovoidi, più antiche, e questo contenitore attestato esclusivamente nel corso del I sec. d.C. (Contino *et al.* 2016: 545, 547-48; Contino 2020: 103) (Figura 11.3).

Ostia LIX

Presso il NMT sono presenti 29 frammenti di orlo, di cui 12 pertinenti ai contesti in esame.

Si tratta di un'anfora a corpo cilindrico, collo troncoconico corto e quasi perfettamente cilindrico, orlo ad anello ingrossato ed arrotondato, che può evolvere anche in profili "a mandorla", brevi anse a nastro ingrossato con striature, impostate sul collo, subito sotto l'orlo, e sulla spalla, piccolo fondo vuoto "a bicchierino". L'anfora presenta una discreta uniformità tipologica, dovuta probabilmente ad una maggiore standardizzazione del tipo rispetto alle precedenti produzioni di anfore Africane Antiche e Dressel 26 e a una notevole semplicità dell'articolazione. Si evidenzia una certa incuria nell'esecuzione.

Le dimensioni medie dell'anfora sono: h. 85-90 cm; diam. max: 32-34 cm; diam. orlo: 13-14 cm. La capacità dell'anfora è di ca. 40 litri (Tavola 11.2.8-10).

L'analisi petrografica, pur all'interno di una certa variabilità, permette di collocare la produzione dell'anfora nella Tunisia Nord-occidentale. È stata rintracciata una famiglia comune tra l'anfora Africana Antica e le Ostia LIX e i loro predecessori e simili (AP3-5), di cui si dirà a breve, che suggerisce una continuità produttiva in alcune zone della Tunisia nordoccidentale interessate dall'affioramento in superfice del Flysh numidico, in particolare verso il confine con l'Algeria.

Fa eccezione un gruppo di impasti, appartenente a Salakta. Si è ipotizzato che lo spostamento della produzione dell'anfora a Salakta abbia segnato l'inizio di un processo di evoluzione del tipo verso le successive forme Africana I e II, con cui condivide la forma cilindrica e, in particolare, con le forme più antiche di Africana I, con orlo a mandorla (Figura 11.3).

L'anfora è attestata dall'età neroniana fino all'inizio del II sec. d.C. (Ostia III: 572; Bonifay *et al.* 2015: 190-92, 207, tab. 1; Contino e Capelli 2016: 547-49, 551-52, 554; Contino 2020: 103-06).

AP3-4-5

Presso il NMT sono presenti 34 frammenti di orlo, di cui 28 pertinenti ai contesti in esame.

Si individuano tipi simili all'anfora Ostia LIX, alcuni leggermente precedenti cronologicamente, che sembrerebbero costituire i precursori della stessa, caratterizzati generalmente da orli più estroflessi, con diametri maggiori e dimensioni maggiori del corpo dell'anfora.

Gli unici esemplari interi utili a sostegno della descrizione tipologica sono quelli provenienti da Pompei, Istres e La Longarina, con alcune reciproche differenze (Marty 2014: 631, fig. 31, n. 1; Contino 2020: 106-07) (Tavola 11.2.1-3).

Presso il NMT si individuano alcuni orli distinti dal tipo Ostia LIX e, in alcuni casi, prossimi agli esemplari sopra descritti: AP3, 4, 5[4]. Si tratta di 32 frammenti di orlo che si concentrano per lo più nei contesti di età tiberiano-neroniana (Contino e Capelli 2016: 550-51) (Tavola 11.2.4-7).

Anfore africane precoci indeterminate

All'interno della categoria delle anfore Africane Precoci indeterminate confluiscono fondi e anse frammentarie (198 frr.)

Tripolitana I

La Tripolitana I è il tipo più rappresentato al NMT: 657 frammenti di produzione tripolitana di cui 647

---

[4] AP3, 4, 5= Africane Precoci tipo 3, 4, 5.

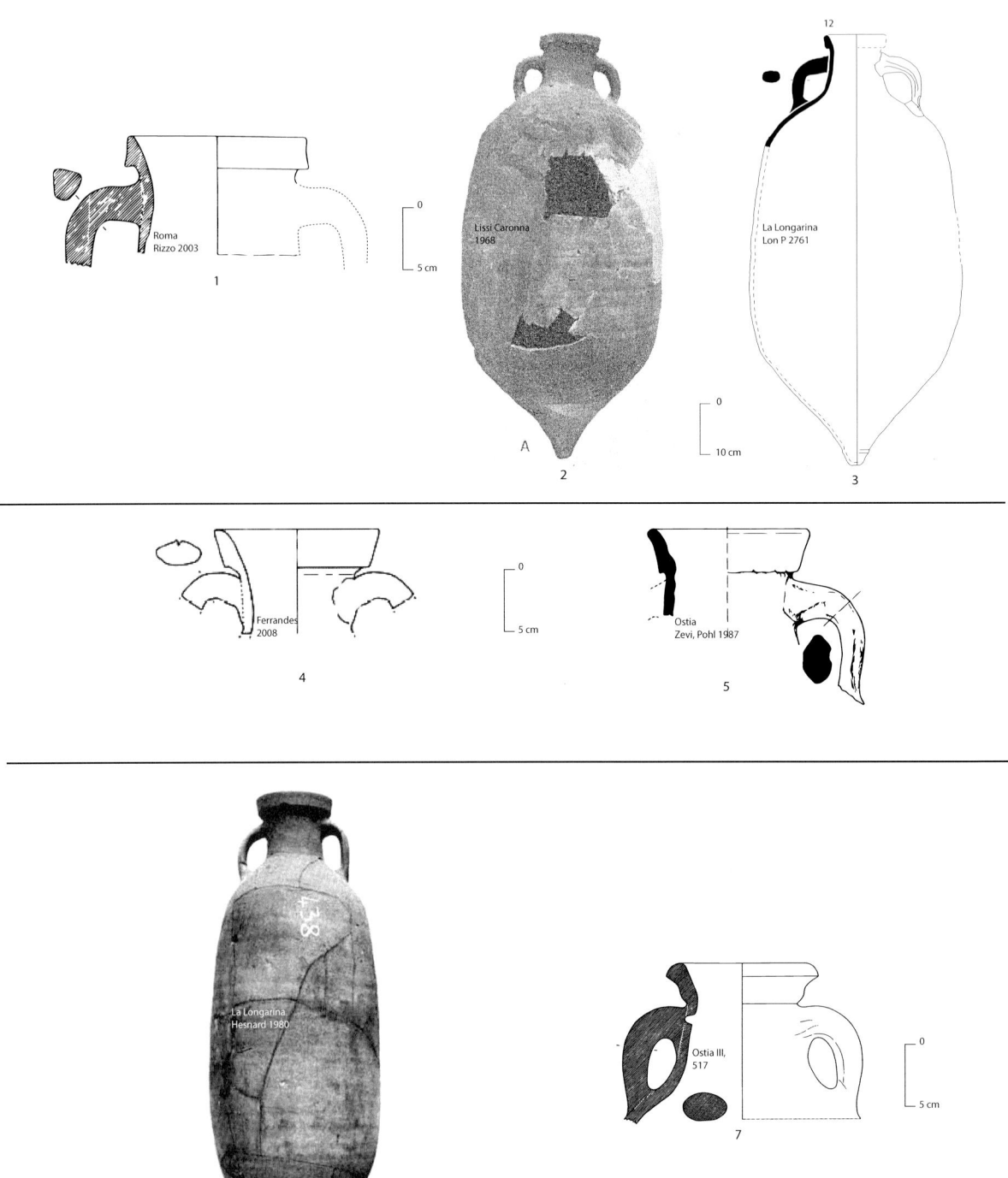

Figura 11.3. Anfore Africane Precoci. Ipotesi di provenienza su base tipo-petrografica. (elaborazione A. Contino)

sono pertinenti all'anfora Tripolitana I. 560 frammenti provengono dai contesti in esame.

L'anfora è caratterizzata da un corpo cilindrico, un collo lungo cilindrico leggermente svasato all'attacco con l'orlo, un orlo a labbro bipartito con diverse varianti legate all' ambito produttivo e cronologico. Sono attestati profili quadrangolari, a "S" o a "doppio gradino", a "*pseudo-casquette*"[5]. Le anse a nastro ingrossato sono impostate sul collo e sulla spalla, spesso con la tipica digitatura all'interno del collo in coincidenza con l'attacco dell'ansa. Il breve puntale conico è cavo.

Le dimensioni medie dell'anfora sono: h. 96-105,5 cm; diam max. 33-37,5 cm; diam orlo 14-16. La capacità dell'anfora è compresa tra 50 e 60,5 litri (Ostia III: 562-71, Bonifay 2004: 105-07).

Le analisi petrografiche mostrano diverse varianti, tuttavia è possibile identificare produzioni provenienti dal territorio controllato da Leptis Magna e dal plateau di Tahruna (Tavola 11.2.11-13).

L'anfora si data tra il terzo quarto del I a.C. e il II d.C.

NMT e contesti romani, ostiensi e portuensi: contesti a confronto

Per poter ricostruire un quadro, se pur non esaustivo, delle anfore africane importate a Roma dall'età tardo repubblicana all'età giulio claudia- traianea, si è proceduto all'analisi comparativa dei dati del NMT con le notizie note per l'area romana, ostiense e portuense.

La selezione dei contesti è avvenuta in primo luogo su base cronologica, quindi in relazione ai dati quantitativi, tipologici e/o topografici. Laddove i contesti non erano perfettamente sovrapponibili cronologicamente, vengono proposte delle tavole comparative tra i diversi siti, in particolare per alcuni materiali di area ostiense. Particolarmente scarsi i dati di età tardo repubblicana, che risulterebbero di grande interesse per le produzioni attestate a NMT in posizione residuale.

A causa della diversa cronologia, purtroppo, non è stato possibile procedere al confronto quantitativo e qualitativo del NMT con i dati del Monte Testaccio (*Estudios I-VI*).

Non si vuole proporre una disamina esaustiva di tutti i ritrovamenti romani, ostiensi e portuensi, che sarebbe peraltro complicata dalla difficoltà di accedere a dati ancora inediti[6], quanto piuttosto una valutazione dei dati del NMT sulla base del confronto con i contesti maggiormente rilevanti.

Da ultimo preme evidenziare prioritariamente la natura e la tipologia del contesto del NMT: un'area di discarica/deposito di materiali, nel quartiere commerciale della città antica, forse in relazione se non dipendenza dalle strutture orrearie. Si tratta quindi di un'occasione importante in cui è possibile avere un'immagine sufficientemente nitida dei beni di consumo che giungevano nell'Urbe approdando all'*Emporium* (sulla scarsità dei dati: Hesnard 2001: 287-88, 298).

Il panorama romano

Età tiberiano-neroniana (NMT-contesto 1)

I dati quantitativi provenienti dal NMT sono in linea con quelli ad oggi noti nell'area urbana e mostrano ancora una prevalenza dei prodotti italici su quelli di importazione ispanica, che supereranno quelli locali, almeno nell'Urbe, solo a partire dagli inizi del I d.C.

Le percentuali di anfore africane (8,7%), pur rispettando in generale la collocazione alle spalle dei contenitori italici ed ispanici, risultano discretamente attestate in relazione ad altri contesti romani (Rizzo 2003: 144-60, 158, 172, 177; Bonifay 2003: 114). Queste sono infatti leggermente più basse nei contesti di età neroniana della *Via Nova* e della *Meta Sudans* (3,96%) e nei contesti di età augustea e giulio-claudia di Via Marmorata (4,2%). Più simili ai dati del NMT le attestazioni dello scavo di Via Sacchi (10,32 %), il cui contesto di riferimento però si colloca nell'età tardo-augustea, dunque leggermente precedente al nostro (Rizzo 2003: 146, 147, 152-54; Bertoldi 2011: 148; Ferrandes 2008: 253).

Appare dunque evidente che lo scavo del NMT presenta percentuali di attestazione maggiori per alcune forme di contenitori altrimenti poco presenti in ambito urbano, in particolare appartenenti alla categoria delle anfore africane precoci e tripolitane (Pergola *et al.* 1987; Rizzo 2003: 146-47, tab. 26b; Ferrandes 2014: 363; 2013: 94, 253; 2008: 256; Bertoldi 2011: 148-49; Cardarelli 2013: 39, Lissi-Caronna 1968: 13, fig. 5) (Tabella 11.3).

Età neroniano-flavia (NMT-contesto 2-3)

Il panorama anforico è ancora dominato dalle produzioni italiche e ispaniche seguite da quelle orientali. Le anfore africane rappresentano il 5,34% dei frammenti significativi. I dati generali sulle produzioni

---

[5] Non si tratta ancora del vero profilo "a casquette" proprio delle anfore Tripolitane III.

[6] Colgo l'occasione per ringraziare gli studiosi e le Istituzioni che hanno favorito l'accesso ai reperti: Soprintendenza Speciale Archeologia, Belle Arti e Paesaggio di Roma; Parco Archeologico di Ostia Antica; Mercati Traianei; Per i contesti del Palatino: Prof.ssa C. Panella.

Tabella 11.3. Anfore Africane Precoci e Tripolitane. Attestazioni a Roma (OAF).

Sito	Età tiberiano-neroniana											Età neroniano-flavia			
	AFRICANA ANTICA	DRESSEL 26	OSTIA LIX	AP3, 4, 5	AFRICANE PRECOCI	AFRICA PROCONSOLARE	TRIPOLITANA I	TRIPOLITANA II	MAU XXXV	TRIPOLITANIA	NON ID	AFRICANA ANTICA	DRESSEL 26	OSTIA LIX	AP3, 4, 5
via Nelli (età augustea)	1, tav. 3.2														
via Marmorata (fase tiberiano-neroniana)							11								
via Sacchi (età tardo-augustea-età giulio-claudia)		1, tav. 3.4	1 (?)											2(?)	
Celio (età neroniano-flavia)														1	
Horti Lamiani (età tardo repubblicana)	1														
Crypta Balbi (fase traianea)															
Forum Transitorium (età flavia)															
Terme di Traiano strato III M (età traianea)															
Vigna Barberini (età neroniano-flavia)												1(?), tav. 3.1		7	1
Palatino nw obliterazione condotto di eta' domizianea															
Palatino nw drenaggio neroniano		no nn.frr													
Terme Elagabalo: domus e tabernae (fase tiberiano-neroniana)									3						
Terme Elagabalo (fase tiberiano-neroniana)							1								
via Nova									11						
Meta Sudans (età tiberiano neroniana)			1			9	1		16	4					
NMT	53, tav. 1.2-3	12	4, tav 2.9	22, tav. 2.4-7	198		174, tav. 2.11-13	2	12		25	8	7, tav. 1.6-7	4, tav 2.10	4

	AFRICANE PRECOCI	AFRICA PROCONSOLARE	TRIPOLITANA I	MAU XXXV/DR 2-4	TRIPOLITANIA	NON ID	Età traianea	AFRICANA ANTICA	DRESSEL 26	OSTIA LIX	OSTIA XXIII	AP 5	AFRICANE PRECOCI	AFRICA PROCONSOLARE	TRIPOLITANA I	MAU XXXV/DR 2-4	NON ID
via Nelli (età augustea)																	
via Marmorata (fase tiberiano-neroniana)																	
via Sacchi (età tardo-augustea-età giulio-claudia)				5													
Celio (età neroniano-flavia)					2												
Horti Lamiani (età tardo repubblicana)																	
Crypta Balbi (fase traianea)		1	3	10											6	14	
Forum Transitorium (età flavia)			1	15													
Terme di Traiano strato III M (età traianea)								4				9	4	39			
Vigna Barberini (età neroniano-flavia)		15		112	9												
Palatino nw obliterazione condotto di eta' domizianea				17	1												
Palatino nw drenaggio neroniano																	
Terme Elagabalo: domus e tabernae (fase tiberiano-neroniana)																	
Terme Elagabalo (fase tiberiano-neroniana)																	
via Nova			1	11						1			4		23		
Meta Sudans (età tiberiano neroniana)																	
NMT	98		126	25		5		10	8	4	1	3	71		205	95	7

africane sono ancora una volta in linea con quanto attestato per la stessa epoca dai contesti di *Via Nova, Crypta Balbi, Forum Transitorium* e Vigna Barberini, benché la maggior parte dei dati provengono dal riempimento del criptoportico della Vigna Barberini.

Per quanto attiene alle indagini effettuate presso via Sacchi il dato è più alto e si attesta intorno al 14 %·. Per lo scavo di Via Marmorata è assente una fase propriamente flavia.

Sul nostro scavo le anfore Tripolitane I e le anfore africane precoci sono quelle maggiormente rappresentate, pur diminuendo in numero assoluto, il che ancora una volta distingue il NMT dagli altri contesti romani (Rizzo 2003: 160-73, tab. 27b; Ferrandes 2008: 256-58; Danti 2006: 432-33, tab. 12) (Tabella 11.2).

Età flavio-traianea (NMT contesti 4-5)

I dati di confronto per questi contesti provengono in particolar modo dai contesti della *Via Nova* e della *Crypta Balbi.* Se i dati sulle produzioni anforiche sono coerenti per quanto riguarda il superamento delle produzioni italiche da parte di quelle ispaniche e il forte incremento delle importazioni di vino gallico, tuttavia al NMT non si registra una flessione nelle importazioni di prodotti egeo-orientali (Casaramona *et al.* 2010; Coletti e Lorenzetti 2010), come accade invece nei due contesti di confronto. La stessa mancata flessione si rileva presso lo scavo della *Porticus Aemilia.* Tale dato sarebbe forse da indagare in relazione alla natura dei contesti, che si caratterizzano specificamente come luoghi di stoccaggio (Rizzo 2003: 173-78; Contino e D'Alessandro 2014a, b). Le anfore africane rappresentano il 4,3% dei frammenti significativi, in questo caso il dato risulta inferiore a quello registrato alla *via Nova* e alla *Crypta Balbi* dove, in totale, si attestano al 10,05% (Rizzo 2003: 139, 174-75, tab. 29; Bertoldi 2008: 465, tav. 4) (Tabella 11.2).

Nel panorama urbano, per quanto è stato possibile sulla base dei dati esaminati, si verifica l'assenza di tipi ormai residuali ancora presenti al NMT. Tale differenza si deve probabilmente alla natura stessa del sito, collocato nell'area di stoccaggio della città e destinato all'accumulo di materiale da reimpiego (Tavola 11.3.1, 2, 4).

NMT e i contesti ostiensi e portuensi

Per taluni aspetti lo scavo del NMT, collocato nell'area portuale e commerciale dell'Urbe, può trovare confronti più puntuali nei contesti ostiensi, poiché Ostia rappresenta, in particolare nei primi decenni dell'impero, la via di ingresso delle derrate a Roma attraverso il Tevere (Pavolini 2006; Keay 2012: 41-44; Bruno 2012).

La tipologia dei dati a disposizione è differenziata, non tutti i contenitori trattati in questo studio avevano infatti già subito un processo di classificazione tipologica al momento dell'edizione dei contesti ostiensi.

Per quanto riguarda alcuni contesti scavati nel corso degli anni 70 (*Taberna* dell'Invidioso, *Domus* dalle Pareti Gialle, Piazzale delle Corporazioni, Caserma dei Vigili-Zevi, Pohl 1970: 93 fig. 97.119, 184, fig. 100, 180, 181 e fig. 88, 89, 194, 312-13, fig. 116.1990-91; Ostia VI, tab. 38 p. 279 -), ci limiteremo a fornire l'indicazione delle attestazioni sulla base dell'analisi di precedenti studiosi e della descrizione tipologica (Tavola 11.3.5).

Di grande interesse per il nostro contesto è il deposito della Longarina 1 (Hesnard 1980: 141-56) (Tavola 11.1.1; Tavola 11.3.3), che restituisce uno dei complessi più interessanti di esemplari integri o ricostruibili in territorio italico. Al momento dell'edizione i contenitori ovoidi di provenienza africana furono identificati come Dressel 26, attribuendo loro un'origine campano-molisana (Venafro) (Zevi 1966: 224-25), si trattava in realtà di Africane Antiche, ma il tipo non era stato ancora identificato e classificato al momento dell'edizione del contesto poiché lo fu solo successivamente, nel 1987 (Empereur e Hesnard 1987: 35-36, 69; Contino *et al.* 2019: 237-41).

Per quanto riguarda pubblicazioni più recenti possono essere fornite indicazioni maggiormente precise, come nel caso della *Domus* del Portico o della *Domus* dei Pesci (Zevi *et al.* 2004: 21-328, Geremia Nucci 2004: 96, fig. 40i-l; Boersma *et al.* 1986: 77-137; Van der Werff 1986: 109-12) e del fondamentale scavo delle Terme del Nuotatore (Ostia III; Rizzo 2014: 273 tab. 37).

Un elemento di difficoltà nel confronto dei dati è stata la non perfetta coincidenza delle fasi cronologiche. Di seguito sono illustrate le comparazioni effettuate sulla base dei periodi attestati nei contesti stratigrafici (Tabella 11.4).

L'analisi comparativa con i dati ostiensi, condotta su base cronologica, ancora una volta rivela due elementi fondamentali.

In primo luogo la bassa attestazione dell'anfora Tripolitana I in strati coevi a quelli del NMT.

In secondo luogo la bassissima attestazione dell'anfora Africana Antica, della Dressel 26, dei tipi AP3-5, in tutti gli altri contesti esaminati (Tabella 11.5) (Tavola 11.3.3, 5, 6, 7).

Per quanto attiene i contesti portuensi, al momento non sono edite stratigrafie direttamente comparabili con i nostri dati cronologici, tuttavia i risultati di *survey,* effettuati tra il 1997 e il 2004 in diversi settori del

Tabella 11.4. Tabelle comparative delle fasi dei diversi siti ostiensi e del NMT.

DOMUS DEI PESCI	DATAZIONE		NMT	DATAZIONE
Periodo I	II a.C.-metà I d.C.		Contesto 1	Età tiberiano-neroniana e residui
Periodo II	ultimi 2 decenni del I d.C. 80-100		Contesto 2-3	Età neroniano- flavia
Periodo III. Fase 1	primi decenni del II d.C.		Contesto 4-5	età traianea
Ostia II	DATAZIONE		NMT	DATAZIONE
Periodo V a-b	età domizianea		Contesto 2-3	Età neroniano- flavia
OSTIA III	DATAZIONE		NMT	DATAZIONE
Periodo Va-b	età flavia		Contesto 2-3	Età neroniano- flavia
Periodo IV a-c	età traiano adrianea		Contesto 4-5	età traianea
OSTIA VI	DATAZIONE		NMT	DATAZIONE
Periodo 1 a e 1b	Età tardo repubblicana-80 d.C.		Contesto 1	Età tiberiano-neroniana e residui
Periodo 2 a e 2b	70-80 d.C.		Contesto 2-3	Età neroniano- flavia

complesso archeologico, permettono di documentare la presenza del materiale ceramico riferibile ai diversi periodi di vita del sito, dalla fondazione del porto di Claudio all'occupazione tardo antica (Keay *et al.* 2005: 71). Questi contenitori documentano la prima fase di vita del sito, al momento della realizzazione del porto di Claudio, e il successivo sviluppo in età traianea (Tabella 11.6).

Altri rari materiali provengono dagli scavi del "Palazzo Imperiale" di *Portus*, ma da contesti cronologici più tardi dei nostri, in posizione residuale. Sembrano assenti dal sito le anfore Africane Antiche e Dressel 26 (Mele 2005: 226-30, tab. 6.18; Zampini 2011).

Da un intervento presso i magazzini cd. Traianei, di fronte alla darsena, in corrispondenza della cella C9 e del tratto del corridoio C12 del portico nord, nell'angolo nord-est del corpo di fabbrica trasversale medio, (Bukowiecki *et al.* 2018; Bukowiecki 2018; 2020; Boetto *et al.* 2010) è stato possibile rinvenire 1 orlo di Ostia LIX-XXIII e 1 orlo di Tripolitana I da contesti di età imperiale, compresi tra la fine del I e il III sec. d.C., un possibile orlo di Ostia LIX da contesti della metà-seconda metà del V sec d.C. in posizione residuale (Contino e Quevedo 2021: fig. 8.3)

Conclusioni

Produzione e origine delle anfore africane precoci

Come noto, l'incremento delle esportazioni africane corrisponde all'apparizione dei tipi Africana I e II: è, infatti, alla metà del II sec. d.C. che l'Africa si sostituisce gradualmente alla *Baetica* nella produzione olearia, oltre a fornire *salsamenta* e vino. A questo incremento produttivo corrisponde una standardizzazione dei processi di produzione dei contenitori anforici, che prevede la collazione dei prodotti dall'entroterra e l'invaso nelle principali città costiere, che divengono anche sede dei maggiori atelier ceramici (Bonifay 2004).

Tuttavia, non si conosce a fondo l'organizzazione della produzione e del commercio dei beni, e la relativa produzione di contenitori da trasporto, nella fase compresa tra la nascita della Provincia d'Africa e la metà del II sec. d.C.

L'apparizione delle forme più antiche di anfore romanizzate a profilo ovoide sembra coincidere con la nascita della *Provincia d'Africa,* nella Tunisia Nord-occidentale, quindi con l'arrivo di coloni italici in numero consistente, e con la presa di Corinto e la

Tabella 11.5. Anfore Africane Precoci e Tripolitane. Attestazioni a NMT e in area ostiense (OAF).

	NMT	TERME NUOTATORE	DOMUS PESCI	DOMUS PROTIRO	TABERNA INVIDIOSO	PIAZZALE CORPORAZIONI	CASA DELLE PARETI GIALLE	LONGARINA
età tardorepubblicana -età tiberiano neroniana								
AFRICANA ANTICA	53	1				5		20, tav. 1.1, 3.3
DRESSEL 26	12			2 (?)	1, tav. 3.5			
OSTIA LIX	4							
AP 3, 4, 5	22							
AFRICANE PRECOCI	198							
AFRICA PROCONSOLARE		1						
TRIPOLITANA I	192	No nn. Frr tav. 3.7		1				4, tav. 3.6
TRIPOLITANIA								
NON ID								
età neroniano-flavia								
AFRICANA ANTICA	8	1						
DRESSEL 26	7	3	1 (?)					
OSTIA LIX	4	32	22					
OSTIA XXIII			3					
AP 4, 5	4		1					
AFRICANE PRECOCI	98							
AFRICA PROCONSOLARE		9						
TRIPOLITANA I	147	1	2					
TRIPOLITANIA			5					
NON ID	5		1					
età traiano-adrianea								
AFRICANA ANTICA	10	1						
DRESSEL 26	8	6						
OSTIA LIX	4	29	11		1 + 2 (?)			
OSTIA XXIII	1							
OSTIA LIX/XXIII		17	9					
AP 5	3							
AFRICANE PRECOCI	71					2		
AFRICA PROCONSOLARE		37						
TRIPOLITANA I	206	3					6	
TRIPOLITANIA		4	5					
NON ID								

Tabella 11.6. *Portus*. Anfore Africane primo-imperiali provenienti da Survey e ritrovamenti presso i magazzini c.d. traianei.

Tipo	OAF SURVEY	OAF MAGAZZINI C.D. TRAIANEI
Ostia LIX	26	1 (?)
Ostia LIX/XXIII	5	1
Tripolitana I	1	1
Tripolitana II	6	
Schoene Mau XXXV	2	
Dressel 2-4	5	

Figura 11.4. Impero romano. Provincia Romana d'Africa 146 a.C.

conseguente diaspora di genti greche nel Mediterraneo, entrambi avvenute nel 146 a.C. (Contino e Capelli 2016: 553-54; Bonifay *et al.* 2023: 207-09) (fig. 4). Sulla base delle recenti analisi petrografiche è possibile collocare le prime produzioni ovoidi, Africane Antiche, inizialmente assegnate alla Tripolitania (Empereur e Hesnard 1987), proprio nella Tunisia Nord-occidentale.

Nota per la produzione ed esportazione del grano oggi questa regione appare, quindi, sotto una nuova luce, e risulta probabilmente coinvolta anche nel commercio dei prodotti liquidi e semiliquidi, fatto

che la renderebbe la prima produttrice di contenitori romanizzati dell'Africa (Contino e Capelli 2016: 553-54).

In questa prima fase produttiva, con l'introduzione del modello greco-romano di anfora ovoide, che costituisce una standardizzazione della forma a livello mediterraneo (Garcia Vargas *et al.* 2019), assistiamo, tuttavia, a un'alta variabilità metrologica e ad un sistema di parcellizzazione degli ateliers, probabilmente legati ai *fundi* agricoli, fatto testimoniato dalla varietà dei profili e degli impasti analizzati (Bonifay *et al.* 2023: 219-22; Contino e Capelli 2016: 551-54). Tale fase

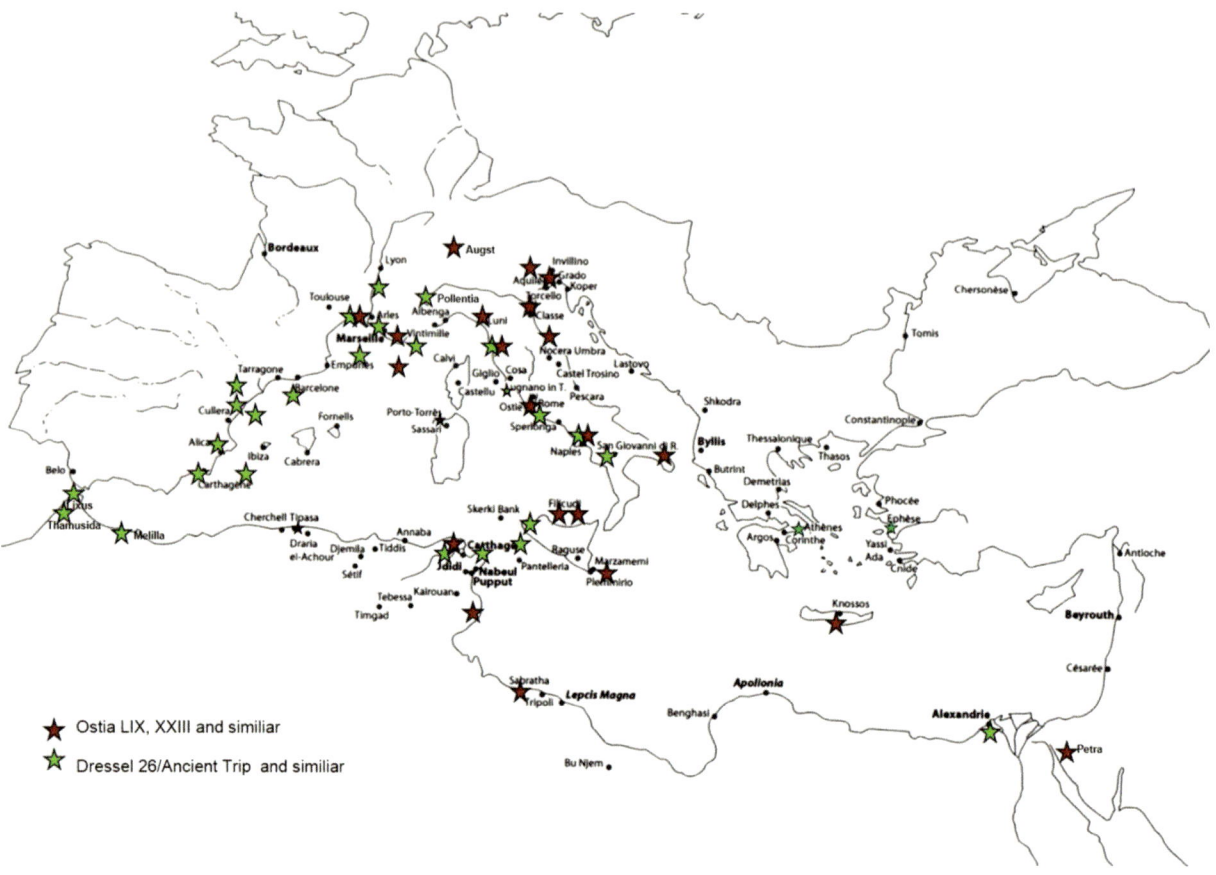

Figura 11.5. Anfore africane precoci. Carta di diffusione. (elaborazione A. Contino)

si caratterizza peraltro per una bassa percentuale di esportazioni, come è evidente dai quantitativi minimi di queste anfore, pur diffuse in numerosi siti del Mediterraneo (Figura 11.5).

Nella Tunisia nord-occidentale, fin da età cesariana, sono attestate, accanto alla ceralicoltura, l'arboricoltura e la policoltura, che prevedevano la coltivazione di olivo, vite e alberi da frutta, attraverso un sistema di ottimizzazione dei terreni (per l'età cesariana: *Bell. Afr.*, 50.1; 67.2; Plin., *Nat. Hist.* 15.17; 17.93; 129; 18.188, che parlano della presenza di produzione olearia e policoltura, accanto alla ceralicoltura, nella Tunisia nord-occidentale). Come noto, la produzione arboricola è caratterizzata da un più alto indice di produttività rispetto alla cerealicoltura e permette la produzione di un surplus da destinare all'esportazione.

I contenitori africani precoci ed in particolare l'anfora Africana Antica costituirebbero l'indicatore materiale di queste prime esportazioni. Complesso definire il contenuto di queste anfore. I dati dei *tituli picti* hanno fatto recentemente proporre, almeno per i tipi Ostia LIX e Dressel 26, che contenessero olio d'oliva o olive a diversi gradi di maturazione (Bonifay *et al.* 2015),

analisi in gascromatografia hanno rilevato la presenza di olio di moringa in anfore Ostia LIX (Djaoui *et al.* 2015). Ulteriori analisi in corso di pubblicazione hanno individuato olio non d'oliva e markers del vino in alcuni contenitori, indipendentemente dai tipi, ad eccezione delle anfore Dressel 26 che mostrano solo tracce di oli vegetali (Pecci *et al.* 2021. 94-96). Sono in corso di studio le analisi effettuate sui contenitori ovoidi rinvenuti presso La Longarina 1, Ostia. È possibile che in questo primo periodo dell'occupazione romana d'Africa, quando ancora non era stato organizzato un sistema standardizzato e specializzato di produzione agricola e dei relativi contenitori da trasporto, si assista ad una polivalenza dei tipi anforici in relazione alla possibilità di trasportare vari contenuti prodotti in diversi periodi dell'anno. Tale ipotesi, al momento del tutto preliminare, meglio si sposerebbe con l'individuazione di differenti contenuti all'interno dei contenitori.

I dati attuali rafforzano quindi l'ipotesi che, nella prima fase della romanizzazione, dalla Provincia d'Africa, nata nel 146 a.C., costituita dalla sola Tunisia nord-occidentale con capitale prima ad Utica e poi a Cartagine, si esportassero, accanto al grano, almeno in parte vino o derivati e oli vegetali, che confermano la rilevanza dell'area non solo per la produzione di cereali ma anche per la coltivazione di prodotti provenienti dalla arboricoltura.

Resta da chiarire quale fosse il principale canale di commercializzazione delle prime anfore africane precoci, data la loro occasionale attestazione sulle sponde del Mediterraneo. Sulla costa e nell'entroterra spagnolo, le anfore Africane Antiche si associano in numero consistente soprattutto alla presenza di strutture militari, colonie di nuova fondazione o complessi "produttivi", come le miniere de La Loba (Mateo 2012; Contino *et al.* 2019). Contesti più consistenti sono stati individuati a Roma (NMT) e Ostia (La Longarina). Rinvenimenti sporadici sono attestati in Francia e nel mediterraneo orientale (Contino e Capelli 2019). Si potrebbe dunque supporre un'organizzazione statale di queste prime importazioni dalla Tunisia Settentrionale, che avrebbero rifornito l'Urbe, e siti di carattere militare o produttivo e colonie sull'opposta sponda dell'Impero, la penisola iberica, che rappresenta anche l'area di più precoce diffusione dei tipi (metà II a.C.), normalmente attestati in altre regioni a partire dal I a.C. La presenza in minor numero sul libero mercato potrebbe derivare da un accantonamento da parte dei *negotiatores* di piccole quantità di beni riversati poi sui siti del Mediterraneo occidentale e orientale.

Anfore africane precoci il panorama romano, ostiense e portuense

La particolare attestazione dei tipi Africana Antica, Dressel 26 e Tripolitana I a NMT ne fanno un'importante tessera per la ricostruzione del mosaico tipologico e produttivo di queste anfore, nonché dei flussi commerciali tra l'Urbe, la Tripolitania e l'Africa del Nord tra l'età tardo repubblicana e primo imperiale.

A partire dall'età tardorepubblicana o almeno augustea, sulla base soprattutto dei materiali in posizione residuale provenienti dai cotesti esaminati, si rileva che giungono nell' Urbe anfore ovoidi africane provenienti da un areale compreso tra la Tunisia nord-occidentale e l'Algeria: le anfore Africane Antiche (Hesnard 1980; Ferrandes 2013; Lissi Caronna 1968). Al passaggio di secolo e in particolare all'inizio del I sec. d.C. ad esse si accompagnano le anfore AP3, 4, 5, le Dressel 26 e infine, dalla seconda metà del I sec. d.C. le Ostia LIX e poi le Ostia XXIII (Contino e Capelli 2016). Tali anfore rappresentano l'indicatore materiale delle esportazioni verso l'Urbe dall'Africa del Nord, tra il I a.C. e l'inizio del II d.C. (Carandini 1970; Panella 1993: 629; Contino e Capelli 2016: 553-54).

Per quando riguarda il volume delle importazioni dall'Africa nord-occidentale, stante l'impossibilità di certezza sul contenuto, l'impressione suscitata dai dati quantitativi è che si tratti di beni che giungono in misura molto bassa nell'Urbe, i quali sembrano avere piuttosto la natura di arrivi sporadici non inseriti in un flusso costante di merci. Tale situazione potrebbe essere l'effetto di una ancora scarsa organizzazione produttiva, che implica una bassa produzione di surplus destinato all'esportazione; di scarse capacità d'inserimento nelle dinamiche commerciali; per alcuni contenitori di una produzione canalizzata piuttosto verso specifici fabbisogni provinciali, viste le più alte attestazioni del tipo Africana Antica nella penisola iberica; in ultimo di una produzione specifica, di minore entità o destinata ad un minor numero di acquirenti.

Per quanto riguarda le ultime produzioni di anfore Africane Precoci, le Ostia LIX, si possono considerare tipologicamente il trait d'union tra le produzioni precoci e le successive forme Africana I e II, che testimoniano la standardizzazione della produzione agricola e anforica africana. L'individuazione di una produzione tarda di anfore Ostia LIX a Salakta conforta tale ipotesi (Nacef 2015: 38-39). Il tipo è in generale maggiormente attestato in fasi successive rispetto a quelle analizzate nell'articolo.

Le produzioni Tripolitane in età primo imperiale

Essendo la Tripolitana I l'anfora più attestata, appare evidente che, almeno sul sito del NMT, il principale bene importato dalla Tripolitania fosse l'olio, sempre superiore in numero di attestazioni rispetto alle anfore vinarie Schoene Mau XXXV, e che esso era anche il prodotto africano più attestato in assoluto.

Questo dato permette forse di chiarire un'annosa questione sul rapporto tra i dati materiali e le fonti antiche circa le importazioni tripolitane. Le fonti infatti affermano che già in età tardorepubblicana e giulio-claudia il bene maggiormente esportato verso l'Urbe dalla Tripolitania fosse l'olio. Tuttavia nei siti romani, perlopiù contesti di consumo, le anfore vinarie Schoene Mau XXXV presentano nella quasi totalità indici di attestazione maggiori rispetto alle anfore Tripolitane I (Bonifay 2003: 114). I dati del NMT, un sito di stoccaggio, testimoniano invece dell'arrivo importante delle anfore Tripolitane I a Roma e forse di una diversa modalità di immagazzinamento e consumo dei beni. Il vino, probabilmente, era commercializzato direttamente nelle piccole anfore vinarie mentre l'olio veniva travasato dai grandi contenitori in recipienti di minori dimensioni. In tal modo si spiegherebbe da un lato la presenza molto più alta delle Tripolitane I in un sito di stoccaggio rispetto ai siti di consumo, e allo stesso tempo si giustificherebbe la più debole presenza delle Schoene Mau XXXV, che probabilmente si limitavano a transitare per l'area di immagazzinamento cittadina, giungendo poi direttamente sui siti di consumo. Probabilmente motivazioni simili potrebbero giustificare l'alta presenza delle Africane precoci sul NMT ma la scarsissima attestazione su altri siti di consumo dell'Urbe.

La presenza predominante delle anfore Tripolitane, già all'inizio del I d.C., testimonia l'importanza, nota dalle fonti, dell'olio tripolitano e delle città esportatrici, in particolare *Leptis Magna* che già in età augustea viene riabilitata e liberata dal tributo imposto da Cesare.

Da un punto di vista produttivo e morfologico le anfore cilindriche prodotte in Tripolitania, le Tripolitane I, rappresentano forse l'imitazione e l'interpretazione tripolitana delle anfore ovoidi prodotte nel Nord (Bonifay 2004: 101; Contino *et al.* 2019: 246).

In conclusione, dal punto di vista dello stoccaggio e della redistribuzione dei beni, la presenza pressoché esclusiva di alcune anfore africane e tripolitane, di età tardo-repubblicana e primo imperiale, sul sito dell'NMT potrebbe indicare che alcuni contenitori non uscissero dal quartiere commerciale e che i relativi prodotti venissero rinvasati prima di essere messi in commercio, come sembra evidenziare la presenza di tipi altrove quasi non attestati, per i medesimi intervalli cronologici, come la Tripolitana I, limitatamente all'età giulio-claudia, l'Africana Antica, la Dressel 26.

Bibliografia

Ben Jerbania, I. 2013. Observations sur les amphores de tradition punique d'après une nouvelle découverte près de Tunis. *Antiquités Africaines* 49: 179-97.

Ben Jerbania, I. 2018. La production des amphores ovoïdes de type "Africaine ancienne" à Utique, avec une annexe de Claudio Capelli, Analyses pétrographiques. *Antiquités Africaines* 53: 175-92.

Bertoldi, T. 2008. Terme di Traiano. I materiali del saggio III M. *Mélanges d'archéologie et d'histoire de l'École française de Rome: Antiquité* 120.2: 447-67.

Bertoldi, T. 2011. Le anfore, in A. Capodiferro e P. Quaranta (eds) *Gli scavi di Via Marmorata*: 151-56. Roma: Electa.

Boersma, J.S., D. Yntema, J. Van der Werff 1986. Excavations in the House of the Porch (V II,4-5) at Ostia. *Bulletin Anticke Beschaving* 61: 77-137.

Bonifay, M. 2003. La céramique africaine, un indice du développement économique?. *Antiquité tardive* 11: 113-28.

Bonifay, M. 2004. *Etudes sur la céramique romaine tardive d'Afrique* (British Archaeological Reports, International Series 1301). Oxford: BAR.

Bonifay, M., E. Botte, C. Capelli, A. Contino, D. Djaoui, C. Panella e A. Tchernia 2015. Nouvelles hypothèses sur l'origine et le contenu des amphores africaines Ostia LIX et XXIII. *Antiquités Africaines* 51: 189-210.

Bonifay, M., C. Capelli, A. Contino, E. Jerray e J. Nacef 2023. Regional amphora standardization in Roman Africa (146 BC - 699+ AD), in H. González Cesteros e J. Leidwanger (eds) *Regional Economies in Action: Standardization of Transport Amphorae in the Roman and Byzantine Mediterranean (Athens 16-18 ottobre 2017)* (Archäologisches Institut. Sonderschriften 63): 207-25. Wien: Österreichisches.

Bruno, D. 2012. Regione XIII. Aventinus, in A. Carandini (ed.) *Atlante di Roma antica*: 388-420. Milano: Electa.

Bukowiecki, E. 2018. L'ambition portuaire de Claude. *Dossiers de l'archéologie* 390, 28-33.

Bukowiecki, E. 2020. Histoire d'un site (1): Portus, les docks high-tech des empereurs romains, in *À l'école de toute l'Italie: carnet de la vie scientifique de l'École française de Rome.* consultato il 7 gennaio 2020, <https://efrome.hypotheses.org/420>.

Bukowiecki, E., M. Mimmo, C. Panzieri e R. Sebastiani 2018. Le système des sols surélevés dans les entrepôts d'Ostie, de Portus et de Rome. Nouvelles découvertes en cours, in V. Chankowski, X. Lafon e C. Virlouvet (eds) *Entrepôts et circuits de distribution en Méditerranée antique: actes du colloque d'Athènes; Athènes, 22-24 octobre 2012* (Bulletin de correspondance hélleniques, Supplément 58): 231-68. Athènes: École française d'Athènes.

Capelli, C. e A. Contino 2013. Amphores tripolitaines anciennes ou africaines anciennes ? *Antiquités Africaines* 49: 199-208.

Capelli, C. e M. Piazza 2013. Analyses en microscopie optique d'amphores de type Maña C et "Tripolitaine ancienne" provenant du dépotoir de Mnihla. *Antiquités Africaines* 49: 193-98.

Carandini, A. 1970. Produzione agricola e produzione ceramica nell'Africa di età imperiale, in *Omaggio a R. Bianchi Bandinelli* (Studi miscellanei 15): 97-119. Roma: L'Erma di Bretschneider.

Cardarelli, V. 2013. Terme di Elagabalo: ceramica romana da contesti di età neroniana, in C. Panella e L. Saguì (eds) *Valle del Colosseo e pendici nord-orientali del Palatino* (Dopo lo scavo. Materiali e contesti 2): 21-42. Roma: Scienze e lettere.

Casaramona A., S. Colantonio, B. Rossi, C. Tempesta e G. Zanchetta 2010. Anfore cretesi dallo scavo del Nuovo Mercato di Testaccio. *Rei Cretariae Romanae Fautorum Acta* 41: 113-22.

Coletti, F. e E.G. Lorenzetti 2010. Anfore orientali a Roma. Nuovi dati dagli scavi della Soprintendenza Archeologica di Roma nell'area del Testaccio. *Rei Cretariae Romanae Fautorum Acta* 41: 155-64.

Contino, A. 2013a. Tripolitana Antica e Dressel 26 a Roma. Il caso del Nuovo Mercato Testaccio. Dati preliminari, in *L'Africa Romana*, XIX (Convegno internazionale di studi, Sassari, 16-19 dicembre 2010): 1471-87. Roma: Carrocci.

Contino, A. 2013b. Anfore africane tra I e II d.C. (Ostia 59, Ostia 23, Uzita): rinvenimenti dall'area del

Nuovo Mercato Testaccio, in D. Bernal, L.C. Juan, M. Bustamante, J.J. Díaz, A.M. Sáez (eds) *Hornos, talleres y focos de produccion alfareraen Hispania*, II: *Sociedad de Estudios de la Cerámica Antigua en Hispania I - ex officina hispana, Congres de Càdiz (3-4 de marzo 2011)*: 317-32. Cadiz: Universidad de Cadiz.

Contino, A. 2020. Anfore Africane Precoci dai Granai del Foro a Pompei: ricerche tipo-petrografiche su alcuni contenitori africani conservati nei depositi pompeiani, in M. Osanna e L. Toniolo (eds) *Fecisti Cretaria: Dal frammento al contesto; studi sul vasellame ceramico del territorio vesuviano* (Studi e Ricerche del parco Archeologico di Pompei 40): 89-99. Roma: L'Erma di Bretschneider.

Contino, A. e L. D'Alessandro 2014a. La Porticus Aemilia in epoca imperiale. Anfore orientali da un contesto orreario, in R. Morais, A. Fernández e M.J. Sousa (eds) *As Produções Cerâmicas de Imitação na Hispania*, II: *Sociedad de Estudios de la Cerámica Antigua en Hispania II - ex officina hispana, Congreso de Braga (3-6 april 2013)*: 141-49. Porto: Universidade do Porto.

Contino, A. e L. D'Alessandro 2014b. Materiali ceramici dai recenti scavi della Porticus Aemilia (Testaccio, Roma). Dati Preliminari. *Rei Cretariae Romanae Fautores Acta* 43: 323-34.

Contino, A., L. D'Alessandro, G.L. Pascual e A. Ribera 2019. Distribution of African and Hispanic ovoid amphorae in Italy: the cases of Pompei and Rome, in E. García Vargas, R.R. De Almeida, H. González Cesteros e A. Sáez Romero (eds) *The Ovoid Amphorae in the Central and Western Mediterranean between the Last Two Centuries of the Republic and the Early Days of the Roman Empire* (Roman and Late Antique Mediterranean Pottery 13): 237-73. Oxford: Archaeopress.

Contino, A., L. D'Alessandro e R. Sebastiani 2022. Il Nuovo Mercato Testaccio: la discarica, in D. Bernal Casasola, A. Contino, R. Sebastiani (eds) *Da Roma a Gades: Gestione, smaltimento e riuso dei rifiuti artigianali e commerciali in ambiti portuali marittimi e fluviali* (Convegno Internazionale Roma 19-20 settembre 2019) (Archaeopress-Access Archaeology 2022): 31-52, <https://www.archaeopress.com/Archaeopress/Products/9781803272986>, 2022

Contino, A. e C. Capelli 2016. Nuovi dati archeologici e archeometrici sulle anfore africane tardorepubblicane e primo imperiali: rinvenimenti da Roma (Nuovo Mercato Testaccio) e contesti di confronto, in *III Congreso International de la Secah, Ex-Officina Hispana, (Tarragona 10-13 dicembre 2014)*: 539-56. Tarragona: Insitut català de arqueologia clàssica.

Contino, A. e C. Capelli 2019. Late republican and early imperial ovoid amphorae: the African production, in E. García Vargas, R.R. De Almeida, H. González Cesteros e A. Sáez Romero (eds) *The Ovoid Amphorae in the Central and Western Mediterranean between the Last Two Centuries of the Republic and the Early Days of the Roman Empire* (Roman and Late

Antique Mediterranean Pottery 13): 42-61. Oxford, Archaeopress.

Contino, A., C. Capelli, M. Milella, F. Pacetti, L. Ungaro e M. Bonifay 2016. L'anfora Dressel 26 del Castro Pretorio. *Antiquités Africanes* 52: 145-56.

Contino, A. e A. Quevedo 2021. Contesti tardoantichi di Portus (Fiumicino–IT): novità dai c.d. Magazzini Traianei. *Papers of the British School of Rome* 90: 139-69.

Danti, A. 2006. Le anfore, in C. Pavolini, Un contesto archeologico flavio da Piazza Celimontana, *Mélanges de l'École française de Rome: Antiquité* 118.3: 430-62.

Djaoui, D., N. Garnier e E. Dodinet 2015. De l'huile de ben identifiée dans quatre amphores africaines de type Ostia LIX provenant d'Arles: difficultés d'interpretation. *Antiquités africaines* 51: 179-87.

Empereur, J. e A. Hesnard 1987. Les amphores Hellénistiques du Bassin Occidental de la Méditerranée, in *Céramiques hellénistiques et romaines*, II (Annales littéraires de l'Université de Besançon 331): 24-71. Paris: Les Belles Lettres.

Estudios I-VI: Blázquez Martínez, J.M. e J. Remesal Rodríguez (eds) *Estudios sobre el Monte Testaccio (Roma)*, 1, (Instrumenta 6, 10, 14, 24, 35-47). Barcelona: Universidad de Barcelona, 1999-2001-2003-2007-2010-2016.

Ferrandes, A. 2008. I contenitori da trasporto, in F. Filippi (ed.) *Horti et Sordes: Uno scavo alle falde del Gianicolo*: 247-83. Roma: Quasar.

Ferrandes, A. 2013. Il drenaggio neroniano, in C. Panella (ed.) *Scavare nel centro di Roma: Storie, uomini, paesaggi*: 91-95. Roma: Quasar.

Ferrandes, A. 2014. Circolazione ceramica e approvvigionamento urbano a Roma nel I secolo a.C. Nuovi dati dall'area degli Horti Lamiani. *Rei Cretariae Romanae Fautores Acta* 43: 353-66.

Gallone, A. e S. Zottis (eds) 2010. *L'archeologia con gli occhi di Silvia: atti della giornata di studio per ricordare Valeria Silvia Mellace (Palazzo Massimo alle Terme, 7 marzo 2009, Roma)*. Catania: Prampolini.

García Vargas, E., R.R. de Almeida, H. González Cesteros e A.M. Sáez Romero (eds) 2019. *The Ovoid Amphorae in the Central and Western Mediterranean between the Last Two Centuries of the Republic and the Early Days of the Roman Empire* (Roman and Late Antique Mediterranean Pottery 13). Oxford: Archaeopress.

Geremia Nucci, R. 2004. Il materiale ceramico, in F. Zevi, R. Geremia Nucci, A. Leone, Ostia. Sondaggio stratigrafico in uno degli ambienti della Domus dei pesci (1995 e 1996). *Notizie degli Scavi di Antichità* 15-16: 21-327.

Hesnard, A. 1980. Un dépôt augustéen d'amphores à la Longarina (Ostie), in J.H. D'Arms e E.C. Kopff (eds) *The Seaborne Commerce of Ancient Rome* (Memoirs of the American Academy in Rome 36): 141-56. Ann Arbor: University of Michigan Press.

Hesnard, A. 2001. L'approvisionnement alimentaire de Rome à la fin de la République et du Haut Empire, in *La ville de Rome sous le Haut Empire: nouvelles connaissances, nouvelles réflexions* (Pallas 55): 285-302. Toulouse: Presses universitaires du Mirail.

Keay, S. (ed.) 2012. *Rome, Portus and the Mediterranean* (Archaeological Monographs of the British School at Rome 21). London: The British School at Rome.

Keay, S., M. Millett e L. Paroli (eds) 2005. *Portus: An Archaeological Survey of the Port of Imperial Rome* (Archaeological Monographs of the British School at Rome 15). London: The British School at Rome.

Lissi-Caronna, E. 1968. Roma, Piccolo deposito di anfore in via Alessandro Nelli. *Notizie degli scavi di antichità* 22: 10-15.

Marty, F. 2014. Faciès céramique de l'agglomération secondaire du chemin du Castellan (Istres, Bouches-du-Rhône) durant le Haut-Empire, in *Actes du congrès de Chartres*: 599-640. Marseille: Société française d'étude de la céramique antique en Gaule.

Mateo Corredor, D. 2012. La importación de aceite tripolitano en Hispania Ulterior durante la época tardorrepublicana, in A. Castro Correa, D. Gómez Castro, G. González Germain, K. Starczewska, J. Oller Guzmán, A. Puy Maeso, R. Riera Vargas e N. Villagra Hidalgo (eds) *Estudiar el pasado: aspectos metodológicos de la investigación en Ciencias de la Antigüedad y de la Edad Media; Proceedings of the First Postgraduate Conference on Studies of Antiquity and Middle Age (Universitat Autònoma de Barcelona, 26-28th October 2010)* (British Archaeological Reports, International Series 2412): 119-27. Oxford: Archaeopress.

Mele, C. 2005. Amphorae, in S. Keay, M. Millett e L. Paroli (eds) *Portus: An Archaeological Survey of the Port of Imperial Rome* (Archaeological Monographs of the British School at Rome 15): 223-34. London: The British School at Rome.

Nacef, J. 2015. *Production de la céramique antique dans la région de Salakta et Ksour Essef, Tunisie* (Roman and Late Antique Mediterranean Pottery 180). Oxford: Archaeopress.

Ostia III: Carandini, A. e C. Panella (eds) 1973. *Ostia*, III: *Le terme del Nuotatore. Scavo degli ambienti III, VI, VII. Scavo dell'ambiente V e di un saggio nell'area SO* (Studi miscellanei 21). Roma: L'Erma di Bretschneider.

Ostia VI: Panella, C. e G. Rizzo (eds) *Le Terme del Nuotatore: i saggi nell'area NE; le Anfore, Ostia e i commerci mediterranei* (Studi miscellanei 38). Roma: L'Erma di Bretschneider.

Panella, C. 1993. Merci e scambi nel Mediterraneo tardo antico, in A. Giardina e A. Schiavone (eds) *Storia di Roma*, III.2: 613-97. Torino: Einaudi.

Pavolini, C. 2006 *Ostia*. Roma: Laterza.

Pecci, A., A. Contino, S. Mileto, C. Capelli, L. Toniolo e P. Reynolds 2021. Anfore africane antiche a Pompei: uso e riuso in base all'analisi dei contenuti. *Rivista di Studi pompeiani* 32: 87-102.

Peña, T.J. 2007. Two groups of *tituli picti* from Pompeii and environs: Sicilian wine, not flour and hand-picked olives. *Journal of Roman Archaeology* 69: 233-54.

Pergola, P., M. Royo, Y. Thébert, H. Broise, J.-P. Morel, F. Villedieu e M.-B. Carre 1987. Rome: le Palatin (Vigna Barberini). *Mélanges de l'école française de Rome* 99.1: 481-98.

Remesal Rodríguez, J. 2019. I provvedimenti annonari: la Baetica, l'olio per Roma e il Monte Testaccio, in R. Rea, C. Panella, A. D'Alessio (eds) *I Severi: Roma Universalis; l'impero e la dinastia venuta dall'Africa*: 232-41. Roma: Electa.

Rizzo, G. 2003. *Instrumenta Urbis*, I: *Ceramiche fini da mensa, lucerne ed anfore a Roma nei primi due secoli dell'impero* (Collection de l'École française de Rome 307). Roma: Ecole française de Rome.

Sebastiani, R. e M. Serlorenzi 2011. Nuove scoperte dall'area di Testaccio (Roma). Tecniche costruttive, riuso e smaltimento dei contenitori anforici pertinenti ad horrea e strutture utilitarie di età imperiale, in J. Arce e B. Goffaux (eds) *Horrea d'Hispanie et de la Méditerranée romaine* (Collection de la Casa de Velázquez 125): 67-96. Madrid: Casa de Velázquez.

Van der Werff, J.H. 1986. The amphora wall in the House of the Porch, in J.S. Boersma, D. Yntema e J. Van der Werff, Excavations in the House of the Porch (V II,4-5) at Ostia. *Bulletin Anticke Beschaving* 61: 109-12.

Zampini, S. 2011. La ceramica dello scavo del 2007 nel Palazzo Imperiale di Portus, in S. Keay e L. Paroli (eds) *Portus and its Hinterland: Recent Archaeological Research* (Archaeological Monographs of the British School at Rome 18): 93-99. London: The British School at Rome.

Zevi, F. 1966. Appunti sulle anfore romane. *Archeologia classica* 18.1: 208-47.

Zevi, F., R. Geremia Nucci e A. Leone 2004. Ostia. Sondaggio stratigrafico in uno degli ambienti della Domus dei pesci (1995 e 1996). *Notizie degli scavi di antichità* 15-16: 21-327.

Zevi, F. e I. Pohl 1970. Ostia (Roma). Casa delle Pareti Gialle, salone centrale. Scavo sotto il pavimento a mosaico. *Notizie degli scavi di antichità* VIII, 24, Supp. I: 43-237.

12. Geuma :
l'échantillon des liquides comestibles et son rôle dans l'organisation des sociétés et des espaces portuaires.

Pascal Arnaud

La vente sur échantillon a suscité durant les dernières années un intérêt croissant de la part de l'érudition, mais reste singulièrement absent de la réflexion d'une partie des historiens du droit même les plus récents (Jakab 2009 : 210-26). Leur attention s'est d'abord focalisée sur le *deïgma*, perçu à la fois comme objet, comme le cœur d'une pratique de l'échange et comme lieu structurant de la cité marchande dans la Grèce classique et hellénistique (Bresson 2008 : 101-05 ; 2016 : 309-13) ; ce furent ensuite les artefacts destinés au transport et à la conservation des échantillons, les inscriptions qu'elles portaient et les procédures qu'elles mettaient en œuvre qui ont aiguisé l'appétit des chercheurs dans un contexte chronologique d'époque romaine impériale et d'expression latine (Liou et Morel 1977 ; Djaoui et Tran 2014; Andreau *et al.* 2017 et 2019). On s'intéressa enfin au rôle de la dégustation dans la procédure d'emptio-venditio (Jakab 2009 ; Mataix 2018 : 65-66 ; 85-87). Les pratiques de la vente sur échantillon n'ont néanmoins jamais réellement été abordées à une échelle chrono-culturelle et disciplinaire large, englobant les mondes grec et romain.

Jusqu'à ce jour, un mot est étrangement resté sous les écrans du radar lexical attaché à ce débat. Il s'agit du mot grec γεῦμα (que nous transcrirons désormais *geuma*), qui caractérise les échantillons de liquides consommables, essentiellement les échantillons de vin. Les formes de la vente du vin sur échantillon ont bien été décrites par Alain Bresson, mais l'existence d'un mot technique pour distinguer deux types d'échantillon – celui du vin et celui du grain – semble avoir échappé à l'attention de l'érudition.

Dans un passage de la *Vie d'Apollonios de Tyane* (6.12),[1] Philostrate met les mots suivants dans la bouche du sage éthiopien Thespesion tentant de contredire Apollonios :

– Suppose que tu sois un marchand (ἔμπορος) ou un armateur (ναύκληρος) qui nous apporte quelque cargaison de là-bas, t'imagines-tu, au prétexte qu'elle viendrait de l'Inde, qu'elle serait mise en vente sans avoir été évaluée, et sans qu'ait été fourni un échantillon à examiner (deïgma) ou à goûter (geuma) ?
Apollonios lui fit cette réponse :
– Je les fournirais à toute personne qui en ferait la demande.

Il oppose ensuite à la démarche, de son point de vue normale, qu'il vient de décrire, consistant à demander de présenter d'un échantillon, *deïgma* ou *geuma*, pour fonder une transaction entre vendeur et acheteur, celle qui consisterait à accuser *a priori* le transporteur et le marchand de débarquer une cargaison frelatée, une accusation qui justifierait, de son point de vue, que le marchand ou l'armateur choisisse de se diriger vers un port moins inamical.

La présentation d'un échantillon, qualifié de *geuma* ou *deïgma*, selon la nature du produit (la métaphore mise dans la bouche d'Apollonios ne vise pas un produit spécifique et évoque donc tous les types d'échantillons) est donc considérée par Philostrate comme la norme du commerce maritime. Cette vaste métaphore était supposée intelligible d'un lecteur habitué aux pratiques du commerce à l'époque de Septime-Sévère. Elle confirme, s'il en était besoin, la familiarité supposée du lecteur de Philostrate avec les deux systèmes d'échantillons en usage dans le commerce maritime sous l'empire. Elle nous incite surtout à enquêter sur le sens du mot *geuma* en tant qu'échantillon des liquides, et tout particulièrement du vin.

Ni Liddle and Scott, ni Bailly ne donnent au mot γεῦμα le sens d'échantillon, qu'il a pourtant à l'évidence, et que lui ont reconnu quelques traducteurs, dans tel ou tel passage. Ce sens est particulièrement clair lorsque ce mot forme un couple avec le mot *deïgma*.

Le couple des *deïgmata* et des *geumata* a alimenté de nombreuses métaphores littéraires, de Plutarque aux Pères de l'Église, pour signifier les deux formes des échantillons produits afin de démontrer la qualité d'un

---

[1] "εἰ δὲ ἔμπορος" εἶπεν "ἢ ναύκληρος ἦσθα καί τινα ἡμῖν ἀπῆγες ἐκεῖθεν φόρτον, ἆρα ἂν ἠξίους, ἐπειδὴ ἀπ' Ἰνδῶν οὗτος, ἀδοκίμαστον αὐτὸν διατίθεσθαι καὶ μήτε γεῦμα παρέχειν αὐτοῦ μήτε δεῖγμα;" ὑπολαβὼν δὲ ὁ Ἀπολλώνιος "παρειχόμην ἂν" εἶπε τοῖς γε χρῄζουσιν, κτλ..."

lot conservé à part : celle que l'on observe et celle que l'on goûte.

Le *deïgma* était en effet la base d'un examen visuel et tactile. Les papyrus nous montrent que les *deïgmata*, conditionnés dans des récipients très normés, et transportés dans des conditions qui ne l'étaient pas moins, permettaient d'évaluer la qualité des céréales. La qualité du fruit et de son degré de sécheresse étaient décrits dans des documents d'accompagnement et parfois peints sur le vase lui-même (Guéraud 1950 ; Liou et Morel 1979 ; Andreau *et al.* 2017 ; 2019). L'examen visuel soumettait également l'échantillon à un test quantitatif dont le but était d'établir la proportion d'éléments extérieurs (terre, orge, etc...) et donc le degré de pureté du blé, et de déterminer ainsi la quotité de blé effectivement à livrer ou à acquérir pour obtenir la quotité escomptée de blé pur à 100% (*P. Oxy* IV. 708 et Mayerson 2002).

Le *geuma*, comme son nom l'indique, permettait à un palais expert de définir une qualité et de comparer un lot à l'échantillon remis en garantie et qui a fondé la transaction. À l'époque romaine, cette qualité est celle qu'affichent les *tituli picti* de façon très détaillée, non dans un but publicitaire, comme on l'a trop écrit, mais comme l'engagement écrit et formel du marchand sur la qualité d'un produit. Par extension, l'édit du maximum de Dioclétien utilise du reste le mot *geuma* au sens de "qualité" éprouvée par le goût, dans les cas où la désignation du produit ne suffit pas à caractériser un goût. "Premier *geuma*" ou "second *geuma*" désignent ainsi première ou seconde qualité d'un produit et s'appliquent à tous les liquides : vin, huile et *garum*.

Le chapitre 2 oppose ainsi au Falerne le "vin vieux de premier choix (goût)" et le "vin vieux de second choix (goût)".

Ch.2.

7 Φαλέρνου Ἰταλ(ικὸς) ξ(έστης) α′ (*denarii*) λ′
8 οἴνου παλαιοῦ πρώτου γεύματος Ἰταλ(ικὸς) ξ(έστης) α′ (*denarii*) κδ′
9 οἴνου παλαιοῦ δευτέρου γεύματος Ἰταλικὸς ξ(έστης) α′ (*denarii*) ιϛ′

7 De Falerne, 1 xeste italique, 30 deniers
8 de vin vieux de premier goût, 1 xeste italique, 24 deniers
9 de vin vieux de second goût, 1 xeste italique, 12 deniers

Le chapitre 3 oppose par ordre de prix décroissant l'huile d'olive de fruit vert à l'huile de second choix (goût), à l'huile de table et à l'huile de radis et à l'huile amère, et le *garum* de première et seconde qualité (goût) :

1 ἐλαίου· ὀμφακίνου Ἰταλ(ικὸς) ξ(έστης) α′ (*denarii*) μ′
2 δευτέρου γεύματος Ἰταλ(ικὸς) ξ(έστης) α′ (*denarii*) κδ′
3 κιβαρίου Ἰταλ(ικὸς) ξ(έστης) α′ (*denarii*) ιβ′
4 ἐλαίου ῥαφανίνου Ἰταλ(ικὸς) ξ(έστης) α′ (*denarii*) η′
5 ὄξους Ἰταλ(ικὸς) ξ(έστης) α′ (*denarii*) ϛ′
6 γάρου γεύματος πρωτίου Ἰταλ(ικὸς) ξ(έστης) α′ (*denarii*) ιϛ′
7 δευτέρου γεύματος Ἰταλ(ικὸς) ξ(έστης) α′ (*denarii*) ιβ′

1 **De l'huile** : d'olives non gâtées, 1 xeste italique, 40 deniers
2 de second goût, 1 xeste italique, 24 deniers
3 de table, 1 xeste italique, 12 deniers
4 de radis, 1 xeste italique, 8 deniers
5 amère, 1 xeste italique, 6 deniers
6 **De la sauce de poisson (garum)** : de premier goût, 1 xeste italique, 16 deniers
7 de second goût, 1 xeste italique, 12 deniers

Certaines catégories se définissent ainsi non par référence à une appellation ou à un processus d'élaboration, mais par un goût, fondateur d'une qualité et d'une catégorie commerciale et éprouvé par un échantillon. On est en droit de penser qu'un goût spécifique était associé en réalité à toutes les qualités de vins, d'huile, et de *garum*.

Les cas où, comme dans le texte de Théophraste d'où est partie notre enquête, *deïgma* et *geuma* sont associés avec une valeur métaphorique sont ceux où le sens d'"échantillon" est le plus clair. C'est le cas notamment dans un passage de la *Vie de Nicias* de Plutarque, où le biographe décrit le goût des Siciliens pour Euripide alors même qu'ils ne le connaissaient que par des morceaux choisis transmis par les voyageurs, comparés à des échantillons désignés des deux noms (δείγματα καὶ γεύματα). Comme les échantillons, ils arrivaient par mer et suffisaient à convaincre de la qualité de l'ensemble d'un lot encore inconnu dans sa totalité. Comme des échantillons ils circulaient ensuite comme du grossiste au détaillant, et comme les échantillons d'un bien précieux, on les faisait circuler avec parcimonie.[2]

Dans un autre passage, le biographe utilise le *deïgma* et le *geuma* pour introduire et filer une métaphore de Théopompe relative à Lysandre

---

2 Plut., *Nicias* 29.3 : μάλιστα γὰρ ὡς ἔοικε τῶν ἐκτὸς Ἑλλήνων ἐπόθησαν αὐτοῦ τὴν μοῦσαν οἱ περὶ Σικελίαν, καὶ μικρὰ τῶν ἀφικνουμένων ἑκάστοτε **δείγματα καὶ γεύματα** κομιζόντων ἐκμανθάνοντες ἀγαπητῶς μετεδίδοσαν ἀλλήλοις. "Il paraît que, de tous les Grecs de l'extérieur, ceux établis en Sicile étaient ceux qui étaient le plus en attente de sa muse, ils en apprenaient par cœur les petits échantillons (*deïgmata* et *getmata*), chaque fois que des voyageurs les leur livraient, et ils les échangeaient entre eux au compte-gouttes".

Il ne donnait pas aux Grecs un échantillon (deïgma) honnête de l'autorité lacédémonienne. Le poète comique Théopompe a donc l'air de plaisanter, lorsque, comparant les Lacédémoniens aux détaillants, il dit qu'après avoir fait goûter aux Grecs le doux breuvage de la liberté, ils leur avaient ensuite versé du vinaigre. Au contraire, le premier échantillon (geuma) qu'ils eurent à goûter de leur gouvernement fut plein d'aigreur et d'amertume ; car Lysandre ne laissa dans aucune ville le peuple à la tête des affaires, et il confia partout l'autorité au petit nombre des nobles les plus audacieux et les plus violents.[3]

Dans ce passage, Plutarque utilise d'abord le mot *deïgma*, auquel il paraît donner une valeur générique, avant de passer au *geuma*, pour filer la métaphore que Théopompe, au IVe s. av. J.-C., empruntait à l'univers des détaillants de vin.

La plus ancienne occurrence du couple **γεῦμα καὶ δεῖγμα** se rencontre en fait au IIIe s. av. J.-C. chez Philochore dans un passage cité par Athénée de Naucratis. Elle prend place dans une discussion relative à l'usage de boire en l'honneur du bon démon une petite quantité – la plupart des sources citées par Athénée insistent sur ce point – de vin pur après le repas. Athénée (*Deipn.* 15. 48 Kaibel) verse à ce dossier un passage de Philochore qui compare le repas et cette petite quantité de vin pur au *deïgma* pour le premier et au *geuma* pour le second qui préfigurent la puissance du dieu.

Philochore au l. 2 d'Atthis écrit "c'était alors la règle de servir à tous après le repas un peu de vin pur, comme un échantillon (geuma kaï deïgma) de la puissance du dieu bienfaiteur, alors que le vin bu avant était, lui, mélangé".

Ici encore *deïgma* semble avoir une valeur générique et *geuma* renvoyer au cas spécifique du vin, ce qui justifie dans le contexte qu'il soit nommé en premier lieu. Le mot *geuma* caractérise ici un échantillon de vin pur de petit volume.[4]

La tradition scripturaire n'échappe pas à l'usage de cette métaphore. On en trouve un bel exemple dans un passage des *Catenae* attribué à Titus de Bostra, évêque de la cité principalement actif dans les années 360 :

On appelle (le démon) de surdité celui qui rend sourd à l'audition de la parole de Dieu. De mauvais démons retirent la capacité d'écoute des convictions des hommes et privent notre âme de son ouïe. C'est précisément pour chasser le démon de surdité et pour que nous entendions le discours de Vérité que le Christ est venu parmi les hommes ; Car celui-là n'était pas rendu sourd par un démon mais il s'est trouvé être à lui seul un échantillon (deïgma) de tous ; et celui-là seul il l'a soigné, pour qu'il fournît l'échantillon générique (geuma katholikos) du salut universel.[5]

Ici le sourd guéri a valeur de *deïgma* de l'humanité ; il en partage les impuretés et il est une partie représentative de la qualité du tout. La métaphore du *geuma* illustre un autre type d'échantillon : celui qui permet d'avoir un avant-goût d'un produit qui sera largement consommé plus tard.

Vers la même époque, Ephrem le Syrien utilise les deux mots comme des synonymes, mais est plus précis dans la métaphore en faisant du *geuma* l'échantillon d'une jarre :

Et ceci est un exemple (deïgma) de sa mauvaise qualité, comme s'il s'agissait de l'échantillon (geuma) d'une jarre pleine...[6]

Une autre série cohérente d'occurrences où le sens d'échantillon est également clair est celle des cas où le mot est attesté au pluriel. L'une des occurrences les plus claires et les plus intéressantes est aussi la plus ancienne. On la trouve dans un passage des *Acharniens* d'Aristophane (*Acharn.* 186-202) où Amphitheus invite Dicéopolis à tester trois *geumata* (187 Ἔγωγέ, φημι, τρία γε ταυτὶ γεύματα) de vins de qualités différentes et de faire son choix. Dans un article consacré aux inscriptions d'Éphèse qui retiendront bientôt notre attention, H. Engelmann (1986) citant ce passage, en tirait la conclusion que le mot οἰνηρὸν γεῦμα dans les inscriptions d'Éphèse désignait "la dégustation du vin" (*das Degustieren von Wein*). L'ensemble du passage montre au contraire que les *geumata* d'Aristophane sont, plus précisément, des échantillons de vin présentés à la dégustation en vue d'un choix, conformément à la pratique coutumière de la vente. C'est en ce sens que s'entend la conclusion de Dicéopolis : δέχομαι καὶ σπένδομαι κἀκπίομαι "je l'accepte, je le ratifie et je le bois

---

[3] Plut., *Lysandre* 13.5 : οὐκ ἐπιεικὲς ἐδίδου τοῖς Ἕλλησι **δεῖγμα** τῆς Λακεδαιμονίων ἀρχῆς, ἀλλὰ καὶ ὁ κωμικὸς Θεόπομπος ἔοικε ληρεῖν ἀπεικάζων τοὺς Λακεδαιμονίους ταῖς καπηλίσιν, ὅτι τοὺς Ἕλληνας ἥδιστον ποτὸν τῆς ἐλευθερίας γεύσαντες ὄξος ἐνέχεαν· εὐθὺς γὰρ ἦν τὸ **γεῦμα δυσχερὲς καὶ πικρόν**, οὔτε τοὺς δήμους κυρίους τῶν πραγμάτων ἐῶντος εἶναι τοῦ Λυσάνδρου, καὶ τῶν ὀλίγων τοῖς θρασυτάτοις καὶ φιλονεικοτάτοις τὰς πόλεις ἐγχειρίζοντος.

[4] FHG I 387= Jacoby F 3b, 328,F, fragment 5a = Athen., *Deipnosophistae* 15.48, 14 Kaibel) : Φιλόχορος δ' ἐν δευτέρῳ Ἀτθίδος 'καὶ θέσμιον, φησίν, ἐτέθη τότε προσφέρεσθαι μετὰ τὰ σιτία πᾶσιν ἀκράτου μὲν ὅσον **γεῦμα καὶ δεῖγμα** τῆς δυνάμεως τοῦ ἀγαθοῦ θεοῦ, τὸν δὲ λοιπὸν ἤδη κεκραμένον (cf. aussi Athen., *Deipnosophistae* (epitome), Peppink 2,2, page 158, line 7 : Φιλόχορος δέ φησι καὶ θέσμιον τεθῆναι προσφέρεσθαι μετὰ τὰ σιτία πᾶσιν ἀκράτου μέρος, γεῦμα δὲ δεῖγμα τῆς ἀγαθοῦ θεοῦ δυνάμεως, τὸν δὲ λοιπὸν ἤδη κεκραμένον)

[5] *Catenae (Novum Testamentum), Catena in Lucam* (typus B) (e codd. Paris. Coislin. 23 + Oxon. Bodl. Misc. 182) (Cramer, Page 92). 39. Κωφὸν καλεῖ, τὸ κωφότητα ἐμποιοῦν πρὸς τὸ μὴ ἀκουσθῆναι λόγον Θεοῦ· δαίμονες γὰρ πονηρότατοι περιελόντες τὸ εὐήκοον τῆς τῶν ἀνθρώπων προαιρέσεως, ἐπήρωσαν ἡμῶν τὴν ἀκοὴν τῆς ψυχῆς· διὰ τοῦτο Χριστὸς παρεγένετο, ἵνα ἐκβάλῃ τὸ δαιμόνιον τὸ κωφόν, καὶ ἀκούσωμεν λόγον ἀληθείας· οὐδὲ γὰρ ἐκεῖνος ἦν ὁ δαιμονιζόμενος κωφός, ἀλλ' ὁ εἷς ἐτύγχανε **δεῖγμα** τῶν πάντων· τὸν δὲ ἕνα θεραπεύει, ἵνα καθολικὸν **γεῦμα** παράσχῃ τῆς οἰκουμενικῆς σωτηρίας.

[6] Ephraem, *Chronicon* 1998-99: Καὶ τοῦτο δεῖγμα τῆς ἑαυτοῦ κακίας, | ὡς ἐκπλέου γένοιτο **γεῦμα τοῦ πίθου**.

d'un trait". La dégustation n'est que la pratique qui accompagne et justifie l'échantillon. Le mot *geumata* désigne donc techniquement ici les échantillons présentés pour la dégustation dans le cadre normé des pratiques qui s'attachent à la vente du vin dès l'époque classique. Ce passage est à rapprocher d'un célèbre passage du *Cyclope* d'Euripide (149-50) :

> *Ul.* *Tu voudrais bien que je goûte d'abord ce vin pur ?*
> *Si.* *C'est conforme au droit. L'échantillon (geuma) appelle l'achat.*[7]

Dès le IVe s. av. J.-C., le mot *geuma* au pluriel caractérise de fait les échantillons de vin pur et les place au centre du processus commercial. Les *geumata* désignent les contenus, sans considération du contenant, au même titre que le *deïgma*, dont les contenants ont par ailleurs pu être normés par l'administration. Le texte le plus ancien qui soit limpide sur ce sens est un fragment des *Adelphes* de Diphile (II 541 K) conservé dans les *Deipnosphistes* d'Athénée (11.100 = 499e).

> *"Oh ! le fripon, qui peut même, ayant une petite cruche (lagynion) cachée sous l'aisselle, aller où l'on goûte le vin (geumata), et le vendre jusqu'à ce qu'il tombe sur le détaillant qui se laisse tromper par le marchand de vin, comme dans un repas où chacun apporte sa contribution".*[8]

Ce texte tiré d'une pièce emblématique de la Nouvelle Comédie montre que *geumata* au pluriel désignait non seulement les échantillons de vins, mais aussi, par extension, le lieu où ces échantillons étaient goûtés, et que ces échantillons étaient habituellement contenus dans un *lagynion* ou « petit *lagynos* ». La forme précise d'un *lagynos* est mal établie avant l'époque hellénistique (Rotroff 2006 : 82-84). À l'époque hellénistique c'est un vase bi-tronconique à col haut et à une anse. Mais parmi les *lagynoï* hellénistiques communs de l'agora deux individus (Rotroff 2006 : 84 et fig. 18, n° 113-14) se distinguent de la série à la fois par leur forme et par leurs petites dimensions. Sur le fondement du fragment de Diphile, nous proposons d'y voir des cruches destinées à contenir des échantillons de vin.

Ce texte fait également des *geumata* la désignation du lieu particulier où les marchands de vin (*oïnopôloï*) vendaient aux détaillants (*kapèloï*). Dès le IVe s. av. J.-C., comme le *deïgma*, les *geumata* auraient donné leur nom à un lieu du commerce dans la cité. Ce point semble confirmé par un passage d'Éphippe, un autre comique attique, qui faisait des *geumata* du vin le pendant des

étables des chevaux et donc sans doute non seulement un lieu mais aussi un bâtiment.[9]

L'échantillon est associé à toutes les étapes de la vente. On le trouve d'abord à l'échelle du cellier, où le vin est acheté en demi-vrac. On se souvient qu'au IVe s. de l'ère chrétienne, Ephrem le Syrien, évoquant un échantillon (*deïgma*) de la méchanceté d'un homme, file la métaphore en comparant cet échantillon à un *geuma* de la jarre (*pithos*) tout entière.

Plusieurs de ces échantillons, en forme d'amphorette, porteurs de *tituli picti* et datés du IIIᵉ s. ont été trouvés dans la région de Tanaïs en mer Noire (Ilyashenko1996 = *SEG* 46, 962.1-14). Ils sont invariablement définis comme γευματηρὰ πίθου, le premier mot étant parfois abrégé γευμ(ατηρὰ). Chaque échantillon mentionne le numéro et la capacité, exprimée en *lagynoï*, de la jarre qu'il représente, sur le modèle formulaire suivant : "Échantillon de la jarre *x* ; *lagynoï* tot". Certains de ces échantillons sont précédés d'un numéro. L'inscription est la garante de l'identification du lot représenté. Il s'agit alors d'échantillons de conformité valant pour un lot.

Les détails de ces inscriptions sont à rapprocher de l'épigraphie des objets désignés en latin comme les *ampullae*,[10] que l'on trouve associés à de gros conteneurs, *dolia* ou barriques.

Il s'agit ici de la même façon d'associer un échantillon, et son conteneur, porteur d'une inscription, à un *dolium* identifié par un numéro et un emplacement dans un chai, mais on trouve également la caractérisation du propriétaire, du domaine et de la qualité du produit. Une célèbre inscription de Rome datée du IVe s. (*CIL* VI, 1785, p. 3174, 4761, 4794) = *CIL* VI, 31931 = *ILMN*-1, 51 = *AE* 2001, 169 = *AE* 2006, 8 = *AE* 2006, 170) nous rappelle que lors du transport des barriques de vin d'État jusqu'à Rome, une fois les barriques livrées à destination, les *ampullae* qui les accompagnaient (et le contenu restant) étaient restituées aux *possessores* après avoir été goûtées par les experts.[11]

Contrairement à l'opinion d'A. Chastagnol (1950 : 169), les *ampullae* n'étaient pas le récipient fourni par le propriétaire avec lequel on puisait dans le tonneau, mais l'échantillon fourni par le vendeur ou le convoyeur,

---

[7] {Ὀδ.} βούληι σε γεύσω πρῶτον ἄκρατον μέθυ; | {Σι.} δίκαιον· ἦ γὰρ γεῦμα τὴν ὠνὴν καλεῖ.
[8] οὐδετέρως δὲ Δίφιλος ἐν Ἀδελφοῖς εἴρηκεν (II 541 K)· ὦ τοιχωρύχον | ἐκεῖνο καὶ τῶν δυναμένων λαγύνιον· ἔχον βαδίζειν εἰς τὰ γεύμαθ' ὑπὸ μάλης, | καὶ τοῦτο πωλεῖν μέχρι ἂν ὥσπερ ἐν ἐράνῳ | εἰς λοιπὸς ἢ κάπηλος ἠδικημένος | ὑπ' οἰνοπώλου.

[9] *Comicorum Atticorum fragmenta*, vol. 2", éd. T. Kock, Leipzig: Teubner, 1884. Fragment 18 : ἔνθ' ὄνων ἵππων στάσεις | καὶ γεύματ' οἴνων. "Il y avait là les écuries des chevaux et des ânes et les *geumata* du vin".
[10] *AE* 1972, 117 = Gasperini 1971 : 206 (Tarente): *Adadinum / Pet(t) iaco st() af pariete / vini ordo secu(ndus) / do[li]um prim(um) / amp(ulla) X misce(llum?)* ; Gasperini 1971 : 197 (Tarentum): *Vappa / in fundo Pettiano / secundum lacum / ordine primo / dolio primo secundo / doli(o) amp(ulla) XXV // Vap(pa) / Pet(tiano)*
[11] *CIL* VI, 1785 (p 3174, 4761, 4794) = *CIL* VI, 31931 = *ILMN*-1, 51 = *AE* 2001, 169 = *AE* 2006, 8 = *AE* 2006, 170: *d<e=F> ampullis placuit ut post degustatio[nem] / possessori reddantur*

échantillon avec lequel était comparé le contenu du tonneau.

L'ensemble de ce corpus documentaire nous montre que dès le IVᵉ s., l'échantillon de vin était associé à toutes les étapes de la vente, du chai au détaillant, en passant par la vente de gros dans les ports. C'est cette dernière situation que paraît illustrer le cas d'Ephèse.

On sait que dans le monde Égéen classique, le *deïgma* n'était pas seulement un échantillon, mais un lieu institutionnel dévolu à la présentation des échantillons et soumis à un contrôle et à des garanties étatiques. Faisant écho à la comédie attique, trois inscriptions d'Éphèse font d'un lieu désigné comme le *geuma* d'Ephèse le centre de l'activité d'une corporation et fournit le premier parallèle d'époque impériale pour un lieu institutionnellement dévolu à la vente sur échantillon.

Elles permettent en effet d'identifier le *geuma* comme le lieu de l'activité de métiers organisés en associations professionnelles. Se fondant sur une interprétation erronée du passage des *Acharniens* évoqué plus haut, Eingelmann, voyait dans la "*synergasia* de ceux qui négociaient au *geuma* sacré du vin" la guilde des marchands du vin produit dans les vignes de la déesse et qui auraient eu leurs boutiques dans les portiques où ont été trouvées deux de ces inscriptions. Cette interprétation, fondée sur une utilisation très partielle de la documentation tant épigraphique que littéraire, résiste mal à l'analyse.

La plus ancienne de ces inscriptions est la dédicace d'une statue votée par le peuple et la *boulè* à P. Vedius Antoninus, fils de Publius, en remerciement son activité édilitaire notamment durant les séjours de L. Vérus en 164 et 166 (*IK* III. 728 = *SEG* 36, 1019 = *AE* 1959, 13). La statue a été érigée par un groupe qui se désigne lui-même comme "ceux qui font du négoce au *geuma*" (οἱ ἐπὶ τὸ γεῦμα πραγματευόμενοι). Kalinowski (2002 : 131), tributaire de l'interprétation d'Engelmann a voulu en faire une "désignation générique pour diverses associations de marchands de produits alimentaires, incluant celle du vin sacré". Cette interprétation ne repose sur aucune comparaison tangible, ni à Éphèse, ni ailleurs. La désignation relativement vague ne suffit certes pas à caractériser à coup sûr une association professionnelle, mais elle indique clairement que le *geuma* était un lieu structurant du négoce où des négociants avaient leur activité. Se fondant sur l'interprétation par Engelmann des inscriptions suivantes, il localise les boutiques dans le portique de Servilius et lie la dédicace à la proximité de ce portique et des bains auxquels Védius Antoninus avait offert l'huile. Cette hypothèse peine à convaincre. Offrir l'huile aux bains est une évergésie d'une grande banalité. Or le point important dans cette affaire est que le *geuma* est

défini comme le lieu autour duquel s'organise l'activité commerciale des dédicants – les *pragmateuomenoï* actifs au *geuma*, qui ne sont pas de simples détaillants, mais des négociants, et sont assez riches pour offrir la statue. Le texte de l'inscription montre que c'est pour l'ensemble des services rendus et des monuments offerts à la cité qu'est honoré le personnage. Un lien particulier avec les *pragmateuomenoï* actifs au *geuma* justifie seul qu'ils aient payé la statue. Parmi d'autres hypothèses, on peut imaginer que le *geuma* avait bénéficié du programme édilitaire financé par le généreux donateur.

Les deux autres inscriptions, toutes deux sévériennes, s'attachent clairement à une association professionnelle (*synergasia*) associée à l'activité du *geuma* et à laquelle ont été concédés des espaces correspondant à deux fois deux entrecolonnements de portiques. La première (*IK* XVI. 2076 = *SEG* 36, 1026), datée des environs de 200, en concédait deux à l'association du *geuma* sacré (συνεργασίᾳ ἱεροῦ γεύματος). La seconde (*JÖAI* 56, 71, no. 1 = *BE* 1987:38 = *SEG* 35, 110) postérieure à 212, lui donnait le titre plus détaillé "d'association au *geuma* sacré du vin" (συνεργασίᾳ οἰνηρῷ ἱερῷ γεύματι) et lui concédait à nouveau deux espaces dans un portique.

Pour comprendre ces deux inscriptions, il faut les réintégrer dans la longue série des textes qui attribuent des entrecolonnements à des associations professionnelles, toujours dans un même portique, et dans un espace compris entre le stade et le théâtre. Contrairement à une idée répandue, le portique dans lequel ont été attribués les entrecolonnements n'est pas le portique dit "de Servilius". L'expression κανναβαρίοις τοῖς ἐν τῇ Σερβει<λ>είου στοᾷ (*IK* XII. 445) sur laquelle elle se fonde caractérise le lieu où était établie l'activité professionnelle des *canabarii* et non celui où ont été attribués les entrecolonnements, comme le montre clairement l'article τοῖς. Le portique dont elles proviennent n'est donc pas nécessairement le portique dit "de Servilius".

La remise en contexte de cette inscription permet de tirer plusieurs conclusions majeures.

Tout d'abord, les entrecolonnements n'ont pas été attribués à des individus pour des boutiques. Ils l'ont tous été à une série d'associations professionnelles caractérisées comme *synergasiaï* : les propriétaires des bains privés [*IK* XIV. 2078], les vendeurs de noix – ou les fabricants de boutons – [*Id.* 2079] ; les fabricants de sandales [*Id.* 2080]) ; les fabricants de saucisses [Knibbe 1985]) ; les utriculaires (*askosmisthaï*, *IK* XII 444), les cordiers, travailleurs de chanvre (*kanabarii*) du portique de Servilius (*IK* XII 445) enfin, qui est le seul groupe à ne pas être caractérisé comme *synergasia*.

Ensuite, ces attributions ont été effectuées sous l'autorité de l'Asiarque M. Fulvius Publicianus

Nikephoros, *advocatus fisci* sous Sévère-Alexandre, avec validation par le *grammateus* (*tou dèmou* ?). Elles l'ont été le long de la voie sacrée sur l'itinéraire montant de la procession, le long du gymnase de Vedius et entre le stade et le théâtre. Trois particularités suggèrent que l'opération s'est étalée sur une durée assez longue, sans doute de plusieurs années : les variations dans la formule onomastique et dans la titulature de cet asiarque, dont la seule constante est le titre d'Asiarque, le fait que certaines colonnes ont été regravées (*IK* XVI 2082) et la présence de plusieurs *grammateïs* différents. On note également que certains emplacements ont été apparemment réattribués (pas nécessairement au même endroit), pour le même nombre d'entrecolonnements, aussi bien aux *pragmateuomenoï* du *geuma* qu'aux fabricants de sandales, à moins que M. Fulvius Publicianus Nikephoros n'ait choisi de doubler l'espace attribuer à ces deux associations. On trouve en effet deux fois chacune de ces *synergasiaï* comme bénéficiaire de deux entrecolonnements, et celle qui nous intéresse plus spécifiquement apparaît dans les deux inscriptions avec une titulature sensiblement différente, ce qui semble exclure que les deux inscriptions aient été synchrones.

Plutôt qu'une restauration en règle du portique comme on le suppose d'ordinaire, il s'agit plutôt à notre sens d'une entreprise de régulation des espaces assignés aux corps constitués à l'occasion des processions de la déesse, comme le suggère le fait qu'une colonne ait été regravée avec une nouvelle inscription, l'ancienne étant déjà due au même M. Fulvius Publicianus Nikephoros.

Il ne peut en tout cas s'agir de boutiques. Les cas des *canabarii* et de nos *pragmateuomenoï* montrent bien que leur activité se déroulait en d'autres lieux. C'est également le cas des *balnearii privati*, exploitants des bains privés, qui n'avaient pas à tenir boutique. Il est douteux qu'il se soit agi de locaux professionnels. En effet, ce ne sont pas des échoppes mais des entrecolonnements qui ont été attribués à ces groupes, sur le modèle des sièges réservés au théâtre. Il s'agit donc très vraisemblablement d'emplacements alloués pour assister aux processions en l'honneur de la déesse. Quant au mot « sacré », à l'époque qui nous intéresse, il définit tout ce qui est placé sous tutelle impériale – parfois sous tutelle d'une cité – et n'implique aucune relation particulière avec Artémis.

Ces inscriptions nous donnent au contraire à notre sens plusieurs informations essentielles. Le *geuma*, lieu institutionnel dévolu à la vente du vin sur échantillons comme le *deïgma* de l'époque grecque classique l'était à la vente des céréales et les *geumata* à celle du vin, était au cœur du négoce du vin à Éphèse, au point de caractériser le lieu d'activité d'une association professionnelle. La précision qu'il s'agissait du *geuma* du

vin laisse entendre que des lieux et pratiques similaires étaient associés à d'autres produits (huile, *garum*). Le *geuma* du vin, lieu de l'activité des *pragmateuomenoi*, était sans doute le marché de gros du vin dans la cité et constituait à Éphèse une institution placée à l'époque sévérienne sous la tutelle institutionnelle et donc sous la garantie de l'empereur ou de la cité. On est en droit de penser que P. Vedius Antoninus monumentalisa le lieu à l'occasion de l'un ou l'autre des passages de Lucius Vérus dans la cité.

L'ensemble de ces témoignages éclaire d'un jour nouveau les pratiques de la vente sur échantillon. Dès l'époque grecque classique, elles s'articulent autour de deux types d'échantillons : ceux qui sont destinés à un examen visuel (*deïgmata*) et ceux qui sont destinés à un test gustatif (*geumata*). Ces deux formes d'échantillon s'attachent à tous les stades de la vente. Dans le cas du vin, on les trouve lors de la vente du producteur au marchand, puis du marchand au négociant et dans la vente du grossiste au particulier. Ces échantillons avaient pour première fonction de permettre à un œil ou à un palais expert d'évaluer la qualité d'un produit et à l'acheteur d'estimer, sur cette base, son juste prix. Ils garantissaient en outre la conformité du produit acquis à celui qui avait fondé l'achat, qui pouvait être conclu à distance. Leur conservation et leur examen en un lieu permanent organisait enfin la topographie des villes portuaires.

Références

Andreau, J., L. Rossi L. and A. Tchernia 2017. *CIL* IV, 9591: un transport de blé entre Ostie et Pompéi. *Mélanges de l'École française de Rome : Antiquité* 129.1: 329-37.

Andreau, J., L. Rossi and A. Tchernia 2019. *CIL* IV, 9591: un transport de blé entre Ostie et Pompéi 2. *Mélanges de l'École française de Rome : Antiquité* 131.1: 201-16.

Bresson, A. 2008. *L'économie de la Grèce des cités*, II : *Les espaces de l'échange*. Paris: Armand Colin.

Bresson, A. 2016. *The Making of the Ancient Economy*. Princeton: Princeton University Press.

Chastagnol, A. 1950. Un scandale du vin à Rome sous le Bas-Empire : l'affaire du préfet Orfitus. *Annales : histoire, sciences sociales* 5.2: 166-83.

Djaoui, D. 2014. Découverte d'un pot mentionnant la société des DD Caecilii dans un contexte portuaire situé entre 50- 140 apr. J.-C. (découverte subaquatique à Arles, Bouches-du-Rhône, France), in R. Rui Morais, A. Fernández Fernández et M.J. Sousa (éd.) *Ex officina Hispana : As produciões cerâmicas de imitação na Hispania*: 161-78. Porto: Faculdade de letras da Universidade do Porto.

Djaoui, D. and N. Tran 2014. Une cruche du port d'Arles et l'usage d'échantillons dans le commerce de vin romain. *Mélanges de l'École française de Rome : Antiquité* 126: 487-94.

Engelmann, H. 1986. Degustation von Götterwein (*IvE* 2076). *Zeitschrift für Papyrologie und Epigraphik* 63: 1078.

Gasperini, L. 1971. *Terza miscellanea greca e romana*. Roma : Istituto italiano per la storia antica.

Guéraud, O. 1933. Deux documents relatifs au transport des céréales dans l'Égypte romaine, 2. Sachet ayant contenu un échantillon d'orge. *Annales du Service des antiquités de l'Egypte* 33 : 62-64.

Guéraud, O. 1950. Un vase ayant contenu un échantillon de blé (ΔΕΙΓΜΑ). *Journal of Juristic Papyrology* 4: 107-18.

Ilyashenko, S.M. 1996. Об одной категории дипинти на светлоглиняных амфорах из Танаиса – On a certain category of dipinti on light-clay amphorae from Tanais. *Vestnik drevnej istorii (Вестник древней истории)* 219: 54-67.

Jakab, E. 2009. *Risikomanagement beim Weinkauf : Periculum und Praxis im Imperium Romanum*. Munich: Beck.

Kalinowski, A. 2002. The Vedii Antonini: Aspects of patronage and benefaction in second-century Ephesos. *Phoenix* 56.1/2: 109-49.

Liou B., and M. Morel 1977. L'orge des Cavares : une amphorette à inscription peinte trouvée dans le port antique de Marseille. *Revue archéologique de Narbonnaise* 10: 189-97.

Mataix Ferrandiz, E. 2018. Explaining the commerce of Roman Mediterranean ports: the evidence from *scripta commercii* and law. PhD dissertation, University of Southampton and Université Lyon 2-Lumière.

Mayerson, P. 2002. *P.Oxy.* IV 708: δείγματα found to be οὐ καθαρά and their implications. *The Bulletin of the American Society of Papyrologists* 39: 111-17.

Rotroff, S.I. 2006. *The Athenian Agora, XXXIII : Hellenistic Pottery: The Plain Wares*. Princeton: Princeton University Press.

13. The Late North African Connection between Barcino and Carthage: Rescue Excavations at Barcelona and the Aiguablava V

Cèsar Carreras and Joan Mayoral

One of the first academic contributions of Simon Keay was the study of late Roman amphorae, which involved the classification of late Roman amphorae assemblages from different sites in Catalonia such as *Barcino* (Barcelona), La Salut (Sabadell), or *Tarraco* (Tarragona). His pioneering work included the study of a selection of amphorae assemblages from old excavations in Barcelona before 1982 (Sant Iu, Tinell, Plaça del Rei, Villa de Madrid, Tapineria, Sant Miquel, etc.). The result was a two-volume publication that included new late Roman amphorae typologies and some conclusions about late Roman trade in this territory (Keay 1984). Almost 80% of the amphora types recorded in these Catalan sites were produced in the North African provinces, showing an exhaustive evolution of African amphorae typologies from the 3rd to the 7th centuries AD. Almost 20 years later, Bonifay (2004) redefined some North African amphorae typologies based on the evidence of the North African workshops and sites, including more conclusive archaeometric data about the content of every type. Nevertheless, with some minor corrections Simon's classification of late North African vessels still remains nowadays the main typological catalogue.

Although the late North African amphorae were important in all the main ports of the western Mediterranean, the Catalan harbours recorded extremely large amounts of amphorae and other coarse and fine wares from North Africa. Some years later, Remolà (2000) completed a study of all the late amphorae evidence from rescue excavations at the site of ancient *Tarraco* (Tarragona) and confirmed the high dependence of the city on North African imports in later periods, which were mainly vessels containing olive oil and fish sauce. Likewise, the excavation of the *cardo maximus* at *Iluro* (Mataró) also reported a large amount of North African vessels together with African Red Slip and coarse ware (Cerdà *et al.* 1998).

1. North African Amphorae at *Barcino*

With reference to *Barcino*, local amphorae from rescue excavations have been studied since 1996 but not fully published. Some partial publications revealed a high percentage of North African amphorae in any late context from the 3rd century AD onwards, reaching values of more than 50% of the overall assemblage in

weight and sherds (Carreras and Berni 2005; Carreras 2012).

The first North African amphorae in *Barcino* arrived in the late 2nd century AD with the classical forms of Africana I, and the most common Africana II in their four versions (A, B, C, and D) that were numerous in urban contexts in the 3rd and 4th centuries AD. Most contexts of this early period such as the excavations of Can Cortada, Sant Pau del Camp, Avinguda de la Catedral, Sant Miquel, Ajuntament 96, Arc Boters, Bones Lletres, Rasa de la Catedral, Sant Honorat, or C/Avinyó 15-16 contained African amphorae, but always in relatively low numbers. All these amphorae types have been understood as being used to import olive oil to the city together with the contemporaneous Baetican Dressel 20 and 23. One of the most notable features of these early Northern African amphora types is the presence of stamps. The number of stamps documented in 2009 (Berni and Carreras 2009) was still low, only four marked vessels, but it has increased in the recent unpublished excavations at Sant Honorat and C/Avinyó 15/16 reaching a total of 11 North African stamps, most of which appeared on Africana II-D amphorae dated between the late 3rd and 4th centuries AD (Carreras 2021).

Three of the latest stamps on Africana II-D recovered at C/Avinyó 15-16 can provide some insight into their origins, and the transport routes selected to carry these vessels (see Figure 13.1).

The first stamp reads **LEPMN/BSCD** (MUHBA- 094/03-1402-1), which stands for LEP(tis) M[i]nor – present Lamta (Tunisia) in the southern part of the Hammamet Gulf. A possible workshop of this production is located at Dahar Slima (Peacock *et al.* 1989: 197-98, fig. 24). This family of stamps presents different variants, but the ones with a second line including BSCD are recorded in places such as Villa de Can Rafart (Mataró), Porto-Torres, Cabrera I, and Cabrera III on the route south-north crossing the Mediterranean. The second stamp **COLN** (MUHBA-094/03-1402-2) does not have any parallel so far, although it is part of a family of African stamps that identify colonies such as *colonia Leptis Magna* (Khom) or *colonia Hadrumentum* (Sousse). In this particular case, the stamp might identify the COL(onia)

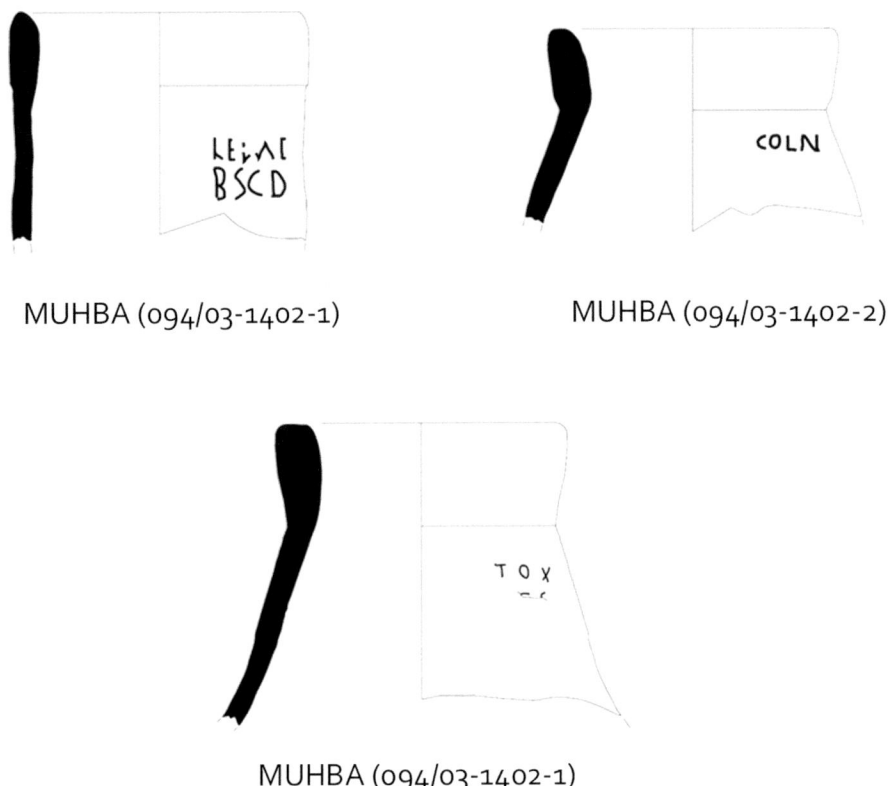

Figure 13.1. Amphora stamps on Africana II-D found at C/Avinyó 15-16.

N(*eapolis*), currently Nabeoul in the Zeugitana region (northern part of the Hammamet Gulf). Lastly, the third stamp **TOP/HCS** (MUHBA-094/03-1402-1) has been found within archaeological contexts at Ostia or the *Nuovo Mercato* of Testaccio (Rome), but its precise origin is still unknown. The evidence of the stamps from *Barcino* suggests that the Africana series were produced in the Gulf of Hammamet and were probably filled with the olive oil produced in the Byzacena region, and perhaps, fish sauces from Zeugitana. In addition to the Africana II-C and II-D, the North African imports in *Barcino* during the 3rd and 4th centuries also included another heterogenous type of amphora known as Keay XXV in its different variants (Carreras and Berni 2005).

The Keay XXV – also known as Africana III or Sullecthum 10 and 11 (Nacef 2015: 48-50) – was a common import in the urban excavations at *Barcino*. Although the specific contents of this type of amphora are still unknown, some samples suggest that they may have contained wine (Woodworth *et al.* 2015). The distribution of this type of amphora inside *Barcino* was concentrated in the central and western quarters of the city where they were used as a recycled construction material in a period of intense building activity. Before the late 3rd century AD, most rubbish deposits containing amphorae within the city were documented outside the city walls. However, from the 3rd century onwards there was a significant development of the construction activity in the town centre and most amphorae sherds were used to raise the street levels and create terraces (Beltran and Carreras 2011). This building work with North African amphorae is recorded in the density maps of late African vessels that also correspond to the Keay XXV distribution (see Figure 13.2) (Beltran and Carreras 2011: 215, fig. 22).

From the end of the 4th century onwards, the numbers of North African amphorae (Keay XXXV, XXXVI, XL, and XLI) increased in the *Barcino* contexts, reaching percentages of more than 50% of the amphora assemblages (Carreras 2012: 42, fig. 2). The success of the North African exports was general in the whole Western Roman Empire probably due to the privileges granted to the African *navicularii* by Theodosius to bring the *annona* to Rome in the year AD 364 (C.Th. 13.5.10), 395 (C.Th. 13.5.24), 400 (C.Th. 13.5.30), and 412 (C.Th. 13.5.36). Such privileges may have favoured the African traders, encouraging them to open new routes and markets such as the eastern ports of the Iberian Peninsula including *Cartago Nova*, *Tarraco*, or *Barcino* (Reynolds 2010: 74).

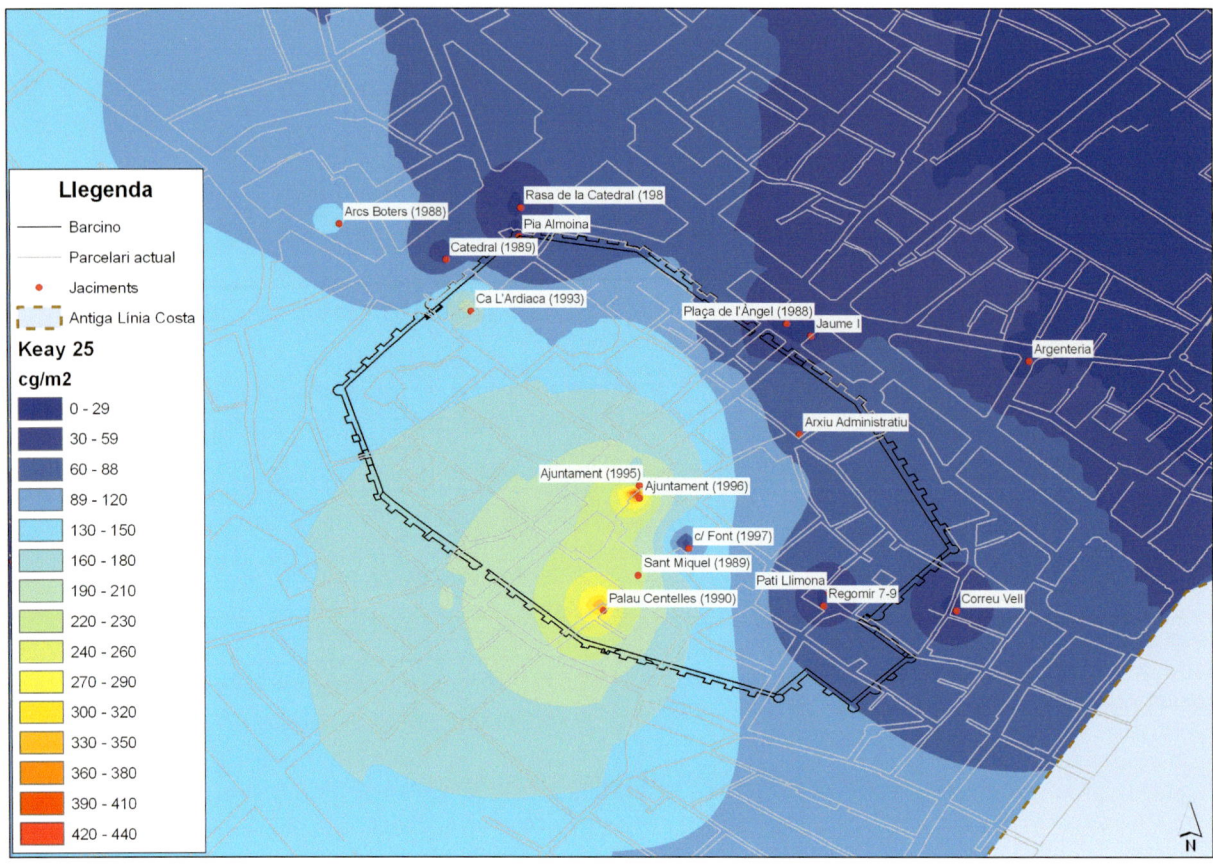

Figure 13.2. Density of North African amphorae at *Barcino* (Beltran and Carreras 2011: 215, fig. 22).

Despite the political changes that occurred in *Hispania* with the arrival of the Visigoths in the 5th century AD and the establishment of the Vandal kingdom in Carthage (AD 430), the commercial flow between *Barcino* and Carthage remained unaltered (Carreras 2012: 46-50). New olive oil amphora types, such as Keay LV and Keay LXI, appeared in good numbers in *Barcino* contexts. Nevertheless, the most popular African vessel was the Keay LXII, which possibly carried either wine or fish sauces (Bonifay 2004: 137-39).

Similarly to earlier periods, North African amphorae were not transported alone but, instead, were usually accompanied by cooking wares and African Red Slip D; forms such as the Hayes 87 A-C, 88, 99, 103, and 104 are characteristic of the end of the 5th century and the beginning of the 6th, while the Hayes 91 D, 104 C, 105, 106, 107, and 108 were more common during the 6th and 7th centuries AD (Járrega 2005).

The importance of North African imports at *Barcino*, as well as across the whole north-eastern coast of *Hispania* in Late Antiquity was clear, reaching percentages of 50% in some amphora assemblages. These strong contacts between *Tarraconensis* and northern Africa were also present during the Republic and Early Empire, although

never as intensely as the later periods. In order to understand such economic phenomena, one should look to the sea routes in some detail.

2. Sea Routes between *Barcino* and Carthage

Commercial contacts between the Catalan coast and the region of Carthage date back to, at least, the 5th-4th centuries BC, when Punic amphorae reached the main Iberian *oppida* of the north-eastern coastal region (Ramon 1995; Martínez HahnMüller 2016). These early commercial contacts were probably arbitrated by Ebussitanian traders through the southern Balearic island of Ibiza, since most amphora assemblages also contain Punic-Ebussitanian vessels. This argument is confirmed in the Augustan period by the overwhelming presence of Punic-Ebussitanian amphorae in 1st century AD contexts at Riudarenes (049/4) and C/Avinyó 2015/6 (046/05) excavations close the ancient Roman port of *Barcino*.

On the one hand, Guerrero (1993) documents the navigation south to north through the northern Balearic Islands (Mallorca and Menorca) from prehistoric times, which took advantage of the currents and winds, allowing contact between northern Africa and north-east Spain through the Balearic ports of call. Moreover, the prevailing regime of winds and currents favoured navigation from the African coasts to southern Gaul, the Balearic Islands, and Levantine Spain as recorded in the *Compasso da navigare* of the 13th century AD (Quaini 2004). Some routes sailed directly from *Thrabaca* to Narbonne or from *Igilgili* to Marseille, while others called at Balearic ports before reaching their final southern European destinations. On the other hand, the inverse route north to south was extremely difficult because ships had to sail against currents and winds, so the stop in the Balearic Islands was even more necessary.

During the Principate, a great number of amphorae from *Tarraconensis* (i.e. Pascual 1 and Dressel 2-4) were documented in the main ports of the northern Balearic Islands such as *Palma*, *Pollentia* (Mallorca) and *Maios* and Sa Nitja (Menorca), but they also reached the city of Carthage in great numbers in the middle of the 1st century AD (Berni and Miró 2020). The only literary evidence of the route between North Africa and the eastern Narbonense coast comes from Strabo (2.5.8), who referred to a distance of 5000 stadia between the Gallic Gulf (Gulf of Leon) and Libya (Africa). This should be understood as the distance between the main port of this gulf, Narbonne, and the North African coast – a place close to *Thrabaca* where the distance reaches 5000 stadia (870km) (Arnaud 2005: 153, route 1).

Although sailing routes south to north was relatively easy on account of the favourable winds regime and sea currents (Ruiz de Arbulo 1997), travelling in the opposite direction was considerably more complicated since it required sailing against both winds and currents. The 19th-century sources (Derrotero general del Mediterráneo 1883) recommended that the route from Argel to Marseille should pass the western side of Menorca or even Mallorca in order to avoid the strong currents of the Gulf of Leon. Additionally, there were also routes that sailed to the south of Sardinia and then to northern Menorca and the Catalan coast. Therefore, in the south to north navigation it was advisable to sail through the Balearic Islands, from which ships could decide the best destination from the Levantine or north-eastern coast of Hispania Tarraconensis or south-eastern Gaul.

In fact, the main ports of the Balearic Islands and some of their shipwrecks provide large quantities and a wide variety of North African amphorae. Marimon (2004) describes the African amphora evidence from the ports of *Pollentia*, Colonia Sant Jordi, and Porto-Pi (*Palma*), concluding that they were regular trading ports on the route from *Africa Proconsularis* to *Hispania Citerior Tarraconensis*. This use of the Balearic ports as stopping points on longer journeys could explain the presence of Baetican, eastern, and Italian amphorae, which reached the Islands from other routes, and appear mixed with African vessels in shipwrecks such as the Cabrera I and III. In the 6th century, two late Roman fortresses were built at Penya de sa Bastida and Alaró castle in Alaró (Serra de Tramuntana) with a significant presence of African pottery.

On the northern coast of Menorca, in the port of Sa Nitja, there is evidence of the presence of Africana II-D amphorae with stamps. One of these stamps was LEPM/BSD, which also appears in *Barcino*, as we have previously indicated. The number of African vessels at this site is considerable (Rita 1994), including amphorae from other origins such as the eastern Mediterranean and Baetica (Marimón 2004: 1060).

While it is true that the surveys carried out so far in the port of Sa Nitja have provided a large quantity of materials from the Roman period, amphorae of African origin in this case (Contreras *et al.* 2013: 119-20), there is no indication that this is the site of one or more wrecks. Instead, the finds seem to point at the continued use of this space as the port of *Sanisera*.

We should not, however, dismiss the significance of this site, because it shows us how long it has been in operation as an anchorage, as well as the periods of greatest and least intensity in its use. Aside from the Aiguablava V site, there are currently no other documented underwater sites along the Catalan coast with cargoes similar to that of Sa Nitja. Even so, the wreck of Aiguablava V is believed to be a vessel that was used to service a redistribution route given that, besides the shipment of African amphorae, it also transported goods from other parts of the Empire. Additionally, there is evidence of isolated finds, both by the CASC[1] and as contributions from individuals.[2] With regard to the Balearic coast, there are more documented underwater sites with African amphorae such as Cap Blanc, Dragonera A, Cabrera I and III (Parker 1992).

Most African workshops producing amphorae and pottery (African Red Slip ware and coarse ware) were located in the Gulf of Hammamet (*Neapolis* – Nabeoul; *Hadrumentum* – Sousse; *Leptis Minor* – Lamta; *Sullecthum* – Salakta), currently eastern Tunisia (Byzacena, Zeugitana). Therefore, African traders sailed from this gulf following the coast and turning west around the Hermaion cape towards the two main harbours of the province: Carthage and Utica. Then, the ships sailing towards the Balearic Islands followed the African coast westwards to Cape Tretum, located between *Thabraca* and *Igilgili*, where they took a north-westerly direction leading them to either Mallorca or Menorca.

---

[1] Centre d'Arqueologia Subaquàtica de Catalunya
[2] Source: CASC database

The advantage of this Balearic route is that sailors did not lose sight of the coast (either African, Balearic, or European) except for a very short time (see Arnaud 2005: 30-31).

With regard to the production region, the recent work by Nacef (2015) illustrates the potential of the North African workshop at Salakta (Sullecthum) with a wide variety of amphorae typologies (Sullecthum series) as well as African Red Slip (ARS) and coarse wares. In addition to this, the local amphorae epigraphy (i.e. ASYL/) reveals the destination of their production towards particular markets. In this case, the stamp ASYL and its variants are documented in Ostia (4 ex.), Rome (15 ex.), Marseille (1 ex.) and the Spanish coast near Alicante (1 ex.).

The stamp LEPMI recorded at *Barcino* and produced at *Leptis Minor* (Lamta), was again directed towards the city of Rome, as revealed by the epigraphy (Ostia: 4 ex.; Rome: 2 ex.; Porto Torres: 1 ex.), as well as other destinations (Cabrera I: 1 ex.; Cabrera III: 1 ex; Sa Nitja: 1 ex.; Mataró: 1 ex.; *Barcino*: 1 ex.) following the Balearic route. Lastly, the stamp TOP – also recorded at *Barcino* – again indicates a preference for the Roman market (Ostia: 14 ex.; Rome: 38 ex.; Gricignano: 1 ex.), although it was also distributed in southern Gaul (Narbonne: 1 ex.; Llupià: 1 ex.; Lussan: 1 ex.), the Balearic Islands (Cabrera I: 1 ex.; Cabrera III: 1 ex.), *Hispania* (Villaricos: 1 ex.; Santa Pola: 1 ex.), and Mauretania (Thamusida: 4 ex.; Banasa: 1 ex.; Volubilis: 1 ex.).

Probably, the arrival of these northern African cargoes was due to a commercial network in different Mediterranean ports, which involved the presence of agents or representatives of African cities or individuals (i.e. *negotiatores*). In the case of *Hispania Citerior Tarraconensis*, three African *negotiatores* (Haley 1991) are documented so far in epigraphic sources. Most people with African *cognomina* in the province lived in *Tarraco* (16 inscriptions) – though most of them had military or administrative careers – and *Barcino* (five inscriptions) – probably with commercial links, of which only *Quintus Ovidius Venusianus* (CIL II.14, 1289) appears to have been born in Africa.

Lastly, once these North African ships reached the ports of *Tarraconensis*, the cargoes could either be consumed in the town and hinterland or redistributed to other ports along the coast through coastal navigation.

3. Aiguablava V: A Shipwreck with a Cargo including North African Amphorae

The final link in this connection between northern Africa and the Catalan coast is a series of shipwrecks with mixed cargoes documented off the north-east coast of Catalonia. One of these examples is the Aiguablava V

shipwreck, which is located in the cove of Aiguablava to the south of Cape Begur in the province of Girona (Figure 13.3). The cove is oriented towards the north-east, being protected to the north by Cape Begur itself, the current port of Fornells and the *Illa Blanca* (White Island), and to the east it is sheltered by the *Punta des Mut*, a raised ledge where the Parador de Aiguablava is currently located. This setting shelters the cove from northern winds, predominant in the area, and reduces its exposure to dangerous eastern storms. Thanks to its location, the cove is ideal for making stopovers on a cabotage route, as well as being a place to stop in the event of adverse weather conditions while crossing the cape or even after passing it on a north-south route. Nevertheless, the cove is completely exposed to north-easterly winds, which could easily surprise a boat anchored there, trapping it with no possibility to exit the cove and even crashing it against the rocks.

The origin of the Aiguablava V ship is not entirely clear. It has been hypothesised that the vessel sailed along a redistribution route, running either from north to south starting at the port of Narbonne or from south to north starting at the port of *Tarraco* or *Barcino*, and made a stop at the cove of Aiguablava where it finally sank. It is likely that such stop at the cove was due to bad weather, or to obtain fresh water from the coast. Therefore, it seems feasible that such a small boat was surprised by an inescapable storm from the north-east that caused her to sink.

The Aiguablava V wreck presents a heterogeneous cargo, indicating that it was a vessel intended for cabotage and redistributive trade, and that it possibly sank while returning to its port of origin. Generally, when ships left a second-order (or third-order) harbour for a first-order one, their cargo was homogeneous, since they came from a specific production area. Therefore, a vessel such as the Aiguablava V would leave a secondary port loaded with a variety of products from its hinterland, heading towards a main port in order to sell the merchandise. As is the case today, the cost of returning with an empty merchant vessel in Roman times was extremely high and not very profitable (Nieto 1989). However, it is still too soon to accept this hypothesis; further, more detailed study of the materials and their chronology is necessary.

The main cargo of the Aiguablava V provides a wide variety of amphorae coming from different origins such as Africa, Baetica, Ebussus, the Aegean, eastern Mediterranean, and Gaul. Such a variety of products suggests that a redistributive port of high order may have been the starting origin of the commercial venture. These containers indicate a rich cargo of wine, salted fish, and olive oil (Mayoral 2016). Furthermore, within the repertoire of African amphorae it is possible to distinguish the following typologies (Figure 13.4):

Figure 13.3. Location of Aiguablava V shipwreck.

Africana 2A (Keay IV and V), 2C (Keay VI), and 3A (Keay XXV variant B and C) (Keay 1984; Bonifay 2004).

The chronology of the Aiguablava V site is still under study. However, currently the evidence seems to point to a date between the 3rd and 4th centuries AD, based on the cargo carried on the boat. This hypothesis is supported by the study of the plan and stratigraphy of the site, where a large quantity of materials with late antique chronology were found in the first layer, whereas the second layer contained less material of an older chronology. However, we must consider several points before reaffirming this hypothesis, such as the fact that the wreck is in a cove which has been continuously used from the Iron Age to present day.

It is also imperative to bear in mind that the site is located in a shallow area (3 to 5 m), and that a wreck is not a closed site and currents can easily move heavy cylindrical/spherical material.

By the time the Aiguablava V sank, the port of *Emporion* had already lost its importance, only *Narbo*, *Tarraco*, or even *Barcino*, which was becoming increasingly relevant, remained as first-rate ports in the area. As for the port of Narbonne, there is evidence of trade during the 3rd and 4th centuries AD; a good example is the case of the Mandirac site discovered by the archaeologists Corinne Sánchez and Marie-Pierre Jézégou. At this site a canal was found, originally built to protect ships entering the port of Narbonne seeking shelter from storms. The

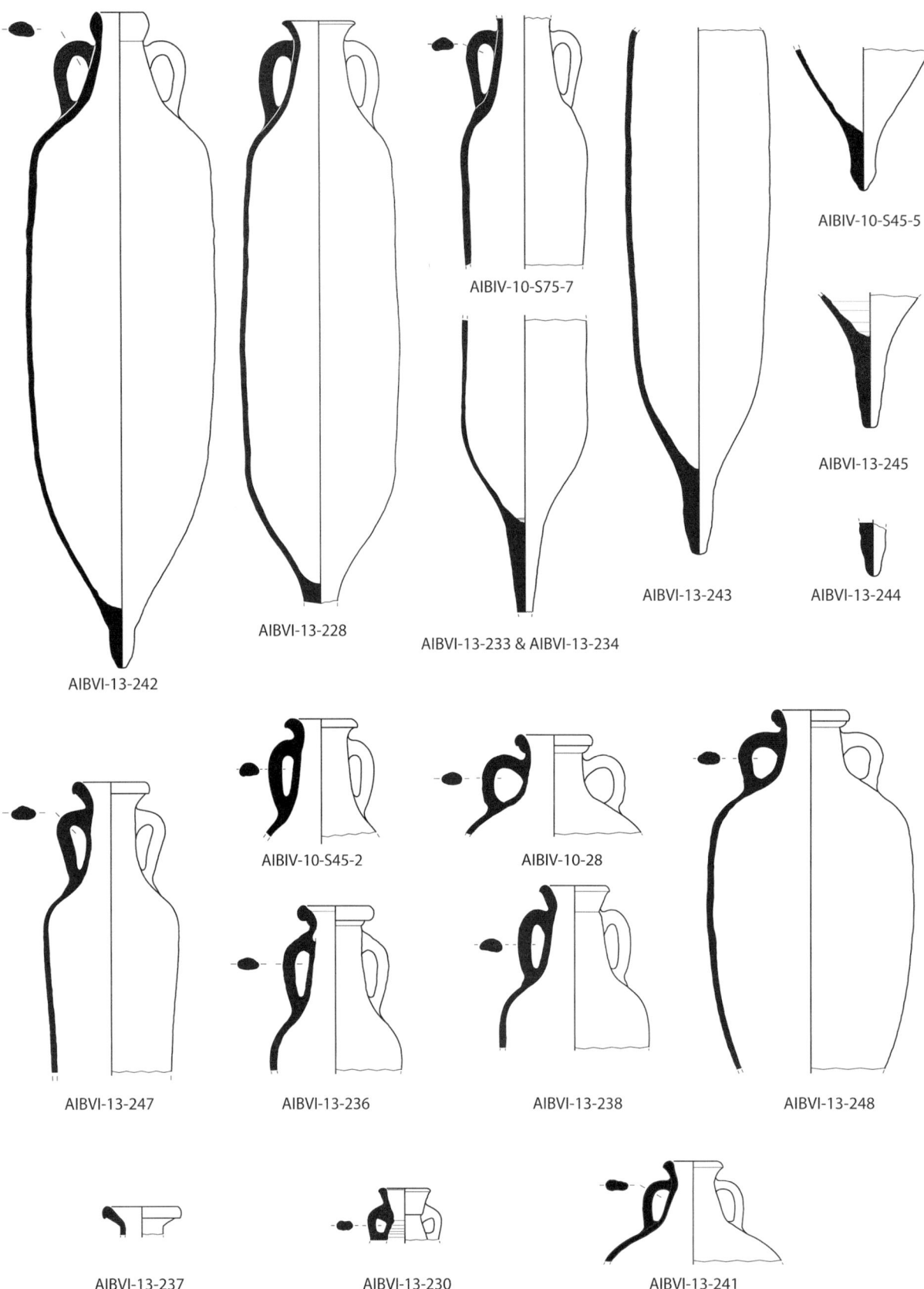

AIBVI-13-242

AIBVI-13-228

AIBVI-13-233 & AIBVI-13-234

AIBIV-10-S75-7

AIBVI-13-243

AIBIV-10-S45-5

AIBVI-13-245

AIBVI-13-244

AIBVI-13-247

AIBIV-10-S45-2

AIBIV-10-28

AIBVI-13-248

AIBVI-13-236

AIBVI-13-238

AIBVI-13-237

AIBVI-13-230

AIBVI-13-241

Figure 13.4. North African amphorae from the Aiguablava V (Africana II-A, II-C, and III-A type).

team excavating the site found a wreck loaded with Lusitanian, Baetican, and African amphorae dating to the 3rd and 4th centuries AD under the foundations of one of the two dikes of the canal (Sánchez and Jézégou 2014). This clearly indicates that, during these centuries, the port of Narbonne continued to be an important first-rate trading point, especially considering the monumental dimensions of the canal. With regard to the port of Tarragona, according to Macias and Remolà (2010), during the second half of the 2nd century AD the city experienced a social crisis. Nevertheless, the port continued to be a space for commercial exchange; new public baths were built on the old site of a large port warehouse, which could imply that the volume of goods had decreased and therefore the former importance of the port was already in decline. Regarding *Barcino*, the remains found in the rescue excavations carried out in the city point towards significant growth, although there is still no evidence for the location of its port and the studies covering this subject are scarce.

4. Final Remarks

We are far from understanding how the commercial circuits between North Africa and north-eastern *Tarraconensis* worked in the late Roman period. However, what the archaeological record clearly reveals is the high dependence of African products (ARS, coarse wares, amphorae) in the coastal towns of the north-east of the Iberian Peninsula. The imported amphora found in *Barcino* are an illustrative example, also employed by S.J. Keay in the mid-80s, to document an important commercial flow between the production centres of the Gulf of Hammamet and the urban centres of the eastern Spanish coast. With the recent developments in our knowledge of the production centres (i.e. particular products) and amphora stamps, reconstructing sailing routes and ports of call has become considerably easier. Some of these routes faced opposing winds and currents and required short stops at ports in the Balearic Islands. In this sense, the Balearic Islands played an important role in the transit between north and south in the late Roman period, as they had previously (i.e. Punic trade, *Tarraconensis* wine). The key Balearic ports have provided North African ceramic assemblages similar to those recorded in the eastern Spanish ports.

Once these North African merchant ships arrived at the destination ports, all their cargo was unloaded there but not all of it was necessarily consumed in the destination town. Underwater archaeology has documented shipwrecks of small vessels loaded with African products together with amphorae and products of other regions that followed coastal routes along the north-east Spanish and south-east Gallic coasts. These small ships completed a redistribution trade between the main ports (i.e. *Tarraco, Barcino, Narbo*) and small coastal towns. We have chosen the Aiguablava

V shipwreck, located in a cove on the Costa Brava, to illustrate this type of watercraft. This shipwreck contained a mixed cargo with products predominantly coming from North Africa, but also amphorae and pottery from other origins such as the Guadalquivir Valley, the island of Ebussus, southern Gaul, the Aegean, and other eastern Mediterranean regions. In light of the above, it is likely that the Aiguablava V vessel departed from either a southern Gallic port such as Narbonne or a north-eastern Spanish port such as *Barcino* to sell their cargo along the coastal route north to south. In conclusion, the partial pieces of evidence available to us reveal an intense commercial traffic between the north and the south of the western Mediterranean, an idea already proposed for the first time by S.J. Keay in his pioneering work in 1984.

Bibliography

Arnaud, P. 2005. *Les routes de la navigation antique: itinéraires en Méditerranée.* Paris: Errance.

Beltrán, J. and C. Carreras 2011. Barcino, in J.A. Remolà and J. Acero (eds) La gestión de los residuos urbanos en Hispania (Añejos del Archivo Español de Arqueología 50): 233-54. Madrid: Consejo superior de investigaciones científicas.

Berni, P. and C. Carreras 2009. Les marques d'àmfores importades o d'altres àrees de la Tarraconense, in C. Carreras and J. Guitart (eds) *Barcino, I: Marques i terrisseries d'àmfores al Pla de Barcelona*: 45-62. Barcelona: Institut d'estudis catalans.

Bonifay, M. 2004. *Études sur la céramique romaine tardive d'Afrique* (British Archaeological Reports, International Series 1301). Oxford: Archaeopress.

Carreras, C. 2012. Circulació amfòrica al port de la Barcino tardoantigua: segles V al VII dC. *Quarhis* 8: 40-54.

Carreras, C. 2021. Nous segells d'àmfora de les excavacions de Barcino (2009-2020). *Faventia* 43: 35-69.

Carreras, C. and P. Berni 2005. Late Roman amphorae in the city of Barcino (Barcelona), in J.M. Gurt, J. Buxeda and M.A. Cau (eds) *LRCW1: Late Roman Coarse Wares, Cooking Wares and Amphorae in the Mediterranean; Archaeology and Archaeometry* (British Archaeological Reports, International Series 1340): 165-78. Oxford: Archaeopress.

Cerdà, J.A., J. García, C. Martí, J. Pujol, J. Pera and V. Revilla 1998. *El cardo maximus de la ciutat romana d'Iluro (Hispania Tarraconensis)* (Laietania 10). Mataró: Museu de Mataro.

Contreras, F., A.J. Talavera and P. Massó 2013. Estudio de las ánforas de la África Bizacena localizadas en el fondo subacuático del puerto de Sa Nitja (Menorca). *V Jornades d'Arqueologia de les Illes Balears*: 119-26.

Guerrero, V.M. 1993. *Navíos y navegantes en las rutas de Baleares durante la Prehistoria.* Palma de Mallorca: El Tall.

Haley, E.W. 1991. *Migration and Economy in Roman Imperial Spain*. Barcelona: Universitat de Barcelona.

Járrega, R. 2005. Los contextos cerámicos tardoantiguos del grupo episcopal de Barcino. *Acta Antiqua Complutensia* 5: 231-52.

Keay, S.J. 1984. *Late Roman Amphorae in the Western Mediterranean: A Typology and Economic Study; The Catalan Evidence* (British Archaeological Reports, International Series 196). Oxford: Archaeopress.

Marimón, P. 2004. Las Insulae Baliares en los circuitos de intercambio africano: la importación de alimentos (123 a.C.-707 d.C.). *L'Africa romana* 15: 1051-76.

Martínez Hahnmüller V. (2016). Una historia del Mediterráneo Occidental. La lucha por el poder en Cartago durante la segunda mitad del siglo III a.C. *Gerión. Revista de Historia Antigua*, 34, 127-144.

Mayoral, J. 2016. Estudio preliminar del pecio Aiguablava v. un barco hundido en la cala de aiguablava en el siglo II d.C., in I. Pinto Coelho, J. Bento Torres, L. Serrão Gil and Tiago Ramos (eds) *Entre ciência e cultura: da interdisciplinaridade à transversalidade da arqueologia; actas das VIII jornadas de jovens em investigação arqueológica* (Colecção ArqueoArte, 4): 429-38. Lisbon: Centro de história d'Aquém e d'Além-Ma.

Nacef, J. 2015. *La production de la céramique antique dans la région de Salakta et Ksour Essef (Tunisie)* (*Roman and Late Antique Mediterranean Pottery 8)*. Oxford: Archaeopress.

Parker, A.J. 1992. *Ancient Shipwrecks of the Mediterranean and the Roman* (British Archaeological Reports, International Series 580). Oxford: Archaeopress.

Peacock, D.P.S., F. Bejaoui and N. Belazreg 1989. Roman amphora production in the Sahel region of Tunisia. *Publications de l'École française de Rome* 114: 179-222.

Quani, M. 2004. Inquadramento geostorico del Mediterraneo occidentale, in L. De Maria and R. Truchetti (eds) *Rotte e porti del Mediterraneo dopo la caduta dell' impero romano d'Occidente: continuità e innovazione tecnologiche e funcionale; Genova, IV Seminario ANSER*: 333-42. Soveria Mannelli: Rubettino.

Ramon, J. 1995. *Las ánforas fenicio-púnicas del Mediterráneo Central y Occidental* (Instrumenta 2). Barcelona: Edicions Universitat de Barcelona.

Remolà, J.A. 2000. *Las ánforas tardo-antiguas en Tarraco (Hispania Tarraconensis)*. Barcelona: Universitat de Barcelona.

Reynolds, P. 1995. *Trade in the Western Mediterranean, AD 400-700: The Ceramic Evidence* (British Archaeological Reports, International Series 604). Oxford: Archaeopress.

Reynolds, P. 2010. *Hispania and the Roman Mediterranean. AD 100-700: Ceramics and Trade*. London: Duckworth.

Rita, MªC. 1994. Ánforas africanas del bajo imperio romano en el yacimiento arqueológico de Sanitja (Menorca), in *III Reunió d'Arqueologia cristiana hispànica, Maó 1988*: 321-32. Barcelona: Institut d'estudis catalans.

Vivar, G. 2013. El derelicte d'Illa Pedrosa. Comerç marítim i xarxes de distribució en època tardorrepublicana al Mediterrani centre-occidental. Unpublished PhD dissertation, Universitat de Barcelona.

Vivar, G. and R. Geli 2015a. *Memòria de l'excavació del derelicte Aiguablava V 2013*. Informe d'excavació inèdit.

Vivar, G. and R. Geli 2015b. *Informe de l'excavació del derelicte Aiguablava V (Begur, Baix Empordà) 2014*. Informe d'excavació inèdit.

Woodworth, M., D. Bernal, M. Bonifay, D. De Vos, N. Garnier, S.J. Keay, A. Pecci, J. Poblome, M. Pollard, F. Richez and A. Wilson 2015. The content of African Keay 25/ Africana 3: initial results of the Coronam Project. *Archaeoanalytics: Chromatography and DNA Analysis in Archaeology*: 41-57. Esposende: Município de Esposende.

14. Simon Keay's Late Roman Amphorae 40 Years Later: An Update on African Amphorae

Michel Bonifay and Claudio Capelli

It is perhaps difficult to imagine today[1] the upheaval represented in 1984 by the publication of Simon Keay's *Late Roman Amphorae in the Western Mediterranean* (Keay 1984, hereafter referred to as *LRAWM*). For all those who, at the beginning of the 1980s, in the context of the development of preventive archaeology, were confronted with massive discoveries of late Roman amphorae, a book suddenly made it possible to name these objects, to have an indication of their provenance and content, and above all to have chronological milestones.

One can certainly draw parallels with John Hayes's *Late Roman Pottery*, published 12 years earlier (Hayes 1972, hereafter referred to as *LRP*). Although the geographical area taken into consideration differed (the whole of the Mediterranean in Hayes's case vs. the Catalan contexts in Keay's), as well as the nature of the documentation (published and unpublished sources in Hayes's case, mostly unpublished data in Keay's case), the aims pursued were substantially similar: constructing typologies and reflecting on the production and distribution of these two different classes of ceramics, in order to tidy up the material culture of late Roman antiquity. The similarity of these two works thus fully justified the correspondence between their two titles, even if in his work Simon Keay paid more attention to economic history, a premise for the evolution of his fields of research until recent years.

Like the *LRP* ('a supplement': Hayes 1980), the *LRAWM* was updated by its author some ten years after its publication (Keay 1998, after a paper presented at the conference in honour of John W. Hayes in 1995). As John Hayes did in 1981, Simon Keay mainly focused on 'advances in chronology and typology' (Keay 1998: 141) and, just like the present one, his paper was exclusively devoted to African amphorae. Finally, Simon Keay's latest contribution to the study of Roman amphorae in 2005 came in the form of the University of Southampton's *Roman Amphorae: A Digital Resource* website, which he initiated with David Williams, giving the floor to a series of specialists in the different classes of Roman amphorae from the whole Mediterranean basin. The aim of this website, one of the first of its kind, was 'to "democratize" amphora studies so that the same range of information could be within reach of all scholars irrespective of country' (Keay and Williams 2005), and make amphorae a powerful tool for research on the economy of the Roman world.

In this short contribution in honour of Simon Keay, taking once again the example of African amphorae, we would like to review the progress made during these almost 40 years in the knowledge of these containers, from the point of view of their typology and chronology, of their origin and content, and finally of their contribution to economic studies.

Simon Keay's African Amphorae

Within the documentation studied by Simon Keay, African amphorae occupy a central position. It is first of all obvious from a quantitative point of view. According to Simon Keay (1984: 392-98), if we put aside the 15 types said of unknown origin, the *LRAWM*'s 93 types are divided into three production areas: the Iberian Peninsula (*Baetica, Lusitania, Tarraconensis*) with 12 types, the eastern Mediterranean with eight types, and Africa (*Mauretania caesariensis, Africa proconsularis,* and *Tripolitania*) with no less than 58 types. This proportion could be explained by the nature of the contexts studied by Simon Keay, mainly large late antique burial cemeteries, the large cylindrical African amphorae being particularly well suited to their reuse as sarcophagi.

Second, most of the Hispanic types classified by Simon Keay were already known in other typologies since the 1950s (Almagro 1955; Beltran 1970: both typologies still used today alongside Keay's), while the eastern Mediterranean amphorae had just been catalogued in the late 1970s and early 1980s by John Riley from the material of Benghazi and then Carthage (Riley 1979 and 1981, both typologies used today in preference to Keay's). On the contrary, the classifications of African amphorae in Spain were less satisfactory and the progress made in Carthage on the knowledge of African ceramics had not yet been fully extended to amphorae. In 1984, the most up-to-date typologies of African amphorae were due to Clementina Panella and Daniele Manacorda, based on the stratigraphy of Ostia, which

---

[1] Paper written in 2022.

Keay Type	Keay Figure	Other Name	suggested Origin	suggested Content	suggested Date
3B sim.	39.4-5	-	Algeria?	Oil?	c. 400-500
3/5	42.4	-	Nabeul	Oil?	c. 400-500
27	26.1	-	Northern Tunisia	Oil?	c. 400-500
36	29.4	-	Northern Tunisia	Oil, wine?	c. 400-500
35A	98.2, 4	-	Nabeul	Oil?	c. 400-500
35B/85	101.1/174.1	-	Nabeul	Salted fish?	c. 400-500
39	107.1	-	Nabeul	Oil?	c. 400-500
40	108.1	-	Northern Tunisia	Oil, wine?	c. 400-500
41	109.1	-	Northern Tunisia	Oil, wine?	c. 400-500
57	128.11	-	Nabeul	Salted fish?	c. 450-500
56	127.3-4	-	Nabeul	Salted fish, wine?	c. 475-530+
55	125.1-3	-	Nabeul	Salted fish, wine?	c. 500-550+
64	164.2	-	Nabeul	?	c. 450-500
59/8B	130.7/48.1-2	-	Southern Byzacena	Oil?	c. 400-550
(11B)	172.2	Malaval 29	Southern Byzacena	?	c. 450-500
11C	174.7	-	Tripolitania?	Oil?	c. 450-500
34	98.1	-	Southern Byzacena	?	500-700
62Q	155.12	Albenga 11-12	Nabeul?/Byzacena?	Oil?	c. 450-500+
62R	156.1	-	Northern Tunisia	?	c. 450-500+
62A/B	135.2/144.4	-	Nabeul/Byzacena	Oil?	500-550+
62D	145.14	-	Byzacena	?	500-550+
62E	147.8	-	Byzacena	?	550-600
61A/D	132.2/133.10	-	Byzacena	?	575-700
61C	133.8	-	Byzacena	Oil?	575-650
(92)	48.7	Bonifay 47	Byzacena	?	575-650
8A	47.3-4	-	Byzacena	?	650-700+
50?	115.1	-	Byzacena?	?	650-700+

Figure 14.1. Simon Keay's main late African amphora types and updates (M. Bonifay and C. Capelli).

did not go beyond the beginning of the 5th century (Panella 1973; Manacorda 1977).

This is why Simon Keay's contribution on African amphorae, 'extending the typology [well] into the 6th century' (Keay 1998: 141), was so fundamental.

Typology and Chronology

First of all, it must be said that Simon Keay's typology of African amphorae proved to be particularly effective, which explains why it was immediately adopted by researchers and remains a solid reference today. However, as a result of an approach developed particularly from the late 1990s, the cross-referencing of typological and petrographic data, workshop surveys and the observation of the distribution of types on the African territory, as well as the multiplication of discoveries in well-dated contexts, made it possible to refine the classification carried out in 1984 on the basis of the Catalan documentation and to continue the

chronological adjustments initiated by Simon Keay in 1998.

Retaining the main types and following the numbering adopted by Simon Keay (we follow the solution adopted by himself in his 1998 article by changing the Roman numerals to Arabic ones), it is possible, in the present state of research, to make the following observations (Figures 14.1 and 14.2):

Types **1A** and **1B** must be clearly distinguished. Type 1A, still preferably called 'Dressel 30', whose production in Africa is now known to be spread over a wide area, not only in *Mauretania caesariensis* in the cities of *Tubusuctu* and *Saldae* (according to the stamps) but also in *Africa proconsularis* at Nabeul and Salakta (according to workshop finds and petrography), must be distinguished from the Keay Type **1B** (current name) whose petrography is different, even though it is probably of Algerian origin (no known workshops) (Capelli and Bonifay 2007: 554-55). While the first type

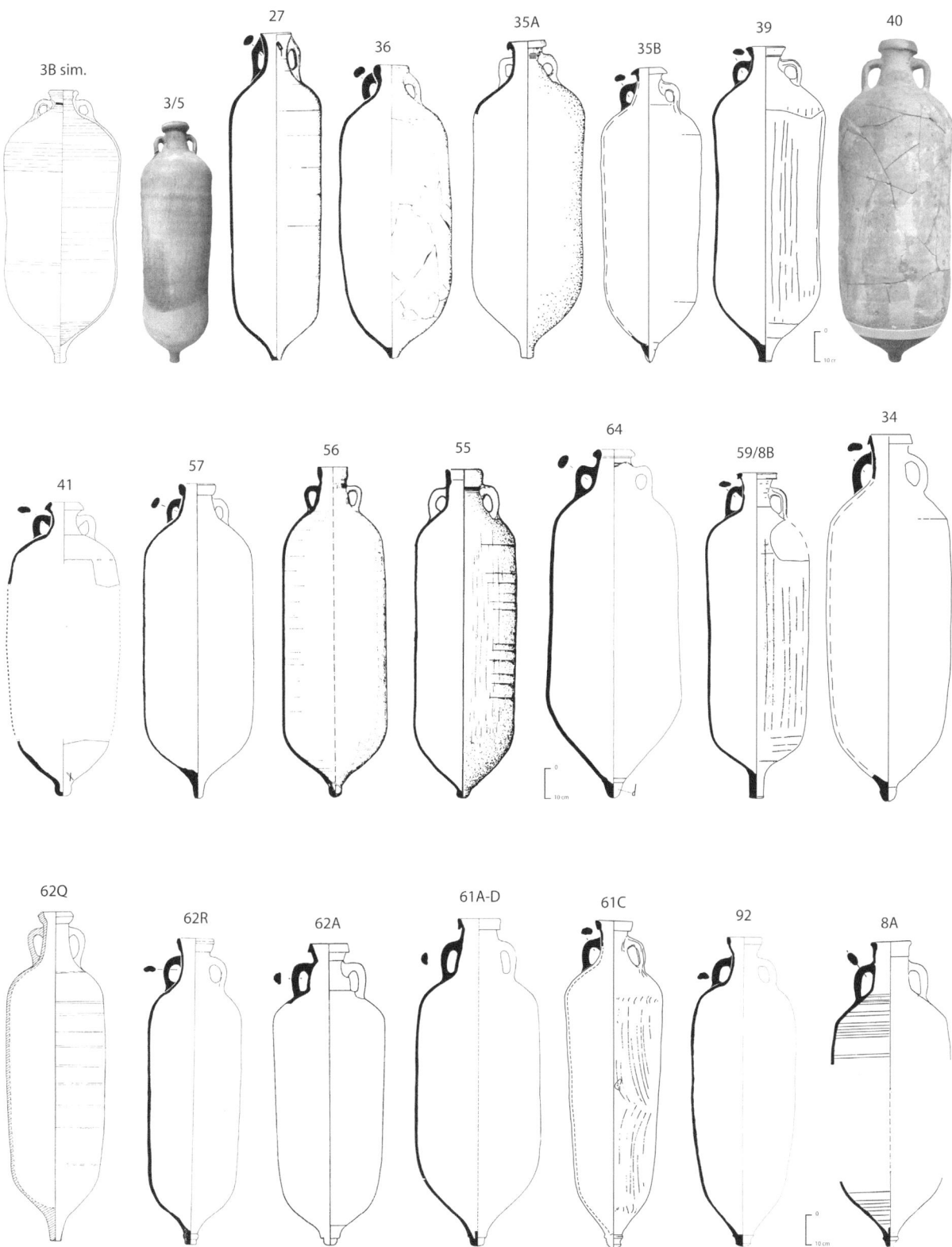

Figure 14.2. Simon Keay's main late African amphora types (credit for illustrations: Albore Livadie 1984 (62A); Aoyagi 1994 (3B sim.); Freed 1995 (62R); Keay 1984 (27, 35A); Liou 1975 (61A-D); Murialdo 1988 (8A); Opaiţ 1997-98 (35A, 55, 56); Pallarès 1987 (62Q); Remolà Vallverdú 2000 (41); Sciallano and Sibella 1991 (57); Wilson 1996 (64); M. Bonifay (other illustrations)).

is attributable to the 3rd century, the second is clearly a largely 4th-century production.

Simon Keay's renumbering of Panella's Africana I, II A, B, C, and D into his Types **3**, **4**, **5**, **6**, and **7** did not add much to our knowledge of these types. It is today even questionable whether some fragments are not related to other types. If some fragments are clearly classical productions, well attested from the workshops of Salakta (Africana I: *LRAWM* fig. 38.1 and 2) and Nabeul (Africana II C: *LRAWM* fig. 45.1), others are more problematic, either because they could belong to already known similar types (*LRAWM* fig. 37.8: type Ostia XXIII?), or because they could come from other unknown workshops (perhaps in regions not yet prospected, for example in Algeria), or because they are new types in the process of being defined. Among the latter is the Type **3B similis** (*LRAWM* fig. 39.4-5 and fig. 107.3), which turns out to be a completely separate type from the Africana I family, of late date (5th century) and possibly of Algerian origin (Bonifay 2004: 129; Bonifay and Capelli 2016). This is also the case for Type **3/5**, which we have recently proposed to link to an amphora produced at Nabeul in the 5th century (Bonifay 2016: 603-04), even if the body of the latter seems to be of a smaller diameter than that illustrated by Simon Keay (*LRAWM* fig. 42.4). In general terms, some of the fragments classified by Simon Keay as Africana I and II may in fact correspond to large late African amphorae, a hypothesis more consistent with the dating of the contexts he studied.

Types **8A** and **8B** pose the double problem of their formal similarity with each other and with the last variant of the previous types. The wide banded rim could indeed lead one to associate Type **8A** with Africana II D (Type 7). Since the work by Giovanni Murialdo (1988), it is known that this amphora is undoubtedly one of the latest of the African production, datable to the second half of the 7th century and the beginning of the 8th century (Bonifay 2019: 302). On the other hand, the petrography and the distribution of the two types on the African territory and within the stratigraphies allowed us to distinguish them both from the point of view of their origin and their chronology. While the production of Type **8A** is now well attested in the Tunisian Sahel (Nacef 2017), that of Type **8B** is to be sought in southern Byzacena, in the hinterland of *Iunca* (Majoura and Meknassi workshops: Nasr and Capelli 2018 and Ben Moussa 2017) but not in *Iunca* itself, contrary to the initial hypotheses, this city being rather the exporting port of these amphorae. The chronology of the latter is also different. It is now assumed that Types **59** and **8B** are grouped together, the former representing an early variant of the latter, between the beginning of the 5th century and the mid-6th century (Bonifay 2004: 132).

Tripolitanian amphorae are classified by Simon Keay in his Types **9** (classical Tripolitana II), **10** (late Tripolitana II), and **11** (Tripolitana III). The fragments attributed to the latter type are, however, not always convincing (the fragments in *LRAWM* fig. 51, except nos 2-4, do not seem to be Tripolitanian). Also noteworthy is Type *LRAWM* **fig. 50.2** (Type 11A), which corresponds to a (non-Tripolitanian) type attested in Rome, Marseilles, Alexandria, etc., datable to the 5th century (Bonifay *et al.* 2017: 848), and the Type *LRAWM* **fig. 172.2**, which may have originated in almost the same regions as Type 8B and can also be dated to the second half of the 5th or beginning of the 6th century. On the other hand, the fragment *LRAWM* **fig. 174.7** (Type **11C**), now known from almost complete examples in Marseille (Bonifay *et al.* 2011: figs 11 and 12.29), may well belong to a late Tripolitanian production of the 5th century.

Type **25**, corresponding to the medium-sized cylindrical amphorae identified at Ostia by Daniele Manacorda (1977), is undoubtedly one of the key types in Simon Keay's classification. No less than 29 variants (A to Z4) of this type have been distinguished in the *LRAWM*, grouped into seven subtypes, of which the first three are enough to gather the bulk of the documentation. In 2004, one of us proposed a new designation (Bonifay 2004: 119-22): Africana III A (= Type **25.1**), B (= Type **25.3**), and C (= Type **25.2**) in a chronological classification that may not be relevant in practice, as Type 25.2 appears to be the successor of Type 25.1, even if Type 25.3 is chronologically intermediate between the first two types. In this respect, one can quite easily identify some early variants of Type 25.1 (*LRAWM* fig. 77.3-10), some late variants of Type 25.2 (*LRAWM* fig. 77.3-10), and the most characteristic example of Type 25.3 (*LRAWM* fig. 77.4), all of them probably coming from the Nabeul workshops. But in general terms, it must be admitted that the grouping of the different fragments which enabled Simon Keay to constitute his variants is not always convincing. In fact, there is great heterogeneity in the profile of the rims and sometimes even in the morphology of the body and bottom of these amphorae, so that the classification of newly exhumed fragments often remains rather difficult as soon as one moves away from the main variants. Such heterogeneity is probably explained by the vastness of the production areas of these amphorae which, in the 4th century, seem to have been produced everywhere in Africa, from *Mauritania Caesariensis* to *Tripolitania*. It should not be forgotten either that these amphorae were imitated in Spain, as the study of the Mazarron workshops has shown (Berrocal Caparrós 2012). Undoubtedly, the entire Catalan documentation on these amphorae studied by Simon Keay would deserve to be revised by comparing typological and archaeometric (petrographic and chemical) data.

Obviously, Keay's proposed Type **26** designation failed to replace the name traditionally given to small cylindrical African amphorae, known as 'spatheia'. The distinction of these containers from the later variants of Type 25.2, based on dimensions, is sometimes rather theoretical. These are in fact the same types of amphorae, declined in different dimensions, probably with the aim, from the 5th century onwards, of optimising ship cargoes in a changing economic context. Most of the sherds classified by Simon Keay are classic examples of the 5th century (*spatheion* 1: LRAWM fig. 90.10-17; *spatheion* 2: LRAWM fig. 91.7), while the *spatheion* 3 of the 7th century (probably without any typological link with the previous ones) seem to be absent. Some fragments are probably of Hispanic production (Type **26C**).

From Type **27** onwards, we enter the heart of Simon Keay's African classification, with the identification of types that remained unknown until 1984. The work carried out over the last 40 years has made it possible to validate the main lines of this classification, to propose new groupings or differentiations, to correct certain dates, and to specify the production areas.

Thus, the cross-referencing of typological and petrographic data has made it possible to propose the grouping of Types **27** and **36**, which clearly came from the same workshops in the 5th century and may have originated in the lower valley of the Mejerda (?) (Bonifay and Capelli 2023). On the other hand, Simon Keay was right to distinguish between Types **40** and **41** because, although their morphology is similar, petrography clearly distinguishes their production, also characteristic of the 5th century (Capelli and Bonifay 2014). Finally, the recently published research on Rougga has made it possible to locate the production of Type **34** (note that only LRAWM fig. 98.1 is consistent with this type) in southern Byzacena and to move its dating to the 6th-7th centuries (Bonifay 2004: 143). But the main contribution of Simon Keay's work concerns a large series of amphorae that research carried out in Tunisia from the 1990s onwards has allowed to be attributed to the workshops of Nabeul. This is the case of Types **35** (/**85**), **39**, **55**, **56**, **57**, and **64**. The discovery in 1996 of the Sidi Zahruni workshop, followed by the prospection by a Tunisian team of about ten other workshops on the territory of the ancient *Neapolis* (Mrabet and Ben Moussa 2007), to which was added the contribution of petrography (Bonifay *et al.* 2010), allow us to have a clear picture of the production of amphorae in this city during the Vandal period, in the 5th century and in the first third of the 6th century.

Types **62** and **61** (the former preceding the latter in chronology), emblematic types of Simon Keay's work and of which the Catalan documentation had provided a hitherto unparalleled quantity of specimens, quickly gave rise to various revisions. Even though it seemed imprudent in the early 1980s to date these two types beyond the central decades of the 6th century (Keay 1984: 309 and 350), it became clear ten years later that the beginning of the production of Type 62 was not earlier than the beginning of that century, while the later variants of Type 61 extended well into the 7th century (Keay 1998: 147-48). On the other hand, distinctions were made in the Type **62** typology (Bonifay 2016: 605). It was thus proposed to partially remove from Type 62 the **variant Q**, similar to amphorae nos 11 and 12 from the dome of the Albenga baptistery and datable to the end of the 5th century, as well as the **variant R**, which was probably contemporaneous with these. On the other hand, minute typological peculiarities in the shape of the rim, combined with petrographic data, have made it possible to distinguish, within **variant A**, the examples produced in Nabeul and those produced in the workshops of the Tunisian Sahel, while the **variant D**, with an internal step, seemed to be characteristic of the latter workshops. Lastly, the **variant E** was considered as belonging to a later period of production. Considering Type **61**, it appeared that the great mass of specimens of **variants A and D** originated from workshops in the Moknine region and were not earlier than the 7th century. On the other hand, **variant C** as well as an amphora identified in Marseille (Bonifay 2004: type 47), but which could perhaps be linked to the small fragments classified under Type **92**, could be attributed with certainty to the workshop of Henchir Chekaf, near Salakta (Capelli and Bonifay 2016: 547).

Finally, research carried out in the 1990s in Rome, Sant'Antonino di Perti, and Marseille brought to light types that were little or not represented in the documentation studied by Simon Keay: late miniature *spatheia* (already mentioned above), globular amphorae with umbilical bottom (Castrum Perti type: Murialdo 2001), amphorae 'con orlo a fascia' (Saguì 1998: 315 and fig. 8.1) and/or amphorae with a wide flared band, close to Type **8A** and (perhaps erroneously?) assimilated to Type **50** (Bonifay 2004: 141-43). The dating of all these types is still open to question, but they probably indicate the continued production of African amphorae even though some territories had already come under Umayyad rule.

Apart from these very late types, few new major types have been added in the last 40 years to Simon Keay's original typology for African amphorae of the 5th century and beyond. On the other hand, some of the types classified by Simon Keay as African production within the Catalan documentation have not, or hardly, been reported in publications from other regions. This is the case of types represented in *LRAWM* by a single specimen (Types **29**, **44**, **46**, **60**, **90**), or of a morphology too generic to ensure identification (Types **30**, **31**, **32**,

89), or even too poorly defined (Types **33**, **37**, **42**, **43**, **45**, **63**, **75**, **77**). It will be necessary to be attentive to the attributions that could in the future be made to these types. Finally, some types also classified as African in the *LRAWM* were found to come from other production regions: the Iberian Peninsula (Type **21**), Ibiza (Types **24** and **79**), or Sicily (Type **81**), while some others remain dubious (Types **28**, **51**, **58**, **71**, **78**, and **84**).

Origin and Contents

Following the 'north European tradition' (Keay 1984: 446), Simon Keay paid close attention to the description of the fabrics of the amphorae he studied. Eight fabrics, divided into two groups, were attributed to Africa on the basis of observations carried out with an ×8 hand lens. Unfortunately, it was not possible to make thin sections.

However, 1984 was also the year in which volume 1 of the British excavations at Carthage was published, under the direction of Michael Fulford and David Peacock, with an important chapter by the latter on the petrography of ceramics, in particular of African production (Peacock 1984). This study represented a considerable advance for the study of African amphorae, but a mistake was to think that this classification of fabrics could be extended to all African productions, whereas it was only valid for the site of Carthage. Indeed, African productions are difficult to distinguish from one another, both from the petrographic and chemical points of view, being rather homogeneous even for geographically very distant areas. This situation can be explained by the low geological and sedimentological variability of the North African regions where almost only sedimentary rocks and aeolian deposits are found, while metamorphic and volcanic rocks are very rare. It follows that the inclusions are mainly composed of quartz grains which clearly show an aeolian origin because of their rounded shape, their high sphericity, and their micro pitted and matt surface (Capelli and Bonifay 2007).

As far as the amphorae are concerned, the real progress came from the implementation, from 1998 onwards (Capelli 2002-03; Capelli and Bonifay 2007; 2014; 2016; 2023), of an integrated archaeological and archaeometric analytical method allowing the typology to be cross-referenced with thin section observations in search of the mineralogical and petrographic characteristics of the fabrics (identification of the components associated with quartz, percentage, degree of sorting and sphericity of quartz and other inclusions, composition of the matrix, other technological characteristics, etc.). Above all, it was necessary to temporarily give up analysing African amphorae from Mediterranean consumer sites, in order to concentrate on the few workshop references that were available to

us at the end of the 1990s, and then to look for others by collaborating in the surveys carried out by Tunisian or international teams working in North Africa.

More than 50 amphora workshops were thus characterised from the double point of view of typology and petrography, mostly located in Tunisia but also in Libya (Figure 14.3). The best-referenced areas are those of Nabeul (nine workshops: Bonifay *et al.* 2010) and Salakta (nine workshops: Nacef 2015) in Tunisia, and the Tarhuna Plateau in Libya (Ahmed 2019: 15 workshops; Alhaddad *et al.* 2023). Other production areas, although not yet located in the field, have been highlighted by the typological and petrographic homogeneity of certain types (Keay Types 27 and 36, 34, 59, and 8B, etc.).

This long-term work, which in fact cannot hope to have an end, has made it possible to gradually complete a large petrographic and typological database on the areas of production of African ceramics, especially amphorae, and to start testing these results on consumption sites outside Africa. A large-scale test was carried out in 2008-09 on the entire Sicilian territory, with the analysis of more than 500 samples in thin sections other than several thousand by a ×10 hand lens (Malfitana and Bonifay 2016). Last but not least, another archaeometric approach has recently been implemented through the use of portable XRF, a mobile, relatively cheap, and non-destructive archaeometric technique, which gives encouraging results.

In terms of contents, however, Simon Keay's view in 1984 was still very much influenced by the discourse of the 'Italian school' of the 1970s on the development of olive growing as a driving force in the economy of Roman Africa. The example of Type 25 is quite revealing. Even though pitched specimens or specimens containing olive stones or shellfish remains were mentioned, the conclusion remained the same: 'given the importance of olive oil in the African economy at this time, it is probable that the majority of these [amphorae] probably contained olive oil' (Keay 1984: 193).

The questioning of oil as the main content of African amphorae, initiated by Robert Lequément at the end of the 1970s, was largely confirmed during the 1990s by systematic investigations carried out on complete specimens in the DRASSM warehouses in Marseille (Bonifay 2007). The evidence of visually visible traces of internal pitch coatings made an oleaginous content unlikely for many amphora series (Garnier *et al.* 2011). Subsequently, mass spectrometry analyses identified other types of content, notably animal fats (salted fish?) and wine. Thus, while it seems clear that the African I (Keay Type 3) and Tripolitana I and III amphorae were intended for the transport of oil, many other types, including Keay 25 amphorae, were mostly devoted

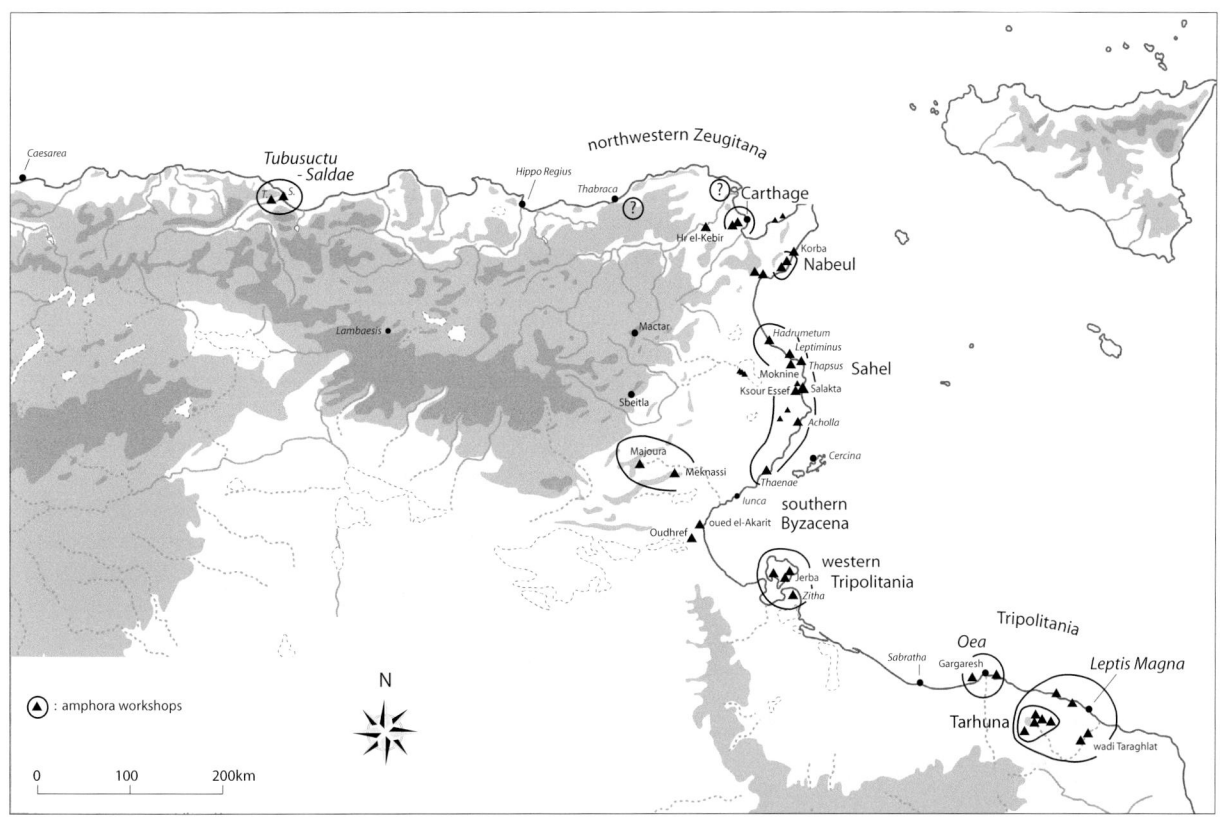

Figure 14.3. Main Roman African amphora workshops (M. Bonifay).

to other contents. Generally speaking, the contents of African amphorae may have been very varied and changed over time (Bonifay 2021).

The Circulation of Late Antique African Amphorae in the Western Mediterranean

Simon Keay's work in classifying and naming late African amphorae in 1984 and the chronological adjustments he proposed in 1998 have made these containers a particularly powerful tool for studying the late antique economy. In addition to Simon Keay (1998: 149-53), several authors have investigated the fluctuating circulation of African amphorae in the 5th-7th centuries and in the western Mediterranean basin, in the context of the geopolitical changes undergone in Africa (Vandal, Byzantine, and Arab conquests) (Panella 1993; Reynolds 1995 and 2010; Bonifay 2003).

While all of these authors agree that the 5th century was a turning point in the spread of African foodstuffs (this is also true for tableware), opinions differ on the precise moment. According to Clementina Panella, the decrease in the arrival of African amphorae did not occur, at least in Rome, before the end of the 5th century, at the beginning of the second Vandal period from AD 475 onwards, while Paul Reynolds sees a change in the middle of the 5th century linked to the end of the

annona system of supply between Africa and Rome. For our part, after having supported the latter hypothesis for a time (Bonifay 2003), we are leaning more towards a break at the very beginning of the 5th century, linked to a crisis in demand in Rome and perhaps in other major consumer centres, or even as early as the end of the 4th century, which the social unrest in Africa from the 360s onwards, more or less instrumentalised by fanatical religious groups, may have announced.

Finally, in line with Simon Keay's vision of Spain's relations with the Mediterranean world on the eve of the Visigothic conquest (Keay 1988: 202 sq.), this date would correspond to the appearance of the family of large cylindrical amphorae (Types 27/36, 59/8B, 35, 40, 41 etc.), with capacities of more than 60 litres, replacing the Type 25 amphorae, which generally contained around 27 litres. Such a change in the way African foodstuffs were packaged must undoubtedly be explained by a change in the way they were transported to the various cities of Spain, Gaul, and Italy, whether or not the latter had already passed under the domination of 'barbarian' kingdoms. In the end, one may wonder whether the key to this change does not lie in the progressive (or brutal?) weakening of Portus, in the first half of the 5th century, as a hub of commercial relations in the western Mediterranean basin. This is what the study of African amphorae from this site, carried out by Pina Franco in the framework of a doctoral thesis directed by Simon Keay (Franco 2012), tends to show, with only 2% of Types 27, 35, 36, 39, and 3B similis, for 30% of Type 25 amphorae and 52% of African I, II, and Tripolitanian amphorae (Franco 2020: fig. 1). The need to bypass Rome in order to supply the cities could have generated more direct maritime connections and the optimisation of cargoes by using large cylindrical amphorae, and *spatheia* as space fillers.

In sum, what the appearance of this family of large African containers in the 5th century could demonstrate, whose classification constitutes the essential contribution of Simon Keay's 1984 work, is the solidity of the networks of traders responsible for meeting the demand of the cities. The latter proved capable of inventing alternative solutions as soon as an obstacle to their mission – consisting of 'transporting what was lacking' (Tchernia 2011: 157-72) – arose, perhaps at the cost of turning to landowners and their (?) amphora producers in order to obtain from them the necessary new packaging. Even if the typological diversity of those amphorae tends to show that the traders had to diversify their supplies, the Nabeul region seemed to dominate the production of containers while the workshops of the Tunisian Sahel seem to completely stop.

What happened afterwards is not clear and also depends on the date assigned to the appearance of the last family of African amphorae represented by Types 62 and 61. In our view, Type 62, which illustrates a last attempt to standardise African containers, seems to appear at the very beginning of the 6th century, i.e. without any link with the Byzantine conquest, but concomitant with the increase in the arrival of eastern amphorae in Africa, the commercial influence perhaps preceding the military conquest. Produced in several workshop areas including Nabeul, Type 62 also marks the revival of workshops in the Tunisian Sahel, notably in the hinterland of Salakta. From the end of the 6th century and throughout the 7th century, this region of production was dominant, with large workshop concentrations at Ksour Essaf and Moknine, producing several variants of Type 61 as well as the umbilical-bottomed amphorae of the Castrum Perti type (Nacef, Capelli 2017). These amphorae were distributed in several parts of the Mediterranean basin, not only to sites belonging to the Byzantine Empire (Cartagena, Koper) but also to cities under Visigothic or Frankish rule (Tarragona, Marseille).

In his paper of 1998, Simon Keay wrote that 'it would be interesting to discover the location of the production area' of those latest African types, 'if, as the historical sources suggest, Byzacena was lost to the Arabs in A.D. 674' (Keay 1998: 149). The cross-referencing of typological and archaeometric analyses, as well as workshop surveys and excavations, allowed us to confirm that these types originate mainly from workshops in the already Umayyad Tunisian Sahel, which exported their production to the western Mediterranean until the end of the 7th century (Rome, Marseille, Tarragona), and even, in the case of Type 8A, in the first quarter of the 8th century.

Conclusion

Unquestionably, Simon Keay's 1984 classification and its chronological update in 1998 have broken the cognitive barrier that prevented us from appreciating the diffusion of liquid or semi-liquid African foodstuffs (oil, salted fish, and wine) beyond the early 5th century. Even if the exact contents of these containers are not yet known with precision, the progress of research over the last 40 years, better structuring the typologies, has made it possible to specify the origin of the containers present on the consumer sites and to trace the fluctuations of their arrival over time.

Evolving from pioneering work on the basis of Catalan documentation into a universally applicable tool, this classification was necessary for Simon Keay to embrace broader questions of Roman economy and port interconnectivity, as demonstrated in his recent ERC PortusLimen project (2014-19). But, by an irony to which history has accustomed us, the amphorae of which Simon Keay proved to be the real inventor, the African amphorae of the 5th-7th centuries, are precisely those that were missing in whole or in part in the Portus stratigraphy. However, their absence from the infrastructure of the imperial port of Rome, contrasting with their presence in the city of Rome itself and in many cities of the western Mediterranean, paradoxically helped us to better understand the networks of African foodstuffs in the classic Roman period (Bonifay and Tchernia 2012), and the role of Portus in the redistribution of these goods in the western Mediterranean before the 'disruption' of the early 5th century (Keay 2012: 19 and n. 71).

Bibliography

Ahmed, M.A.M. 2019. *Rural Settlement and Economic Activity: Olive Oil and Amphorae Production on the Tarhuna Plateau during the Roman Period* (Open Access Monograph 1). London: Society for Libyan Studies.

Alhaddad, M., M. Bonifay, C. Capelli, J. Doret† and E. Jerray 2023. Preliminary archaeological and archaeometrical characterisation of Roman pottery workshops on the Tarhuna Plateau (Libya). *Libya antiqua* 16: 35-68.

Albore Livadie, C. 1984. Relitto Porto A di età tardoimperiale, in *Archeologia subacquea*, II: *Isole Eolie*

(Bollettino d'arte, Supplemento 29): 95-97. Rome: Istituto poligrafico e zecca dello stato.

Almagro, M. 1955. *Las necrópolis de Ampurias*, II: *Necrópolis romanas y necrópolis indígenas* (Monografías ampuritanas 3). Barcelona: Museo Arqueológico.

Aoyagi, M. 1994. *The Roman Site of Cazzanello (Tarquinia): Archaeological Research; Preliminary Report, 2* (Annual Report of the Institute for the Study of Cultural Exchange 10). Tokyo: University of Tokyo (in Japanese).

Beltrán Lloris, M. 1970. *Las ánforas romanas en España* (Anejos de Caesaraugusta. Monografías arqueológicas 8). Zaragoza: Deputacion provincial.

Ben Moussa, M. 2017. Nouvelles découvertes d'ateliers de céramique antique en Tunisie, in A. Mrabet (ed.) *Le peuplement du Maghreb antique et médiéval*: 165-76. Sousse: Université de Sousse.

Berrocal Caparrós, M.d. C. 2012. Producciones anfóricas en la costa meridional de Carthago-Spartaria, in D. Bernal-Casasola and A. Ribera i Lacomba (ed.) *Cerámicas hispanorromanas*, II: *Producciones regionales*: 255-78. Cadiz: Universidad de Cádiz.

Bonifay, M. 2003. La céramique africaine, un indice du développement économique ? *Antiquité Tardive* 11: 113-28.

Bonifay, M. 2004. *Études sur la céramique romaine tardive d'Afrique* (British Archaeological Reports, International Series 1301). Oxford: Archaeopress.

Bonifay, M. 2007. Que transportaient donc les amphores africaines ?, in E. Papi (ed.) *Supplying Rome and the Empire* (Journal of Roman Archaeology Supplement 69): 8-32. Portsmouth (RI): Journal of Roman Archaeology.

Bonifay, M. 2016. Amphores de l'Afrique romaine : nouvelles avancées sur la production, la typo-chronologie et le contenu, in R. Járrega and P. Berni (eds) *Amphorae ex Hispania: Paisajes de producción y consumo, III Congreso internacional de la SECAH - ex officina hispana (Tarragona, 10-13 de diciembre de 2014)* (Monografías Ex Officina Hispana 3): 595-611. Tarragona: Institut català d'arqueologia clàssica.

Bonifay, M. 2019. Marqueurs céramiques de l'Afrique byzantine tardive, in R. Bockman, A. Leone and Philipp von Rummel (eds) *Africa-Ifrīqiya: Continuity and Change in North Africa from the Byzantine to the Early Islamic Age; Papers of a Conference Held in Rome 28 February-2 March 2013* (Palilia 34): 295-313. Rome: Deutsches Archäologisches Institut Rom.

Bonifay, M. and C. Capelli 2016. Recherches sur l'origine des cargaisons africaines des épaves du littoral français (II) : Port-Vendres 1 et Pointe de la Luque B, in D. Djaoui (ed.) *Histoires matérielles: terre cuite, bois, métal et autres objets; des pots et des potes; mélanges offerts à Lucien Rivet* (Archéologie et histoire romaine 33): 537-50. Montagnac: Éditions Monique Mergoil.

Bonifay, M., C. Capelli, A. Drine and T. Ghalia 2010. Les productions d'amphores romaines sur le littoral tunisien: archéologie et archéométrie. *Rei Cretariae Romanae Fautorum Acta* 41: 319-27.

Bonifay, M., C. Capelli and M. Moliner 2011. Les amphores africaines de la basilique de la rue Malaval à Marseille (Ve siècle), in *SFECAG: Actes du congrès d'Arles*: 235-54. Marseille: SFECAG.

Bonifay, M., C. Capelli and K. Şenol 2017. Amphores africaines tardives à Alexandrie : archéologie et archéométrie, in D. Dixneuf (ed.) *LRCW 5: Late Roman Coarse Wares, Cooking Wares and Amphorae in the Mediterranean; Archaeology and Archaeometry* (Études alexandrines 43): 845-58. Alexandria: Centre d'études alexandrines.

Bonifay, M. and A. Tchernia 2012. Les réseaux de la céramique africaine (Ier - Ve s.), in S.J. Keay (ed.) *Rome, Portus and the Mediterranean* (Archaeological Monographs 21): 315-36. London: The British School at Rome.

Capelli, C. 2002-2003. Ricerche petrografiche preliminari sulle ceramiche 'eoliche', in M. Bonifay, C. Capelli, T. Martin, M. Picon and L. Vallaury, Le littoral de la Tunisie: Étude géoarchéologique et historique (1987-1997): la céramique. *Antiquités Africaines* 38-39 [2005]: 178-83.

Capelli, C. and M. Bonifay 2007. Archéométrie et archéologie des céramiques africaines : une approche pluridisciplinaire, in M. Bonifay and J.-C. Tréglia (eds) *LRCW 2: Late Roman Coarse Wares, Cooking Wares and Amphorae in the Mediterranean; Archaeology and Archaeometry* (British Archaeological Reports International Series 1662): 551-67. Oxford: Archaeopress.

Capelli, C. and M. Bonifay 2014. Archéométrie et archéologie des céramiques africaines : une approche pluridisciplinaire, 2. Nouvelles données sur la céramique culinaire et les amphores, in N. Poulou-Papadimitriou, E. Nodarou and V. Kilikoglou (eds) *LRCW 4: Late Roman Coarse Wares, Cooking Wares and Amphorae in the Mediterranean; Archaeology and Archaeometry; The Mediterranean; A Market without Frontiers* (British Archaeological Reports, International Series 2616): 235-53. Oxford: Archaeopress.

Capelli, C. and M. Bonifay 2016. Archeologia e archeometria delle anfore dell'Africa romana. Nuovi dati e problemi aperti, in A.F. Ferrandes and G. Pardini (eds) *Le regole del gioco: tracce archeologi racconti; studi in onore di Clementina Panella* (Lexicon Topographicum Urbis Romae Supplementum 6): 535-57. Rome: Quasar.

Capelli, C. and M. Bonifay 2023. Archéométrie et archéologie des céramiques africaines : une approche pluridisciplinaire, 3, in *LRCW 6: Late Roman Coarse Wares, Cooking Wares and Amphorae in the Mediterranean; Archaeology and Archaeometry* (Roman and Late Antique Mediterranean Pottery): 243-57. Oxford: Archaeopress.

Franco, P. 2012. African amphorae from Portus. Unpublished PhD thesis, University of Southampton.

Franco, P. 2020. North Africa and Portus through the amphora. Quantifying trade relationships, in C. Panella and M. Bonifay (eds) *North Africa: Territories, Centers of Production and Trade in Ancient Mediterranean*, in M.T. D'Alessio and C.M. Marchetti (eds) *RAC IN ROME: atti della 12a Roman Archaeology Conference (2016); le sessioni di Roma*: 339-46. Rome: Quasar.

Freed, J. 1995. The late series of Tunisian cylindrical amphoras at Carthage. *Journal of Roman Archaeology* 8: 155-91.

Garnier, N., T. Silvino and D. Bernal-Casasola 2011. L'identification du contenu des amphores : huile, conserves de poissons et poissage, in *SFECAG: Actes du congrès d'Arles*: 397-416. Marseille: SFECAG.

Hayes, J.W. 1972. *Late Roman Pottery*. London: The British School at Rome.

Hayes J.W. 1980. *Supplement to Late Roman Pottery*. London: The British School at Rome.

Keay, S.J. 1984. *Late Roman Amphorae in the Western Mediterranean: A Typology and Economic Study; The Catalan Evidence* (British Archaeological Reports International Series 196). Oxford: British Archaeological Reports.

Keay, S.J. 1988. *Roman Spain*. London: British Museum Publications.

Keay, S.J. 1998. African amphorae, in L. Saguì (ed.) *Ceramica in Italia: VI-VII secolo; atti del convegno in onore di John W. Hayes (Roma, 11-13 maggio 1995)*: 141-55. Florence: All'Insegna del Giglio.

Keay, S.J. 2012. Introduction, in S.J. Keay (ed.) *Rome, Portus and the Mediterranean* (Archaeological Monographs 21): 1-32. London: The British School at Rome.

Keay S.J. and D. Williams (eds) 2005. Roman amphorae: a digital resource. York: Archaeology Data Service, viewed 8 March 2022, <https://doi.org/10.5284/1028192>.

Liou, B. 1975. Informations archéologiques. *Gallia* 33-2: 572-605.

Malfitana, D. and M. Bonifay 2016 (eds). *La ceramica africana nella Sicilia romana: la céramique africaine dans la Sicile romaine* (Monografie dell'Istituto per i beni archeologici e monumentali, C.N.R. 12). Catania: Istituto per i beni archeologici e monumentali.

Manacorda, D. 1977. Le anfore, in A. Carandini and C. Panella (eds) *Ostia*, IV: *Le Terme del Nuotatore: scavo dell'ambiente XVI e dell'area XXV* (Studi miscellanei 23): 117-285. Rome: De Luca.

Mrabet, A. and M. Ben Moussa 2007. Nouvelles données sur la production d'amphores dans le territoire de l'antique Neapolis (Tunisie), in A. Mrabet and J. Remesal Rodríguez, *In Africa et in Hispania: études sur l'Huile Africaine* (Instrumenta 25): 13-40. Barcelona: CEIPAC.

Murialdo, G. 1988. Necropoli e sepolture tardo-antiche del Finale. *Rivista di Studi Liguri* 54: 221-42.

Murialdo, G. 2001. Le anfore da trasporto, in T. Mannoni and G. Murialdo (eds) *S. Antonino: un insediamento fortificato nella Liguria bizantina* (Collana di monografie preistoriche ed archeologiche 12): 255-96. Bordighera: Istituto internazionale di studi Liguri.

Nacef, J. 2015. *La production de la céramique antique dans la région de Salakta et Ksour Essef (Tunisie)* (Roman and Late Antique Mediterranean Pottery 8). Oxford, Archaeopress.

Nacef, J. with a contribution by C. Capelli 2017. Moknine 2. Nouvelles données sur un atelier d'époque tardive en Byzacène, in D. Dixneuf (ed.) *LRCW 5: Late Roman Coarse Wares and Amphorae in the Mediterranean; Archaeology and archaeometry* (Études alexandrines 43): 491-515. Alexandria: Centre d'études alexandrines.

Nasr, M. and C. Capelli 2018. Archéologie et archéométrie des productions de l'atelier de Majoura (Tunisie). *Rei Cretariae Romanae Fautorum Acta* 45: 765-70.

Opaiţ, A. 1997-98. North African and Spanish Amphorae in Scythia Minor. *Il Mar Nero: Annali di archeologia e storia* 3: 47-95.

Pallarès, F. 1987. Alcune considerazioni sulle anfore del Battistero di Albenga. *Rivista di studi Liguri* 53: 269-306.

Panella, C. 1973. Le anfore, in A. Carandini and C. Panella (eds) *Ostia, III: Le Terme del Nuotatore, Scavo degli ambienti III, VI, VII, Scavo dell'ambiente V e di un saggio nell'area SO* (Studi miscellanei 21): 463-633. Rome: De Lucca.

Panella, C. 1993. Merci e scambi nel Mediterraneo tardoantico, in A. Carandini, L. Cracco Ruggini and A. Giardina (eds) *Storia di Roma*, III.2: *I luoghi e le culture*: 613-97. Turin: Einaudi.

Peacock, D.P.S. 1984. Petrology and origins, in M.G. Fulford and D.P.S. Peacock (eds) *Excavations at Carthage: The British Mission*, I.2: *The Avenue du Président Habib Bourguiba, Salammbo: The Pottery and Other Ceramic Objects from the Site*: 6-20. Sheffield: University of Sheffield.

Remolà Vallverdù, J.A. 2000. *Las ánforas tardo-antiguas en Tarraco (Hispania tarraconensis): siglos IV-VII d. C.* (Instrumenta 7). Barcelona: Universitat de Barcelona.

Reynolds, P. 1995. *Trade in the Western Mediterranean AD 400-700: The Ceramic Evidence* (British Archaeological Reports, International Series 604). Oxford: Tempus Reparatum.

Reynolds, P. 2010. *Hispania and the Roman Mediterranean, AD 100-700: Ceramics and Trade*. London: Duckworth.

Riley, J.A. 1979. The Coarse Pottery from Berenice, in J.A. Lloyd (eds) *Excavations at Sidi Khrebish-Benghazi (Berenice)* (Lybia Antiqua supplement 2). Tripoli: Department of Antiquities.

Riley, J.A. 1981. The pottery from the cistern 1977.1, 1977.2 and 1977.3, in J.H. Humphrey (ed.) *Excavations at Carthage Conducted by the University of Michigan, VI*: 86-124. Ann Arbor: Kelsey Museum.

Saguì, L. 1998. Il deposito della Crypta Balbi: una testimonianza imprevidibile sulla Roma del VII secolo ?, in L. Saguì (ed.) *Ceramica in Italia: VI-VII secolo; atti del convegno in onore di John W. Hayes (Roma, 11-13 maggio 1995)*: 305-30. Florence: All'Insegnia dell'Giglio.

Sciallano, M. and P. Sibella 1991. *Amphores: comment les identifier?* Aix-en-Provence: Edisud.

Tchernia, A. 2011. *Les Romains et le commerce*. Naples: Centre Jean Bérard.

Wilson, R.J.A. 1996. Rural life in Roman Sicily: excavations at Castagna and Campanaio, in R.J.A. Wilson (ed.) *From River Trent to Raqqa: Nottingham University Archaeological Fieldwork in Britain, Europe and Middle East, 1991-1995*: 24-41. Nottingham: University of Nottingham.

15. A Bibliographic Network Study of Roman Amphora Epigraphy

Tom Brughmans, Jordi Pérez González and José Remesal Rodríguez

Introduction

Archaeologists study material culture to generate knowledge about the past and typically document this process in publications, citing how specific sources led to specific insights about the past. Citation of previously published works is the most common way of formally acknowledging that authors were influenced by it to generate new knowledge or insights. Citation analysis tools in bibliometrics allow for mapping out these flows of influence (Börner *et al.* 2004; Brughmans 2013; Sinclair 2016). But what about the citation of objects used in the process: does the citation of specific objects themselves reveal this knowledge creation process? To some extent it must do, because archaeological subdisciplines and particular research topics commonly tend to use large published or observable collections of material culture, such as topical publication series, museum collections, or topical databases of objects. But this is a particularly challenging question to address empirically for a specific research topic, because the explicit citation of sets of individual objects is far less systematically presented in archaeological publications than a bibliographic list of references. However, extracting such citations of specific objects for an entire research topic is possible for disciplines with a long research tradition in systematically documenting and indexing objects, and collecting citations of them. Moreover, the analysis of object citation practices using bibliometric techniques requires this information to be digitally available.

This paper outlines a proof-of-concept, demonstrating that it is feasible to explore published expression of influence by specific objects on a discipline-wide scale. We show that Roman epigraphy is such a discipline with a strong tradition of the highly systematic documentation and publication of individual objects. This is uniquely demonstrated by the database of CEIPAC (*Centro para el Estudio de la Interdependencia Provincial en la Antigüedad Clásica*). The CEIPAC database includes for the case of epigraphy on Roman amphorae a digital record of the citation of individual objects in individual publications. This unique combination allows us to explore how archaeological material culture networks are intertwined with bibliometric networks. Who cites what objects and for what purpose? Do we see communities in the citation practices of particular sets of objects, can these be explained by different national

or language traditions, and what is the impact of the publication of a new large corpus of objects on object citation practices?

We first describe the CEIPAC database and how the bibliographic information in it is structured. We subsequently present a method for creating network representations of this bibliographic information and for visually exploring the resulting object-publication networks. We analyse the bibliographic information of several major works that have been included into the CEIPAC database over the last 30 years. The aim of our analysis is to understand how research has developed in a field as distinguished as that of Latin epigraphy with regard to *instrumenta domestica* such as amphorae. To this end, different works have been selected as case studies that can offer a general picture of the research throughout the last decades. We include case studies of compilations of modern authors such as Keay and Remesal, specific noteworthy sites such as Augst and Mainz, amphora typologies such as Dressel 1, and publication languages such as Catalan. We additionally include studies focused on key catalogues in the field: Carré *et al.* (1995: Series I); Blanc-Bijon *et al.* (1998: Recueil II); and Etienne and Mayet (2004). We discuss and interpret the networks within the context of Roman epigraphy studies and its rich history of research, focusing in particular on the role of large corpora and language-based scholarly communities.

Bibliographic Information in the CEIPAC Database

The CEIPAC database currently has about 50,000 records[1] corresponding to the surviving epigraphic information, especially concerning amphorae (Aguilera Martín and Berni Millet 1991: 249; Remesal Rodríguez *et al.* 2008; Remesal Rodríguez 2012; Remesal Rodríguez *et al.* 2015: 248-49). The largest number of included inscriptions are stamps, painted inscriptions (*tituli picti*) and graffiti written on amphorae found throughout the Roman Empire. The entry of epigraphic information focuses mainly on Latin epigraphy, although we have recently expanded the sample of Greek epigraphy in the digital corpus (Remesal Rodríguez *et al.* 2013; Remesal Rodríguez *et al.* 2017).[2] The database has also been organised independently of the significance of

---

[1] <http://ceipac.ub.edu>.
[2] <http://romanopendata.eu/greek> (available online).

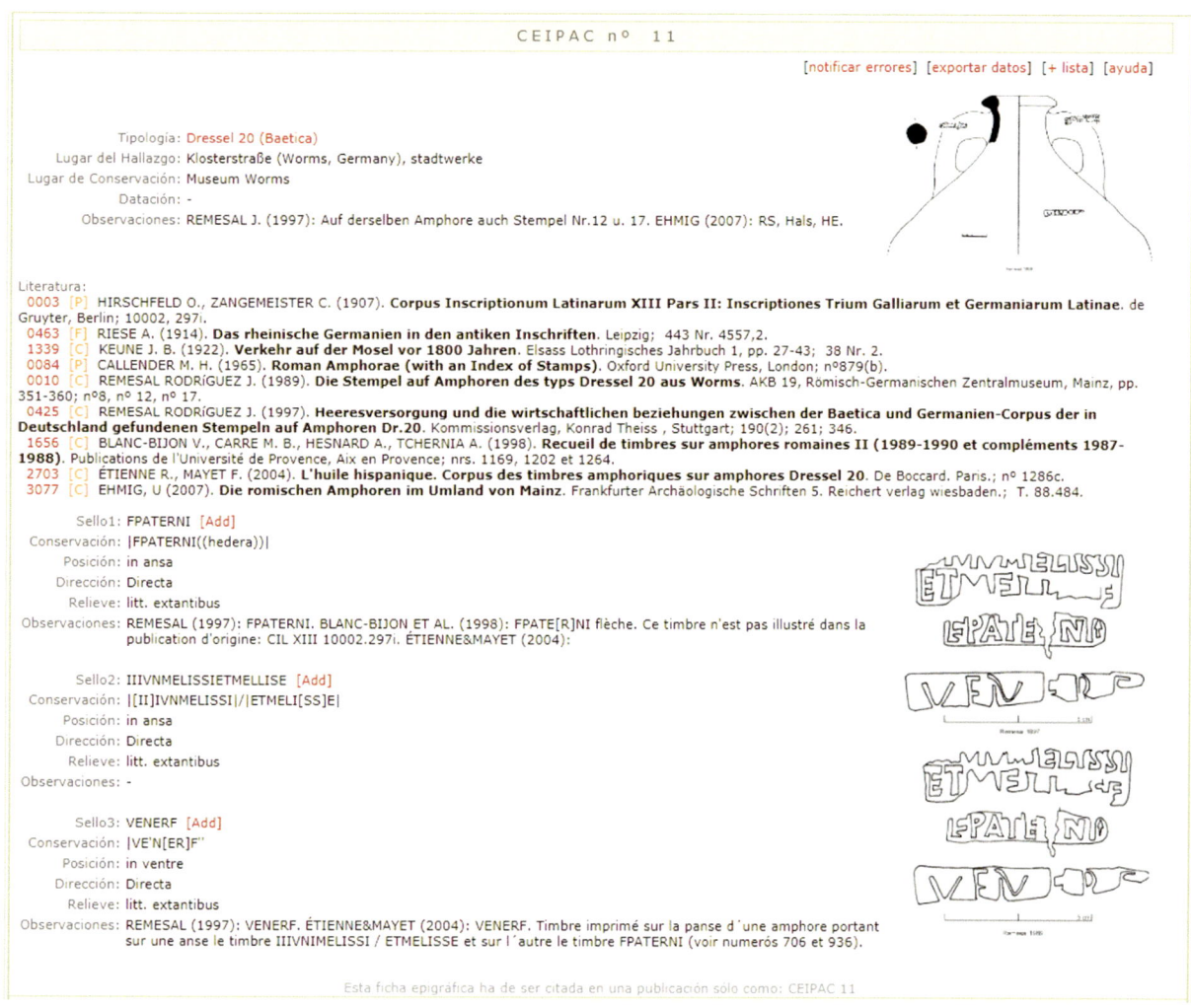

Figure 15.1. Bibliographic chain of the CEIPAC file n.11.

each of the aforementioned inscriptions and through a relational system which distinguishes between objects, stamps, *tituli picti*, and graffiti. On the significance of the stamp, see Remesal Rodríguez (1986; 2011; 2016; 2022; 2024); Berni Millet (2008; 2021); Moros (2014; 2021; 2022; 2024); Rubio-Campillo *et al.* (2017); Remesal Rodríguez and Moros Díaz (2019); Mataix (2019). On *tituli picti* see Rodríguez Almeida (1989; 1994); Remesal Rodríguez (1997; 2008); Remesal Rodríguez and Aguilera Martín (1999; 2001; 2003; 2007; 2010; 2014); Aguilera Martín (2001; 2002; 2007); Aguilera Martín and Berni Millet (1998); Liou and Marichal (1978); Pérez González (2014); Remesal Rodríguez *et al.* (2019: 180 n. 29); González Tobar and Estévez (2021). On graffiti in general, see Rodríguez Almeida (1993); Casulleras *et al.* (1999); García Brosa *et al.* (2001); Rovira Guardiola (2007); Remesal *et al.* (2003; 2007; 2010; 2014); Ozcáriz (2024); Ozcáriz *et al.* (2020); Ozcáriz (2023); González Tobar *et al.* (2023) and Bermúdez and Caballero (2024).

The bibliographic information we rely on for this study is stored in the literature field of the 'objects' section. In addition to information related to the amphoric type, this object section includes other noteworthy data such as that studied here. Literature is here understood to include all those bibliographic sources which publish and describe the object. The literature around an object can be made up of one or more bibliographic references.

The data is structured in two parts: the bibliographic pattern and the references to the object in the publication. The literature value is encoded with a bibliographic text pattern which consists of a number, is enclosed in parentheses, and is followed by an equals sign, e.g. '(84) = Callender (1965)'. The number is given by the bibliographic catalogue of the database, which to date includes more than 4200 publications relating to amphorae epigraphy.

One of the most interesting aspects about the epigraphic literature is the well-known 'bibliographic chain' reflecting aspects of the knowledge creation process: when an object has several sources of literature, they form a bibliographic chain, e.g. '(84) = No. 40. (1664) =

No. 43.1' (item (1664) = Carreras and Funari 1998). This bibliographic concatenation allows the user to identify those published works in which the consulted object entry has been cited. This is why users are urged to use the CEIPAC reference, in order to facilitate future consultations without the need to repeat all the references linked to the text. An example is shown in Figure 15.1 for the file for the Dressel 20 amphora found in Klosterstraße (Worms, Germany) with the stamps FPATERNI, IIIVNMELISSIETMELLISE, and VENERF (CEIPAC 11). In it, one can see in a chronological order the bibliographic chain of the publications where the consulted epigraphy has been cited.

Materials and Methods

Data

All results presented here were based on the data in the CEIPAC database in June 2019. The total dataset consists of 43,149 objects cited by 4113 publications. As discussed above, an 'object' refers to a unique object in the CEIPAC database, representing a single amphora object that can be individually cited by a publication and can have evidence of stamps, *titulu picti*, and/or graffiti in the CEIPAC database (Figure 15.2). A publication refers to a scholarly publication that has published and/or cited

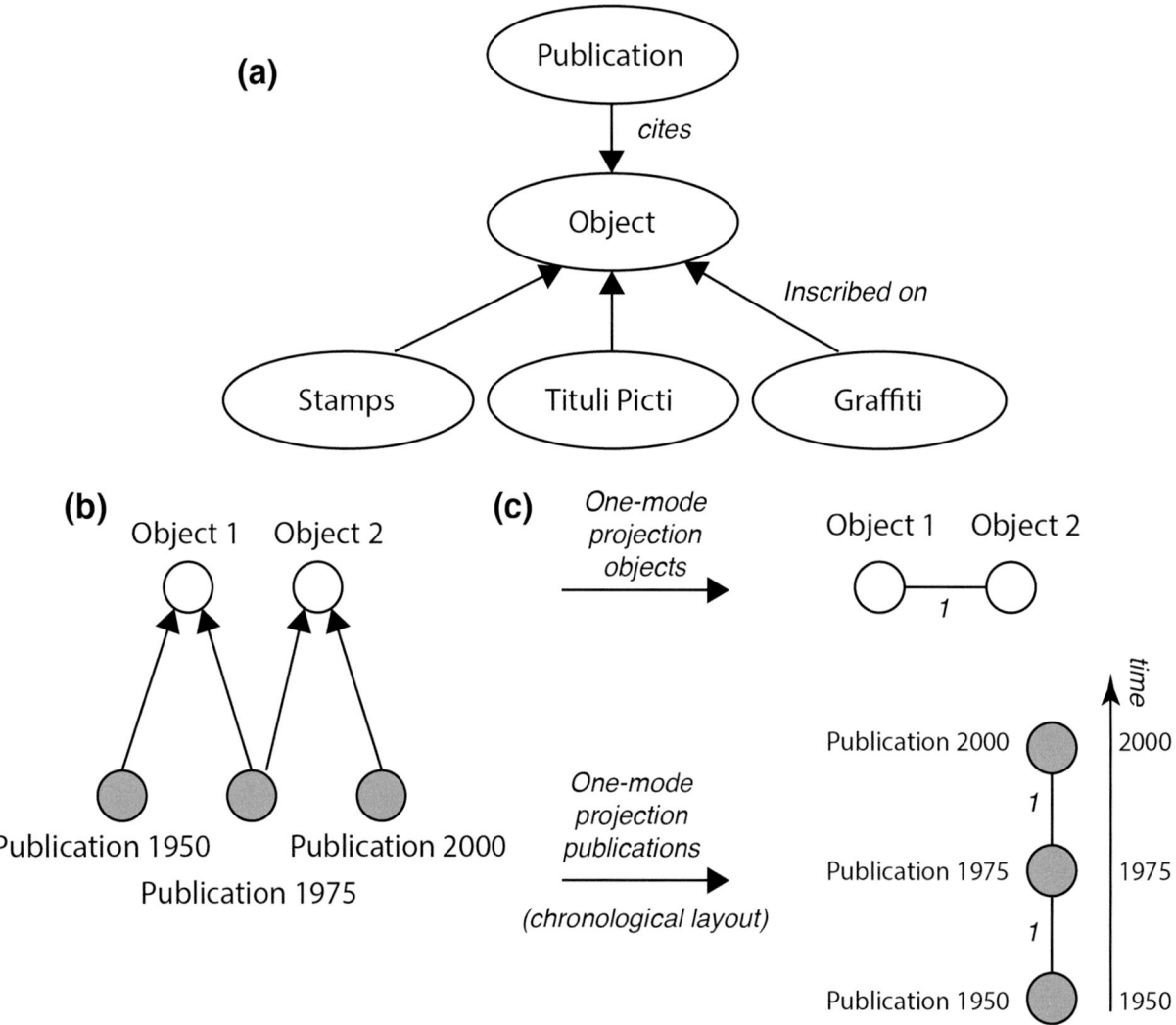

Figure 15.2. (a) Schematic representation of a selection of the data types and their relationships in the CEIPAC database used here; (b) abstract example two-mode network representation; (c) abstract example one-mode network projection and chronological layout.

an amphora object included in the CEIPAC database. The data used to generate all networks is openly available as an adjacency list, an attribute table with additional information on the objects, and an attribute table with additional information on the publications, all in comma separated value (.csv) format (Online Supplementary Material).

Summary Network Method

The network method used here consists of four steps:

1. The entire dataset was represented as a two-mode network;
2. eight subsets were extracted from this overall two-mode network to explore eight substantive case studies;
3. each case-study subset was projected as a one-mode network of publications and laid out chronologically;
4. the one-mode networks were visually explored within the context of the history of research of Roman amphora epigraphy studies.

This method is described in more detail in the remainder of this section. All network research was performed with the network software Visone v2.18 (Project Team Visone 2019).

Two-Mode Network Representation

We imported into Visone an adjacency list 'Brughmans_etal_CEIPAC_adjacency-list.csv' (Supplementary Online Material) including a row for each object followed by the publications citing it. This resulted in a two-mode network of 45,296 nodes consisting of 43,150 objects with 2146 publications (note these numbers are smaller than those of the total dataset because uncited objects and publications on Roman epigraphy not citing objects are not included in an adjacency list). These nodes are connected by 122,679 edges representing as many citations of objects in publications. The two-mode network formed the overall dataset (Figure 15.3) from which subsets were extracted to create one-mode networks representing the case studies.

Case Studies

Eight case studies were selected to explore diverse aspects of the history of research of Roman amphora epigraphic studies, including a combination of key catalogues, amphora types, sites, individuals, and language. A further consideration motivating the selection of these case studies was the need to make subsets that were small enough such that they could be computed and would facilitate a visual exploration of the networks. For example, creating a subset of all data published in the English language would result in a massive network that would lie outside of the computational resources of this study to produce and that would be too big as to enhance a visual exploration. We selected the following case studies:

1. Recueil: annual collection of epigraphy (Carre *et al.* 1995; Blanc-Bijon *et al.* 1998).
2. Étienne and Mayet (2004): a key corpus of amphoric epigraphy.
3. Remesal: the publications included in CEIPAC authored by J. Remesal-Rodríguez.
4. Keay: the publications included in CEIPAC authored by S. Keay.
5. Catalan: a limited number of amphoric epigraphy publications are written in Catalan and allow for visual exploration.
6. Mainz: all objects in the database from the city of Mainz.
7. Augst: all objects in the database from the city of Augst.
8. Dressel 1: all objects in the database of the amphoric type Dressel 1.

We extracted the data for each case study from the two-mode network. For the publication-based case studies 1-5 this is done by (i) selecting the relevant publications of the case study (e.g. selecting 'Étienne and Mayet 2004' for case study 3); (ii) selecting all objects cited by these publications; (iii) selecting all other publications that cite these same objects. For the object-based case studies 6-8 this is done by (i) selecting the relevant objects for the case study (e.g. all objects from Mainz); (ii) selecting all publications that cite these objects. Making these data selections for each case study allows us to study specific groups of publications that were influenced by specific groups of objects.

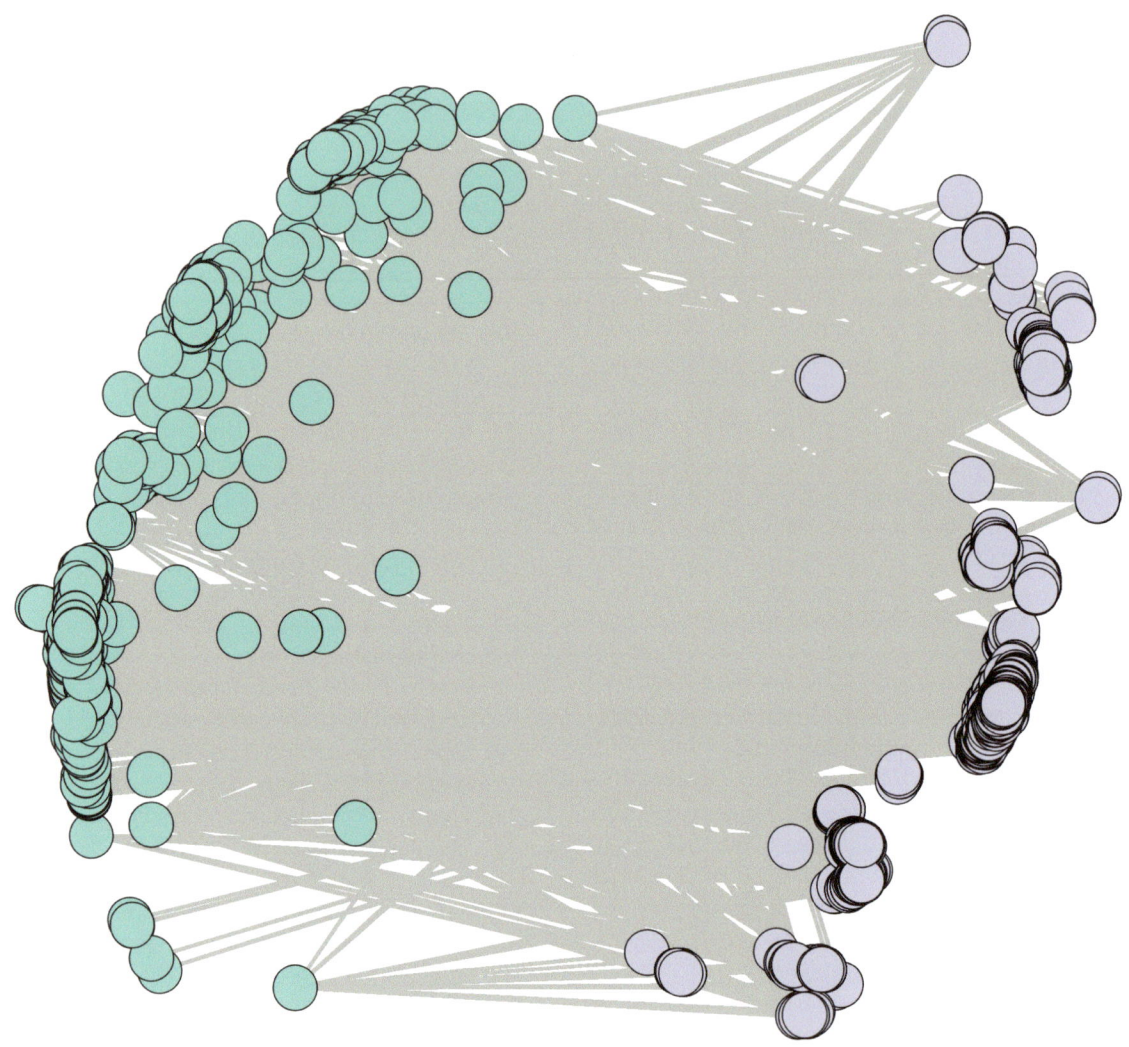

Figure 15.3. The two-mode network of the entire dataset connecting 2146 publications (left, green) to 43,150 objects (right, purple) through 122,679 citations (grey lines).

One-Mode Network Representation and Visual Exploration

We need to place a focus on the publications to allow us to explore flows of influence between them and the knowledge creation process through time. For this purpose, we created for each case study a so-called one-mode network representing publications as nodes. A pair of nodes is connected in the case that they both cite the same object or multiple objects (Figure 15.2c). This network therefore represents the similarity of publications based on how they were influenced by particular material culture objects.

Because publications and the objects are published in a particular year, we have a growing corpus of objects that can be cited throughout time: e.g. a publication from 1890 can only cite objects published before that date, whereas a publication from 2017 can cite all

objects published from the 19th century up to 2017. This means our one-mode networks of publications reflect an incremental growth of the published knowledge of amphora epigraphy objects, and a changing ability to be influenced by objects and publications published at different times. Were recent publications mostly influenced by recently published epigraphy objects or did they draw equally strongly on much older published objects? How do the sets of objects that are typically cited change through time? And do we see communities of publications (and the authors behind them) that tend to cite different sets of published objects?

To allow us to address these kinds of questions in a visual exploration, we lay out the one-mode networks chronologically with the oldest publication at the bottom. The label of a node reflects the author of the publication, and the node's location reflects its date (indicated by the blue horizontal lines and the label on the y-axis). Moreover, we colour code the nodes based on the language of the publication (see legend included in each figure).

These visualisations of the one-mode networks per case study formed the basis for all visual explorations presented and interpreted in the remainder of this paper. These visualisations are large and complex tangles, and need to be explored by interactively zooming in and out to explore the details. For this reason, we provide high-resolution versions of the figures for all case studies as downloadable supplementary online materials.

Context: The Development of Amphora Epigraphy Studies

It is our aim to explore and interpret these object and bibliographic networks within the context of the long-standing history of research of Roman amphora epigraphy, which we sketch in this section.

Throughout the 18th and 19th centuries, various corpora projects were created in order to gather as many inscriptions as possible for study. The creation of these corpora was linked from its origin to the European academies. Thus, as Buonopane (2009) describes, when Barthold Georg Niebuhr (1776-1831) drew up the project of a *Corpus inscriptionum* in which all the Greek and Roman inscriptions were to be collected, he requested the approval of the *Königlich Preussischen Akademie der Wissenschaften di Berlino*. Because the project itself was vast, Niebuhr, August Böckh (1785-1867), Olaus Kellermann (1805-37), and Abel-François Villemain (1790-1870) decided to review the original concept and present sections of it individually. This fell under the patronage of the *Académie des Inscriptions di Parigi*. Later, Theodor Mommsen (1817-1903) proposed to the *Königlich Preussischen Akademie der Wissenschaften di Berlino* the creation of a corpus comprising all Latin inscriptions (*Über Plan und Ausführung eines Corpus inscriptionum Latinarum*). The first point of Mommsen's project was to collect all the known epigraphic texts and carry out a critical and rigorous autopsy of them. The second section emphasised how the corpus should be ordered, the third point focused on the false epigraphs and the development of the transcripts, the fourth on the indexes, and the fifth on the methods of how the corpus should be implanted in draft form. Determined to complete this colossal undertaking, he secured the collaboration of notable scholars of his day, such as Giovan Battista de Rossi, Eugen Bormann, Heinrich Dressel, Herman Dessau, and Karl Zangemeister (Pérez González 2018: 5-16).

These works were key to the subsequent development of the humanities. The great names of the time, their original research, and the support of their institutions all energised these studies among the scientific community. These were years of movement. Large collections of monuments were moved around the world, universities, academies, and other like-minded institutions were created, and it was then that the need arose to gather as much information as possible in archives, libraries, catalogues, and so on. The compilation of these references in the various corpora marked a profound change for the development of historical studies. From the publication of these catalogues, their consultation was facilitated and the analysis of the texts was promoted.

More than a hundred years later, some of these projects, such as the *Corpus Inscriptionum Latinarum* (CIL), are still active and their cumulative nature is essential when preparing studies, whether in detail or as a whole. To date, the *CIL* has more than 17 volumes divided into 70 parts with about 180,000 inscriptions.

In the particular case of the CIL, the work of Dressel from 1899 stands out, which categorises the epigraphy on the *instrumenta domestica* of the city of Rome, and especially that which relates to amphorae and lamps.[3] The incorporation of all this information into the CEIPAC amphoric epigraphy database allows us to know in detail the value of the total number of inscriptions collected and their bibliographic relationship with the works both prior to their publication and their subsequent impact. Of Dressel's work, for example, the database includes 6512 objects with epigraphy, of which 4797 are stamps, 5811 are *tituli picti*, and 35 are graffiti. Dressel's research resulted in the compilation of about 80 different works, ranging from L. Peto's work of 1699 (cited by Dressel as *L. Paetus*) to Gardner's catalogue of Greek vases from 1989. Moreover, this compilation involved the incorporation of more than 1200 objects with epigraphy into his total work. Regarding the impact of his work, he is mentioned only three years after the catalogue's publication in Bonsor's studies on the ancient towns of the Guadalquivir extending into the present day; he also serves as an example in the 2010 work of Mani, who used the *CIL* to describe the stamps found in Hadrumentum. According to the data collected in the CEIPAC database, there are 48 works which have made mention of Dressel's work, citing or reviewing his inscriptions up to 4971 times (Figure 15.4).[4]

The decades after the publication of these epigraphic collections gave way to a number of **specialised and independent publications**, which reported the materials found in the different archaeological

---

[3] Cf. The supplementary materials noted in n. 1. The visualisation was obtained at romaopendata.eu of the bibliographic search of Dressel's publication in 1899 (*CIL*). It shows a higher concentration of inscriptions in the city of Rome.
[4] Cf. the supplementary materials in n. 2 (Dressel table CEIPAC).

1708 1733 1758 1783 1808 1833 1858 1883 1908 1933 1958 1983 2008

Figure 15.4. Timeline of the bibliographic chain of Dressel's work from 1889 in the *Corpus Inscriptionum Latinarum* vol. XV. Dressel's work has been marked in red. Pérez González 2018: 8, fig. 2.

excavations. These regional studies were generally connected by the use of **national languages** during the first decades of the 20th century, with the exception of a small number of works such as those developed by Bonsor (1888; 1901; 1931a; 1931b) and Callender (1948; 1965) in English and Spanish respectively, who collected the inscriptions of the Roman pottery of the Guadalquivir, and the various works in French such as that by Thouvenot in Morocco (Thouvenot 1941; on Mauretania Tingitana see Pons and Pérez 2018).

However, it was not until 1965 and the publication of Callender's book *Roman Amphorae (with an Index of Stamps)* that we witness a significant compilation of amphoric epigraphy which revitalised the field. His work collects more than 7700 stamps of 75 different types, of which about 6600 inscriptions were found on Dressel 20. Of these, more than 4600 copies come directly from the materials of Rome published by Dressel in 1899, while the rest of the inscriptions belong to the copies which he collected from his epigraphic missions and/or from other publications distributed

throughout western Europe. Callender also took into account works from the mid-18th century (e.g. Lupi 1734; Cecconi 1756; Morcelli 1781; Petrini 1795) up to three years before the publication of the volume (e.g. Gillam and Daniels 1961; Susini 1962).

In parallel, and through the use of the romanopendata. eu interface in its exploratory section of bibliographic data (Giménez *et al.* in press), we can observe how Dressel's publication of 1899 focused his interest on the materials from Rome, which served as the basis for Callender's work in 1965. Callender also added the unpublished materials from his missions, from which the epigraphic compilation was later elaborated by Etienne and Mayet, although they did not make full use of the corpora of their predecessors (Figure 15.5) (Etienne and Mayet (2004) only employ 576 inscriptions from Callender and 34 from Dressel. Data source: CEIPAC).

It was from the last third of the 20th century that a series of catalogues began to be published on a continuous

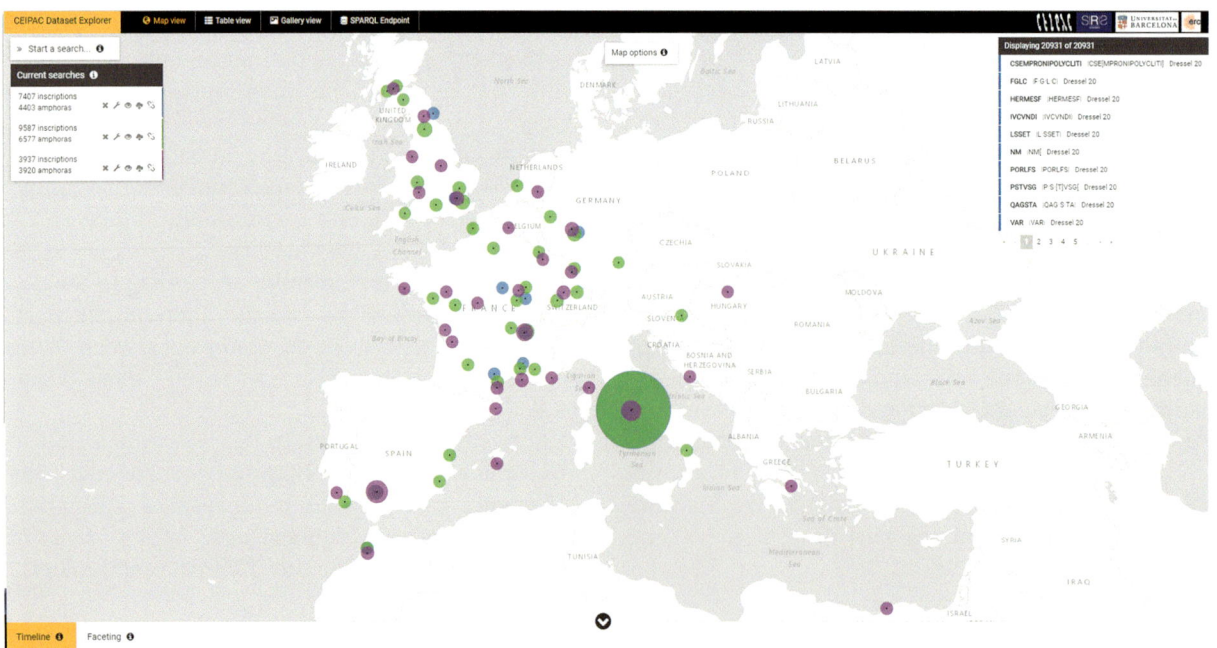

Figure 15.5. Visualisation obtained from romanopendata.eu of the bibliographic search of the publications of Dressel 1899 (green), Callender 1965 (blue), and Etienne and Mayet 2004 (purple).

basis, once again accelerating scholarly investigations. For example, the publication of regional and/or local monographs has served to stimulate studies on amphora epigraphy and promote knowledge about ceramic productions and food consumption throughout Roman territory. After the works of the 1980s such as Remesal Rodríguez (1986); Martin-Kilcher (1987-94); and Amar and Liou (1984), research on amphora epigraphy has intensified. Among the studies on the commercialisation of amphorae and epigraphy on French territory, one may count the works of Baudoux (1990; 1996); Olmer (1997); Laubenheimer and Marlière (2010); Garrote Sayó (2016); Marimon (2017) and Corbeel (2018). In progress, a work by Dubler will place special attention on the diffusion and commercial circuits of Baetican oil in the provinces of Gaul and Germania; (cf. Dubler 2019). In the case of the German border, particularly in Germania Superior, the works of Remesal Rodríguez (1986; 1997); Martin-Kilcher (1987-94); Ehmig (2003; 2007); Schimmer (2009) may be noted. For the studies carried out on present-day Austria, the works published by Bezeczky (1997; 1998) should be highlighted. In the case of Raetia, cf. Bermúdez Lorenzo (2017; 2021). For the study of Germania Inferior, a notable work in recent years by Mayer (2016) stands out; Montfort and van den Berg (2017); Remesal Rodríguez (2018); and González Cesteros and Berni Millet (2018). The case of Britannia has been studied by Funari (1996); Carreras Montfort and Funari (1998) and its northernmost border by Ayllón *et al.* (2019). Regarding the commercialisation and production of amphorae in North Africa, on the Mediterranean side, see Mayet (1978) and Pons Pujol (2009). On the distribution of food in Egypt, cf. Rovira Guardiola (2004). As for works that define epigraphy resulting from studies on the producing centres in Baetica, the works of Clark Maxwell (1899); Callender (1948); Beltran (1970); Remesal Rodríguez (1977-78); Ponsich (1979); Chic García (1985); Étienne and Mayet (2004); Berni Millet (2008); Barea *et al.* (2008); and Moros Díaz (2019) can be mentioned. In parallel, the most recent works of the Oleastro project directed by S. Mauné are noteworthy: Mauné *et al.* (2014); González Tobar *et al.* (2018); González Tobar and Mauné (2018); Bourgeon (2018; 2022); Desbonnets (2018). Another work in preparation by Ivan González Tobar will pay special attention to the productions of the Corduba *conventus*: González Tobar (2023).

Results and Discussion: A Journey through the Bibliographic Tangle

Case Study Catalogue: *Étienne and Mayet 2004*

We start our visual exploration of the networks with the work of Étienne and Mayet (2004) since it is one of the most recent general corpora of amphoric epigraphy, with a focus on inscriptions relating to olive

oil amphorae of the Dressel 20 type, which are the most popular type in our database (Rubio-Campillo *et al.* 2018a; 2018b: 39) (Figure 15.6). Their study presents a general picture of the structure of the data and the bibliographic relationships between the authors, especially for the last two centuries. The number of stamps on Dressel 20 amphorae amounts to 4000 inscriptions, with a total of 274 bibliographic items in a chronological frame that falls between 1836 and 2017.[5] As the authors mention in their introduction to the corpus, they have selected the stamps on Dressel 20 known at the date of publication.[6] This catalogue therefore omits some material that has subsequently been added to the CEIPAC database: unpublished collections including the materials from the epigraphic missions in Morocco (1973), the prospections of G.E. Bonsor during the late 19th century in the region of Seville, the late epigraphy of Rome and Ostia from the end of the 2nd and 3rd centuries AD, and a part of the Lyon-Vienne materials. It is also important to note the section of unpublished stamps which E. Rodríguez Almeida found in the decade between 1960 and 1970 on Monte Testaccio (Rome, Italy).[7]

Despite these biases and omissions, this is still the most recent compilation of this epigraphy and best allows for visualisation of the bibliographic sequence linked to the development of this research topic. For example, in the network drawn up from the work of Étienne-Mayet in 2004 the data from several corpora stand out, especially the works of Dressel from 1899 for the CIL XV of Rome and Callender from 1965. Consequently, corpora of Latin inscriptions from the end of the 19th century appear to be linked by the beginning of the 20th century to the *CIL* (lower part of the network). Here, the works carried out in Latin and those which specialised in Roman regions or provinces stand out, such as A. Hübner (1873), E. Hübner (1903), Hirschfeld (1888), Zangemeister (1906), and Hirschfeld and Zangemeister (1907). All of them offered an ideal initial basis for the further development of future

---

[5] The information can be consulted in the CEIPAC bibliographic file, n. 2703. See: <http://ceipac.ub.edu>.

[6] 'Le *corpus* des timbres d'amphore Dressel 20 qui fait l'object de ce volumen ne vise nullement à l'exhaustivité dans ce domaine: il est tout destiné à illustrer le chapitre sur les fabricants de ce type d'amphore en Bétique; les exemples choisis comme les pourcentages qui sont donnés proviennent de ce corpus. Tenter l'exhaustivité reviendrait à repousser la publication pour toujours; or, nous voyons combien nous sont útiles le *CIL* XV, 2 de Dressel et *l'Index of Stamps de Callender*, même si nous en voyons les limites [---]. Contrariament aux *Recueils de timbres* publiés par l'Université d'Aix-en-Provence, nous n'avons pas effectué un dépouillement systématique des revues qui demandait un trop gros investissement en temps, mais nous incorporé dans notre *corpus* tous les poinçons, récemment publiés dans les monographies avec leur dessin, quand nous ne les avions pas déjà dans notre fichier'. Étienne and Mayet 2004: II, 7-8.

[7] Cf. The supplementary materials noted in n. 3. See also the visualisation obtained in romaopendata.eu of the bibliographic search of Etienne and Mayet 2004. It shows a greater concentration of materials from the published and unpublished inscriptions.

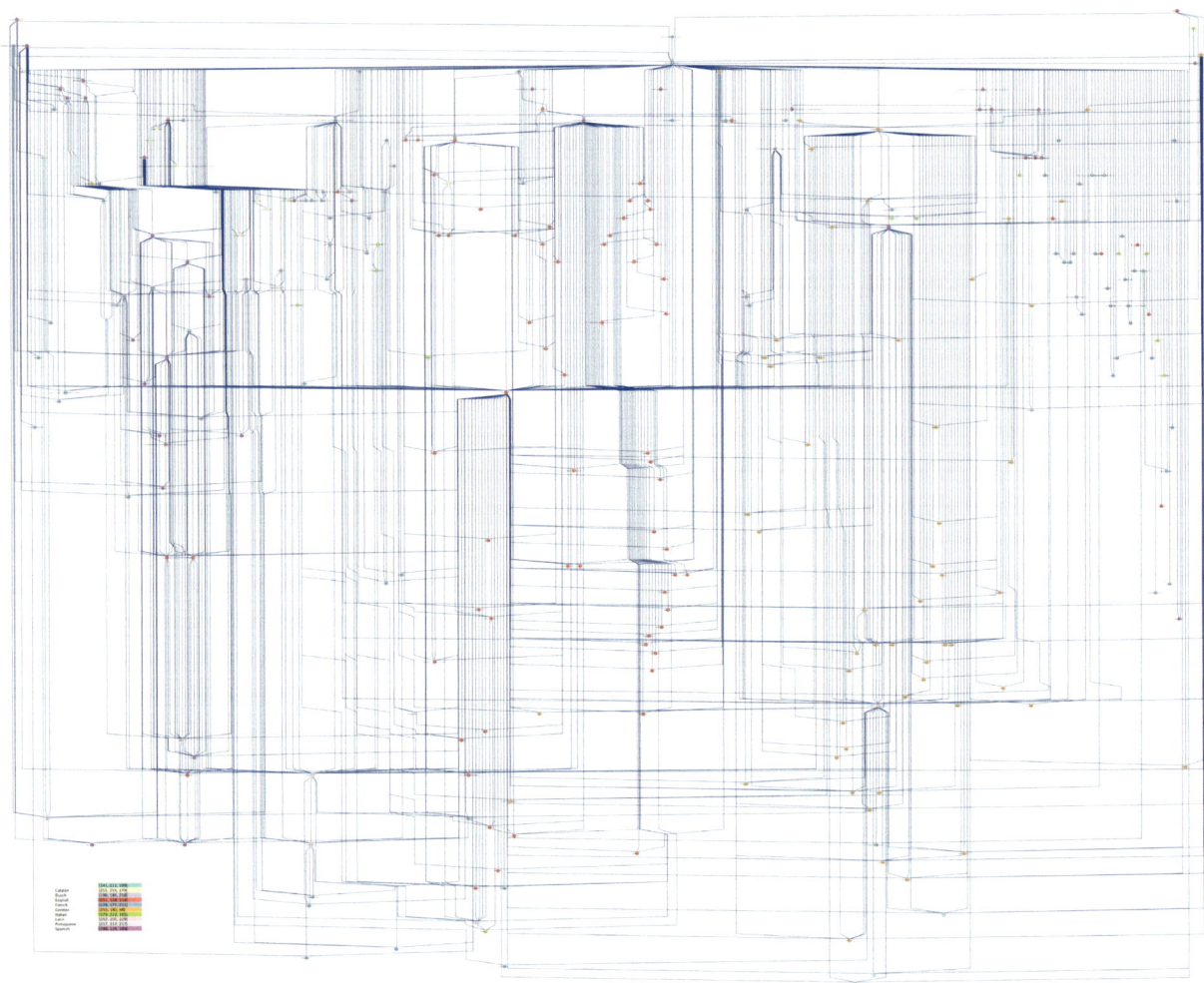

Figure 15.6. One-mode network for case study focused on the Étienne and Mayet (2004) catalogue (high-resolution version in online supplementary material). For Figures 15.6-15.12: nodes represent publications, node colour represents publication language (see figure legend), edges represent citation of at least one object in common, edge colour represents number of objects in common (dark = high), chronological layout from old (bottom) to recent (top), publication dates on y-axis.

regional research. Indeed, different regional traditions can be clearly observed in specialised works on the study of a Roman region or province, such as those of Mauretania Tingitana, Baetica, Hispania Citerior Tarraconensis, Britannia, and Germania (these regions stand out in the networks below through the different colours representing different publication languages). Unpublished works whose subsequent mentions are unknown or recent catalogues whose impact cannot yet be measured are usually grouped on the margins of the network (see the section to the right of the network or the corpora on Monte Testaccio (Rome)) (Blázquez *et al.* 1994; Blázquez and Remesal 1999; 2001).

Case Study Scholar: Remesal

These general catalogues (as well as some monographs such as the *Recueils de timbres* (Carre *et al.* 1995; Blanc-

Bijon *et al.* 1998) – to which we turn in the next section) have become key resources in Roman amphora epigraphy studies. They can be considered hubs in this network. It is normal that in most of these epigraphic compilations part of the materials tend to be reproduced which were previously published in catalogues such as those of the *Corpus Inscriptionum Latinarum* or Callender. As a rule, these catalogues usually combine series of minor works and unpublished materials by the editors. Examples of this are the two catalogues published by Remesal which focus exclusively on Dressel 20 olearian amphorae found on the Germania frontier (Figure 15.7). In his 1986 publication up to 55 different bibliographic sources were used, while in the 1997 edition 221 references were provided. Like other works dedicated to the specific study of a region, the resulting network is very homogeneous, with almost all works being composed in the same language, with the exception of

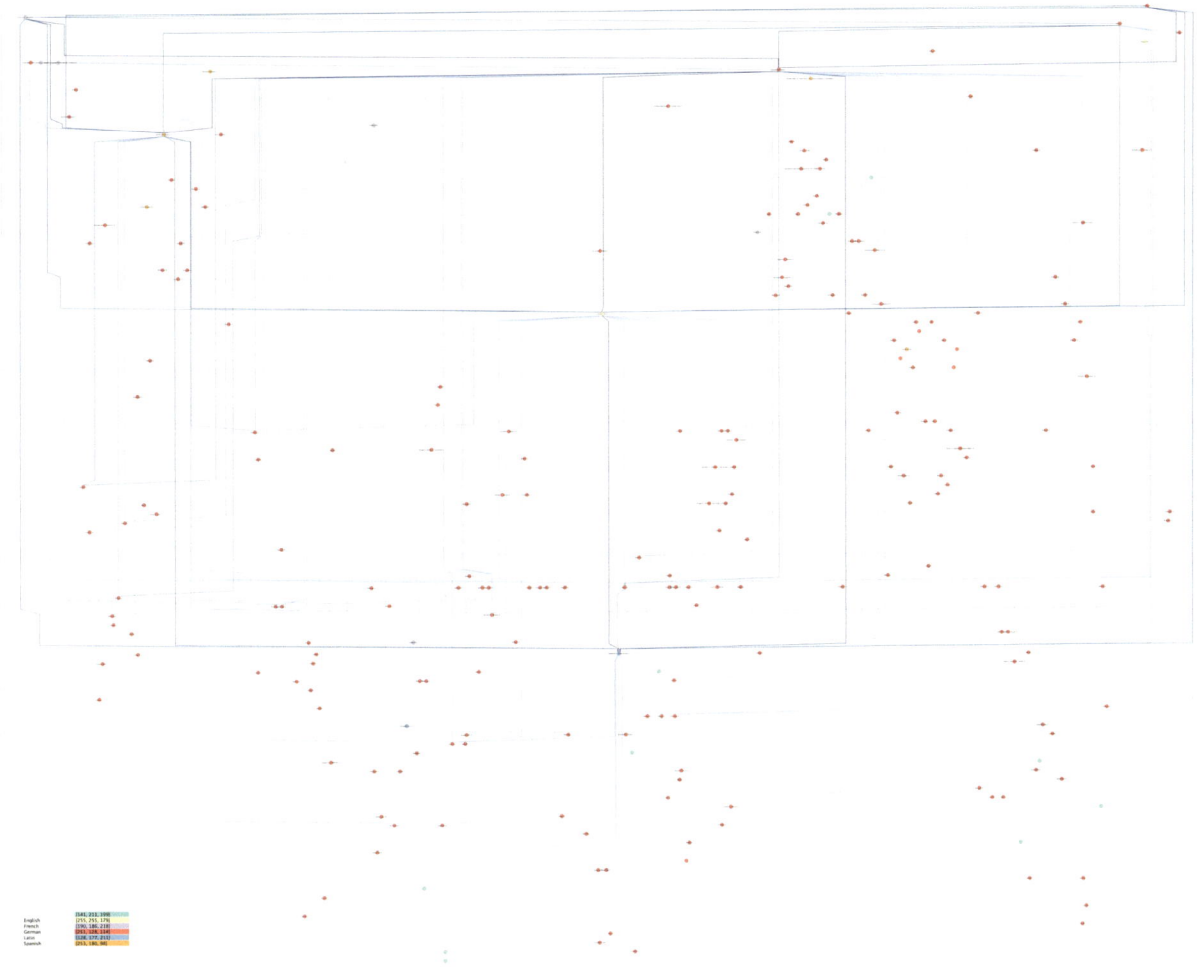

Figure 15.7. One-mode network for case study focused on the catalogues by Remesal (high-resolution version in online supplementary material).

some corpora from the early 20th century (Hirschfeld and Zangemeister 1907 (CIL 13.2)). This made Remesal's works indispensable for future study in the region, such as those by Etienne and Mayet (2004), and by Ehmig (2003; 2007), just as the works of Callender and Hirschfeld and Zangemeister previously were for him. Another example of specialised catalogues in a specific place would be the recent publication of Mongardi's book on the amphoric epigraphy of *Mutina*, who, in addition to publishing a corpus of previously unpublished inscriptions, incorporated materials from 57 different works on the city (Mongardi 2018). Other amphora productions that are well known for the publication of prolific catalogues are those of the Brindisi area (cf. Mananorda and Pallecchi 2012; Palazzo 2013); those of the Laietanian region (cf. Pascual Guasch 1977; 1991; Comas i Sola 1997; Carreras *et al.* 2009; 2013; 2019); those of Lusitania (cf. Fabiao and Guerra 2016); or the various collaborative works by S. Cipriano and S. Mazzocchin on northern Italian productions in Dressel 6 types (e.g. 1998; 2016).

Case Study Catalogue: Recueils

Another catalogue, the *Recueils de timbres* (Carre *et al.* 1995; Blanc-Bijon *et al.* 1998), is an attempt by the *Université d'Aix-en-Provence* to collect epigraphy annually in the style of the *Année Épigraphique* (Figure 15.8). The presentation of these collections as catalogues containing a very varied epigraphy in terms of origin, as well as the amphoric type, have allowed a greater dissemination of its contents among various specialists (Network 3. Carre *et al.* 1995 and Blanc-Bijon *et al.* 1998 in Roman Open Data (https://romanopendata.eu). Cf. Supplementary materials n.4) (Figure 15.9); hence they have been referenced in a corpus on Brindisian amphorae (Palazzo 2013), one on Laetanian productions, and one on the study of materials from the eastern part of the Iberian Peninsula (Márquez and Molina 2005). Although the impact of the two catalogues has lasted over time (see Dressel 1 (Network 11) and Catalan Bibliography (Network 12)), the lack of the project's

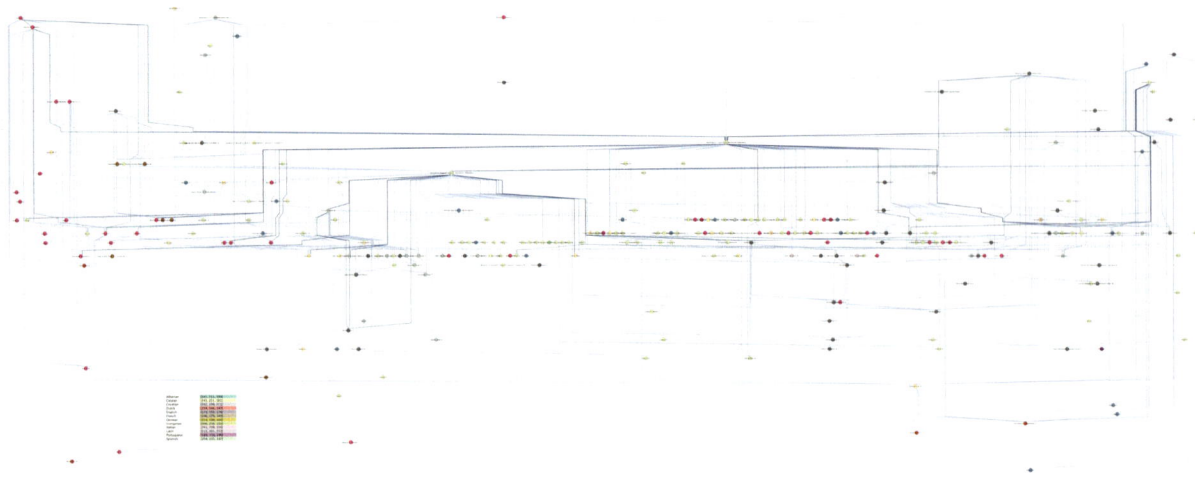

Figure 15.8. One-mode network for case study on the *Recueils* catalogues (high-resolution version in online supplementary material).

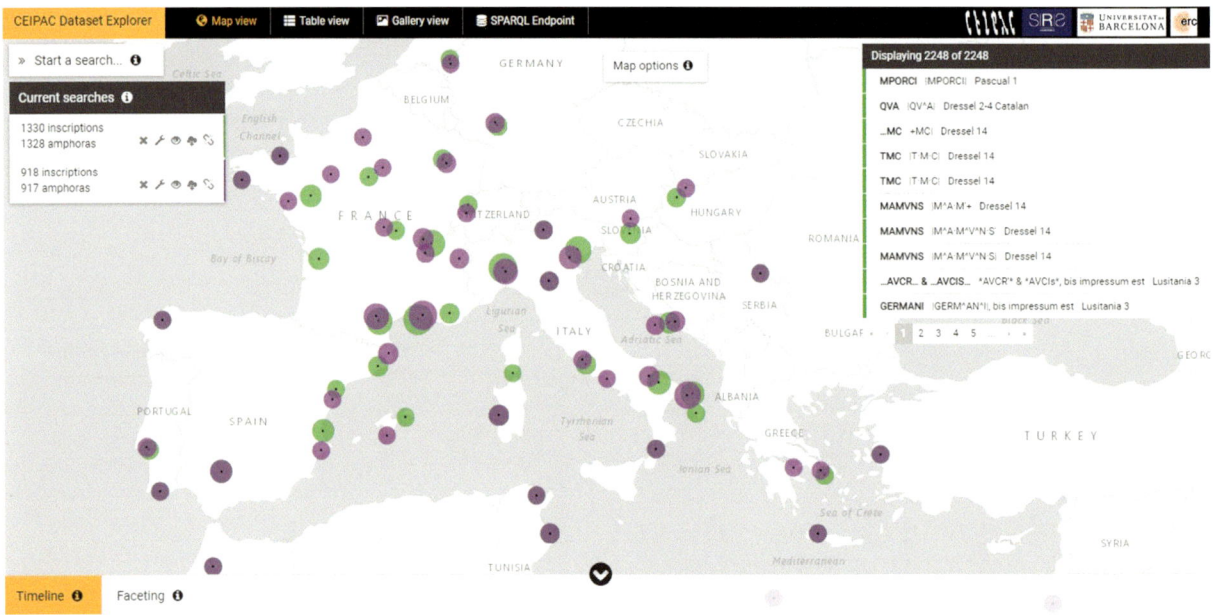

Figure 15.9. Visualisation obtained from romaopendata.eu from the search by *Recueils des timbres* = Carré *et al.* 1995 (green) and Blanc-Bijon *et al.* 1998 (purple).

continuity only brought together the materials from the years 1987-90, when the project ended.

Despite the interruption of the project, the fact that they are both heterogeneous and largely unpublished materials means that their impact is prolonged over time, and interest in them is dispersed among researchers specialised in different types and origins. This is clearly reflected in the broad branched structure of the network and the clear influence among different language communities. It is worth remembering that

from the work of Carré *et al.* 1995 stamps of up to 44 different amphoric types were published and 112 bibliographic entries are known (94 before p. X 17 post p.). By the time of Blanc-Bijon *et al.* 1998 up to 59 typologies and 203 bibliographic entries were known (179 before p.p./ 32 p.p.).

With regard to the impact on this field of research, can we say that this represents a 'winning formula' that guarantees a greater bibliographic impact? Possibly, for it appears that by bringing together many different amphoric types, well-known typologies, or different places of discovery, one generates a continuous interest to review the materials of this type of catalogue.

Case Study Scholar: Keay

Another example that can help us answer this question is observed by the visualisation of the network of Keay's works, especially that of 1984. His study on the typologies and economy of late amphorae focuses on the particular case of the north-east of the Iberian Peninsula (Catalonia, Spain). He combined what was already published in 1983 with unpublished materials and drew on 16 other bibliographic references. This resulted in a varied set of citations (21) which, perhaps due to the diversity of typologies and because it was a region with one of the longest research traditions on the topic, fostered continuous interest in the subject.

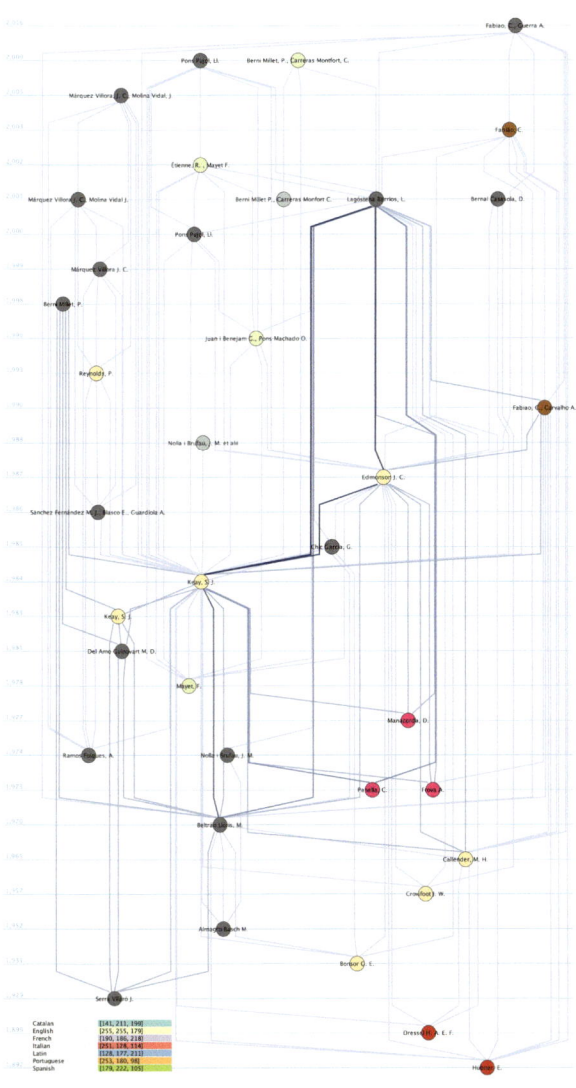

Figure 15.10. One-mode network for case study on Keay's publications (high-resolution version in online supplementary material).

This network does not have a dominant publication language, but represents a clear example of the multilingualism that has characterised these studies in recent decades. For example, while Keay translated the findings in Ostia from the original publications of Panella and Manacorda (1913 and 1977) from Italian to English, a decade later they served Edmonson to discuss Lusitanian productions in English (1987) and they were used a decade later by Lagóstena to describe the production of Hispanic fish sauce (2001; in Spanish).

Case Studies Sites: Mainz and Augst

The networks created from objects from a specific place, such as those developed for the cities of Mainz and Augst, repeat the network structures already observed. The preferential use of large corpora as a hub is prioritised, with a more homogenous publication language dependent on the studied region, in this case German, but without neglecting those references in other languages that are significant for the study of the place. It is also worth noting the appearance of publications other than these catalogues, which are represented as isolated nodes and lack an internal relationship in the configuration of the network, and which may be the result of specific findings in the city.

While the results in the elaboration of these networks may show similar patterns to date, due to their relatively closed structures, when starting from the language or the typology, networks of greater dynamism and richness can appear in which there is no clear dominant axis or patterning, and sometimes also without temporal continuity.

Case Study Language: Catalan

As a sample of the bibliographic network linked to languages, we have selected Catalan. The first thing we see is a greater ramification of the network which showcases a varied investigation that is linked to different types or areas of study. This is followed by a temporary increase in the use of the language in academic production, with a greater presence in research from the late 1970s to the present day. This was exemplified by a great proliferation of studies on archaeology, epigraphy, and ancient history in Catalan-speaking regions that encouraged the dissemination of their research. An overview of the network shows a great connection with two other languages, Spanish and French, which are widely represented and with a lesser presence of Italian and English. Regarding the structure of the network, we can differentiate three sections. The first is centred on the studies by Pascual (1977; 1991) and Comas (1985), who were responsible for the initial effort to gather the epigraphy of Catalonia in their catalogues. Before them, only individual works of these

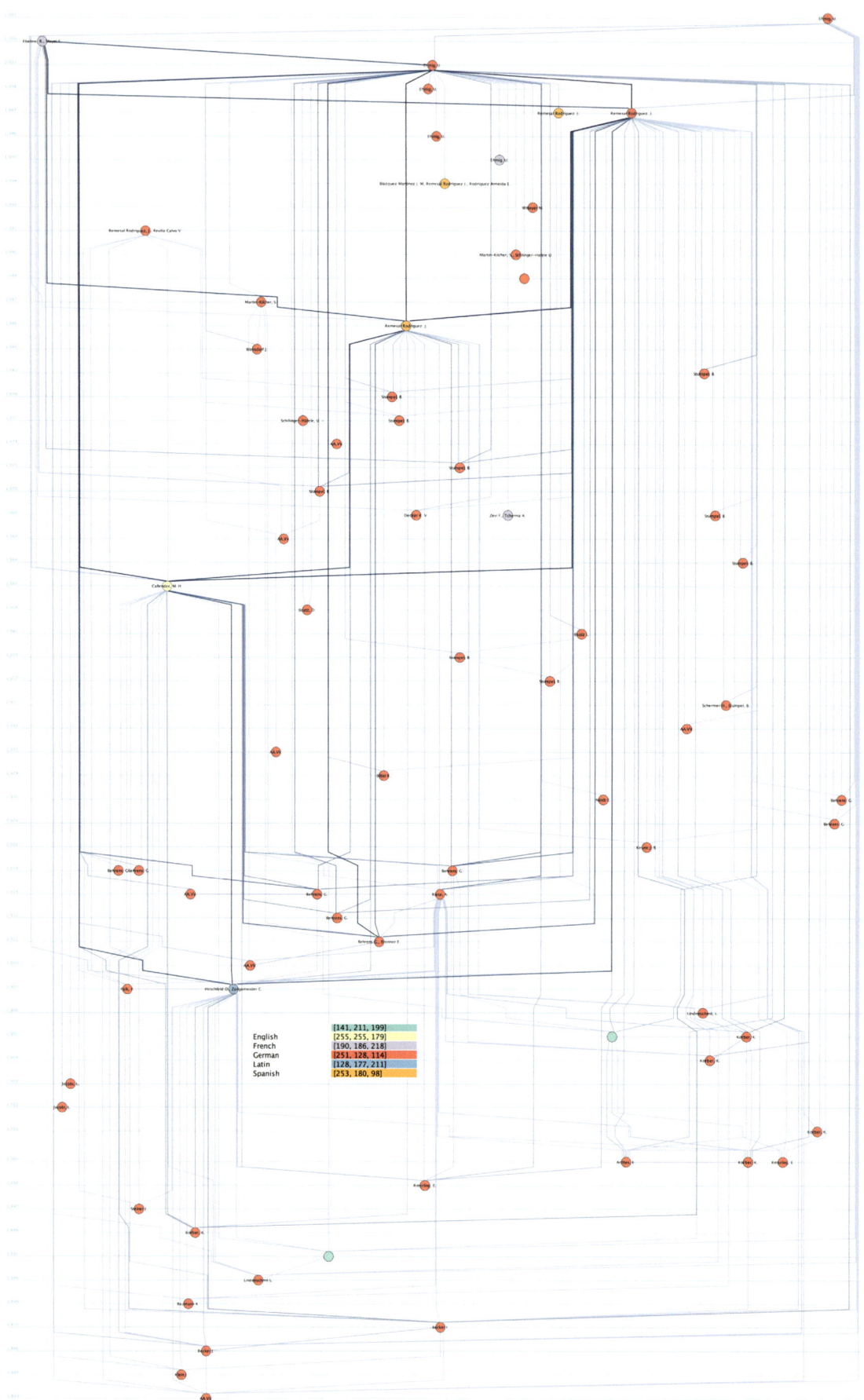

Figure 15.11. One-mode network for case study on objects from Mainz (high-resolution version in online supplementary material).

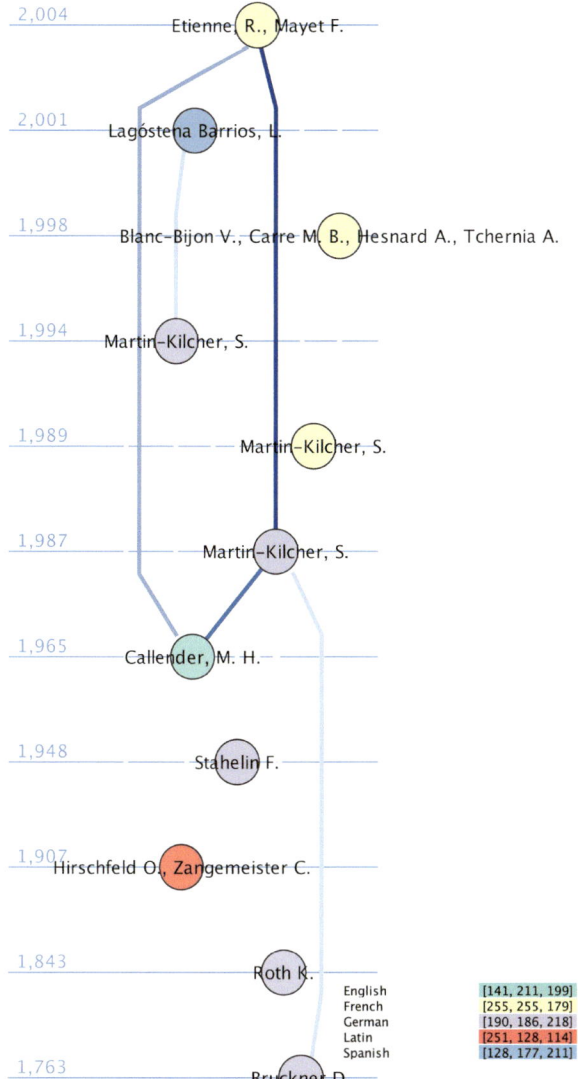

Figure 15.12. One-mode network for case study on objects from Augst (high-resolution version in online supplementary material).

On the historiographic production in the region, see Palacín *et al.* 2020). Consequently, this network gives the impression of being the inheritor of traditional works in the region and the success of its impact may be linked to the continual increase of publishing large sets of materials in specialised corpora, in this case those from the area of the Llobregat-Besòs, with *Barcino* and *Baetulo* being used as references. Apart from this, a third and more isolated dataset is represented (upper left margin of the network). Although it is true that this indicates a constant and well-represented bibliographic production, it shows a more remote connection with the rest of the network's publications, perhaps because it contains little information regarding the specific findings of epigraphy in other regions of Catalonia, especially those of Girona.

Case Study Amphora Type: Dressel 1

Finally, a bibliographic-typological network has been created focused on publications of one of the most represented amphoric types: Dressel 1. The resulting network shows one of the characteristics of this type, namely its large number of variants. Here, in addition to representing the three variants that Lamboglia differentiated in 1955, Dressel 1, a, b, and c,[8] we must add the subvariants derived from the place of production of these types: Italic (a, b, c), Tyrrhenic (a, b, c) Tarraconensis (b), Betic (c), and Lugdunenses (b). In this regard, the result shows a very heterogeneous network, with three or four different structures as well as with some nodes lacking continuity, links, or transcendence as a result of the complexity of the type. Broadly speaking, the networks that are derived from the *Recueils de timbres* are differentiated and samples are collected from previous years without taking into account the place, the subtype, or the language. Thanks to the networks established in recent works by Laubenheimer and Marlière from 2010, or Lagóstena 2001, each one represents the findings of the materials from the study region.

Conclusion

This paper presents a formal method for exploring the interrelationship between researchers and the objects they study. Specifically, we have focused on how researchers have been influenced by specific sets of objects, through citing them in publications. A study of this phenomenon was made possible for the case of Roman amphoric epigraphy, thanks to the use of the CEIPAC database which uniquely, records both objects and published citations to them. We have argued that research communities, networks, and research traditions are revealed when scholars are explored through the sets of objects they study and cite. This

finds were known in several languages – especially in French and Italian – and some epigraphic sets, such as those collected by Almagro Basch in Empúries (1952) or that of the Spanish amphorae by Beltrán Lloris (1970). Soon, these works, due to their foundational nature, became the reference publications for future research, generating the extension of a new branch in the network, which showcased varied and continuous diffusion (upper right margin), with the sum of some of their inscriptions in the *Recueils de timbres* mentioned above, or more recently in the publications edited by the *Institut Català d'Arqueologia Clàssica* (ICAC) in the *Corpus internacional des timbres amphoriques*, where Berni Millet and Carreras Monfort have revitalised research in recent years (Carreras 2009; Berni and Carreras 2013. Recently and outside the study: Carreras 2019.

---

8 ADS Collection: 463. DOI: <https://doi.org/10.5284/1028192>.

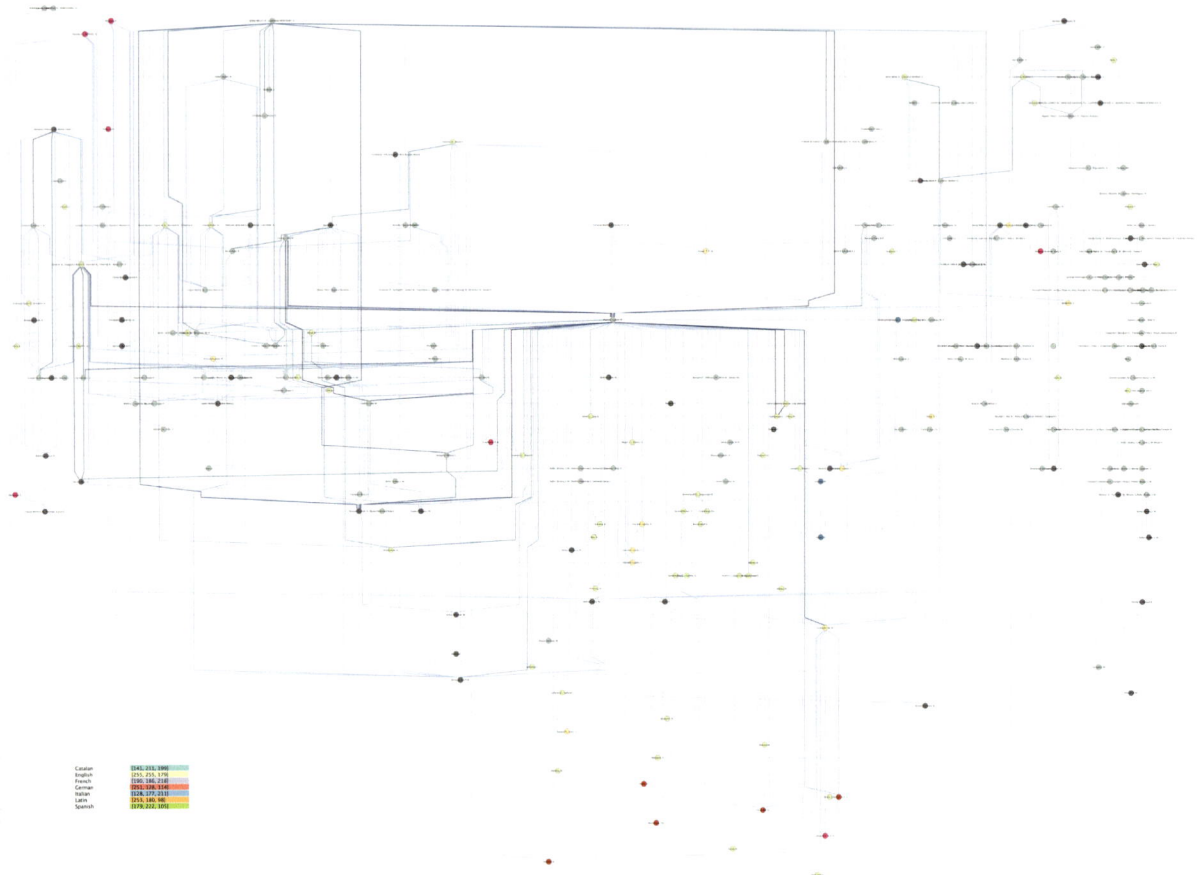

Figure 15.13. One-mode network for case study on publications written in Catalan (high-resolution version in online supplementary material).

current paper focused on demonstrating the feasibility of the method and was restricted to a visual exploration of the results, and we argue future work should explore the wider implications of the method and of object citation practices on the archaeological knowledge creation process.

Our results allow us to identify both the major trends in the research tradition of Roman epigraphy, and the particular objects, people, and publications these trends are composed of. A dominating trend is the structuring effect on publication and citation patterns of the major catalogues. At the end of the 19th century, with the publication of several epigraphic catalogues from projects by different European academies, the foundations were laid for the development of this research topic. These catalogues became timeless works which had to be consulted by researchers until the present day. During the first half of the 20th century, a series of smaller works appeared which were linked to national studies and published in the languages of each country. From the middle of the 20th century, when interest in large corpora was reactivated, the work of Callender took on special relevance, as it facilitated

the subsequent development of regional monographs, many of which were derived from research works linked to a doctoral thesis or a specialised monograph. It is also not surprising that in these networks the works related to the CEIPAC project stands out (Remesal *et al.* 2015) as its long-running database has been a catalyst for the growing interest in this field. In recent years, this approach is complemented by other projects such as OLEASTRO.[9]

The bibliographic networks presented here can also help us identify and understand smaller patterns, such as research topics and interests, the formation of various schools of thought, and the development of language-specific research communities. Originally, studies on the subject were published in Latin at the end of the 19th century and the beginning of the 20th century. But gradually the language of the country or region of origin of the researcher or the analysed materials has become preferential. As such we saw the dominance of the German language in the network surrounding

---

9 <https://archimede.cnrs.fr/index.php/102-programmes-scientifiques/programmes-scientifiques-3/717-oleastro>.

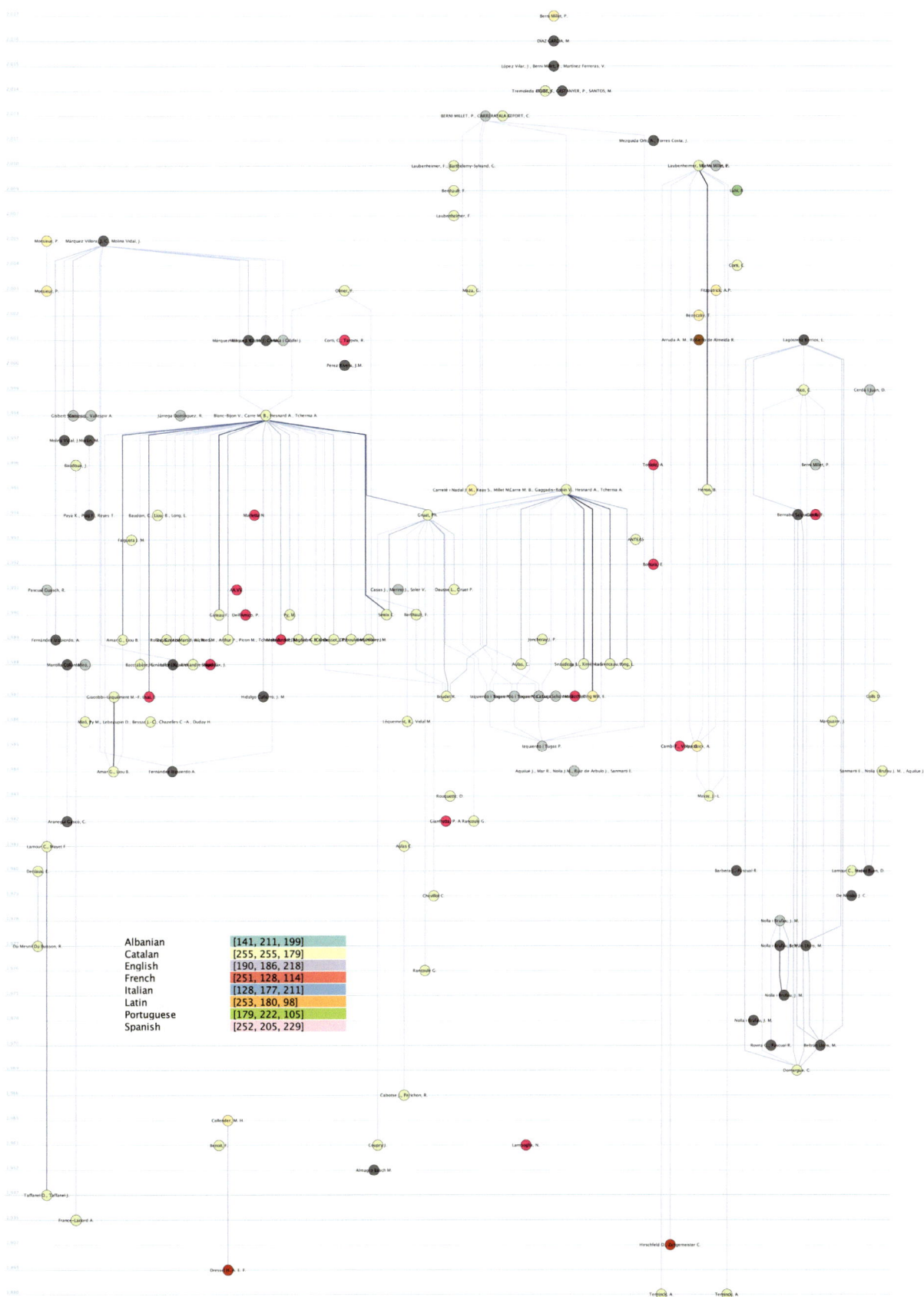

Figure 15.14. One-mode network for case study on objects of the Dressel 1 amphora type (high-resolution version in online supplementary material).

the objects from Augst and Mainz, we highlighted the Catalan research tradition, and we emphasised the impact on redrawing national research networks by scholars such as Simon Keay who embraced the multilingualism that distinguishes the field.

Online Supplementary Materials

All network data to generate the two-mode network and replicate the published results, and high-resolution figures of all one-mode networks, can be downloaded as online supplementary material from http://doi.org/10.32028/9781805831785-15-Online SupplementaryMaterials.

Acknowledgements

TB's work was performed in the context of project SIMREC made possible thanks to European Union's Horizon 2020 research and innovation programme Marie-Skłodowska-Curie Actions agreement 791948, and in the context of project MINERVA made possible thanks to a Sapere Aude Research Leadership grant awarded by the Independent Research Fund Denmark (DFF) under grant agreement 0163-00060B.

Bibliography

Aguilera Martín, A. and P. Berni Millet 1991. Programa Testaccio. *Activitat científica de la Universitat de Barcelona*, II època 2: 6-7.

Aguilera Martín, A. and P. Berni Millet 1998. Las cifras hispánicas. *Calligraphia et tipographia. Arithmetica et numerica. Chronologia*. Barcelona: Universitat de Barcelona.

Almagro Basch, M. 1952. *Las inscripciones ampuritanas griegas ibéricas y latinas*. Barcelona: CSIC.

Amar, G. and B. Liou 1984. Les estampilles sur amphores du golfe de Fos. *Archaeonautica* 4: 145-211, viewed 1 May 2025, <www.persee.fr/doc/nauti_0154-1854_1984_num_4_1_956>.

Ayllón Martín, R., J. Pérez González and J. Remesal Rodríguez 2019. Olive oil at the border of the Roman Empire. Stamps on Baetican Dressel 20 found on the Tyne-Solway Isthmus, in S. Günther, T. Mattern, R. Rollinger, K. Ruffing and C. Schäfer (eds) *Marburger Beiträge zur Antiken Handels-. Wirtschafts- und Socialgeschichte*, XXXVI (2018): 121-45. Rahden: Leidorf.

Barea, J.S., J.L. Barea Solís and J. Moros 2008. *Figlina Scalensia: un centro productor de ánforas Dressel 20 de la Bética*. Barcelona: Universitat de Barcelona.

Baudoux, J. 1990. Les amphores d'Alsace et Lorraine. Contribution a l'historie de l'économie provinciale sous l'Empire Romain. Unpublished PhD thesis, Université Marc Bloch (Strasbourg).

Baudoux, J. 1996. *Les amphores du nord-est de la Gaule*. Paris: Editions de la Maison des Sciences de l'homme.

Beltrán Lloris, M. 1970. *Las Ánforas Romanas en España*. Zaragoza: Institución Fernando el Católico (CSIC), Fundación Pública de la Excma. Diputación de Zaragoza.

Bérmudez Lorenzo, J.M. 2017. *Raetia*: las relaciones socioeconómicas de una provincia romana centroeuropea con las provincias mediterráneas. Unpublished PhD thesis, Universitat de Barcelona <http://hdl.handle.net/2445/121332>.

Bermúdez Lorenzo, J.M. 2021. *Economía de Raetia (s. I-III d.C.): Epigrafía anfórica* (Instrumenta 76). Barcelona: Universidad de Barcelona.

Bermúdez Lorenzo, J.M. and D. Caballero Payá 2024. En cuadrilla: los grafitos como fuente para el estudio del ámbito laboral en la producción anfórica de la Bética. Una nueva aproximación metodológica. Huarte de San Juan. *Geografía e Historia* 31 (May 2024): 165-80, viewed 1 May 2025, <https://doi.org/10.48035/rhsj-gh.31.8>.

Berni Millet, P. 2008. *Epigrafía anfórica de la Bética: Nuevas formas de análisis*. Barcelona: Publicacions i Edicions Universitat de Barcelona.

Berni Millet, P. 2021. Producción anfórica en Hispania. La evidencia de la epigrafía. L'épigraphie sur céramique, in W. Broekaert, A. Delattre, E. Dupraz and Mª.J. Estarán Tolosa (eds) *L'instrumentum domesticum, ses genres textuels et ses fonctions dans les sociétés antiques* (Hautes Etudes du monde gréco-romain 60): 19-39. Geneva: Droz.

Berni Millet., P. and C. Carreras Montfort 2013. Corpus epigràfic de segells en àmfores, dolia, tegulae i gerres de ceràmica, in C. Carreras Montfort, A. López Mullor and J. Guitart i Duran (eds) *Barcino*, II: *Marques i terrisseries d'àmfores al Baix Llobregat*: 127-285. Barcelona: ICAC.

Bezecky, T. 1997. Amphorae from the auxiliary fort of Carnuntum, in H. Stiglitz (ed.) *Das auxiliarkastell Carnuntum*, I: *Forschungen 1977-1988*: 147-78. Vienna: Österreichisches Archäologisches Institut.

Bezecky, T. 1998. Amphora types of Magdalensberg. *Arheoloski Vestnik = Acta archaeologica* 49: 225-42.

Blanc-Bijon, V., M.B. Carré, A. Hesnard and A. Tchernia 1998. *Recueil de timbres sur amphores romaines II (1989-1990 et compléments 1987-1988)*. Aix en Provence: Publications de l'Université de Provence.

Blázquez Martínez, J.M. and J. Remesal Rodríguez 1999. *Estudios sobre el Monte Testaccio (Roma)*, I. Barcelona: Servei de publicacions de la Universitat de Barcelona.

Blázquez Martínez, J.M. and J. Remesal Rodríguez 2001. *Estudios sobre el Monte Testaccio (Roma)*, II. Barcelona: Servei de publicacions de la Universitat de Barcelona.

Blázquez Martínez, J.M., J. Remesal Rodríguez and E. Rodríguez Almeida 1994. *Excavaciones arqueológicas en el Monte Testaccio (Roma): memoria de la Campaña de 1989*. Madrid: Ministerio de Cultura.

Bonsor, G.E. 1888. Marcas de alfareros romanos. *Memorias de la Sociedad Arqueológica de Carmona* 1: 56-62.

Bonsor, G.E. 1901. Los pueblos antiguos del Guadalquivir y las alfarerias romanas. *Revista de archivos, bibliotecas y museos* 12: 837-57

Bonsor, G.E. 1931a. *An Archaeological Sketch-Book of the Roman Necropolis de Carmona*. New York: Hispanic Society of America.

Bonsor, G.E. 1931b. *The Archaeological Expedition along the Guadalquivir*. New York: The Hispanic Society of America.

Börner, K., J.T. Maru and R.L. Goldstone 2004. The simultaneous evolution of author and paper networks. *PNAS* 101: 5266-5527.

Bourgeon, O. 2018. La production d'amphores oléicoles dans la basse vallée du Genil (Ecija, Séville, Espagne). Contribution à l'histoire socio-économique de la Bétique romaine (Ier s.-IVe s. ap. J.-C.). Unpublished PhD thesis, Université Paul Valéry-Montpellier III, viewed 1 May 2025, <http://www.theses.fr/2018MON30054>.

Bourgeon, O. 2022. *La production d'amphores à huile dans la vallée du Genil (Ier-Ve s. ap. J.-C.): contribution à l'histoire socio-économique de la Bétique romaine*. Barcelona: Publicaciones y ediciones de la Universidad de Barcelona.

Brughmans, T. 2013. Networks of networks: a citation network analysis of the adoption, use, and adaptation of formal network techniques in archaeology. *Literary and Linguistic Computing* 28.4: 538-62, <https://doi.org/10.1093/llc/fqt048>.

Buonopane, A. 2009. *Manueale di epigrafía latina* (Beni culturali 33). Rome: Carocci editore.

Callender, M.H. 1948. Las Ánforas del Sur de España y sus sellos. *Cuadernos de Historia Primitiva del Hombre* 3.2: 139-42.

Callender, M.H. 1965. *Roman Amphorae (with an Index of Stamps)*. London: Oxford University Press.

Carre, M.B., V. Gaggadis-Robin, A. Hesnard and A. Tchernia 1995. *Recueil de timbres sur amphores romaines (1987-1988)*. Aix en Provence: Publications de l'Université de Provence.

Carreras Montfort, C. 2009. Les marques d'àmfores produïdes als tallers de Barcino, in C. Carreras Monfort and J. Guitart i Duran (eds) *Barcino, I: Marques i terrisseries d'àmfores al pla de Barcelona*: 21-44. Barcelona: Institut d'estudis catalans. Institut català d'arqueologia clàssica.

Carreras Montfort, C. 2019. *Catàleg de marques d'àmfora, tègula, dolia i signacula del Vallès Occidental i Oriental*. Barcelona: Institut d'estudis catalans.

Carreras Montfort, C. and P.P.A. Funari 1998. *Britannia y el Mediterráneo: estudios sobre el abastecimiento de aceite bético y africano en Britannia*. Barcelona: Servei de Publicacions de la Universitat de Barcelona.

Carreras Montfort, C. and J. van den Berg (eds) 2017. *Amphorae from the Kops Plateau (Nijmegen): Trade and Supply to the Lower-Rhineland from the Augustan Period to AD 69/70*. Oxford: Archaeopress.

Carreras Montfort, C. and J. Guitart i Duran (eds) 2009. *Barcino, I: Marques i terrisseries d'àmfores al pla de Barcelona*. Barcelona: ICAC.

Carreras Montfort, C., A. López Mullor and J. Guitart i Duran (eds) 2013. *Barcino, II: Marques i terrisseries d'àmfores al Baix Llobregat*. Barcelona: ICAC.

Carreras Montfort, C., J. Folch, and J. Guitart i Duran (eds) 2019. *Laietània Interior: Marques i terrisseries d'àmfores al Vallès Occidental i Oriental*. Barcelona: ICAC.

Casulleras Calvo, J., M. García Brosa García Morcillo and R. Rovira Guardiola 1999. Los Grafitos del Siglo II (Campañas de 1989 y 1990), in J.M. Blázquez and J. Remesal, *Estudios sobre el Monte Testaccio (Roma)*, I: 53-74. Barcelona: Publicacions de la Universitat de Barcelona.

Cecconi, L. 1756. *Storia di Palestrina città del prisco Lazio*. Ascoli: Niccola Ricci.

Chic García, G. 1985. *Epigrafía anfórica de la Bética, I: Las marcas impresas en el barro sobre ánforas olearias (Dressel 19 20 23)*. Sevilla: Universidad de Sevilla.

Cipriano, S. and S. Mazzocchin 1998. I bolli di 'C.LAECANIUS BASSUS': un aggiornamento alla luce di nuovi dati da 'PATAVIUM'. *Aqvileia Nostra* 69: 362-78.

Cipriano, S. and S. Mazzocchin 2016. Le Produzioni di anfore adriatiche della Gens Iulia, in F. Mainardis (ed.) *'Voce concordi' Scritti per Claudio Zazzaria* (Centro di Antichità altoadriatiche 85): 217-46. Trieste: Editreg.

Comas i Sola, M. 1985. *Baetulo: les Àmfores*. Badalona: Museu de Badalona.

Comas i Sola, M. 1997. *Baetulo: les marques d'àmfora*. Barcelona: Institut d'estudis catalans.

Coorbel, S. 2018. Les producteurs de matériaux de construction en terre cuite et d'amphores en Gaule Narbonnaise: l'apport des estampilles à la connaissance des structures socio-économiques d'une province romaine (fin Ier s. av. - fin IIIème s. ap.). Unpublished PhD thesis, Montpellier 3, viewed 1 May 2025, <https://www.theses.fr/2018MON30046>.

Clark Maxwell, W.E. 1899. The Roman towns in the valley of the Baetis between Cordoba and Sevilla. *The Archaeological Journal* 56: 245-305.

Desbonnets, Q. 2018. Les ateliers d'amphores à huile du conventus d'Hispalis (Séville, Espagne). Caractérisation et étude d'une zone de production de la province romaine de Bétique (Ier s. av. J.-C.-Ve s. ap. J.-C.). Unpublished PhD thesis, Université Paul Valéry-Montpellier III, viewed 1 May 2025, <http://www.theses.fr/2018MON30041>.

Dubler, C. 2019. Commerce et diffusion de l'huile de Bétique dans les provinces des Gaules et des Germanies (Ier-IIIe s. ap. J.-C.). Unpublished PhD thesis, Université Paul Valéry-Montpellier

III, viewed 1 May 2025, <https://www.theses.fr/s139316>.

Dressel, H.A.E.F. 1899. *Corpus inscriptionum Latinarum, XV: Inscriptiones Urbis Romae Latinae: instrumentum domesticum Pars 2 fasc. 1. Adjectae sunt tabulae duae amphorarum et lucernarum formas exprimentes.* Berlin: De Gruyter.

Edmonson, J.C. 1987. *Two Industries in Roman Lusitania: Mining and Garum Production* (British Archaeological Reports, 362). Oxford: Archaeopress.

Ehmig, U. 2003. *Der römischen Amphoren aus Mainz* (Frankfurter Archäologische Schriften 4). Möhnesee: Bibliopolis.

Ehmig, U 2007. *Die romischen Amphoren im Umland von Mainz* (Frankfurter Archäologische Schriften 5). Wiesbaden: Reichert.

Etienne, R. and F. Mayet 2004. *L'huile hispanique: corpus des timbres amphoriques sur amphores Dressel 20.* Paris: De Boccard.

Fabiao, C. and A. Guerra 2016. *Marcas de* ânforas *romanas na Lusitânia (do Museu Nacional de Arqueologia de Lisboa ao Museo Nacional de Arte Romano de Mérida).* Lisbon: Academia das Ciências de Lisboa

Funari, P.P.A. 1996. *Dressel 20 Inscriptions from Britain and the Consumption of Spanish Olive Oil: With a Catalogue of Stamps.* Oxford: Tempvs Reparatvm.

García Brosa, G., M. García Morcillo, P. Ozcáriz and R. Rovira Guardiola 2001. Los Grafitos del Siglo III (Campañas de 1989, 1991 y 1992), in J.M. Blázquez and J. Remesal (eds) *Estudios sobre el Monte Testaccio (Roma)*, II: 305-66. Barcelona: Publicacions de la Universitat de Barcelona.

Garrote Sayó, E. 2016. *La presència de l'Oli Bétic a la Gallia Narbonensis.* Unpublished PhD thesis, Universitat de Barcelona, viewed 1 May 2025, <http://hdl.handle.net/2445/104754>.

Giménez, X., A. Mosca, J. Pérez, J. Remesal and G. Rull. in press. RomanOpenData: An application of semantic technologies to Roman amphora epigraphy. *Semantic Web.*

Gillam, J.P. and C.M. Daniels 1961. The Roman mausoleum on Shorden Brae, Beaufront, Corbridge, Northumberland. *Archaeologia Aeliana* 4th Series 39: 50.

González Cesteros, H. and P. Berni Millet 2018. *Roman Amphorae in Neuss: Augustan to Julio-Claudian Contexts* (Roman and Late Antique Mediterranean Pottery 12). Oxford: Archaeopress.

González Tobar, I. 2021. La production d'amphores à huile dans le Conventus Cordubensis (Province de Bétique, Espagne) à l'époque romaine. Nouvelles perspectives socio-économiques. Unpublished PhD thesis, Université Paul Valéry-Montpellier III, viewed 1 May 2025, viewed 1 May 2025, <http://www.theses.fr/s163320>.

González Tobar, I. 2023. *La production d'amphores à huile dans la moyenne vallée du Guadalquivir* (Instrumenta 84). Barcelona: Universitat de Barcelona Edicions.

González Tobar, I. and S. Estévez de la Mata 2021. Novedades sobre etiquetado y expedición del aceite bético: los tituli picti del alfar romano de El Sotillo (Almodóvar del Río, Córdoba). *SPAL: Revista de prehistoria y arqueología*, 30.1: 241-57.

González Tobar, I. and S. Mauné 2018. Un atelier rural inédit d'amphores à huile augusto-tibériennes. Fuente de los Peces (Fuente Palmera, province de Cordoue). *Mélanges de la Casa de Velázquez* n.s. 48.2: 203-34.

González Tobar, I., S. Mauné, O. Tiago-Seoa ne, E. García Vargas and F. Levêque 2018. L'Atelier d'amphores Dressel 20 et Haltern 70 d'El Mohíno à Palma del Río (Prov. de Cordoue, Espagne), Ier-IIe s.apr. J.-C. *SFECAG: Actes du Congrès de Reims*: 319-44.

González Tobar, I., A. Soler i Nicolau and P. Berni Millet 2023. Las Geórgicas de Virgilio in figlinis: a propósito de un grafito ante cocturam sobre un ánfora olearia bética. *Journal of Roman Archaeology* 36.1: 1-22, <https://doi.org/10.1017/S1047759423000156>.

Hirschfeld, O. 1888. *Corpus inscriptionum latinarum, XII: Inscriptiones Galliae Narbonensis Latinae.* Berlin: De Gruyter.

Hirschfeld, O. and C. Zangemeister 1907. *Corpus inscriptionum latinarum, XIII.2: Inscriptiones Trium Galliarum et Germaniarum latinae.* Berlin: De Gruyter.

Hübner, A. 1873. *Corpus inscriptionum latinarum, VII: Inscriptiones Britanniae Latinae.* Berlin: De Gruyter.

Hübner, Ae.1903. *Additamenta nova ad Corporis* vol. II, EE IX, Fasc. I, Berlin 1903, 12-185.

Keay, S.J. 1983. The import of olive oil into Catalunya during the third century A.D., in J.M. Blázquez Martínez and J. Remesal Rodríguez (eds) *Producción y comercio del aceite en la Antigüedad: segundo congreso internacional*: 551-68. Madrid: Universidad Complutense de Madrid.

Keay, S.J. 1984. *Late Roman Amphorae in the Western Mediterranean: A Typology and Economic Study; The Catalan Evidence*, 2 pts (British Archaeological Reports 196). Oxford: Archaeopress.

Lagóstena Barrios, L. 2001. *La producción de salsas y conservas de pescado en la Hispania romana (II a. C.-VI d. C.)* (Col·lecció instrumenta 11). Barcelona: Servei de publicacions de la Universitat de Barcelona.

Laubenheimer, M. and E. Marlière 2010. Échanges et vie économique *dans le Nord-Ouest des Gaules: le témoignage des amphores du IIe siècle avant J.-C. au IVe siècle après J.-C.*, 2 vols. Besançon: Presses universitaires de Franche-Comté.

Liou, B. and R. Marichal 1978. Les inscriptions peintes sur amphores de l'anse Saint-Gervais a Fos-sur-Mer. *Archaeonautica* 2: 109-81, viewed 1 May 2025, <https://doi.org/10.3406/nauti.1978.870>; <www.persee.fr/doc/nauti_0154-1854_1978_num_2_1_870>.

Lupi, A.M. 1734. *Dissertatio et animadversiones ad nuper inventum Severae Martyris epitaphium.* Palermo: ex typographia Stephani Amato.

Manacorda, D. 1977. Anfore spagnole a Pompei, in *L'instrumentum domesticum di Ercolano e Pompei nella prima età imperiali* (Quaderni di cultura materiali 1): 121-33. Rome: L'Erma di Bretschneider.

Manacorda, D. and S. Pallecchi 2012. *Le Fornaci Romane di Giancola (Brindisi)*. Bari: Edipuglia.

Mauné, S., E. García, O. Bourgeon, S. Corbeel, C.H. Carrato, S. García, F. Bigot and J. Vázquez 2014. L'atelier d'amphores à huile Dr. 20 de Las Delicias à Ecije (Prov. de Séville, Espagne). *SFECAG: Actes du Congrès de Chartres* 2014: 419-44.

Mayer, D. 2016. *Stempel auf amphoren aus Köln* (Kölner Jahrbuch 49. Band. Sonderdruck). Berlin: Mann.

Marimon, P. 2017. Entre el Mediterráneo y el limes germánico: el río Ródano como factor de comunicación e integración económica. Unpublished PhD thesis, Universitat de Barcelona, viewed 1 May 2025, <http://hdl.handle.net/2445/116487>.

Márquez Villora, J.C. and J. Molina Vidal 2005. *Del Hiberus a Carthago Nova. Comercio de alimentos y epigrafía anfórica grecolatina* (Instrumenta 18). Barcelona: Universitat de Barcelona.

Martin-Kilcher, S. 1987-94. *Die römischen Amphoren aus Augst und Kaiseraugst: Ein Beitrag zur römischen Handels und Kulturgeschichte*, I: *Die Südspanischen Ölamphoren (Gruppe 1)*; II: *Die Amphoren für Wein, Fischsauce, Südfrüchte (Gruppen 2-24) und Gesamtauswertung*; III: *Archäologische*. Augst: Römermuseum Augst.

Mataix, E. 2019. Rethinking the Roman epigraphy of merchandise: a metapragmatic approach. *Maarav* 23.1: 177-205.

Mayet, F. 1978. Marques d'amphores de Maurétanie Tingitane (*Banasa, Thamusida, Volubilis*). *Mélanges École française Rome: antiquité* 90: 357-406.

Mongardi, M. 2018. Firmissima et splendidissima populi Romani colonia: *L'epigrafia Anforica di Mutina e del suo territorio* (Instrumenta 62). Barcelona: Universitat de Barcelona.

Morcelli, S.A. 1781. *De stilo inscriptionum latinarum libri III. ex officina Giunchiana*. Rome: Ex officina Giunchiana.

Moros Díaz, J. 2014. La intervención Severiana en la producción del aceite bético, in J.M. Blázquez Martínez and J. Remesal Rodríguez (eds) *Estudios sobre el Monte Testaccio Roma*, VI: 773-860. Barcelona: Publicacions de la Universitat de Barcelona.

Moros Díaz, J. 2019. *Análisis epigráfico de los sellos olearios béticos hallados en centros de producción: el caso de la zona productora de la Scalensia*. Universitat de Barcelona. Unpublished PhD thesis, Universitat de Barcelona, viewed 1 May 2025, <http://hdl.handle.net/10803/666949>.

Moros Díaz, J. 2021. *Organización productiva de las ánforas olearias béticas (Dressel 20, ca. 30-270 d.C.)* (Instrumenta 77). Barcelona: Universitat de Barcelona.

Moros Díaz, J. 2022. Esquemas organizativos de la producción anfórica olearia bética (Dressel 20, *ca.* 30-270 d.C.), in J. Remesal Rodríguez and J. Pérez

González (eds) *Arqueología y téchne: métodos formales, nuevos enfoques / Archaeology and Techne: Formal Methods, New Approaches* (Access Archaeology): 98-112. Oxford: Archaeopress.

Moros Díaz, J. 2024. Las unidades productivas de las ánforas olearias béticas (Dressel 20, ca.30-20 d.C.). *Epigraphica* 86: 213-34, <https://doi.org/10.48255/0013-9572.EPIGR.86.2024.16>

Olmer, F. 1997. Les amphores romaines en Bourgogne. Contribution à l'histoire économique d'une région de La Téne finale au Haut-Empire, 4 vols. Unpublished PhD thesis, Université de Burgogne.

Ozcáriz, P. 2023. Los grafitos 'ante cocturam' de las ánforas Dressel 20: Propuesta de sistematización para la elaboración de un corpus, in M. Bentz and M. Heinzelmann (eds) *Archaeology and Economy in the Ancient World: Sessions 4-5, Single Contributions; Proceedings of the 19th International Congress of Classical Archaeology, Cologne/Bonn 2018*: 385-95. Heidelberg: Propylaeum, <https://doi.org/10.11588/propylaeum.1005.c13505>.

Ozcáriz, P. 2024. Los grafitos históricos como voz de los desfavorecidos. *Huarte de San Juan. Geografía e historia* 31 (May 2024): 7-17, <https://doi.org/10.48035/rhsj-gh.31.1>.

Ozcáriz Gil, P., J. Pérez González and J. Heredero Berzosa 2020. The logistics of marking in the Baetic amphoras. The use of numerals in the organizational systems of ceramic productions. *Studia antiqua et archaeologica* 26.2: 231-47.

Palacín Copado, C., J. Pérez González and G. Rull Fort 2020. Epigrafia amfòrica i roman open data: Les àmfores del litoral central de Catalunya com a cas d'estudi. *Laietania: Estudis d'historia i d'arqueología de Mataró i del Maresme* 21: 97-130.

Palazzo, P. 2013. *Le anfore di Apani (Brindisi)*. Rome: Scienze e lettere.

Panella, C. 1973. Le anfore, in A. Carandini *et al., Ostia*, III: *Studi miscellanei*: 463-633. Rome: De Luca.

Pascual Guasch, R. 1977. Las ánforas de la Layetania, in *Méthodes classiques et méthodes formelles dans l'étude des amphores actes du colloque de Rome 27-29 mai 1974*: 47-96. Rome: Ecole française de Rome.

Pascual Guasch, R. 1991. *Index d'Éstampilles sobre Àmfores Catalanes*. Barcelona: Edicions Servei del Llibre L'Estaquirot.

Pérez González, J. 2014. La base de datos *on line* del Ceipac. Los *tituli picti*. *Ar@cne: Revista electrónica de recursos en internet sobre geografía y ciencias sociales* 190 (1 November 2014), viewed 1 May 2025, <http://www.ub.es/geocrit/aracne/aracne-190.htm>.

Pérez González, J. 2018. Epigrafía lapidaria en la era digital. *Boletín del archivo epigráfico* 2: 5-16, viewed 1 May 2025, <http://archivoepigraficodehispania.es/data/documents/BAE-2.a.J.Perez.pdf>.

Petrini, P. 1795. *Memorie prenestine disposte in forma di annali*. Rome: Pagliarini.

Pons Pujol, Ll. 2009. *La economía de la Mauretania Tingitana (s.I-III d.C.): aceite, vina y salazones* (Instrumenta 34). Barcelona: Universitat de Barcelona.

Pons Pujol, Ll. and J. Pérez González 2018. La presencia del aceite bético en *Mauretania Tingitana*. Nuevos métodos de análisis. *Studia antiqua et archaeologica* 24.2: 279-302, viewed 1 May 2025 <http://saa.uaic. ro/articles/SAA.24.2.2018.279-302.pdf>.

Ponsich, M. 1979. *Implantation rurale antique sur le Bas-Guadalquivir*. Paris: De Boccard.

Project Team Visone 2019. Visone v.2.19, viewed 1 May 2025, <http://visone.info>.

Remesal Rodríguez, J. 1977-78. La economía oleicola bética: nuevas formas de análisis. *Archivo español de arqueología* 50-51: 87-142.

Remesal Rodríguez, J. 1986. *La annona militaris y la exportación de aceite betico a Germania.* Madrid: Ediciones de la Universidad Complutense.

Remesal Rodríguez, J. 1997. *Heeresversorgung und die wirtshaftlicjen beziehungen zwischen der Baetica und Germanien-Corpus der in Deutschland gefundenen stempell auf amphoren Dr.20.* Stuttgart: Theiss.

Remesal Rodríguez, J. 2011. *La Bética en el concierto del Imperio Romano.* Madrid: Real academia de la historia.

Remesal Rodríguez, J. 2012. Corpus versus Catalog, propuestas sobre una vieja cuestión, in M.E. Fuchs, R. Sylvestre and C.S. Heidenreich (eds) *Inscriptions mineures: nouveautes et reflexions; actes du premier colloque Ductus (19-20 juin 2008, Université de Lausanne).* Bern: Lang.

Remesal Rodríguez, J. 2016. Sellar para qué?, in M. Buora and S. Magnani (eds) *Le iscrizioni con funzione didascalico-esplicativa: committente, destinatario, contenuto e descrizione dell' oggetto nell' Instrumentum Inscriptum; atti del Vi incontro Instrumenta Inscripta. Aquileia (26-28 marzo 2015)*: 73-89. Trieste: Editreg.

Remesal Rodríguez, J. (ed.) 2018. *Colonia Ulpia Traiana (Xanten) y el Mediterráneo: El comercio de alimentos* (Instrumenta 63). Barcelona: Universitat de Barcelona, viewed 1 May 2025, <http://hdl.handle. net/2445/128515>.

Remesal Rodríguez, J. 2022. *Heinrich Dressel y el Testaccio. Nuevos datos sobre los materiales y la formación del Corpus Inscriptionum Latinarum, XV* (Instrumenta 82). Barcelona: Universitat de Barcelona.

Remesal Rodríguez, J. (2024). *Oleum Baeticum: Economía y política en el Imperio Romano.* Real Academia de la Historia.

Remesal Rodríguez, J. and A. Aguilera Martín 1999. *Addenda et corrigenda* a los *tituli picti* y a los sellos de la campaña de 1989. Indices de los tituli de la campaña de 1989, in J.M. Blázquez Martínez and J. Remesal Rodríguez (eds) *Estudios sobre el Monte Testaccio,* I: 101-27. Barcelona: Universitat de Barcelona.

Remesal Rodríguez, J. and A. Aguilera Martín 2001. Los *tituli picti*, in J.M. Blázquez Martínez and J. Remesal Rodríguez (eds) *Estudios sobre el Monte Testaccio (Roma)*, II. Barcelona, 45-203.

Remesal Rodríguez, J. and A. Aguilera Martín 2003. Los *tituli picti*, in J.M. Blázquez Martínez J. Remesal Rodríguez (eds) *Estudios sobre el Monte Testaccio (Roma)*, III: 45-196. Barcelona: Universitat de Barcelona.

Remesal Rodríguez J. and A. Aguilera Martín 2007. Los *tituli picti*, in J.M. Blázquez Martínez J. Remesal Rodríguez (eds) *Estudios sobre el Monte Testaccio (Roma)*, IV: 27-182. Barcelona: Universitat de Barcelona.

Remesal Rodríguez J. and A. Aguilera Martín 2010. Los *tituli picti*, in J.M. Blázquez Martínez J. Remesal Rodríguez (eds) *Estudios sobre el Monte Testaccio (Roma)*, V: 41-166. Barcelona: Universitat de Barcelona.

Remesal Rodríguez, J. and A. Aguilera Martín 2014. Los *tituli picti*, in J.M. Blázquez Martínez J. Remesal Rodríguez (eds) *Estudios sobre el Monte Testaccio (Roma)*, VI: 39-414. Barcelona: Universitat de Barcelona.

Remesal Rodríguez, J., P. Berni Millet and A. Aguilera Martín 2008. Amphoreninschriften und ihre elektronische Bearbeitung, in M. Hainzmann and R. Wedenig (eds) *Instrumenta inscripta latina*, II: *Akten des 2. internationalen Kolloquiums, Klagenfurt, 5-8 Mai 2005*: 247-64. Klagenfurt: Verlag des Geschichtsverein für Kärnten.

Remesal Rodríguez, J., M. García Sánchez and G. Rull 2017. La banque de données d'épigraphie amphorique grecque du CEIPAC et EPNet Project, in *Protection and Enhancement of Cultural Heritage: The Case of Transport Amphorae; Proceedings of the Scientific Conference; Rhodes, 30 September 2017*: 171-83. Rhodes: Ministry of Culture and Sports Ephorate of Antiquities of the Dodecanese.

Remesal Rodríguez, J. and J. Moros Díaz 2019. Los negocios de Caius Iuventius Albinus en la Bética. *Journal of Roman Archaeology* 32: 224-49 <https://doi. org/10.1017/S1047759419000138>.

Remesal Rodríguez, J., V. Porcheddu and M. García Sánchez 2013. *Sodales Adiuvate!* Il contributo dell'informatica al progresso dell'epigrafia anforaria greca. *Epigraphica* 75.1-2: 309-36.

Remesal, J., R. Rovira, G. García and P. Ozcáriz 2003. Los grafitos, in J.M. Blázquez and J. Remesal (eds) *Estudios sobre el Monte Testaccio (Roma)*, III: 363-98. Barcelona: Universitat de Barcelona.

Remesal, J., P. Marimón, R. Rovira and J. Torres 2007. Los grafitos del siglo III (campañas de 1995, 1996 y 1997), in J.M. Blázquez, J. Remesal (eds) *Estudios sobre el Monte Testaccio (Roma)*, IV. Barcelona: Universitat de Barcelona: 233-316.

Remesal, J., S. Calzada, R. Rovira and J. Soria 2010. Los grafitos, in J.M. Blázquez and J. Remesal (eds) *Estudios sobre el Monte Testaccio (Roma)*, V: 243-372. Barcelona: Universitat de Barcelona.

Remesal Rodríguez J., A. Aguilera Martín, M. García Sánchez, D.-J. Martín-Arroyo Sánchez, J. Pérez

González and V. Revilla Calvo 2015. Centro para el Estudio de la Interdependencia Provincial en la Antigüedad Clásica (CEIPAC). *Pyrenae: Revista de prehistòria i antiguitat de la Mediterrània Occidental* 50, special volume: 245-75.

Remesal, J., R. Ayllón, S. Calzada, J. Moros and R. Rovira Guadiola 2014. Los grafitos, in J.M. Blázquez and J. Remesal (eds) *Estudios sobre el Monte Testaccio (Roma)*, VI: 465-536. Barcelona: Universitat de Barcelona.

Remesal Rodríguez, J., Ll. Pons Pujol, J. Pérez González and J.M. Bermúdez Lorenzo 2019. Nuevas Propuestas de datación de la epigrafía anfórica a través de la cronología de los asentamientos militares del *limes* renano-danubiano. *Espacio, tiempo y forma, serie II, historia antigua* 32: 173-214, <https://doi.org/10.5944/etfii.32.2019.24343>.

Rodríguez Almeida, E. 1989. *Los* Tituli picti *de las Anforas Olearias de la Betica:* Tituli picti *de los Severos y de la* Ratio Fisci. Universidad Complutense de Madrid. Madrid 1989. *L'antiquité classique* 199: 433-34, viewed 1 May 2025, <www.persee.fr/doc/antiq_0770-2817_1993_num_62_1_1176_t1_0433_0000_2>.

Rodríguez Almeida, E. 1993. Graffiti e produzione anforaria della Betica, in W.V. Harris (ed.) *The Inscribed Economy*: 95-106. Ann Arbor: University of Michigan.

Rodríguez Almeida, E. 1994. Scavi sul Monte Testaccio: novità dei *Tituli picti. Publications de l'École Française de Rome* 193: 111-31, viewed 1 May 2025, <www.persee.fr/doc/efr_0000-0000_1994_act_193_1_3073>.

Rovira Guardiola, R. 2004. *Las Relaciones comerciales entre Hispania y las provincias orientales durante el Alto Imperio Romano*. Unpublished PhD thesis, Universitat de Barcelona, viewed 1 May 2025, <http://hdl.handle.net/10803/2589>.

Rovira Guardiola, R. 2007. Grafitos ante cocturam sobre ánforas Dressel 20: una propuesta de evolución cronológica, in *Acta XII Congressus internationalis epigraphiae Graecae et Latinae (Barcelona, 3-8 Septembris 2002)* (Monografies de la secció històrico-arqueològica 10): 1255-62. Barcelona: Institut d'estudis catalans.

Rubio-Campillo, X., J.M. Bermúdez Lorenzo, J.-M. Montanier, J. Moros Díaz, J. Pérez González, G. Rull and J. Remesal Rodríguez 2018. Provincias, sellos e hipótesis nulas: la identificación de rutas de comercio a través de medidas de distancia cultural, in J. Remesal Rodríguez (ed.) *Cuantificar: qué, cómo y para qué; Quantification in Classical Archaeology; Objects, Methodologies and Aims*: 237-49. Barcelona: Universitat de Barcelona.

Rubio-Campillo, X., M. Coto-Sarmiento, J. Pérez-Gonzalez and J. Remesal Rodríguez 2017. Bayesian analysis and free market trade within the Roman Empire. *Antiquity* 91.359: 1241-52, <https://doi.org/10.15184/aqy.2017.131>.

Rubio-Campillo, X., J.-M. Montanier, G. Rull, Bermúdez J.M. Lorenzo, J. Moros Díaz, J. Pérez González and J. Remesal Rodríguez 2018. The ecology of Roman trade. Reconstructing provincial connectivity with similarity measures. *Journal of Archaeological Science* 92: 37-47 <https://doi.org/10.1016/j.jas.2018.02.010>.

Schimmer, F. 2009. *Amphoren aus Cambodunum/Kempten: Ein Beitrag zur Handelsgeschichte der römischen Provinz Raetia* (Münchner Beiträge zur provinzialrömischen Archäologie. 1). Wiesbaden: Reichert.

Sinclair, A. 2016. The intellectual base of archaeological research 2004-2013: a visualisation and analysis of its disciplinary links, networks of authors and conceptual language. *Internet Archaeology* 42 <https://doi.org/10.11141/ia.42.8>.

Susini, G.C. 1962. *Fonti per la storia greca e romana del Salento*. Bologna: Accademia delle scienze dell'Istituto di Bologna.

Thouvenot, R. 1941. Marques d'amphores romaines trouvées au Maroc. *Publications du Service des antiquités du Maroc* 6: 95-98

Zangemeister, C. 1906. *Corpus inscriptionum latinarum*, XIII: *Inscriptiones Trium Galliarum et Germaniarum Latinae, Pars II, fasc. 1, Inscriptiones Germaniae superioris*. Berlin: De Gruyter.

16. Moldes de silicona y dendrogramas en el análisis de los sellos anfóricos olearios béticos

(Dressel 20, *ca.* 30/270 d.C.)

Juan Moros Diaz

Introducción

El estudio de los sellos de las ánforas olearias béticas cuenta con una larga tradición bibliográfica. Desde que Dressel diera a conocer los materiales del *CIL* XV a finales del s. XIX, se ha realizado un notable esfuerzo por parte de los investigadores para comprender su significado y extraer de los sellos información válida. Pero la investigación desarrollada sobre estos documentos presenta, aún hoy en día, serias carencias técnicas y metodológicas.

Por un lado, la reproducción de los sellos en las publicaciones ha supuesto un problema que hemos tardado en solucionar. Las imágenes de los sellos son un aspecto básico de la información que éstos nos aportan. En las ánforas Dressel 20, los sellos se desarrollan sobre superficies curvas de diversas partes de los envases. Esta circunstancia ha sido determinante a la hora de reproducirlos de manera fidedigna y los métodos de representación tradicionalmente utilizados: transcripciones tipográficas, dibujos con diversos convenios gráficos, calcos o fotografías, presentaban una serie de limitaciones que han lastrado el avance de la investigación, haciendo de la clasificación de los sellos una tarea subjetiva difícilmente sostenible.

Por otro lado, los sellos se suelen presentar en los trabajos a partir de *corpora* o catálogos que pueden seguir diversos convenios de organización interna. Una vez establecida esta organización, sea cual sea, se van presentando sello tras sello en forma de fichas, donde se consignan una serie de datos asociados a cada sello, que pueden variar de autor a autor. Pero, esta manera de presentar la información está condicionada por la paginación y presenta un alto grado de fragmentación. En estas condiciones resulta arduo llegar a tener una imagen de conjunto de los sistemas de sellado de los talleres.

En este trabajo presentamos dos nuevas herramientas que nos ayudarán a resolver estos problemas: una nueva manera de representar los sellos (apartado 1) y un modelo epigráficamente lógico que nos permitirá optimizar la organización del material (apartado 2). En este segundo apartado, el más extenso, presentamos una explicación detallada sobre la confección de los dendrogramas (MRE) o mapas de relaciones epigráficas de una familia de sellos (2.2) o de las familias de sellos de un determinado centro productor (2.3). Finalmente, en el apartado 3 incluimos una interpretación general sobre la función de los sellos de las ánforas olearias béticas, que nos permitirá extraer todo el potencial de las nuevas herramientas de análisis presentadas.

1. La representación gráfica del material: los moldes de silicona

La investigación de los sellos de Dressel 20 se ha visto condicionada decisivamente por las limitaciones que presentaban los métodos usados en la propia representación gráfica del material, a pesar de contar con una solución óptima a este problema desde sus inicios. Dressel había conseguido realizar unos calcos de los sellos en papel de muy buena calidad (Figura 16.1b). Estos calcos no llegaron a publicarse debido a que las técnicas de impresión de finales del s. XIX no lo permitían, pero posibilitaron que Dressel clasificara los sellos incluidos en el *CIL* XV de manera muy precisa, sin tener que volver a recurrir al material. Desgraciadamente, la técnica usada por Dressel no llegó a los investigadores y durante los siguientes 100 años se usaron diversos métodos para representar gráficamente los sellos que, por uno u otro motivo, presentaban limitaciones que han dificultado el avance de la investigación. Los más usados han sido los dibujos realizados a partir de calcos en papel y en menor medida las fotografías. Como hemos visto, los sellos de las Dressel 20 se presentan sobre superficies curvas, generalmente sobre las asas de los envases. Esta circunstancia impide que una fotografía de los sellos sea una buena forma de representarlos, pues la imagen aparece deformada debido a la perspectiva y será imposible obtener de ella unas simples medidas del epígrafe. Para conseguir una imagen plana se utilizaron calcos en papel y sus dibujos, pero el sistema presentaba un alto grado de subjetividad. Dibujos de un mismo ejemplar realizados por distintos investigadores producían resultados diferentes (Barea *et al.* 2008: 173, fig. 6 y 7).

a

b

c

Figura 16.1 Transcripción tipográfica de Dressel (a), calco de Dressel (b) y molde de silicona (c) de un mismo ejemplar CIL XV 2571. (Imágenes del calco y molde: CEIPAC)

Siento éste el estado de la cuestión, en 2008 presentamos una nueva técnica para representar gráficamente los sellos anfóricos basada en la confección de moldes de silicona (Figura 16.1c), que no era más que una puesta al día de la técnica utilizada por Dressel (Barea *et al*. 2008: 167-80). Ambos métodos nos permiten contar con una imagen plana, neutra y objetiva de los epígrafes.

La técnica presenta evidentes ventajas:

- Facilidad y rapidez de ejecución.
- La información que se aporta es neutra, objetiva y reproducible.
- Dado que las fotografías de los sellos se obtienen en condiciones de laboratorio, esto ayuda a facilitar la lectura de sellos que se presentan mal impresos, deteriorados o faltos de relieve
- Permite afrontar dos nuevas líneas de investigación: la clasificación de las matrices y el estudio del diseño de los sellos.

En estos años, la técnica de los moldes de silicona ha pasado a ser el estándar de publicación de los sellos de las Dressel 20[1]. Sin embargo, no ha trascendido a

otros tipos anfóricos o a otros objetos del llamado *instrumentum domesticum inscriptum*, lo que pone de relieve la compartimentación que todavía hoy presentan los estudios dedicados a estos documentos.

2. La clasificación y organización de los sellos: los dendrogramas (MRE)

Cuando estudiamos los sellos de un determinado centro de producción debemos describir los sistemas de sellado utilizados y cómo éstos evolucionaron en el tiempo (Remesal 1977-78: 89). Con los sistemas de organización de los sellos tradicionalmente utilizados, *corpora* y catálogos, resulta arduo obtener una imagen de conjunto que nos permita comprender la serie y establecer sus pautas, ya que, por su propia naturaleza y por la paginación, la información se presenta muy fragmentada. Entendemos que sería más conveniente utilizar un sistema de organización de los sellos en forma de diagrama de árbol, que condense y resuma en una sola imagen, por muy grande que resulte, todas las

---

[1] Un nutrido grupo de publicaciones ya incluyen esta técnica de representación: Barea *et al*. 2008; Moros *et al*. 2010; Moros 2014;

Remesal en Testaccio 2010; 2014; Berni 2015: 173-207; 2017: 185-282. Esta técnica ha sido adoptada por los investigadores franceses y españoles que trabajan en los centros productores de la Bética dentro del proyecto OLEASTRO de las Universidades de Montpellier 3 y Sevilla (p. ej. Bourgeon *et al*. 2016; González Tobar *et al* 2018).

Tabla 16.1. Cuadro simplificado de los contenidos de los sellos y sus marcadores.

JERARQUÍA CONTENIDO	Elementos principales	Elementos secundarios (ATRIBUTOS).
Nombres de personas	Personajes principales **TRIA NOMINA** (P+N+C1)	**(A1)** *clarissimus vir, pater et filius, numerales*
	Personajes subordinados **COGNOMINA** (C2)	**(A2)** *servus, libertus, fecit*
Nombres de personas	**TOPÓNIMOS** (T)	**(A3)** *figlinae, officinae, fundi, coloniae, portus.*
Símbolos	**SÍMBOLO** (s)	

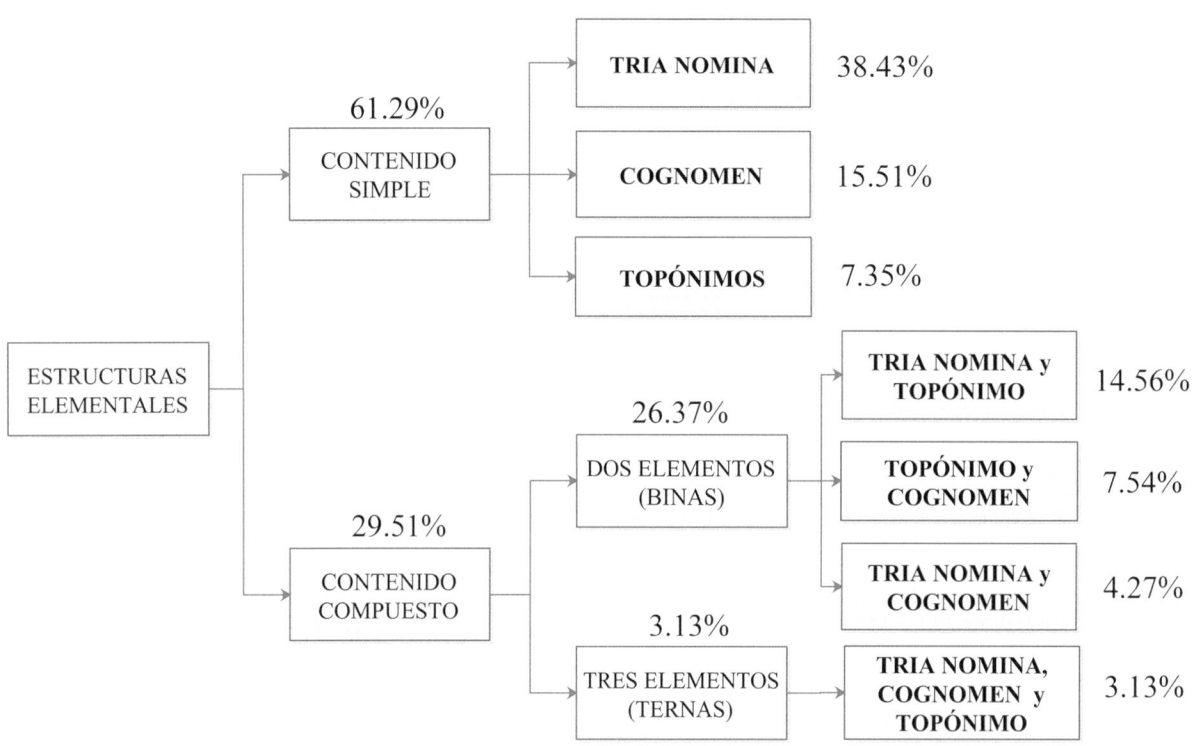

Figura 16.2 Estructuras elementales y su incidencia en el sellado

características de los sellos que debemos conocer para describir los sistemas de sellado del taller.

Con este objetivo hemos desarrollado una idea de Berni sobre la clasificación de los sellos (Berni 2008: 140). El sistema agrupa los sellos por sus contenidos y los ordena a partir de cuatro niveles de clasificación:

FAMILIA → ESTRUCTURA → LECTURA → MATRIZ

A este sistema de organización de los sellos lo denominamos técnicamente dendrogramas (MRE) o mapas de relaciones epigráficas. Antes de pasar a

describir este nuevo sistema debemos conocer algunos aspectos básicos de los sellos de las Dressel 20.

2.1. Conceptos básicos de los sellos de las ánforas olearias béticas

2.1.1. El contenido de los sellos

Los sellos están compuestos por uno o varios elementos simples que clasificamos por su "jerarquía" y "contenido". En esencia, por su jerarquía en la inscripción, los elementos de los sellos se pueden dividir entre elementos principales y sus ATRIBUTOS

Tabla 16.2. Nivel II: Fórmulas epigráficas de la familia de sellos de *C.Ennius Hispanus* de Huertas del Río

| Fórmula epigráfica | Personaje principal. | | | Topónimo |
	Praenomen (P)	Nomen (N)	Cognomen (C1)	Topónimo (T)
C1+T			X	X
P+N+C1+T	X	X	X	X

(columnas de la Tabla 16.1). Por su contenido, a su vez, se pueden dividir entre nombres de personas y nombres de lugares (filas de la Tabla 16.1).

2.1.2. Características básicas del sistema de sellado bético

En nuestra opinión, la composición del texto de los sellos de las ánforas olearias béticas, que a primera vista se nos presenta como un verdadero galimatías, en esencia resulta extremadamente simple. Contamos con tres elementos principales, denominados genéricamente: TRIA NOMINA, COGNOMEN y TOPÓNIMO, que pueden aparecer en los sellos solos (como elementos simples), asociados por parejas (lo que hemos llamado binas) o los tres juntos (que llamamos ternas). De modo que el sistema de sellado se puede reducir a siete estructuras elementales[2], tres de contenido simple y cuatro de contenido compuesto. En la Figura 16.2 presentamos un cuadro que recoge la incidencia de cada una de estas estructuras elementales en el sistema de sellado de las ánforas olearias béticas[3].

2.2. Los dendrogramas (MRE): familia, estructura, lectura, matriz

Una vez que conocemos las características básicas de los sellos de las Dressel 20 podemos pasar a definir la confección de los dendrogramas. En la Figura 4 incluimos el dendrograma de la familia de sellos de *C.Ennius Hispanus* de Huertas del Río[4], que nos va a servir de ejemplo para describir sus cuatro niveles de clasificación.

- **Nivel I "Familia":** El concepto de familia de sellos fue redefinido[5] por Berni (2008: 139 ss.) para mostrar el criterio usado por Dressel al agrupar sellos en el *CIL* XV. Una familia está constituida por un grupo de sellos que comparten un elemento común, ya sea éste unos Tria Nomina, un Cognomen o un Topónimo.

  En la serie que nos ocupa (Figura 16.3), estudiamos la familia de sellos de *C. Ennius Hispanus"*.

- **Nivel II "Estructura":** Los sellos están compuestos por uno o varios elementos simples en una disposición determinada a la que denominamos "estructura del sello". Cada estructura viene representada por su "fórmula epigráfica". El concepto de fórmula epigráfica fue acuñado por Berni (2008: 134). Sería el esquema de la estructura de cada sello expresada como suma de los marcadores que representan a sus elementos simples. Los marcadores que representan a cada uno de los elementos simples que componen los sellos podemos verlos en la Tabla 16.1.

  En esta serie, tenemos dos estructuras representadas por sendas fórmulas epigráficas (Tabla 16.2). El personaje principal se asocia al TOPÓNIMO, y puede aparecer con todos los elementos de la onomástica romana (*praenomen, nomen y cognomen*) o únicamente con su *cognomen*.

- **Nivel III "Lectura":** Denominamos lectura al texto que presenta el sello resolviendo los posibles nexos y sin consignar los puntos ni los elementos decorativos. Sellos de una misma familia y estructura, pueden obedecer a diversas lecturas, es decir, diversos desarrollos del

---

[2] En las estructuras de los sellos (*vide* apartado 2.2) recogemos todos sus elementos, los elementos principales y sus Atributos, en la disposición que presentan en la inscripción. En las estructuras elementales solo consideramos sus elementos principales, sea cual sea la forma que tienen los sellos de expresarlos, y sin considerar el orden en que éstos aparecen en los epígrafes.

[3] En el cuadro de la Figura 3 están recogidas las estructuras que presentan una incidencia superior al 0.5% sobre el total de las lecturas conocidas y representan al 90 % de los sellos. Para elaborar estas estadísticas se estudiaron más de 2500 lecturas distintas y sus resultados pueden consultarse en el capítulo 1 de la publicación de nuestra tesis doctoral: Moros Diaz 2021: 19-56.

[4] Referencias básicas del yacimiento: Clark-Maxwell 1899: 268 ("Las Huertas del Río"); Bonsor 1931: 51 ("Huertas del Río"), lám. XXXIV (133-47); Ponsich 1979: 43 nº 79 ("Huerta del Río"), fig. 13 y lám. VIII. Chic 2001: 167 ("La Manteca"); Remesal 1977-78: 113 ("Huerta de Nicasio"), 2001: 52.

[5] El término "familia de sellos" fue acuñado por Remesal con otro sentido: "sellos diversos, pero que al llevar el mismo *nomen*, y a veces del mismo *cognomen* o *praenomen*, podía proponerse que pertenecieran a individuos de la misma familia" (Remesal 2000: 378). En nuestros trabajos, a este concepto de Remesal lo denominamos: "grupos familiares" (Remesal 1977-78: 110).

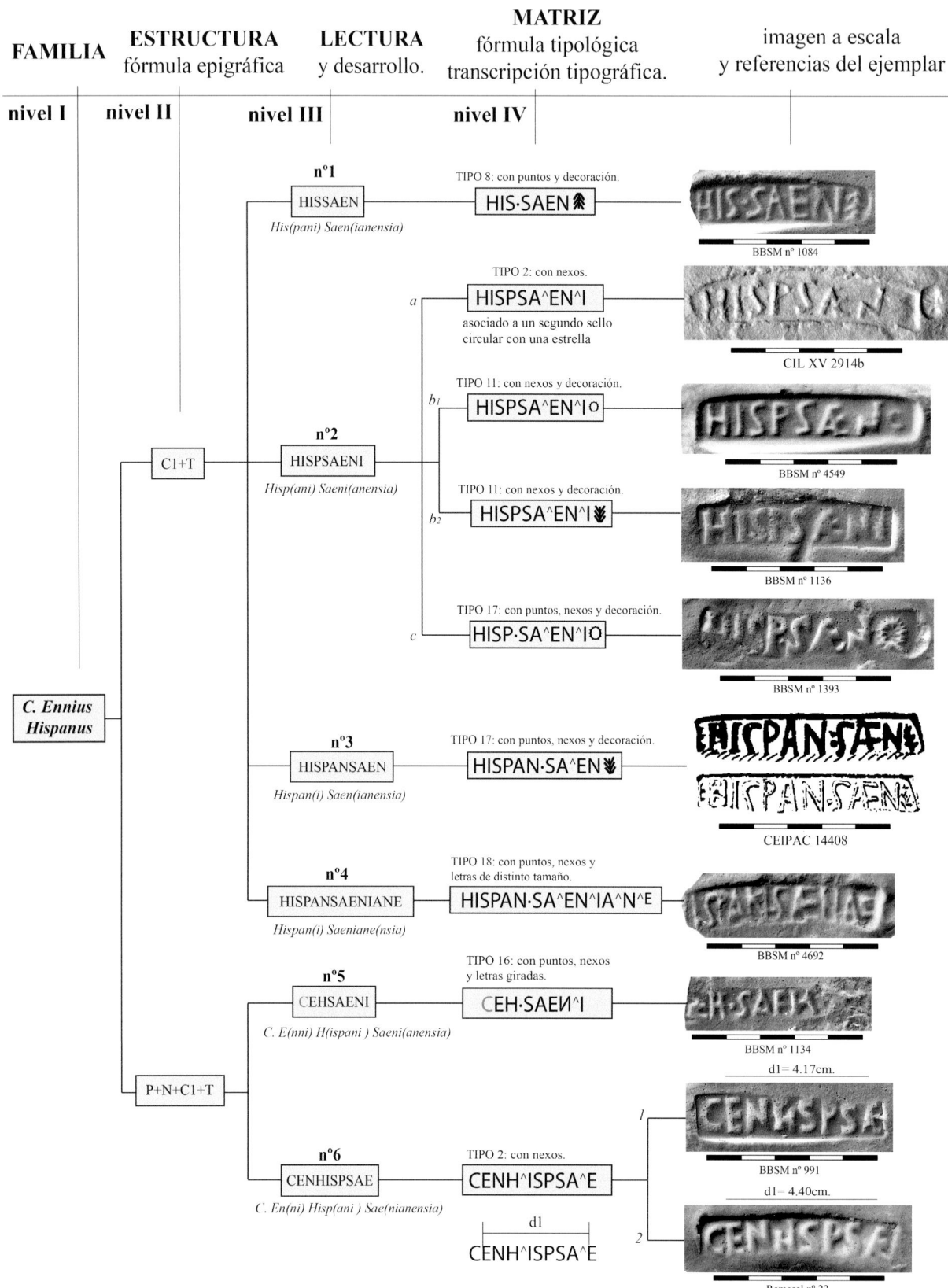

Figura 16.3 Dendrograma de la familia de sellos de *C. Ennius Hispanus* de Huertas del Río

Figura 16.4. **Composición de la fórmula tipológica de las matrice**s

Tabla 16.3. Nivel III: Organización de las lecturas de la familia de**de *C.Ennius Hispanus* de Huertas del Río**

| Estructura. | Nº | Lectura | Personaje principal. | | | Topónimo |
			Praenomen (P)	*Nomen* (N)	*Cognomen* (C1)	Topónimo. (T)
C1+T	1	HISSAEN			His(pani)	*Saen(ianensia)*
	2	HISPSAENI			Hisp(ani)	*Saen(ianensia)*
	3	HISPANSAEN			Hispan(i)	*Saen(ianensia)*
	4	HISPANSAENIANE			Hispan(i)	*Saen(ianensia)*
P+N+C1+T	5	CEHSAENI	C	E(nni)	H(ispani)	*Saeni(anensia)*
	6	CENHISPSAE	C	En(ni)	Hisp(ani)	*Saeni(anensia)*

texto. Las 6 lecturas que componen la serie que tratamos quedan reflejadas en la Table 16.3.

- **Nivel IV "Matriz"**: Sellos con una misma lectura pueden derivar de matrices diversas[6]. Las clasificamos por su "fórmula tipológica". Sellos que presentan la misma fórmula tipológica se clasifican por su "transcripción tipográfica". Finalmente, sellos que obedecen a una misma trascripción tipográfica se clasifican por el tamaño de la matriz, de menor a mayor.

Veamos con más detenimiento el sistema adoptado para clasificar las matrices de los sellos.

2.2.1. Fórmula tipológica.

Está compuesta por cuatro elementos o niveles de clasificación: nivel 1 (forma de la cartela), nivel 2 (relieve del texto), nivel 3 (dirección de lectura) y nivel 4 (elementos caracterizadores del texto, tipos 0-31) (Figura 16.4).

- **Forma de la cartela.** Nivel 1 de la fórmula tipológica (Figura 16.4). Campo o caja de escritura donde se encuentra contenida la inscripción. Pueden presentar distintas formas (rectangulares, cuadradas, circulares u ovaladas...) y diseños (simples, dobles, enmarcadas, festoneadas...). Podemos ver un cuadro de la clasificación adoptada en Moros Diaz 2021: figura 50. Otra clasificación en Berni 2008: figura 17.

- **Relieve del texto.** Nivel 2 de la fórmula tipológica (Figura 16.4). Los sellos pueden presentarse impresos con letras excisas (*litteris extantibus*) (95%), incisas (*litteris cavis*) (4.8%) o ambas al mismo tiempo (*litteris simul extantibus et cavis*) (0,09%) (Berni 2008: 65-69).

- **Sentido de la lectura.** Nivel 3 de la fórmula tipológica (Figura 16.4). Los sellos pueden presentarse impresos con una lectura directa, de izquierda a derecha (91,8%), o retro, de derecha a izquierda (8,2%) (Berni 2008: 65-69).

- **Clasificación de las matrices por los elementos caracterizadores del texto (Tipos 0-31).** Nivel 4 de la fórmula tipológica (Figura 16.4). Clasificación de las matrices de los sellos que resulta de las combinaciones posibles que pueden adoptar los cinco elementos caracterizadores del texto seleccionados: puntos, nexos, letras giradas y reflejadas, elementos decorativos y

---

[6] Remesal 1977-78: 102. Sobre la mecánica del sellado de las ánforas olearias béticas: Remesal 1977-78: 98; Moros 2020.

TIPOS.	Puntos.	Nexos	Letras giradas	Decoración	Letra ≠ tamaño.	
0						-
1	X					1 elemento.
2		X				
3			X			
4				X		
5					X	
6	X	X				2 elementos
7	X		X			
8	X			X		
9	X				X	
10		X	X			
11		X		X		
12		X			X	
13			X	X		
14			X		X	
15				X	X	
16	X	X	X			3 elementos
17	X	X		X		
18	X	X			X	
19	X		X	X		
20	X		X		X	
21	X			X	X	
22		X	X	X		
23		X	X		X	
24		X		X	X	
25			X	X	X	
26	X	X	X	X		4 elementos
27	X	X	X		X	
28	X	X		X	X	
29	X		X	X	X	
30		X	X	X	X	
31	X	X	X	X	X	5 elementos

Figura 16.5 Tipos de matrices por los cinco elementos caracterizadores del diseño de su texto

letras de distinto tamaño. Estos elementos han sido seleccionados por su representatividad en el sellado y presentan incidencias de entre el 40% y el 3% sobre el total de los ejemplares de la base de datos CEIPAC. Como resultado de estas combinaciones posibles obtenemos 32 tipos diferentes. Así, una matriz "tipo 0" no presentaría ningún elemento caracterizador y la "tipo 31" contendría los cinco. Con un elemento caracterizador tendremos los tipos 1 a 5, con dos los tipos 6 a 15, con tres los tipos 16 a 25 y con cuatro los tipos 26 a 30 (Figura 16.5).

En la serie que nos ocupa tenemos las siguientes fórmulas tipológicas (Tabla 16.4)

En las ánforas olearias béticas, la inmensa mayoría de los sellos presentan cartelas del tipo A1 (cartela simple rectangular), letras excisas (*litt. extantibus*) y lectura directa. Solo vendrán indicadas en la fórmula tipológica si cambian alguno de estos datos. De modo que, si no se indica nada, y en la fórmula tenemos por ejemplo "Tipo 2", debemos sobrentender que la fórmula es "A1/*Litt. extantibus*/Directa/Tipo 2".

2.2.2. Transcripción tipográfica.

Son esquemas donde se recogen, además del texto, los elementos caracterizadores del diseño de los sellos: puntos, nexos, letras giradas o reflejadas, elementos decorativos y letras de distinto tamaño. Orientan al lector sobre las características básicas que nos llevan a diferenciar las matrices. Se trata de una simplificación de las transcripciones tipográficas establecidas por Dressel en el *CIL* XV (Figura 16.1a). Veamos algunas convenciones adoptadas en las trascripciones tipográficas:

- Los puntos (triangulares, circulares y ondulados) se esquematizan y se colocan en la posición que adoptan en la inscripción.
- Los nexos se esquematizan con un acento circunflejo (^) entre las letras involucradas y un guion ondulado (~) si se trata de una ligadura.

Tabla 16.4. Nivel IV: Fórmulas tipológicas de las matrices de la familia de sellos de *C. Ennius Hispanus* de Huertas del Río

Fórmula tipológica.	Forma de la cartela	Relieve del texto.	Sentido de la lectura	Elementos del texto (tipos 0-31)
Tipo 2	(A1) Rectangular	*Litt. extantibus.*	Directa	Con nexos
Tipo 8	(A1) Rectangular	*Litt. extantibus.*	Directa	Con puntos y decoración
Tipo 11	(A1) Rectangular	*Litt. extantibus.*	Directa	Con nexos y decoración
Tipo 16	(A1) Rectangular	*Litt. extantibus.*	Directa	Con puntos, nexos y letras giradas
Tipo 17	(A1) Rectangular	*Litt. extantibus.*	Directa	Con puntos, nexos y decoración
Tipo 18	(A1) Rectangular	*Litt. extantibus.*	Directa	Con puntos, nexos y letras de distinto tamaño

- Las letras giradas o reflejadas se recogen en la posición que adoptan en el texto.
- Los elementos decorativos se esquematizan con la forma aproximada que presentan.
- Las matrices de lectura retro se recogen tal cual aparecen en el epígrafe.
- No se incluyen las formas particulares de las letras, dado que contamos con una imagen del sello.
- Otros elementos caracterizadores no considerados en las fórmulas tipológicas quedan recogidos no obstante en la transcripción tipográfica, por ejemplo: letras en griego, letras borradas, etc.

Una vez clasificadas tipológicamente y determinadas sus transcripciones tipográficas, nos quedan pocas herramientas para individualizar las matrices, ya que varias matrices distintas pueden obedecer a una misma transcripción tipográfica. Esto sucede, por ejemplo, en el sello CENHISPSAE (nº6 de la Figura 16.3). En cada uno de los grupos resultantes debemos dilucidar internamente y por comparación, qué ejemplares pertenecen a cada matriz concreta.

El criterio que usamos para separar matrices distintas es tomar las medidas de ciertas partes del sello, que se recogen en un diagrama adjunto a la tipología correspondiente (Figura 16.3, nº6), y procedemos a ordenar los ejemplares, dentro de cada trascripción tipográfica, por su tamaño (de menor a mayor). Si los sellos presentan diferente tamaño, obedecerán a matrices distintas. En este punto, debemos tener en cuenta las tolerancias dimensionales que son admisibles entre dos sellos procedentes de la misma matriz, que hemos estudiado en otro trabajo (Moros 2020: 689).

Con esta clasificación, la familia de sellos de *C.Ennius Hispanus* de Huertas del Río está compuesta, hasta el momento, por 2 estructuras, 6 lecturas y 10 matrices distintas (Figura 16.3).

2.3.- Los dendrogramas de las familias de sellos de un centro productor: el caso de la *figlina Saenianensia*

Acabamos de ver los criterios adoptados para confeccionar el dendrograma de la familia de sellos de *C.Ennius Hispanus* de Huertas del Río. Ahora podemos trabajar sobre todas las familias de sellos de este centro productor. En Huertas del Río desarrolló su actividad la *figlina Saenianensia*, que se sitúa en el *conventus* de *Hispalis* junto a la localidad de Lora del Río, en la orilla derecha del Guadalquivir. El sellado de las ánforas en este centro productor se desarrolla entre Nerón-Vespasiano y el final de Marco Aurelio-Cómodo.

Dado que incluimos todos los sellos del taller, el tamaño del dendrograma resultante impide su publicación en papel, aunque se puede descargar de una dirección web[7].

A la hora de acometer el dendrograma de un taller, en primer lugar, debemos establecer el orden de prioridades de los elementos que componen los sellos. Veamos este asunto más desarrollado.

---

[7] Para seguir la explicación, los investigadores interesados pueden descargar el dendrograma de la *figlina Saenianensia* en formato PDF en la siguiente dirección web: <https://ub.academia.edu/JuanMorosDiaz> en el apartado dedicado a los dendrogramas (MRE): Huertas del Río, versión 01 (2021). Otros ejemplos, con los dendrogramas de Cerro de los Pesebres, El Mohíno, Cortijo de Romero y la serie de *C. Iuventius Albinus* de Malpica, pueden descargarlos en esa misma página o en el repositorio de la Universidad de Barcelona: <http://diposit.ub.edu/dspace/handle/2445/133685>.

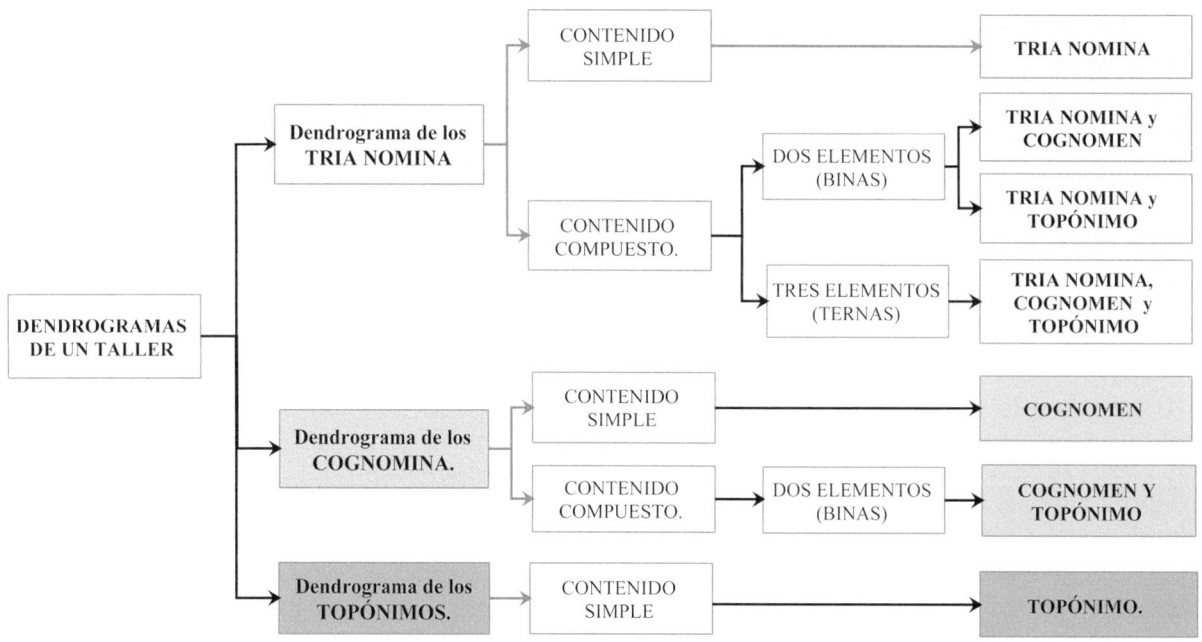

Figura 16.6 Distribución de las estructuras elementales entre los tres árboles que forman el dendrograma de un centro productor para un orden de prioridades: Tria Nomina→Cognomen→Topónimo

Como hemos comentado anteriormente, una familia de sellos estará formada por ejemplares que contienen un elemento común. De modo que podemos formar familias a partir de cualquiera de los elementos que los componen: TRIA NOMINA, COGNOMINA O TOPÓNIMOS. Bajo estas condiciones, en un taller tendríamos, en general, tres dendrogramas, uno para las familias creadas a partir de los TRIA NOMINA, otra para los COGNOMINA, y finalmente otra para los TOPÓNIMOS. Pero un sello que contenga los tres elementos puede incluirse en cualquiera de las tres familias. Como no queremos repetir los sellos en los dendrogramas, debemos establecer un orden de prioridades. En nuestro caso, como trabajamos desde los centros de producción, el orden de prioridades adoptado será: TRIA NOMINA → COGNOMEN → TOPÓNIMO[8], con la distribución de estructuras elementales de la Figura 16.6.

Una vez establecido el orden de prioridades de los elementos y con los criterios de clasificación descritos en este trabajo, tenemos que el dendrograma de la *figlina Saenianensis* presenta por el momento: 12 estructuras, 78 lecturas y 103 matrices distintas (ver nota 7).

3.-Discusión

En este trabajo se ha descrito una nueva técnica de representación de los sellos y un nuevo sistema para clasificar y organizar el material epigráfico. Sin embargo, en ausencia de una base interpretativa previa, en realidad no tenemos del todo claro para qué sirven las nuevas y sofisticadas herramientas de análisis que estamos presentando. En este punto, se hace necesario plantear una hipótesis sobre la función de los sellos de las ánforas olearias béticas.

En nuestra opinión, las ánforas se sellaban para controlar y coordinar la actividad desarrollada en *figlinae* que presentaban una división interna de su organización productiva. Los contenidos de los sellos representarían a los diversos elementos del sistema organizativo que participaron en la producción de las ánforas. Desde este punto de vista, el sello sería un identificador, necesariamente codificado, que sitúa al objeto manufacturado en una rama concreta del árbol general que describe el esquema organizativo básico del taller en una fase concreta de su actividad[9].

A nadie se le escapan las ventajas que supone para un sistema organizativo de cierta complejidad tener identificados los objetos manufacturados que produce, máxime cuando estamos hablando de producciones en masa donde los objetos son muy parecidos a nivel morfológico, ya que esta circunstancia resulta básica para la contabilidad, control y organización de las hornadas, manipulación y control de la calidad de la producción, organización del almacenaje, etc. Veamos

---

[8] Sobre los distintos criterios adoptados al establecer el orden de prioridades en la clasificación de los sellos de las Dressel 20: Moros Diaz 2021: 140-43.

[9] Otra visión sobre la función de los sellos puede consultarse en Remesal 2016.

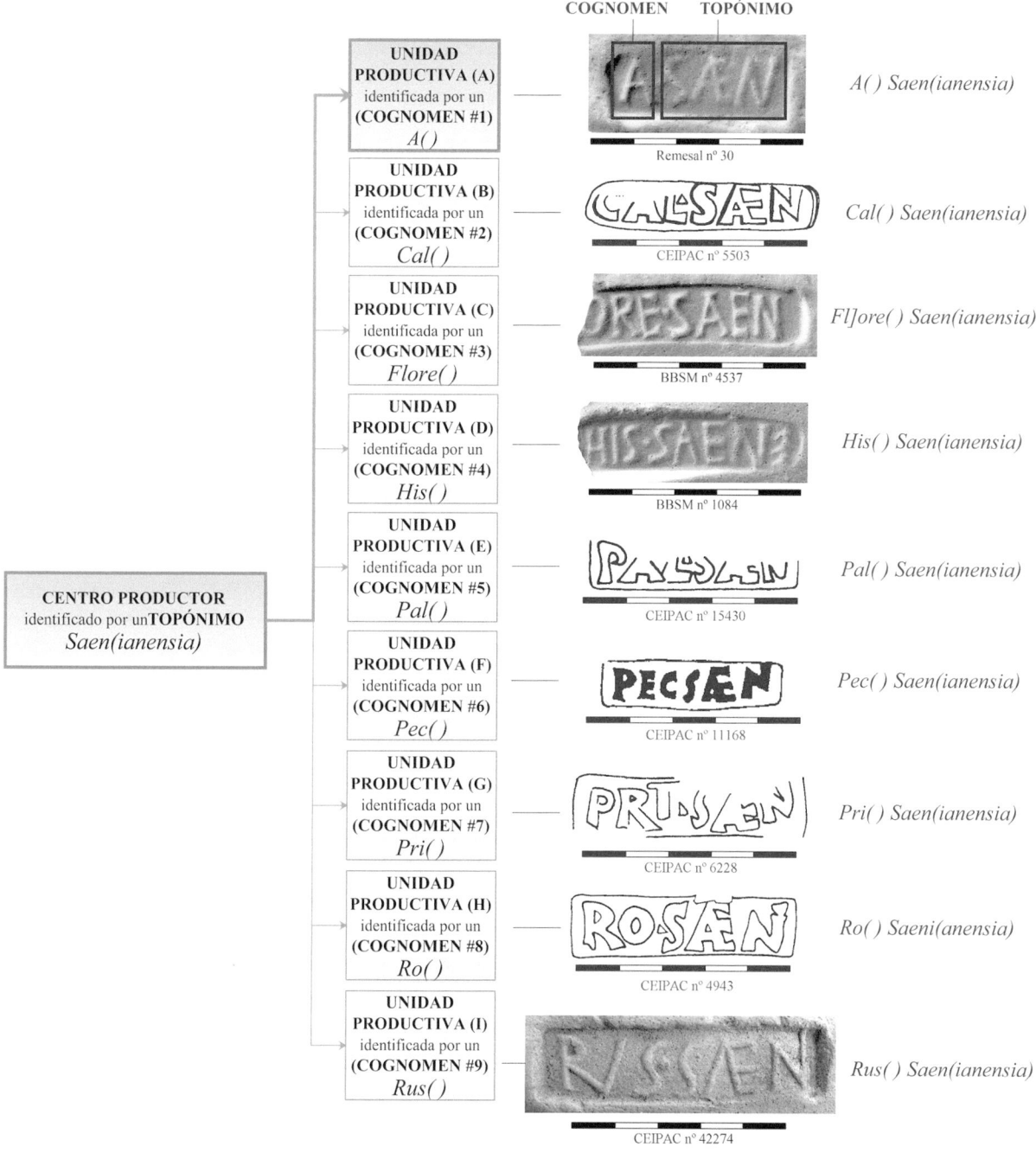

Figura 16.7 Esquema organizativo básico de la *figlina Saenianensia* en una fase de su actividad desarrollada en época flavia

un ejemplo concreto que nos ayudará a entender la hipótesis.

En la Figura 16.7, recogemos nuestra interpretación de cómo se articulan los elementos que componen los sellos, es decir, los distintos elementos que componen el identificador de las ánforas, en el esquema organizativo[10] básico de la *figlina Saenianensia*

que venimos estudiando en este trabajo. En nuestra opinión, en esa fase de su actividad desarrollada en época flavia, este centro productor estaría compuesto por varias "unidades productivas" identificadas por los nombres de sus responsables: *A( ), Cal( ), Flore( ), His( ), Pal( ), Pec( ), Pri( ), Ro( ) y Rus( )*. En estas unidades productivas se manufacturaban las ánforas en crudo, que luego pasarían por el resto del proceso productivo: cocción, control de calidad, contabilidad y almacenaje. Las unidades productivas estarían compuestas por cuadrillas de trabajadores: barreros, alfareros, personal

---

10 Sobre los esquemas organizativos de la producción de las ánforas olearias béticas, tenemos un trabajo monográfico: Moros Diaz 2022.

auxiliar para la manipulación de los envases, etc., gestionados por el personaje que aparece en el sello.

Como vemos, los distintos elementos que componen el identificador nos van concretando cada vez más la situación de las ánforas en el árbol general formado por las diversas producciones del taller. Cada sello nos marcará una ruta concreta en dicho esquema organizativo. Los contenidos de los sellos pueden precisar la procedencia del objeto manufacturado hasta el nivel de "unidad productiva". El siguiente nivel de precisión, el referente al "lote" concreto al que pertenece el ánfora, viene determinado por la matriz del sello. Cada matriz concreta identifica a un lote de ánforas producido en la alfarería[11].

De ser correcta la hipótesis -si efectivamente los sellos identifican la procedencia de los objetos manufacturados dentro del sistema organizativo que los produjo-, estudiando todas las series de un determinado centro productor, podríamos llegar a reconstruir dicho esquema organizativo y describir cómo evoluciona en el tiempo, ya que tendríamos la misma información que crearon y usaron los propios gestores de los alfares para controlar el proceso productivo. Desgraciadamente, esto no es posible por el momento. Al estudiar los sellos individuales de un determinado centro productor, tendremos necesariamente lagunas e imprecisiones sobre su composición organizativa: primero, porque no contamos con todos los sellos que se usaron en el centro productor, segundo, porque no tenemos las dataciones exactas de los sellos y, tercero, porque, en el caso de la Dressel 20, debido al fenómeno del doble y triple sellado del ánfora, habremos perdido parte de las relaciones que se establecieron entre los diversos elementos que componían su organización productiva.

De modo que no podemos reconstruir todo el esquema organizativo de los centros productores, pero podemos aproximarnos reconstruyendo partes de éste. Con este tipo de organización de los datos que nos proponen los dendrogramas, tendremos desplegados todos los elementos que necesitamos conocer para interpretar la serie y reconstruir, al menos, los elementos del sistema organizativo que han llegado hasta nosotros. A partir de estos fragmentos podemos plantear hipótesis sobre la organización productiva de cada centro productor y de su evolución en el tiempo.

Conclusiones

Entendemos que el modelo de estudio propuesto podría aplicarse al conjunto del llamado *instrumentum domesticum inscriptum*, es decir, que podría aplicarse a cualquier taller que hubiese sellado sus objetos manufacturados producidos en masa durante época romana, fuesen éstos del tipo que fuesen. De modo que las nuevas herramientas de análisis, debidamente adaptadas, nos pueden permitir plantear hipótesis para reconstruir la organización productiva de talleres artesanales emplazados en un territorio muy amplio, que produjeron objetos manufacturados de muy diversa índole y que desarrollaron su actividad durante un periodo de casi mil años.

Bibliografía

Barea, J.S., J.L. Barea, J. Solís, J. y J. Moros 2008. *Figlina Scalensia: un centro productor de ánforas Dressel 20 de la Bética* (Col·lecció instrumenta 27). Barcelona: Universitat de Barcelona.

Berni Millet, P. 2008. *Epigrafía anfórica de la Bética, nuevas formas de análisis* (Col·lecció Instrumenta 29). Barcelona: Universitat de Barcelona.

Berni Millet, P. 2015. Viaje en el tiempo por la producción y el comercio del aceite bético con la iconografía romana, en *Amphorae ex Hispania: paisajes de producción y consumo: III congreso internacional de la Sociedad de Estudios de la Cerámica Antigua (SECAH), Tarragona, 10 - 13 de diciembre de 2014*, (Monografías Ex Officina Hispana 3): 49-62. Tarragona: Institut català d'arqueologia clàssica.

Berni Millet, P. 2017. Amphorae-epigraphy: stamps, graffiti and *tituli picti* from Roman Nijmegen, en C. Carreras Monfort y J. van den Berg (eds) *Amphorae from the Kops Plateau (Nijmegen): Trade and Supply to the Lower-Rhineland from the Augustan Period to AD 69/70* (Archaeopress Roman Archaeology 20): 185-282. Oxford: Archaeopress.

Bonsor, G. 1931. *The Archaeological Expedition along the Guadalquivir (1889-1901)*. New York: Hispanic Society of America (traducción castellana de G. Chic García y A. Padilla Monge: "Expedición arqueológica a lo largo del Guadalquivir". Ecija).

BOURGEON, O., E. GARCÍA VARGAS, S. MAUNÉ, S. CORBEEL, C.H. CARRATO, S. GARCÍA DILS Y J. VAZQUEZ PAZ 2016. Investigación arqueológica en el alfar de las Delicias (Écija, Sevilla) 2013-2015: un primer balance, en *Amphorae ex Hispania: paisajes de producción y consumo: III congreso internacional de la Sociedad de Estudios de la Cerámica Antigua (SECAH), Tarragona, 10 - 13 de diciembre de 2014* (Monografías Ex Officina Hispana 3): 310-33. Tarragona: Institut català d'arqueologia clàssica.

Chic García, G. 2001. *Datos para un estudio socioeconómico de la Bética: Marcas de alfar sobre ánforas olearias*, 2 vol. Écija: Graficas Sol.

Clark-Maxwell, W.G. 1899. The Roman towns in the valley of Baetis between Cordoba and Sevilla. *Archaeological Journal of London* 56: 245-305.

GONZÁLEZ TOBAR, I., S. MAUNÉ, O. TIAGO SEOANE, E. GARCÍA VARGAS Y F. LEVÊQUE 2018. L'atelier d'amphores à huile et d'amphores à vin d'El Mohino

---

[11] Todas estas hipótesis sobre la función de los sellos se desarrollan en el capítulo 3 de nuestra Tesis Doctoral (Moros Diaz 2021: 109-35).

(Ier s.-début du IIe s.) à Palma del Río (prov. de Cordoue, Espagne), en *Actes du Congrès international de la SFECAG de Reims*: 319-44. Marsella: Société française d'étude de la céramique antique en Gaule.

MOROS DÍAZ, J. 2014. La intervención Severiana en la producción del aceite bético, en *Estudios sobre el Monte Testaccio Roma*, VI (Col·lecció instrumenta 47): 773-860. Barcelona: Universitat de Barcelona.

MOROS DÍAZ, J. 2020. La mecánica del sellado de las ánforas olearias béticas, en *Ex Baetica Romam: Homenaje a José Remesal Rodríguez*: 681-700. Barcelona: Universidad de Barcelona.

MOROS DIAZ, J. 2021. *Organización productiva de las ánforas olearias béticas (Dressel 20, ca.30-270 d.C.): un modelo de análisis e interpretación de los sellos del instrumentum domesticum* (Col·lecció instrumenta 77). Barcelona: Publicaciones de la Universidad de Barcelona.

MOROS DÍAZ, J. 2022. Esquemas organizativos de la producción anfórica olearia bética (Dressel 20, *ca.* 30/270 d.C.), en J. Remesal Rodríguez y J. Pérez González (eds) *Arqueología y Téchne: métodos formales, nuevos enfoques / Archaeology and Techne: Formal Methods, New Approaches* (Access Archaeology): 98-112. Oxford: Archaeopress.

Moros Díaz, J., J.S. Barea Bautista, J.L. Barea Bautista y J. Solis Siles 2010. Propiedades de los Severos en la Bética: la figlina Paterna, en *Estudios sobre el Monte Testaccio (Roma)*, V (Col·leció instrumenta 35): 495-511. Barcelona: Universitat de Barcelona.

Ponsich, M. 1979. *Implantation rurale antique sur le Bas-Guadalquivir*, II (Publications de la Casa de Velazquez, sér. Archéologie 3). París: De Boccard.

Remesal Rodríguez, J. 1977-78. La economía oleícola bética: nuevas formas de análisis. *Archivo Español de Arqueología* 50-51: 87-142 = *Saalburg Jahrbuch* 38 (1982): 30-71.

Remesal Rodríguez, J. 2000. Oleum Baeticum. Consideraciones y propuestas para su estudio. *Ex Baetica Amphorae: Conservas, aceite y vino de la Bética en el Imperio Romano (Congreso Internacional, Sevilla-Écija, 1998)*: 373-92. Écija: Editorial Gráficas.

Remesal Rodríguez, J. 2001. Lora del Río en la Antigüedad. *Lora del Río: Revista de Estudios Locales* 11 (2000-01): 50-57.

Remesal Rodríguez, J. 2016. ¿Sellar para qué? *Atti del VI incontro Instrumenta Inscripta, Aquileia (26-28 marzo 2015). Antichità Altoadriatiche* 83: 73-90.

Testaccio 2010 = Blázquez Martínez, J.M. y J. Remesal Rodríguez (eds) 2010. *Estudios sobre el Monte Testaccio (Roma)*, V (Col·lecció instrumenta 35). Barcelona: Universitat de Barcelona.

Testaccio 2014 = Blázquez Martínez, J.M. y J. Remesal Rodríguez (eds) 2014. *Estudios sobre el Monte Testaccio (Roma)*, V (Col·lecció instrumenta 47). Barcelona: Universitat de Barcelona.

Relación de imágenes:

Transcripción tipográfica (a), calco de Dressel (b) y molde de silicona (c) de un mismo ejemplar *CIL* XV 2571

Estructuras elementales y su incidencia en el sellado

Dendrograma de la familia de sellos de *C. Ennius Hispanus* de Huertas del Río

Composición de la formula tipológica de las matrices

Tipos de matrices por los cinco elementos caracterizadores del diseño de su texto

Distribución de las estructuras elementales entre los tres árboles que forman el dendrograma de un centro productor para un orden de prioridades: TRIA NOMINA→COGNOMEN→TOPÓNIMO

Esquema organizativo básico de la *figlina Saenianensia* en una fase de su actividad desarrollada en época flavia

17. A Consideration of the Level of Distribution Reciprocity Based on Amphorae Frequencies: The Case Study of *Berytus*

Naseem Raad

Introduction

Beirut, the modern-day capital of Lebanon, lies on the northern side of a wide coastal plain along the central portion of the Levantine coast (Figure 17.1). In the Roman period (beginning in the Levant around 64 BC), it was an active and well-connected mid-sized port city, particularly after its elevation to the status of *colonia* around 15 or 14 BC by the emperor Augustus, and its designation as *Colonia Iulia Augusta Felix Berytus* (henceforth referred to as *Berytus*) (Hall 2004: 46). Augustus also granted land in the hinterland of *Berytus* to veterans who had served him at the Battle of Actium (31 BC) (Hall 2004: 46). The period coinciding with this settlement is characterised by an increase in public and private construction and a refurbishing of harbour installations in the urban centre, a rise in the frequency of wine and oil pressing installations in the hinterland of the colony's new territory, and the production of a new kind of amphora, or ceramic storage jar, used primarily to package wine (Elayi and Sayegh 2000: 231-32; Fischer-Genz 2016; Perring *et al.* 2003: 209). This economic expansion contrasts sharply with the economic stagnancy observed in the city between 150 and 50 BC, as seen in the lack of public and private construction throughout the city, likely associated with the reported destruction of the city in 143 BC (Perring *et al.* 2003: 203-04).

This paper traces the export of wine from the new Roman colony through the identification and quantification of exported amphorae from *Berytus* between the 2nd century BC and the 5th century AD at other port sites throughout the eastern Mediterranean. This allows for a consideration of the change in the capacity of exports over time from Beirut, and a comparison of patterns across several important political and cultural shifts in the city's history. Most pertinently, this includes the transition from a Seleucid settlement to a Roman colony, providing valuable insight into the potential correlation between economic expansion and Roman colonisation. These distribution patterns are then compared to an assemblage of imported amphorae uncovered in Beirut, specifically at residential contexts

and from bathhouses in the centre of the city. This is done to explore the reciprocity of trade between *Berytus* and other port sites throughout the eastern Mediterranean. Finally, these considerations are contextualised within regional socio-political factors as a preliminary step in shedding light on the maritime economy of *Berytus*.

Background and Methodology

An amphora is a pottery container utilised for the non-local and typically maritime transportation primarily of agricultural products (Hayes 1997; University of Southampton 2014). It was initially utilised in the northern Levant as far back as the 15th century BC and became increasingly common during the early 1st millennium BC (Peacock and Williams 1986: 20). Its use became more widespread and developed into the standard vessel for the maritime transportation of a variety of products, primarily olive oil, wine, and fish sauce (Hayes 1997: 27; Peacock and Williams 1986: 1). Thus, while ceramic vessels are often analysed as archaeological objects in themselves, amphorae are unique in the sense that they represent an economic transaction involving a packaged agricultural good. This allows them to be utilised as an index of economic activity and seaborne distribution (University of Southampton 2014). When quantified on a larger scale, they can be used as a reflection of long-term economic trends, especially through the collation of multiple assemblages and the use of a large sample size.

This paper focuses on one index acquired from such analyses, which is here labelled as the degree of reciprocity in distribution levels between two sites. Certain economic relationships between port cities in the Mediterranean appear to have had a large difference in the distribution balance of products packaged in amphorae. In other words, certain products seem to have been primarily leaving from one port and arriving at another. In some circumstances, the skew is clear and marked by a large sample of available data, such as in the one-sided and highly directional exportation of olive oil from Spain and North Africa

Figure 17.1. Beirut, the modern-day capital of Lebanon (map by author).

to Rome (Keay 2012: 38). This imbalance is sometimes associated with large-scale state contracting for the provision of subsidised agricultural products (Aldrete and Mattingly 1999: 178; Peña 1998). It can also serve as an indication of regional specialisation resulting in intensive and extensive growth (Mattingly 1988a; 1988b). This involves the contextualisation of production and distribution trends within geopolitical patterns and policies, cultural norms and tastes, social networks, and maritime distribution networks, among numerous other factors. However, at sites where ceramic studies are still at a nascent stage, and thorough examinations of the above-mentioned aspects are largely missing, an effective first step in exploring maritime economies is collating the available amphora data, conducting preliminary statistical analyses, and identifying highly directional distribution patterns.

Economic Trends and Distribution Reciprocity at *Berytus*

This is precisely the case in the port city of *Berytus*, where a new type of amphora began to be produced at workshops within the urban centre in the late Hellenistic and early Roman periods (Reynolds 2000b). Known simply as the Beirut Type amphora, this ceramic vessel was used to package wine from the late 2nd century BC to the mid-7th century AD (Table 17.1). This paper summarises part of the author's doctoral research that traces the vessel's distribution at other port sites throughout the eastern Mediterranean to shed light on the scope and scale of wine exports from the colony of *Berytus* from the 2nd century BC to the 5th century AD. There are also extensive publications on the amphora assemblages observed at the sites of BEY 006 (residential context), 007 (residential context adjacent to the harbour), and 045 (baths complex in the centre of the city) (Table 17.3) from excavations in the Beirut Central District undertaken in the 1990s (Reynolds 1999; 2000b). This makes possible a comparison of imports with exports to begin putting together a picture of *Berytus*'s maritime economy.

Since the Beirut Type amphora was unknown prior to the excavations of the 1990s, and not widely recognised to this day, ceramicists publishing reports before 2000 have sometimes grouped examples of the Beirut Type under the general term 'eastern Mediterranean', mistakenly attributing it to another eastern Mediterranean source (most prevalently the Agora M334 type, which closely resembles Beirut Types 5-7 in its handles), or categorised it simply as Lebanese (Adan-Bayewitz 1986). For this reason, I have re-examined ceramic reports that included photographs and/or drawings from port sites in the eastern Mediterranean to identify previously mislabelled or unrecognised specimens. However, many ceramic reports did not provide photographs or drawings for all vessels, making identification near impossible, which might suggest that the Beirut Type is underrepresented in the frequencies specified. Furthermore, due to the typological similarities between each type, differentiating between handle sherds of the Beirut Type from those of an Agora M334 amphora is difficult solely through written reports (Reynolds 2005: 572). For these reasons, it must be clarified that the trends observed, and the subsequent proposals made, are preliminary and subject to revision when the quantity and quality of data improve. Finally, as this study marks the first effort to quantify exports from *Berytus*, the author has surveyed only port sites in the eastern Mediterranean to maintain a consistent database and minimise bias in statistical analyses. Future examinations should consider a wider variety of contexts, including shipwrecks, smaller maritime sites or anchorages, and rural sites.

Late 2nd Century BC to Early 1st Century AD

In Hellenistic Beirut, most imported wine packaged in amphorae (roughly 64% of quantified imports) come from Sidon in southern Lebanon (Reynolds 2005: 570). These forms drop in frequency drastically around 175 to 150 BC (Wicenciak 2016: 645), possibly coinciding with the beginning of the production of the Beirut 1 Type amphora, which was produced roughly between the late 2nd century BC and the early 1st century AD in Beirut. Imports were also arriving from Tunisia, most commonly in the 2nd century BC, though the observed forms most likely transported olive oil or fish sauce, not wine (Reynolds 2000a: 1040-41).

The Beirut Type 1 amphora appears to have been exclusively consumed locally, as a review of ceramic reports from eastern Mediterranean port sites has revealed a limited distribution of the type (Table 17.2 and Table 17.4). The only confirmed identifications come from Jiyeh, a coastal site which lies roughly 30km south of Beirut, and Paphos in Cyprus, though

Table 17.1. Outline of the Beirut Type typology with associated phases of production (after Reynolds 2000b).

Beirut Type	Date of Production	Production Sites
1	late 2nd BC to early 1st AD	Beirut
2	first half of 1st AD to beginning of 2nd AD	Beirut, Jiyeh, Khalde
3	end of 1st AD to mid-2nd AD	Beirut
4	end of 2nd AD to mid-3rd AD	Beirut
5	second half of 4th AD	Beirut
6	mid-4th AD to 5th AD	Beirut
7	mid-5th AD to mid-6th AD	Beirut, Khalde
8	second half of 5th AD to mid-7th AD	Beirut, Bekaa Valley?

Table 17.2. Imported amphora sherds uncovered at BEY 006, 007, and 045, and categorised based on source (after Reynolds 2000b: 1056, table 1).

BEY 006 (Residential), BEY 007 (Residential and Adjacent to Port), and BEY 045 (Baths) Amphora Assemblages				
Sherds (diagnostics)	% of Total Imports	Source	Date Range	Contents
111	4,62%	Spain	Late 1st BC - 7th AD	Mixed
78	3,25%	Tunisia	3rd BC to late-1st BC; 2nd AD to 6th AD	Mixed, primarily oil and/or fish sauce? Reuse?
28	1,17%	Italy	1st AD - 3rd AD	Primarily wine
4	0,17%	Gaul	2nd AD to early 3rd AD	Primarily wine
134	5,58%	Sidon	4th BC to 3rd BC	Unknown
109	4,54%	Sidon	2nd BC to 1st BC	Unknown
83	3,45%	Tyre	2nd BC to 2nd AD	Unknown
49	2,04%	North Lebanon	2nd AD	Unknown
72	3,00%	Amrit	4th BC to 3rd BC	Probably wine
119	4,95%	Amrit	1st AD to 5th AD	Probably wine
532	22,14%	Gaza	2nd AD to 6th AD	Probably wine
265	11,03%	Akko	2nd AD to 6th/7th AD	Probably wine
27	1,12%	Cilicia	2nd AD to 3rd AD	
249	10,36%	Cilicia or Cyprus	4th AD to 6th AD	Wine or oil, wine more likely
21	0,87%	Crete	1st AD to 4th AD	
162	6,74%	Greece	2nd AD to 6th AD	
6	0,25%	Greece	Hellenistic Period	
83	3,45%	Greece	Undated	
36	1,50%	Unknown		
29	1,21%	Asia Minor	3rd/2nd - 1st BC; 4th-5th AD	
59	2,46%	Pontus (Black Sea)	2nd AD to 6th AD	
131	5,45%	Eastern Med.		
16	0,67%	Egypt		
2403	100,00%			

this example could also potentially be a Sidon 3 Type (Megaw and Hayes 2003: 467; Wicenciak 2016: 655). Sidon 2 amphorae were also produced in Beirut from the 3rd century BC to the 1st century BC, though it is unclear whether the majority of forms uncovered in Beirut are local products or imports from southern Lebanon (Reynolds 2005: 570). Adding to this issue, there does not currently exist any quantified data regarding the capacity of distribution of the Sidon 2 or Tyre types, and so it is difficult to contextualise the patterns observed in Beirut with regional markets. The reciprocity of transactions between Beirut, Tyre, and

Sidon also remains unclear since we lack quantified ceramic data from specific contexts at the sites of Tyre and Sidon.

In the late Iron Age and early Hellenistic period, Beirut was likely under Sidonian rule, or at least, it was a dependent of Sidon (Perring *et al.* 2003: 199). This political relationship is potentially revealing in terms of the production of Sidon 2 Type amphorae in Hellenistic Beirut. Specifically, it has been proposed that the production of parallel forms in both sites is an indication of centralised control of wine production

Table 17.3. The total number of port sites where Beirut Type amphorae were observed organised by type.

Beirut Type Amphora Presence (1) or Absence (0) at Regional Commercial Port Sites									
Site	Type 1	Type 2	Type 3	Type 4	Type 5	Type 6	Type 7	Type 8	Source
Akko	0	0	1	0	0	0	0	1	Silberstein *et al.* 2017: 143, 154
Alexandria	0	1	0	0	0	0	0	0	Wicenciak 2016: 656
Amathous	0	0	1	0	0	0	0	1	Kaldeli 2013: 421, 456
Apollonia	0	0	0	0	1	0	0	0	Grossman 2001: 81-93
Ashkelon	0	0	1	0	0	0	0	0	Johnson 2008: 152
Athens	0	1	0	0	0	0	0	1	Hayes 2000: 290, 296
Berenice (Libya)	0	1	0	0	0	0	0	0	Riley 1979: 367, 369, 372
Berenike (Egypt)	0	0	1	0	0	0	0	0	Hayes 1996: 159
Bodrum	0	0	1	0	0	0	0	1	Reynolds 2000b: 391
Caesarea	0	0	1	0	1	0	0	1	Blakely and Horton 1987: 44; Tomber 1999: 299
Carthage	0	0	1	0	0	0	0	0	Reynolds 2000b: 391
Dor	0	0	0	0	0	0	0	0	Stern 1996
Jaffa	0	0	0	0	0	0	0	0	Gendelman 2018
Kition	0	1	0	0	0	0	0	0	Frangié-Joly 2017
Knossos	0	0	1	0	0	0	0	0	Forster 2009: 92
Kourion	0	1	0	0	0	0	0	1	Kaldeli 2013: 426, 463
Limyra	0	0	0	0	0	0	0	0	Vroom 2004; 2007
Marina El-Alamein	0	1	1	0	0	0	0	0	Daszewski *et al.* 1990: 47
Paphos	1	1	1	0	0	0	0	1	Kaldeli 2013: 411, 448; Megaw and Hayes 2003: 467
Posideion/ Ras el Bassit	0	0	0	0	0	0	0	0	Mills and Beaudry 2010; Mills and Reynolds 2014
Sabratha	0	0	1	0	0	0	0	0	Reynolds 2000b: 391
Salamis	0	0	0	0	0	0	0	1	Diederichs 1980: Pl. 20.207-210
Sidon	0	1	0	0	0	0	0	0	Wicenciak 2016: 655
Tyre	0	0	0	0	0	0	0	1	Gatier *et al.* 2010: 73
Total Mentions	1	8	11	0	2	0	0	9	
Total Percentage	4%	33%	46%	0%	8%	0%	0%	38%	

Table 17.4. Distribution of all Beirut Types at quantified contexts with frequencies based on total sherd count.

Observed Frequencies of Beirut Type Amphorae at Quantified Assemblages in the Eastern Mediterranean									
Site	Context	Type 1	Type 2	Type 3	Type 4	Type 5	Type 6	Type 7	Type 8
Akko		0	0	0,6	0	0	0	0	0,4
Amathous	Agora (early)	0	0	4	0	0	0	0	0
	Agora (late)	0	0	0	0	0	0	0	2,3
	Palaea Lemesos	0	0	0,4	0	0	0	0	0
Antioch		0	0	0	0	0	0	0	0
Apollonia		0	0	0	0	3,4	0	0	0
Ashkelon		0	0	0,6	0	0	0	0	0
Caesarea	Harbour	0	0	0	0	?	0	0	0,9
	Area LL	0	0	0	0	0	0	0	0
	Vault 1	0	0	5	0	0	0	0	0
	Late Byzantine Building	0	0	0	0	0	0	0	1,5
Jaffa		0	0	0	0	0	0	0	0
Jiyeh		0	40	?	0	0	0	0	0
Kourion	Early	0	0,9	0	0	0	0	0	0
	Late	0	0	0	0	0	0	0	1,4
Paphos	SK Castle	1	2	1	0	0	0	0	0,3
	House of Orpheus	0	0	1,9	0	0	0	0	0
	Theatre (early)	0	0	0,8	0	0	0	0	0
	Theatre (late)	0	0	0	0	0	0	0	0,9
Salamis		0	0	0	0	0	0	0	4
Yavneh-Yam		0	0	0	0	0	0	0	0
Limyra		0	0	0	0	0	0	0	0
Aphrodisias		0	0	0	0	0	0	0	0
Elaiussa Sebaste		0	0	0	0	0	0	0	0
Antiochia Ad Cragum		0	0	0	0	0	0	0	0

(Wicenciak 2016: 644). This might also have included the supervision of the stamping of vessels with manufacturer names, personal names, and dates following the Sidonian calendar (Ala Eddine 2003: 112-14). However, it must be clarified that while it is quite likely that the municipality played a role in some step of the supply chain of wine in Hellenistic Beirut, this does not imply that the same entity played a role in *every* step. Rather, the stamping of amphorae at this time could have fulfilled some role related to municipal fiscal policy, perhaps to signify that taxes had been paid on the product, and it had been approved for consumption or shipping (Rauh *et al.* 2013: 150). This procedure would not necessarily be tied to the production of the wine itself, or its subsequent distribution, which should be regarded as entirely separate processes.

Early 1st Century AD to 3rd Century AD

This period in the history of *Berytus* marks a phase of an increase in the distribution of wine produced in the colony and packaged in the Beirut Type amphora. During this time, the Beirut Type 2 amphora came into production, a form that was significantly different from the earlier Sidonian and Beirut 1 types. The vessels are larger than their predecessors and were sometimes stamped 'COL BER' (*Colonia Berytus*) to specify them as products of the Roman colony (Perring *et al.* 2003: 208).

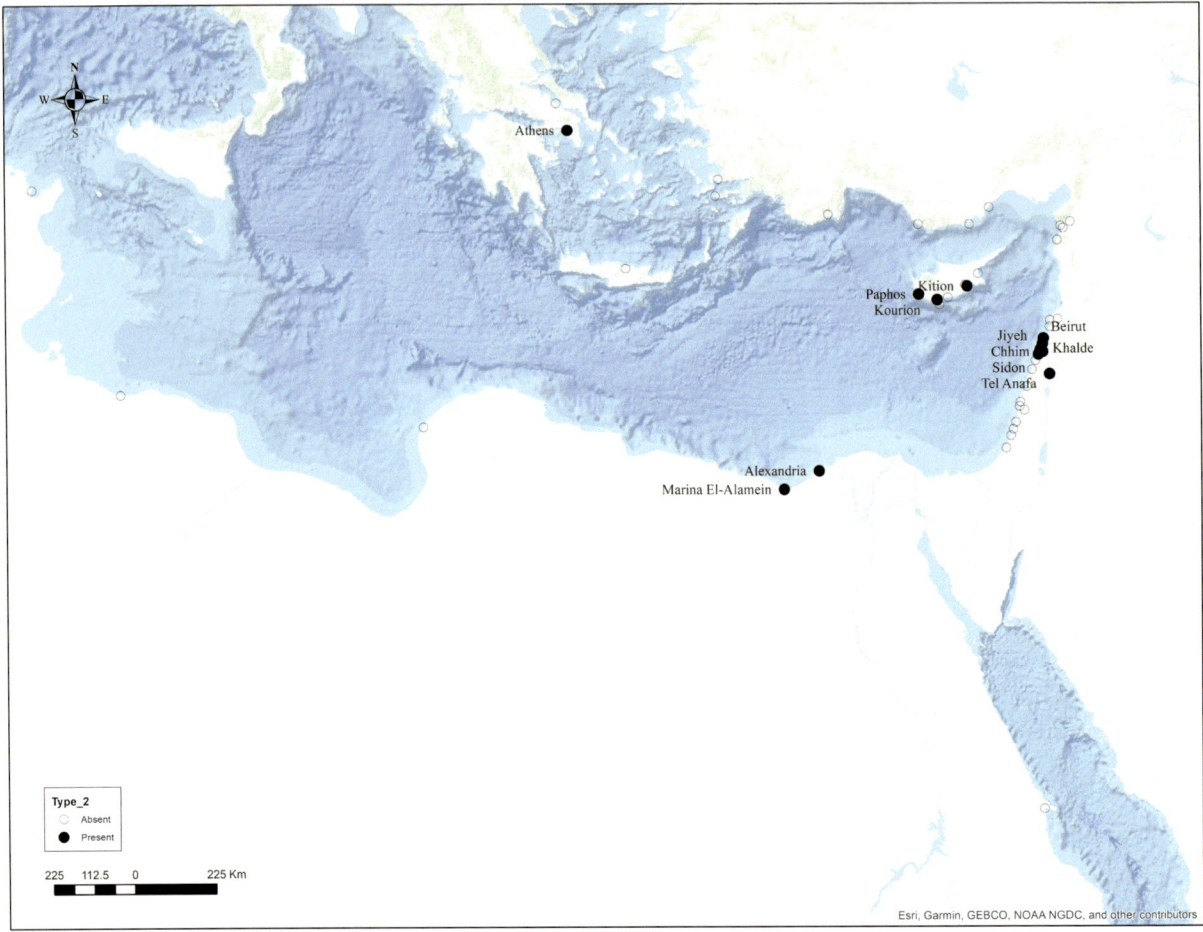

Figure 17.2. All observed instances (Presence/Absence) of the Beirut Type 2 amphora in the eastern Mediterranean (map by author).

The production of Beirut Type 2 coincides with the settlement of Augustus's veterans in the colony, and it seems likely that the two developments are correlated.

Beirut Type 2 is observed much more extensively than its predecessor at port sites throughout the eastern Mediterranean (Figure 17.2). Along the Levantine coast, it has been noted at Beirut, Khalde, Jiyeh, and Sidon (Wicenciak 2016: 656). In Cyprus, Beirut Type 2 amphorae have been seen at Kition, Amathous, and Paphos, where a stamped sherd was uncovered (Hayes 1991: pl. XXIII.14; Kaldeli 2013: 408, 421, 426). Though the range of exports is wider than that of the Beirut 1 amphora, the quantities observed are still quite low. Outside of the production centres, where it makes up between 45% and 65% of the total assemblage, it consistently represents less than 5% of the quantified assemblages in the regional market. Outside of the Levant and Cyprus, it has been observed at Berenice in Libya, Marina el-Alamein and Alexandria in Egypt, and Athens in Greece (Reynolds 2000b: 391; Wicenciak 2016: 656). As in the case of sites along the Levantine coast and in Cyprus, this seems to have been limited

to several sherds in each region. Beirut Type 3 came into production at the end of the 1st century AD, and is the most widely distributed form produced in *Berytus* (Figure 17.3). However, Type 3 also never represents more than 5% of any imported assemblage at the studied port sites, though it pops up at a variety of sites throughout the eastern Mediterranean and North Africa.

At this time, the imported assemblage at *Berytus* is quite diverse, with the imports from Tunisia halting and new imports arriving from Italy, Gaul, Spain, and the southern Levant (Reynolds 2000a: 1056). These developments might be associated with the influx of settlers, with the change in the amphora assemblage reflecting the tastes of a new clientele in the colony. There are no significant discrepancies in the degree of reciprocity of exchanges, apart from the disappearance of North African amphorae in *Berytus* during the production and distribution of Beirut Types 2 and 3 to Berenice, Carthage, and Sabratha (Reynolds 2000a: 1037, 1041-42; Wicenciak 2016: 656). However, the frequencies observed are quite low, and do not allow

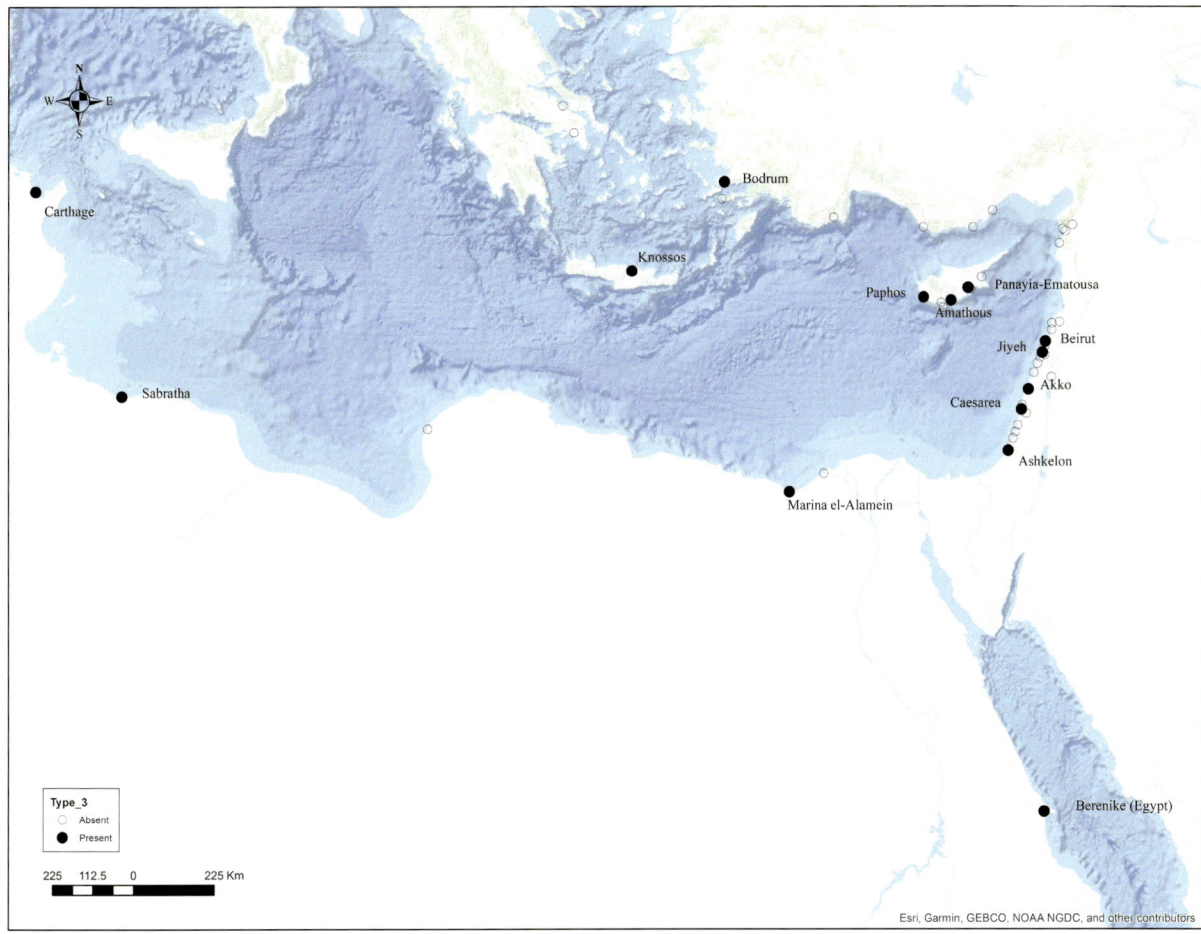

Figure 17.3. All observed instances (Presence/Absence) of the Beirut Type 3 amphora in the eastern Mediterranean (map by author).

for the proposal of any definitive patterns. *Berytus* seems to have been a well-connected port, attracting products from a wide variety of sources, but in minimal quantities. This might be indicative of opportunistic economic exchanges as opposed to consistent, specific, and highly directional distributions.

After Beirut Type 3 went out of production in the mid-2nd century AD, the Beirut Type 4 was produced roughly from the end of the 2nd century AD to the mid-3rd century AD, but is markedly absent throughout the eastern Mediterranean (Table 17.2). This comes at a time when southern Levantine imports increase dramatically in Beirut, specifically from the regions of Akko, Caesarea, and Ashkelon, eventually dominating the assemblage of imported amphorae in *Berytus* (Reynolds 1999: 54). This high directionality in the flow of products might best be explained by geopolitical changes at the colony of *Berytus*, specifically in the independence and separation of *Heliopolis* in modern-day Baalbek (Figure 17.4; Perring *et al.* 2003: 212-13). The site of *Heliopolis*, initially included within the territory of *Berytus*, was a major producer of wine in the

Roman period (Fischer-Genz 2016), and was connected to *Berytus* by a road through the Bekaa Mountains along the road markers depicted in Figure 17.4 at Fyadieh, Karak Nuh, and Hizzin (Abou Diwan and Doumit 2017). In AD 193, Severus granted *Heliopolis* its independence as a separate *colonia* (Millar 1993: 218, 221), coinciding with the sharp drop in the export of Beirut Type 4 amphorae. It seems likely that at this time, *Heliopolis* might have established different regional networks that saw a decrease in the supply of wine to the urban centre of *Berytus*, reducing the capacity of exports from the port city (Hamel 2014: 69-70). Furthermore, the contemporaneous rise in southern Levantine imports seems to have served to help fill this gap in the supply of wine at *Berytus* for local consumption as well. This discrepancy in the degree of reciprocity speaks to the importance of *Heliopolis* in the wine industry of *Berytus*.

3rd Century AD to 5th Century AD

The import of southern Levantine forms appears to have increased in the 4th and 5th centuries AD, at which time Cypriote and Cilician imports also increase, all of

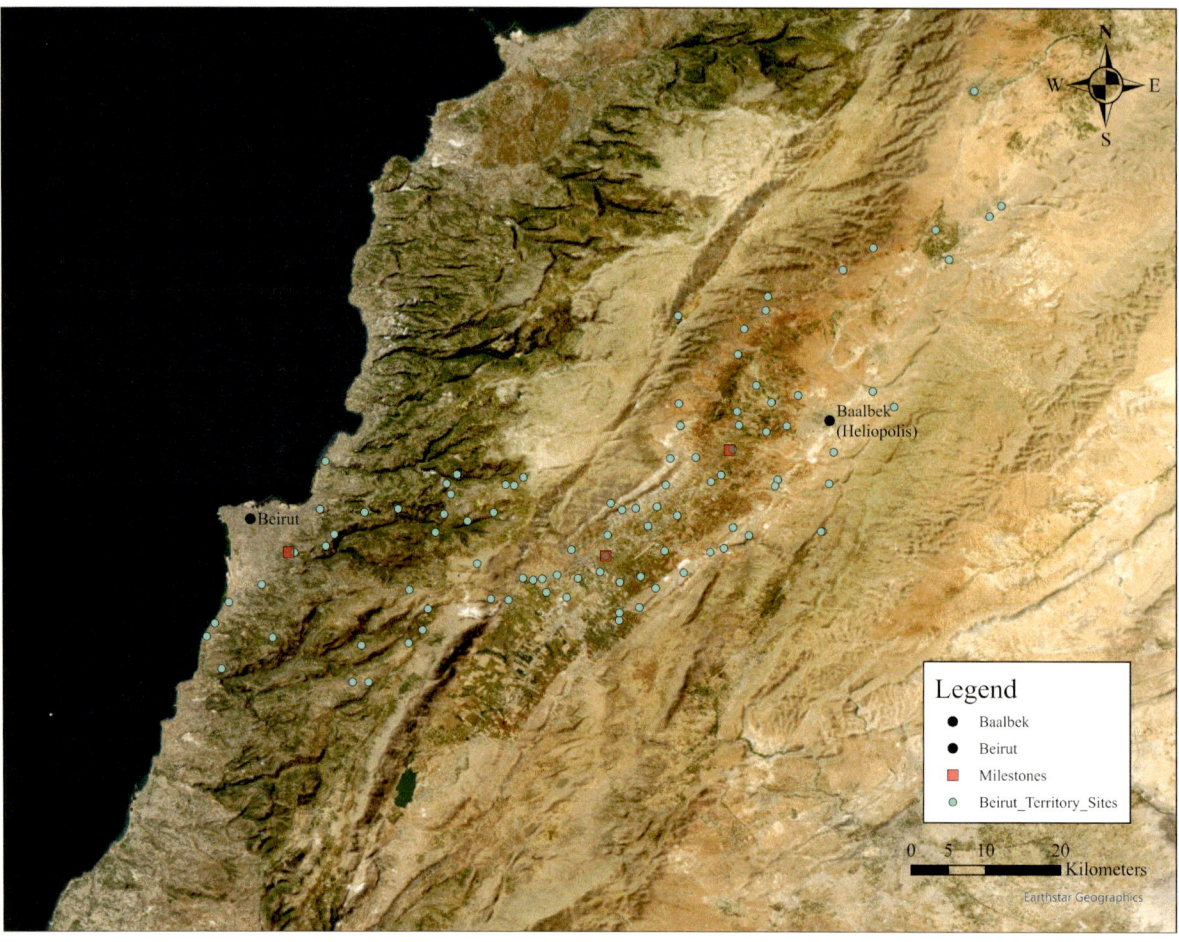

Figure 17.4. Roman sites in the hinterland of *Berytus*, milestones of the Roman road connecting *Berytus* with *Heliopolis* (Baalbek) marked by a red cross (map by author).

which are believed to have been used to package wine (University of Southampton 2014). These imports come specifically from Akko and Caesarea in Late Roman Amphora (LRA) 5 and Almagro 54 amphorae, with a particularly high concentration between the 2nd and 4th centuries AD, and Agora M334 amphorae from Akko in the 4th century AD (Reynolds 1999: 41, 54, 109; 2005: 574). They dominate the assemblage of imported amphorae at this time, comprising over 60% of the total imported specimens. The amphorae from Cilicia and Cyprus come in LRA 1 containers, and comprise around 20% of the total imported assemblage from this time period, and have been dated roughly to the 4th and 5th centuries AD (Reynolds 1999: 41, 54, 109; 2005: 574).

The export of wine at this time from *Berytus* is extremely limited. Although Beirut Type 5 amphorae, produced around the late 4th century AD, are observed at Caesarea and Apollonia, these were identified in harbour contexts and might represent a shipment in transit or even discarded forms (Grossman 2001: 81-93; Tomber 1999, fig. 6.1). Conversely, as mentioned

earlier, the assemblage of imported amphorae in *Berytus* studied in this paper come from residential and urban contexts, presumably after the products had been unloaded and processed. Thus, the distribution of wine from the southern Levant to *Berytus* seems to have grown even more highly directional in this period. Furthermore, the frequency of Beirut Type amphorae within the urban centre of *Berytus* also seems to have decreased at this time (Reynolds 1999: 54).

Given the lack of reciprocity between southern Levantine sites and Beirut in the distribution of wine, it seems likely that merchants from the southern Levant consistently travelled to *Berytus* with the intention of distributing wine packaged in Almagro 54 and LRA 5/6 containers. After unloading cargo, merchants might have then loaded a heterogeneous cargo composed largely of products not packaged in amphorae from *Berytus*. This could have included textiles and garments, which were commonly produced in Beirut as at a number of other Syrian cities, as well as the famous purple dye of the Levantine coast (Hall 2001-02: 153-54; Millar 1993: 266).

A Brief Note on Causative Factors

These patterns and considerations must also be framed within the nuances of regional markets involving small cargoes, multiple distinct products, and an intricate network of agents, shipowners, suppliers, and consumers (Leidwanger 2014: 33; Rathbone 2003). Thus, the propositions made in previous sections should be further contextualised in the context of socio-economic relationships on a small scale between *Berytus*, its neighbouring anchorages and 'opportunistic ports' as Leidwanger calls them (2014: 35), other regional port cities, and ultimately, the wider Mediterranean. Moreover, it must be recalled that the movement of products by maritime transportation is dictated largely by harbour accessibility and wind patterns, which fluctuate on a daily and seasonal basis (El-Safadi 2016). This is especially true along the Levantine coast, where much of the shore is westward facing and exposed to dominant winds (Marriner *et al.* 2008: 2497). In this way, wind patterns are quite important in determining the optimal times and points of departure and arrival, and are inherently relevant to the distribution of amphorae in the eastern Mediterranean.

Conclusion

There appears to have been a fairly stable distribution reciprocity between *Berytus* and other port cities in the eastern Mediterranean from the 1st century AD to the 3rd century AD. During this time, the Beirut Type amphora was exported with a fairly wide range but at low frequencies, indicating that wine from *Berytus* might have been a high-value product transported as part of a heterogeneous cargo. After the independence of *Heliopolis* in AD 193, the frequency of these exports decreased, while southern Levantine imports at *Berytus* increased dramatically. This high directionality and low reciprocity indicates that southern Levantine wine might have filled the gap in the market after wine from *Heliopolis* ceased to arrive at *Berytus* in the same capacity as earlier periods.

Shedding light on distribution patterns solely through the reciprocity – or lack thereof – of exchange is not, by itself, an effective methodology. Regardless, the initial collation and statistical analysis of amphora assemblages allows for a recognition and quantification of economic shifts in understudied areas. This has been undertaken in this paper by starting with the imported amphora assemblage from *Berytus*, and by subsequently comparing it to the frequency and range of exports from the port city. By tracing and quantifying the distribution of the Beirut Type amphora throughout the eastern Mediterranean, and comparing these figures to the imported assemblage at *Berytus* itself,

this paper signifies a preliminary step in outlining the maritime exchange networks within which *Berytus* was involved, and suggesting correlative geopolitical and social developments.

Bibliography

Abou Diwan, G. and J. Doumit 2017. The Berytus-Heliopolis Baalbak road in the Roman period: A least cost path analysis. *Mediterranean Archaeology and Archaeometry* 17.3: 225-41.

Adan-Bayewitz, D. 1986. The pottery from the late Byzantine building (stratum 4) and its implications, in L.I. Levine and E. Netzer (eds) *Excavations at Caesarea Maritima 1975, 1976, 1979: Final Report (Qedem 21)*: 90-129. Jerusalem: Hebrew University of Jerusalem.

Ala Eddine, A. 2003. Hellenistic stamped amphorae from Beirut. *Archaeology and History in Lebanon* 17: 109-19.

Aldrete, G.S. and D.J Mattingly 1999. Feeding the city: The organization, operation, and scale of the supply system for Rome, in D.S. Potter and D.J. Mattingly (eds) *Life, Death, and Entertainment in the Roman Empire*: 171-204. Ann Arbor: University of Michigan Press.

Blakely, J.A. and Horton, F.L. 1987. *The Pottery and Dating of Vault 1: Horreum, Mithraeum, and Later Usage.* Joint Expedition to Caesarea Maritima Excavation Reports 4. Lewiston (NY): Edwin Mellen.

Daszewski, W.A., G. Majcherek, Z. Sztetyłło and I. Zych 1990. Excavations at Marina el-Alamein 1987-88. *Mitteilungen des Deutschen Archäologischen Instituts Abteilung Kairo* 46: 15-51.

Diederichs, C. 1980. *Salamine de Chypre IX céramiques hellénistiques, romaines et byzantines.* Paris: De Boccard.

Elayi, J. and H. Sayegh 2000. *Un quartier du port phénicien de Beyrouth au Fer III / Perse: Archéologie et histoire* (Transeuphratène Supplement 7). Paris: Gabalda.

Fischer-Genz, B. 2016. Ancient wine and oil presses from the Bekaa Valley. *Journal of Eastern Mediterranean Archaeology and Heritage Studies* 4.1: 57-71.

Forster, G. 2009. Roman Knossos: The pottery in context: A presentation of ceramic evidence provided by the Knossos 2000 Project (1993-95), 2 vols. Unpublished PhD thesis, University of Birmingham.

Frangié-Joly, D. 2017. *Le site de Bey-144: Fouilles et étude de la céramique (période hellénistique-début de l'ère romaine)* (British Archaeological Reports, International Series 2881). Oxford: BAR.

Gatier, P.-L., A. Baud, D. Cahu, G. Charpentier, A. Devillechaise, C. Duvette, M. El-Masri Hachem, P. Ferreira, A. Flammin, N. Haidar-Vela, X. Husson, H. Kahwagi-Janho, C. Piaton, D. Pieri, A. Schmitt and T. Zaven 2010. Mission archéologique de Tyr: Rapport Préliminaire 2008-2009. *Bulletin d'archéologie et d'architecture Libanaises* 14: 135-240.

Gendelman, P. 2018. Roman amphorae, in O. Tsuf (ed.) *Ancient Jaffa from the Persian to the Byzantine Period: Kaplan Excavations (1955-1981)*: 417-44. Munster: Zaphon.

Grossmann, E. 2001 *Maritime Tel Michal and Apollonia: Results of the Underwater Survey 1989-1996* (British Archaeological Reports, International Series 915). Oxford: BAR.

Hall, L.J. 2001-02. Berytus through the classical texts: From *Colonia* to *Civitas*. *ARAM* 13-14: 141-69.

Hall, L.J. 2004 *Roman Berytus: Beirut in Late Antiquity*. London: Routledge.

Hamel, H. 2014. Roman pottery in Baalbek/*Heliopolis*, in B. Fischer-Genz, Y. Gerber and H. Hamel (eds) *Roman Pottery in the Near East. Local Production and Regional Trade; Proceedings of the Round Table Held in Berlin, 19-20 February 2010* (Roman and Late Antique Mediterranean Pottery 3): 67-78. Oxford: Archaeopress.

Hayes, J.W. 1991. *Paphos*, III: *The Hellenistic and Roman Pottery*. Nicosia: Dept of Antiquities of Cyprus.

Hayes, J.W. 1996. The pottery, in S.E Sidebotham and W.Z. Wendrich (eds) *Berenike 1995: Preliminary Report of the Excavations at Berenike (Egyptian Red Sea Coast) and the Survey of the Eastern Desert*: 147-78. Leiden: Centre for Non-Western Study.

Hayes, J.W. 1997. *Handbook of Mediterranean Roman Pottery*. London: British Museum Press.

Hayes, J.W. 2000. From Rome to Beirut and beyond: Asia Minor and eastern Mediterranean trade connections. *Rei Cretariae Romanae Fautorum Acta* 36: 285-97.

Kaldeli, A. 2013. Roman amphorae from Cyprus: Integrating trade and exchange in the Mediterranean. Unpublished PhD dissertation, University of College London.

Keay, S.J. 2012. Introduction, in S.J. Keay (ed) *Rome, Portus and the Mediterranean*: 1-32. London: The British School at Rome.

Leidwanger, J. 2014. Maritime networks and economic regionalism in the Roman eastern Mediterranean. *Analyse des réseaux sociaux en archéologie* 135: 32-38.

Marriner, N., C. Morhange, and M. Saghieh-Beydoun 2008. Geoarchaeology of Beirut's ancient harbour, Phoenicia. *Journal of Archaeological Science* 35: 2495-2516.

Mattingly, D.J. 1988a. The olive boom. Oil surpluses, wealth and power in Roman Tripolitania. *Libyan Studies* 19: 21-41.

Mattingly, D.J. 1988b. Oil for export? A comparison of Libyan, Spanish and Tunisian olive oil production in the Roman Empire. *Journal of Roman Archaeology* 1: 33-56.

Megaw, A.H.S. and J.W Hayes 2003. Hellenistic and Roman pottery deposits from the 'Saranda Kolones' castle site at Paphos. *Annual of the British School at Athens* 98: 447-516.

Millar, F. 1993. *The Roman Near East, 31 B.C.-A.D. 337*. Cambridge (MA): Harvard University Press.

Mills, P.J.E. and N. Beaudry 2010. Pottery from late Roman Ras el Bassit, Syria, in S. Menchelli, S. Santoro, M. Pasquinucci and G. Guiducci (eds) *LRCW3: Late Roman Coarse Wares, Cooking Wares and Amphorae in the Mediterranean; Archaeology and Archaeometry; Comparison between Western and Eastern Mediterranean* (British Archaeological Reports, International Series 2185.1): 857-66. Oxford: BAR.

Mills, P.J.E. and P. Reynolds 2014. Amphorae and specialized coarsewares of Ras al Bassit, Syria: Local products and exports, in N. Poulou-Papadimitriou, E. Nodarou and V. Kilikoglou (eds) *LRCW4: Late Roman Coarse Wares, Cooking Wares and Amphorae in the Mediterranean; Archaeology and Archaeometry; The Mediterranean; A Market without Frontiers* (British Archaeological Reports, International Series 2616.1): 133-42. Oxford: BAR.

Peacock, D.P.S. and D.F. Williams 1986. *Amphorae and the Roman Economy: An Introductory Guide*. London: Longman.

Peña, J.T. 1998. The mobilization of state olive oil in Roman Africa: The evidence of late 4th-c. Ostraca from Carthage, in J.T. Peña, J.J. Rossiter and A.I. Wilson (eds) *Carthage Papers: The Early Colony's Economy, Water Supply, a Public Bath, and the Mobilization of State Olive Oil* (Journal of Roman Archaeology Supplementary Series 29): 116-238. Ann Arbor: Journal of Roman Archaeology.

Perring, D., P. Reynolds, and R. Thorpe 2003. The archaeology of Beirut: A report on work in the insula of the House of the Fountains. *The Antiquaries Journal* 83: 195-229.

Rathbone, D. 2003. The financing of maritime commerce in the Roman Empire I-II AD, in E. Lo Cascio (ed) *Credito e moneta nel mondo romano: atti degli Incontri capresi di storia dell'economia antica: Capri, 12-14 ottobre 2000*: 197-229. Bari: Edipuglia.

Rauh, N., C. Autret and J. Lund 2013. Amphora design and marketing in Antiquity, in M. Frass (ed.) *Kauf, Konsum und Markte, Wirtschafts-welten im Fokus - Von der römischen Antike bis zur Gegenwart, Wiesbaden*: 145-81. Wiesbaden: Harrassowitz.

Reynolds, P. 1999. Pottery production and economic exchange in 2nd century Berytus: Some preliminary observations of ceramic trends from quantified ceramic deposits from the Anglo-Lebanese excavations in Beirut. *Berytus Archaeological Studies* 43: 35-110.

Reynolds, P. 2000a. Baetican, Lusitanian and Tarraconensian amphorae in classical Beirut: Some preliminary observations of trends in amphora imports from the western Mediterranean in the Anglo-Lebanese excavations in Beirut (BEY 006, 007, and 045). *Congreso Internacional 'Ex Baetica Amphorae' (Sevilla-Écija, December 1998)*: 1035-65. Écija: Editorial Gráficas.

Reynolds, P. 2000b. The Beirut amphora type, 1st century BC-7th century AD: An outline of its formal development and some preliminary observations of regional economic trends. *Rei Cretariae Romanae Fautorum Acta* 36: 387-95.

Reynolds, P. 2005. Levantine amphorae from Cilicia to Gaza: A typology and analysis of regional production trends from the 1st to 7th centuries, in J. Buxeda i Garrigós and M.A. Cau Ontiveros (eds) *LRCWI: Late Roman Coarse Wares, Cooking Wares and Amphorae in the Mediterranean; Archaeology and Archaeometry*: 563-611. Oxford: Archaeopress.

Riley, J.A. 1979. Coarse pottery, in J.A. Lloyd (ed.) *Excavations at Sidi Khrebish, Benghazi (Berenice) II* (Libya Antiqua Supplements 5): 91-467. Tripoli: Department of Antiquities, People's Socialist Libyan Arab Jamahirya.

Safadi, C. 2016. Wind and wave modelling for the evaluation of the maritime accessibility and protection afforded by ancient harbours. *Journal of Archaeological Science: Reports* 5: 348-60.

Silberstein, N., E. Galili and J. Sharvit 2017. Hellenistic, Roman and Byzantine ceramics from the Akko Marina, in E. Galili (ed.) *The Akko Marina Archaeological Project* (British Archaeological Reports, International Series 2862): 35-162. Oxford: BAR.

Stern, E. (ed). 1996. *Excavations at Dor, Final Report*, I.B: *Areas A and C: The Finds* (Qedem Reports 2). Jerusalem: Hebrew University of Jerusalem.

Tomber, R. 1999. Pottery from the sediments of the inner harbour, in K.G. Holum, A. Raban and J. Patrich (eds) *Caesarea Papers*, II: *Herod's Temple, the Provincial Governor's Praetorium and Granaries, the Later Harbor, a Gold Coin Hoard, and Other Studies* (Journal of Roman Archaeology Supplementary Series 35): 295-322. Ann Arbor: Journal of Roman Archaeology.

Vroom, J. 2004. Late antique pottery, settlement and trade in the east Mediterranean. A preliminary comparison of ceramics from Limyra (Lycia) and Boeotia, in W. Bowden, L. Lavan and C. Machado (eds) *Recent Research on the Late Antique Countryside*: 281-330. Leiden: Brill.

Vroom, J. 2007. Limyra in Lycia: Byzantine/Umayyad pottery finds from excavations in the eastern part of the city, in S. Lemaître (ed.) *Céramiques antiques en Lycie, VIIe s. a.C.-VIIe s. p.C.: les produits et les marchés; actes de la table-ronde de Poitiers, 21-22 mars 2003*: 261-92. Paris: De Boccard.

University of Southampton 2014. *Roman Amphorae: A Digital Resource*, Archaeology Data Service, viewed 15 August 2021, <https://doi.org/10.5284/1028192>.

Wicenciak, U. 2016. Ceramic patchwork in Hellenistic to Byzantine Phoenicia: Regionalization and specialization of vessel production. *Polish Archaeology in the Mediterranean* 25: 619-90.

18. Late Roman Amphorae in the Western Mediterranean. A Typology and Economic Study: La evidencia anfórica del siglo VII e inicios del siglo VIII en Tarragona 40 años después.

Francesc Rodríguez Martorell

1. Introducción

La publicación del trabajo del S. Keay, *Late Roman Amphorae in the Western Mediterranean. A typology and economic study: the catalan evidence* (1984), representa uno de los mayores hitos en el estudio de los recipientes anfóricos mediterráneos de época tardorromana. En este sentido, dicha monografía definió un gran número de contenedores bajo un mismo sistema cronotipológico estandarizado que, con ligeras modificaciones, siguen utilizándose hoy en día en los análisis ceramológicos (véanse, por ejemplo, las obras de referencia de Bonifay, 2004; Pieri, 2005; Reynolds, 2010; Bernal, 2019, así como las distintas ediciones del congreso internacional *Late Roman Coarse Ware, Cooking Ware and Amphorae*).

Para el caso de la ciudad de Tarragona (Catalunya), objeto de estudio del presente artículo, el trabajo de S. Keay también puede considerarse la piedra angular sobre la que se ha cimentado la tradición de los estudios ceramológicos posteriores (TEd'A, 1989; Aquilué, 1992a; Macias, 1999; Remolà, 2000; Rodríguez, 2020). Durante estos últimos 40 años, J. A. Remolà ha ido ampliando las informaciones, la identificación y el catálogo de los envases destinados al transporte marítimo para el siglo V, gracias al hallazgo de importantes basureros cerámicos como el Vila-Roma y depósitos cerámicos con mayor fiabilidad estratigráfica (Remolà, 1993; 1998; 2000; 2013 y 2016; Remolà y Abelló, 1989; Remolà y Uscatescu, 1998).

A pesar de los abundantes estudios de estos dos investigadores, queda aún pendiente por conocer el nivel de abastecimiento anfórico de Tarragona durante los siglos VI y VIII. Esta laguna se encuentra justificada en parte debido a las limitaciones de la documentación estratigráfica que se tenía hasta este momento. Del mismo modo afectan las interpretaciones hegemónicas según las cuales Tarragona perdería influencia frente a la vecina Barcelona, la marginación de la ciudad respecto de los circuitos comerciales mediterráneos tras la formación del reino visigodo de Toledo y el abandono ante la llegada de la conquista árabe (Keay, 1984: 14; Remolà, 2000: 300-307 y 2013: 327; cfr. Rodríguez, 2020: 13-32; Lasheras y Rodríguez, en prensa).

El presente trabajo tiene como objetivo retomar las investigaciones desarrolladas por S. Keay en la ciudad de Tarragona, y presentar las novedades generadas al respecto de los recipientes anfóricos más tardíos localizados en el área portuaria. El estudio ceramológico, llevado a cabo en el marco de nuestra reciente tesis doctoral, ha permitido individualizar un conjunto de hasta 15 nuevos depósitos cerámicos, datados entre la segunda mitad del siglo VII e inicios del VIII (Rodríguez, 2020). Los envases detectados suman un total de más de 576 ejemplares estimados, los cuales han sido a su vez catalogados por áreas geográficas, tipos y subvariantes, siguiendo la sistematización que introdujo Keay en su monografía. Esta información revela una nueva imagen para Tarragona, alejada del tradicional panorama recesivo, de pérdida de protagonismo y veloz abandono.

2. El conocimiento anfórico de Tarragona: 40 años después.

Cuando S. Keay publicó su monografía sobre los contenedores anfóricos en 1984, junto a los casos de Barcelona, Empúries, Girona y Terrassa, en Tarragona sólo se habían documentado diez contextos cerámicos con suficiente detalle para establecer una primera sistematización anfórica amplia (Figura 18.1). En cuanto a los depósitos, abarcan principalmente los situados en la zona más elevada de la ciudad –Parte Alta–, además de algunos hallazgos anfóricos en el cementerio cristiano de la basílica de San Fructuoso, en el área de la Calle Pere Martel y en el interior de las *fossae* del anfiteatro (Keay 1984: 14-27).

El desarrollo de la arqueología urbana en Tarragona a partir de los años 80 y hasta la década del 2000, supuso un incremento exponencial del número de depósitos encontrados en la ciudad, y modificó sustancialmente el panorama defendido hasta ese momento por S. Keay (Remolà, 2000) (Figura 18.1). Buena prueba de ello son los depósitos cerámicos más conocidos por la investigación especializada: los contextos de la calle *Vila-Roma* y del *Antic Hospital de Santa Tecla,* fechados *grosso modo* entre los años 425-450/460 (TEd'A 1989 y 1990; Aquilué 1992a y b; Reynolds 1995: 281; Macias 1999; Remolà 2000; Járrega 2000: 468; Reynolds et al 2011).

Figura. 18.1: Mapa base de Tarragona con la ubicación de los principales contextos cerámicos tardo-antiguos analizados por S. J. Keay (amarillo), X. Aquilué, J. M. Macias y J. A. Remolà (rojo) y F. Rodríguez (verde) (elaboración a partir de Keay, 1984; Aquilué, 1992; Macias, 1999; Remolà, 2000; Rodríguez, 2020).

Estos extraordinarios contextos destacan por mantener una relación porcentual casi idéntica entre las tres principales categorías cerámicas estudiadas (vajilla fina de mesa, ánforas y cerámica común), así como por la constante presencia de material importado procedente de amplias áreas del Mediterráneo occidental y oriental (Remolà, 2000: 294s y gráfico 3).

Según el análisis de estos depósitos realizado por J. A. Remolà, se confirma la preeminencia de los envases norteafricanos de tradición grecorromana, en particular, los contenedores cilíndricos de pequeñas (Keay 26F), medianas (Keay 25 y 27) y grandes dimensiones (Keay 35, 36 y 41) (Remolà, 2000: 297). Del mismo modo, se documenta una alta presencia de recipientes de origen bético y lusitano (Keay 13A, C-D, 16B-C, 19A-B, 19C,

21, 23, 68, 91(?) y 78) (Remolà, 2000: 297). Al igual que ocurre en otros enclaves del Mediterráneo occidental – por ejemplo, en el sur de la Galia (Pieri 2005)–, destaca la inusitada presencia de envases procedentes de Chipre, Antioquía, Palestina y Asia Menor (LRA 1A, 3 y 4A; Ágora de Atenas M-273; Remolà Tardía A y H) e itálicas (Ánfora de Empoli; Remolà Tardía C, D y E) (Remolà, 2000: 298) (Figura 18.2).

A partir del último cuarto del siglo V y de la primera mitad del siglo VI –momento en el cual *Tarraco* se integra en el reino visigodo de Toledo y pasa a denominarse *Tarracona*, tal y como se desprende de la evidencia numismática conservada (Benagés, 2007)– el panorama es incierto y el conocimiento ceramológico escaso, por lo que se requieren más estudios especializados. La

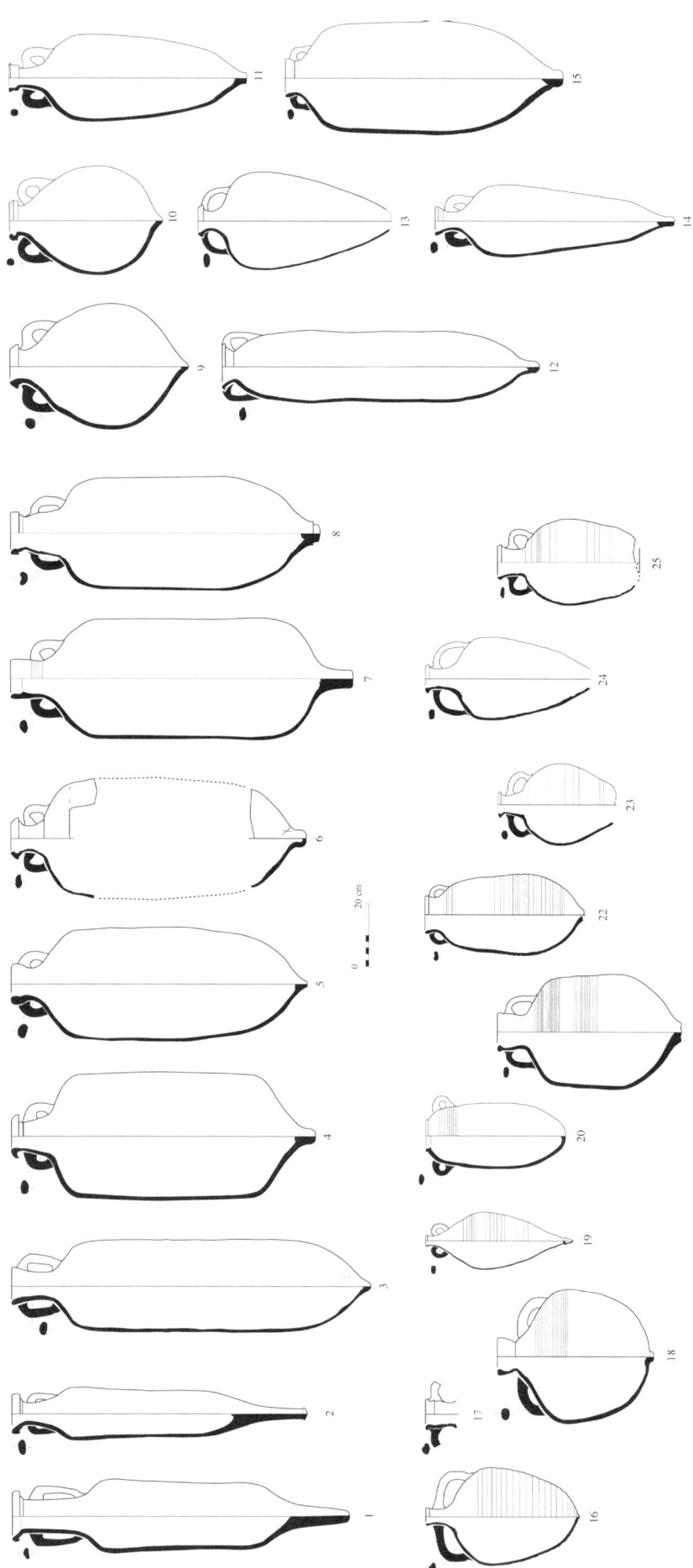

Figura. 18.2: Principales recipientes anfóricos localizados en las estratigrafías tarraconenses de los siglos V y VI. 1: Keay 25. 2: Keay 26F. 3: Keay 27B. 4: Keay 35B. 5: Keay 36B. 6: Keay 41. 7: Keay 55. 8: Keay 62. 9: Keay 13A. 10: Keay 13C-D. 11: Keay 19B. 12: Keay 16B-C. 13: Keay 23. 14: Keay 21. 15: Keay 78. 16: LRA 1A. 17: LRA 1B1. 18: LRA 2A. 19: LRA 3. 20: LRA 4A. 21: Agora Atenas M-273. 22: *Samos Cystern Type.* 23: Remolà Tardía A. 24: Ánfora Empoli. 25: Remolà Tardía B (a partir de Keay, 1984 y Remolà, 2000).

mayoría de los contextos del siglo VI analizados en estos últimos 40 años proceden de niveles de amortización de antiguas estructuras romanas altoimperiales, rellenos con enterramientos asociados y niveles constructivos con alta fragmentación cerámica y escaso número de ejemplares (Key, 1984: 14-21; Remolà, 2000: 300). En este sentido, la investigación a menudo ha recurrido al extenso vertedero documentado por P. M. Berges en el cuerpo "A" de la *Torre de l'Antiga Audiència*; si bien no resulta útil para caracterizar con precisión el panorama cerámico del siglo VI, debido a graves e irremediables problemas estratigráficos durante la excavación y mezcla de los horizontes fechados entre finales del siglo V e inicios del VIII (Keay, 1984: 18-19; Aquilué, 1992a: 342-441; Macias, 1999: 206-214; Remolà, 2000: 52-54).

Por el momento, los análisis apuntan para el siglo VI un aparente "retorno" a la situación del siglo IV, con un aumento de los productos locales en cerámica común y una disminución del porcentaje de ánforas, con respecto al siglo V. A ello se suma la aceptación generalizada de ciertas interpretaciones historicistas, que han promovido la tesis de una supuesta pérdida de poder urbano de *Tarracona* frente a la vecina *Barcinona* (Barcelona), o de una falta de abastecimiento tras la entrada del imperio romano de Oriente en la esfera peninsular (Keay, 1984: 14; 1987: 394; Aquilué, 1992a: 419; Macias, 1999: 284-285; Remolà, 2000: 298-330 y 2013: 327).

Sin embargo, este aparente retorno no debe traducirse en un retroceso en el abastecimiento cerámico de la ciudad, sino en un reajuste de los porcentajes cerámicos importados frente a la distorsión provocada en el siglo V por el abastecimiento preferente a las tropas imperiales arribadas a *Tarraco* para recuperar los territorios peninsulares ocupados por los suevos, vándalos y alanos (Remolà y Pérez, 2013; Remolà, 2016; Remolà, Lasheras y Pérez, 2020).

Mientras no dispongamos de nuevos contextos que amplíen las valoraciones preliminares, durante el siglo VI se observa la sustitución gradual de los tipos anfóricos del siglo V y la introducción de nuevos envases, como los contenedores norteafricanos Keay 62 y Keay 55, 56, 57, 63, 64, 77 o 85 (Remolà, 2000: 302). Este proceso transicional también se aprecia en envases del Mediterráneo oriental, como los contenedores LRA 1A, 2A y 4A, que son reemplazados por la siguiente generación de recipientes LRA 1B1, 2B y 4B, al tiempo que la Agora de Atenas M-273 desaparece en favor del tipo *Samos Cystern Type*. Una cuestión aún por dilucidar en Tarragona es la marcada reducción, a lo largo del siglo VI, de las producciones béticas y lusitanas –muy reconocibles en las estratigrafías del siglo V– y su posible sustitución por otros contenedores menos visibles en el registro ceramológico. De igual forma,

falta por definir mejor la presencia y los ritmos de las primeras 'ánforas de imitación bizantina' en el Mediterráneo occidental, especialmente las vinculadas al modelo hegemónico de la LRA 1B1 de Cilicia, como son el caso de los contenedores Ech Chekaf IV, la Keay 72 del área valenciana y la Remolà Tardía B, entre otras (Remolà, 2000: 237; Nacef, 2007; Ribera y Rosselló, 2012: 394) (Fig. 18.2).

Por lo que respecta a los tipos anfóricos más tardíos documentados en Tarragona, la ausencia de secuencias estratigráficas fiables había provocado interpretaciones desiguales para las últimas centurias de la Antigüedad tardía (Remolà, 2000: 304). A modo de ejemplo, en el contexto del Mausoleo de la Calle *Sant Auguri,* datado entre el siglo VII e inicios del siglo VIII, únicamente se conservaban 60 individuos estimados, de los cuales apenas un ejemplar podía atribuirse a un recipiente anfórico (Macias y Remolà, 2005: 5, tav. 1). Las excavaciones arqueológicas llevadas a cabo dentro del plan de ampliación urbanística conocido como PERI-2, objeto de estudio en el siguiente apartado, se desarrollaron en paralelo a la publicación de los trabajos ceramológicos de J. A. Remolà (2000: 96-98), lo que impedía mayores precisiones. Algunos datos de gran interés se obtienen gracias al estudio preliminar presentado en el marco del congreso de Arqueología Cristiana de Cartagena del año 1998 y de la publicación de un reducido lote cerámico adscrito a la segunda mitad del siglo VII (Macias y Remolà, 2000). Los contenedores anfóricos estudiados en dicho artículo ampliaban considerablemente la escasa información publicada hasta entonces sobre los últimos envases detectados por S. Keay en 1984, aunque se limitaban a enumerar su presencia en las estratigrafías portuarias. Lo más destacable de la publicación era la aparición de los primeros envases globulares con fondo umbilicado procedentes del norte de África, fenómeno que empezaba a documentarse también en otros yacimientos mediterráneos como Sant'Antonino di Perti o la Crypta Balbi (Saguì 1998; Keay 1998; Murialdo 2001; Bonifay 2004: 152, fig. 83).

3. Novedades anfóricas de la segunda mitad del siglo VII e inicios del siglo VIII: el área portuaria de *Tarracona.*

En los últimos años, el área portuaria se ha convertido en una de las zonas arqueológicas más activas para el conocimiento urbano, económico y social de la ciudad de *Tarraco*(*na*) durante la Antigüedad tardía. Recientemente, se ha presentado un estudio en profundidad de la evolución de esta área, tanto a nivel de estratigrafía, arquitectura y urbanismo (Lasheras, 2018). En este sentido, las informaciones arqueológicas apuntan a que tras una fase de ampliación urbana producida durante el siglo V, a partir del siglo VII se configura un nuevo modelo de ocupación, centrado en la construcción cerca de la línea de costa de un conjunto de espacios productivos, para el servicio portuario o el intercambio comercial (Lasheras, 2018: 654-662; Rodríguez *et al.* 2020). El conocimiento de este gran conjunto de edificios ha coincidido con un amplio estudio ceramológico que ha puesto de relieve hasta 15 depósitos cerámicos inéditos, que certifican el mantenimiento de los flujos de abastecimiento comercial mediterráneo durante las últimas etapas de la Antigüedad tardía (Rodríguez y Macias, 2016, 2018 y 2023; Rodríguez, 2020) (Figura 18.3).

La localización de estos contextos ha permitido agrupar distintos datos cerámicos en una misma horquilla cronológica y aportar información sobre las pautas de consumo y de distribución –tanto en términos compositivos como porcentuales– de la ciudad entre los siglos VII y VIII. Por el momento se han podido diferenciar en el área portuaria hasta 4 períodos u horizontes concatenados. El primero, denominado H1, se ubica al entorno del año 650 y reúne una serie de contextos suficientemente significativos y con un total de 265 individuos estimados, de los cuales 100 corresponden a envases para el transporte marítimo. El segundo de los períodos, o H2, data entre los años 675/700 y 715, engloba 5 de los contextos más representativos del área portuaria y conserva un total de 1084 individuos (342 de los cuales corresponden a ánforas). El horizonte H3 está datado exclusivamente en el siglo VIII, *circa* 700 - 715, y se diferencia del anterior periodo al situarse estratigráficamente por encima del anterior. Este último está formado por un total de 449 individuos, 134 contenedores dirigidos al transporte de víveres. Por último, el horizonte H4, el más tardío detectado hasta el momento, dispone de un único contexto cerámico y una muestra reducida de 26 individuos anfóricos que, probablemente, sean materiales residuales con un uso secundario y prolongado, por lo que no serán tomados en consideración en el análisis.

Los contenedores con mayor número de individuos registrados en el puerto tarraconense provienen del Norte de África, seguidos de la extensa área que ocupaba el Mediterráneo oriental. A bastante distancia de éstos, encontramos los recipientes locales, denominados Remolà tipo tardío B. Por último, situamos los envases de origen indeterminado (Fig. 18.4.1).

La distribución por horizontes constata un predominio en el horizonte H1 (*circa 650*) de las mercancías de origen oriental. Esta alta incidencia se encuentra reconocida en parte gracias al alto número de recipientes anfóricos de los tipos LRA 1B1 (16,49%), LRA 5 (16,49%) y LRA 4C (10,31%). En menor número, se documentan los contenedores LRA 6 (3,09%) y LRA 7(4,12%), junto con ejemplares del tipo Samos Cystern (2,06%) y LRA 2C/13 (2,06%). En cambio, de los ejemplares del norte de África incluidos en este primer horizonte destaca por encima del resto de recipientes la forma Keay 61 (13,40%), mientras que el resto – Bonifay Globular tipo 2 y 3, "Orlo a Fascia" /Bonifay type 52, Ech Chekaf IV, Keay 8A y las "*Spatheion*" 3 de pequeñas dimensiones –mantienen un porcentaje relativamente bajo y uniforme (del 3,09% al 7,22%). El horizonte anfórico del H1 incorpora la presencia de hasta 7 ejemplares de la forma Remolà tipo tardío B, un posible recipiente fabricado local y/o regionalmente a partir de la segunda mitad del siglo VI y que continúa muy presente a mediados del siglo VII, así como de 3 individuos indeterminados (Figuras 18.4 y 18.5).

El horizonte H2 muestra un cambio de tendencia en los suministros anfóricos, donde el predominio del abastecimiento oriental queda sustituido por la hegemónica presencia de los contenedores tunecinos. Continúa llegando un amplio surtido de mercancías de la otra orilla del Mediterráneo y, a nivel tipológico, se detecta una disminución relativa de la presencia de recipientes como la Samos Cistern type (de un 2,06 a un 1,53%, la LRA 1B1 (de un 16,49 a un 12,23%) y la LRA 7 (de un 4,12 a un 2,75%). Por primera vez en Tarragona, se detecta la presencia de ejemplares globulares orientales sin una clara adscripción geográfica, pero que entroncan con realidades difíciles de detectar a nivel general en el occidente del Mediterráneo (Figura 18.7). En cambio, por lo que respecta al repertorio tunecino, se evidencia un mayor porcentaje de la forma Keay 61, que pasa de un 13,40% a un 33,03%; así como del Bonifay Globular tipo 2 que aumenta hasta 12 puntos porcentuales su representatividad (del 4,12% al 16,51%). El contenedor Bonifay Globular tipo 3 y el Keay 8A también aumentan levemente (del 3,09% al 3,36% el primero y del 3,09% al 3,67% el segundo). El resto de los recipientes norteafricanos reducen su representatividad en cuanto al porcentaje general del horizonte, si bien su número de individuos es mayor: "Orlo a Fascia" /Bonifay type 52 (del 3,09% al 0,92%), "*Spatheion*" tipo 3 (del 1,03% al 0,92%) y el envase Ech Chekaf IV (del 3,09% al 3,06%) (Figura 18.6). Por último, los envases Remolà tipo tardío B reducen considerablemente su presencia en este horizonte, hasta volverse meramente testimoniales, un hecho que pudiera indicar su posible final productivo (del 7,22% al 2,75%).

El H3 se inicia con la ausencia de nuevos repertorios y con una clara reducción porcentual de muchas de las ánforas evidenciadas en horizontes anteriores. No se constatan, por tanto, las producciones de tendencia globular oriental ni las LRA 2C/13, mientras que los contenedores orientales "tradicionales" parecen retrotraerse a la tendencia observada durante el H1. La presencia de la forma LRA 1B2, así como de la Samos Cistern y de una posible variante tardía del ánfora Ágora M334 son relevantes en términos generales, aunque su aparición en este momento permite

Listado de contextos cerámicos s. VII – VIII analizados en Rodriguez, 2020

Núm.	Codi	Carrer	Fragments	I.E.	I.E. Coetanis	Cronologia
1	P2-7-22a/1	Felip Pedrell, 10–12	315	112	42	650-675
	P2-7-22b/1	Felip Pedrell, 12–Vidal i Barraquer 44–46	500	352	126	650/660-675
2	P2-7-22b/2	Felip Pedrell, 12–Vidal i Barraquer 44–46	1278	727	155	675-700/715+
	P2-7-22b/3	Felip Pedrell, 12–Vidal i Barraquer 44–46	1006	614	85	675-700/715+
	P2-7-22b/4	Felip Pedrell, 12–Vidal i Barraquer 44–46	1374	911	152	700-715+
3	P2-7-24/1	Felip Pedrell, 11	232	157	67	650-700
	P2-8-25/1	Smith, 88	454	127	30	650-660/675
4	P2-8-25/2	Smith, 88	858	344	50	700-715+
5	P2-6-TVB001/1	Vidal i Barraquer, s/n	200	80	60	700-715+
	TVB27/1	Vidal i Barraquer, 27	8231	1928	258	675-700
	TVB27/2.1	Vidal i Barraquer, 27	1153	776	180	675/700-715
	TVB27b/2.1	Vidal i Barraquer, 27	2887	1210	406	675/700-715
6	TVB27/2.2	Vidal i Barraquer, 27	723	480	98	700-715+
	TVB27/2.3	Vidal i Barraquer, 27	377	222	90	700-715+
	TVB27b/2.3	Vidal i Barraquer, 27	689	554	138	715-725+
		TOTAL	**20277**	**8594**	**1937**	

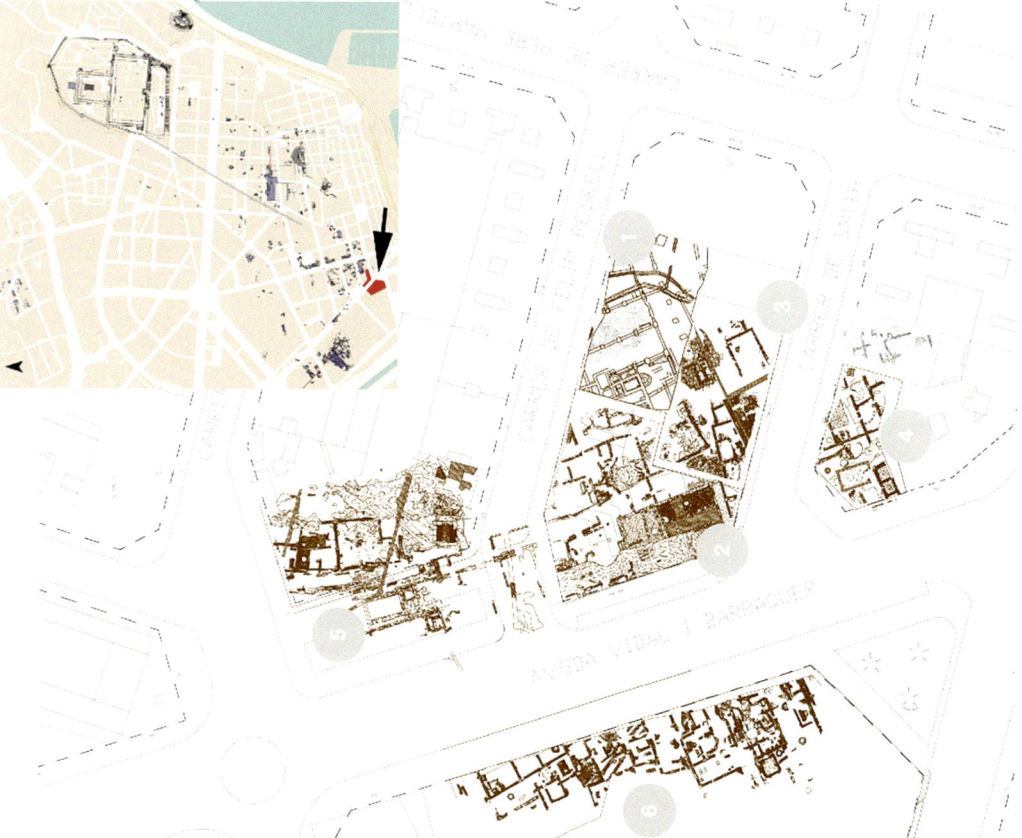

Figura. 18. 3: Planta arqueológica del área portuaria de *Tarraco(na)*, con indicación de los contextos cerámicos analizados en la tesis doctoral (elaboración propia a partir de la documentación gráfica del archivo CODEX – Arqueologia i Patrimoni).

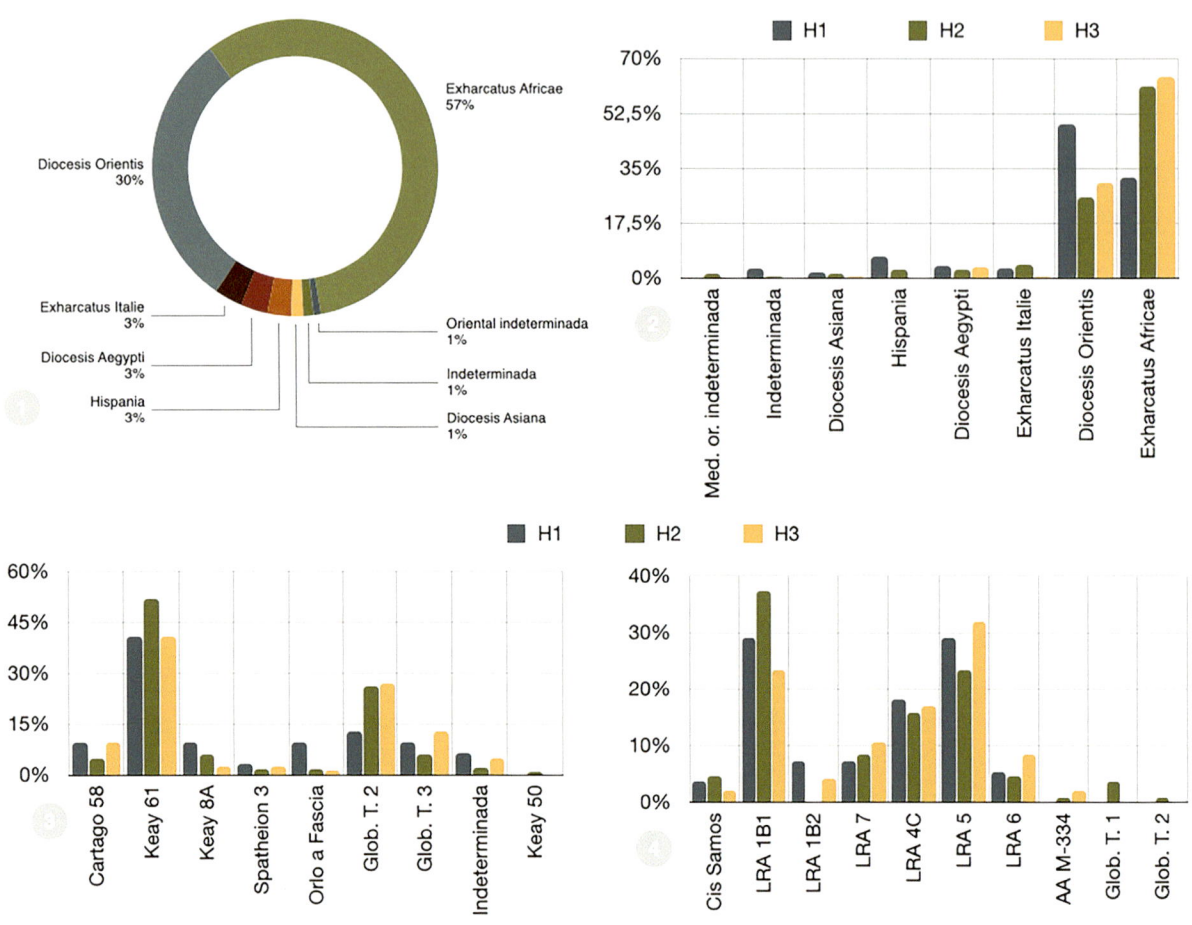

Figura 18.4: Síntesis de los recipientes anfóricos del área portuaria. **1 y 2:** Distribución porcentual por procedencias y por cada horizonte. **3:** Distribución porcentual de las principales formas norteafricanas. **4:** Distribución porcentual de las principales formas del Mediterráneo oriental.

interpretarlas como residuales. Este comportamiento a la baja también parece reflejarse en el abastecimiento norteafricano, aunque sigue predominando dentro del conjunto del período. En este sentido, los envases Keay 61 siguen constituyendo el ejemplar mayoritariamente identificado (26,32%), así como el ánfora Bonifay Globular tipo 2 (18,05%) y el tipo 3 (7,52%). En menor medida se documentan los últimos recipientes de Ech Chekaf IV (6,02%), los tipos Keay 8A (1,5%) y "*Spatheion*" tipo 3 (1,5%), así como un posible ejemplar de "Orlo a Fascia" /Bonifay type 52 (0,75%) (Figura 18.8).

4. Consideraciones finales

Con el presente artículo, hemos pretendido realizar un repaso al conocimiento anfórico generado en estos 40 años en la ciudad de Tarragona, con especial mención a los hallazgos más recientes que permiten actualizar el balance ceramológico precedente. Del mismo modo, se pretende presentar las últimas novedades relativas a los contenedores de transporte localizados en el área

portuaria y datados entre el siglo VII e inicio del siglo VIII.

A la vista está que la tradición ceramológica generada en estos últimos 40 años se ha nutrido, e incluso se nutre hoy en día, de la excelente publicación de S. Keay sobre los contenedores anfóricos tardorromanos del área catalana. El trabajo *Late Roman Amphorae in the Western Mediterranean. A typology and economic study: the catalan evidence* (1984) constituyó un magnífico catalizador para la realización de una serie de tesis doctorales exclusivamente dedicadas a los estudios ceramológicos, que generaron un conocimiento económico, histórico y social fundamental, en unas centurias con escasa visibilidad arqueológica y sobre todo, documental (Aquilué, 1992a; Macias, 1999; Remolà, 2000; Rodríguez, 2020). Igualmente, todas estas investigaciones han ofrecido a la comunidad científica nuevos datos para una correcta comparación con otros enclaves mediterráneos de idéntica cronología, aportando nuevas perspectivas dentro del complejo y aún abierto debate científico sobre el final de la Antigüedad tardía.

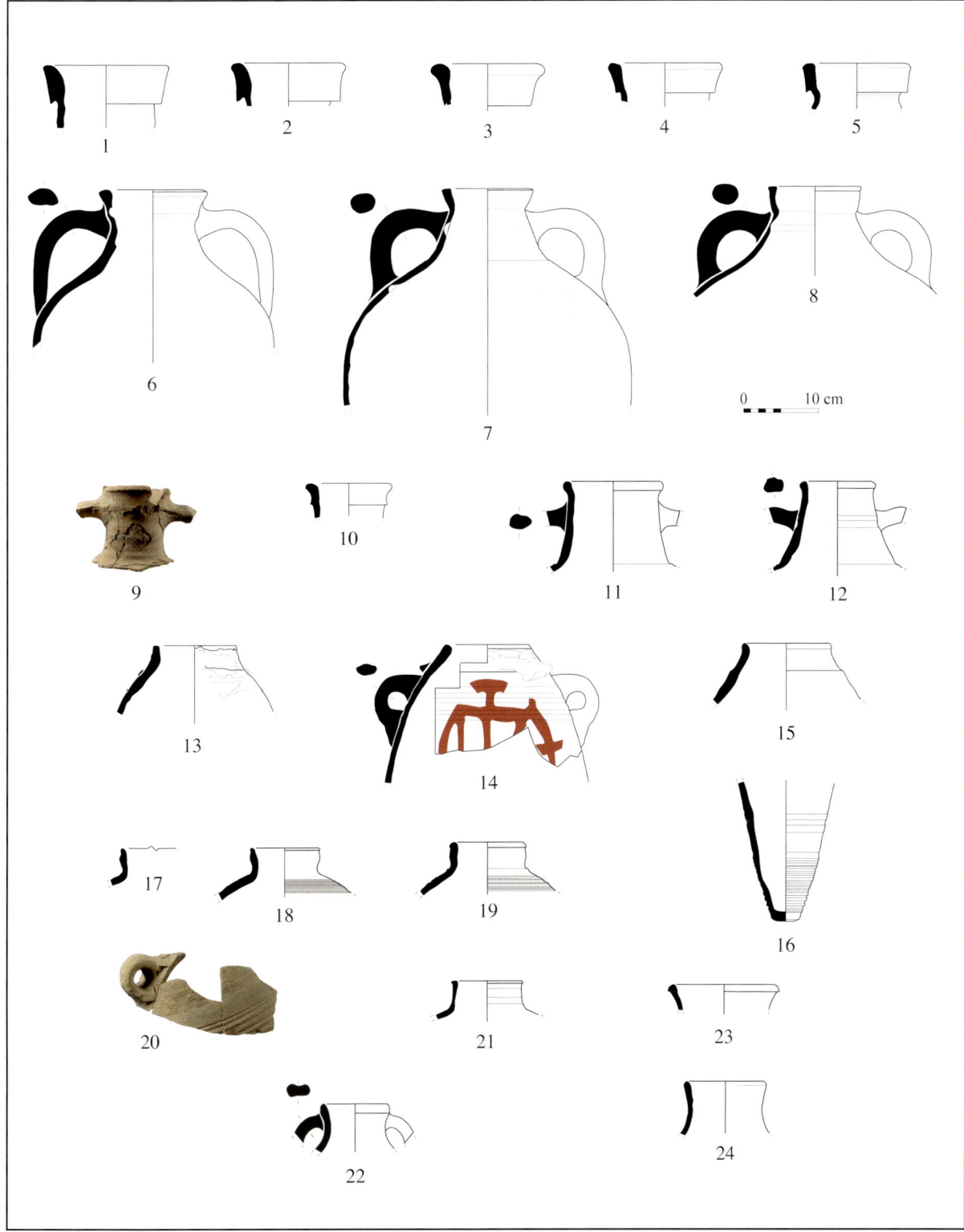

Figura. 18.5: Principales recipientes anfóricos documentados en el Horizonte H1. **1 y 2:** Keay 61A. **3:** Keay 61/8A. **4 y 5:** "Orlo a Fascia" / Bonifay type 52. **6:** Ech Chekaf IV. **7 y 8:** Bonifay Globular type 2. **9 y 10:** LRA 1B1. **11 y 12:** LRA 2C. **13-16:** LRA 4C. **17-20:** LRA 5. **21:** LRA 6. **22:** *Samos Cystern Type.* **23 y 24:** Remolà Tardía B.

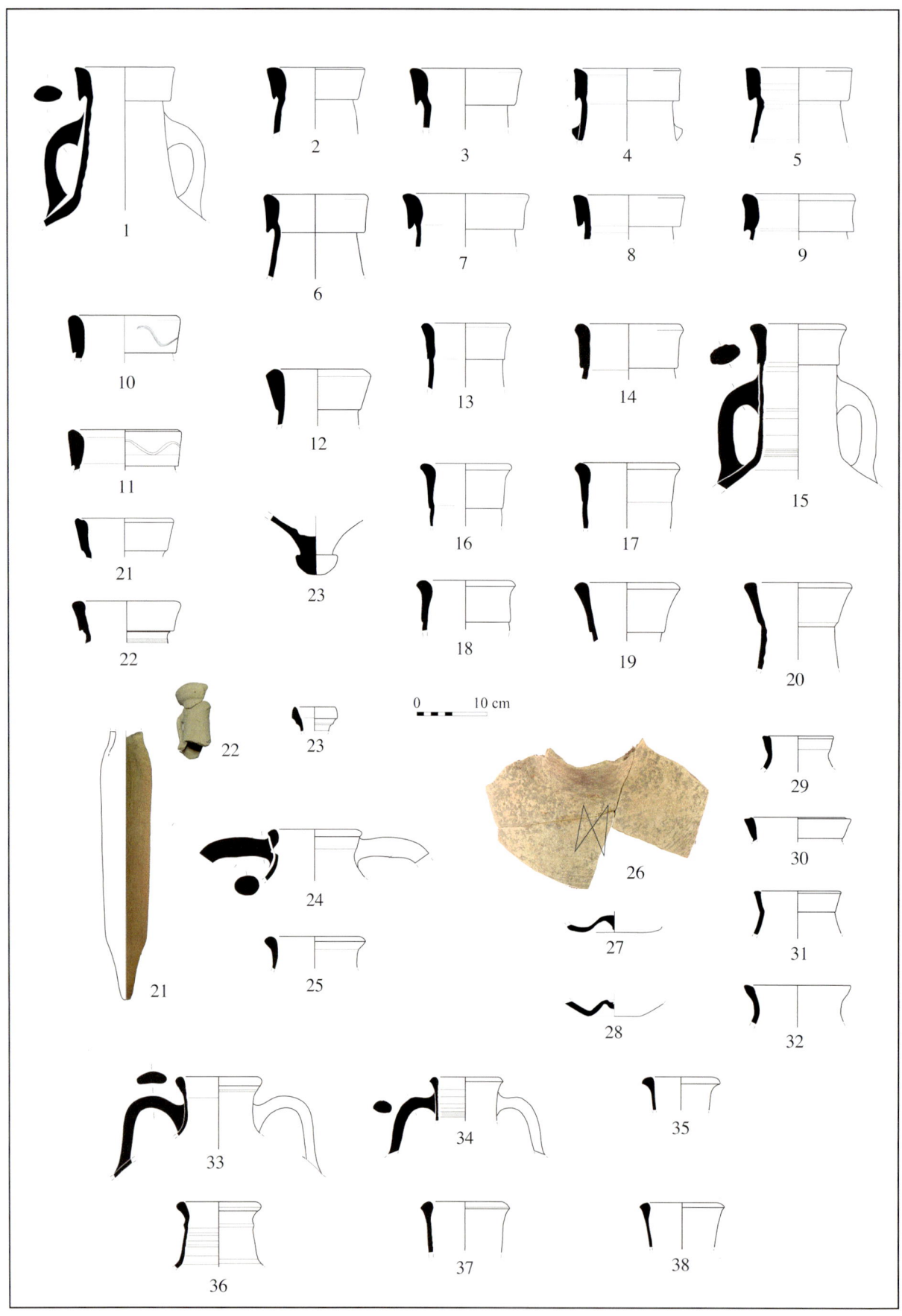

Figura. 18.6: Principales recipientes anfóricos norteafricanos documentados en el Horizonte H2. **1-9:** Keay 61A. **10 y 11:** Keay 61B tardía. **12:** Keay 61 var. Tarragona. **13-15:** Keay 61/8A. **16-18:** Keay 8A. **19 y 20:** Keay 50. **21-23:** "*Spatheion*" type 3. **24-25:** Ech Chekaf IV. **26-32:** Bonifay Globular type 2. **33-38:** Bonifay Globular type 3.

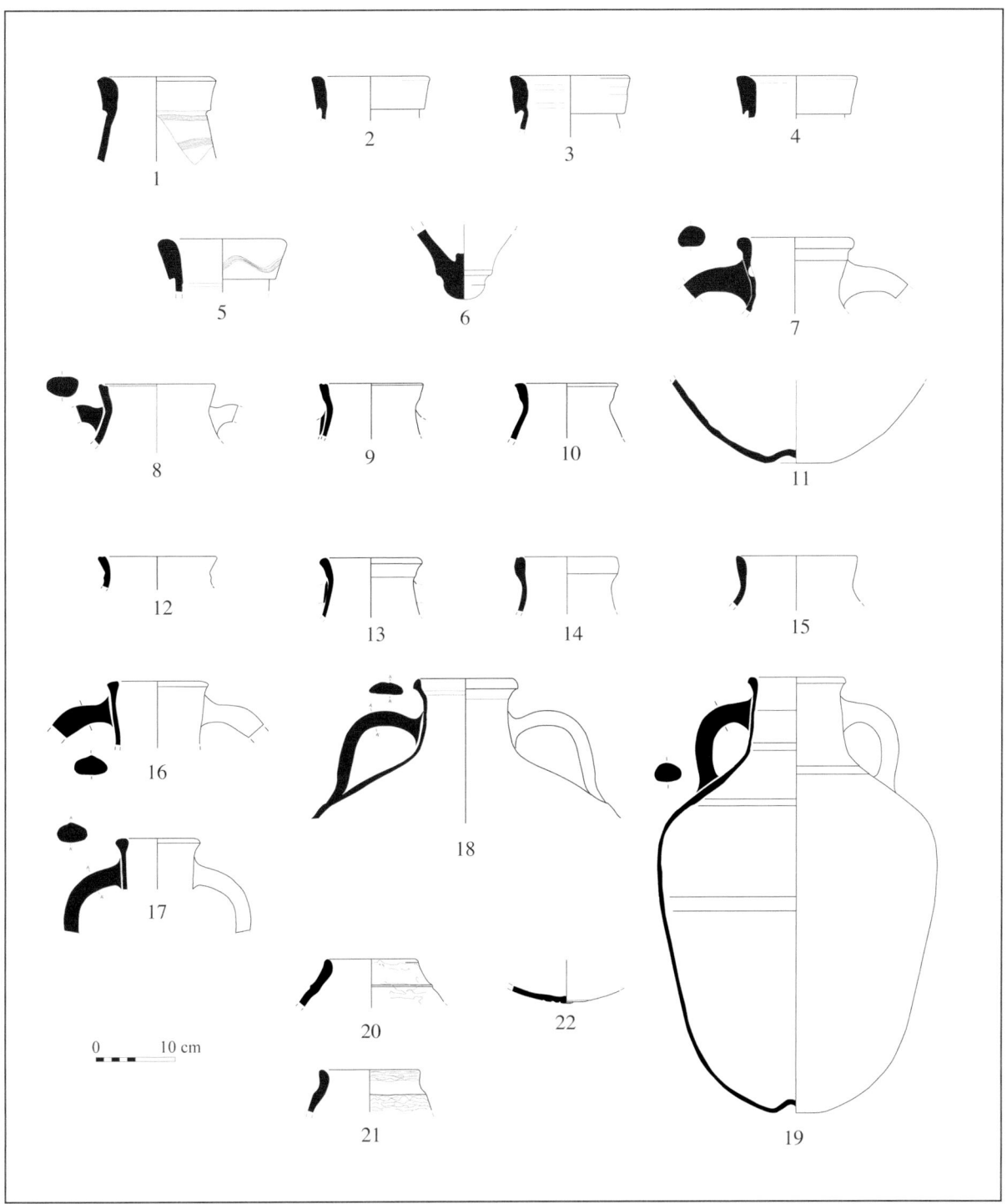

Figura. 18.7: Principales recipientes anfóricos orientales e indeterminados documentados en el Horizonte H2. **1-7:** LRA 1B1. **8-10:** LRA 2C/13. **11-19:** LRA 4C. **20-26:** LRA 5. **23 y 27:** LRA 6. **28:** LRA 7. **29 y 31:** Globular indeterminada.

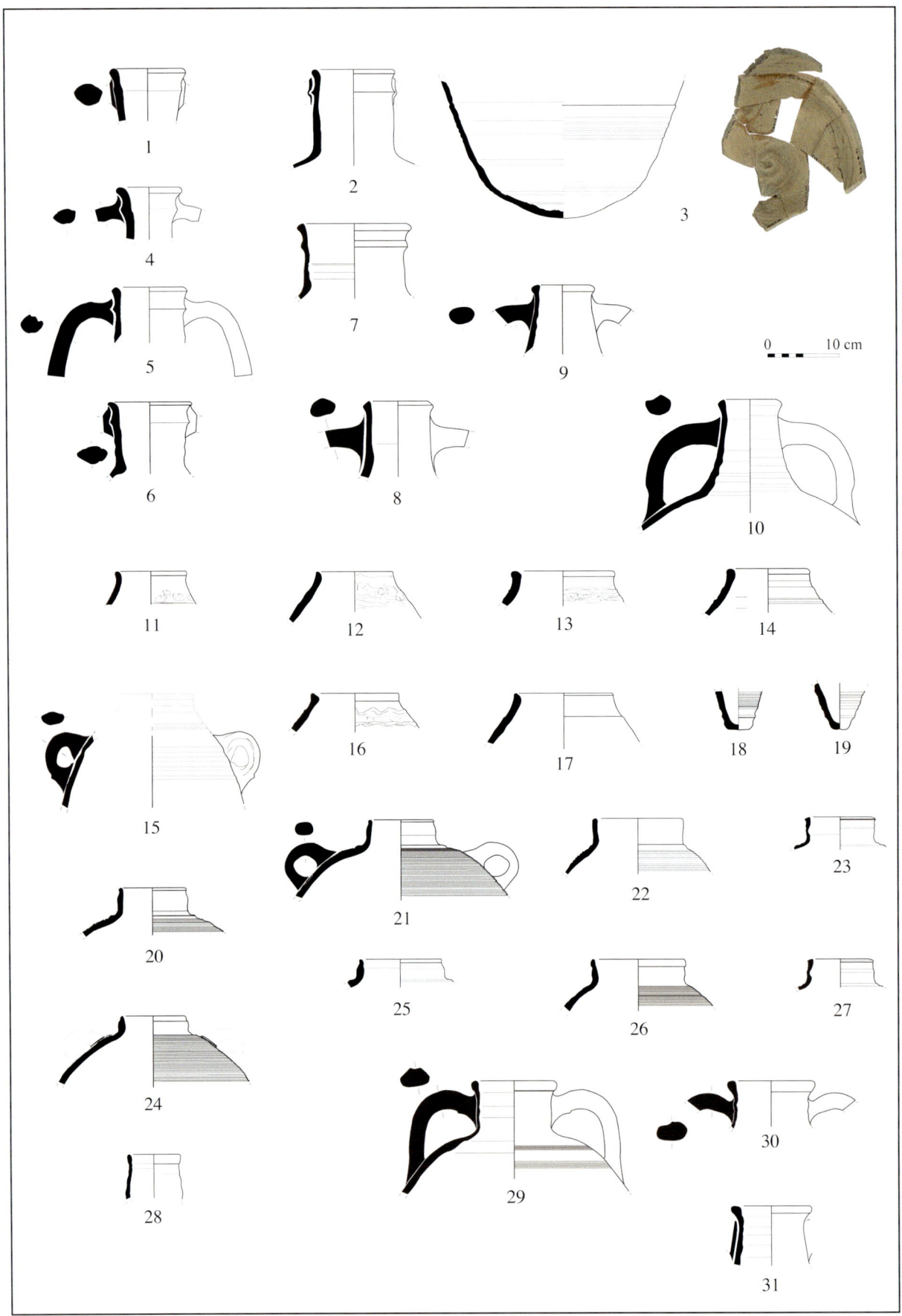

Figura. 18.8: Principales recipientes anfóricos documentados en el Horizonte H3. **1-6:** Keay 61. **5:** Keay 61B Tardía. **7:** Ech Chekaf IV. **8-15:** Bonifay Globular type 2. **16-19:** Bonifay Globular type 3. **20-21:** LRA 4C. **22:** LRA 5.

Aún queda por desentrañar la evolución del comercio mediterráneo durante la transición romano-visigoda de *Tarraco*(na) o el papel que jugó la ciudad durante el interregno ostrogodo y la unificación de los territorios hispanos e itálicos. Del mismo modo, otro tema pendiente es conocer en qué posición quedó la ciudad tras la conquista de amplios espacios occidentales por parte del imperio romano de oriente. Factores como el volumen de excedente disponible para comercializar, la capacidad económica de las ciudades satélites no imperiales para comprar y las diferentes rutas comerciales público-privadas entre el Mediterráneo occidental y oriental empezarían a desempeñar un papel muy importante en este período, tal y como parece constatarse posteriormente durante los siglos VII e inicios del VIII.

5. Bibliografía

Aquilué, X. 1992a. Relaciones económicas, sociales e ideológicas entre el Norte de Africa y la Tarraconense en época romana. Las cerámicas de producción africana procedentes de la Colonia Iulia Urbs Triumphalis Tarraco, Tesis Doctoral inédita, Universitat de Barcelona.

Aquilué, X. 1992b.Comentaris entorn a la presència de les ceràmiques de producció africana a Tàrraco, in X. Dupré (coord.) Miscel·lània Arqueològica a J. M. Recasens: 25-33. Tarragona.

Bernal, D. 2019. Ánforas tardorromanas en *Hispania*. Claves de identificación, in C. Fernández Ochoa, Ángel Morillo Cerdán y M. Zarzalejos Prieto (eds.) Manual de cerámica romana IV. Producciones cerámicas de época medio-imperial y tardorromana: 551-670. Alcalá de Henares: Museo Arqueológico Regional.

Bonifay, M. 2004. Études sur la céramique romaine tardive d'Afrique. Oxford: British Archaeological Report.

Keay, S. J. 1984. Late Roman Amphorae in the Western Mediterranean. A tipology and economic study: the Catalan evidence. Oxford: British Archaeological Report.

Keay, S. J. 1998. African amphorae. in L. Saguì, (eda.) Ceramica in Italia: V-VII secolo. Atti del Convegno in onore di John W. Hayes (Roma 1995): 141-155. Florencia: Biblioteca di Archeologia Medievale 14.

Járrega, R. 2000. Las cerámicas de importación en el Noroeste de la Tarraconense durante los siglos VI y VII dC. V Reunión de Arqueología Cristiana Hispánica, Cartagena 1998: 467-483. Barcelona.

Macias, J. M. 1999. La ceràmica comuna tardoantiga a Tàrraco. Anàlisi tipològica i històrica (segles V-VII). Tarragona.

Macias, J. M. y Remolà, J. A. 2000. Tarraco visigoda: caracterización del material cerámico del siglo VII dC. in J. M. Gurt y N. Tena (eds.) V Reunió

d'Arqueologia Cristiana Hispànica, Cartagena (1998): 485-497. Barcelona: Institut d'Estudis Catalans.

Macias, J. M. y Remolà, J. A. 2005. La cultura material de *Tarraco-Tarracona* (*Hispania Tarraconensis - Regnum Visigothorum*): cerámica común y ánforas, in J. M. Gurt, J. M. Buxeda y M. A. Cau (eds.) LRCW1: Late Roman Coarse Wares, Cooking Wares and Amphorae in the Mediterranean. Archaeology and Archaeometry: 125-136. Oxford: British Archaeological Report..

Murialdo, G. 2001. Le anfore di transporto, in T. Mannoni y G. Murialdo (dir.) S. Antonino: un insedimento fortificato nella Liguria bizantina: 255-296. Bordighera.

Nacef, J. 2007. Nouvelles données sur l'atelier de potiers de Henchir ech Chekaf (Ksour Essef, Tunisie), in M. Bonifay y J.C. Tréglia (eds.) LRCW 2: Late Roman Coarse Ware, Cooking Ware and Amphorae in the Mediterranean. Archaeology and Archaeometry: 581-591. Oxford: British Archaeological Report.

Lasheras, A. 2018. El suburbi portuari de Tarraco a l'Antiguitat tardana (segles III-VIII dC), Tesi doctoral inédita. Tarragona: Universitat Rovira i Virgili.

Lasheras, A. y F. Rodríguez. en prensa. Tarragona in the 8th century: new issues for discussion, in S. Esders, F. Krueger, S. Polla, T. S. Richter y C. Wickham (eds.), The 8th Century. Patterns of Transition in Economy and Trade Throughout the Late Antique, Early Medieval and Islamicate Mediterranean in Multidisciplinary Perspectives. Berlín - New York: De Gruyter.

Pieri, D. 2005. Le commerce du vin oriental à l'époque Byzantine (V - VII siècles). Le témoignage des amphores en Gaule. Beirut.

Remolà, J. A. 1993. Un tipo de ánfora tardo-romana poco conocido (VLR 8.198). Archivo Español de Arqueología, 66: 300 - 310.

Remolà, J. A.1998. Ánforas y modelos de aprovisionamiento en la ciudad tardo-antigua de Tarraco (*Diocesis Hispaniarum),* in L. Saguì (eda.) Ceramica in Italia: VI - VII secolo, Atti del Convegno in onore de John W. Hayes, Roma, 11-13 maggio 1995: 797-808. Florencia: Biblioteca di Archeologia Medievale..

Remolà J. A. 2000 Las ánforas tardo-antiguas en Tárraco (Hispania Tarraconensis). Barcelona: Col·lecció Instrumenta.

Remolà, J. A. 2013. Ánforas orientales tardías en *Tarraco* (siglos V - VII), in M. P. de Hoz y G. Mora (eds.) El Oriente griego en la Península Ibérica. Epigrafía e Historia: 307-330. Madrid: Bibliotheca Archaeologica Hispana 39.

Remolà, J. A. 2016. Lusitanian Amphorae in Tarraco (3rd - 5th century AD), in I. V. Pinto, R. de Almeida, A. Martin (eds.) Lusitanian Amphorae: Production and Distribution: 333-342. Oxford: Roman and Late Antique Mediterranean Pottery 10.

Remolà, J. A. y Abelló, A. 1989. Les àmfores, in: TEd'A [Taller Escola d'Arqueologia] Un abocador del segle

V dC en el fòrum provincial de Tàrraco: 249-323. Tarragona: Memòries d'excavació 2.

Remolà, J. A., Lasheras, A. y Pérez, M. 2020. Tarraco, una base de operaciones de los ejércitos imperiales (ca. 420 - 470 dC), in N. Christie, P. Diarte y A. Carneiro (eds.) Urban transformations in the Late Antique West: from materials to models: 135-154. Coimbra: Imprensa da Universidade de Coimbra.

Remolà, J. A. y Pérez, M. 2013. Centcelles y el *praetorium* del *comes Hispaniarum* Asterio en *Tarraco*. Archivo Español de Arqueología, 86:161-186.

Remolà, J. A. y Uscatescu, A. 1998. El comercio de ánforas orientales en Tarraco (siglos V - VII dC), in El vi a l'Antiguitat, Economia, Producció i comerç al Mediterrani occidental. Actes del Col·loqui d'Arqueologia Romana (Badalona, 28 de novembre - 1 de desembre de 1985): 553-562. Barcelona: Monografies Badalonines 9.

Reynolds, P. 1995. Trade in the Western Mediterranean, AD 400 - 700: The ceramic evidence. Oxford: British Archaeological Report.

Reynolds, P. 2010 Hispania and the Roman Mediterranean, AD 100-700. Ceramics and Trade. Oxford: Duckworth.

Reynolds, P., Bonifay, M. y Cau, M. Á. 2011.Key contexts for the dating of late Roman Mediterranean fine wares: a preliminary review and 'seriation, in M. A. Cau, P. Reynolds i M. Bonifay (eds.) Late Roman Fine Wares: solving problems of typology and chronology. Volume 1. A review of the evidence, debate and new contexts: 15-32. Oxford: Roman and Late Antique Pottery 1..

Ribera, A. y Rosselló, M. 2012. Anforas tardías de *Valentia*, *Rei Cretariae Romanae Favtorum* 42: pp. 385-396.

Rodríguez, F. 2020. El comerç mediterrani a Tarracona a les portes de l'Islam (ss. VII - VIII dC), Tesi doctoral inédita. Tarragona: Universitat Rovira i Virgili.

Rodríguez, F., Díaz, M., Macias, J. M., Roig, J. F. y Teixell, I. 2020. Los últimos edificios domésticos, de servicio portuario y productivos del suburbio de *Tarracona* (s. VII-VIII), in C. Doménech y S. Gutiérrez (eds.) El sitio de las cosas: la Alta Edad Media en contexto: 67-82. Alacant: Universitat de Alacant.

Rodríguez, F. y Macias, J. M. 2016. Nuevo contexto cerámico de la segunda mitad del s. VII en *Tarraco* (*Tarraconensis, Regnum Visigothorum*), in R. Járrega y P. Berni (eds.) Amphorae ex Hispania: paisajes de producción y consumo (Tarragona, del 10 al 13 de desembre de 2014): 936-952. Tarragona: ICAC.

Rodríguez, F. y Macias, J. M. 2018. Buscando el siglo VIII en el puerto de *Tarracona*: entre la residualidad y el desconocimiento, in I. Martín Viso; P. Fuentes, J. C. Sastre y R. Catalán (coords.) Cerámicas altomedievales en Hispania y su entorno (s. V -VIII dC): 573-587. Madrid: L'Ergastula.

Rodríguez, F. y Macias, J. M. 2023. *Tarracona*: Pottery and trade in the 7th and 8th centuries, in V. Caminneci, E. Giannitrapani, M. Concetta Parello y M. Serena Rizzo (eds.) LRCW 6. 6th International Conference on Late Roman Coarse Ware, Cooking Ware and Amphorae in the Mediterranean: Archaeology and Archaeometry. Land and sea: pottery routes: 27-39. Oxford: Roman and Late Antique Mediterranean Pottery 19.

Saguì, L. 1998. Il deposito della Crypta Balbi: una testimonianzza imprevedibile sulla Roma del VII secolo?, Ceramica in Italia: V-VII secolo. Atti del Convegno in onore di John W. Hayes (Roma 1995): 305-330. Florencia: Biblioteca di Archeologia Medievale 14.

TEd'A [Taller Escola d'Arqueologia] 1989. Un abocador del segle V dC en el fòrum provincial de Tàrraco. Tarragona: Memòries d'excavació 2.

TEd'A [Taller Escola d'Arqueologia]1990. Taller Escola d'Arqueologia 1987-1990: Tarragona.

19. Ánforas tardorromanas de la *Carthaginensis* en Mallorca: primera valoración del cargamento del pecio de ses Fontanelles

Darío Bernal-Casasola
Miguel Ángel Cau-Ontiveros
José Luis Portillo Sotelo
José Alberto Retamosa Gámez
Leandro Fantuzzi
Sebastià Munar i Llabrés

Carlos de Juan
Jaume Cardell Perelló
Alessandra Pecci
Alejandro Valenzuela
Enrique García Riaza
Piero Berni Millet

Estas páginas están dedicadas a Simon Keay, amigo y maestro.
Amante de las ánforas y de la economía romana,
y el primero que "encauzó" las producciones tardorromanas de *Hispania*,
quien habría disfrutado reflexionando sobre el origen y el destino
—quizás a su querido *Portus*— del pecio de Ses Fontanelles

1.- Introducción: un excepcional pecio tardorromano mallorquín con un singular cargamento anfórico[1]

En julio de 2019 se produjo un hallazgo casual en la Playa de Palma, en la isla de Mallorca, consistente en un pecio naufragado a escasa distancia de la costa actual (a unos 60 m) y a muy poca profundidad (apenas 2 m), junto a un antiguo humedal costero, actualmente desecado, no lejos del importante yacimiento de origen indígena de Son Oms (Figura 19.1A). La importancia del hallazgo propició una primera actuación arqueológica de urgencia encargada por el Consell de Mallorca, cuyos resultados evidenciaron el notable estado de conservación del casco de la embarcación y del cargamento (Figura 19.1B), que se encontraban prácticamente intactos (Munar 2019). Ante esta singular situación, el Consell de Mallorca decidió promover un proyecto de investigación conjuntamente con las universidades de Barcelona, Cádiz e Islas Baleares, que se inició con una primera valoración científica, arqueológica y arqueométrica del mobiliario recuperado en la primera campaña de excavaciones, parte de cuyos resultados constituyen la base de este trabajo (Bernal-Casasola y Cau 2020).

Desde el año 2021 se está desarrollando el proyecto de investigación ARQUEOMALLORNAUTA, resultado de un convenio entre las cuatro instituciones citadas, que incluye entre sus objetivos la finalización de la excavación del pecio de Ses Fontanelles (de aquí en adelante citado como DSF = *Derelicte de Ses Fontanelles*), el estudio integral de su cargamento y de la arquitectura naval de esta embarcación de mediano tamaño (12 x 6 m de eslora aproximadamente), de cara a su futura musealización. Hasta la fecha, se han realizado diversos avances de los hallazgos, aún en prensa parcialmente, como es el caso de una síntesis general de la campaña de 2019 (Munar *et al.* 2022), la presentación del proyecto de investigación (Cardell *et al.* 2022), una primera valoración de las inscripciones pintadas —*tituli picti*— (Soler *et al.* 2021), sobre las que luego volveremos; y los primeros resultados de una aproximación *multiproxi* al estudio del yacimiento, incluyendo el análisis de las maderas y el abarrote, así como de las ánforas utilizando arqueozoología, análisis petrográfico de las fábricas cerámicas, análisis de residuos orgánicos… (Cau *et al.* 2022 a). Recientemente se han dado a conocer sendos trabajos sobre las ánforas en general (Cau *et al.* 2022 b), uno específico sobre las producciones olearias (Bernal-Casasola *et al.* 2024 a) y otro sobre las vinarias (Bernal-Casasola *et al.* 2024 b), que se completan con una visión general, actualizada, sobre el pecio, en clave de alta divulgación (Bernal-Casasola *et al.* 2023).

[1] Este trabajo es resultado del proyecto de investigación *ARQUEOMALLORNAUTA*, promovido por el Consell de Mallorca en colaboración con la Universitat de Barcelona, la Universidad de Cádiz y la Universitat de les Illes Balears. Asimismo, se inscribe en el marco de desarrollo de los proyectos GARVM IV (PID2022-138814OB-I00/MCIN/AEI), "Garum en diacronía: aproximación interdisciplinar a la tipología de las salsas fermentadas romanas en el Círculo del Estrecho", del Gobierno de España/Feder; y MEDUSA (PCM_00031) del Plan Complementario de Ciencias Marinas de la Junta de Andalucía; y ARQCERPOL (PID2021-123223NB-I00), financiado por MCIN/AEI/10.13039/501100011033/ y "FEDER Una manera de hacer Europa". Este estudio es también parte de las actividades del Equip de Recerca Arqueològica i Arqueomètrica, Universitat de Barcelona (ERAAUB), Grup de Recerca Consolidat (2017 SGR 1043), gracias a la ayuda del Comissionat per a Universitats i Recerca, DIEU, Generalitat de Catalunya.

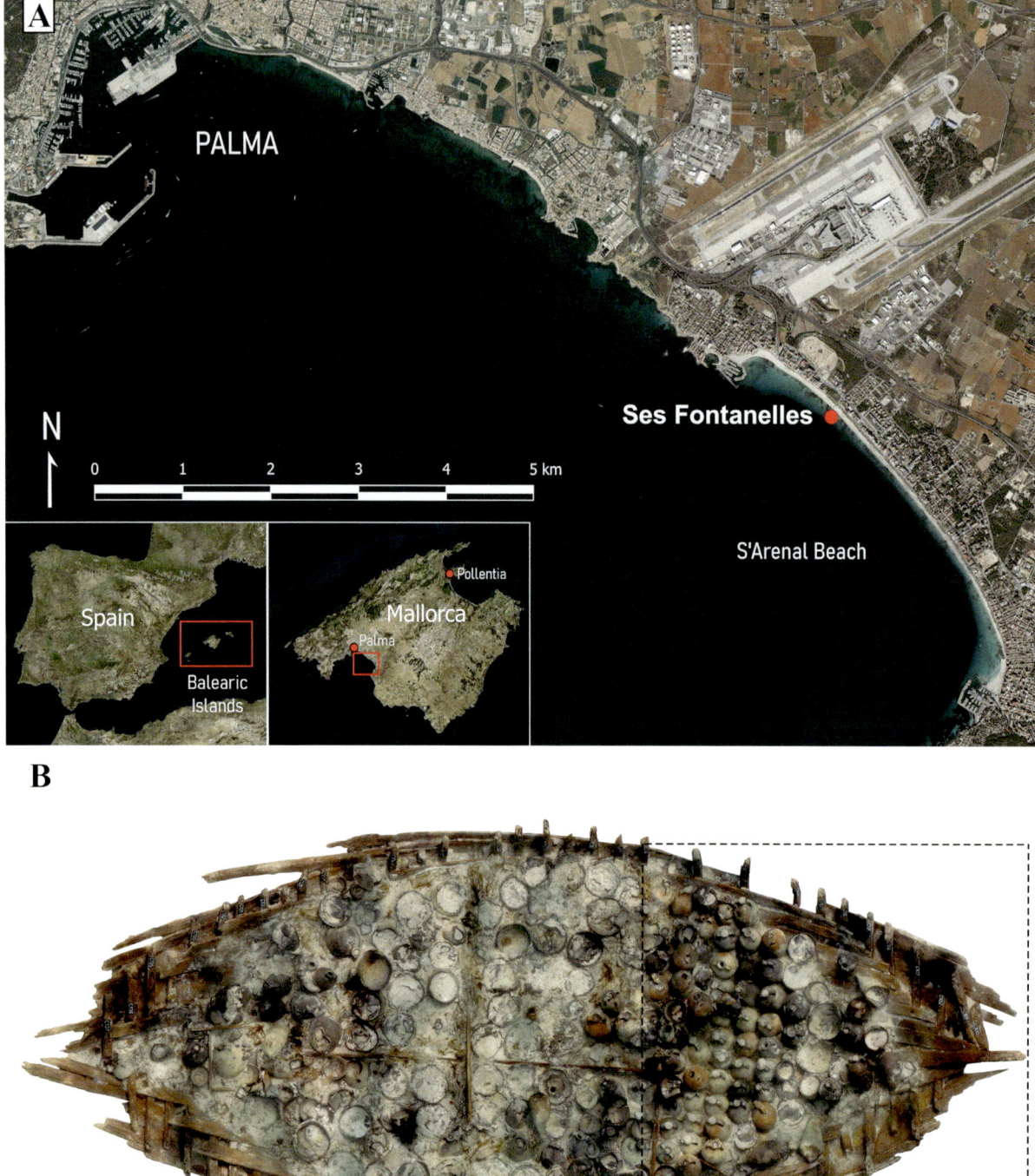

Figura 19.1. Localización del pecio de Ses Fontanelles en las Baleares y en la bahía de Palma (Mallorca) (A), con detalle del proceso de excavación del tercio de proa del barco de donde proceden las ánforas objeto de estudio (B.- Fotogrametría de K. Yamafune).

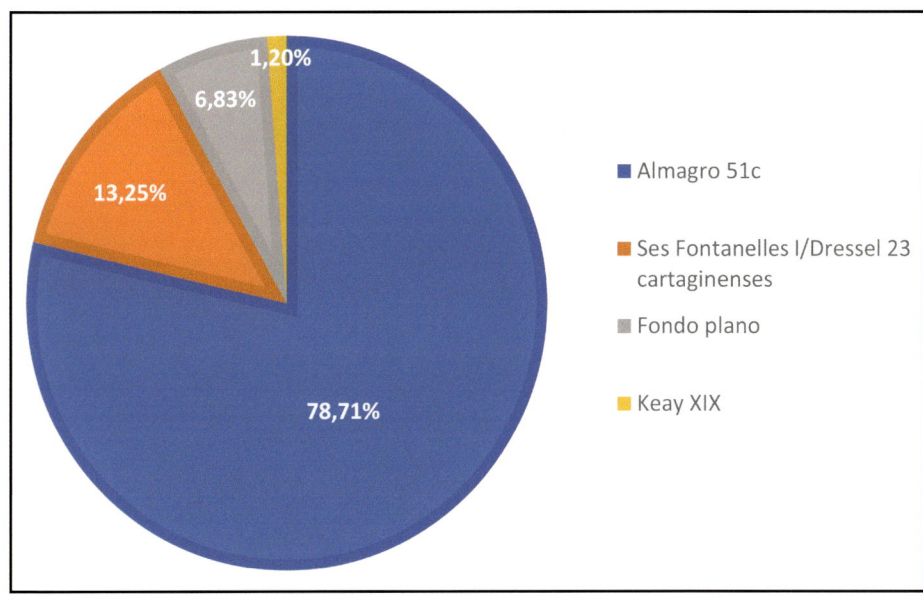

Gráfico 19.1. Representación porcentual de las diversas familias identificadas.

En este trabajo presentamos una primera valoración del cargamento basada en el estudio de las ánforas procedentes de la primera campaña de excavación realizada en el pecio[2], planteando las líneas de investigación advertidas, a desarrollar en futuros ensayos.

2.- Valoración preliminar del cargamento excavado

Por lo que sabíamos gracias a la excavación del tercio de proa del cargamento (Figura 19.1B), el pecio de Ses Fontanelles está conformado con exclusividad por ánforas de transporte, a lo que habría quizás que unir la posible existencia de un producto perecedero no conservado, como se advirtió durante la excavación, al detectar un posible hueco en parte de la bodega.

En la actuación del año 2020 se procedió a la ejecución del inventario de todo el mobiliario recuperado hasta entonces, que ascendió a 290 elementos diagnosticables[3]: de ellos el 95,52 % son ítems cerámicos (277 exactamente), que podrían reducirse a 249 si no

se consideran los ejemplares indeterminados, que se corresponden con paredes con elementos de interés relacionables con alguna de las formas reconocidas, siendo esta última cifra la que utilizamos para la cuantificación preliminar que tratamos en estas páginas.

Como se verá de manera detallada a continuación (Figura 19.2A), los tres tipos de ánforas que componen el cargamento son las conocidas ánforas salsarias del tipo Almagro 51c, completadas con otras de tipología desconocida (y que denominamos Ses Fontanelles I = SF I/ Dressel 23 cartaginenses) y, en menor medida, ánforas de fondo plano para el comercio de vino o productos derivados de la uva: los mostos reducidos térmicamente, conocidos como *defrutum/sapa/caroenum*. Como se aprecia en el Gráfico 1, cada una de ellas alcanza unos porcentajes respectivos del 78,71 % (Almagro 51c, con 196 individuos), del 13,25 % (SF I, con 33 individuos) y del 6,83 % (17 ánforas de fondo plano); a las que hay que añadir tres fragmentos de Keay XIX, que parece que no formaron parte de las mercancías objeto de comercio (1,2 %), sino que posiblemente constituyeran vituallas de la tripulación; valores todos ellos que hay que tomar de forma preliminar y con cautela, ya que no corresponden, como hemos indicado, a la totalidad del cargamento sino únicamente al tercio de proa excavado en la primera campaña[4].

De todas las ánforas recuperadas se realizó una primera aproximación detallada de una selección de 25 ejemplares, los mejor conservados y con más

[2] Tras la realización de este trabajo se ha podido ultimar la excavación del cargamento (noviembre de 2021 – febrero de 2022), cuyos resultados se han dado a conocer en algunos eventos congresuales a lo largo del año 2022 (*VI Congreso Internacional de la SECAH* -Zaragoza, marzo-; *El Ví a l'Antiguitat* -Badalona, octubre-; *Under the Mediterranean II* -Valletta, noviembre-). Remitimos a la bibliografía final para la ampliación de información.

[3] El criterio de ordenación adoptado durante la reorganización del mobiliario, basado en el inventario preliminar realizado durante la excavación arqueológica de 2019 que se centró en las ánforas recuperadas en buen estado de conservación y georreferenciadas (Munar 2019: 84-88, Anexo II) incluye un código alfanumérico individualizado para cada pieza, consistente en las siglas del yacimiento (DSF) seguido de un número creciente que no implica consideraciones topográficas, tipológicas o de cualquier otra naturaleza. Esta denominación es la que se ha utilizado para referirnos a cada una de las piezas a título particular.

[4] Remitimos a las precisiones realizadas con posterioridad en otros trabajos, tras la valoración general de todos los hallazgos (Bernal-Casasola *et al.* 2024 a).

Tabla 19.1. Dimensiones (en cm) de una selección de 25 ánforas completas del cargamento (Bernal-Casasola y Cau 2020: 25-43).

Tipología	Numeración	Altura total	Anchura máxima	Diámetro interior de la boca
Almagro 51c	DSF-179	68,5	31,2	8
	DSF-180	70,2	28	8
	DSF-181	70,1	29,6	8,8
	DSF-182	64	28	8,4
	DSF-184	63,6	27,2	8,4
	DSF-187	66	27	8
	DSF-188	68,2	30,8	8,6
	DSF-189	69,2	31	8
	DSF-191	70,5	30,6	8,2
	DSF-192	69,7	30	8,4
	DSF-193	70	31	8,2
	DSF-200	65,2	29,2	10
	DSF-202	69	28,2	8,8
	DSF-204	70	31	10
	DSF-207	66,5	33	8
	DSF-210	68	32	9
	DSF-211	66,5	30	8,6
	DSF-212	68	28	8
	DSF-213	70,5	29,4	8,6
	DSF-214	64	31	7,4
	DSF-215	68,5	27	8,2
	DSF-217	66	31	8,2
Ses Fontanelles I/Dressel 23 cartaginenses	DSF-002	64,5	43	8
Ánforas de fondo plano	DSF-265	57,5	37	14
	DSF-266	56	40,6	12

potencialidad museográfica (Bernal-Casasola y Cau -Ontiveros 2020), que conforman aproximadamente el 10 % del total recuperado en la primera campaña, y que constituyen una muestra representativa a todos los niveles de su composición. De ellas se ilustran en este trabajo, por cuestiones de espacio, una veintena, que combinan parte de las citadas anteriormente con otras más fragmentarias, pero muy representativas, de manera que esta selección pueda ser usada como botón de muestra para los futuros análisis histórico-arqueológicos sobre este singular yacimiento subacuático (Figura 19.2-6, Tabla 19.1). Las presentamos agrupadas por familias, y de ellas tratamos aspectos tipológicos, epigráficos y del paleocontenido, dejando los aspectos tecnológicos y de proveniencia para los siguientes apartados del trabajo.

2.1.- Ánforas del tipo Almagro 51c

Constituyen la forma mayoritaria de todas las identificadas hasta la fecha. Este tipo de ánfora se adecúa a un intervalo cronológico muy amplio, ya que las de producción bética se fechan genéricamente entre el 175 y el 500/525 (Bernal-Casasola 2019: 584, fig. 15),

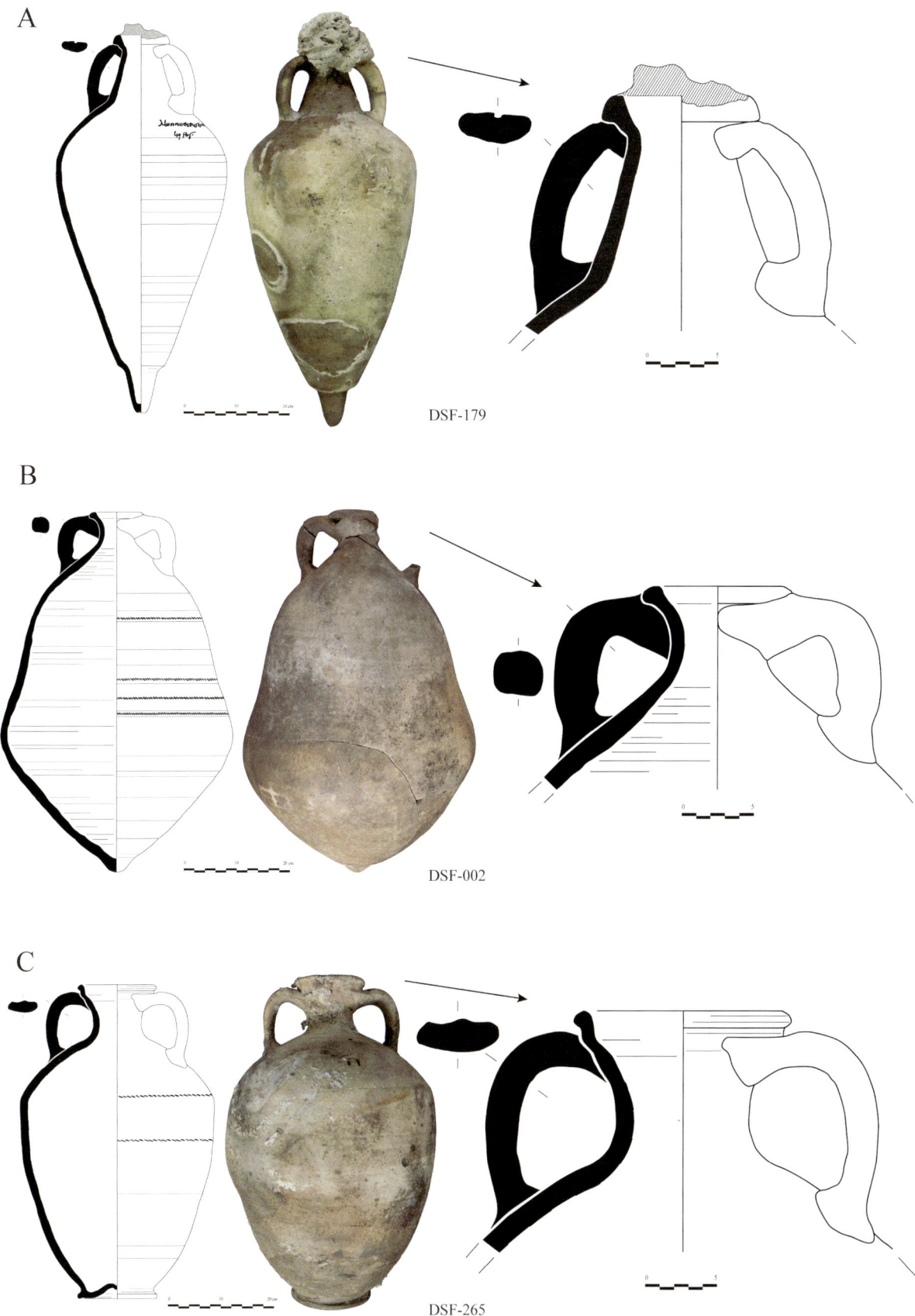

Figura 19.2. Tipos de ánforas que constituyen los componentes identificados del cargamento del pecio de Ses Fontanelles (A.-Almagro 51c; B.- Ses Fontanelles I/Dressel 23 cartaginenses; C.- Ánfora de fondo plano).

las producidas en el Algarve entre el 200 y el 500 (Viegas 2016) y las manufacturadas en la *Lusitania* occidental entre el 175-450 (Viegas *et al.* 2016).

En el DSF presentan una cierta diversidad tipológica (o si se prefiere una reducida estandarización microrregional), derivada de su manufactura artesanal, aunque no existen evidencias incontestables de que las mismas respondan a talleres diferenciados o a diversos artesanos dentro de la misma *figlina*. Son recipientes de dimensiones medias, que rondan los 68 cm de altura[5], con ciertas variaciones, oscilando desde los 63,6 (DSF-184) a los 70,5 (DSF-191, DSF-213); y con una anchura media de 30 (29,74 exactamente), con poca oscilación (entre los 27 cm de las DSF-187 y DSF-215 a los 31,2 de la DSF-179): estos parámetros se sitúan en el estándar de las producciones de la *Lusitania* occidental, cuyos valores se sitúan entre 65-77 y 25-42 cm (Viegas *et al.* 2016), siendo por ello algo más bajas y menos anchas que las mismas. Al mismo tiempo, son de dimensiones algo mayores que las Almagro 51c fabricadas en el Algarve portugués, que oscilan entre los 55-59 cm de altura y los 27,5 de anchura (Viegas 2016). Atendiendo a parámetros globales, y conscientes de la dificultad de comparación con ejemplares completos de todas las áreas productoras, podemos indicar que algunas ánforas de Ses Fontanelles guardan notables similitudes con las del taller lusitano de la Quinta di Rouxinol en Seixal (Raposo *et al.* 1995: fig. 4, 4).

Las bocas sí parecen diferenciarse de las producciones lusitanas y béticas[6], tanto por su diámetro más reducido (8,45 cm de media), frente a los valores entre 8,5 y 11 propios de las producciones del Tajo y del Sado (Viegas *et al.* 2016) y 8,4-12,3 cm de las manufacturadas en el sur de Portugal (Viegas 2016). Los bordes presentan asimismo un corto desarrollo en altura, siendo normalmente de sección circular o subcircular, con extremo superior redondeado. Si, además, consideramos la delgadez de las paredes, son parámetros que nos han animado a considerar a estas ánforas del pecio de Ses Fontanelles como "Almagro 51c gráciles". Los cuellos son cortos, de forma troncocónica o de hipérbole, con las características asas de cinta, de sección recta o curva, tanto lisas en su zona dorsal como con una o doble acanaladura: precisamente la morfología de las asas apunta a un estadio evolutivo intermedio de estas ánforas, en el cual aún no se han reducido de dimensiones y engrosado, como acontece en los ejemplares más tardíos.

Respecto al cuerpo de las ánforas, da la impresión de que se sitúan en un estadio evolutivo intermedio

entre las "Almagro 51c piriformes" y las "fusiformes", atendiendo a la nomenclatura de Mayet[7], pues no son tan anchas como las primeras ni con fondos tan amplios y cortos en altura; y sobre todo aún presentan el pivote netamente distinguido de la parte baja de la panza, y no macizado todavía, como pasa en las segundas. De ahí que las consideremos como "Almagro 51c fusiformes iniciales" o precedentes de las Almagro 51c, de la variante C de Mayet. No se conoce bien la fecha de tránsito entre las morfologías piriformes y fusiformes, aunque el consenso de la investigación es que dicha mutación formal debió producirse en algún momento del s. IV d. C., no necesariamente de manera uniforme en todas las regiones productoras de esta forma en *Hispania*.

Tipológicamente destaca el detalle de que todos los pivotes documentados en Ses Fontanelles son cilíndricos y huecos, de base plana, notándose algunas ocasiones un carácter troncocónico invertido de su sección (DSF-179, 180), aunque mayoritariamente son de paredes paralelas o sensiblemente convergentes. Es importante destacar que esta constatación permite relacionarlos con los denominados de la variante B, propios desde mediados del s. III hasta finales del s. IV d. C.: en el caso de los del pecio mallorquín, su fondo plano con escasa convexidad, sus dimensiones moderadas y su cierta altura permiten emparentarlos con los del taller de Pinheiro, característicos de la segunda mitad del s. III o de la primera mitad del s. IV d. C. (Viegas *et al.* 2016: fig. 3, nº 10-17 y 18-20 respectivamente).

Respecto a los *tituli picti*, es importante destacar que aproximadamente la mitad de todas las ánforas recuperadas presentaban inscripciones en tinta negra (*atramentum*). El estudio monográfico realizado hasta la fecha, al cual remitimos para la ampliación de la información, ha permitido identificar al menos dos tipos de inscripciones asociadas a las Almagro 51c: las mayoritarias (36) presentan dos líneas, habiendo sido interpretada la primera de ellas como alusiva a una *societas* comercial integrada por dos personajes, nombrados en genitivo: *Alunnii et Ausonii* NN(); reflejando la segunda línea el nombre del producto conservado, *liq(uaminis) fl(o)s*; solamente un ejemplar (DSF-187) presenta un *titulus* diverso, compuesto por anotaciones de carácter ponderal en libras romanas (327 gr) relativas al peso del recipiente vacío (30 libras = 9,810 kg) y al contenido neto de la salsa piscícola (60 libras = 19,620 kg)[8] (Soler *et al.* 2021: 291-98). La única

---

[5] Exactamente 67,83 de media, teniendo en cuenta los 22 ejemplares analizados en la Tabla 19.1.
[6] De las manufacturas béticas es difícil aportar estimaciones cuantitativas claras ante el reducido grado de cuantificación de los talleres conocidos, debido a la fragmentariedad de los materiales.

[7] Investigadora que diferenció entre las Almagro 51c de la variante A (=actualmente denominadas Lusitana 3) y especialmente de la variante B y C, respectivamente (Mayet y Silva 1998: 143-46 y 202-23).
[8] El cubicaje de los ejemplares se ha estimado a través de cuatro ánforas estudiadas íntegramente (DSF-179, 182, 189 y 204), teniendo en cuenta el peso del recipiente vacío, en kg (9,7; 8,2; 8,1; 10,9); el peso del ánfora llena de agua (17,8; 16; 18,7; 18,3) y su peso global (27,5; 24,2; 26,8; 29,2) (Bernal-Casasola y Cau 2020: 50, 52 y 54, tabla 4.1).

inscripción ponderal procede de un ánfora extraída de la parte central de la embarcación, lo cual, unido a la diversidad en el rótulo pintado, tendería a hacernos pensar en una posible divergencia tipológica en el envase, aspecto este que no se percibe en el estudio arqueológico de la pieza. Todo ello denota que estas ánforas, procedentes de al menos dos lotes diversos asociables con *mercatores* o *societates* diferenciados, usaron ánforas procedentes de los mismos talleres o, si eran diversos, arqueológicamente no somos capaces de diferenciarlos con claridad, siendo esta una de las líneas de investigación a desarrollar en el futuro.

En relación con el paleocontenido, la homogeneidad de las inscripciones pintadas alusivas a la flor de *liquamen* no dejaban duda alguna sobre el contenido piscícola de las Almagro 51c de Ses Fontanelles. Pero no solo esto, sino que además parecían responder a un cargamento homogéneo con un único producto haliéutico -aspecto este que ha podido ser descartado con la continuidad de la investigación, tratándose de un flete mixto compuesto mayoritariamente por aceite, salsas fermentadas de pescado y en menor medida vino-. La *flos liquaminis* es un producto poco citado en los *tituli picti*, conociéndose unos 10 ejemplos, con variantes[9], de los 69 registrados alusivos al *liquamen* (Curtis 1991: 195-96), frente a las 136 alusiones a la *flos gari,* en todas sus variedades[10]. Su asociación con ánforas béticas es evidente, estando documentadas dos veces en Dressel 14 y una en Dressel 9 y Dressel 10, además de las fórmulas encomiásticas *liquamen flos excellens* -dos veces en Dressel 14-, *liquamen flos primum* en Pompeji XIV y *liquamen scombri flos excellens* tanto en Pompeji XIV como en Dressel 12 (Ehmig 2003: 64-65, tab. 9).

La documentación de muchas de estas ánforas con su sistema de hermetización totalmente intacto (*opercula,* tanto de corcho como de madera, y en menor medida de cerámica), a lo que han contribuido las concreciones de abarrote y de arena que en ocasiones occluían la totalidad de la boca (Figura 19.2, DSF-179; Figura 19.3, DSF-182, 185), ha permitido también un detallado análisis del paleocontenido de estas ánforas. Aún en fase de estudio, adelantamos los resultados de dos ejemplares (Figura 19.3, DSF-220 y DSF-231) de los ocho estudiados en el año 2020[11]: en el primero de ellos, se recuperaron 15 ml de un sedimento oscuro con inclusiones arenosas

y múltiples restos ictiológicos, mientras que en el segundo los residuos correspondían a algunos restos ictiológicos adheridos tanto a las paredes internas como a la parte basal interior del pivote hueco del ánfora. Tras el procesado del sedimento con agua y tamices con mallas de 4 mm, 2 mm, 500 μm, 250 μm, 125 μm, 63 μm y secado al aire, con excepción de la muestra DSF-231, que presentaba los huesos adheridos en las paredes, se procedió a su triaje mediante una lupa binocular (Valenzuela 2020). En relación con la composición taxonómica, las muestras se componen casi de forma exclusiva por una única especie, el boquerón (*Engraulis encrasicolus*), a excepción de un único hueso hiomandibular en la muestra DSF-231, correspondiente a la sardina (*Sardina pilchardus*). La identificación anatómica ha permitido señalar la presencia de restos casi exclusivos de boquerón: dentarios derechos (12 en DSF-220 y 12 en DSF-231) e izquierdos (14 y 15), articulares (2 y 2), fragmentos del neurocráneo (7 y 11), del maxilar (18 y 19), de cleitros (14 y 14), hiomandibulares (12 y 18), vértebras (9 y 64) y escamas (menos de 25 y entre 50-100, respectivamente). Por tanto, los otros elementos cuantificados que componen la región craneal son los predominantes, apareciendo el resto del esqueleto apendicular infrarrepresentado, en mayor o menor medida, según el caso. Aun siendo tentador sugerir que los contenidos de las ánforas Almagro 51c de Ses Fontanelles estaban compuestas casi exclusivamente por cabezas de boquerón, el contenido adherido en las paredes internas del pivote de la muestra DSF-231 mostraba una realidad más compleja, ya que aparecieron diversos esqueletos de boquerón en conexión anatómica, verificando que los peces fueron introducidos enteros, quedando adheridos en la resina de las paredes del ánfora: posteriormente, con su micronización definitiva, los elementos craneales se desprendieron del cuerpo y, por decantación, fueron a parar al fondo del contenedor, donde se acumularon. Para la estimación del tamaño de los peces, y utilizando como referencia los criterios osteométricos definidos en otros casos (Assis y Amaro 2006), se ha podido estimar una población explotada de boquerones de entre 7 y 12,5 cm, si bien la gran mayoría eran individuos con tallas comprendidas entre 8 y 10 cm. En el caso de la sardina de la muestra DSF-231, se estima, a partir de la longitud de la región dorsal del hiomandibular, que su tamaño rondaría 11,4 cm (Valenzuela 2020).

Con estos datos, si bien preliminares, es posible identificar los ingredientes del producto contenido: una salsa realizada mayoritariamente con boquerones, con la intrusión puntual de sardinas, que a veces se pescan accidentalmente junto a los primeros y terminan como ingredientes de las salsas piscícolas[12]. La escasez de restos permite excluir que se trate de

---

[9] Según Curtis, estando atestiguada la fórmula *liquamen flos* (2 veces), *liquamen flos excellens* (2), *liquamen flos primum* (2), *liquamen flos flos –floris-* (2), *liquamen flos excellen scombri, liquamen flos optimum* (1991: 195-96).

[10] *Garum flos* (52), *Garum flos scombri* (44), *Garum flos per se* (10), *garum flos geminum* (9), *garum scombri flos* (8), *garum flos scombri optimum* (4), *garum flos scombri romulianum* (3), *garum flos flos -o floris-* (1), *garum flos scombri excellens vetus* (1), *garum flos flos murenae* (1), *garum flos scombri lunense* (1), *garum flos romulianum* (1), *garum flos lucretianum* (1) (Curtis 1991: 195).

[11] DSF-220, 226, 231, 235, 256, 257, 266, 272 (Valenzuela 2020: 123-31, tabla 8.1).

[12] En otros casos conocemos una situación inversa: salsas realizadas con clupeidos (sardinas), con la introducción puntual de engráulidos

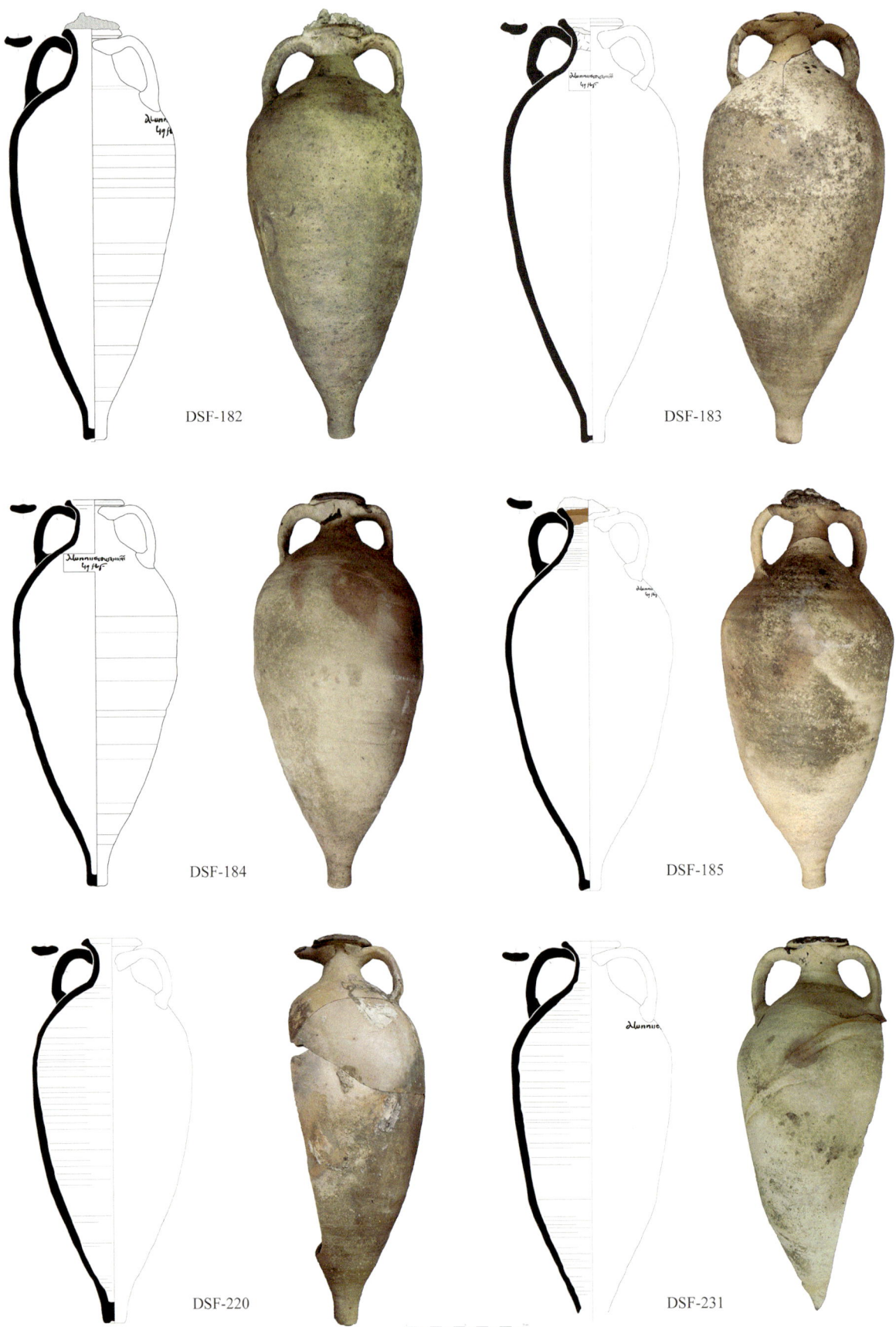

DSF-182

DSF-183

DSF-184

DSF-185

DSF-220

DSF-231

Figura 19.3. Selección de ánforas del tipo Almagro 51 c, tanto completas (DSF-182 a DSF-185) como fragmentadas (DSF-220, DSF-231), estas últimas con restos de paleocontenidos.

pescados en salazón, pues de lo contrario se habrían recuperado kilos de sedimento íctico, no siendo este el caso. De manera que la interpretación es que debió tratarse de una salsa fermentada de pescado, líquida, que por otro lado es la definición que conocemos del *liquamen* por las fuentes clásicas (García Vargas *et al.* 2014; recientemente Grainger 2021: 32, 35 y 227) y por su propio lexema. La interpretación de que haya pocos restos y que en buena parte aparezcan sin conexión anatómica deriva de que se trata de salsas mal filtradas de estos pequeños boquerones —*pisciculi*—, que a pesar de haber quedado en buena parte hidrolizados durante la maceración de la salsa aún se habrían "colado" al rellenar las ánforas con el producto en las *cetariae* de la Cartaginense. Impurezas ícticas, involuntarias, que nos permiten identificar el contenido de estos envases.

Por último, cabe indicar que el vaciado controlado de varios de estos ejemplares ha verificado el empleo de aromatizantes, actualmente en proceso de estudio, visibles a través del registro carpológico. Además de todo esto, se han realizado análisis de residuos orgánicos por cromatografía de gases / espectrometría de masas a un ejemplar (Figura 19.3, DSF-220), el cual ha confirmado la presencia de compuestos identificables con resina de coníferas —usada en la impermeabilización[13], además de azufre— posiblemente usado para hermetizar los envases, y ácidos de diversa naturaleza que sugieren un contenido de productos animales (Pecci 2020: 113-21, muestra 4), aunque si no fuese por los hallazgos ictiológicos y las inscripciones pintadas la interpretación no sería unívoca.

2.2.- Ses Fontanelles I – Dressel 23 cartaginenses

El segundo grupo porcentual en la muestra de la primera campaña de excavación es el representado por un tipo nuevo de ánfora, que ha sido posible definir gracias a la existencia de un ejemplar completo, el único íntegro identificado en 2019, caído tras el hundimiento de la hilera superior de ánforas de la bodega, y recuperado por ello en el entorno perimetral del casco del barco (Figura 19.2, DSF-002).

Se trata de un ánfora de dimensiones medias, con 64,5 cm de altura, y una panza irregular, pero extremadamente ancha, alcanzando los 43 cm. Su peso es de 13,9 kg. La boca es también estrecha (8 cm aprox.), caracterizada por una pared oblicua y exvasada, con borde de sección semicircular exterior rematado en un extremo apuntado (Figura 19.2, DSF-002; Figura 19.4), que en estado fragmentario se confunde con las bocas de las Almagro 51c, pues la parte superior de

las asas arranca también del plano superior del borde. Especialmente importante para su reconocimiento son las asas, de sección circular o subcircular, elemento que las singulariza: de carácter macizo, presentan una trayectoria vertical para facilitar su aprehensión, y un acusado giro en su parte alta para adherirse a la parte superior del cuello. Presentan amplias rebabas en la unión con el cuerpo del recipiente, y en ocasiones digitaciones para facilitar las uniones de ambas partes durante la fase de torneado y secado. El cuello es corto y troncocónico, con paredes muy oblicuas que reducen rápidamente la amplitud de los hombros. La panza, a tenor del único ejemplar completo conservado, es irregular, de tendencia "alimonada", aunque con un torneado deficiente que define al menos, tres sectores: un tercio superior de sección triangular, realizado de una sola pieza, como confirman en ocasiones las abruptas carenas con la parte central del cuerpo (Figura 19.4, DSF-003); la zona central del cuerpo presenta una trayectoria troncocónica poco acusada, con pareces sensiblemente cóncavas; y el tercio inferior, muy característico, es como el superior, de tendencia triangular, rematado en un pezón o apéndice de botón, que en ocasiones está bien diferenciado (Figura 19.2, DSF-002) y en otras es prácticamente imperceptible (Figura 19.4, DSF-056, 095). Este último detalle tipológico es la segunda característica de este envase, el fondo apuntado, que remite a la conocida tradición alfarera de las olearias del Valle del Guadalquivir.

Como indicamos, en estado fragmentario son fácilmente confundidas con las Almagro 51c, que fabricadas en los mismos talleres presentan múltiples similitudes formales: precisamente, en el único taller alfarero en el cual se conoce su manufactura, El Mojón, en la zona costera al sur de Cartagena (entorno de Mazarrón), se han identificado algunos bordes y asas de esta tipología que han sido considerados como "Almagro 51c fusiformes" (Berrocal 2012: 264).

No conocemos en la bibliografía de referencia ánforas con esta tipología que hayan sido definidas como tales, de ahí la conveniencia de proceder a su bautismo. Son evidentes las similitudes tipológicas con las ánforas béticas de la forma Dressel 23, que son un poco más grandes[14], especialmente la forma alimonada del cuerpo, las asas de sección circular y el fondo, apuntado y abotonado, cuya producción se sitúa entre el 280 y el 600 d. C. (Berni y Moros 2017), si bien son diversos los detalles, anteriormente descritos, que las singularizan. Es por ello que se ha optado por otorgar la denominación Ses Fontanelles I, al ser el pecio de Palma el primer lugar donde se han identificado; aunque al unísono se las considera Dressel 23 cartaginenses, al

---

(boquerones), como sucede en *Augusta Emerita* (Bernal-Casasola *et al.* 2016).

[13] La mayor parte de ánforas de esta tipología presentan un revestimiento resinoso interior, en ocasiones de apariencia "caramelizada" y con burbujas estalladas.

[14] Entre 45-54 cm de altura total y 33-37 cm de anchura máxima, eso sí, con una boca algo más amplia, entre 12 y 14,5 cm (Berni y Moros 2017).

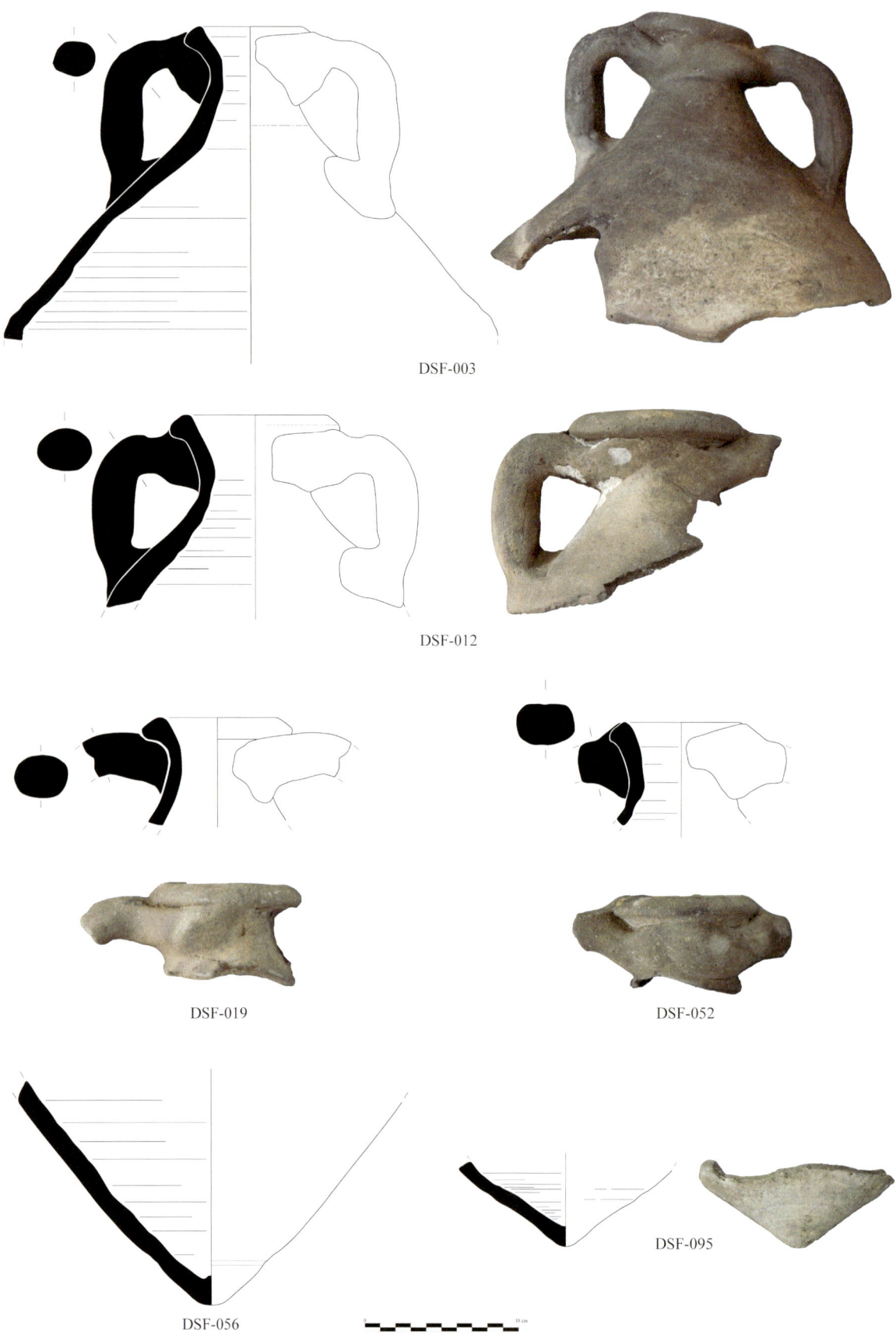

Figura 19.4. Detalle de algunos ejemplares de bocas (DSF-003, 012, 019, 052) y fondos (DSF-056, 095) de Ses Fontanelles I / Dressel 23 cartaginenses.

tratarse esta su zona de manufactura, como veremos a continuación, y al inspirarse tipológicamente en los conocidos envases olearios del valle del Guadalquivir[15].

Frente a los demás tipos de ánforas del cargamento, todos ellos con paredes resinadas claramente visibles macroscópicamente, las SF I/Dressel 23 cartaginenses no presentaban resina visible, un detalle como sabemos compatible con un posible contenido oleario. Para confirmarlo se realizó un análisis de residuos orgánicos en el ejemplar DSF-002, que confirmó una elevada presencia de ácido oleico ($C_{18:1}$), seguido de ácido palmítico ($C_{16:0}$), entre los ácidos grasos, además del $C_{9:0}$ entre los de cadena corta. Los ácidos dicarboxílicos, entre los que el ácido azelaico es el más profuso, son asimismo muy abundantes, y el β- sitosterol está presente solo en trazas (Pecci 2020: 114). En general, el perfil químico de los tres extractos analizados sugiere un contenido de aceite vegetal; sin embargo, los análisis realizados no han permitido la identificación de los triacilgliceroles (TAGs), por lo que no podemos confirmar al 100 % que dicho sea de oliva. Además, la muestra analizada de la pared interior del ánfora SF I es la única muestra, entre las cinco analizadas, en la que no aparece ácido tartárico en el primer extracto, lo cual refuerza la idea de que este tipo de ánfora contuvo un aceite vegetal. A diferencia de las otras ánforas analizadas, donde los biomarcadores de resina/pez son realmente abundantes, en la DSF-002 el ácido dehidroabiético solo está presente en trazas y tampoco se han constatado marcadores del proceso de producción de la resina aplicada al ánfora (Pecci 2020: 115).

En definitiva, el análisis de residuos orgánicos cuadra con las variables tipológicas (morfología ovoide de la panza, asas de sección circular y extremo apuntado del fondo) y con la "inspiración" en los citados modelos del valle del Guadalquivir, cuyo contenido es claramente oleario.

Por último, cabe indicar que no se han recuperado *tituli picti* asociados a este tipo anfórico: la totalidad de ánforas recuperadas procede del piso superior de la bodega, el peor conservado, como confirma la mayor fragmentariedad de los ítems recuperados y la pérdida de las inscripciones, si es que existieron[16].

2.3.- Ánforas de fondo plano

El tercer grupo es el conformado por las ánforas de fondo plano, que es la característica común que presentan una serie de envases del pecio (Figura 19.2A). Se decidió inicialmente utilizar esta perífrasis porque se detecta una notable variabilidad de formas que corresponden a tipos diversos, actualmente en fase de estudio y caracterización. Consideramos más prudente en su momento esperar a la ultimación de la excavación integral del cargamento, para generar una nueva propuesta tipológica que ha sido recientemente dada a conocer (Bernal-Casasola *et al.* 2024 b), aunque esta denominación ha demostrado ser muy útil y operativa al tratar de clasificar material en estado fragmentario.

Por una parte contamos con algunas piezas que presentan bordes con sección triangular o subtriangular, y sobre todo ranurados o acanalados en su parte exterior (Figura 19.5, DSF-057 y 058), con amplias asas de cinta, detalles todos ellos que permiten considerarlas afines a las denominadas Matagallares I por el alfar epónimo de la costa granadina - Bética oriental- (Bernal-Casasola 2019: 598, fig. 25C), de las cuales se conoce también una producción en la Tarraconense meridional (Berrocal 2012: 266, fig. 9). También se cuenta al menos con dos formas completas, la primera de ellas con el borde escalonado, corto cuello y asas de cinta muy desarrolladas, con doble acanaladura dorsal (Figura 19.2, DSF-265), que encuentra múltiples concomitancias con la línea evolutiva terminal de las Gauloise 4 francesas, imitadas por doquier y también en época medio imperial y tardorromana en *Hispania*, y que se encuentra emparentada formalmente con las denominadas Matagallares II (Bernal-Casasola 2001). Y la segunda es un ejemplar completo de perfil más achatado, con cuerpo de tendencia bitroncocónica -con carena en el tercio superior-, fondo plano, asas de cinta acanaladas dorsalmente y corto cuello rematado en un corto borde de extremo exterior redondeado y sensiblemente apuntado (Figura 19.5, DSF-266). Como decimos, la clasificación tipológica es compleja aún, pero es cierto que esta forma recuerda al tipo denominado Mojón III, de amplio cuello, borde poco desarrollado, asas de cinta y tercio superior de la panza de sección triangular (Berrocal 2012: 262-63, fig. 7), aunque del mismo no se conoce en el mencionado taller ningún fondo asociado esta forma que permita precisiones al respecto. Precisamente las ánforas documentadas en el DSF parecen ajustarse a una cierta variabilidad, aunque con algunas características comunes: bases cóncavas o muy cóncavas en su parte interior; remate central del fondo normalmente umbilicado, con botón central; y reborde perimetral exterior, a modo de rebaba, que en ocasiones no apoya directamente sobre el suelo (Figura

---

[15] Recientemente se ha reflexionado sobre la nomenclatura de los tipos anfóricos de nueva definición, considerando que si se trata de formas ya conocidas en la bibliografía es mejor mantener dicho apelativo seguido del calificativo de la región de manufactura: una dinámica fosilizada desde hace décadas para algunas formas (Dressel 1 itálicas, tarraconenses...) y que facilita la comprensión por parte de la comunidad científica (Bernal-Casasola 2019: 561-67). La tendencia a medio plazo es que prevalezca en la bibliografía la segunda de las denominaciones propuestas.

[16] Trabajos posteriores han verificado que a las mismas se asocia un amplio aparato epigráfico pintado y sellado sobre los *opercula*, como verificaron los materiales recuperados en las últimas campañas en la

zona central y de la popa de la embarcación (Bernal-Casasola *et al.* 2024 a).

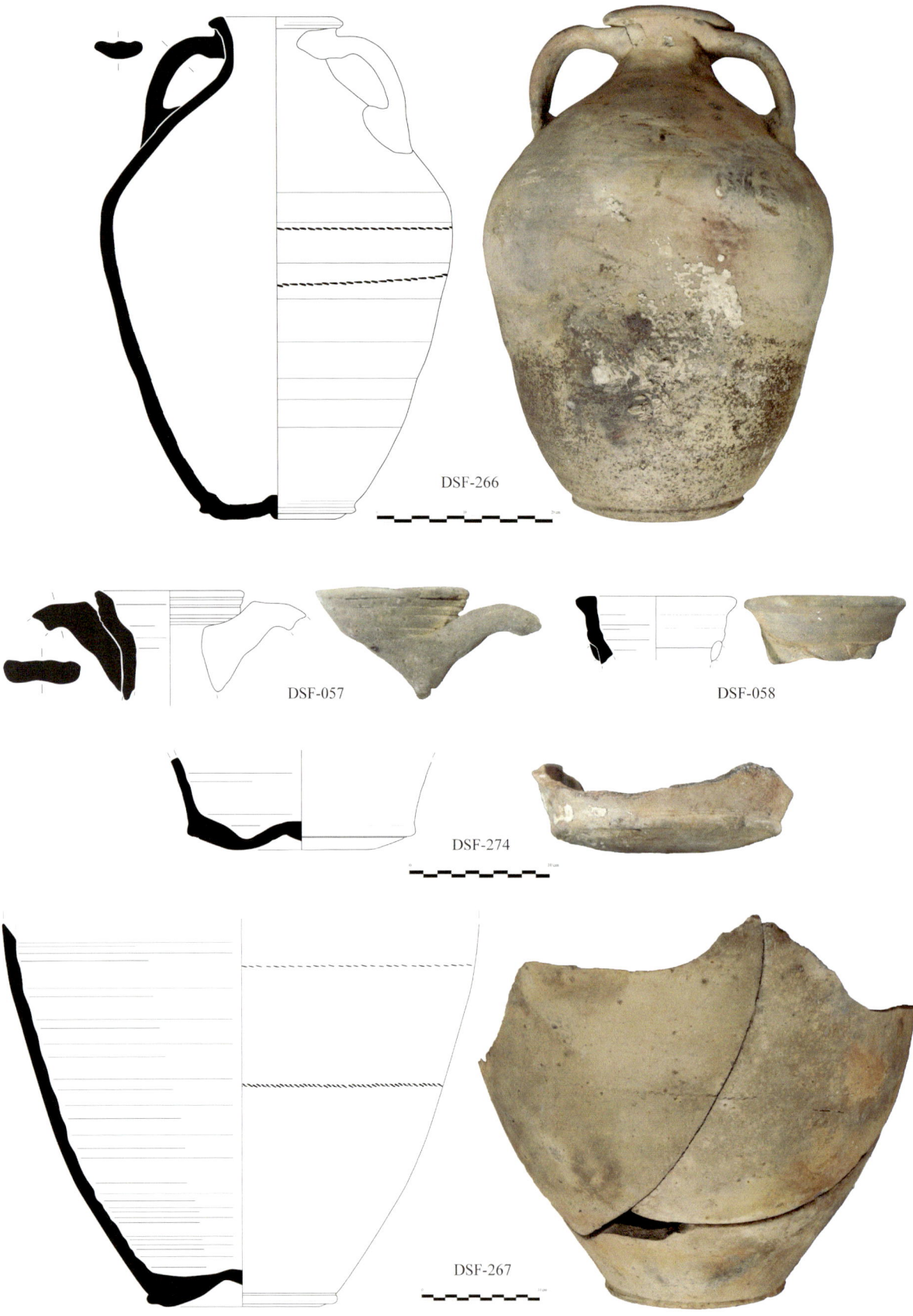

Figura 19.5. Detalle de un ejemplar completo (DSF-266) y de bocas (DSF-057, 058) y fondos (DSF-267, 274) de ánforas de fondo plano cartaginenses.

19.5, DSF-266, 267, 274), aspecto este que le confiere notable inestabilidad al envase. En el estado actual de la investigación no resulta posible atribuir a cada una de las formas identificadas un tipo de fondo específico.

Estos envases de fondo plano son considerados tradicionalmente como vinarios por su relación con las ánforas de mesa destinadas al consumo de caldos fermentados y hunden sus raíces en una antigua tradición itálica tardorrepublicana, con talleres desde *Florentia* a Naxos (Menchelli 2021: 267-68, figs 6, 4 y 5): inspirándose en ellos nace en época augustea la conocida producción de la Narbonense estudiada por Fanette Laubenheimer, que es la que triunfa durante el Alto Imperio. En *Hispania* se conocen muy bien desde época augustea gracias a las Oberaden 74 tarraconenses, y a las Dressel 28 y las "tipo *urceus*" en la Bética. A continuación, tenemos las Gauloise 4 y otros tipos afines de fondo plano producidos en toda la costa peninsular, desde Llafranc a Bueu, con los conocidos talleres de *Dianium* y de Los Matagallares y Los Barreros en Salobreña, delimitando por el norte y sur, respectivamente, nuestra zona de referencia. No se trata, por tanto, de una novedad ni una rareza la aparición de ánforas de fondo plano en la zona de influencia de *Carthago Spartaria* en los siglos III y IV d. C. como tímidamente se han ido dando a conocer en los últimos años con los llamados tipos Cartagena 1, 2 y 3 de producción local-regional cartagenera o de su entorno, que, aunque conocidos únicamente en estado fragmentario, se sitúan en esta línea (Quevedo 2021). En fechas más recientes se acaba de definir un nuevo tipo, denominado Cartagena 4, que es muy similar a las ánforas de Ses Fontanelles, en cronología —al proceder de los niveles de abandono de la habitación 13 del Edificio del Atrio en El Molinete, fechado a finales del s. III d. C.—, identificado por dos ejemplares de fondo plano (con 42,5 y 24,74 litros de capacidad respectiva), ambos de fondo plano y, el de menor tamaño, con restos de resina al interior (García Aboal 2021). Resulta de gran interés el carácter hibrido de ambos ejemplares en relación a las ánforas del DSF, pues ambas son de fondo plano y, al mismo tiempo, presentan asas de sección circular (García Aboal 2021: 227, figs 3 y 4). A nuestro entender estos aspectos ilustran la variedad de talleres productores de este tipo de ánforas en los ss. III y IV d. C., constituyendo los hallazgos conocidos (Cartagena 4 y los tipos nuevos en el pecio DSF) únicamente la punta del iceberg de una importante producción alfarera que ha pasado desapercibida hasta nuestras fechas a los ojos de la investigación especializada, y que dará muchas novedades en el futuro.

Para intentar avanzar al respecto, se han analizado tres ejemplares por cromatografía de gases acoplada a espectrometría de masas (GC-MS)[17], cuyos resultados —que no detallamos aquí por cuestión de espacio—, han permitido identificar componentes relacionados con árboles de la familia de las Pinaceae (ácidos dehidroabiético, abiético, metildehidroabietato y 7-oxodehidroabiético), y sobre todo ácido tartárico y succínico —y también siríngico normalmente vinculado al vino tinto—que en la época y contexto estudiados se consideran los marcadores del vino o vinagre (Pecci 2020: 116-17). Además, una de ellas al menos (Figura 19.6A, DSF-267), ha conservado restos *in situ* de un residuo "caramelizado" sobre el fondo, en el cual se aprecian, incrustados, huesos de posibles aceitunas, pendientes de caracterización carpológica[18].

Si indirectamente se planteó que las ánforas de fondo plano del pecio de Ses Fontanelles pudieran relacionarse con el vino y sus derivados (por los fondos planos y por el aspecto resinado de sus paredes), los análisis arqueométricos realizados, si bien preliminares, confirman su relación con el vino/vinagre; además, la presencia de restos carpológicos en algún ejemplar —la mayor parte de restos de fondos estudiados no se caracterizan por ello— permite plantear que algunas, muy pocas aparentemente, llevarían frutas en conserva. Por el momento, los *tituli picti* asociados a estas ánforas, de los cuales se conocen únicamente dos ejemplares fragmentarios (Soler *et al.* 2021: 298-300, DSF-265 y 266), parecen remitir a fórmulas ponderales relacionadas con el contenido vínico y, al mismo tiempo, a la referencia EX, quizás relacionable con las aceitunas en arrope (*olivae ex defruto* o similar).

2.4.- Ánforas del tipo Keay XIX: vituallas de la tripulación

Por último, es necesario recordar que completan el elenco tipológico recuperado en Ses Fontanelles dos partes superiores de ánforas del tipo Keay XIX (Figura 19.6, B y C). En ambos casos han aparecido en estado fragmentario y no hay evidencias de que estuviesen estibadas con la parte restante de la carga. Ello, unido como veremos en los siguientes apartados al estudio minero-petrográfico que ha permitido proponer un origen para las mismas en la costa malacitana, permiten considerarlas parte de las mercancías que los tripulantes llevaban para consumo propio - salazones béticas en esta ocasión-.

---

[17] Además de las ánforas DSF-267 y 274 (Figura 19.5), se ha analizado la DSF-272, no ilustrada.

[18] Durante el análisis de residuos orgánicos de esta pieza también se han identificado otros ácidos (esteárico, palmítico y oleico; además de trazas de β-sitosterol), lo cual podría indicar —conscientes del citado residuo sólido en el fondo— que, si las citadas aceitunas se conservaron en un medio de vino/vinagre/*defrutum*, no liberaron grasas abundantes o que los ácidos grasos se degradaron (Pecci 2020: *passim*).

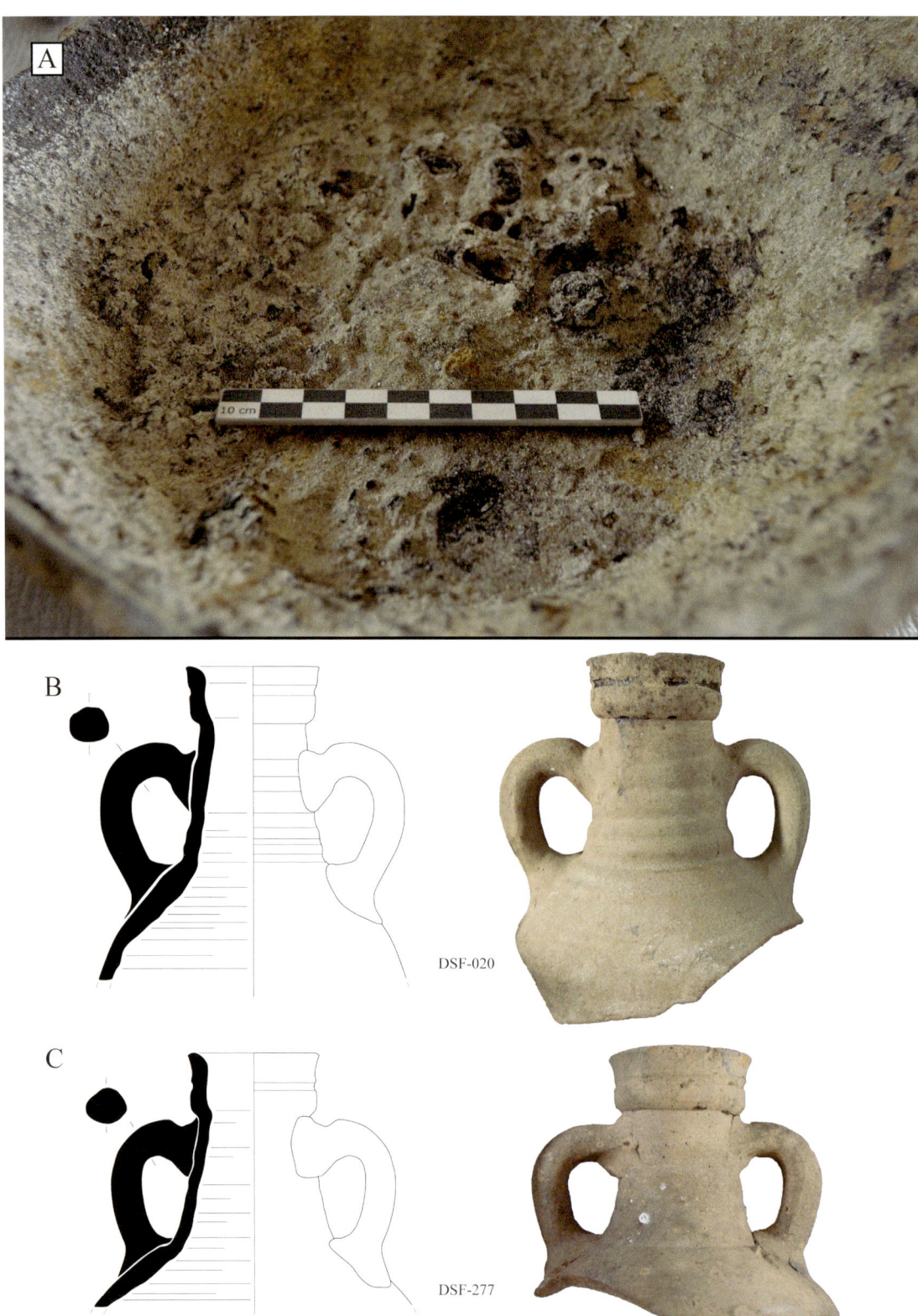

Figura 19.6. Detalle del interior de una de las ánforas de fondo plano (A.- DSF-267) con una costra de paleocontenido endurecido y restos carpológicos, y sendas bocas de Keay XIX béticas (B.- DSF-020; C.- DSF-277).

Desde un punto de vista formal constituyen ejemplares evolucionados dentro de esta familia, la cual se fecha entre el 250-500 d. C. para la producción bética (Bernal-Casasola 2001: 282-84; 2019: 594-95) y entre el 375 y el 500 d. C. para la lusitana (Pinto y Magalhães 2016). Así lo indica la escasa anchura del cuerpo y la progresiva estilización del cuello, que da lugar a formas muy alargadas. Destaca la profunda acanaladura que presentan ambas en la zona intermedia del borde, similar a las que encontramos en algunas Keay XXI en fechas posteriores (Remolà 2000: 191, fig. 64, 4). Al no encontrarse publicadas en detalle las *figlinae* productoras de estas formas en el litoral malagueño (Finca del Secretario, Huerta del Rincón...) no resultan posibles ulteriores precisiones.

3.- Un cargamento homogéneo: apuntes tecnológicos

Un aspecto que consideramos importante destacar aquí es la constatación de aspectos de carácter tecnológico característicos de las producciones anfóricas del DSF (Figura 19.7). Y lo que es más importante aún: todos estos detalles se han constatado en las tres grandes familias definidas (Almagro 51c, SF I y fondo plano) lo cual constituyó, *ab origine*, un detalle fundamental para considerar una procedencia homogénea de todo el cargamento, cuyos envases habían sido fabricados en la misma región productora, como posteriormente confirmaron los análisis arqueométricos, que resumimos en el siguiente apartado.

Se trata de aspectos técnicos que afectan a varios momentos de producción de los envases en los talleres: el torneado y el montaje/ensamblado/secado. Por motivos de espacio presentamos estas constataciones a continuación de manera sintética.

En primer lugar, diversos indicios permiten valorar que el torneado de las ánforas fue bastante defectuoso, resultado de la ausencia de pericia en los alfareros, constatación que quizás responda a una ausencia de tradición previa o a la necesidad de adquisición de una maestría artesanal en poco tiempo. Se constata, al menos, en los siguientes elementos.

Durante la fase de torneado:

- Líneas de torno muy visibles en la parte exterior (Figura 19.7 A), pero distribuidas de manera totalmente irregular a lo largo del cuerpo del envase, lo cual genera apariencias heterogéneas (desde algunas en las cuales casi no se detectan —DSF-183, 185, 220, 231— a otras en las cuales se espacian por todo el cuerpo —DSF-002, 184, 266— o se concentran en algunos puntos —DSF-182—).

- Deficiente ejecución al torno, generando rebabas de arcilla, deformaciones en algunos ejemplares y especialmente fondos irregulares que no permiten un apoyo firme de las piezas, especialmente en las ánforas de fondo plano (Figura 19.7 B).

- Acentuadas marcas de sutura a la hora de proceder a la unión de las diversas partes del envase, especialmente en la unión del cuello con los hombros y en las diversas partes ensambladas de la panza, sobre todo en la unión con el pivote (Figura 19.7 C).

Durante la fase de ensamblaje y secado:

- Habitual empleo de cuerdas para garantizar la sujeción de las diversas partes del cuerpo. Esta técnica se constata en todas las familias recuperadas (Figura 19.7 D, E), tanto en las olearias (DSF-002) como en las vinarias (DSF-265, 265) y en menor medida en las salazoneras. No obstante, son especialmente abundantes en las SF I/ Dressel 23 cartaginenses, sin duda alguna por su mayor peso. Se trata del empleo de cabos finos para reforzar las uniones durante la fase de secado para evitar deformaciones y roturas. A veces solo se constatan una o dos, aunque en otras se han contabilizado hasta cinco líneas subparalelas de cuerda, no siempre horizonzales como en la DSF-002. Se detectan también anudamientos entre cabos horizontales para reforzar las presiones en dichos puntos. Es importante destacar que parece una característica técnica de la citada zona de producción cartaginense, como ha sido recientemente identificado en el alfar de la parcela de Renfe en Águilas en el caso de imitaciones de ánforas africanas, y como también se cita que acontece, de manera ocasional, en el taller de El Mojón (Quevedo 2021: 208 y 212, fig. 13). Se trata de una interesante línea de investigación a rastrear en futuros trabajos[19], pues constituye una especificidad de la región, junto al mundo púnico-ebusitano, zona desde la cual se pudo haber importado esta técnica al ser mucho más antigua y longeva[20].

- En ocasiones, se aprecian una serie de aparentes "brochazos" exteriores resultado de la aplicación de engobe, o de "peinados" tras el torneado (DSF-234).

---

[19] De manera combinada con el estudio de la cabullería y los restos textiles aparecidos en el pecio, para intentar detectar además las fibras usadas y los sistemas de trenzado, y utilizando modelos aplicados en otros yacimientos (Ulanowska 2020).

[20] Donde está ampliamente constatada esta práctica desde época púnica hasta, al menos, el Alto Imperio con su presencia en la forma PE-41 (Ramon 1991: lam. XXXI).

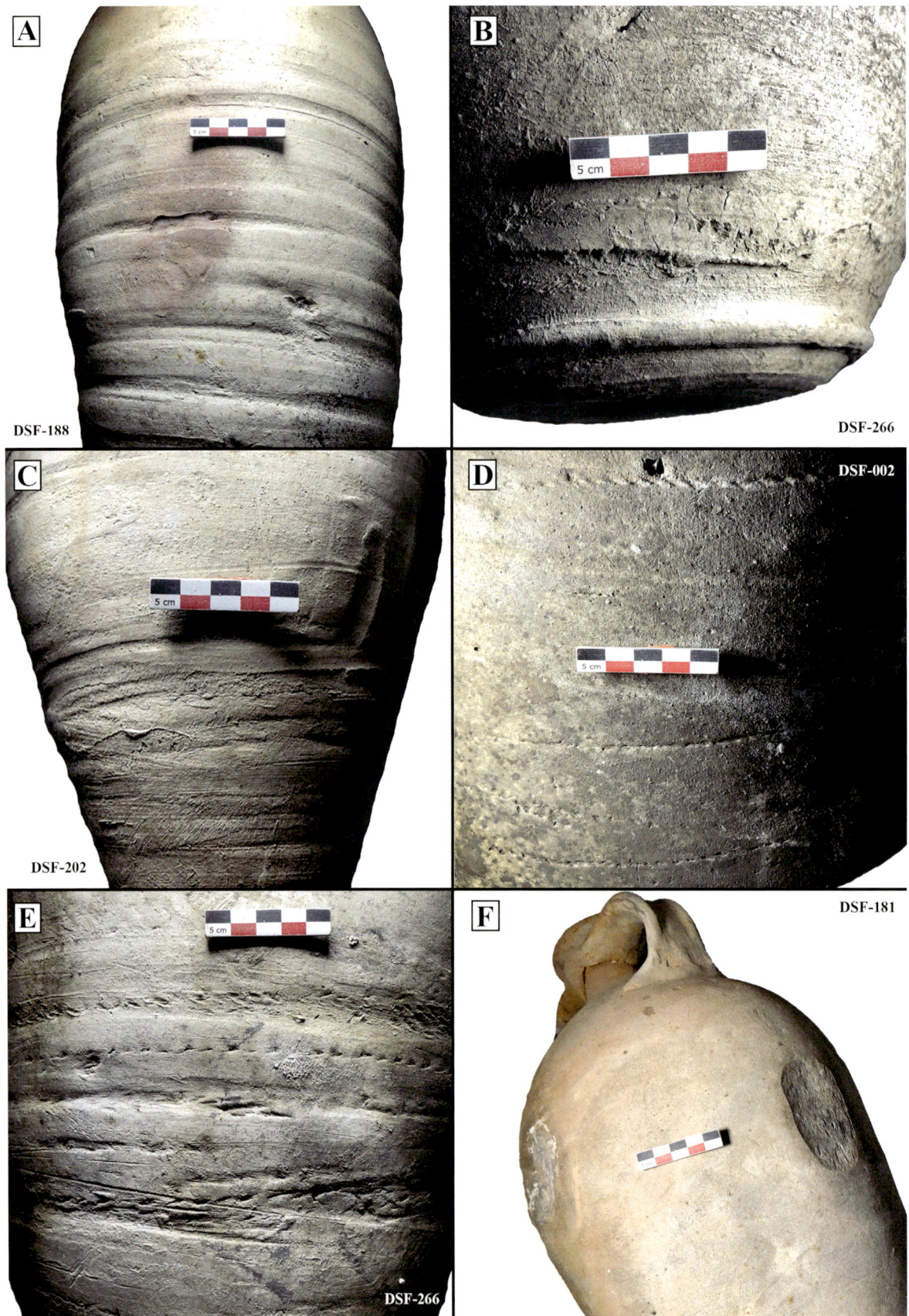

Figura 19.7. Detalles tecnológicos de las ánforas del pecio de Ses Fontanelles, con indicación de las acusadas marcas de torno (A.- DSF-188), las rebabas arcillosas y los fondos irregulares (B.- DSF-266), las marcas de sutura entre las partes (C.- DSF-202), las improntas de cuerda para asegurar el ensamblaje (D.- DSF-002; E.- DSF-266) y las marcas subcirculares de usura postdeposicional (F.- DSF-181).

Durante la cocción, da la impresión de que se alcanzaron temperaturas reducidas, lo que les confiere a muchos ejemplares una alta friabilidad. Es posible que el enterramiento subacuático en el pecio haya magnificado esta cuestión, que tendrá que ser estudiada en detalle, pero la realidad es que el estado de conservación de muchas de estas ánforas es deficiente, siendo muy frecuente su diaclasado horizontal, especialmente en los envases olearios. Ello ha provocado la abundancia en estos envases cerámicos de "marcas de usura subcirculares", en las zonas de contacto entre las ánforas, resultado más que probable de la fase postdeposicional, tras el hundimiento y posterior enterramiento, con concavidades a veces de notables dimensiones y varios milímetros de profundidad (Figura 19.7 F), que en ocasiones terminan perforando la pasta cerámica.

Todos estos aspectos no fueron disimulados por los alfareros, lo cual constituyen útiles indicadores arqueológicos para rastrear el origen geográfico de estas producciones a través del análisis tecnológico de su manufactura y cocción[21]. Actualmente está en fase de elaboración un catálogo detallado de estas patologías.

4.- De la *Carthaginensis*: síntesis de los estudios mineralo-petrográficos de las "pastas" cerámicas

Para poder determinar la proveniencia de las ánforas se realizó en 2020 un primer estudio arqueométrico de las fábricas cerámicas, consistente, tras un análisis preliminar macroscópico *de visu* con microscopio digital y lupa binocular, en el estudio petrográfico de una decena de individuos de las familias identificadas (SF I/Dressel 23: DSF-002, 003; Almagro 51c: DSF-183, 185, 186, 195, 263; Fondo plano: DSF-263, 266, 270; Keay XIX: DSF-277), las cuales fueron analizadas mediante Microscopía Óptica (MO) a través del estudio de láminas delgadas, para su caracterización petrográfica y mineralógica (Figura 19.8).

Además de las observaciones macroscópicas, que desvelaron la elevada frecuencia en todas ellas del característico componente micáceo, el estudio por MO permitió la definición de dos grupos (Fantuzzi *et al.* 2020):

- Grupo Petrográfico 1: caracterizado por fábricas ricas en moscovita, con contribución metamórfica (cuarcitas/esquistos), al que se adecuaban todas las muestras menos la DSF-277. Aunque entre las 9 muestras pueden detectarse ligeras variaciones de fábrica, la naturaleza de estas variaciones no resulta incompatible con un origen geológico común. Respecto a la identificación de dicha área, se realizó una comparativa con la geología local del sur peninsular, con la colección de referencia del ERAAUB de la Universitat de Barcelona y con muestras de Águilas y Mazarrón, habiéndose concluido que de los potenciales candidatos la zona al sur de Cartagena es la más probable, conociéndose en dicha región fábricas en alfares locales en las que predominan las inclusiones de cuarzo, moscovita y los fragmentos de rocas metamórficas ricas en cuarzo y moscovita, además de óxidos de hierro (Berrocal 2012: 256-57).

- Grupo Petrográfico 2: con múltiples rocas metamórficas de grado bajo-muy bajo (filitas), integrado únicamente por la muestra DSF-277. La fábrica observada en lámina delgada indica claramente una proveniencia de un área con contribución metamórfica dominante, diferente del área de producción anterior, siendo las áreas del Complejo Maláguide y Alpujárride las potencialmente más probables, si bien el estudio comparativo con análisis previos parece indicar que es el litoral malacitano el candidato más probable para el ánfora del tipo Keay XIX analizada (Fantuzzi *et al.* 2020: 108-10).

Estas primeras conclusiones petrográficas, ampliadas en otros trabajos (Fantuzzi *et al.* 2020; Cau *et al.* 2022 a) parecen confirmar que los tres grupos de ánforas del pecio de Ses Fontanelles, con abundante moscovita y fragmentos de roca metamórfica visibles en sus fábricas, podrían haber sido manufacturadas en alfares de la microrregión de Cartagena, en sentido amplio. Estas conclusiones coinciden con la restante evidencia arqueológica disponible (talleres productores de estas formas y analogías tecnológicas en alfares del sureste, entre Águilas y Mazarrón). Es necesario realizar estudios adicionales (muestreo más numeroso tanto de ánforas del mismo pecio, como de la potencial área de proveniencia; y análisis químicos complementarios) con el fin de obtener evidencias más sólidas para confirmar esta hipótesis.

5.- Balance y perspectivas de investigación.

El pecio de Ses Fontanelles, hundido en aguas de Palma (Mallorca), es de gran relevancia para el conocimiento de la economía y el tráfico marítimo en los primeros siglos de la Antigüedad Tardía, tal y como hemos indicado en trabajos previos y que no reiteramos aquí: por su excepcional estado de conservación —embarcación y cargamento— y por la singularidad de las mercancías transportadas (Bernal-Casasola y Cau 2020; Munar *et al.* 2022).

---

[21] Parece que el torneado irregular es una característica de las producciones anfóricas locales del área de Cartagena también en momentos precedentes (Quevedo 2021: 215).

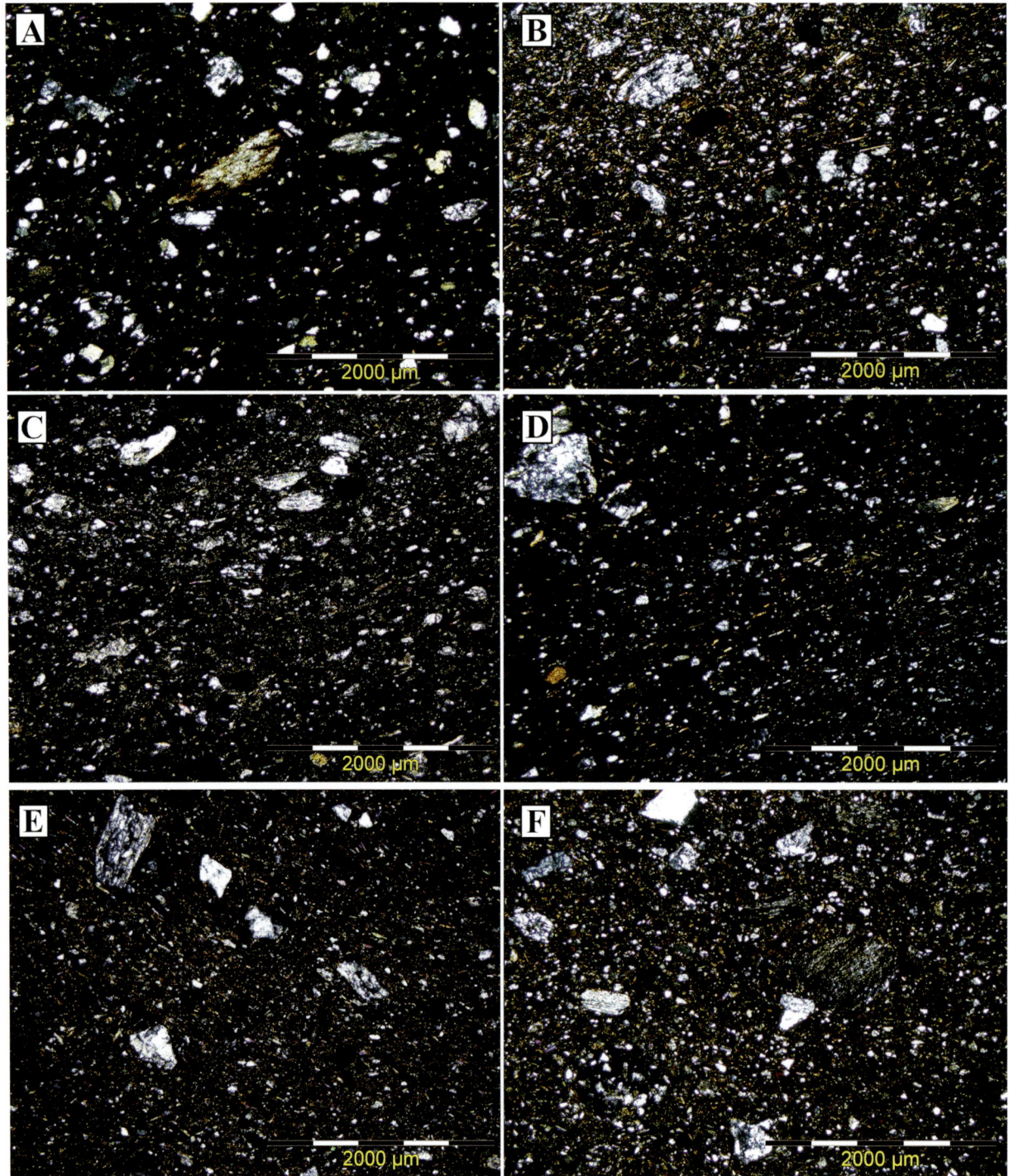

Figura 19.8. Fotomicrografías de las láminas delgadas tomadas a 40x en nícoles cruzados de algunas ánforas del Grupo Petrográfico 1: Almagro 51c (A.- DSF-183; B.- DSF-185), Ses Fontanelles I/Dressel 23 cartaginenses (C.- DSF-002; D.- DSF-003) y de fondo plano (E.- DSF-270); y del Grupo Petrográfico 2: Keay XIX (F.- DSF-277).

Respecto a la cronología, fechamos el hundimiento en momentos avanzados del s. IV d. C. (Bernal-Casasola y Cau 2020; Soler *et al.* 2021: 310; Munar *et al.* 2022), posiblemente en torno a mediados de dicha centuria. Por lo que se refiere a las ánforas, las mismas cuadran bien en la citada propuesta sin mayores precisiones, más allá de la datación *post quem* del 280 d. C. que se deriva de las Ses Fontanelles I/Dressel 23 cartaginenses, al imitar las Dressel 23 béticas, conocidas solo a partir de entonces.

En lo que atañe directamente a las ánforas, destacamos los siguientes aspectos:

- Constituye el primer pecio con un cargamento procedente procedente de la *Carthaginiensis* bien documentado bien documentado en todo el Mediterráneo, reforzando una línea de investigación tímidamente conocida hasta la fecha gracias a la constatación de algunas ánforas, aisladas, en contextos de consumo mediterráneos (Quevedo 2021).
- Permiten cubrir un vacío en la producción anfórica de la microrregión de Cartagena (Berrocal 2012; Bernal-Casasola 2019: 650 y 609; García Aboal 2021; Quevedo 2021), especialmente en el s. IV d. C., pues en ella se conocía con claridad la producción a partir del s. V d. C., con los conocidos *spatheia*. Este hallazgo mallorquín confirma el comercio transmediterráneo de algunos tipos anfóricos conocidos en alfares (Berrocal 2012); y se presentan por primera vez perfiles completos (= ánforas de fondo plano) que contribuyen a su conocimiento y mayor precisión.
- La definición de un nuevo tipo de ánfora olearia (Ses Fontanelles I/Dressel 23 cartaginense) permite valorar la importancia del comercio marítimo de aceite del sureste hispano, línea de investigación totalmente inédita hasta la fecha. Habrá que combinar futuros estudios con almazaras cartageneras para ampliar esta cuestión.
- Ses Fontanelles constituye, con 39 *tituli picti* conservados (Soler *et al.* 2021), el yacimiento subacuático con más inscripciones pintadas de *Hispania* (seguido de lejos por el almeriense de Pecio Gandolfo, con 25 *dipinti*, y por el de La Albufereta I, con 11). Cuando se ultime la excavación arqueológica de los dos tercios restantes (central y popa) del pecio es muy probable que esta cifra se multiplique. Su importancia se magnifica por su cronología, al no haber prácticamente epigrafía pintada en producciones hispanas en estas fechas; y al asociarse a formas anepígrafas hasta la fecha (Almagro 51 c).
- La presencia de numerosos *tituli* en las ánforas permite reabrir el debate científico sobre si estos envases comerciales se etiquetaban puntualmente (por lotes) o bien si todas llevaban *dipinti*, como parece suceder en Ses Fontanelles y en otros yacimientos con buenas condiciones de conservación (como la *Bottega del Garum* de Pompeya).
- El pecio de Ses Fontanelles constituye una posibilidad única para estudiar conjuntamente los restos de alimentos en las ánforas aparecidas, en las cuales coinciden inscripciones alusivas al producto con restos físicos de paleocontenidos en envases completos y taponados. Una ocasión única a nivel atlántico-mediterráneo.

Esperamos con la continuidad de los trabajos de campo y laboratorio poder contribuir en los próximos años a dar respuesta a algunos de estos interrogantes.

Bibliografía

Assis, C., y C. Amaro 2006. Estudo dos restos de peixe de dois sitios fabris de Olisipo. *Setúbal Arqueológica*, 13: 123-44.

Bernal-Casasola, D. 2001. La producción de ánforas en la Bética en el s. III d.C. y durante el Bajo Imperio, en *Congreso internacional Ex Baetica Amphorae: conservas, aceite y vino de la Bética en el imperio romano*, I: 239-72. Écija: Editorial Gráficas.

Bernal-Casasola, D. 2019. Ánforas tardorromanas en Hispania. Claves de identificación, en C. Fernández Ochoa, A. Morillo Cerdán, Mar Zarzalejos Prieto (eds) *Manual de cerámica romana*, IV: *Producciones cerámicas de época medio-imperial y tardorromana*: 549-670. Madrid: Comunidad de Madrid.

Bernal-Casasola, D. y M.A. Cau 2020. *Estudio preliminar del cargamento del pecio tardorromano de Ses Fontanelles (Palma de Mallorca): inventario, catalogación y primeras analíticas*. Memoria inédita depositada en el Consell de Mallorca.

Bernal-Casasola, D., M.A. Cau-Ontiveros, P. Berni, A. Pecci, J.A. Retamosa, J.L. Portillo-Sotelo, J. Oviedo, E. Fernández Tudela, M. Goñalons Lapiedra, E. García Riaza, J. Cardell 2024 a. Ánforas tardorromanas, crismones y el oleum dulce: reflexiones sobre el pecio mallorquín de Ses Fontanelles. *Romula* 21: 29-84.

Bernal-Casasola, D., M.A. Cau-Ontiveros, J. Cardell, E. García Riaza, A. Pecci, J.A. Retamosa, J.L. Portillo-Sotelo, L. Fantuzzi, J. Oviedo, C. De Juan, C. Munar, P. Berni y J.A. Moya 2024 b. Ánforas vinarias de la Cartaginense: aportaciones del pecio mallorquín de Ses Fontanelles, en *III Col·loqui internacional d'arqueologia: el vi a l'antiguitat; economia, producció i comerç al Mediterrani; actes (Badalona 19, 20 i 21 d'octubre de 2022)*: 550-68. Badalona: Museu de Badalona.

Bernal-Casasola, D., M.A. Cau-Ontiveros, C. De Juan Fuertes, S. Munar Llabrès, J. Cardell Perelló, E. García Riaza, J.A. Moya Montoya, J. Oviedo Callealta, J.L. Portillo Sotelo, J.A. Retamosa Gámez y L. Fantuzzi 2023. Repensando el comercio marítimo de Carthago Spartaria: acerca del pecio tardorromano de Ses Fontanelles (Mallorca). *Drassana* 31: 156-85.

Bernal-Casasola, D., R. Marlasca, C.G. Rodríguez Santana, B. Ruiz Zapata, M.J. Gil y M. Alba 2016. Garum de sardinas en *Augusta Emerita*. Caracterización arqueológica, epigráfica, ictiológica y palinológica del contenido de un ánfora Beltrán IIB. *Rei Cretariae Romanae Fautorum Acta* 44: 737-49.

Berni, P. y J. Moros Díaz 2017. Dressel 23 (Valle del Guadalquivir). Amphorae ex Hispania. Paisajes de producción y de consumo, <http://amphorae.icac.cat/amphora/dressel-23-guadalquivir-valley>, 23 mayo, 2017.

Berrocal, M.C. 2012. Producciones anfóricas en la costa meridional de Carthago-Spartaria, en D. Bernal-Casasola y A. Ribera (eds) *Cerámicas hispanorromanas, II: Producciones regionales*: 255-77. Cádiz: Universidad de Cádiz.

Cardell Perelló, J., D. Bernal-Casasola, M.A. Cau Ontiveros y E. García Riaza 2022. Arqueomallornauta. Un proyecto de investigación sobre el comercio y el tráfico marítimo mallorquín en la Antigüedad Tardía, en F. Cerezo Andreo, C. Pérez-Reverte Mañas y S. Solana Rubio (eds) *Actas del I Congreso iberoamericano de arqueología náutica y subacuática*. Cádiz: Editorial Universidad de Cádiz, en prensa.

Cau Ontiveros, M.A., D. Bernal-Casasola, L. Fantuzzi, J.A. Retamosa, J.L. Portillo, A. Pecci, A. Valenzuela, S. Munar Llabrés, P. Berni, J. Cardell Perelló, y E. García Riaza 2022 b. Primera aproximación a la tipología y procedencia de las ánforas del pecio de Ses Fontanelles (Mallorca, Islas Baleares), en *Los cursos fluviales en Hispania, vías de comercio cerámico: actas del VI Congreso internacional de la SECAH (Zaragoza, 2022)* (Monografías Ex Officina Hispana 6): 401-14. Zaragoza: SECAH.

Cau Ontiveros, M.A., D. Bernal-Casasola, A. Pecci, L. Fantuzzi, Ll. Picornell-Gelabert, A. Valenzuela, J.A. Retamosa, J.L. Portillo, J. Cardell Perelló, S. Munar Llabrés, C. de Juan Fuertes y E. García Riaza 2022a. Multianalytical approach to the exceptional late Roman shipwreck of Ses Fontanelles (Mallorca, Balearic Islands). *Archaeological and Anthropological Sciences* 16, artículo 58: 16-58.

Curtis, R.I. 1991. *Garum and salsamenta: Production and Commerce in materia medica*. Leiden: Brill.

Ehmig, U. 2003. *Die römischen Amphoren aus Mainz* (Frankfurter archäologische Schriften 4). Möhnesee: Bibliopolis.

Fantuzzi, L., M.A. Cau Ontiveros y D. Bernal-Casasola 2020. Observación macroscópica y caracterización petrográfica de las ánforas, en D. Bernal-Casasola y M.A. Cau (eds) *Estudio preliminar del cargamento del pecio tardorromano de Ses Fontanelles (Palma de Mallorca): inventario, catalogación y primeras analíticas*: 91-112. Memoria inédita depositada en el Consell de Mallorca.

García Vargas, E., D. Bernal-Casasola, V. Palacios, A. Roldán, A. Rodríguez y J. Sánchez 2014. Confectio gari pompeiani. Procedimiento experimental para la elaboración de salsas de pescado romanas. *Spal* 23: 65-82.

García-Aboal, M.V. 2021. Un nuevo tipo de ánfora tardorromana en Cartagena. *Spal* 30.1: 222-40.

Grainger, S. 2021. *The Story of Garum: Fermented Fish Sauce and Salted Fish in the Ancient World*. Abingdon: Routledge.

Mayet, F. y C. Tavares da Silva 1998. *L'atelier d'amphores de Pinheiro (Portugal)*. París: De Boccard.

Menchelli, S. 2021. Italian and sicilian amphorae and their contents: a general overview, en D. Bernal-Casasola, M Bonifay, A. Pecci y V. Leitch, *Roman Amphora Contents: Reflecting on the Maritime Trade of Foodstuffs in Antiquity* (Roman and Late Antique Mediterranean Pottery 17): 259-72. Oxford: Archaeopress.

Munar Llabrés, S. 2019. *Informe/Memoria Final de l'excavació arqueológica d'urgencia al derelicte de la Platja de Palma*. Original inédito depositado en el Consell de Mallorca.

Munar Llabrés, S., J. Cardell, C. De Juan, M.A. Cau, D. Bernal-Casasola, L. Picornell y E. García Riaza 2022. Ses Fontanelles shipwreck (Mallorca, Balearic Islands): an exceptional late Roman vessel and its cargo. *Journal of Maritime Archaeology* 17: 487-505 <https://doi.org/10.1007/s11457-022-09331-6>.

Pecci, A. 2020. Análisis de residuos orgánicos de ánforas, en Bernal-Casasola D. y Cau M.A. (ed.) *Estudio preliminar del cargamento del pecio tardorromano de Ses Fontanelles (Palma de Mallorca): inventario, catalogación y primeras analíticas*: 113-22. Memoria inédita depositada en el Consell de Mallorca.

Pinto, I. Vaz. y A.P. Magalhães 2016. Almagro 51A-B (Lusitania Occidental), Amphorae ex Hispania. Paisajes de producción y de consumo <http://amphorae.icac.cat/amphora/almagro-51a-b-western-lusitania>, 08 julio, 2016.

Quevedo, A. 2021. La producción anfórica de *Carthago Nova* y su territorio: estado de la cuestión. *Spal* 30.1: 196-221.

Ramon, J. 1991. *Las ánforas púnicas de Ibiza*. Eivissa: Museo Arqueológico de Ibiza.

Raposo, J.M.C., A.J.G. Sabrosa y A.L.C. Duarte 1995. Ânforas do vale do Tejo. As olarias da Quinta do Rouxinol (Seixal) e do Porto dos Cacos (Alcochete), en *Actas do 1º congresso de arqueologia peninsular (Porto, 1993)*: 331-43. Porto: Sociedade portuguesa de antropologia e etnologia.

Remolà, J.A. 2000. *Las ánforas tardo-antiguas en Tarraco (Hispania Tarraconensis)* (Col.lecció instrumenta 7). Barcelona: Universitat de Barcelona.

Soler, A., A. Font, P. Berni, E. García Riaza, D. Bernal-Casasola, M.A. Cau, J. Cardell y S. Munar 2021. El singular conjunto de tituli picti del pecio de Ses Fontanelles (Mallorca, islas Baleares) y su contribución a la epigrafía anfórica tardorromana hispánica. *Cupauam* 47.1: 287-317.

Ulanowska, A. 2020. Textile uses in administrative practices in Bronze Age Greece: new evidence on textile impressions from the undersides of clay sealings, en M. Bustamante-Álvarez, E.H. Sánchez López y J. Jiménez Ávila (eds) *Redefining Ancient*

Textile Handcraft: Structures, Tools and Production Processes (Purpureae Vestes 7): 413-24. Granada: Universidad de Granada.

Valenzuela, A. 2020. Primer análisis arqueozoológico de los restos ictiológicos de ánforas, en D. Bernal-Casasola y M.A. Cau, *Estudio preliminar del cargamento del pecio tardorromano de Ses Fontanelles (Palma de Mallorca): inventario, catalogación y primeras analíticas*: 123-32. Memoria inédita depositada en el Consell de Mallorca.

Viegas, C. 2016. Almagro 51C (Lusitania Meridional), Amphorae ex Hispania. Paisajes de producción y de consumo <http://amphorae.icac.cat/amphora/almagro-51c-meridional-lusitania>, 08 julio, 2016.

Viegas, C., J.M.C. Raposo y I.V. Pinto 2016. Almagro 51C (Lusitania Occidental), Amphorae ex Hispania. Paisajes de producción y de consumo <http://amphorae.icac.cat/amphora/almagro-51c-western-lusitania>, 20 julio, 2016.

20. Connecting Rome, Ostia, and Portus by Land: Understanding the Road Network in the Lower Tiber Valley through Archaeological and Computational Approaches

Dragana Mladenović and Maria del Carmen Moreno Escobar

1. Introduction

Simon Keay always found it paradoxical that ports have often been studied in geographical isolation, although they occupy a privileged liminal position between land and sea and are connected to networks of land-based towns and other ports. He has thus made sure that his own project at Portus does not fall into the same trap: *Portus Romae* has been extensively contextualised, within its immediate hinterland, the port-system of Imperial Rome, and the Mediterranean network of Roman ports and Imperial supply systems.[1] Furthermore, the connectivity and movement between the Imperial capital, its maritime port of Portus, the fluvial port of Ostia, and the River Tiber has lately received due scholarly attention, with the main focus resting on the networks created by natural and artificial waterways, and the workings of the riverine traffic.[2]

In this paper we would like to add an additional element to the picture by concentrating on the land connection between the nodes of this system, i.e. the roads linking Rome, Ostia, and Portus: the *via Campana/Portuensis*, the *via Ostiensis*, and the *via Flavia* (Figure 20.1). By taking into account the physical geography and archaeological remains, the authors wish to explore the dynamic relationship between the roads, the settlements which they served and the River Tiber, and to tease out the roles that these communication links played in the Lower Tiber Valley port and settlement network. It is hoped that through this process some of the rationale that guided the choice of when and which terrestrial route to take between the mouth of the Tiber and Rome will be revealed, reflecting not only practices but perhaps also contemporary perceptions of these alternative communication lines.

The authors will restrict their enquiry to the early and middle Imperial period (late 1st century BC to early 3rd century AD), aiming to understand specifically the impact that the key episode in the development of the port system of Rome – the construction of the harbour complex at Portus – had on the existing communication

networks. Widening the chronological span would certainly reveal broader complexity of the changing relationship between Rome and its maritime front; due to the constraints of this paper, such an analysis remains outside of its scope.

2. The Dataset

The present study is based on an earlier data compilation that was used for analysing the occupation of the Lower Tiber Valley in relation to the development of Rome's port system.[3] It resulted from an extensive archival and publication review and includes 494 entries, comprising archaeological sites found on both banks of the Tiber between the city walls of Rome and the mouth of the river, as well as on the Isola Sacra, dated between the late Republic and the late Empire. The data was compiled into a database, georeferenced, and included in an associated Geographic Information System, constituting the *Ager et Portus Tiberis* information resource (APT).[4] In order to analyse the developments across time we classified the evidence into five periods, based on the dating provided by original publications (Table 20.1). The application of this chronological classification results in the restriction of the dataset to 164 sites for which we have enough temporal resolution to define their occupation with this level of detail, thus leaving aside sites for which defining specific enough chronology was not possible. Though not used in the quantitative analysis, the excluded sites are at times brought in to discuss an observed phenomenon, if their features are particularly well suited to further elucidate it.

---

[1] Keay and Paroli 2011; Keay 2012; 2016; Keay *et al.* 2020.
[2] Boetto 2016; Keay *et al.* 2021; Moreno Escobar 2022.
[3] Initial data gathering for the *via Portuensis* area was conducted by D. Mladenović in 2007-08, during the research stay in Rome that was funded by a grant from the Craven Committee (Faculty of Classics) and the Meyerstein fund (School of Archaeology) of the University of Oxford. This author would like to thank Laura Cianfriglia of the Soprintendenza Speciale per i Beni Archeologici di Roma for her kind support and help in this process. The dataset was further refined and significantly expanded by M.C. Moreno Escobar as a part of her postdoctoral research project 'Exploring the Port System of Imperial Rome' at the British School at Rome in 2016-17. The archaeological and spatial analysis of this dataset, however, was conducted while Moreno Escobar was working on the project 'Beyond Ports: Movement and Connectivity in the Roman Mediterranean', funded by the Swedish Research Council (grant application: 2020-01621).
[4] Moreno Escobar 2022.

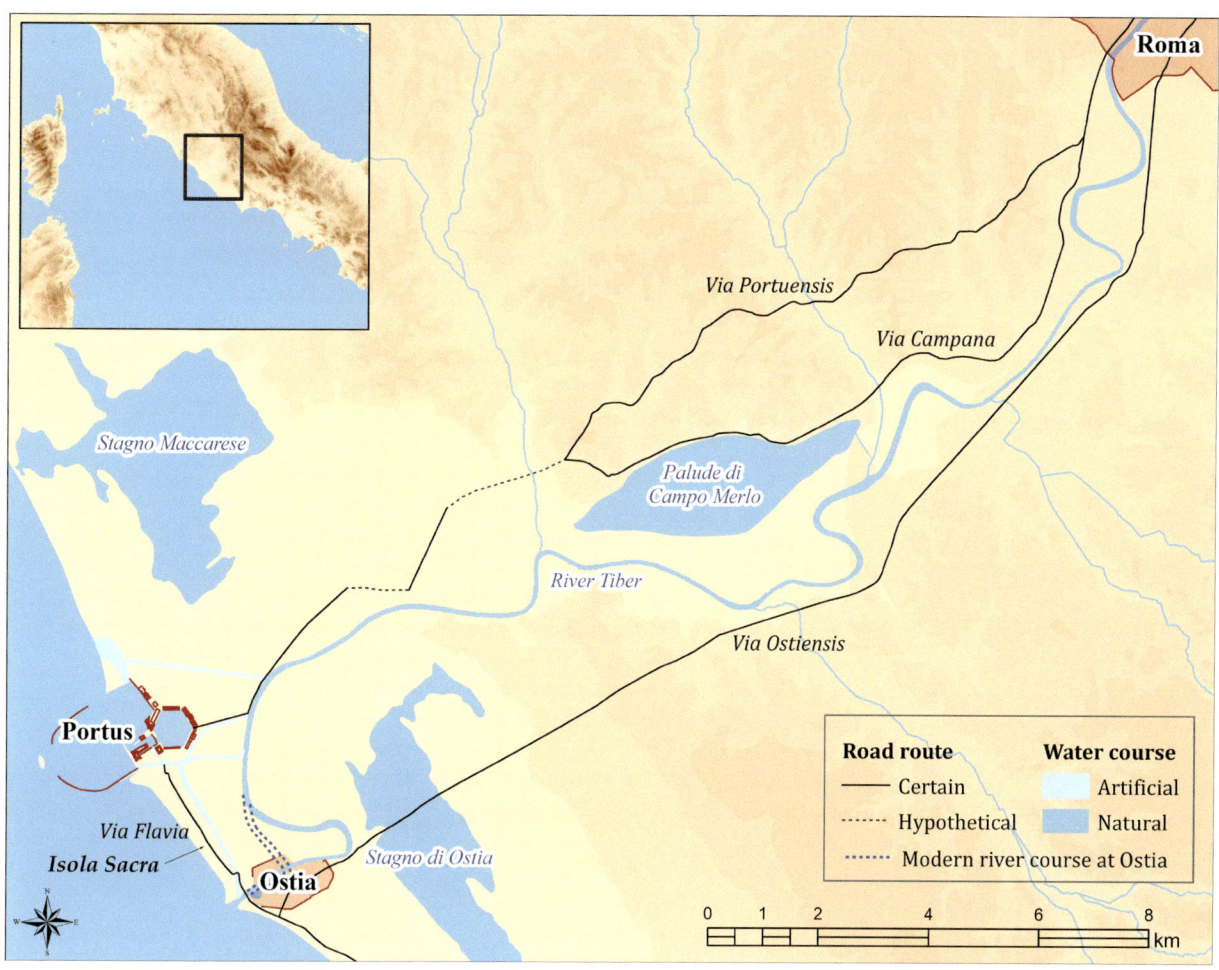

Figure 20.1. Main axes of communication between Rome, Ostia, and Portus in imperial times
(source: M.C. Moreno Escobar).

Table 20.1: Chronological periods used to classify archaeological evidence in this study (Moreno Escobar
2022, Table 1).

Chronological period	Temporal extent
Period 1	Augustan to pre-Claudian (c. 27 BC to 40 AD)
Period 2	Claudian to Flavian (c. 40 to 100)
Period 3	Trajanic and Hadrianic (c. 100 to 140)
Period 4	Antonines (c. 140 to 190)
Period 5	Severan (c. 190 to 235)

A new layer of interpretation was added to this data through re-evaluating the typology and/or functionality of sites, distinguishing 12 site types (Table 20.2).

The courses of the roads under study have been reconstructed following those traditionally accepted in modern scholarship, amended to align with remains of road stretches known from archaeological evidence.[5]

In order to explore how the different regions in the

[5] Tomassetti 1979a, b; Venditti 1992; Serra 2007. It should be noted that we are following the traditional identification of the *via Campana* route with the modern course of the Via della Magliana, despite Scheid 1976 who believed Via della Magliana to be significantly more modern and proposed the identification of the haulage road along the Tiber with the *via Campana*. Our decision is based on the fact that no archaeological evidence has emerged since the 1970s that would place the *via Campana* closer to the river, while the excavations at Ponte Galeria demonstrated that the *via Campana* could not have been used for ship towing, at least not on its last stretch (Serlorenzi *et al.* 2004).

Table 20.2: Functional typologies used to classify the archaeological evidence in this study (Moreno Escobar 2022, Table 2).

Generic typology	Specific typology
Settlement	Cities, towns, *villae*, rural settlements...
Funerary	Necropolis, isolated burials, funerary monuments...
Sacred structures and places	Temples, sacred locations, sacred complexes...
Productive activities	Glass workshops, kilns, quarries, fish farming facilities...
Storage and trade	Warehouses, storerooms, *tabernae*...
Port infrastructure	Structures enhancing connectivity between land and water, usually placed at locations where the two environments meet: moles, landings, quays, lighthouses...
Road infrastructure	Road sections, *stationes*, bridges...
Infrastructure	Territorial markers (*e.g. cippi*)
Urban infrastructure	Gates, city walls...
Water infrastructure	Cisterns, water drainage...
Other	Inscriptions, honorific monuments, dumping sites...
Undefined	Building structures and surface scatters offering insufficient information for reliable interpretation

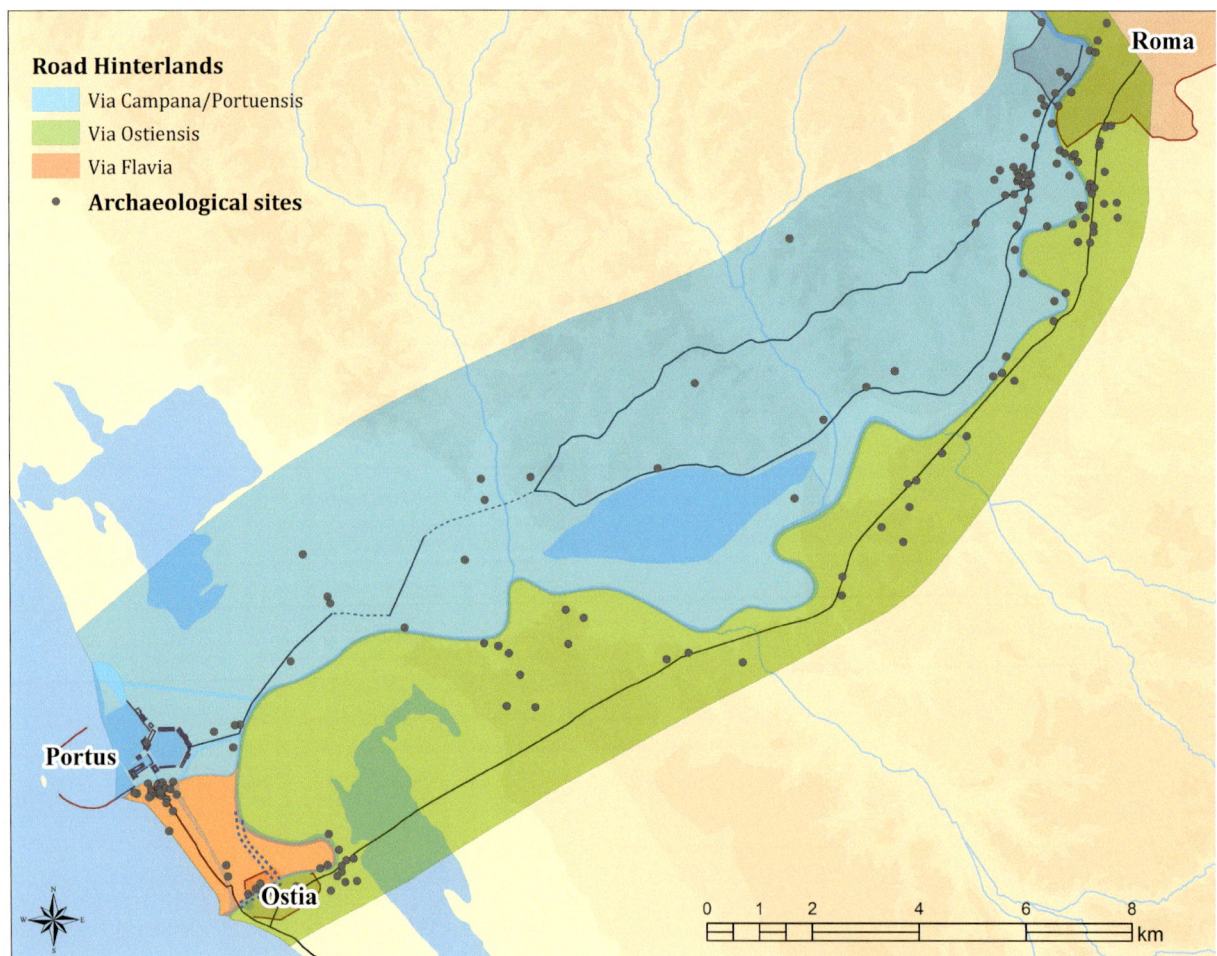

Figure 20.2. The study area divided into road hinterlands and the distribution of archaeological sites of the early and middle Imperial period (source: M.C. Moreno Escobar, with data from APT).

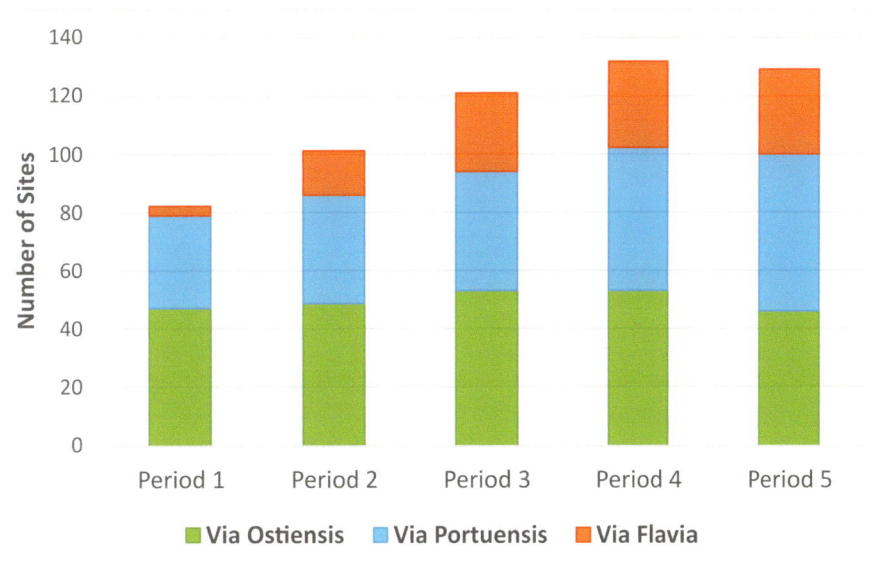

Figure 20.3. Number of sites identified in the hinterlands of the via *Campana/Portuensis*, via *Ostiensis*, and via Flavia in the periods under study (source: M.C. Moreno Escobar).

Lower Tiber Valley were occupied we have divided the study area into sections associated with each of the roads, defined as road hinterlands: the *via Campana/Portuensis*, the *via Ostiensis*, and the *via Flavia* hinterland (Figure 20.2). In the following sections, we will use different techniques of quantitative and spatial analysis to explore the articulation between the occupation evidence and the road communication axes.

3. Intensity and Spatial Distribution of Occupation along the Road Network through Time

Our first analyses focus on the number (Figure 20.3) and the spatial distribution (Figure 20.4) of sites that existed in each of the roads' hinterlands at the different periods under consideration.

In the time of the early Empire substantial occupation existed in the Ostiensis and Portuensis hinterlands (Figure 20.3), with the Claudian foundation of Portus having very little impact on the settlement numbers along these two roads, though they both experienced modest occupation growth in Periods 2 and 3 (Period 2: two additional sites on the Ostiensis and five on the Portuensis, Period 3: four additional sites on each road). Instead, the foundation of the *Portus Romae* had a greater impact on Isola Sacra where occupation significantly increased between the mid-1st and the mid-2nd centuries AD (Periods 2 and 3). The Isola Sacra stretch of the *via Flavia* has been dated to the Flavian period,[6] and our analysis offers further support to the proposition

that the original bridge at the location of the later *Ponte di Matidia* should also be dated to the same period,[7] as it is hard to imagine that the establishment of Portus would have had such a significant and immediate impact on Isola Sacra had a link between the two not already been in place. The spatial distribution of sites on the Isola Sacra shows two distinct groupings at either end of the *via Flavia* (Figure 20.4), the larger one gravitating towards the imperial port, and the smaller one towards the urban community at Ostia. The new settlements and structures at the Portus end are clearly limited to the south side of the *Fossa Traiana* canal in all periods under consideration,[8] leading us to conclude that the controlled environment of the imperial port did not allow for such developments on its territory.

We would like to briefly turn to the contested question of the *via Campana/via Portuensis* duality. Traditional scholarship maintains that the *via Portuensis* was constructed by Claudius to serve the port, with the pre-existing road on the same bank, the *via Campana*, becoming a hauling road at this point.[9] They are believed to partly share a route: for the first two miles the *via Portuensis* follows the *via Campana*, branching off at Pozzo Pantaleo (present Via Q. Majorana) and crossing through the valley of Monteverde, before the roads join again around the 11th mile, at Ponte Galeria.

---

[6] By coin evidence from excavation, Baldassarre 1996: 13-14.

[7] Keay *et al.* 2020, in particular p. 151.
[8] Though one should also allow for a possibility of a bias in the dataset due to the extensive works in this area by Germoni *et al.* 2011 and more recently Keay *et al.* 2020.
[9] Cf. s.v. Campana, via in *LTURS* II, 56-58 (J. Scheid).

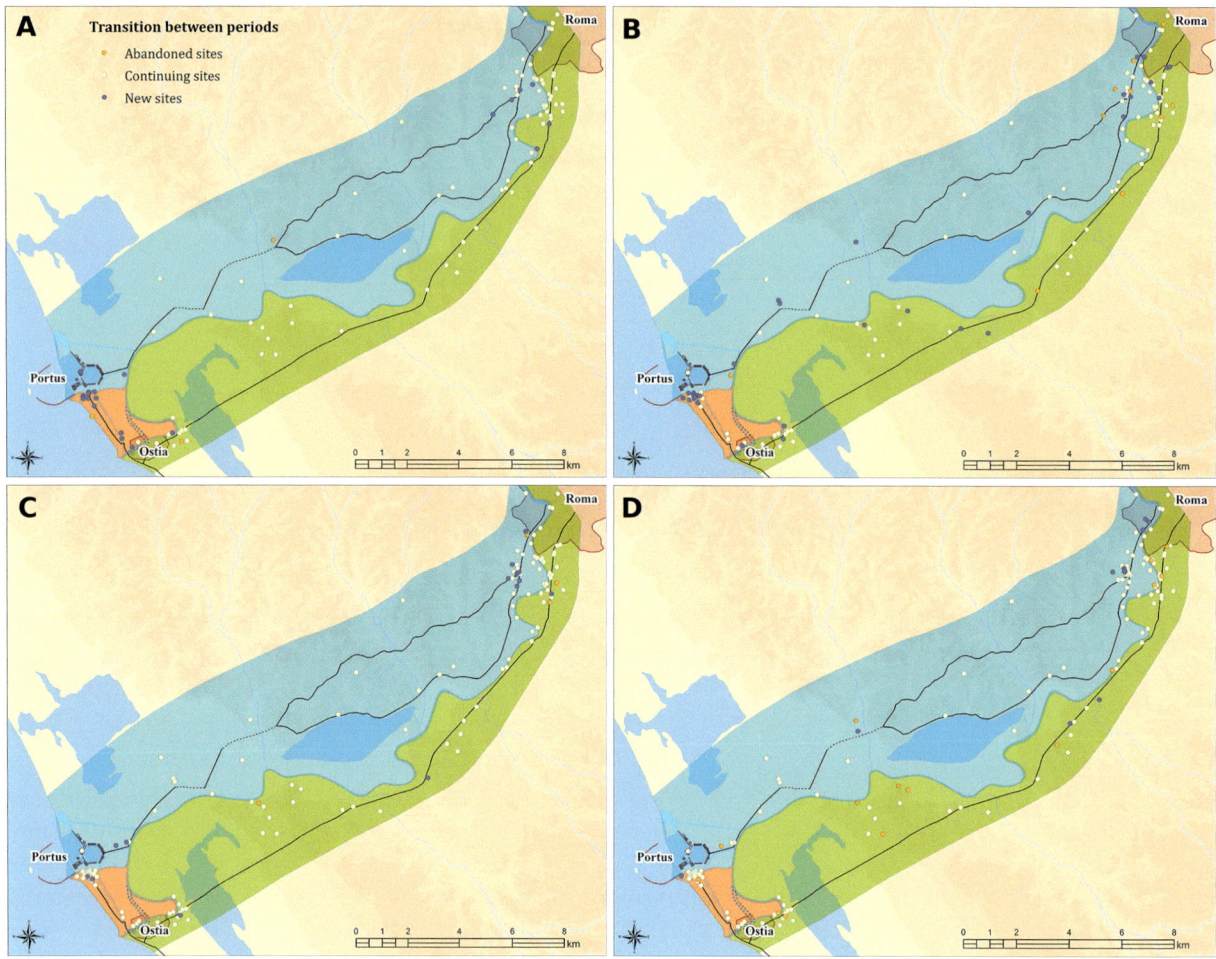

Figure 20.4. Maps showing the continuity, abandonment, and new foundation of sites in the transitions between Period 1 to Period 2 (A), Period 2 to Period 3 (B), Period 3 to Period 4 (C), and Period 4 to Period 5 (D) (source: M.C. Moreno Escobar, data from APT).

Looking at the changes in occupation between Period 1 and Period 2 (Figure 20.4A), one can indeed observe new sites appearing in Claudian-Flavian times along the course of the *via Portuensis*,[10] mainly around the bifurcation with the *via Campana*, which seems to support the hypothesis of the Claudian construction of this section of the road.[11] Though the numbers are small, one should note the existence of sites in the vicinity of the *via Portuensis* that were active already in Period 1, and earlier, i.e. before the construction of Portus,[12] leading us to speculate about the existence of a communication link on this route already in previous

periods, connecting Rome with the *Campus Salinarum* along the higher ground than the *via Campana*. On the other hand, not only is there no decline of occupation observable along the post-Claudian *via Campana*, but from the time of Trajan and Hadrian occupation along it intensifies (Figure 20.4B), while the newly built northern branch, the *via Portuensis*, sees sites being abandoned. From this moment on (Figure 20.4C and Figure 20.4D), new sites in the Portuensis hinterland concentrate in and around the bifurcation of the *via Campana* and the *via Portuensis* at Pozzo Pantaleo (mainly reflecting a growth of the urban necropolis) and along the *via Campana*. It would therefore seem that despite the Claudian construction of the *via Portuensis* branch, the southern *via Campana* route remained as the main axis of communication with Portus. Further implications of these observations will be explored in the Discussion section.

While the Antonine period (Period 4) sees further growth of occupation in the Portuensis hinterland

---

[10] E.g. the funerary structures at Site 9 at Vigna Pia (Cianfriglia *et al.* 2002: 349-53; Cianfriglia 2006: 501, 505-10) and the family tomb at Vigna Jaconini (Tomassetti 1979b: 357-61).

[11] Recently, a Trajanic date has been put forward for the construction of the *via Portuensis* (Arnoldus Huyzendveld *et al.* 2009: 600); the analysis here described speaks in favour of the traditional Claudian date.

[12] Such as the republican fortification at Ponte Galeria-La Chiesola (Cianfriglia *et al.* 2002: 354-56), a republican villa at Via delle Vigne (L. Cianfriglia, pers. comm.), and an early imperial villa at the Grande Raccordo Anulare, svincolo AlItalia (L. Cianfriglia, pers. comm.).

(eight additional sites) and Isola Sacra (three additional sites), the occupation of the Ostiensis side seems to have plateaued (Figure 20.3). Finally, Period 5 witnesses several new trends: firstly, a further intensification of the occupation of the Portuensis hinterland (five additional sites), and the decrease in the intensity of occupation in the Ostiensis area (seven sites less), whereas the occupation of Isola Sacra remains practically unchanged (one site less). The trends in the occupation between the Portuensis and Ostiensis hinterlands in Periods 4 and 5 may be early signs of the increasing importance of Portus, culminating with it gaining its municipal status at the beginning of the 4th century AD,[13] and the dwindling influence of Ostia which saw the reduction of its population and urban infrastructure from the early and middle 3rd century AD.[14] The decline of Ostia was felt also on the city territory, particularly in the plains next to the river (Figure 20.4D), where three *villae* and a sanctuary were abandoned, with funerary structures being the only new sites in the area.[15]

4. Changes in the Mode of Occupation along the Road Network across Time

Expanding the chronological analysis to consider types of sites provides further insight into the observed trends, allowing for different uses and organisation of the study areas to be traced (Figure 20.5).

The importance of the vicinity of the River Tiber and its role as a transport axis is clear across the whole study period and for all three hinterlands, as evidenced by the presence of port infrastructure.[16] The establishment of the port infrastructure and its eventual disuse fall mainly outside our study period in the Campana/Portuensis and the Ostiensis hinterlands, with little change in the number of sites over time. The Isola Sacra port infrastructure, on the other hand, gets established only after the foundation of Portus and grows over Periods 2 and 3. The modest numbers for this type of evidence seem surprising, bearing in mind the Isola Sacra is an island further traversed by an artificial channel (the Portus-to-Ostia canal), and are likely due to unequal survival and intensity of study: evidence on the eastern side of the island was most likely obliterated by the lateral movement of the Tiber,

while little is known about the infrastructure linked to the Portus-to-Ostia canal, likely completed during the time of Hadrian, which remains poorly investigated. The greatest concentration of port infrastructure was to be found on the Portuensis side instead (nine-ten sites, against seven-eight on the Ostiensis, and one-two on the Isola Sacra) and port infrastructure there has the highest relative importance when compared with other types of occupation (20-30%, against 15-17% on the Ostiensis and 7-8% on Isola Sacra), which may point to a port service role of this river bank.

While storage facilities increase over time in the Ostiensis and Isola Sacra hinterlands, curiously no such trend is observable on the Portuensis bank, despite its port infrastructure and proposed role in river transport. Between the 1st and the 3rd century AD both Ostia and Portus witnessed outstanding increases in storage capacity through construction of warehouses at both sites,[17] but clearly this was not enough and the growing presence of storage infrastructure outside Portus, Ostia, and Rome is indicative of the need to expand the storage capacity of the port system. The exclusion of the Portuensis hinterland from such developments is curious. It could be that the massive increase of the storage capacity at Portus itself made any further development on this side of the river redundant, or storage was simply not the designated function of this Tiber bank before goods reached the capital itself.

Other categories of occupation reveal additional trends. Settlement numbers remain relatively stable across all areas and periods (in the case of Isola Sacra after its establishment and increase in Period 2), with the exception of the Ostiensis hinterland where between Periods 4 and 5 there is a 33% decrease. Interestingly, other types of sites in the Ostiensis area do not decline as sharply, or not at all (e.g. the quantity of port and storage infrastructure remains constant), which seems to suggest a depopulation of the countryside rather than reduced importance of the lower Tiber's left bank within the port and transport system. Funerary evidence, conversely, shows a distinctive trend of general growth across time, which in the case of Ostiensis and Portuensis hinterlands can clearly be linked to the growth of the metropolitan cemeteries along the routes of the two roads.

5. Linking Occupation and Communication Axes in the Lower Tiber Valley

Due to the strategic importance that the Lower Tiber Valley played in connecting Rome to its maritime and fluvial ports, and via them the wider Empire, the area contained a number of important axes of

---

[13] Keay and Millett 2005a, 13.

[14] Pavolini 2002; Pensabene 2007: 434-38.

[15] The mentioned sites include two *villae* in Ficana (Cordano 1981: 108-10; Fischer-Hansen 1990: 63-85 and one at Dragoncello (Pellegrino 1983), a possible temple (Pellegrino 1984; Zevi 2002: 18), and funerary structures, such as the tomb of *M. Antonius Antius Lupus* (s.v. *M. Antonii Antii Lupi Sepulcrum* in *LTURS* I, 72-74 (A. Bianchi)), and the tombs mentioned in Vaglieri 1907: 285.

[16] Port infrastructure is taken to incorporate all structures enhancing the connectivity between land and water, usually placed where the two environments meet. Examples include landing facilities such as moles and quays, as well as other support port infrastructure (e.g. lighthouses).

[17] Keay and Millett 2005b, in particular, table 9.1, pp. 302-03; Boetto *et al.* 2016.

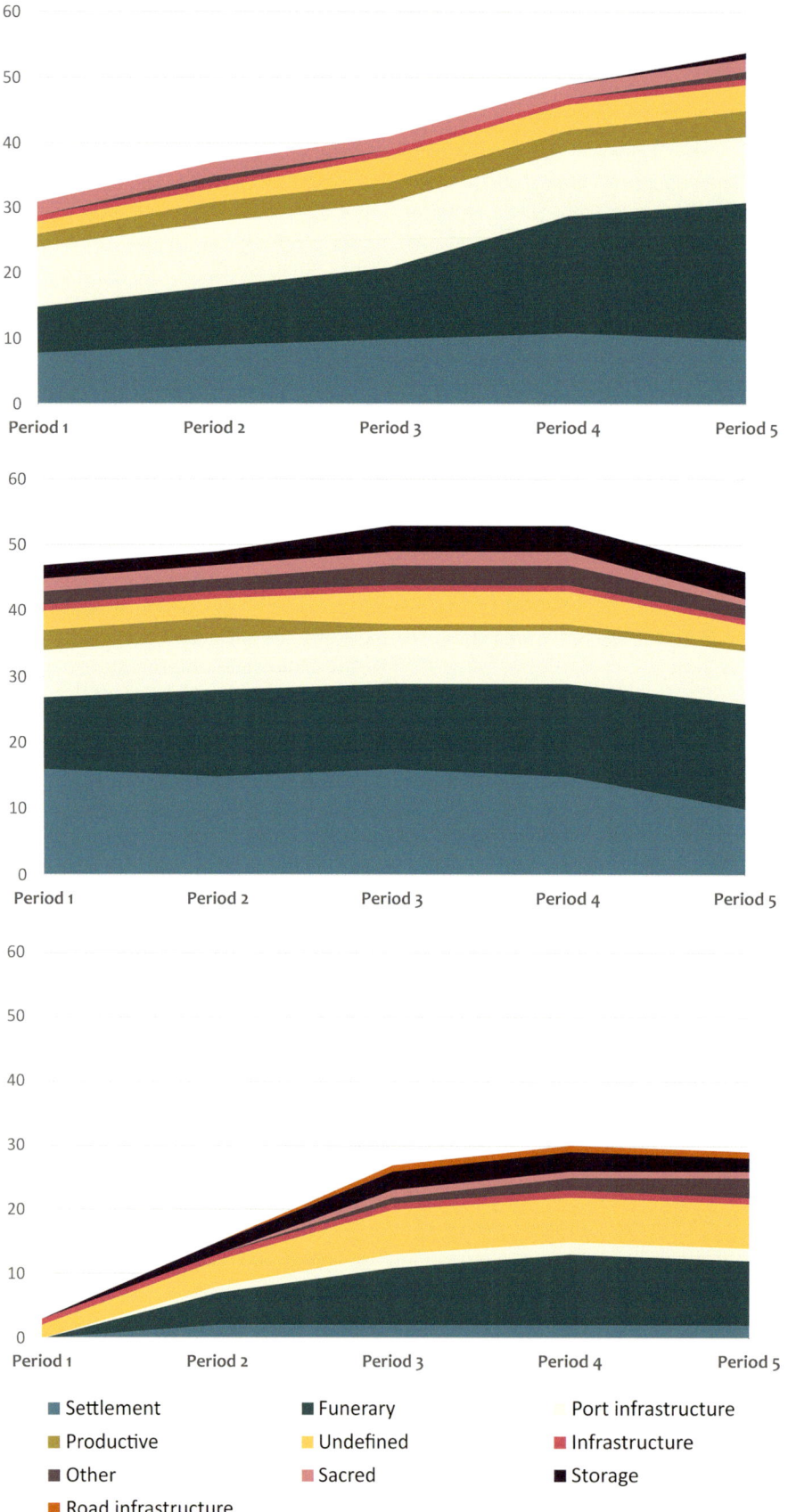

Figure 20.5. Development of occupation in the *via Campana/Portuensis* (upper), the *via Ostiensis* (centre), and the *via Flavia* (lower) hinterlands through time (source: M.C. Moreno Escobar).

communication on a fairly small territory. The following analyses aim to clarify the influence of these axes on how the area was occupied. The potential relationship between communication axes and occupation will be explored using two different parameters: first, the proximity between communication axes and sites (based on Euclidean distance), and second, the visibility from the communication axes to sites in the area.

a. Exploring Proximity

The visual inspection of the maps in Figures 20.2 and 20.4 hints at the influence of roads in articulating the occupation of the Lower Tiber Valley. This possibility remains strong even after discounting the relatively high proportion of funerary sites present in the dataset (33%), as these are known to have been roadside by design.[18] In order to achieve a more integrated picture, alongside roads we will include the River Tiber as a communication axis in our proximity analysis. Our focus will be on the areas in the immediate surroundings of roads and the river, defined as a distance of up to 100m from each.

The analysis thus conducted revealed a close relationship between archaeological sites and communication axes (Figure 20.6): of the 164 sites, 50 (30%) are found within the 100m buffer zone of the Tiber, and 57 (35%) within 100m of the roads. More interestingly, there are 14 sites (9%) within 100m of both the river and the roads, pointing at potential transhipment locations. Contextualising these figures historically reveals several trends (Figure 20.6). The river had a stronger pull on the occupation of the valley than the roads between Periods 1 and 3. This situation changes in Period 4 when road-orientated sites overtake those in the vicinity of the river, a trend that continues into Period 5. It is also interesting that the potential locations of transhipment (understood as sites placed in the intersection areas of the road and river buffers) increased from the time of the Claudian foundation of Portus (from seven in Period 1 to ten in Period 2 and 13 in Periods 3 to 5) (Table 20.3) and that the majority are located on the Ostiensis side of the Tiber Valley. This is unsurprising bearing in mind that the *via Ostiensis* is closer to the Tiber along longer stretches than the *via Portuensis*, but is also likely linked with this side hosting more storage facilities, more settlements that some of these transhipment points likely served, and offering links to a number of secondary roads.[19] Ammianus Marcellinus describes one such transhipment

operation: the transport of a 32m obelisk for the Circus Maximus in 357, which was brought by ship till *vicus Alexandri*, then transported along the *via Ostiensis* for *c.* 4km to the city.[20] It is interesting to note that although the Portuensis side had more port infrastructure, it has less in terms of transhipment points, which coupled with the storage facilities also being grouped on the Ostiensis side, underscores once more the functional duality of the two river margins.

While the cited figures speak clearly of a close association between the occupation of the area and the vicinity of the river and the roads, proximity alone, however, may not be the most appropriate means to explore these relationships. A high number of funerary sites, traditionally located along the roads, and locations of port infrastructure that are inherently situated in close proximity to the river could be largely boosting these trends. A more nuanced approach would be to use visibility as a means to explore the impact of these communication axes in the territorial configuration of the Tiber Valley, under the assumption that if the communication axes were indeed factors influencing the territorial organisation, the sites would appear in the areas visible from these axes.

b. Exploring Visibility

In order to explore the intervisibility between the sites on the one hand, and the roads and the Tiber on the other, we will rely on the application of the concept of fuzzy viewsheds[21] and its implementation within GIS environments,[22] which in contrast to other ways of estimating visibility (e.g. binary viewsheds)[23] allows for the decay in visual acuity related to the increasing distance between the observer and the features in the landscape to be accounted for, as well as to take into consideration the size of the elements seen. Using this approach, we calculated multiple fuzzy viewsheds from observers distributed every 200m along the communication axes active in the periods under study (i.e. the *via Campana/Portuensis*, the *via Ostiensis*, and the River Tiber),[24] with an exception of the *via Flavia*

---

18 Cf. Hesberg and Zanker 1987.
19 In addition to the *vicus Alexandri* discussed below, another example of a possible transhipment point can be found mid-way along the *via Ostiensis* in Torrino Mezzocammino where we find remains of few structures close to both the river and the road, in the vicinity of an intersection between the *via Ostiensis* and a secondary road, with several settlements within a 1.5km radius (Mancini 1913).

20 *Rerum gestarum libri* XXVII, 4.14; s.v. *Alexandri Vicus* in *LTURS* I, 42-43 (P.M. Barbini).
21 A fuzzy viewshed represents (cartographically) how visible an object is depending on its size and the distance from the observer (Rášová 2014). For an introduction to this topic, see also Fisher 1994.
22 For its implementation within GIS, see Ogburn 2006; Rášová 2014; Moreno Escobar 2022.
23 A binary viewshed represents the visible and non-visible areas from the location of one or more observers. For an introduction on the topic, see Wheatley and Gillings 2002: 204-06.
24 The analyses were carried out using the ESRI ArcGIS 10.1 software. Observers were placed every 200m, with a defined height of 1.60m, representing the height of the eyes of an adult walking along the roads, and at 2.60m to represent an individual sailing along the Tiber on a *navis caudicaria* (accounting for 1m of air draught). Given the diversity of archaeological sites and structures present the height of the features observed was set conservatively at 2m above the surface, reflecting the height of standing architectural structures,

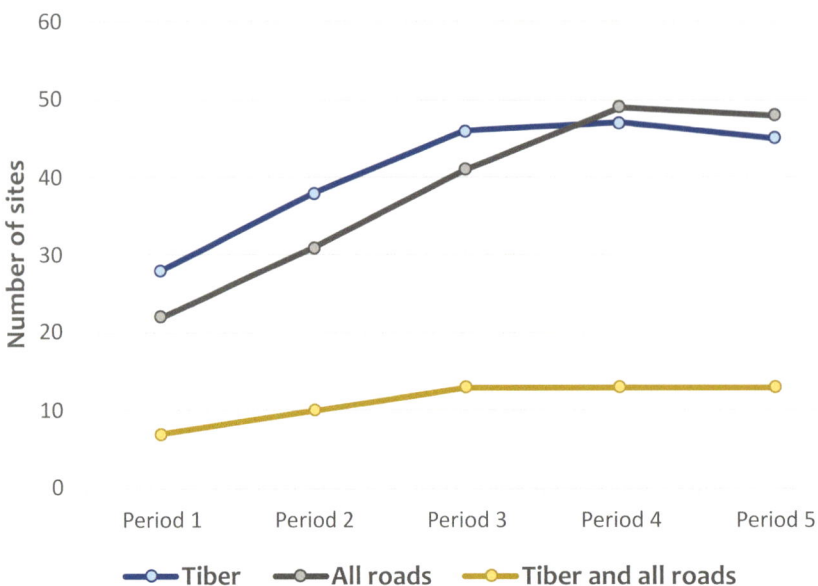

Figure 20.6. Number of sites within 100m of the Tiber, the roads, and both the Tiber and the roads across time (source: M.C. Moreno Escobar).

Table 20.3. Number of sites with a potential role as transhipment location in the *via Campana/Portuensis*, the *via Ostiensis*, and the *via Flavia* hinterlands through time (source: M.C. Moreno Escobar).

Hinterland	Period 1	Period 2	Period 3	Period 4	Period 5
Campana/Portuensis	0	1	2	2	2
Ostiensis	7	7	7	7	7
Flavia	0	2	4	4	4
Total	7	10	13	13	13

which was left out due to the insufficient quality of the Digital Elevation Model[25] for Isola Sacra to guarantee representative results. This procedure resulted in the calculation of *c.* 500 individual fuzzy viewsheds from the Tiber and the roads for each of the periods under study, which were then added up to calculate cumulative fuzzy viewsheds[26] for each of the communication axes

in each of the periods (for an example[27] of the viewshed from the *via Ostiensis*, see Figure 20.7). Based on this data we were able to estimate the visual ranges of individual communication axes (i.e. how far you could see from each of them), and then compare them against the distribution of known archaeological sites in each period, enabling us to identify which sites were visible and which not. These findings were then converted into summaries showing the relative proportions of visible/non-visible sites from each axis (Figure 20.8), and in order to explore if the observable trends are a reflection of a change in the organisation of these areas, we further disaggregated this data by period

as well as the active use of port infrastructure by individuals. These analyses were performed over a modified DEM that removed the main modern road infrastructure in the Tiber Valley and modified the modern course of the river to represent the known situation from the antiquity (more details in Moreno Escobar 2022).

[25] The model combined the LiDAR-based DTM of the Ministero dell'Ambiente e della Tutela del Territorio e del Mare (2013 version) and data from the TIN Italy raster dataset (Tarquini *et al.* 2012). This model has been used for all analyses and in all the figures in this paper.

[26] Cumulative fuzzy viewsheds could be considered as the sum of several fuzzy viewshed maps; they represent how clearly an object can be seen by multiple observers, depending on the size of the object and the distance from the observers.

[27] Given the limitations of this paper, it is not possible to show all cumulative fuzzy viewsheds calculated for each period and route of communication (one viewshed per route (3) per period (5), a total of 15). This multiplicity of viewsheds is derived from the need to acknowledge the diachronic changes in the topography occurring in the Lower Tiber Valley between Period 1 and 3; for more details on this, see Moreno Escobar 2022.

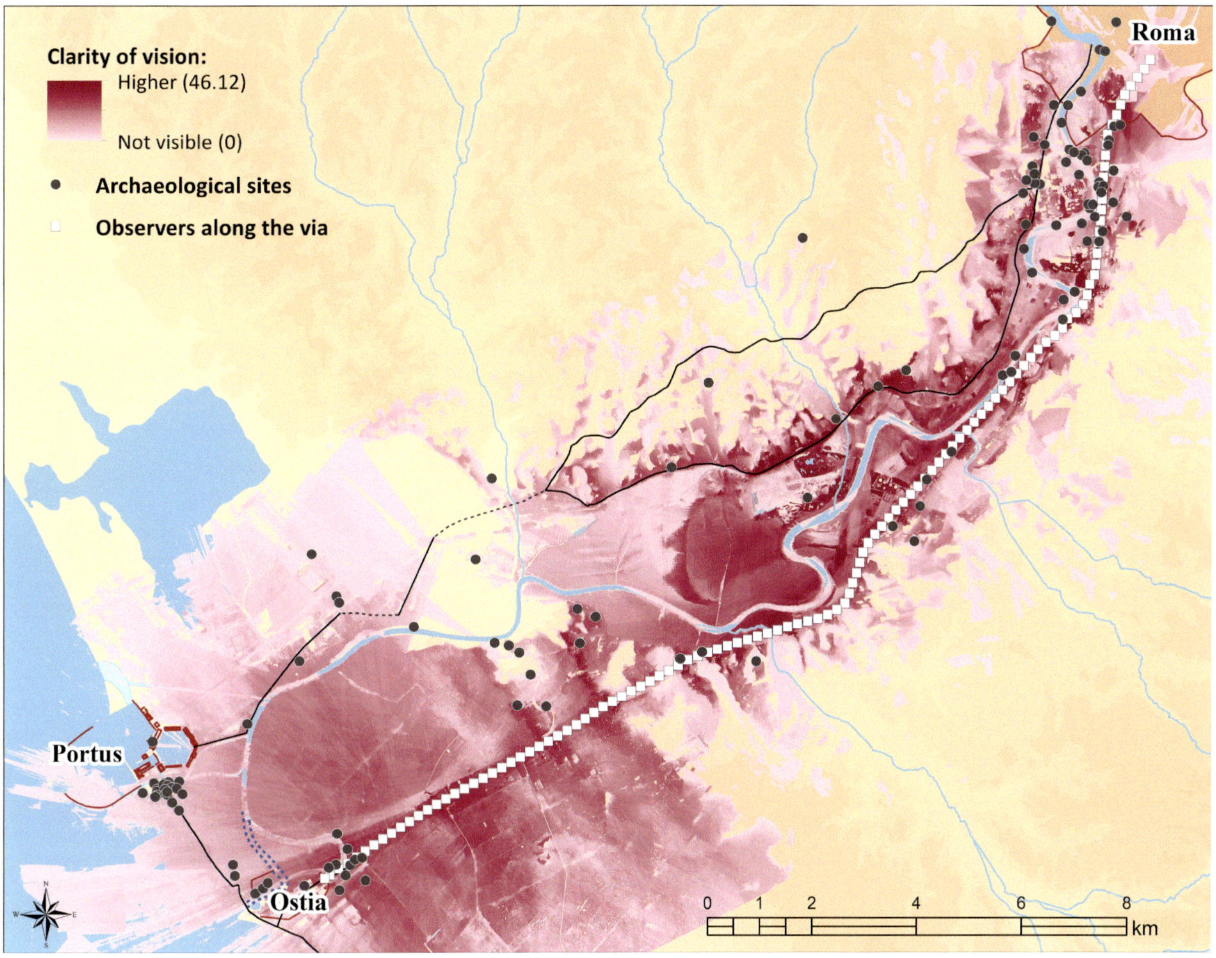

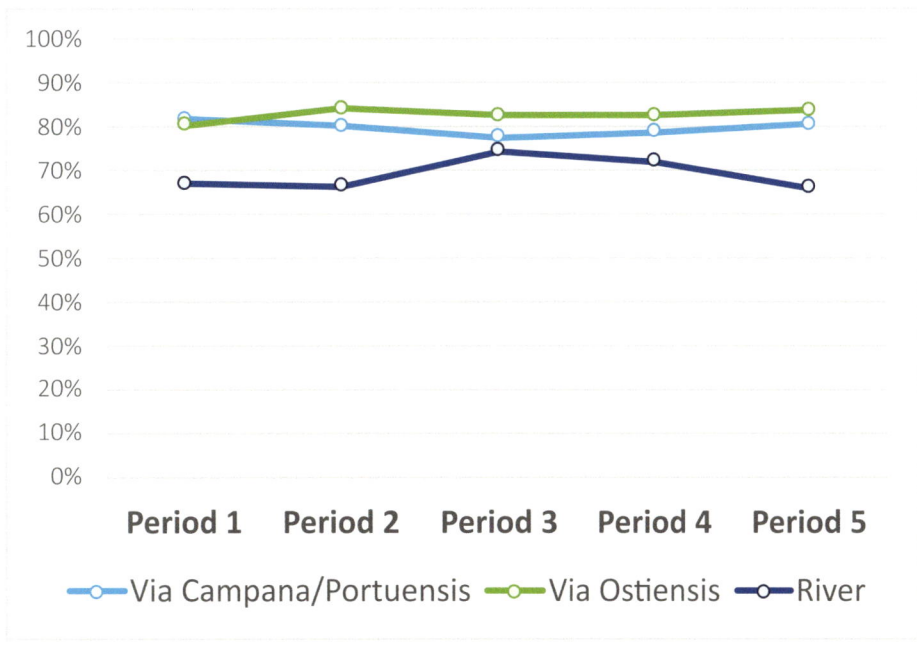

Figure 20.7. Example of a cumulative fuzzy viewshed along the *via Ostiensis* in Period 3 (source: M.C. Moreno Escobar).

Figure 20.8. Percentage of visible sites from the via *Campana/Portuensis*, the via *Ostiensis*, and the
River Tiber through time (source: M.C. Moreno Escobar).

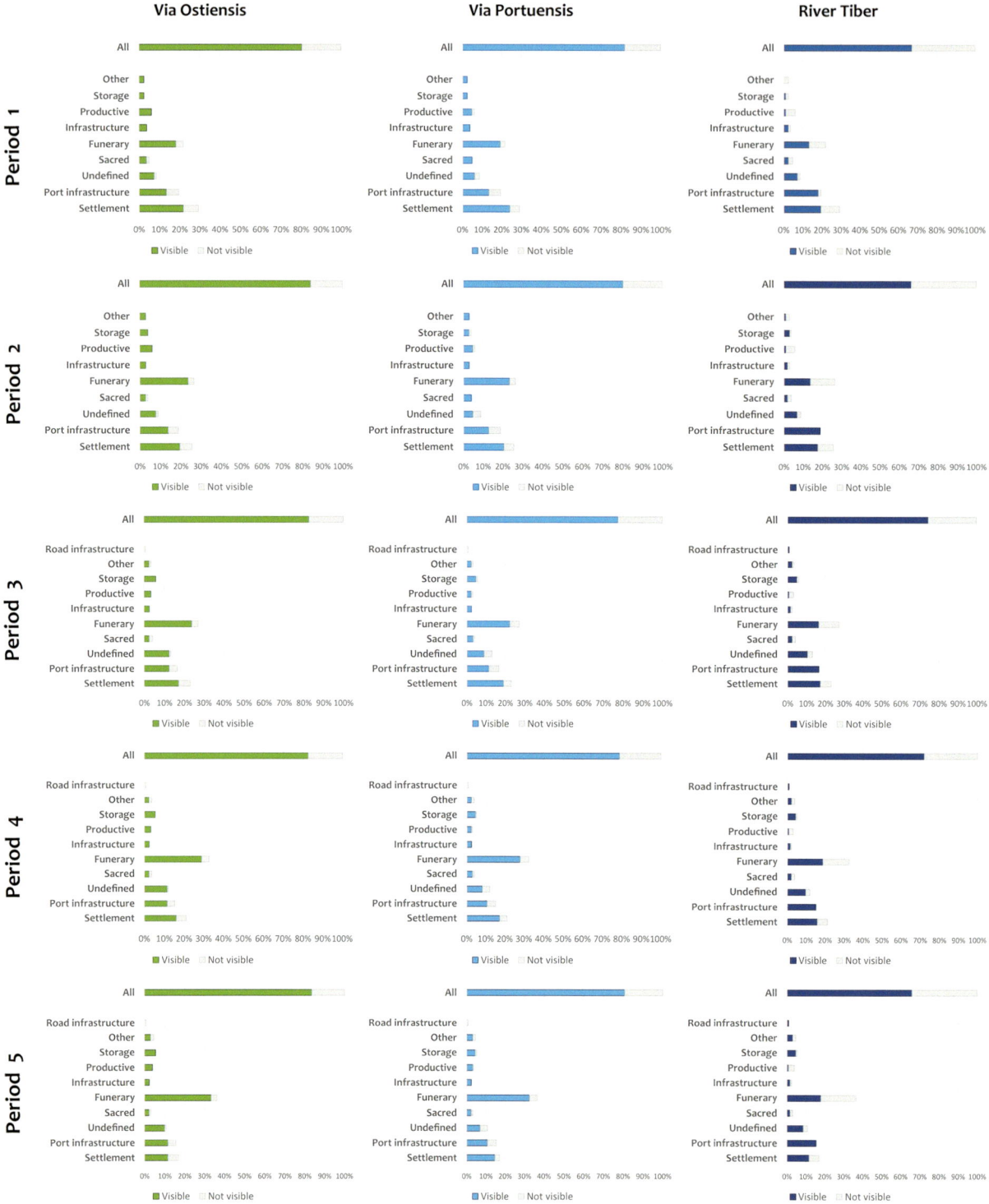

Figure 20.9. Relative proportion of sites visible and not visible from the via *Campana/Portuensis*, the via *Ostiensis* and the River Tiber in the periods under study (source: M.C. Moreno Escobar).

and type of occupation (Figure 20.9). These analyses together with individual viewshed results informed the discussion that follows.

As we can observe in Figure 20.8, the larger proportion of sites was visible from the roads than from the river through time, and the trend holds across all site types (Figure 20.9). In Period 1 the highest percentage of sites visible from the road is found in the Portuensis hinterland (82%), marginally higher than of the Ostiensis (80%). This trend inverts in Period 2, when the *via Ostiensis* becomes the one with the highest percentage of sites visible (84%), mainly due to the higher number of visible funerary sites (cf. Figure 20.9), the primacy it will keep for the rest of the study period. In Period 3 it will have 5% more visible sites than the Portuensis, even though at this precise moment the percentage of visible sites from both roads decreases. The percentage of sites visible from the roads will increase again from the Period 4 onwards, and those visible from the river will decrease.

While the percentages related to road visibility vary almost negligibly, the situation with the Tiber is a little different. The Tiber visibility registers the highest fluctuation: after remaining stable in Periods 1 and 2, when the proportion of visible sites was 67% and 66% respectively, Period 3 sees a marked increase to 74% of sites visible from the river. This rise is attributed to new storage facilities, funerary, and undefined sites.

The increase in storage facilities is made up of newly founded sites on the riverfront related to the transhipment activities discussed earlier, and underscores once more the rising importance of river transport after the construction of Portus and the further development of Rome's port system.

The change in the number of funerary sites visible from the river, on the other hand, could be taken as evidence of the revaluation of the river as a communication axis between the city of Rome and its maritime front. Roman tombs have a long history of being positioned along the thoroughfares, designed to catch a passer-by's eye, with epitaphs that directly engage with the observer, all in an effort to perpetuate memory.[28] In all periods we find tombs of well-off Romans being positioned in locations visible from the river, often in a place where they would be much less visible from the nearby road (and sometimes not visible at all), clearly showing that the river is a more prestigious thoroughfare. Thus, we find a riverside mausoleum at Santa Passera, turned into a defensive tower for the local dock in the Middle Ages, while at Idrovore della Magliana the 'il Trullo dei Massimi' mausoleum is still visible to the passing river

traffic.[29] It is highly likely that these tombs were located on the land owned by the deceased, but knowing that visibility was an important factor in tomb location, the choice to position them towards the river rather than facing a road or an entrance to their properties, as was a preference at the time,[30] clearly indicates the prestige of the riparian location. From Period 2 it is no longer just the elite burials, but also necropoleis that favour visibility from the river than from the road, in particular those located in the wider area of the Tiber delta,[31] where the traffic along the natural and artificial waterways would have been particularly lively. Despite the general decrease in the proportion of visible sites, this trend seems to continue into Period 4 (58% of the funerary sites are visible from the river in Period 4, compared to 61% in Period 3), although the increase in the proportion of non-visible funerary sites likely indicates that the river's prestige is starting to decrease, a trend that continues in Period 5.

6. Discussion

The three roads featured in this study have very different histories. The *via Campana/Portuensis* and the *via Ostiensis* are roads of great antiquity, both possibly starting off as a southern continuation of the *via Salaria*,[32] facilitating transport of salt collected at the mouth of the Tiber further into Lazio. Along the course of both roads there were extraction activities, mainly tufa and pozzolana quarries,[33] with their output likely being transported both along the roads and via the river. The initial transport function of both roads is underlined by the choice of their routes. A cost surface analysis for the *via Campana/Portuensis* has shown both branches of the road taking the highly efficient route through the topography of the right bank of the Tiber,[34] and while there was no space in this paper to conduct the same analysis for the *via Ostiensis*, it seems extremely likely that the same rationale was followed. Their shared function, as well as geographical proximity, was likely the reason why the same official was in charge of the *via Campana* and the *via Ostiensis*,[35] clearly designating them as a part of a joint system.

We would like to return briefly to the proposed duality of the *via Campana/Portuensis* at this point. The presented analyses, as well as recent archaeological excavations at Ponte Galeria, indicate that Claudius's mid-1st-century AD 'construction of the *via Portuensis*' most

---

[28] Koortbojian 1996; Hope 2009: 151-82.

[29] For the Santa Passera mausoleum, see Kammerer-Grothaus 2000; for il Trullo dei Massimi, Tomassetti 1979b: 347, 372-75.

[30] Griesbach 2007: esp. 28-30, 50-56, 146-49; Borg 2019: 24-27.

[31] Buzzetti and Virgili 1985: 435, 438-40; Keay *et al.* 2020, G16, G19, G20, G32, G34, G35, G39, G40.

[32] Quilici 1990: 69, 89.

[33] Cianfriglia and Filippini 1987; Roggio 2012: UC 73, UC 76, UC 83, UC 104, UC 113; Buccellato and Coletti 2014.

[34] Moreno Escobar 2009.

[35] *CIL* VI 1610, *CIL* X 1795.

likely represented merely an addition of a road section connecting the new imperial port and the *via Campana* (which originally terminated in the salt pans north-east of Portus),[36] a partial restoration of the *via Campana*,[37] and a consolidation of a pre-existing northern branch of the road between present-day Pozzo Pantaleo and Ponte Galeria. This northern branch was only around 1km shorter than the old *via Campana* section, and in addition more rugged,[38] making it unlikely that it was conceived merely as a short-cut. Instead, this section offered a hillside alternative to the *via Campana* during floods,[39] a concern further addressed by the construction of viaducts on the final stretches of the road towards Portus.[40] The existence of sites along the northern branch that predate Portus reveals that this stretch was already in use as an alternative route in times of floods at least since the Republican period, now being formalised and consolidated under Claudius and Trajan rather than constructed from scratch. The low-lying branch of the *via Campana* seems to have remained the primary route though whenever conditions allowed it, as sites continue to gravitate primarily towards it. The fact that no source actually distinguishes between the *via Campana* and *via Portuensis*, with the later name coming into use at some point before the 3rd century AD,[41] points to the two branches with a common course at the origin and terminus being viewed as a single communication route. It is now equally clear that though lying relatively low in the Tiber Valley the *via Campana* could not have served as a hauling road, as some have suggested,[42] since its known stretches are too far from the river.[43] As on the Ostiensis site, that function was instead fulfilled by a '*strada delle bufale*'/'*via del tiro delle barche*', a route closely hugging the riverbank that has been attested as separate from the *via Campana/Portuensis*/Via della Magliana in cartography till the late medieval period,[44] and it is this road, perhaps little

more than a dirt path, that the sources are referring to in reference to ship hauling,[45] and not the *via Campana*.

Though both the *via Ostiensis* and the *via Campana/ Portuensis* start off as transport and commercial links between Lazio/Rome and the Tyrrhenian coast, their development trajectories diverge at one point, likely from the time of the establishment of Rome's first maritime colony – Ostia.[46] The *via Ostiensis* is now linking two settlements and, with Ostia becoming Rome's maritime gateway, also supporting overseas traffic. A towpath would have been presently constructed, facilitating the transfer of goods via hauled rivercraft to the growing facilities at *Emporium* and *Portus Tiberinus*.[47] Numerous individuals have departed from the capital down the *via Ostiensis*, possibly most famously Paul who is believed to have walked the road to sail out of Ostia, leading to the *via Ostiense* becoming a pilgrimage route in later centuries.[48] In the Imperial period Ostia enjoyed imperial patronage and that of Roman senators and knights, as did its wider hinterland.[49] The area just south of Ostia became popular with wealthy men in the Republic, with the number of villas increasing in the 2nd century AD, and the villa owners used the *via Ostiensis* and the *via Laurentina* (which branched off from the *via Ostiensis* at two different locations),[50] to reach their properties. Pliny the Younger, who himself had a villa near Laurentum, describes this scenic and pleasant road journey and highlights the role that Ostia played in attending to the villa owners' needs.[51] The *via Ostiensis* was clearly a route that served several metropolitan elite networks, making it an attractive location for the well-off suburban *domus*, *horti*, and villas, as well as burials.[52] Even after the intensity of occupation in the

---

[36] The original course of the last section of the *via Campana* is not clear, see Serlorenzi and Di Giuseppe 2009.

[37] A section of the *via Campana* excavated at Ponte Galeria testifies to this intervention, as well as to further significant rebuilding work by Trajan (Serlorenzi *et al.* 2004; Arnoldus Huyzendveld *et al.* 2009).

[38] The length of the upper branch, as reconstructed in our model, is 11,866m, while the lower branch measures 13,043m; the mean slope of the northern route is 5.3°, while that of the southern one is 4.5°.

[39] As there are no hydrology models for the Lower Tiber Valley known to the authors that take into account palaeotopography outside of the city of Rome, it is not possible to decisively prove this hypothesis. Bearing in mind, however, that the lateral extent of the valley is still fairly constrained on that section of the Tiber causing the flood water to rise higher, and that during some of the recorded floods water levels reached even the modern Via Portuense (Bersani and Bencivenga 2001, fig. 8), it seems inevitable that the lower branch of the road would have suffered from regular flooding. The authors would like to thank Ferréol Salomon (CNRS) for the helpful discussion of the topic.

[40] Arnoldus Huyzendveld *et al.* 2009.

[41] Scheid 1976: 645; Serra 2007: 19.

[42] Originally suggested by R. Lanciani in Henzen 1868: 106, later championed by Scheid 1976 and followed by many.

[43] Cf. Arnoldus Huyzendveld *et al.* 2009; Serlorenzi and Di Giuseppe 2009 for the Ponte Galeria section.

[44] Serra 2007: 19; Tella 2018: 56 and fig. 16.

[45] Procopius (*Goth.* 1.26) describes the process on the Portuensis side of the river. For a full list of ancient sources that refer to ships being towed up the Tiber along both banks, see Malmberg 2015: n. 12.

[46] Unfortunately, we are not in a position to offer settlement analysis in support of this hypothesis as the events fall outside of the chronological scope of this paper.

[47] For a proposed reconstruction of the towing route on the Ostiensis bank, see Aguilera Martín 2012, esp. 111-13. For a concise bibliography on the commercial and storage facilities at the *via Ostiensis* terminus, see s.v. *Emporium* in *LTUR* II, 221-23 (C. Mocchegiani Carpano), s.v. *Porticus Aemilia* in *LTUR* IV, 116-17 (F. Coarelli), Aguilera Martín 2002: 54-104; Serlorenzi and Sebastiani 2008; Bisconti and Ferri 2018: 20-42.

[48] *The Apocryphal Acts of Peter*, chapter 3; on the Christianisation of the *via Ostiensis*, see Bisconti and Ferri 2018: 75-87, 101-38.

[49] For the town, see Meiggs 1973: 41-82; in the hinterland, the *vicus Laurentium Augustanorum* counted members of the Ostian council and a procurator *annonae* (*CIL* XIV 341, 2045) among its patrons.

[50] At the third and the eleventh mile of the *via Ostiensis*, cf. Tomassetti 1979a.

[51] Plin., *Ep.* 2.17.

[52] E.g. the tomb of Ser. Sulpicius Galba (*CIL* I 695 = *ILS* 863), a suburban *domus* of Marco Annio Vero (Roggio 2012: UC 11), several villas in the area of the later Basilica San Paolo fuori le Mura (Roggio 2012: UC 21, UC 90, UC 94), the *horti olitorii* owned by the *collegium magnum arkarum Faustinarum matris et Piae* (*CIL* VI 33840 = *ILS* 7455), multiple villas in the vicinity of Tenuta del Torrino, Vitinia and Dragoncello (De Franceschini 2005: nos 87-92), the property belonging to Symmachus was likely located in Ficana (*Epistulae* 2.52.2; 3.82; 6.72), a large mausoleum at *vicus Alexandri* belonged to M. Anonius Antius Lupus (s.v. *M. Antonii Antii Lupi Sepulcrum* in *LTURS* I, 72-74 (A. Bianchi)), a

Portuensis hinterland surpasses that of the Ostiensis side in Period 5, the well-to-do still opted for the left Tiber bank location for their residences.[53]

The *via Campana/Portuensis* hinterland seems to have attracted much less elite attention. The area at the outskirts of the *horti Caesaris* hosted several sanctuaries,[54] and further down the road the collegium of the *Fratres Arvales* maintained the Dea Dia cult,[55] founded according to tradition by Romulus himself. A number of private estates can be identified along the road, some through *fistulae* providing names of their owners,[56] while others are known from excavation; the latter reveal properties that could be described as comfortable production farms, not on par with the luxury suburban villas found in the Ostiensis hinterland.[57] Rural settlements seem to have been more common on this side of the river instead, with one epigraphically attested in the area of Janiculum,[58] and several known from archaeological evidence in the area of Ponte Galeria.[59] A relative lack of activity along the *via Campana/Portuensis* is not surprising for the Republican period when the road led to the salt pans at the mouth of the Tiber and not much else, but it is interesting that no great changes are observable after the road received an imperial harbour installation at its marine terminus in the mid-1st century AD. Rural

settlements and farms seem to in fact decline during the 2nd century AD,[60] at least in the area closest to Portus. While the rising number of funerary sites primarily relates to the metropolitan necropolis outside Porta Portese expanding into the disued republican tufa quarry,[61] mirroring the contemporary development of the *via Ostiensis* necropolis, the only observable growth along the *via Campana/Portuensis* following the establishment of Portus is an increase in the port infrastructure, reflecting the growing importance of the Tiber traffic.[62] The already-mentioned increase in the Tiber-facing position of the funerary monuments on the Portuensis bank further highlights the importance of the river communication corridor in comparison to the road, which clearly gained no prestige following the establishment of Portus. Signs of reversal of fortunes observable through the intensification of settlement in the Portuensis hinterland start from Period 4 and are likely linked to the growth and a legal recognition of the civilian settlement at Portus in the early 4th century.

Instead of the *via Campana/Portuensis*, it was the *via Flavia* that gained from Portus's foundation. Clearly built for the purpose of linking Portus and Ostia, the *via Flavia* likely had two primary roles. Research at Portus has thus far provided no evidence of living quarters and while one can think of a number of alternative living arrangements and locations,[63] these are unlikely to amount to significant numbers and the large workforce that would have been required at Portus likely commuted to the site instead. A few possibly came from the Portuensis hinterland, where some burial but no settlement evidence attests to their presence,[64] but the majority likely used the *via Flavia*. Moreover, apart from those arriving on important imperial business, it is unlikely that Portus offered any facilities for those coming to or through the port. Instead, those that had to linger at the port would have had to proceed to Isola Sacra, where immediately south of the *Fossa Traiana* we find a set of *thermae* (di Matidia) and further remains that might indicate a *statio*, as well as another *thermae* in the north-western corner of the island,[65] or continue to Ostia, which had facilities for visitors with any paying power. Commuters and visitors travelling

---

property of the Acilii Glabriones family was located in the vicinity of Acilia (*CIL* VI 809 = *CIL* XIV 74), and an imperial family sarcophagus from the first half of the 3rd century that was found in a secondary position near Casal Palocco came from Acilia too (Andreae 1969). For further epigraphic evidence attesting to elite properties in the Ostiensis hinterland, see Bisconti and Ferri 2018: 45-48.

[53] In Period 1 we find only three villas in the Campana/Portuensis hinterland, compared to 13 in the *Ostiensis*. By period 4 there are still only five villas on the Campana/Portuensis side (the maximum number reached), compared to 12 on the *Ostiensis*. Even as settlement density on the Ostiensis drops off in Period 5, it still has seven villas compared to four in the Campana/Portuensis hinterland. In Franceschini's survey of villas on the wider territory of Rome, she links only two villas to the *via Campana/Portuensis*, compared with seven related to the *via Ostiensis* (De Franceschini 2005: 347).

[54] E.g. two sanctuaries of Hercules (*Herculis Hesychiani sacellum* (*AE* 1924, 15) and *Herculis Victoris aedes* (*CIL* VI 332 = *ILS* 1135)). Another sanctuary to Hercules was made in the wall of the quarry further down the road (*CIL* VI 30891 a-b, 30892). Existence of a sanctuary to Bel and Dea Syria is postulated based on inscription finds (s.v. *Beli Aedes* in *LTURS* I, 217-19 (E. Equini Schneider), s.v. *Deae Syriae templum* in *LTURS* II, 191-96 (S. Ensoli)), while Fors Fortuna sanctuaries were to be found on the first and the sixth mile of the road (s.v. *Fortis Fortunae fanum, templum* in *LTURS* II, 271-72 (F. Coarelli)).

[55] Broise *et al.* 1987; Scheid 1990

[56] E.g. *Grapti praedium* (*CIL* XV 7466), *Candidae praedium* (*CIL* XV 7634), *Caedicii Crescentis praedium* (*LTURS* II, no. 167, p. 23 (W. Eck)), *Cocceiani et Titiani horti* (*CIL* VI 8675, 29772), *domus L. Valerius Paetus* (Iacopi 1943: 44).

[57] E.g. villas at Colle dell'Infernaccio, Magliana Vecchia (De Franceschini 2005, nos 79 and 86), and Ospedale della Vittoria (Mancini 1924).

[58] *Ianicolensis pagus*, attested on inscriptions from the late 2nd/early 1st century BC (*CIL* VI 2219, 2220). It has been recently proposed that another rural settlement, *vicus Septem Caesaris* (*CIL* IX 4680; XIV 2886; VI 712), was also located along the *via Campana* (Aguilera Martín 2012: 115), but its location is highly uncertain.

[59] Petriaggi *et al.* 1995; Serlorenzi *et al.* 2004: 49; Morelli *et al.* 2011, Sito 4.

[60] cf. Petriaggi *et al.* 1995: 366-68; Serlorenzi *et al.* 2004: 49.

[61] Tomassetti 1979b: 327-31, 339-43, 354; Cianfriglia 2006.

[62] On the increase of Tiber traffic following the development of Portus, see Malmberg 2015.

[63] One could envisage e.g. workers residing in living quarters on the upper floors of warehouses, some sleeping on ships, or in shanty towns in the vicinity of the port that have left no trace.

[64] Two Imperial-period necropoleis have been excavated north-east of Portus, at Castel Malnome and at Tenuta de Ducca (Cianfriglia *et al.* 2003; Fabrizio Felici, pers. comm.). Most graves were of adult males whose skeletal remains revealed a life of hard manual labour. The Castel Malnome burials have, however, been associated with the workforce of the nearby salt pans, with osteological material displaying work-specific stress markers.

[65] For the mentioned Isola Sacra sites, see Keay *et al.* 2020, G7, G10, G12.

between Portus and Ostia could have completed the journey on foot in under an hour,[66] with the necropolis of Isola Sacra that rapidly developed along the *via Flavia* providing the 'street front' for parts of their journey, attesting to the growing importance of this communication route.

At the time of the foundation of Portus, the functionality of Ostia's own port was significantly diminished; recent geological research seems to suggest that from some time in the 1st century AD the harbour at the river mouth could serve only small craft thus precluding it from receiving large cargos, though opinions on the speed and the extent of the port's demise vary.[67] The *via Ostiensis*, however, never quite loses the transport function, due to transhipment logistics that we discussed earlier, and it is likely that some ship towing still took place on this bank to facilitate these operations. With the main transhipment of goods from maritime to fluvial craft now taking place at Portus and entering the Tiber along the right bank via *Fossa Traiana* and Canale Romano, it is the Portuensis side towpath that becomes the principal, and ultimately the only, ship hauling route into Rome.[68]

It is clear that the Ostiensis and the Campana/Portuensis hinterlands had slightly different functions in the transport system between the ports, the Tiber, and Rome. While the Ostiensis had a number of transhipment locations, all established in the period when Ostia handled Rome's maritime imports and kept in operation since, the Portuensis side had more general port facilities, but next to no points where goods from river craft could be transhipped onto land before reaching the city. Furthermore, the majority of the Portuensis port facilities have been established or significantly enlarged only after the establishment of Portus; clearly this bank had limited involvement with the river traffic between the mouth of the Tiber and Rome before that. The operation of the above-mentioned towpath, likely only constructed after the establishment of Portus, could be what predicated the functional difference between the two banks: men and animals needed to rest and spend a night during the several days that it took to pull the ships upstream to Rome,[69] for which landing facilities would have been required; at the same time, the transhipment activities

might have been avoided on this bank not to cause disruption to hauling operations.

It is also conceivable that some goods were transported from Portus to the capital directly along *via Campana/Portuensis*, never entering the river system. This would have certainly been the case when summer droughts and high waters and floods in autumn/winter disrupted navigation on the river,[70] but those might not have been the only times. The remains of the *via Campana/Portuensis* reveal it as very solidly built and in heavy use,[71] and its terminus in Trastevere, though less well known and investigated than the *Emporium* area on the left bank, had significant warehouse capacities with inscriptions attesting to a wealth of commercial and storage activities.[72] Some facilities were clearly designed to receive the goods transported on river craft, with extensive urban fluvial port and dock structures extending downstream for about 2km,[73] but their clear concentration around Porta Portese, both inside the city and for at least till the first milestone of the *via Campana/Portuensis* (where the marble fragment of Forma urbis from which these features are known ends),[74] points to the road being a significant transport artery into the capital. Furthermore, a cart could reach Rome in several hours, while we know it took three days to haul a boat from the seaport to Rome,[75] making the road a preferable route when speed rather than cost was of the essence.

While we can use different classes of evidence to discuss the transport of goods, the movement of people in this ports-roads-river-capital system leaves insufficient trace, allowing one only to speculate. One would assume that overseas passengers used roads to complete their voyage, given a significant difference in journey time. While those that moved from Portus to use the facilities at Ostia might have continued along the *via Ostiensis* into Rome, it is to be expected that the majority of people sailing via Portus would have used the *via Campana/Portuensis* for their journey, it being the significantly shorter route.[76] With Portus being a closely controlled piece of imperial infrastructure rather than a commercial port, and the operations at

---

[66] Keay *et al.* 2020: 168.

[67] Goiran *et al.* 2014, *contra* Vött *et al.* 2020.

[68] Aguilera Martín 2012: 111 is of the same opinion; *contra* Malmberg 2015: 192 who proposes three-lane traffic on the Tiber with both tow paths in operation and the middle lane being used by ships travelling downstream on the river's current. The width of the Tiber is, however, not sufficient to allow safe three-lane navigation of the *naves caudicariae* (Keay *et al.* 2021: 402-04), leading us to opt for the single tow path scenario.

[69] On the logistics of towing the ships up the Tiber in antiquity and later periods, see Le Gall 1953: 226-28, 257-58; Eckoldt 1980: 24-25; Malmberg 2015: 190-92; Tella 2018.

[70] Malmberg 2015: 189-90; Boetto 2016: 274-76.

[71] L. Borsari, *NSc* 1893: 519; *NSc* 1897: 147; Cianfriglia and Corsini 1986/87; Petriaggi *et al.* 2001; Catalli 2006.

[72] E.g. *CIL* VI 1152, 29702, 36954, s.v. *cella Civiciana* in *LTUR* I, 256 (L. Chioffi).

[73] Remains were investigated at Ponte de Mattatoio, Pietra Papa, the vicinity of Santa Passera, and in Zona della Magliana, cf. Castagnoli 1980; Mocchegiani Carpano 1984: 30-31; Tucci 2004.

[74] Lanciani 1988: 34.

[75] The three-day journey is attested in Philostr., *Vit. Apoll.* 7.16; see also Le Gall 1953: 255, 257.

[76] Based on our road reconstructions, the journey from Portus via Isola Sacra and then *via Ostiensis* to Rome is almost 27km long, while the same journey along the *via Campana/Portuensis* is 23.4km along the northern branch, and 24.6km on the southern branch. All distances are calculated with journeys terminating at the city walls.

Ostia's river port declining, it is unlikely that great numbers of private travellers came via this route. Ostia in its heyday mainly served those travelling from the western Mediterranean,[77] with some coming from Spain or Gaul now likely opting for disembarking at Centumcellae and continuing along the *via Aurelia* to the capital. Travellers from Greece normally arrived at Brindisi, and many from the East or Alexandria used Puteoli, both reaching Rome along the *via Appia*.[78]

As for those arriving through Portus on official business, we can only ponder at the numbers and the variety of these travellers. Using the quickest route into the city would have been essential for imperial messengers and couriers carrying information and post. We can be certain that the military was among the road's regular users. The fleets from Misenum and Ravenna had barracks in Rome that they used mainly in winter (the Misenum fleet was stationed on the *via Labicana*, while the *Castra Ravennatium* was in Trastevere).[79] Soldiers of both fleets likely went through Portus, and in the case of the Misenum fleet, this is confirmed by a letter from a sailor to his mother describing the journey.[80] Both Belisarius and Totila were certainly equally appreciative of the ease and speed of reaching Rome along the *via Portuensis* when manoeuvring their armies.[81] Imperial officials and likely emperors themselves travelled through Portus and along the *via Campana/Portuensis*, but we hear of no *profectiones* or *adventus* celebrated in relation to such travel.[82] If an emperor wanted to make a conspicuous entrance when travelling via the Tiber mouth to Rome, arriving by river seems to have been the approach of choice, with the upstream river journey adding a symbolic dimension to their voyage.[83] The *via Campana/Portuensis* – and Portus itself – clearly served the business rather than the ceremonial side of the imperial affairs. It is possible that the state and military use, the transport of goods along the road, and the hauling of ships on the right bank, cemented the perception of the former salt and agricultural produce road and its hinterland as less prestigious, further shaping the development of settlement patterns described in this study.

In this paper, we explore the dynamic relationship between people in the past and the regions they inhabited, aiming to ultimately cast new light onto the key period in the changing organisation of Rome's port system, its communication network, and the people that used it routinely. We approached this objective through a compilation and re-evaluation of a dispersed body of data, followed by a quantitative method involving computational and spatial analyses of the thus collected dataset to reveal patterns, and rounded off with a qualitative discussion where by integrating historical, epigraphic, archaeological, and geoarchaeological evidence we provided contextualisation and offered an interpretation of the observed patterns. It is our hope that the paper goes some way to demonstrate the potential that integrative approaches and interdisciplinary collaborations hold, and we offer it here in memory of a scholar who not only pioneered, championed, and excelled in such inquiry, but has also profoundly reshaped the scholarship on Roman ports, thus creating the proverbial shoulders that this study aspires to stand on.

Bibliography

Aguilera Martín, A. 2002. *El monte Testaccio y la llanura subaventina: topografía extra portam Trigeminam.* Madrid: Consejo Superior de Investigaciones Científicas.

Aguilera Martín, A. 2012. La sirga en el Tíber en época romana, in S.J. Keay (ed.) *Rome, Portus and the Mediterranean*: 105-23. London: The British School at Rome.

Andreae, B. 1969. *Processus Consularis*. Zur Deutung des Sarkophags von Acilia, in P. Zazoff (ed.) *Opus nobile: Festschrift zum 60. Geburtstag von Ulf Jantzen*: 1-13. Wiesbaden: Steiner.

Arnoldus Huyzendveld, A., A. Carbonara, C. Ceracchi and C. Morelli 2009. La viabilità nel territorio portuense, in C. Pavolini, V. Jolivet, M.A. Tomei and R. Volpe (eds) *Il suburbio di Roma dalla fine dell'età monarchica alla nascita del sistema delle ville (V–II secolo a.C.)*: 599-619. Rome: Ecole française de Rome.

Baldassarre, I. 1996. *Necropoli di Porto: Isola Sacra*. Rome: Istituto poligrafico e zecca dello stato, Libreria dello stato.

Bersani, P. and M. Bencivenga 2001. *Le piene del Tevere a Roma dal V secolo a.C. all'anno 2000*. Rome: Servizio Idrografico e Mareografico Nazionale, viewed 1 May 2025, <https://speleology.files.wordpress.com/2012/06/piene_tevere_roma.pdf>.

Bisconti, F., and Ferri, G. 2018. *La strada di Paolo: la via Ostiense dalle origini alla cristianizzazione*. Padua: Esedra.

Boetto, G. 2016. Portus, Ostia and Rome: a transport zone in maritime/land interface, in H.G. Kerstin, A. Brita and L. Adam (eds) *Ancient Ports: The Geography of Connections, International Conference at the Department of Archaeology and Ancient History*: 269-87. Uppsala: Uppsala Universitet.

---

[77] Plin., *HN* 19.1.

[78] Cf. Meiggs 1973: 56; Noy 2000: 141-44. The *Historia Augusta* claims that Septimius Severus built the Septizodium facing the *via Appia* for the sole purpose of greeting those arriving from Africa (SHA *Sev.* 24).

[79] *Castra Misenatium*: Lanciani 1988: 30 and *CIL* VI 1091; *Castra Ravennatium*: Giorgetti 1977.

[80] *P.Mich.* 8 490-91.

[81] Cf. Procop., *Goth.* 3.19.

[82] Lehnen 1997; 2001. For Claudius's underwhelming *adventus* at Ostia that predates the construction of Portus, see Suet., *Claud.* 38.1.

[83] Suet., *Tib.* 72.1; *Calig.* 15.1. On the symbolism of such an act, see Görler 1993.

Boetto, G., É. Bukowiecki, N. Monteix and C. Rousse 2016. Les Grandi Horrea d'Ostie, in B. Marin and C. Virlouvet (eds) *Entrepôts et trafics annonaires en Méditerranée: antiquité-temps modernes*: 177-226. Rome: École française de Rome.

Borg, B. 2019. *Roman Tombs and the Art of Commemoration: Contextual Approaches to Funerary Customs in the Second Century CE*. Cambridge: Cambridge University Press.

Broise, H., J. Scheid, and C. Brenot 1987. *Recherches archéologiques à La Magliana: le balneum des Frères Arvales*. Rome: École française de Rome, Soprintendenza archeologica di Roma.

Buccellato, A. and F. Coletti 2014. Attività di cava dal suburbio sud ovest di Roma, in J. Bonetto, S. Camporeale and A. Pizzo (eds) *Arqueología de la construcción, IV: Las canteras en el mundo antiguo: sistemas de explotación y procesos productivos, Actas del congreso de Pavoda, 22-24 de noviembre de 2012*: 105-15. Merida: Taravilla.

Buzzetti, C. and P. Virgili 1985. Via Ostiense. *Bullettino della Commissione Archeologica Comunale di Roma* 90.2: 432-35.

Castagnoli, F. 1980. Installazioni portuali a Roma, in J.H. D'Arms and E.C. Kopff (eds) *The Seaborne Commerce of Ancient Rome: Studies in Archaeology and History*: 35-42. Rome: American Academy in Rome.

Catalli, F. 2006. Rinvenimenti archeologici lungo la via Portuense, in M.A. Tomei (ed.) *Roma, memorie dal sottosuolo: ritrovamenti archeologici, 1980/2006*: 512-13. Milan: Electa.

Cianfriglia, L., M. Clementini, M.C. Grossi, V.S. Mellace, L. Giacopini, D. Mantero and M. Serlorenzi 2002. Via Portuense. *Bullettino della Commissione Archeologica Comunale di Roma* 103: 344-64.

Cianfriglia, L. and A.L. Corsini 1986/87. Roma. Via Portuense, loc. Pozzo Pantaleo. La strada basolata. Relazione preliminare della prima campagna di scavo (1984). *Notizie degli Scavi di Antichità*: 155-74

Cianfriglia, L., A. De Cristofaro, and M. Di Mento 2003. La necropoli imperiale di Castel Malnome (Ponte Galeria): risultati preliminari. Il sepolcreto dei saccarii salarii? *Bullettino della Commissione Archeologica Comunale di Roma* 114: 414-23.

Cianfriglia, L., and P. Filippini 1987. Via Portuense. *Bullettino della Commissione Archeologica Comunale di Roma* 92.2: 533-43.

Cianfriglia, L. 2006. Portuense Magliana (Municipio XV): inquadramento topografico, in M.A. Tomei (ed.) *Roma, memorie dal sottosuolo: ritrovamenti archeologici, 1980/2006*: 499-511. Milan: Electa.

Cordano, F. 1981. *Ficana: una pietra miliare sulla strada per Roma; Mostra itinerante degli scavi italo nordici a Ficana (Acilia), 1975-1980*. Rome: Viella, Libreria editrice.

De Franceschini, M. 2005. *Ville dell'Agro romano*. Rome: L'Erma di Bretschneider.

Eckoldt, M. 1980. *Schiffahrt auf kleinen Flüssen Mitteleuropas in Römerzeit und Mittelalter*. Hamburg: Oldenburg.

Fischer-Hansen, T. 1990. *Scavi di Ficana, I: Topografia generale*. Rome: Istituto poligrafico e zecca dello stato.

Fisher, P. 1994. Probable and Fuzzy Models of the Viewshed Operation, in M. Worboys (ed.) *Innovations in GIS: Selected Papers from the First National Conference on GIS Research UK*: 161-75. London: Taylor & Francis.

Germoni, P., M. Millett, S.J. Keay and K. Strutt 2011. The Isola Sacra: reconstructing the Roman landscape, in S.J. Keay and L. Paroli (eds) *Portus and its Hinterland: Recent Archaeological Research*: 231-60. London: British School at Rome.

Giorgetti, D. 1977. Castra Ravennatium: indagine sul distaccamento dei classiari Ravennati a Roma. *Corsi di cultura sull'arte ravennate e bizantina* 24: 223-53.

Goiran, J.-P., F. Salomon, I. Mazzini, J.-P. Bravard, E. Pleuger, C. Vittori, G. Boetto, J. Christiansen, P. Arnaud, A. Pellegrino, C. Pepe and L. Sadori 2014. Geoarchaeology confirms location of the ancient harbour basin of Ostia (Italy). *Journal of Archaeological Science* 41: 389-98.

Görler, W. 1993. Tiberaufwärts nach Rom. Ein Thema und seine Variationen. *Klio* 75: 228-43.

Griesbach, J. 2007. *Villen und Gräber: Siedlungs- und Bestattungsplätze der römischen Kaiserzeit im Suburbium von Rom*. Rahden: Leidorf.

Henzen, W. 1868. *Scavi nel bosco sacro dei Fratelli arvali*. Rome: Dalla tipografia tiberina.

Hesberg, H. von and P. Zanker 1987. *Römische Gräberstrassen: Selbstdarstellung, Status, Standard. Kolloquium in München vom 28. bis 30. Oktober 1985*. Munich: Verlag der Bayerischen Akademie der Wissenschaften.

Hope, V.M. 2009. *Roman Death: The Dying and the Dead in Ancient Rome*. London: Continuum.

Iacopi, G. 1943. Scavi in Prossimità del porto fluviale di S. Paolo. Località Pietra Papa. *Monumenti Antichi* 39: 2-178.

Kammerer-Grothaus, H. 2000. S. Passera – ein Grabbezirk an der Via Portuensis. *Rom: Mitteilungen des Deutschen Archäologischen Instituts, Römische Abteilung* 107: 341-49.

Keay, S.J. 2012. *Rome, Portus and the Mediterranean*. London: The British School at Rome.

Keay, S.J. 2016. Portus in its Mediterranean context, in K. Höghammar, B. Alroth and A. Lindhagen (eds) *Ancient Ports: The Geography of Connections; Proceedings of an International Conference at the Department of Archaeology and Ancient History, Uppsala University, 23-25 September 2010*: 292-322. Uppsala: Uppsala Universitet.

Keay, S.J., P. Campbell, K. Crawford and M.d.C. Moreno Escobar 2021. Space, accessibility and movement at the Portus Romae, in F. Vermeulen and A. Zuiderhoek (eds) *Space, Movement and the Economy in Roman Cities in Italy and Beyond*, 375-417. London: Routledge.

Keay, S.J., and M. Millett, 2005a. The historical background, in S.J. Keay, M. Millett, L. Paroli and K. Strutt (eds) *Portus: An Archaeological Survey of the Port of Imperial Rome*: 11-14. London: British School at Rome.

Keay, S.J., and M. Millett 2005b. Portus in context, in S.J. Keay, M. Millett, L. Paroli and K. Strutt (eds) *Portus: An Archaeological Survey of the Port of Imperial Rome*: 297-314. London: British School at Rome.

Keay, S.J., M. Millett, K. Strutt and P. Germoni 2020. *The Isola Sacra Survey: Ostia, Portus and the Port System of Imperial Rome*. Cambridge: McDonald Institute for Archaeological Research.

Keay, S.J., and L. Paroli 2011. *Portus and its Hinterland: Recent Archaeological Research*. London: British School at Rome.

Koortbojian, M. 1996. *In commemorationem mortuorum*: text and image along the 'street of tombs', in J. Elsner (ed.) *Art and Text in Roman Culture*: 210-33. Cambridge: Cambridge University Press.

Lanciani, R.A. 1988. *Forma urbis Romae*. Rome: Edizioni Quasar.

Le Gall, J. 1953. *Le Tibre: fleuve de Rome dans l'Antiquité*. Paris: Presses universitaires de France.

Lehnen, J. 1997. *Adventus principis: Untersuchungen zu Sinngehalt und Zeremoniell der Kaiserankunft in den Städten des Imperium Romanum*. Frankfurt am Main: Lang.

Lehnen, J. 2001. Profectio Augusti: Zum kaiserlichen Zeremoniell des Abmarsches. *Gymnasium* 108: 15-33.

Malmberg, S. 2015. 'Ships are seen gliding swiftly along the sacred Tiber': the river as an artery of urban movement and development, in I. Östenberg, S. Malmberg and J. Bjørnebye (eds) *The Moving City: Processions, Passages and Promenades in Ancient Rome*: 187-202. London: Bloomsbury.

Mancini, G. 1913. Roma. Nuove scoperte di antichità nella città e nel suburbio. Via Ostiense. *Notizie degli Scavi di Antichità* 10: 443.

Mancini, G. 1924. Via Portuense. *Notizie degli Scavi di Antichità* 21: 55-60.

Meiggs, R. 1973. *Roman Ostia*, 2nd ed. Oxford: Clarendon Press.

Mocchegiani Carpano, C. 1984. Il Tevere: archaeologia e commercio. *Bollettino di numismatica* 2/3: 21-81.

Morelli, C., A. Carbonara, V. Forte, M.C. Grossi and A. Arnoldus Huyzendveld 2011. La topografia romana dell'Agro Portuense alla luce delle nuove indigini, in S.J. Keay and L. Paroli (eds) *Portus and its Hinterland: Recent Archaeological Research*: 261-86. London: The British School at Rome.

Moreno Escobar, M.d.C. 2009. The Via Portuensis Project. The application of cost surface analysis to a Roman road. Unpublished Master of Science in Archaeological Computing (Spatial Technology), Archaeology, University of Southampton.

Moreno Escobar, M.d.C. 2022. Roman ports in the Lower Tiber Valley: computational approaches to re-assess Rome's port system. *Papers of the British School at Rome* 90: 109-38.

Noy, D. 2000. *Foreigners at Rome: Citizens and Strangers*. London: Duckworth.

Ogburn, D. 2006. Assessing the level of visibility of cultural objects in past landscapes. *Journal of Archaeological Science* 33: 405-13.

Pavolini, C. 2002. La trasformazione del ruolo di Ostia nel III secolo d.C. in *Villes et avant-ports: l'exemple de Rome et Ostie; Nouvelles recherches à Ostie*, 325-52. Rome: École française de Rome.

Pellegrino, A. 1983. Ville rustiche a Dragoncello. *Archeologia Laziale V = Quad AEI* 7: 76-83.

Pellegrino, A. 1984. Scavi a Dragoncello e a Casalbernocchi (Acilia). *Archeologia Laziale VI = Quad AEI* 8: 194-97.

Pensabene, P. 2007. *Ostiensium marmorum decus et decor: studi architettonici, decorativi e archeometrici*. Rome: L'Erma di Bretschneider.

Petriaggi, R., A. Carbonara and C. Vittori 1995. Scavi a Ponte Galeria: nuove acquisizioni sull'acquedotto di Porto e sulla topografia del territorio portuense. *QuadAEI* 24: 361-73.

Petriaggi, R., M.C. Vittori and P. Vori 2001. Un contributo alla conoscenza del tracciato della Via Portuense e della viabilità tra Roma e Porto, in L. Quilici and S. Quilici Gigli (eds) *Urbanizzazione delle campagne nell'Italia antica*: 139-50. Rome: L'Erma di Bretschneider.

Quilici, L. 1990. *Le strade. Viabilità tra Roma e Lazio*. Rome: Quasar.

Rášová, A. 2014. Fuzzy viewshed, probable viewshed, and their use in the analysis of prehistoric monuments placement in western Slovakia, in J.N. Huerta Guijarro, S. Schade and C. Granell Canut (eds) *Connecting a Digital Europe through Location and Place: Proceedings of the AGILE 2014 International Conference on Geographic Information Science, Castellón, June, 3-6*: 47-65. Castelló de la Plana: Springer.

Roggio, B. 2012. *Archeologia e GIS: uno studio diacronico delle trasformazioni dell'area Ostiense di Roma*. Rome: UniversItalia.

Scheid, J. 1976. Note sur la Via Campana. *Mélanges de l'École française de Rome: Antiquité* 88.2: 639-68.

Scheid, J. 1990. *Romulus et ses frères: le Collège des frères arvales, modèle du culte public dans la Rome des empereurs*. Rome: École française de Rome.

Serlorenzi, M. and H. Di Giuseppe 2009. La via Campana. Aspetti topografici e rituali, in C. Pavolini, V. Jolivet, M.A. Tomei and R. Volpe (eds) *Suburbium, II: Il suburbio di Roma dalla fine dell'età monarchica alla nascita del sistema delle ville (V–II secolo a.C.)*: 573-98. Rome: Ecole française de Rome.

Serlorenzi, M., G. Ricci, A. De Tommasi, H. Di Giuseppe, E. Spagnoli, B. Amatucci and C. La Rocca 2004. Nuove acquisizioni sulla viabilità dell'Agro Portuense. Il rinvenimento di un tratto della via Campana e della via Portuense. *Bullettino della Commissione Archeologica Comunale di Roma* 105: 47-114.

Serlorenzi, M. and R. Sebastiani 2008. Il progetto del Nuovo Mercato di Testaccio. *Workshop di archeologia classica* 5: 137-71.

Serra, S. 2007. *Via Ostiense, via Portuense*. Rome: Istituto poligrafico e zecca dello stato, Libreria dello stato.

Tarquini, S., S. Vinci, M. Favalli, F. Doumaz, A. Fornaciai and L. Nannipieri 2012. Release of a 10-m-resolution DEM for the Italian territory: comparison with global-coverage DEMs and anaglyph-mode exploration via the web. *Computers & Geosciences* 38.1: 168-70.

Tella, F. 2018. Dagli helciarii ai pilorciatori: il trasporto delle merci sul Tevere a valle dell'Isola Tiberina, dall'età romana alle soglie del Novecento. *Bollettino della Unione storia ed arte* 13: 45-59.

Tomassetti, G. 1979a. *La campagna romana antica, medioevale e moderna*, ed. by L. Chiumenti and F. Bilancia. Nuova ed. Vol. V: Via Laurentina-Ostiense. Florence: Olschki.

Tomassetti, G. 1979b. *La campagna romana antica, medioevale e moderna*. Nuova ed. Vol. VI: Vie Nomentana e Salaria, Portuense, Tiburtina. Florence: Olschki.

Tucci, P.L. 2004. Eight fragments of the marble plan of Rome shedding new light on the Transtiberim. *Papers of the British School at Rome* 72: 185-202.

Vaglieri, D. 1907. Via Ostiense. *Notizie degli Scavi di Antichità*: 285.

Venditti, E. 1992. *La Via Portuense e il suo territorio: tra leggenda storia e archeologia*. Rome: Tipolitografia Trullo.

Vött, A., T. Willershäuser, H. Hadler, L. Obrocki, P. Fischer and M. Heinzelmann 2020. Geoarchaeological evidence of Ostia's river harbour operating until the fourth century AD. *Archaeological and Anthropological Sciences* 12.4: 88, viewed 17 March 2020, <https://doi.org/10.1007/s12520-020-01035-z>.

Wheatley, D. and M. Gillings 2002. *Spatial Technology and Archaeology: The Archaeological Applications of GIS*. London: Taylor & Francis.

Zevi, F. 2002. Appunti per una storia di Ostia repubblicana. *Mélanges de l'école française de Rome* 114.1: 13-58.

21. Producción, trabajo y comercio. Una aproximación a las mujeres en profesiones portuarias en época romana.

Patricia Terrado Ortuño

Cuando inicié mis estudios predoctorales sobre el puerto de *Tarraco*, conocía bien los trabajos del Profesor Simon J. Keay. Estudié a fondo los resultados del proyecto *Portus* para poder comprender cómo era un puerto en la antigüedad y seguí sus trabajos sobre ciudades portuarias como referente para mi investigación. Las casualidades a veces existen y cuando obtuve un contrato de Formación de Personal Investigador (Ministerio de Economía y Competitividad) para realizar mi tesis, el proyecto *Rome's Mediterranean Ports - Portus Limen* también se ponía en marcha. Tuve la suerte de poder asistir al primer encuentro en la British School el año 2015 en Roma como asistente al seminario *Roman Port Societies through the evidence of inscriptions*[1], del cual recuerdo haber aprendido muchísimo en el estadio inicial de mi tesis. Y aunque ésta no se centró específicamente en los oficios[2], el mundo de la epigrafía portuaria despertaba en mi un interés académico con muchas posibilidades de investigación. Después de asistir a los siguientes encuentros organizados por Simon y su equipo, participé en dos ocasiones como ponente en los mismos junto a otros colegas investigadores. Como colofón, Simon formó parte de mi tribunal de tesis en enero de 2018, cerrando mi etapa como estudiante y habiendo aprendido de uno de los más grandes expertos en puertos romanos[3].

Este artículo pretende recoger un poco de la ilusión de ese primer congreso internacional y agradecer el trabajo de Simon, una persona académicamente brillante, paciente y comprensiva, capaz de aportar al mundo un poco más de humildad y trabajo en equipo.

Los estudios sobre oficios portuarios

Son muchos los estudios que se han realizado sobre trabajo en época romana. Los más recientes incluyen la necesaria relectura desde una perspectiva de género, situándolas al mismo nivel que las aportaciones anteriores y haciendo una interpretación más global e inclusiva de la historia (Cid-López 2015).

En nuestro caso, nos hemos centrado en los oficios ejercidos por mujeres en relación con el puerto para realizar una primera aproximación a este aspecto poco tratado hasta ahora. Para ello, la epigrafía constituye una de las fuentes principales de nuestro estudio, dado que permite identificar las ocupaciones femeninas e identidades profesionales representadas, y también ver cómo pueden narrar sobre los roles y estructuras de género en la sociedad romana (Larsson Lovén 2016: 200).

De este modo, nuestro objetivo no es realizar un corpus epigráfico exhaustivo de los oficios femeninos hallados en puertos, sino ofrecer una visión general de las posibilidades de esta rama de estudio, dado que permite analizar los roles socioeconómicos de la mujer en un contexto de trabajo portuario.

El principal problema a la hora de realizar este trabajo consiste en definir adecuadamente qué es una profesión portuaria. Si bien el hecho de definir el término "puerto" aún genera debate entre los académicos, en lo que respecta al aspecto del trabajo portuario ocurre algo parecido. Así, ¿deberíamos considerar como oficio portuario a aquél relacionado directamente con la actividad portuaria, como es la carga y descarga de mercancías o el mantenimiento de naves? ¿O también debería incluir profesiones de transporte que no necesariamente tenían lugar en un puerto, como pueden ser los oficios de *negotiatores*?[4]

---

[1] Los resultados de este seminario se han publicado recientemente en una monografía (Arnaud y Keay 2020).

[2] Una síntesis sobre este aspecto centrado en Tarraco puede verse en Terrado 2016.

[3] Los resultados de esta tesis, dirigida por los drs. Joaquín Ruiz de Arbulo y Diana Gorostidi en la Universitat Rovira i Virgili (Tarragona) pueden hallarse en Terrado 2019/ ORCID ID: 0000-0001-9554-1237. Este artículo se ha desarrollado dentro de los proyectos de investigación *Vivere in urbe. Arquitectura residencial y espacio urbano en Emporiae y Tarraco. Investigación y socialización* (PID2019-103576 GB C42/ IP: Joaquín Ruiz de Arbulo) y *SULMARE: Sulcato marmore ferro. Canteras, talleres, artesanos y comitentes de las producciones artísticas en piedra en la Hispania Tarraconensis* (PID2019-106967GB-I00/ IP: Diana Gorostidi y Pilar Lapuente). Agradezco asimismo a las doctoras Diana Gorostidi y Ada Lasheras los comentarios y correcciones acerca de esta aportación.

[4] La bibliografía ha tratado este aspecto en sendas publicaciones, especialmente recogiendo los testimonios epigráficos. Así, mientras Rougé fue quien asentó las bases de estos estudios analizando los oficios relacionados con los puertos, navegación y comercio (Rougé 1966), posteriormente varios autores y autoras se han focalizado en estudiar los oficios portuarios de zonas concretas. Ver, por ejemplo: Casson 1971; Tran 2008; 2016; Rohde 2012; Martelli 2013; Rougier 2015; 2016.

Figura 21.1. Relieve que muestra vendedora en una tienda de animales y verduras procedente de Ostia (fuente: Wikimedia Commons (autor: Chescargot) <https://commons.wikimedia.org/wiki/File:OstiaRelief.jpg?uselang=es>).

Esta línea está poco definida dadas las múltiples causalidades y distintos escenarios que envuelven a los oficios portuarios. Por un lado, las evidencias epigráficas conservadas sobre estos oficios son muy escasas, ya excepción de Ostia, Roma y *Portus*, las referencias a trabajos relacionados con puertos son más bien dispersas y se encuentran localizadas en varios enclaves portuarios o fluviales. Por otro lado, importantes ciudades portuarias, como por ejemplo *Tarraco*, no poseen todavía ninguna referencia a un oficio portuario, y no por ello debería considerarse que no existen[5].

Con la intención de despejar estas dudas, nos hemos centrado por un lado en los trabajos artesanales que tendrían lugar en zonas portuarias y, por otro, en los oficios relacionados con las grandes empresas comerciales que, aunque tenían como escenario principal el puerto, esto no implica necesariamente que el oficio tuviera que realizarse necesariamente en el puerto.

Así, el estudio de la epigrafía es fundamental para la identificación de mujeres en el ámbito laboral portuario, y resulta especialmente útil el testimonio de los epitafios. A pesar de la escasa documentación sobre la actividad laboral de la mujer en zonas portuarias, las inscripciones conservadas permiten plantear un paisaje epigráfico en los puertos en el cual varios actores ejercían sus actividades para que el engranaje comercial funcionara y en cuyos espacios la mujer participaba activamente.

Uno de primeros estudios sobre el artesanado femenino lo encontramos en Le Gall, que asentaba una primera relación de trabajos ejercidos por mujeres, así como el artículo de Treggiari en el que ya se incorporaban estudios de mujeres y trabajo (le Gall 1969; Treggiari 1979). La introducción de los estudios de género en estos estudios vino de la mano de Joshel, Dixon o Holleran, y más recientemente de estudiosos como Knapp o Salvaterra (A.A.V.V. 1994; Dixon 2001; Holleran 2013; Joshel 1992; Knapp 2011; Salvaterra 2006).

Del mismo modo, las referencias de *tituli picti* y *signacula* son esenciales para trazar las rutas comerciales de ánforas y establecer qué mujeres participaban en el comercio del aceite y el vino (Berni 2008; Bourgeon 2018; Chic García 1985; 1988). Por último, las fuentes literarias y la iconografía ofrecen más datos para poder identificar estos oficios (Casson 1971; Morais 2010; Pensa 1999; Schmidts 2011; Zimmer 1982) (Figura 21.1).

En el caso de los oficios, cuando se trata de trabajos ejercidos por hombres, la mayor parte de los epígrafes indican la profesión al lado del nombre de quien la ejercía; por el contrario, cuando se trata de identificar los oficios ejercidos por mujeres no siempre se cumple este requisito, dado que en muchas ocasiones trabajaban en el ámbito familiar y aparecen en inscripciones referentes a este entorno. Así, por ejemplo, destacamos el caso de *negotiatrices*[6] dedicadas al comercio de vino y del aceite, como es el caso de las inscripciones CIL XV, 3691, 3729 y 3845-7, las cuales habrían heredado de su padre o marido barcos dedicados al comercio de vino.

---

[5] Sobre este aspecto, consultar Keay y Arnaud 2016.

[6] Ver apartado siguiente.

Continuar con la explotación del negocio familiar, por ende, les permitía seguir recibiendo beneficios (Lázaro 2003: 167; Loane 1979: 23).

Si nos centramos en el trabajo realizado en puertos, los oficios realizados por hombres siguen esta dinámica, pero en el caso de las mujeres la búsqueda es más difícil ya que a menudo el oficio aparece citado en masculino a pesar de que lo realicen mujeres – por ejemplo, el caso de una mujer ejerciendo de *navicularius* o *mercator*[7] –; además, en muchos casos las mujeres ejercían el oficio en empresas familiares, con lo cual el oficio citado en el epitafio englobará a varios sujetos.

Estos estudios epigráficos sobre oficios ejercidos por mujeres también ha permitido clasificarlos en dos clases (Gallego Franco 1993: 113). Por un lado, los oficios ejercidos a gran escala, es decir, existían mujeres involucradas en una actividad mercantil en la que no trabajaban de forma manual y en la que eran parte activa económica. Por otro, nos encontramos con los trabajos propios del artesanado y trabajos manuales que ejercerían de forma directa en pequeños talleres en las zonas portuarias

Las siguientes líneas se centran en el estudio de esta última clasificación.

Negotiatrices y mujeres a cargo de un negocio familiar

Uno de los casos mejor documentados en la epigrafía romana es la presencia de mujeres en posiciones económicas elevadas y como parte activa en la administración de un negocio como es el caso de las *negotiatrices*. También son bien conocidas las mujeres latifundistas y propietarias de fincas que administraban las tierras; o bien hay algunos casos de propietarias de talleres cerámicos o *figlinae*, según referencias en la epigrafía doliar (Chic García 1985; 1988; Taglietti 1994). Sin embargo, en el tema que nos ocupa, son las referencias al papel de *negotiatrix*, recogido en la epigrafía y en las fuentes literarias, las que más información aportan sobre su cometido en el comercio de la *annona*, es decir, como agentes comerciales en la producción, transporte y venta de aceite y vino, especialmente procedente de la Bética (Berni 2008; Berni y García Vargas 2012; Berni 1998; Chic García 1985; 1988).

Así, término *negotiator* implica varias definiciones, dado que puede tratarse o bien de aquel que ejerce una actividad comercial o bien a las acciones ejercidas por éste que implican ingreso y especulación con dinero, e involucra a la disponibilidad de capital (A.A.V.V. 1900: s.v. *negotiator*; Fernández Uriel 2011: 383; Garcia Brossa

1999; Morretta 1999: 232; Valencia Hernández 1990; Verboven 2007). Se refiere a la persona que se dedica al comercio, generalmente en las grandes empresas comerciales marítimas y a gran escala, pero también a trabajos a una escala más pequeña, como las finanzas y gestión de empresas de transportes terrestres y marítimas, la explotación de *tabernae*, la construcción y empresas inmobiliarias (Garcia Brossa 1999: 184; Andreau 2015; Tchernia 2016).

Pese a que la designación habitual para la persona que ejerce como empresario se usa este término, existen otras fórmulas para definirlo, usadas tanto en la epigrafía como en las fuentes. Aunque las designaciones habituales eran *qui negotiantur, qui consistunt, negotia,* etc. Así, encontramos ejemplos del uso de *negotians* en algunos autores, como en Suetonio (*quaestoris negotiantis ex consuetudine*; *Dom.* 9.23) o Petronio (*familiae negotiantis,* 101.4)[8].

En lo que concierne al término *negotiatrix,* es común encontrarlo en femenino, aunque también se han documentado mujeres en negocios junto a su padre, marido o familia, es decir, trabajando en la empresa familiar sin necesidad del uso de este término[9]. De este modo, en muchos casos el título no aparece expresado en femenino, dada la costumbre de usar el masculino de forma genérica en las inscripciones que incluyan grupos mixtos. Asimismo, la dedicación de la mujer al comercio se realiza, en la mayoría de ocasiones, a través de un tercero, con lo cual las referencias a mujeres comerciantes y empresarias son escasas (Fernández Uriel 2011; Lázaro 2003).

Así, la epigrafía indica concretamente quienes son miembros, fundadoras y continuadoras de asociaciones en el ámbito comercial. En consecuencia, se encuentran mujeres propietarias y administradoras de empresas comerciales - aunque a priori no estaba permitido por la legislación (Cantarella 1991; Cid-López 2015; Lázaro 2003) - ya que el desarrollo de la actividad se realiza en el ámbito de la familia: en muchos casos son mujeres que trabajan con sus padres o maridos, o bien que han heredado de éstos el negocio familiar y le dan continuidad (Broekaert 2012)[10].

Estas *negotiatrices* tendrían, a la par que los *negotiatores*, dos ámbitos de actuación. En primer lugar, en empresas de alta escala social y económica como empresarias

---

[7] Cf. Infra.

[8] Para el resto de las referencias, ver Broekaert 2013, n. 43.
[9] Un ejemplo sería la inscripción del siglo II dC procedente de Sevilla, en la que *Aelia Optata* honra con una inscripción a su marido e hijo, los cuales eran propietarios de tierras y talleres cerámicos en el contexto del comercio a lo largo del río *Hispalis* (CIL II, 2329 y 5492). Sobre esta inscripción, véase Gallego Franco 1993.
[10] Un ejemplo sería el epitafio procedente de Pompeya que recoge la existencia de la sede de un *collegium* en un edificio en el cual *Iulia Felix* alquilaba y vendía locales comerciales (Fernández Uriel 2011: 386-87; Gallego Franco 1993: 114; CIL VI, 9148 = ILS 7333; CIL, IV, 1136).

con alta capacidad económica, y en segundo lugar, en la pequeña empresa, disponiendo de menos liquidez y a menudo ejerciendo ellas mismas el oficio[11]. Los testimonios epigráficos las sitúan muy a menudo en actividades comerciales relacionadas con la producción y transporte del cereal, el vino o el aceite (Fernández Uriel 2011: 386). En las inscripciones, junto al término *negotiatrix* se indica generalmente la mercancía con la que se comerciaba, como por ejemplo *Abundia Magiste*, que comerciaba con cereales y legumbres (*negotiatrix frumentaria et leguminaria*). En el caso que no se indique el material con el que comerciaba, éste solía ser el cereal[12] (Eichenauer 1989: 23).

Así, en las inscripciones es habitual encontrar especialmente a *negotiatrices* en el ámbito de la explotación vitivinícola y olearia, liderando negocios a gran escala que ponen de relieve que, o bien participan con su padre o marido en la producción y distribución en el comercio naval de estos productos, o que habían heredado la empresa y continuaban con el negocio familiar.

El mejor ejemplo donde se documentan a *negotiatrices* en estos ámbitos es en el comercio del aceite. El producto exportado por excelencia de la Bética era el aceite, un producto anonario que llegaba a Roma por mar. Desde su embarque a orillas del Guadalquivir, el aceite se desembarcaba a orillas del Tíber, desechando sus envases, las ánforas Dressel 20 (Berni 2008; Blázquez y Remesal Rodríguez 2010; Chic García 1985; 1988; Rodríguez Almeida 1984). Estas ánforas, acumuladas en el Monte Testaccio, contienen tanto en los sellos como en los *tituli picti* información sobre las profesiones involucradas no solo en el transporte del aceite, sino también en su producción y distribución, a saber: los ya mencionados *negotiatores*, los *mercatores*, los *diffusores olearii* y los *navicularii*, profesiones inevitablemente ligadas al puerto (Gallego Franco 1993: 114; Garcia Brossa 1999; Rico 2003; Rodríguez Almeida 1984).

Los *tituli picti* de las ánforas Dressel 20 además proporcionan un importante testimonio de su papel en el comercio marítimo del aceite (Mataix 2022). Así, a pesar de que son pocas las evidencias halladas en ellos de nombres femeninos, la búsqueda de estos nombres tanto de hombres y mujeres ha permitido localizarlos geográficamente, siendo la mayoría procedentes de ciudades costeras o cercanas a la costa, o de regiones fluviales navegables, hecho que sitúa a estos oficios en zonas clave debido a la necesidad de disponer de una red marítima para el transporte que permitiesen

exportar sus productos (Berni 2001; 2008; Bourgeon 2018; Morales Muñoz 2005: 266).

En algunos de estos *tituli picti* aparecen nombres de mujer que formarían parte de familias dedicadas al comercio y a la producción de aceite. Un ejemplo que muestra este trabajo conjunto con sus familias es el de *Caecilius Onesimus* y *Caecilia Charitosa*, padre e hija, que trabajaban en Roma como *negotiatores* en la misma sociedad, tal y como testimonia un *titulus pictus* hallado en una Dressel 20 en Testaccio (s. II dC)[13].

Encontramos también nombres femeninos entre los *diffusores olearii* y los *mercatores*, cuyo cometido era comprar el aceite hispano y conducirlo a distintas partes del imperio. Mientras que los primeros hacen referencia a los agentes intermediarios en el comercio de la *annona*, los segundos se refieren a comerciantes que ejercen a cualquier escala (Garcia Brossa 1999; Mattingly y Aldrete 2000; Rougé 1966; Valencia Hernández 1990). A modo de ejemplo, contamos con el caso de un epígrafe hallado en Roma y datado en la segunda mitad del siglo II dC. En él, *Coelia Mascellina* dedica una inscripción a su padre *Cneus Coellius Masculus* y a su madre, cuyo nombre no se conserva, que fue *negotiatrix olearia ex provincia Baetica item vini,* es decir, que comerciaba con aceite y vino[14]. Además, la dedicante *Coelia Mascellina* aparece documentada en un sello de bronce con inscripción bilingüe en griego y latín, dando fe que habría seguido los pasos de sus progenitores como negociante de aceite y vino Bético (Morretta 1999; Taglietti 1994; Panciera 1980)[15]. Estos testimonios ponen de relieve que no solamente su madre ejercería de *negotiatrix*, sino que la misma *Coelia Mascellina* usaría este sello para marcar las ánforas de su propio negocio (Becker 2016: 926).

Otro ejemplo es de *Aelia Marciana,* hija de *Aelius Marcianus,* que fue procónsul de la provincia *Baetica* durante el reinado de Antonino Pío. Sabemos que fue *negotiatrix* porque en el pecio de Saint-Gervais 3, datado a mediados del siglo II d.C. y situado cerca de Marsella, se hallaron dos ánforas con su sello, dando fe que el aceite que contenían procedía de su propiedad en Hispania (Becker 2016: 926; Nantet 2015: n. 61)[16].

También existían *negotiatrices* a la cabeza de un negocio de escala más modesta, como propietarias y trabajadoras de su propia empresa, tal y como reza el epígrafe hallado en Roma en la cual *Abudia Magiste* ejercía de *negotiatrix frumentaria et leguminaria ab scala mediana* (Figura 21.2). En este caso, su marido era su

---

[11] En el *Digesto* aparece la voz *negotiatrix* en el contexto de actividades de venta (D. 34.2.32.4. (Paul 2 *ad Vit*.)).

[12] En el caso del *negotiator* y del *mercator*, suele ocurrir lo mismo: siempre se indica la materia con la que comercian. Véase, por ejemplo, le Gall 1969.

[13] Rodríguez-Almeida 1979: nº 33; Testaccio: BC-9/1934. *Caecilius Onesimus* se documenta también en dos inscripciones también trabajando solo en el negocio del aceite (*CIL* XV, 3782 y 3783). Véase Chic García 1988: n. 18-19 y Rodríguez-Almeida 1979: 923, no 33.

[14] *AE* 2001, 518 = *AE* 1973, 71.

[15] *CIL* XV, 8166.

[16] *AE* 1981, 634 y *AE* 1991, 1189d.

Entendemos como *navicularius* la persona que explota comercialmente un navío, ya sea propietario de éste o no, asumiendo las ganancias y pérdidas (D. 14.1.1.15 (Ulp. 28 *ad ed.*). El *naviculiarius* no tenía por qué que navegar en el barco de su propiedad, y por este motivo confiaba a un *magister navis* la tarea de los contratos de transporte y de la organización de todo lo necesario para el viaje (Broekaert 2013; de Robertis 1937; de Salvo 1992; Rougé 1966; Sirks 1991; Waltzing 1895).

A pesar de que no se documenta este oficio con el adjetivo en femenino ((D. 14.1.1.16 (Ulp. 28 *ad ed.*); Orsi 1907:767; Jouguet 1931:3), la presencia de mujeres a la cabeza de industrias navales queda documentada en las fuentes, concretamente Suetonio. El historiador narra que durante el reinado de Claudio se produjeron una serie de revueltas debido a las malas cosechas y falta de víveres (Suet., *Cl.* 18-19). Para sofocarla, el emperador promulgó la *Lex Papia Poppea,* que, entre otras cosas, ofrecía facilidades al transporte naval para lograr el abastecimiento de víveres asumiendo cualquier pérdida causada por temporales y otras prerrogativas destinadas a armadores o *navicularii* (Lázaro 2003: 160). En este contexto, la ley también concedió a las madres de más de cuatro hijos la emancipación de sus tutores, es decir una medida para favorecer la natalidad. A partir de la interpretación de Suetonio, Rougé sugiere que la mujer naviera estaría en relación con la navegación comercial pero no tenía la obligación de navegar en sus naves (Rougé 1966: 245). Según Rougé (1966: 245), gracias a esta ley también sería posible que las mujeres explotaran comercialmente barcos, es decir, tenían la posibilidad de unirse a empresas de transporte vinculadas a la *annona,* convirtiéndose en una parte activa de la industria naval (García Garrido 2001: 64). Estas mujeres se encargarían de distribuir sus productos gracias de la navegación convirtiéndose en inversoras, una tipología de empresarias navales que Rougé denomina para sus homólogos masculinos *navicularii honorarii*[18]. Son, por lo tanto, mujeres navieras que podían ejercer como propietarias de barcos o bien como inversoras, las cuales exponían en capital con fines comerciales (Rougé 1966: 245). De este modo, éstas no se embarcarían, sino ejercerían de agentes comerciales que fletarían el barco y cuyo manejo recaería en manos de un *magister navis*. En este sentido, su grado de responsabilidad jurídica era el mismo que los hombres, de modo que las mujeres que participarían en estas empresas poseerían una alta capacidad económica (Lázaro 2003: 162).

De nuevo nos encontramos con un oficio portuario que no necesariamente tenía que desplegarse en el mismo puerto, pero que sin embargo no podía desarrollarse sin la existencia de éste.

Figura 21.2. Inscripción de *Abudia Magiste* (fuente: Epigraphik-Datenbank Clauss / Slaby).

patrono y contaba con varios libertos trabajando para esta empresa (Fernández Uriel 2011: 386; le Gall 1969)[17].

Mujeres en la dirección de naves comerciales

Si bien el caso de las *negotiatrices* incide directamente en el panorama de oficios relacionados directamente con la actividad comercial portuaria, existe otro caso en el cual las mujeres ejercían el papel de armadores.

---

[17] *CIL* VI, 9683 = *ILS* 748839

[18] Rougé clasifica a los *navicularii* en dos tipos: los activos, que son los que poseen barcos, y los honorarios, que son los inversores en empresas navieras (Rougé 1966: 245).

Figura 21.3. Inscripción dedicada a *Zosima* (fuente propia).

Sin embargo, sí que existía un pequeño grupo de oficios situados en áreas portuarias, es decir, los relacionados directamente con el mantenimiento de equipamientos y barcos, las labores de artesanado vinculadas a la venta y el comercio y las tareas de vigilancia y control.

Trabajos artesanales y responsables de talleres

En esta categoría se incluye el trabajo servil, que no requería preparación, y el de las profesiones liberales que requerían unos conocimientos previos para poder ejercerlo. Así, se conservan numerosas inscripciones de trabajo femenino en talleres de artesanado y de construcción. De este modo, podían ser las dueñas o dirigir el taller y no realizar el trabajo más pesado como tal, o bien ejercer el oficio. Las mujeres comerciantes, además, tenían además una doble vertiente: regentar un negocio y/o ejercer el trabajo de éste.

Un ejemplo sería el de la *piscatrix Aurelia Nais*, una liberta que trabajaba en un área mercantil cerca del Tíber, en los almacenes horrea Galbana (Boscolo 2005; Rodríguez Almeida 1984: 94-97)[19]. Así, el oficio de *Aurelia Nais* sería

el de vendedora de pescado y no el de pescadora, debido a la indicación de su puesto de trabajo bien en estos almacenes o bien en lugar cercano a éstos, y que como liberta habría trabajado por cuenta propia (Boscolo 2005: 184-85).

En la misma línea, encontramos a la liberta *Zosima*. Recientes investigaciones apuntan a que se trataría de una mujer ejerciendo de descargadora o *saccaria*, posiblemente en Roma o *Portus*, siendo así el primer testimonio de una mujer ejerciendo este trabajo (Martelli 2013: 8) (Figura 21.3). Sin embargo, en un estudio y análisis en profundidad del epígrafe, creemos que la inscripción en cuestión no hace referencia a su oficio, sino a su gentilicio, proveniente del *collegium saccariorum* que la habría liberado (Martelli 2013 cf. Terrado Ortuño, *en prensa*)[20].

Conclusiones

Si bien es cierto que los estudios más recientes sobre epigrafía nos han aportado datos nuevos sobre el panorama de trabajo que se desarrollaba en los puertos,

---

[19] *CIL* VI, 9801 = ILS 7500

[20] *CIL* VI, 25737 = Epigraphica-1990-135 = *AE* 1981, 148; 1990, 24.

todavía existen algunas lagunas por estudiar, como es el caso de las mujeres tratado en esta contribución. La definición ambigua de oficio portuario pone en relieve la necesidad de establecer qué se considera como tal: si a los trabajos artesanales y manuales llevados a cabo en sus muelles y orillas, o también a las empresas comerciales que no necesariamente tenían sede en los puertos.

A pesar de que son pocos los ejemplos de mujeres trabajando en puertos, existe una dificultad añadida, dado que en la mayor de epígrafes o bien aparecen trabajando en el núcleo familiar o bien no se documentan con el nombre del oficio. Así, cuando se trata de estudiar oficios mediante la epigrafía, muchos de ellos escapan de la mirada del epigrafista, y rara vez aparecen en los relieves o pinturas, ya que el epigrafista sólo percibe aquello que las inscripciones sugieren (Tran 2016: 268).

En conclusión, los citados casos arrojan un poco de luz sobre este tema, poniendo de relieve la presencia de mujeres con un papel activo en la producción y el comercio, así como acerca de las diferentes fases de transporte marítimo y actividades artesanales llevas a cabo en los puertos. La epigrafía presenta a mujeres trabajando en ámbito familiar con un rol activo y a menudo principal en empresas comerciales, como se ha visto el caso de la producción de aceite y vino. Por otro lado, las inscripciones corroboran la presencia de mujeres establecidas en áreas portuarias como tenderas y realizando actividades artesanales y de producción.

De este modo, utilizar todas las fuentes disponibles nos acercará a identificar estos oficios que sin lugar a duda debían existir pero que aparecen de forma fragmentaria en las inscripciones, permitiendo analizar los roles socioeconómicos de la mujer en el trabajo portuario.

Bibliografía

A.A.V.V. 1900. *Thesaurus linguae Latinae*. Leipzig: Teubner.

A.A.V.V. 1994. *Epigrafia della produzione e della distribuzione: actes de la VIIe Rencontre franco-italienne sur l'épigraphie du monde romain (Rome, 5-6 juin 1992)*. Roma: Ecole française de Rome.

Andreau, J. 2015. *The Economy of the Ancient Mediterranean*. Michigan: Michigan Classical Press.

Arnaud, P. y S. Keay 2020. *Roman Port Societies*. Roma: British School at Rome.

Becker, H. 2016. Roman women in the urban economy. Occupations, social connections, and gendered exclusions, en J. Turfa y S. Budin (eds) *Women in Antiquity: Real Women across the Ancient World*: 915-31. London: Routledge.

Berni, P. 1998. *Las ánforas de aceite de la Bética y su presencia en la Cataluña romana*. Barcelona: Universitat de Barcelona.

Berni, P. 2001. Producción anfórica en Hispania. La evidencia de la epigrafía, en W. Broekaert, E. Delattre, E. Dupraz y M.J. Estarán Tolosa (eds) *L'épigraphie su céramique: l'instrumentum domesticum, ses genres textuels et ses fonctions dans les sicíetes antiques*: 19-46. École pratique des hautes études.

Berni, P. 2008. *Epigrafía anfórica de la Bética: nuevas perspectivas de análisis*. Barcelona: Universitat de Barcelona.

Berni, P. y García Vargas, E. 2012. Dressel 20 (Valle del Guadalquivir). 2012, viewed 10 August 2023, <>.

Blázquez, J.M, y J. Remesal Rodríguez (eds). 2010. *Estudios sobre el Monte Testaccio (Roma)*, V (Col·lecció instrumenta 35). Barcelona: Universitat de Barcelona.

Boscolo, F. 2005. Aurelia Nais, piscatrix de horreis Galbae e i "piscatores" di Roma. *Rivista storica dell'antichità* 35: 181-88.

Bourgeon, O. 2018. La production d'amphores à huile dans la basse vallée du Genil : contribution à l'histoire socio-économique de la Bétique à l'époque romaine (Ier s. av. J.-C.- Ve s. ap. J.-C.). Montpellier 3/Universidad de Sevilla.

Broekaert, W. 2012. Welcome to the family!: marriage as a business strategy in the Roman economy. *Marburger Beiträge zur antiken Handels-, Wirtschafts- und Sozialgeschichte* 30: 41-66

Broekaert, W. 2013. *Navicularii et negotiantes: A Prosopographical Study of Roman Merchants and Shippers*. Rahden: Leidorf.

Cantarella, E. 1991. *La mujer romana*. Santiago de Compostela: Universidad Santiago de Compostela.

Casson, L. 1971. *Ships and Seamanship in the Ancient World*. Princeton: Princeton University Press.

Chic García, G. 1985. *Epigrafia anfórica de la Betica, I: Las marcas impresas en el barro sobre anforas olearias*. Sevilla: Universidad de Sevilla.

Chic García, G. 1988. *Epigrafía anfórica de la Bética, II: Los rótulos pintados sobre ánforas olearias: consideraciones sobre la annona*. Sevilla: Universidad de Sevilla.

Cid-López, R.M. 2015. El género y los estudios históricos sobre las mujeres de la Antigüedad. Reflexiones sobre los usos y evolución de un concepto. *Revista de Historiografía* 22.1: 25-49.

Dixon, S. 2001. *Reading Roman Women: Sources, Genres, and Real Life*. Londres: Duckworth.

Eichenauer, M. 1989. *Untersuchungen zur Arbeitswelt der Frau in der roemischen Antike*. Frankfurt: Lang.

Fernández Uriel, P. 2011. Obreras y empresarias en el Periodo Romano Alto Imperial. *Espacio, tiempo y forma*, Serie II, *Historia antigua* 24: 367-90.

Gall, J. le 1969. Métiers de femmes au Corpus Inscriptionum Latinarum. *Révue des études latines* 47: 123-30.

Gallego Franco, M.H. 1993. La mujer hispanorromana y la actividad socioeconómica: las profesiones. *Minerva: Revista de filología clásica* 7: 111-28.

Garcia Brossa, G. 1999. Mercatores y negotiatores: ¿simples negociantes? *Pyrenae* 30: 173-90.

García Garrido, M. 2001. *El comercio, los negocios y las finanzas en el mundo romano*. Madrid: Fundación Estudios Romanos.

Holleran, C. 2013. Women and retail in Roman Italy, en E. Hemerlrijk y E. Wolf (eds) *Women in the Roman City of the Latin West*. Leiden: Brill.

Joshel, S.R. 1992. *Work, Identity and Legal Status at Rome: A Study of the Occupational Inscriptions*. Norman: University of Oklahoma Press.

Jouguet, P. 1931. Dédicace grecque de Médamoud. *Bulletin de l'Institut français D'archéologie orientale* 31: 1-30.

Keay, S. y P. Arnaud (eds) 2016. *The Epigraphy of Port Societies*. Cambridge: Cambridge University Press.

Knapp, R. 2011. *Invisible Romans*. Cambridge (MA): Harvard University Press.

Larsson Lovén, L. 2016. Women, trade and production in urban centres of Roman Italy, en A. Wilson y M. Flohr (eds) *Urban Craftsmen and Traders in the Roman World*: 200-21. Oxford: Oxford University Press.

Lázaro, C. 2003. Mujer, comercio y empresa en algunas fuentes jurídicas, literarias y epigráficas. *Revue internationale des droits de l'Antiquité* 50: 155-93.

Loane, H.J. 1979. *Industry and Commerce of the City of Rome (50 B.C - 200 A.D)*. New York: Arno.

Martelli, E. 2013. *Sulle spalle dei saccarii: le rappresentazioni di facchini e il trasporto di derrate nel porto di Ostia in epoca imperiale* (British Archaeological Reports, International Series). Oxford: Archaeopress.

Mataix Ferrándiz, E. 2022. Distribution management, punishment and protection in public works in the Roman Empire. On Dressel 20 and beyond, en P. Candy y E. Mataix Ferrándiz (eds) *Roman Law and Maritime Commerce*: 77-108. Edinburgh: Edinburgh University Press.

Mattingly, D.J. y G.S. Aldrete 2000. The feeding of imperial Rome: the mechanics of the food supply system, en J. Coulston y H. Dodge (eds) *Ancient Rome: The Archaeology of the Eternal City*: 142-65. Oxford: Oxford University School of Archaeology.

Morais, R. 2010. Trade and the means of transportation, en C. Carreras y R Morais (eds) *The Western Roman Atlantic Façade: A Study of the Economy and Trade in the Mar Exterior from the Republic to the Principate*: 21-30. Oxford: BAR.

Morales Muñoz, C. 2005. La relación entre el registro "Beta" de la epigrafía anfórica olearia bética y la onomástica de la inscripciones gaditanas altoimperiales. *Gerión* 23.1: 251-69.

Morretta, S. 1999. Donne imprenditrici nella produzione e nel commercio dell'ollio Betico (I-III SEC. D.C.). *Saitabi* 49: 229-45.

Nantet, E. 2015. *Phortia: Le tonnage des navires de commerce en Méditerranée*. Rennes: Presses universitaires de Rennes.

Orsi, P. 1907. *Notizie degli scavi di antichità*. Milano: Real Accademia dei Lincei.

Panciera, S. 1980. Olearii, en J.H. D'Arms y E.C. Kopff (eds) *The Seaborne Commerce of Ancient Rome: Studies in Archaeology and History* (Memoirs of the American Academy in Rome 36): 235-349. Michigan: American Academy in Rome.

Pensa, M. 1999. Moli, fari e pescatori: la tradizione iconografica della città portuale in età romana. *Rivista di archeologia* 23: 94-130.

Rico, Ch. 2003. Mercatores, negotiatores et diffusores olearii et le commerce de l'huile de Bétique à destination de Rome aux I et II siècles de notre ère. *Revue des études anciennes* 2: 413-33.

Robertis, F.M. de 1937. Il corpus naviculariorum nella stratificazione sociale del Basso Impero. *Rivista del diritto della navigazione* 3: 115-41.

Rodríguez-Almeida, E. 1979. Monte Testaccio: i mercatores dell'olio della Betica. *Mélanges de l'Ecole française de Rome: Antiquité* 91.2: 873-975.

Rodríguez Almeida, E. 1984. *Il monte Testaccio*. Roma: Quasar.

Rohde, D. 2012. *Zwischen Individuum und Stadtgemeinde. Die Integration von Collegia in Hafenstädten*. Mainz: Verlag Antike.

Rougé, J. 1966. *Recherches sur l'organisation du commerce maritime en Mediterranée sous l'Empire romain*. Paris: École pratique des hautes études.

Rougier, H. 2015. La saisonnalité des activités portuaires dans l'Occident romain sous le Haut-Empire. *Pallas* 99: 209-26.

Rougier, H. 2016. L'identité professionnelle et l'expression du métier dans l'épigraphie portuaire occidentale: différents niveaux de codification. *Dialogues d'histoire ancienne* 42.2: 103-21.

Salvaterra, C. 2006. Labour and identity in the Roman world: Italian historiography during the last two decades, en B Walldijk (ed.) *Professions and Social Identity: New European Historical Research on Work, Gender and Society*: 15-38. Pisa: Edizioni Plus.

Salvo, L. de 1992. *Economia privata e pubblici servizi nell'imperio romano: i corpora naviculariorum*. Messina: Kleio.

Schmidts, T. 2011. *Akteure und Organisation der Handelsschifffahrt in den nordwestlichen Provinzen des Römischen Reiches*. Mainz: Römisch-Germanischen Zentralmuseums.

Sirks, B. 1991. *Food for Rome: The Legal Structure of the Transportation and Processing of Supplies for the Imperial Distributions in Rome and Constantinople*. Amsterdam: Gieben.

Taglietti, F. 1994. Un inedito bollo laterizio ostiense ed il commercio dell'olio betico, en *Epigrafia della produzione e della distribuzione: actes de la VIe Rencontre franco-italienne sur l'épigraphie du monde romain (Rome, 5-6 juin 1992), École française de Rome*, 157-93. Roma: Publications de l'École française de Rome.

Tchernia, A. 2016. *The Romans and Trade* (Oxford Studies on the Roman Economy). Oxford: Oxford University Press.

Terrado Ortuño, P. 2016. *Officia portuensia: Vida i treball al port a través de l'epigrafia i les fonts textuals; una aproximació a Tarraco*, IX. Tarragona: Autoritat Portuària de Tarragona.

Terrado Ortuño, P. 2018. La vida portuaria en Tarraco. Organización y gestión del trabajo a través de las fuentes arqueológicas y documentales. *Cuadernos de Arqueología de la Universidad de Navarra* 26: 49-73

Terrado Ortuño, P. 2019. *El puerto de Tarraco en época romana (s. II aC - III dC). Fuentes, historiografía y arqueología*. Tarragona: Servei de publicacions del Port de Tarragona.

Terrado Ortuño, P. *en prensa*. Acerca de CIL VI, 25737: una saccaria en Roma?

Tran, N. 2008. Les collèges d'horrearii et de mensores, à Rome et à Ostie, sous le Haut-Empire. *Mélanges de l'Ecole française de Rome Antiquité* 120.2: 295-306.

Tran, N. 2016. The social organization of commerce and crafts in ancient Arles: heterogeneity, hierarchy, and patronage, en A. Wilson y N. Flohr (eds) *Urban Craftsmen and Traders in the Roman World*: 255-67. Oxford: Oxford University Press.

Treggiani, S. 1979. Lower class woman in the Roman economy. *Florilegium* 1: 65-83.

Valencia Hernández, M. 1990. Mercator y negotiator. Ambigüedad y realidad económica en la obra de Cicerón. *Caesaraugusta* 66/67: 195-216.

Verboven, K. 2007. Ce que negotiari et ses dérivés veulent dire, en J. Andreau y V. Chankowski (eds) *Vocabulaire et expression de l'économie dans le monde antique*: 89-118. Bordeaux: Ausonius.

Waltzing, J.P. 1895. *Étude historique sur les corporations professionnelles chez les romains depuis les origines jusqu'à la chute de l'Empire d'Occident*, 3 vol. Louvain: Peeters.

Zimmer, G. 1982. *Römische Berufdarstellungen*, XII. Berlin: Deutsches Archäologisches Institut.

22. Un bronzo provinciale di Traiano della zecca di Amisus (Pontus) rinvenuto a Porto

Emanuela Spagnoli

Questo contributo verte sull'inquadramento di un raro bronzo di Traiano di zecca romano-provinciale proveniente da un saggio di scavo diretto da Simon Keay a Porto nel 2009. Il dato si collega alla più ampia riflessione sugli esiti dei collegamenti mediterranei documentati dal sito nella media età imperiale, un tema a cui Simon ha dedicato molti anni di intensa ricerca.

La responsabilità dello studio numismatico dei contesti mi lega da lungo tempo e con profonda amicizia all'equipe del *Portus Project* coordinato da Simon Keay (*Portus Project*: <https://www.portusproject.org/>; cf. Keay *et al* 2021).

A partire dall'incontro di Roma del 2008 (Keay *et al.* 2011), questa collaborazione scientifica si è giovata di un interesse condiviso per la moneta, che per Simon risaliva agli anni della sua formazione numismatica con Richard Reece. Positiva occasione di confronto sui materiali è stata, ancor prima, l'edizione del ripostiglio monetale (2003) rinvenuto in un deposito granario nel corso di scavi alla cinta urbica di Porto, condotti dalla allora Soprintendenza archeologica di Ostia antica: un contesto che sotto un diverso profilo ha valorizzato, tra fine V e inizi del VI secolo, un dato relazionale con l'Africa vandala e bizantina prospettato sulla base anche di altre evidenze materiali e della storia del territorio (Spagnoli 2001; 2013: 527-28; Keay 2005: 177).

Sui risultati di una disciplina specialistica quale è la Numismatica, nei suoi aspetti quantitativi e qualitativi, si è quindi utilmente fondato lo studio di questo importante distretto costiero. La ricostruzione del peso economico di Roma nel Mediterraneo antico, non solo come città-consumatrice, ha appunto costituito uno dei grandi ambiti di ricerca che Simon Keay ha mirato a investigare negli aspetti molteplici e variegati della cultura materiale, integrati nella dimensione della topografia storica del porto imperiale e del distretto funzionale anche sotto il profilo politico-amministrativo. Emergono dal suo lavoro appassionato su questo territorio la pluralità e la ricchezza delle sue linee di indagine.

In omaggio alla sua memoria e alla sua spiccata sensibilità per le dinamiche socioeconomiche di età romana, ho scelto pertanto di soffermarmi su un ritrovamento inedito dagli scavi condotti sotto la sua direzione nel settore PTXI, nell'area del Palazzo Imperiale (Keay 2018: 149; 2020: 45; Keay *et al.* forthcoming). Il complesso delle evidenze contestuali di questi saggi di scavo è di particolare interesse per la storia monetaria del territorio portuense anche perché si aggancia al quadro di carattere generale del distretto ostiense-portuense che ho avuto modo di documentare in altre sedi (Spagnoli 2023).

La moneta qui in esame viene da contesti datati al III secolo d.C. Si tratta di un nominale in bronzo di taglio medio, molto usurato, con tracce evidenti di impiego prolungato e dunque solo parzialmente leggibile, ma lo studio numismatico ne consente un preciso inquadramento in area provinciale (Figura 22.1). È presente, infatti, una contromarca a profilo circolare con monogramma in legamento, ben classificata, impressa dalla zecca di *Amisus,* città del comparto pontico nella provincia imperiale di *Pontus et Bithynia* (RPC III: 147, 149), Figg. 22.2-22.3. Si ricorda in proposito che *Amisus* è città autonoma nella provincia romana istituita fin da tarda età repubblicana e che la zecca, attiva da età giulio-claudia alla prima età flavia (Vespasiano), riprende la sua produzione con Traiano (97/98) in modo discontinuo fino al 113/114 (Per la cronologia delle emissioni di Traiano di zecca imperiale cf. Woytek 2010; sulle emissioni provinciali, da ultimo: Zajac 2022).

In bibliografia questa contromarca è documentata, sempre sul dritto, da almeno altri sette esemplari riferibili ad uno stesso nominale tutti della stessa zecca, ma di tre serie distinte: RPC III, 1231 (98 d.C.: 1 esemplare); 1234 (98/99 d.C.: 4 esemplari); 1236 (106-07 d.C.: 2 esemplari). Per residui caratteri del tipo di rovescio si propone in questo caso una attribuzione alla serie RPC III, 1234 che è anche quella più intensivamente contromarcata, con una consistenza complessiva di quattro monete su un totale di sette esemplari censiti, in collezione pubblica (<https://rpc.ashmus.ox.ac.uk/coins/3/1234>: Paris, BNF; London, BM; Bucharest; Warsaw.), cfr. Figura 22.2.

Come ipotizzato in altri casi da C. Howgego (1985: 8), la contromarca sembrerebbe applicata su uno stock di monete a breve distanza di tempo dalla loro coniazione: essa consente di fissare l'emissione nella tarda età traianea, a partire dal sistema di datazione della zecca

Figura 22.1. Emissione romana-provinciale, Traiano (AD 98-99), zecca di *Amisus* (*Pontus et Bithynia*), D/ Tracce illeggibili della leggenda; busto laureato, a d.; sotto al mento: contromarca PME (in legamento); R/ Tracce illeggibili della leggenda; capricorno con cornucopia, a d.; AE 11,63 g, 28 mm; RPC III, 1234; Howgego 1985: 635: contromarca PME (142 = AD 113-14), cf. <https://rpc. ashmus.ox.ac.uk/countermark/758>; © MIC, PaOnt: da *Portus*, PT XI, Periodo 4 (età severiana), area B2: peristilio industriale (*Building 3*), US 2324 (anno 2009), 30063-SF 415, n. 107 (© Portus Project); foto Autrice: fuori scala.

che prende avvio dalla battaglia di Azio (32/31 a.C.) in chiaro collegamento con Roma (PME=145=113/114 d.C.) (Howgego 1985, n. 635; RPC III: 147, 149: <https://rpc. ashmus.ox.ac.uk/countermark/758> (consultato il 28 marzo 2022); Højte 2006: 20). Un picco delle emissioni in questa provincia si porrebbe dopo il 102, forse in relazione al vasto programma di opere pubbliche (Plino il Giovane, *Ep.* X.23, 37, 39: lo scrittore è presente in *Bithynia* dal 109).

Non mi soffermo in questa sede sulle problematiche produttive della zecca, ma ricordo che sotto il profilo tipologico e formale si evidenziano caratteri peculiari e distintivi: il ritratto di Traiano sul D/ sembra derivato da prototipi monetali imperiali semplificati e la leggenda, in greco, mostra varianti e abbreviazioni della titolatura ufficiale. La coniazione procede inoltre secondo uno standard locale che si addensa su un peso di circa 10 g, con modulo di circa 29 mm. Per dati tecnici e metrologici questo nominale risulta dunque assimilabile al taglio dell'*as* battuto da Roma nella media età imperiale e pertanto la affermazione di questo bronzo nelle stratigrafie portuensi risulta pienamente compatibile con il quadro di circolazione locale della moneta corrente, di basso taglio.

Per il bronzo romano provinciale si ipotizza tuttavia un impiego, in genere, strettamente regionale, anche se i dati di circolazione extra-regionale di questo numerario sono in via di precisazione (Zając 2019: 127-29, 131).

La attestazione di questa moneta a Porto, peraltro da un contesto stratigrafico interamente noto, fornisce quindi un nuovo e importante elemento di giudizio, non solo per delineare l'ampiezza del raggio di diffusione di questi materiali, ad oggi ancora poco documentato in area romana, ma anche per verificarne i tempi di arrivo e le eventuali funzionalità nel profilo socioeconomico e monetario che si determina in questa regione costiera con lo sfruttamento intensivo del bacino traianeo.

L'esemplare proviene da un deposito archeologico scavato nella parte orientale del peristilio industriale del Palazzo Imperiale e, più in dettaglio, esso è stato localizzato nell'area di una rilevante officina vetraria, dentro a uno strato di riempimento ricco di molti residui e di scarti di lavorazione (Lepri e Saguì 2019: 8), Figg. 22.4-22.5. Come si è accennato in apertura, l'epoca di formazione del contesto, basata sulla globalità degli indicatori archeologici è circoscritta in età severiana (Periodo 4) e fornisce dunque un limite cronologico coerente per fissare la dispersione di questo pezzo nel terreno in epoca non distante dalla emissione (PT XI, area B2, Periodo 4, US 2324: cf. Keay 2018: 149; 2020: 45; Keay *et al.*, forthcoming).

Sulla base dello studio della globalità del deposito numismatico stratificato, i due rinvenimenti risultano in fase: essi sono relativi a serie pienamente coerenti sotto il profilo cronologico e funzionale. Oltre a questo bronzo traianeo di *Amisus*, si segnala infatti la presenza

Figura 22.2. *Amisus* (*Pontus et Bithynia*), emissione romana-provinciale, Traiano (AD 98-99), D/ ΤΡΑΙΑΝΟΣ ΣΕΒΑΣΤΟΥ, busto laureato a d., in basso contromarca PME (in legamento) R/ ΑΜΙΣΟΥ ΕΛΕΥΘΕΡΑΣ ΕΤΟΥΣ ΡΛ, capricorno a d.; © Paris Bibliothèque National de France, Inventory no. N 7223/1137 (ex Grand Duc): AE, g 10,90 (0053-0117_btv1b85606127_1-2; <https://gallica.bnf.fr/ark:/12148/btv1b85606127>) fotografia fuori scala.

di un asse di Commodo battuto da Roma (RIC III, 554) da un altro settore di scavo, ma sempre da un contesto di III secolo d.C. e che peraltro consente di datare la costruzione dell'anfiteatro (PT XI, Area A, US 1111). Il dato si rispecchia all'interno di un parametro regionale che per i materiali stratificati di età imperiale raggiunge percentuali non elevate (6,8 % delle emissioni fino ad età severiana). Nel segmento temporale tra Traiano e Commodo, tuttavia, si delinea un picco secondario dell'istogramma popolato da esemplari consunti, ma integri e leggibili, benché non sempre datanti (sei assi/dupondi).

Analogie si riscontrano nel comportamento dei dati monetari tratti da altri saggi di scavo della medesima regione portuense, ad esempio nell'area della Basilica cristiana (Spagnoli 2013: 521, 523-24) o nella necropoli di Isola sacra, dove in fasi di III secolo è stata osservata la significativa incidenza delle valute di avanzato II secolo e in particolare di quelle databili in tarda età antonina (Camilli e Taglietti 2018: 28, fig. 18). Il quadro complessivo delle attestazioni monetali risulta infine comparabile nelle sue linee di tendenza con i risultati dello studio numismatico elaborati per le stesse fasi nella vicina Ostia (Spagnoli 2023: tabella 2).

In questa situazione, restano purtroppo in ombra i dati analitici della circolazione a Roma. Dopo lo studio di Reece (1982: 119, 120, 2 bronzi "greco-imperiali" di Adriano) è però possibile ricavare almeno alcuni dati sparsi, per lo più privi di indicazioni di contesto,

dall'esame di un database disponibile online, comprensivo di schede dei reperti numismatici di oltre trecentotrenta interventi di scavo in città e nel suburbio, anche non programmati e di emergenza, negli anni 1956-2013 (Cf. http://www.catanumilli.it/ElencoScavi.aspx (consultato il 29.3.2022)). Su un totale 9741 monete classificate è stato quindi estrapolato un campione di bronzi provinciali pari al 0,1% delle evidenze, con una peculiare incidenza delle emissioni databili tra l'avanzato II secolo e l'età severiana: tra i materiali di zecca allogena si segnala la presenza di nominali enei delle zecche di *Alexandria* (*Aegyptus*): Adriano (1), Marco Aurelio (1), Caracalla (2), incerto (1); di *Laodicaea* (*Syria*): Caracalla (1); di *Pautalia* (*Thracia*): Geta; di *Nicaea* (*Bythinia*): Geta (1). Si aggiungono a questi, alcuni nuovi dati di circolazione tratti da uno studio preliminare sul bronzo provinciale della tarda età severiana dalle zecche di *Cyzicus* (*Mysia*) e di zecca non classificabile della *Phrygia* (RPC VII.1, 783.1) in *Asia*, restituiti da alcuni contesti di necropoli urbane del tardo III secolo, ancora in corso di studio (Genovese e Spagnoli 2023). A questo quadro, pur lacunoso, manca infine anche il riscontro di altre aree di circolazione e in particolare del grande complesso urbano e portuale di *Puteoli*, di peculiare incidenza per la storia dei transiti legati all'approvvigionamento annonario (Spagnoli *et al.* 2024).

Limitando l'attenzione a questo punto all'esame al campione portuense esaminato anche in rapporto ai dati elaborati per Ostia, si osserva che le emissioni

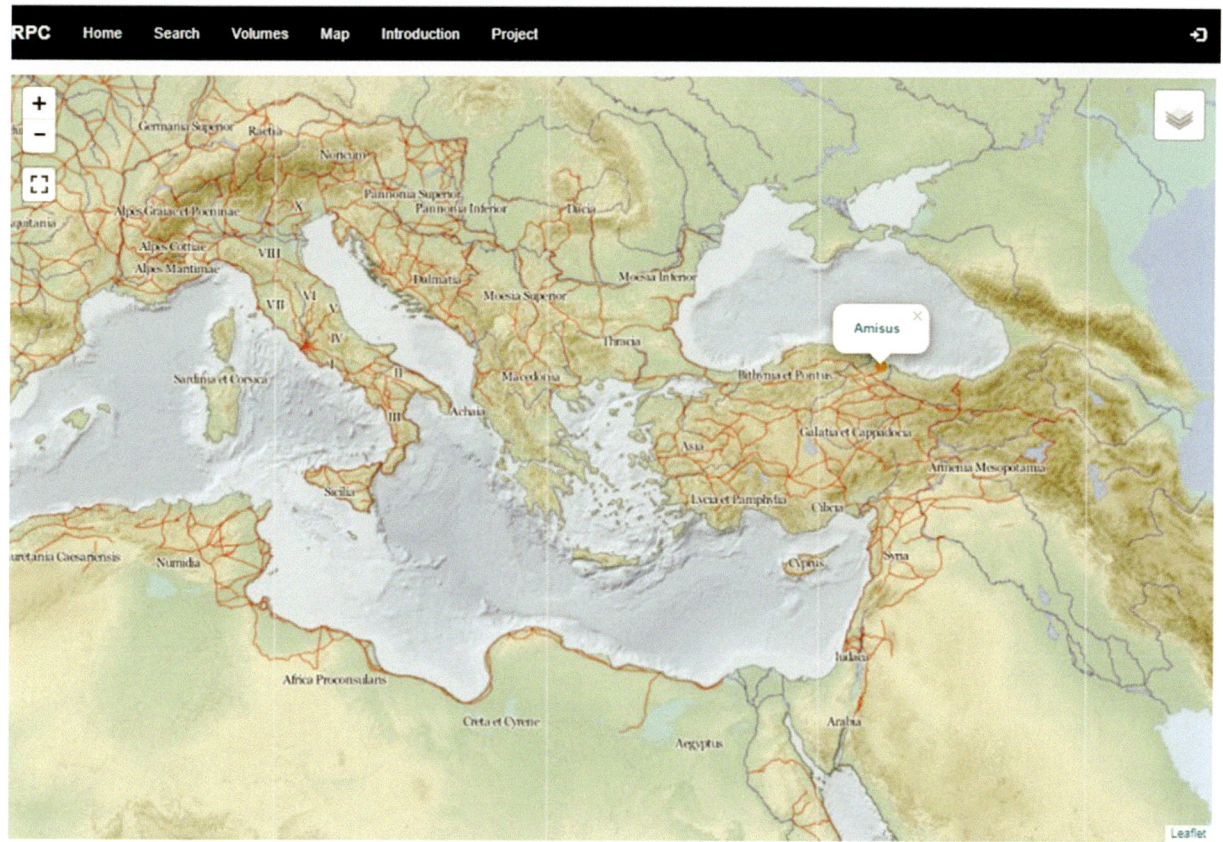

Figura 22.3. Localizzazione della città di *Amisus*, in *Bithynia* (© RPC online: <https://rpc.ashmus.ox.ac.uk/search/map?q=amisus>, rielaborazione dell'Autrice).

enee inquadrabili da Traiano alla prima età severiana si dispongono nei due comparti territoriali in sostanziale parallelismo. Soprattutto ad Ostia si intensifica il carattere eterogeneo degli arrivi di valuta "straniera" e, pur nella assoluta preminenza delle serie enee di zecca imperiale, spicca il nucleo delle emissioni di zecche provinciali, pari al 2,5% su un complesso di materiali di varia provenienza esaminati per uno studio di area (Spagnoli 2023: tabelle 1-2). Non tutti i reperti ostiensi sono ancorati ai contesti, ma si recuperano alcuni importanti dati da depositi archeologici in settori centrali della città la cui formazione si pone in epoca non distante dalla emissione: ad esempio nei saggi al Caseggiato IV, II,5 o alle Terme del Nuotatore V,X,3. A questi depositi archeologici si collega, in fase, una suggestiva localizzazione del bronzo provinciale nell'area del porto fluviale in *Regio* III e nel quadro extramuraneo della *Regio* IV, a ridosso della via Severiana (Spagnoli 2023). Altre indicazioni assumono invece un valore solo topografico, come è nel caso dei reperti restituiti dallo sterro del 1938 nel *Thermopolium* sulla via di Diana I,II,5 (Spagnoli 2022: tabella 2, nn. 300, 302, 440, 543, 546, fig. 3).

A rafforzare questi segnali intervengono poi altri fattori specifici del quadro monetario di questa regione costiera, per cui va dato uno sguardo alle zecche

(Tabella 22.1). Significativa, infatti, risulta in città e nel suburbio la rappresentanza di numerario coevo di area greca e greco-orientale, di *Athenae* e *Corinthus* (*Achaia*), di *Perinthus* e *Byzantium* (*Thracia*), di *Neoclaudiopolis* (*Galatia*), di *Chios* e forse di *Ephesus* (*Ionia*), di *Caesarea* (*Cappadocia*), di *Gaza* (*Syria*); si aggiunge inoltre una limitata attestazione della zecca di *Alexandria* (*Aegyptus*) (RPC IV.4, 14749) la cui moneta sembra porsi in continuità con arrivi di serie della tarda età flavia.

Ragionare in dettaglio sull'indice di permeazione delle valute provinciali, può apparire infine problematico sulla base del limitato campione di studio disponibile, ma la varietà e la congruenza delle serie consolidano nel corso dell'avanzato/fine II secolo una linea di tendenza, con indici in crescita rispetto al raccolto numismatico della prima età imperiale di questo territorio (Spagnoli 2021: 398). Queste monete di scarso valore intrinseco sono di fatto una preziosa spia per la ricostruzione della storia minuta del sito nella sua dimensione ordinaria e documentano una molteplicità di contatti extra-regionali su percorsi non sempre lineari e dai contorni ancora sfumati. Ne emerge una situazione che ha più sfaccettature.

Si delinea infatti, più specifica, una traiettoria che si origina dalle zecche provinciali del versante centrale e

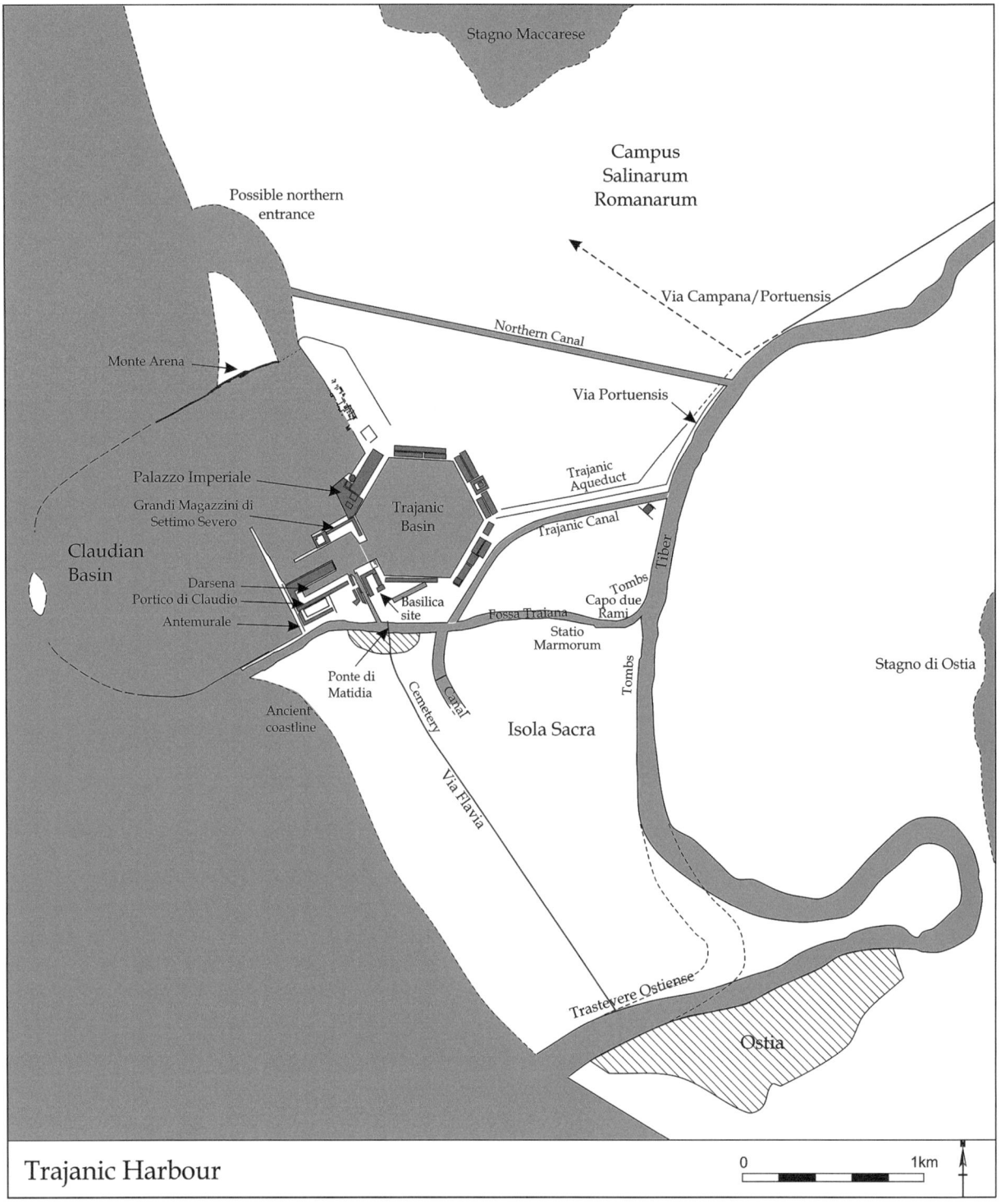

Figura 22.4. Da Keay 2012: 40, fig. 2.5. Plan of Ostia and Portus (© Portus Project).

costiero dell'*Asia Minor* e della *Syria* e *Palaestina*, oltre che dal comparto egeo nord-orientale, articolata secondo più direttrici che dal *Pontus Euxinus*, oltrepassato il Bosforo, lambiscono le coste greche peninsulari e peloponnesiache, il *Sinus Saronicus*, trascinando le valute di zecca greca prima delle chiusure dell'avanzato III secolo (Johnston 2012: 454, 461-65). Si tratta di numeri contenuti, ai quali si unisce però anche un fenomeno,

più circoscritto, di contromarche di probabile area provinciale, non sempre pienamente leggibili (Spagnoli 2022: tabella 2, nn. 163, 560, 573; per i contesti: Heinzelmann 2020: 203, 250-51, 404-05). L'evidenza si conferma a Porto, sia pure con piccolissimi numeri: al caso qui in esame, del bronzo di *Amisus* (*Pontus*), si aggiunge l'evidenza offerta dalla necropoli di Isola Sacra che ha restituito un bronzo di *Antandrus* (*Troas*) in

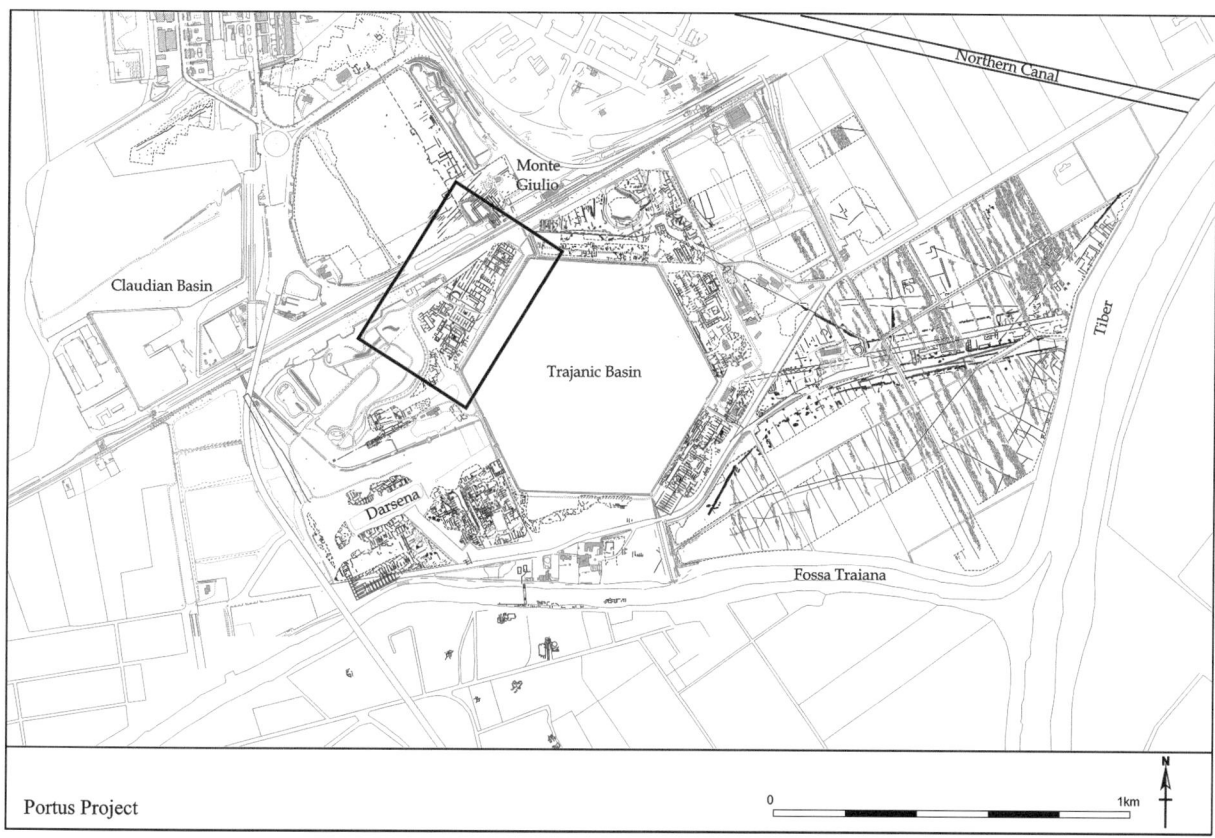

Figura 22.5. Da Keay 2012: 45, fig. 2.7. Plan of Portus, with the focus of fieldwork 2007–12 (indicated by the box)
(© Portus Project).

tomba (Tabella 22.1, n. 8). Il computo globale è però da ritenersi probabilmente sottostimato per le condizioni in genere di cattiva conservazione dei reperti.

In sintesi, emergono tra i due distretti di Ostia e di Porto situazioni diversificate nei numeri assoluti ma coerenti nei dati percentuali. Compatibilmente con la lunga storia della ricerca archeologica di queste aree, il campione ostiense della media età imperiale si mantiene infatti su livelli assoluti più elevati di quelli ad oggi documentati a Porto e in particolare il bronzo di taglio medio si dimostra infiltrato con percentuali variabili ma significative nell'uso pubblico, o in ambito semi-pubblico, anche domestico e privato, o personale (necropoli). Il profilo monetario sembra pertanto indicare in termini quantitativi un persistente sbilanciamento delle attività mercantili di piccolo livello nel quadrante cittadino di Ostia e nel suburbio.

Accanto ad un sintomatico segnale di crescita del bronzo di Roma si consoliderebbe inoltre il consumo delle valute provinciali probabilmente anche in risposta a condizioni situazioni di crescente richiesta di circolante minuto. La dispersione del numerario di basso valore si evidenzia d'altro canto lungo percorsi d'uso ormai profondamente monetarizzati. Questi parametri distributivi danno, infatti, corpo ad un flusso valutario che si attua con rapido trasferimento oltre che con pieno assorbimento della valuta corrente nel comparto territoriale, a Ostia come a Porto. Il fenomeno si delinea in risposta ad una richiesta di bassi tagli valutari che promana da una comunità articolata su una larga e variegata base sociale.

Si innesta in questo quadro anche il ricorso all'uso intensivo di specie non monetali. Si tratta di alcune serie di piombi monetiformi che attestano, specialmente in area ostiense, produzioni locali forse legate a gruppi di *mercatores*, se non specificamente destinate a esigenze amministrative o per il consumo interno, a supporto e/o a integrazione di circuiti economici chiusi o prefissati (Spagnoli 2017: 271). A questi materiali si possono correlare, da ultimo, alcuni peculiari reperti in bronzo definibili come piccole tessere di forma squadrata con soggetti figurati, noti dal mercato antiquario e dubitativamente ricondotti a questo territorio costiero per finalità legate probabilmente al sistema dei transiti navali e marittimi (Stannard 2015; Keay 2018: 191, fig. 29). Una conferma della esistenza di un circuito locale di queste tessere enee giunge da un dato contestuale dell'area PT III, da indagini del 1991 (Spagnoli 2019: 202, n. 28).

L'affluenza di bronzo romano-provinciale, che è di fruizione tendenzialmente regionale, trova infine un buon rapporto di attestazione con le provenienze della ceramica entro la prima età severiana: il dato si coglie in concomitanza con l'accresciuto ritmo dei transiti marittimi e con l'espansione delle strutture di servizio e di magazzino, quindi in sintonia con la richiesta di beni di importazione documentati nei depositi archeologici di Ostia o in quelli portuensi. Si cita ad esempio la peculiare attestazione a Ostia di anfore istro-pontiche e dati più specifici si raccolgono su materiali di tarda età antonina dalla provincia di *Pontus et Bithynia,* se posti in relazione al ricco complesso delle importazioni mercantili che alla stessa epoca giungono dal bacino mediterraneo (Rizzo 2012: 93, fig. 4.3). Questo quadro reca il segno di una prosperità che sembra riflettersi nel famoso elogio di Roma di Elio Aristide (*Orationes* 26.11-13).

La numerosità delle zecche sembra peraltro rispecchiata anche dalla variegata provenienza degli attori economici nei vari comparti produttivi e infrastrutturali e che, chiamati in causa dalle testimonianze epigrafiche, si rivelano quali inurbati di differente estrazione sociale. E' ad esempio ben nota epigraficamente l'esistenza di un luogo di culto e quindi di una struttura associativa dei cittadini di Gaza che sotto Gordiano III risiedevano o soggiornavano a *Portus* (Van Haeperen 2021: 202-01). Anche a Ostia si afferma, nel corso del II-III secolo, una forte presenza di stranieri fino ai vertici dell'amministrazione cittadina (Licordari 2020; Keay 2018: 154-58).

Questa fase di avanzato II- inizi III secolo ci parla pertanto, inequivocabilmente, dello intenso spostamento di uomini e merci secondo una mappa di arrivi che illumina le traiettorie greco-orientali e pontiche, note anche alle fonti. Carichi di legno, metalli e pigmenti dal nord dell'Anatolia o speciali e costose forniture di salse pontiche di pesce sono ad esempio ricordate da Plinio il Vecchio (*HN* 9,18) o da Diodoro Siculo (*Bibl.* 37.3.5). È inoltre documentato archeologicamente l'arrivo di vino, grano, salse di pesce oppure di spezie e tinture, così come di prodotti per l'edilizia: legname, marmo o altre merci esclusive, compresa la materia prima lavorata in sede per l'*instrumentum* di vetro (Bruno *et al.* 2012; Keay 2018: 158-64; Spagnoli 2018, plate 1-5; Lepri e Saguì 2018: figg. 15, 17).

Quantitativi non marginali di bronzi provinciali si infiltrano in questi ambiti economici come una moneta di "accompagno", lungo le rotte dei carichi alimentari e di pregio diretti a Roma dal più vasto bacino mediterraneo, dall'Asia *Minor,* dall'Egitto. Il consumo di valuta "straniera" non è dunque un fenomeno isolato nel quadro locale, ma esso assume uno speciale rilievo con la disamina dell'imponente e variegato campione

documentale ad oggi ricostruito dal più vasto disegno interpretativo del *Portus Project*, finemente elaborato da Simon Keay.

Bibliografia

Bruno, M., H. Elci, A.B. Yavuz e D. Attanasio 2012. Unknown ancient marble quarries of western Asia Minor, in A. Gutierrez Garcia, M.P. Lapuente Mercadal e I. Roda de Llanza (eds) *Interdisciplinary Studies on Ancient Stone*: 562-72. Tarragona: Institut català d'arqueologia clàssica.

Camilli, L. e F. Taglietti 2018. Sepolture e monete: il prezzo dell'Ade? A proposito dei rinvenimenti monetali in tombe della necropoli di Porto all'Isola Sacra, in M. Cébeillac-Gervasoni, N. Laubry e F. Zevi (eds) *Ricerche su Ostia e il suo territorio Atti del Terzo Seminario Ostiense (Roma, École française de Rome, 21-22 ottobre 2015)* (Collection de l'École française de Rome). Roma: Publications de l'École française de Rome, consultato 17 gennaio 2021, <http://www.openedition.org/6540>.

Fabbricotti, E. 1969. Considerazioni su alcune monete trovate recentemente in Ostia. *Rivista Italiana di Numismatica* 17: 61-66

GIC =   Howgego, C.J. 1985

Heinzelmann, M. 2020. *Ostia, I: Forma urbis Ostiae: Untersuchungen zur Entwicklung der Hafenstadt Roms von der Zeit der Republik bis ins frühe Mittelalter.* Wiesbaden: Harrassowitz.

Højte, J.M. 2006. From kingdom to province: reshaping Pontos after the fall of Mithridates V, in T. Bekker-Nielsen (ed.) *Rome and the Black Sea Region: Domination, Romanisation, Resistance*: 15-30. Aarhus: Aarhus University Press.

Howgego, C.J. 1985. *Greek Imperial Countermarks: Studies in the Provincial Coinage of the Roman Empire* (Royal Numismatic Society (Great Britain), Special publication 17). London: Royal Numismatic Society.

Johnston, A. 2012. The provinces after Commodus, in W. Metcalf (ed.) *The Oxford Handbook of Greek and Roman Coinages*: 453-67. Oxford: Oxford University Press.

Keay, S. (ed.) 2012. *Rome, Portus and the Mediterranean* (Archaeological Monographs of the British School at Rome 21). London: British School at Rome.

Keay, S. 2018. The role played by the *Portus Augusti* in flows of commerce between Rome and its Mediterranean ports, in B. Woytek (ed.) *Infrastructure and Distribution in Ancient Economies, Proceedings of a Conference Held at the Austrian Academy of Sciences, 28-31 October 2014* (Denkschriften der phil.-hist. Klasse 506): 147-92. Wien: Verlag der österreichischen Akademie der Wissenschaften.

Keay, S., G. Earl e F. Felici (forthcoming). *Uncovering the Harbour Building: Excavations at Portus 2007-2012, I: The Surveys, Excavations and Architectural Reconstructions* of the Palazzo Imperiale and Adjacent Buildings (British School at Rome Studies). Cambridge: Cambridge University Press.

Keay, S., M. Millett, L. Paroli e K. Strutt 2005. *Portus: An Archaeological Survey of the Port of Imperial Rome* (Archaeological Monographs of the British School at Rome 15). London: British School at Rome.

Keay, S. e L. Paroli (eds) 2011. *Portus and its Hinterland: Recent Archaeological Research* (Archaeological Monographs of the British School at Rome). London: British School at Rome.

Lepri, B. e L. Saguì 2018. Vetri e indicatori di produzione vetraria a Ostia e a Porto. *Mélanges de l'École française de Rome: Antiquité [Online]* 130, Messo online il 03 settembre 2019, consultato il 26 marzo 2022 <http://journals.openedition.org/mefra/6506>.

Licordari, A. 2020. The population of Ostia: composition and working activities, an analysis of inscriptions, in A. Karivieri (ed.) *Life and Death in a Multicultural Harbour City: Ostia Antica from the Republic through Late Antiquity*: 165-72. Roma: Institutum Romanum Finlandiae.

Necropoli di Ostia 1999 = Messineo, G. e A. Pellegrino 1999 *Dalle necropoli di Ostia, riti ed usi funerari: Ostia Antica, Castello di Giulio II, marzo 1998-luglio 1999*. Roma: Soprintendenza archeologica di Ostia.

Pardini, G. 2014. Le monete, in C. Panella e G. Rizzo (eds) *Ostia*, VI: *Le Terme del Nuotatore di Ostia, i saggi nell'Area NE; le anfore, Ostia e i commerci mediterranei* (Studi miscellanei 38). Roma: L'Erma di Bretschneider.

Reece, R. 1982. A collection of coins from the centre of Rome. *Papers of the British School at Rome* 50: 116-45.

Rizzo, G. 2012. Roma e Ostia, un binomio ancora possibile? Di alcuni generi trasportati in anfora in età tardo-antonina, in Keay 2012: 87-104.

RPC = Roman Provincial Coinage, consultato il 26 marzo 2022 <https://rpc.ashmus.ox.ac.uk/>.

RPC III = From Nerva to Hadrian (AD 96–138); RPC IV.1 = From Antoninus Pius to Commodus (AD 138–192): Cyrenaica to Bithynia-Pontus; RPC IV.2= From Antoninus Pius to Commodus (AD 138–192): Asia; RPC IV.3= From Antoninus Pius to Commodus (AD 138–192): Lycia-Pamphylia to Arabia; RPC IV.4 =From Antoninus Pius to Commodus (AD 138–192): Egypt.

SNG ANS = *Sylloge nummorum Graecorum, USA: The Collection of the American Numismatic Society, Part 6; Palestine - South Arabia*. New York: The American Numismatic Society, 1981.

Spagnoli, E. 2001. Ripostiglio monetale da Porto (Fiumicino - Roma). 277 ae post 445/450 d. C. *Annali dell'Istituto italiano di numismatica* 48 (2001 [2003]): 119-56.

Spagnoli, E. 2011. Materiali numismatici da contesti portuensi, in S. Keay e L. Paroli (eds) *Recent Research at Portus and in its Hinterland: Recent Archaeological Research* (Archaeological Monographs of the British School at Rome): 211-30. London: British School at Rome.

Spagnoli, E. 2013. I contesti della Basilica Portuense: il quadro economico-monetario, in M. Maiorano e L. Paroli (eds) *La Basilica Portuense: Scavi 1991-2007*: 521-58. Borgo S. Lorenzo: All'Insegna del Giglio.

Spagnoli, E. 2017. Piombi monetiformi da Ostia e Porto: problematiche interpretative, in M. Caccamo Caltabiano (ed.) *Proceedings XV International Numismatic Congress (Taormina, 21-25 settembre 2015)*: 269-72. Messina: Arbor Sapientiae.

Spagnoli, E. 2018. A new item of Roman imperial lead seal from Portus excavations (2015). *West&East* 3: 4-8.

Spagnoli E. 2019, Piombi *figurati* e *scritti* di età romana. Riflessioni su alcuni aspetti del fenomeno antico e della ricezione settecentesca a partire da un catalogo recente, in *Annali dell'Istituto Italiano di Numismatica*, 65, 2019, 197-227.

Spagnoli, E. 2021. Denari di Vespasiano con marchio di zecca di Efeso in area vesuviana, in M. Osanna (ed.) *Studium erga populum*: *Studium erga sapientiam; Atti del convegno internazionale (Napoli-Pompei, 12-13 luglio 2018)*: 395-409. Roma: L'Erma di Bretschneider.

Spagnoli, E. 2023. Presenze monetali del II secolo a Ostia antica, in M.L. Caldelli, N. Laubry e F. Zevi (eds) *Atti del 6° seminario ostiense, Roma, École française de Rome-Parco Archeologico di Ostia antica, 10-11 aprile 2018)* (Collection de l'École française de Rome): 195-242. Roma: Publications de l'École française de Rome/OpenEdition Books.

Spagnoli, E., I.S. Pagano e A. Pecorella 2024. La moneta nel contesto archeologico. Dati preliminari dalle ricerche in corso in area flegrea (Campania, Italia), in R. Brancato (ed.) *Come Federico opera sul campo 2022: scavi e ricerche archeologiche dell'Università di Napoli Federico II; atti del Convegno organizzato dalla Scuola di Specializzazione in Beni Archeologici, Dipartimento di Studi Umanistici (Napoli 17-18 novembre 2022)*: 115-30. Roma: Quasar.

Stannard, C. 2015. Shipping tesserae from Ostia and Minturnae. *The Numismatic Chronicle* 175: 147-54.

Zając, B. 2019. The Roman imperial coinage model for some provincial coins of Bithynia and Pontus struck during the Reign of Trajan (98–117). *Notae numismaticae*: 123-48.

Zając, B. 2022 (forthcoming). Countermarks on the coins of Bithynia and Pontus in the Roman period, in ACIN XVI Warsaw 2022 (in press).

Van Haeperen, F. 2021. I culti associativi di Portus, in F. Fontana e E. Murgia (eds) Sacrum facere: *Atti del VI Seminario di archeologia del Sacro; forme associative e pratiche rituali nel mondo antico, Trieste* (Polymnia 11): 197-210. Trieste: Edizioni Universita di Trieste.

Woytek, B. 2010. *Die Reichsprägung des Kaisers Traianus (98–117)*. Wien: Verlag der Österreichischen Akademie der Wissenschaften.

Part 3:
Roman Landscapes
and Urban Centres

23. Surveying the Roman Empire

Sophie Hay and Stephen Kay

This paper charts the advent and growth of the application of geophysical prospection by the British School at Rome and University of Southampton to investigate Roman towns in central Italy and the eastern Mediterranean. Over the last two decades, numerous Roman towns in central Italy, northern Africa, and Turkey have been investigated with some form of geophysical technique, most often fluxgate gradiometry due to its speed and effectiveness in recording sub-surface structures. The survey of Falerii Novi led by Simon Keay and Martin Millett, his close colleague throughout his career whom he met at the Institute of Archaeology (Millett 2021), represents a key moment and catalyst for the large-scale investigation of sites in Italy with geophysical prospection. Whilst previously, surveys had been conducted at a number of sites in the central region through the pioneering work of the *Fondazione Lerici* (i.e. Tarquinia, Vulci) as well as by the *Istituto per le Tecnologie Applicate ai Beni Culturali* (ITABC) of the Italian *Consiglio Nazionale delle Ricerche* (CNR), the survey at Falerii Novi illustrated how large greenfield sites could be quickly and relatively inexpensively fully investigated.

SH, SK

Falerii Novi (Fabrica di Roma, Viterbo)

The survey at Falerii Novi, part of the Roman Towns in the Middle and Lower Tiber Valley Project, began in 1997 under the umbrella of the British School at Rome's new Tiber Valley Project (Keay and Millett 2016; Patterson *et al.* 2020). The site immediately lent itself to geophysical prospection, with an open area of *c.* 32ha enclosed by the impressive, preserved city wall. The results of the magnetometry survey revealed in stunning detail the regular orthogonal grid plan of the town, with many buildings typical of a Roman city visible in the data (Keay *et al.* 2000).

The survey season in 1998 was the first geophysics project of the author with Simon and Martin (Figure 23.1).[1] Having completed several surveys with Nicola Terrenato in the Cecina Valley in the early part of the summer (Kay 2003), Nicola and I joined the team for the second season of survey at Falerii Novi. The most popular instrument at the time for large-scale magnetic survey was the Geoscan Fluxgate Gradiometer FM36, results from which the previous season, when compared with resistivity which was also trialled (Keay *et al.* 2000: 5), had been tantalising. Data was collected at a standard interval, 0.5m with a traverse interval of 1m, with data collected in parallel traverses in the same direction. With the advent of multi-sensor carts, looking back it seems incredible such energy was expended in constantly walking back at the end of each 30m traverse, but such was the methodology at the time. Whilst the work was monotonous and conducted under the burning sun of mid-August in Italy, such was the conviviality of the team that it largely went unnoticed. The enthusiasm expressed by Simon was infectious, as well as his inquisitiveness to immediately download the data to see the detailed city plan that was being revealed day by day.

The results of the magnetometry, despite being at what is now considered a coarse resolution, have stood the test of time and are regularly referenced in discussions of Roman urban planning. The recent results of a re-survey using a multi-antenna Ground-Penetrating Radar (GPR) array have shown the plan of the site in depth as well as at a greater resolution (Verdonck *et al.* 2020). The GPR revealed buildings that were too disturbed to interpret in the magnetic data, illustrating how a combined approach with different techniques can extract greater amounts of information, but also how the different geophysics techniques are complementary.

In 2021 the British School at Rome, together with the Universities of London, Harvard, and Toronto, in collaboration with the *Università degli studi di Firenze* and the University of Ghent began excavations at Falerii Novi.[2] The results of the fluxgate gradiometry survey together with the GPR have provided a template of the town plan, but much still remains to be understood about the city. Was there a pre-existing

---

[1] Stephen Kay. The other members of the 1998 team were Letizia Ceccarelli, Graeme Earl, Nick Holland, Simon Keay, Martin Millett, Sarah Poppy, Julia Robinson, Jeremy Taylor, and Nicola Terrenato.

[2] The excavations are conducted under an excavation permit issued by the Ministero della Cultura (Decree 608 of 10/06/2021; Decree 299 of 19/03/2024) and the Soprintendenza Archeologia, Belle Arti e Paesaggio per la provincia di Viterbo e per l'Etruria Meridionale.

Figure 23.1. Simon Keay at Falerii Novi with a trailer of surface material (photo BSR).

Faliscan settlement? What is the chronology and spatial development of the city's infrastructure? And what can be known about Falerii's decline and later urban phases? The new Falerii Novi Project seeks to address these and related questions through targeted stratigraphic excavation and multidisciplinary scientific study. The aim is to evaluate urban changes within a broader regional context, drawing upon the investigation of specific buildings, such as a *macellum*, *domus*, and *tabernae* (Andrews *et al.* 2023). The commencement of the excavations owes a great debt to Simon and Martin as it is their groundbreaking work at the site that paved the way to the new research, and it remains of great personal sadness to the author that Simon is not on hand to share and discuss these exciting developments at Falerii Novi.

The methodology of rapid assessment by magnetometry supported by surface survey and topographical modelling was also employed at the nearby site of Otricoli (Hay *et al.* 2013, see below). However, in the same year as the large survey at Falerii Novi, a further geophysical survey was commenced that was to shape Simon's research and the archaeological activity of the BSR for the next 20 years.

Portus Geophysical Survey 1998-2004 (Fiumicino, Lazio)

Whilst a very different site to Falerii Novi, the Roman imperial harbour of Portus was initially investigated with the same successful methodology (Figure 23.2). The first season of fieldwork took place in the winter of 1998 with magnetometry around the Trajanic harbour which revealed a dense layout of warehouses on four sides of the hexagonal harbour. Over the course of the following seasons the survey extended to include the Claudian harbour to the north and west, and the hinterland of the port towards Rome to the east, in total covering around *c.* 173ha of the harbour complex.[3] The results revealed the unique infrastructure that was built to service the port and aid its connectivity to Rome (Keay *et al.* 2005).

The magnetic survey of Portus revealed a different form of Roman urbanism, where the plan was designed to assist in the functioning of the trade and commerce

---

[3] Other members of the survey team were Letizia Ceccarelli, Frances Condron, Giuseppe Garbati, Nic Holland, Sophie Hay, Paul Johnson, Simon Keay, Fiona Lewis, Martin Millett, Doug Murphy, Louise Revell, Julia Robinson, Tim Sly, Kelly Spradley, Kristian Strutt, Katherine Thomas, and Helen Woodhouse.

Figure 23.2. Frances Condron using a Fluxgate gradiometer Geoscan FM36 with manual logger alongside the Trajanic harbour (photo Doug Murphy).

rather than daily life. The port had to serve a rapidly changing community whose presence was dictated by the tides and economy. The urbanscape of Portus was also closely tied with Ostia Antica, as many of the amenities typical of a Roman town, such as baths and a theatre were at Ostia rather than Portus. The survey, as well as the more recent investigations of Isola Sacra (Keay *et al.* 2020) showed how the two sites should be analysed as one integrated complex network.

The geophysical prospection at Portus also included other forms of survey alongside magnetometry, principally Ground-Penetrating Radar (GPR) and Electrical Resistance Tomography (ERT). The extensive site incorporates areas less suitable for magnetometry, such as roads and modern infrastructure, as well as more deeply buried contexts, therefore the methodology was adapted to include these other techniques. The adaptation of the methodological approach to Roman towns was key to the success of the work of Simon and Martin, as it became clear that each site required a tailored approach in order to extract the most information. The area of the Palazzo Imperiale at Portus proved an important testing ground for these techniques, as well as advancing other forms of

geophysical research such as the data fusion of varying datasets (Keay *et al.* 2009).

SK

Ocriculum (Otricoli, Umbria)

The Roman settlement of *Ocriculum* (Hay *et al.* 2013) lies below the modern hilltop town of Otricoli in Umbria and is a complex urban site straddling an undulating topography of hills, saddles of land, and a small valley that opens up to the water's edge of the River Tiber. Peaking in the first and second centuries AD, the town was an important centre of commence on the *via Flaminia*, and acted as a port and road station for travellers and goods passing up and down Italy. The approach to *Ocriculum* by boat is a less considered theme and one that can no longer be experienced as the river has changed course dramatically. But we should imagine the monumental architecture of *Ocriculum* spoke just as much to traders arriving along the River Tiber, as to those arriving by road.

Ocriculum was partly excavated in the 18th century by the Vatican under the patronage of Pope Pius VI. As

Figure 23.3. Simon Keay and Jeremy Taylor conducting a resistivity survey at Otricoli (photo BSR).

a result many of the finely crafted statues, including Jupiter, Augustus, and members of the Julio-Claudian family are on display in the galleries of the Vatican Museum. The glorious polychrome mosaic, once adorning the floor of the bathhouse, now endures the endless footfall of tourists in the Vatican Museum's Sala Rotonda.

Today, the major monuments of *Ocriculum* still stand, giving an air of grandeur to the site. The theatre nestles against the slope of a hill, the bath complex sits proud in an infilled valley, a monumental vaulted substructure props up one side of a steep ridge to support a temple above, and the amphitheatre – almost invisible from most angles of approach – is partially hewn into an outcrop of rock. The topography defines the settlement of *Ocriculum* in every sense.

The success of the gradiometry survey at Falerii Novi, only 20km south-west of *Ocriculum*, held much promise for the reprise of the collaboration of Simon and Martin who, after preliminary investigations in 1997, began fieldwork in earnest in 2002. By this point, Simon had founded the Archaeological Prospection Service of Southampton (APSS) within the Department of Archaeology at the University of Southampton, led

by Kristian Strutt and Sophie Hay (Millett 2021). The survey of *Ocriculum* was one of the first projects to see the collaboration of APSS and the British School at Rome, a partnership that endured until 2016.[4]

Ocriculum, however, did not deliver the equivalent spectacular results as Falerii Novi. A combination of the underlying tuff bedrock, the poor survival of archaeological remains on the upper slopes, and the deep alluvial deposits in the valleys meant the magnetic fields of the buried archaeology detected by gradiometry were obscured or simply absent. Even traces of the course of the *via Flaminia*, of which a section had been excavated and the robust Roman basalt paving found intact complete with tombs flanking its edges, resisted detection due to the depth of the overburden.

It is testimony to the diverse methodological approach adopted by Simon and Martin that the limited picture of the urban layout produced by the gradiometry and

---

[4] Other major settlements investigated in central Italy include Vignale (Carlucci *et al.* 2007), Fregellae (Ferraby *et al.* 2008), Gabii (Kay 2013), Teano (Hay *et al.* 2012) and Lucus Feroniae (Kay *et al.* 2023). Several minor settlements were also investigated by the Roman Towns in the Middle and Lower Tiber Valley Project (Johnson *et al.* 2004).

Figure 23.4. Martin Millett, Jeremy Taylor, and Simon Keay (left to right) visiting Otricoli, 1997 (photo BSR).

resistivity (Figure 23.3) was so richly complemented by the close-contour topographical survey, led by Tim Sly, that revealed the transformation of the settlement over time. *Ocriculum* proved to be yet another town that did not display the orthogonal layout traditionally associated with Roman settlements and though it boasted monumental architecture the evidence for human habitation was sparse. The natural instinct of the project directors to rummage in the undergrowth, inspect the sections of sunken trackways for inconspicuous archaeological remains, and consider the Vatican plans of the site (Figure 23.4) is an abiding memory of those who worked at Otricoli. The fact that part of a Roman temple was discovered after brushing aside a caking of chicken droppings in their coop, is but one example. Simon, donning his stout walking boots and zip-laden field trousers, was regularly seen striding across the ploughed fields stopping only to examine pottery sherds lying on the surface; quietly and diligently determined to understand the site through its artefacts as well as its landscape.

Leptis Magna (Libya)

Simon's indefatigable fascination for the connectivity of Roman ports around the Mediterranean prompted

a collaboration with *Università degli studi Roma Tre* at Leptis Magna, Libya to investigate the state of preservation of ancient remains along the coastal zone as part of a wider project to manage the conservation of this area. Leptis Magna was one of four eventual Roman *coloniae* in Tripolitania together with Oea, Sabratha, and Tacapae (in modern Tunisia). Leptis enjoyed a wealth of building activity in the reign of Augustus and the remains of edifices from this period still stand today. In AD 203 the Emperor Septimius Severus, a native of Leptis, bestowed his hometown with the prestigious honour of *ius Italicum*, setting it apart from and above the other cities with a monumental building programme to further impress upon the architectural splendour of the city. This included a newly remodelled port area with a lighthouse constructed on its western quay and a probable extension to the eastern quay. But perhaps most famous of all, a visit to Leptis by Severus was commemorated by the construction of a monumental quadriform arch adorned with marble reliefs standing at the junction of the main *decumanus* and *cardo* (Figure 23.5).

Prior to starting fieldwork in 2009 a reconnaissance mission was organised and Simon's relish at being amongst the remains of such a well-preserved Roman

Figure 23.5. Simon accompanied by the local guide walking towards the Arch of Septimius Severus, Leptis Magna. (photo Sophie Hay).

later sea wall defence along the beach. Unfortunately, the beach at the eastern extreme of the city known to be occupied by the luxury Roman coastal villas - *villae maritimae* - was heavily contaminated with modern surface debris so it was the topographic survey of the extant remains that provided the best documentation of this area. But it was immediately above this beach, in the area between the eastern quay of the Severan port and the amphitheatre, where the gradiometry survey produced the most conclusive and rewarding results.

Traces of the late Roman wall and its ditch bisected the survey area north to south and on its eastern flank remains of mausolea podia were seen in abundance. The cemetery was already well documented but was circumscribed to an area immediately east and south of the standing remains of the mausoleum of Gasr Shaddad. The gradiometry survey results clearly indicated that the extent of the cemetery extended north of this area and that the density of mausolea was high. The layout of mausolea in distinct rows was comparable to that found in the western cemetery and there was an observable difference in the size of the mausolea increasing from west to east. Many of the funerary remains in the western part of the survey near the late Roman wall, measured only a few metres but in the eastern part of the survey they were up to 12m in length.

In terms of evaluating the archaeological remains at risk from encroaching coastal erosion these discoveries proved vital, but they also play a fundamental role in understanding the evolution of the urban reaches of this port settlement. The timeliness of this project and Simon's tenacity for undertaking it should not be underestimated either; a couple of years later the Arab Spring began and research work in Libya was halted.

Due to Simon's extraordinary vision and capacity to understand the wider picture he successfully applied for ERC Advanced Grant (Grant no. 339123) for Rome's Mediterranean Ports Project (RoMP).[5] Simon brought together numerous scholars whose research projects focused on Roman ports around the Mediterranean in an attempt to better understand the nature of the harbours that served Roman maritime trade. Harnessing information from the ancient sources, archaeological evidence, and geomorphological data the project sought to chart port development in the first three centuries AD (Keay 2012).

Connectivity was a word used regularly in relation to the Mediterranean port network study but it is also a word that best described Simon's work ethic – effortlessly and generously connecting people, their ideas, and their research.

town was palpable. He was as curious about the layout of the port structures as he was when crouching down and listening to our guide as he explained the rules of a Roman board game that was carved into paving of the forum. Gently engaging with our guide, Simon listened as much as he asked questions and all the while the shutter of his camera barely paused for a moment (Figure 23.6).

The impressive state of preservation of Leptis Magna did not make it a likely candidate for geophysical survey but Simon accepted the challenge of concentrating on the coastal zone. The marine erosion at Leptis Magna is pronounced and the fabric of the ancient city is gradually crumbling into the sea. The varied terrain along this liminal zone required a combination of topographic and gradiometer surveys to record the remains.

At the city's most westerly extent the surveys recorded the course of the late Roman defensive wall dating to the 3rd/4th century AD as well as a section of the

---

[5] https://cordis.europa.eu/project/id/339123.

Figure 23.6. Simon Keay at the port of Leptis Magna, Libya (photo Sophie Hay).

Rome's Mediterranean Ports project: Utica (Tunisia)

The Roman city of Utica lay near the estuary of Tunisia's only perennial river, the Medjerda. It served as one of the most important ports in Roman North Africa as it controlled the riverine corridor to the rich imperial estates to the south producing grain and olive oil for export. With its origins as a Phoenician settlement, the city flourished under republican annexation and developed further in the Imperial period. The gradual silting up of the Medjerda River and estuary diminished Utica's importance and Carthage superseded it.

As with most geophysical surveys that start in unassuming looking fields, it is hard to imagine what lies beneath the soil. The work at Utica was no different. The overall plan of the ancient city of Utica has been a constant focus of study since the first investigations of the site. While the earliest 19th-century accounts often bore little resemblance to reality, excavations in the early and mid-20th-century provided a more detailed recording of the monumental core and a few adjacent city *insula* blocks. The wider extent of the urban area had only ever been theorised by Alexandre Lézine in the 1950s (Lézine 1968) and was largely speculative. What lay beneath those fields was to change that (Hay *et al.* 2010).

Funded by the RoMP project, a combined team of the BSR and APSS joined *the Intstitut National du Patrimoine* – Oxford Utica Project and covered an area of 30ha with gradiometry. In the area north of the Roman circus the results revealed an extensive plan of *insulae* blocks delimited by an orthogonal road system. Each *insula* block measured 90m by 40m and of the 60 *insulae* identified, 40 of those were revealed in their entirety. Within each block regular subdivisions could be detected, providing a clear layout of individual houses, commercial properties, and open spaces, some presumably used for urban agriculture (Figure 23.7).

The survey demonstrated the city was notably larger than Lézine's estimate, and it was only the increased depth of silt deposits overlying the buried remains as the topography sloped down towards the course of the Medjerda River that prevented the gradiometer survey from detecting even more of the urban layout. A core sample taken at the extreme south-eastern limit of the gradiometer survey demonstrated that up to 6m of material has accumulated over the archaeological remains (Pleuger 2020).

Drawing on his wealth of experience of studying Roman towns, Simon was in his element helping to identify and interpret the results of the survey which had provided one of the most coherent orthogonally laid out Roman

Figure 23.7. Results and interpretation of the gradiometry survey at Utica, Tunisia (image Sophie Hay).

towns since the enduring plan of Falerii Novi. It is these moments of camaraderie – the animated discussions, the problems wrestled with, and the interpretations laboured over that never make it onto the page of academic publications but that endure in the memory of the survey team.

Rome's Mediterranean Ports Project: Kane and Pitane (Turkey)

One of the distinct advantages of the RoMP project was that it could provide supplementary survey work to ongoing research projects around the Mediterranean. A long-term study of the Kane Peninsula on the western coast of Turkey in the region of Pergamon by the *Deutsches Archäologisches Institut* (DAI) Istanbul was one such project. To complement the intensive field walking, excavations, geological surveys, and topographical mapping of this area by the DAI, the BSR/APSS team contributed gradiometer and GPR surveys of two port towns: Kane and Pitane.

The military port of this area was based in nearby Elaia, but the strategic locations of Kane and Pitane on the peninsula meant they played an important role in the local sea trade and economy of the area. Defining the extent of the settlement associated with the port at Kane was one objective of the geophysical surveys. On the slope of the hill overlooking the harbour a small area was covered by gradiometry and identified the course of the large enclosing wall. In other areas the gradiometer survey failed to detect structures associated with the port but the underwater exploration

together with geomorphological data from the harbour revealed much about the nature of the port layout. Likewise, at the Roman settlement of Pitane the surface finds suggesting a pottery production site documented during field walking complemented the interpretation of the gradiometer results which provided substantial evidence for the presence of pottery kilns. Simon was an enthusiastic exponent of integrated surveys and the adoption of this approach, particularly at these sites, was paramount in drawing out a better understanding of the archaeological remains.

SH

Portus Project (Fiumicino, Lazio)

The surveys conducted as part of the Rome's Mediterranean Ports project took place against the backdrop of the ongoing Portus Project excavations that began in 2007 following the extensive geophysical survey discussed above. The project was designed to incorporate many aspects of non-invasive survey, both in their extensive use as well as furthering the methodologies and advancing their application in archaeology. Areas such as the *navalia* and Imperial Palace were intensively surveyed in order to extract the maximum possible information to assist with the following excavations. As part of the Portus Project, an extensive geophysical survey was also conducted at the outer limits of the Claudian harbour, with the aim of mapping the western end of the northern mole and locating the site of the famous lighthouse that stood at the entrance.

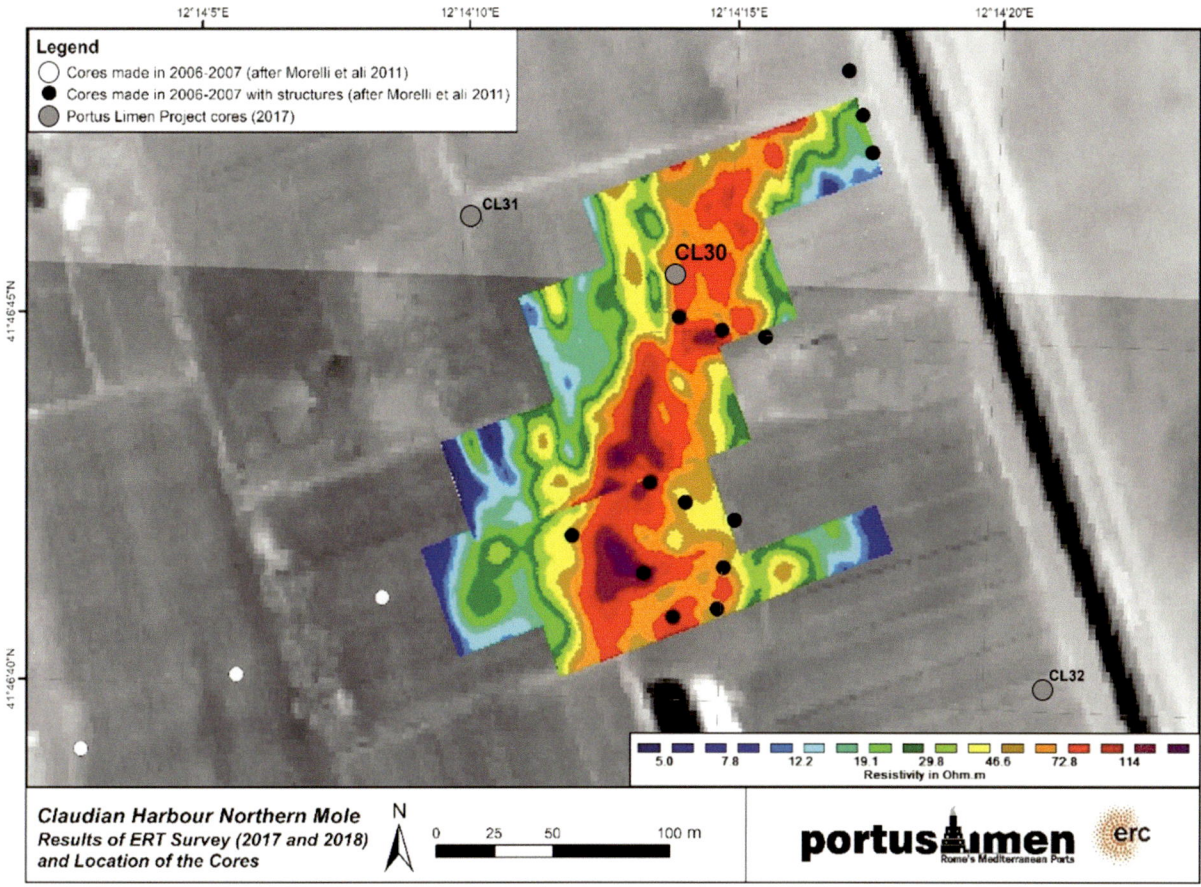

Figure 23.8. ERT survey results from the investigations of the northern mole of the Claudian harbour at Portus (image Elena Pomar).

The area to the west of Viale Coccia di Morto, parallel to the western runway at Rome's Fiumicino airport, was partly investigated by the *Soprintendenza per i Beni Archeologici di Ostia* between 2006 and 2007 with the drilling of 33 mechanical cores, 26 of which intercepted archaeological deposits (Morelli *et al.* 2011). The new research encompassed the area of these investigations, initially using GPR and subsequently ERT, as the high saline content in the soil led to significant attenuation of the radar signal. The most prominent feature in the results was a high resistivity anomaly, crossing the area on a north-east/south-west angle at a depth between 5m and 15m. The feature was subsequently investigated through three cores which were positioned either side of the anomaly as well as above the feature. Analysis of the cores indicated that core CL31 lay in a marine environment, CL32 in a harbour area, and CL30 immediately above the mole, recorded as starting at a depth of 4.3m (Figure 23.8). It was built of pozzolana, basalt, tuff and continued to a depth of approximately 15m where cobbles lay immediately on top of fine sand (Kay *et al.* 2019). The successful identification of the precise location and trajectory of the Claudian mole in this area encouraged further seasons of investigation to the south, with the aim of identifying the area of the lighthouse. Despite potential indications from the earlier cores, no traces of a solid structure were recorded, suggesting that the construction may lie beneath modern buildings to the south.

SK

Over 20 years have passed since the publication of the magnetometer survey results of Falerii Novi and the notion that an investigation of Roman urbanism could be conducted at the scale of a townscape. In the intervening years Simon's research continued to adopt a landscape-wide approach to understanding Roman urbanism. There is no blueprint to the layout of Roman towns; individually dictated by topography, economics, function, and chronology, Roman settlements are diverse in plan and layout. Simon's long-term research has demonstrated that the picture is far more nuanced, as factors such as regional traditions and belief can also affect urban development. The geophysical survey work described in this paper has had a significant impact on our understanding of Roman urbanism and much of that is due to Simon's capacity to have embraced the importance of examining entire cities and their hinterlands.

Acknowledgements

This paper is dedicated to the late Professor Simon Keay. The projects discussed above were directed (or co-directed) by Simon and were a result of his desire and enthusiasm to learn more about the Mediterranean Roman world, from the large complex systems of trade across the Empire to individual households and everyday ceramics. Much of the survey work cited above was conducted by graduates from the University of Southampton (including the two authors) as well as research assistants at the British School at Rome where Simon was a Research Professor (2006-18) and later Chair of Archaeology. The authors are grateful for the work, dedication, and lasting friendships of the wonderful team brought together by Simon.

SH, SK

Bibliography

Andrews, M., S. Bernard, E. Dodd, B. Fochetti, S. Kay, P. Liverani, M. Millett and F. Vermeulen 2023. The Falerii Novi Project. *Papers of the British School at Rome* 91: 9-34.

Carlucci, C., A.M. De Lucia Brolli, S. Keay, M. Millett and K.D. Strutt 2007. An archaeological survey of the Faliscan settlement at Vignale, Falerii Veteres (Province of Viterbo). *Papers of the British School at Rome* 75: 39-121.

Ferraby, R., S. Hay, S. Keay and M. Millett 2008. Archaeological survey at Fregellae, in C. Corsi and E. Polito (eds) *Dalle sorgenti alla foce: il bacino del Liri-Garigliano nell'antichità; culture contatti scambi*: 125-32. Rome: Edizioni Quasar,.

Hay, S., E. Fentress, N. Kallala, J. Quinn and A. Wilson 2010. Utica. *Papers of the British School at Rome* 78: 325-29.

Hay, S., S. Keay and M. Millett 2013. *Ocriculum (Otricoli): An Archaeological Survey* (Archaeological Monographs of the British School at Rome 22). London: British School at Rome.

Johnson, P., S. Keay and M. Millett 2004. Lesser urban sites in the Tiber Valley: Baccanae, Forum Cassii and Castellum Amerinum. *Papers of the British School at Rome* 72: 69-99.

Kay, S. 2003. An integrated approach to the application of geophysical survey to the Cecina Valley Survey Project. *Archeologia e calcolatori* 14: 199-215.

Kay, S. 2013. Geophysical survey of the city of Gabii, Italy, in P. Johnson and M. Millett (eds) *Archaeological Survey and the City* (University of Cambridge Museum of Classical Archaeology Monograph 2): 283-302. Oxford: Oxbow.

Kay, S., S. Hay and C.J. Smith 2023. From sanctuary to settlement. Mapping the development of Lucus Feroniae through geophysical prospection, in A. Launaro (ed.) *Roman Urbanism in Italy: Recent Discoveries and New Directions*: 121-37. Oxford: Oxbow.

Kay, S., E. Pomar, S. Keay, K. Strutt, S. Chapkanski and J.-P. Goiran 2019. Integrating geophysical and geoarcheological surveys for the reconstruction of a Roman port infrastructure: the Claudian harbour at Portus, in J. Bonsall (ed.) *New Global Perspectives on Archaeological Prospection*: 99-103. Oxford: Archaeopress.

Keay, S. 2012. *Rome, Portus and the Mediterranean* (Archaeological Monographs of the British School at Rome 21). London: The British School at Rome.

Keay, S. and M. Millett 2016. Republican and early imperial towns in the Tiber Valley, in A. Cooley (ed.) *A Companion to Roman Italy*: 357-77. Chichester: Wiley.

Keay, S., M. Millett, L. Paroli and K. Strutt 2005. Portus. An archaeological survey of the port of Imperial Rome (Archaeological Monographs of the British School at Rome 15). London: British School at Rome.

Keay, S., M. Millett, J. Robinson, J. Taylor and N. Terrenato 2000. Falerii Novi: a new survey of the walled area. *Papers of the British School at Rome* 68: 1-94.

Keay, S., M. Millett, K. Strutt and P. Germoni 2020. *The Isola Sacra Survey: Ostia, Portus and the Port System of Imperial Rome*. Cambridge: McDonald Institute for Archaeological Research.

Keay, S., G. Earl, S. Hay, S. Kay, J. Ogden and K. Strutt 2009. The role of integrated geophysical survey methods in the assessment of archaeological Landscapes: the case of Portus. *Archaeological Prospection* 16: 1-13.

Lézine, A. 1968. *Carthage, Utique: études d'architecture et d'urbanisme*. Paris: Éditions du Centre national de la recherche scientifique.

Millett, M. 2021. Simon Keay. *Papers of the British School at Rome* 89: 1-8.

Morelli, C., A. Marinucci and A. Arnoldus-Huyzendveld 2011. Il porto di Claudio: nuove scoperte, in S. Keay and L. Paroli (eds) *Portus and its Hinterland* (Archaeological Monograph of the British School at Rome 18): 47-65. London: British School at Rome.

Patterson, H., R. Witcher and H. Di Giuseppe 2020. *The Changing Landscapes of Rome's Northern Hinterland* (Archaeopress Roman Archaeology 70). Oxford: Archaeopress.

Pleuger, E. 2020. Evolution paléoenvironnementale du delta de la Medjerda et géoarchéologie du site d'Utique (Tunisie). unpublished PhD thesis, viewed 1 July 2024, <https://theses.fr/2020LYSE2017>.

Verdonck, L., A. Launaro, F. Vermeulen and M. Millett 2020. Ground-penetrating radar survey at Falerii Novi: a new approach to the study of Roman cities. *Antiquity* 94.375: 705-23.

24. Roman Walls? Keep Calm and Keep on Digging: Acerca de las murallas de *Hispalis* (Sevilla, España)

Fernando Amores and Álvaro Jiménez Sancho

El legado científico del profesor Keay en la arqueología romana del Suroeste de la Península Ibérica se ha centrado principalmente en el estudio de la ciudad. El proyecto de investigación que dirigió en el yacimiento de *Celti* (Peñaflor, Sevilla), donde participó un extenso equipo de profesionales de diferentes universidades británicas y españolas, es un referente metodológico en nuestro país. Poco después llevó a cabo las prospecciones superficiales y geofísicas en Itálica, en vastas zonas de la ampliación adrianea cuyos resultados son fundamentales para el conocimiento del urbanismo del siglo II d.C. Desafortunadamente, las dificultades burocráticas imposibilitaron el desarrollo de otro proyecto de mayor alcance, "Proyecto Ciudades Romanas y Enclaves Urbanos en la Provincia de Sevilla". Una vez centrado en la investigación de *Portus*, siempre estuvo al tanto de las novedades arqueológicas de Itálica y Sevilla (Figura 24.1).

Sus publicaciones significaron un gran revulsivo a la hora de abordar los estudios de los yacimientos romanos de la Bética y en este sentido, este trabajo quiere reconocer su influencia en una cuestión que refleja bien las diferentes aproximaciones al problema de las murallas de *Hispalis* (Sevilla). Por avatares del destino, a los pocos días de su fallecimiento, descubrimos los primeros restos fehacientes de la cerca hispalense, en concreto la fechada en el siglo III d.C. Queremos, pues, que este homenaje sirva para dar a conocer esta primicia.

Si existe un elemento arquitectónico que reúna en sí mismo el carácter urbano de un yacimiento romano, ese es la muralla. Este elemento supera sus claras funciones defensivas al delimitar un ámbito residencial, económico, administrativo y religioso sometido a leyes y con personalidad diferenciada de las demás. La historia urbana se desarrolla usualmente desde una perspectiva particularista, esto es, cada ciudad – sus historiadores– analiza "su" pasado protagonizado por la sucesión de sus habitantes, quienes han venido asumiendo las historias de las diferentes sociedades pasadas como algo propio.

En el caso de Sevilla, la crónica de Juan II, de 1454, proyectaba el pasado clásico identificando la cerca andalusí del siglo XII como romana. Esta tradición medieval fue mantenida por la historiografía durante los siglos XVI a XIX y llegó sin mayor conciencia de contradicción hasta inicios del siglo XX. Todo ello pone en evidencia la fuerza del principio de autoridad y el recurso de usar indicadores básicos en la obsesión por distinguir la cerca romana como paso inicial para realizar cualquier acercamiento al urbanismo de época clásica. De la vieja ciudad romana no asomaban en el bajo medievo más que los famosos fustes de granito de la calle Mármoles. Desde la tardoantigüedad, la ciudad se surtió del fuerte expolio de sus recursos pétreos que fueron reutilizados para la construcción de las nuevas ciudades, que varias veces ostentaron capitalidad política. En el caso de Sevilla, este proceso fue muy intenso, evitando la supervivencia de elementos emergentes del momento romano, cuyos restos se encuentran a unos 4 m de profundidad. La transformación de la ciudad fue tan intensa hasta los siglos XI-XII que tampoco quedan restos de otras cercas que debieron existir entre aquella que hubiera en el s. I d.C., por poner un momento concreto, y la muralla del siglo XII.

Sintetizamos en estas páginas el estado de la cuestión sobre el trazado de la muralla o murallas romanas de *Hispalis*, poniendo de relieve, por un lado, la ausencia de evidencias materiales contrastables científicamente y, por otro, a raíz del citado descubrimiento que damos a conocer, las dificultades a la hora de abordar la reconstrucción de la cerca partiendo de dos premisas insalvables: la ingratitud del registro estratigráfico, que caracteriza la arqueología urbana sevillana, y la intensa destrucción de los contextos previos al desarrollo de la capitalidad almohade durante el siglo XII.

No es este el trabajo que analice pormenorizadamente las diferentes propuestas, pues ha sido un tema ya desarrollado en extensión (Jiménez y Pérez 2015). Nuestra intención es reflexionar sobre la capacidad que tiene la investigación de abordar la reconstrucción de las murallas de época romana (Figura 24.2). Los nuevos restos que presentamos reúnen y ejemplifican lo inconsistente de las distintas hipótesis existentes y el mantenimiento velado en general en la arqueología urbana sevillana.

Figura 24.1. Los profesores Keay y Amores en las excavaciones del solar de la Encarnación en 2005.

La primera propuesta fue la de Thouvenot (1940: 384-85). En el marco de un estudio general de la Bética el investigador francés dedica dos páginas a la cerca de *Hispalis*. Su aproximación puede considerarse un preludio de los trabajos posteriores, ya que recurre a restos conocidos por noticias antiguas y datos de primera mano de arqueólogos del momento (González Acuña 2011: 55). Su hipótesis, no dibujada, establecería un recinto urbano de planta rectangular.

Sin embargo, las hipótesis más divulgadas y también asumidas son las de Collantes de Terán Delorme (1977) y sobre todo, de Campos Carrasco (1993), existiendo algunas propuestas que matizaban una y otra, como las de Blanco (1979), Corzo (1997) y Tabales Rodríguez (2001). A partir del siglo XXI, algunos estudios han desechado la posibilidad de aventurar un trazado preciso y se ha optado por representar una planimetría más basada en manchas que en líneas[1]; de la forma

triangular imperante se ha pasado a un área urbana tendente al rectángulo. Los últimos acercamientos son los de González Acuña (2011) y Jiménez y Pérez (2015)[2] quienes analizan críticamente los trabajos precedentes incorporando la nueva información arqueológica, como los restos de la Encarnación que veremos.

Para el caso de Sevilla, como otras, el conocimiento de sus murallas antiguas se ha ido gestando de manera acumulativa. Inicialmente, aplicando las características estándares de una colonia romana ideal, se entendía que hubo de estar amurallada, en nuestro caso Julio César lo menciona y sus restos habrían de ser reconocibles de algún modo. Sobre esa base filológica, determinados

---

[1] Este punto de vista fue iniciado por el arquitecto Alfonso Jiménez. Este investigador, el único no arqueólogo que ha tratado las murallas de Sevilla, ha ido evolucionando en sus planteamientos a medida que el aumento de la documentación arqueológica ponía en crisis

las propuestas tradicionales: "... la seriedad de una propuesta queda maltrecha desde el momento en que se dibuja y sencillamente se evapora en cuanto se publica, pues, en las actuales circunstancias de la investigación, cualquier trazado general de murallas, calles o manzanas, es simplemente una apuesta personal a partir de datos dispersos, fragmentarios, incongruentes e imprecisos" (Jiménez Martín 2002: 474).

[2] Ambos análisis representan gráficamente un hipotético trazado de mayor anchura que los casos anteriores, evitando así conjeturas indemostrables.

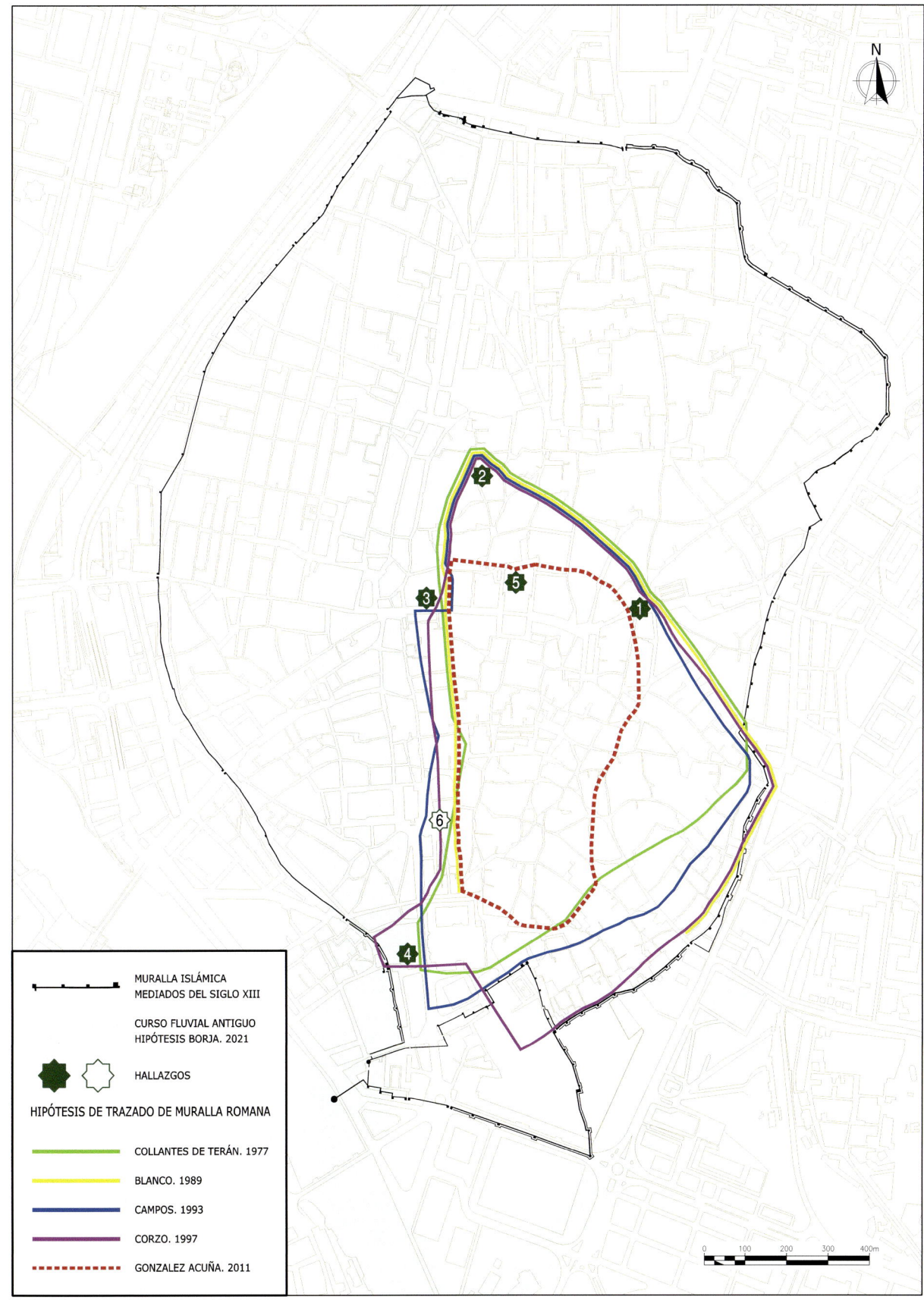

Figura 24.2. Plano del centro histórico de Sevilla con las distintas propuestas del trazado de la muralla y los principales restos tratados.

restos monumentales hallados casualmente desde el siglo XVII se han identificado repetidamente con la muralla. Así, tanto hallazgos como hipotéticos trazados se retroalimentaban sin posibilidad de contrastación científica desde el principio de autoridad.

Posteriormente, gracias a la tesis doctoral de Valencia Rodríguez (1988), las reconstrucciones de topografía urbana han incorporado las referencias a las murallas que se citan en distintos acontecimientos ocurridos a partir de la conquista islámica y transmitidas por diferentes fuentes árabes posteriores. En este sentido, se consideraba que dicha información debía aludir a la cerca romana que pervivía tras el año 712.

Dado que las fuentes filológicas y los hallazgos antiguos no aportaban una información concreta y precisa sobre la que reconstruir un recorrido, se buscaron otros indicadores indirectos a la hora de señalar el trazado defensivo. Por un lado se analizó la disposición del callejero, aplicando principios que en otras ciudades se mostraban eficientes, sobre todo para periodos medievales. Sin embargo, en el caso sevillano se asumía que existían pervivencias y fosilizaciones romanas en la trama urbana actual de determinadas zonas. Este es el caso de la identificación de supuestas puertas en el entorno de las iglesias de San Martín o de Santa Catalina. Ello tuvo su culmen en la formulación de propuestas en las que se dibujaban recorridos muy precisos con localización de accesos, derivando incluso a sostener pervivencias del parcelario, ubicando viarios y otros espacios urbanos bien definidos de época republicana y altoimperial, como publicara Campos en repetidas ocasiones (1993)[3].

Centrados en las diferentes propuestas, los tramos norte y oeste de la cerca serían los que más coincidencias muestran. El elemento fundamental sobre el que se arman casi todas las hipótesis es la noticia del descubrimiento en el siglo XVIII de restos identificados con la muralla en la iglesia de Santa Catalina (Figura 24.2 Punto 1). Desde Collantes de Terán se ha dado por sentado que era así y la disposición de determinadas calles que confluían en este punto apoyaba incluso la existencia de una puerta de la ciudad. Que a finales del siglo XX se asumiera la identificación de unos restos de los que no conocemos el más mínimo detalle[4] resulta cuando menos frustrante. Claramente, sin esta premisa no hay un punto desde el que comenzar el trazado. Aun descartando el valor científico de esa noticia, la investigación arqueológica llevada a cabo en la totalidad de la planta de dicha iglesia en 2014

no alcanzó restos identificables o que indirectamente sugieran la existencia de la muralla[5].

Desde ese punto urbano se traza la muralla hasta enlazar con la iglesia de San Martín (Figura 24.2 Punto 2), donde Campos recurrió a una supuesta pervivencia de restos de la cerca en el basamento del campanario (González Acuña 2011: 57). De una manera bastante simple y *ad hoc*, se llevaba la muralla entre ambas parroquias a través de las actuales calles Gerona, San Juan de la Palma y Viriato. Una vez en el hipotético vértice norte del recinto, el trazado paralelo al cauce viejo del río parece más sencillo de imaginar. En este sentido, se argumenta que la gran diferencia de cotas entre las calles Cervantes y Amor de Dios sería el eco topográfico de la cerca. La proximidad al río y su orilla, y por tanto al límite de la ciudad, explicaría *a priori* el recorrido de la muralla. Sin embargo, estos argumentos tampoco invalidan un desnivel de origen natural o incluso posterior al periodo romano, es decir, que exista esa anomalía topográfica no se explica únicamente por la posible muralla romana (Jiménez y Pérez 2015: 98).

Otros restos fundamentales para vertebrar la reconstrucción del trazado son los descubiertos en las calles Orfila y plaza de Villasís (Figura 24.2 Punto 3). En este caso, la información parece más cualificada pues se trata de los resultados de la vigilancia arqueológica de obras de infraestructuras realizada por el propio Collantes de Terán. Sin duda, la coherencia espacial con la hipótesis de trazado antes descrita tendrá un peso importante a la hora de unir los dos puntos como partes del recinto. Asimismo, nadie dudaría de la solvencia científica de Collantes de Terán. Sin embargo, el problema reside en la interpretación de aquellos restos como pertenecientes a la muralla, algo que debe estar sujeto a debate, aunque la información disponible no permita demasiado. Un aspecto a destacar es que los restos de la plaza de Villasís aparecieron a -1 m, lo cual a la vista de las excavaciones en el entorno invalida que sea una estructura romana. Como en el caso anterior, nuevas excavaciones han demostrado que el paramento descubierto en la calle Orfila está construido en tapial, fechándose en el siglo XI, además se conserva prácticamente bajo el asfalto[6]. Del mismo modo, en un sondeo realizado delante del número 3 de Martín Villa se documentaron dos muros de sillares reutilizados dispuestos perpendicularmente con datación islámica[7].

---

[3] Una crítica a la pervivencia del urbanismo republicano en (Rodríguez Temiño 1991).
[4] Solamente se conoce que era una obra de sillares de más de 2.5 m de anchura aparecida en la cabecera de la iglesia.

[5] Alegar que no se alcanzaron niveles romanos en extensión no valida la interpretación tradicional en modo alguno.
[6] Esta intervención ha permitido analizar de primera mano aquellos restos que documentó Collantes de Terán y contrastar sus conclusiones analizando los mismos restos. Comunicación oral de P. Oliva.
[7] Se trata de dos muros construidos con sillares reutilizados y algunos ladrillos romanos en las llagas. Uno orientado norte-sur, de 1.7 m de altura y 3 m de longitud. Se adosa perpendicularmente a otro, de 2 m de altura y 2.40 m de longitud. No se pudo documentar la anchura. Se fecharon en el siglo X (Jiménez Sancho 2020).

En este punto queremos remarcar que un muro de gran anchura y robustez no implica que se trate de la muralla. En Santiponce, se han documentado recientemente estructuras destinadas a aterrazar determinadas manzanas y calles (Jiménez Sancho 2021). Por tanto, la leve topografía elevada que hoy se percibe en la zona nuclear de Sevilla sería más pronunciada y requeriría de aterrazamientos y contenciones importantes.

Con respecto al trazado de la muralla por la calle Cuna, dos intervenciones, separadas unos 30 m a ambos lados de la vía, presentan secuencias estratigráficas muy distintas que podrían sugerir un límite urbano en este punto (Beltrán y Rodríguez 2014: 160, 205).

Para el tramo sur, casi todas las hipótesis sitúan otro vértice del triángulo en torno al límite sur de la manzana de la Catedral. Sin embargo, la propuesta más anómala viene de la mano de Corzo (1997) quien interpreta la existencia de un apéndice que llega hasta el Postigo del Aceite, ya que considera como restos romanos unas estructuras descubiertas en una obra de los años 60 (Figura 24.2 Punto 4). Realmente, las fotos conservadas muestran unas cimentaciones monumentales de hormigón[8]; sin embargo, los estudios geoarqueológicos basados en decenas de perforaciones geotécnicas indican que el cauce del río discurriría, *grosso modo*, a lo largo de la actual Avenida de la Constitución (Borja 2021).

Para el resto del recorrido que cierra la ciudad por el Este, las propuestas se apoyan en cotas topográficas y alineaciones viarias sin ninguna evidencia material (Jiménez y Pérez 2015: 91-97).

A partir de los años 90 se incorporaron al discurso distintos indicadores que permitiesen discriminar espacios intramuros o extramuros (González Acuña 2011). Los enterramientos serían en principio el factor más fiable, máxime cuando su reconocimiento ofrecía pocas dudas. Como consecuencia, las necrópolis derivadas sugerían zonas a las que la cerca no llegaría, corroborando a grandes rasgos las propuestas de trazado amurallado. La existencia de enterramientos localizados dentro o fuera de esa cerca imaginaria, permitían establecer contracciones o expansiones del espacio intramuros (Jiménez y Pérez 2015: 74-77). Algo parecido sucede con evidencias de usos industriales, aunque en este caso nada concluyentes por sí mismos, entendiendo que las limitaciones legales de época romana no eran un aspecto infalible (Jiménez y Pérez 2015: 78-82).

La enorme cantidad de intervenciones realizadas durante la primera década del siglo XXI ha suministrado un mayor volumen de información; sin embargo, no han aportado evidencias claras, ratificando en cierta medida la extensión de esa corona periurbana que restringe el hipotético recinto amurallado al área que se venía barajando. Ante este panorama, la tendencia actual de la investigación es el desarrollo de hipótesis que se materializan en planos donde destacan manchas y zonas funcionales según su consideración intra o extramuros. Sin embargo, se vislumbra el peso del principio de autoridad, pues en algunos casos se siguen representando trazados muy precisos, combinados con vanguardistas modelados digitales del terreno (Beltrán y Rodríguez 2014)[9].

Como se destaca en las páginas anteriores, la identificación de ciertos restos con la muralla es la cuestión esencial sobre la que se basa la mayoría de reconstrucciones del recinto y precisamente lo que hace, desde nuestra opinión, que todas las propuestas presentadas no pasen de ser conjeturas. En primer lugar, tras varias décadas de numerosas excavaciones urbanas, no es sostenible bajo ningún concepto defender hoy día que en la ciudad actual se mantengan ordenaciones urbanísticas de época romana. El problema radica en establecer el valor científico de las distintas propuestas. En nuestra opinión, no es posible sostener unos trazados sin ninguna evidencia clara que los refrende[10]. Deben existir unos mínimos exigibles sobre los que elaborar hipótesis y en este caso todo el discurso se basa en una premisa que es una falacia (epistemológicamente hablando)[11]: que el urbanismo de época romana está fosilizado en el actual y es posible reconstruirlo[12].

Para el caso de Sevilla, se constata una orientación urbana predominante norte-sur que se mantiene en el tiempo y que se explica por la subordinación de la ciudad al cauce del río[13]. El único caso en el que ha sido posible

---

[8] Las imágenes publicadas evidencian la monumentalidad de la estructura. Sin embargo, destacamos que la cota superior es prácticamente la actual y que gran parte del paramento parece cimiento por lo cual resulta muy improbable que sea de época romana.

[9] Esta publicación, que presenta un panorama actualizado donde fusiona la historiografía con la enorme cantidad de nuevos datos, es un ejemplo de esta disparidad.

[10] Bastante contundente es la tradicional localización del foro en el entorno de la plaza de la Alfalfa por supuestas continuidades funcionales sin resto conocido alguno. El hallazgo del *castellum aquae* (García García 2007), jamás intuido, y el estudio de los restos del entorno (González Acuña 2011: 170-73) han desechado radicalmente aquella idea.

[11] Que un argumento sea falaz no implica que sus premisas o su conclusión sean falsas o verdaderas. Lo falaz de un argumento es la invalidez del argumento en sí. En este caso, se trataría de *argumentum ex silentio*, por el cual la falacia ocurre cuando se dice que algo *debe de ser* cierto simplemente porque no se ha probado su falsedad.

[12] Hasta hoy, solo en un caso se ha podido documentar la correspondencia directa entre una vía romana y otra actual. En calle Ángeles, 1 se excavó una calzada del siglo II con el mismo trazado que la de hoy, pero por dentro del inmueble. Sin embargo, el resto de estructuras romanas excavadas no seguían dicha orientación (Jiménez Sancho et al. 2006).

[13] Hasta mediados del siglo XX, la expansión urbana no se extiende hacia el Este.

documentar varios miles de metros cuadrados de trama urbana desde el siglo I d.C. hasta la actualidad es la intervención en el antiguo mercado de la Encarnación (Figura 24.2 Punto 5) (Amores 2020). Se evidenció que, aún predominando un parcelario ortogonal, hacia el siglo VI d.C. el callejero formalizado a mediados del siglo I d.C. ya estaba difuminado y que en el siglo XI, cuando se vuelve a consolidar el caserío, las calles no se corresponden para nada con el viario antiguo, incluso el callejero andalusí era irreconocible hacia el siglo XV-XVI. Por tanto, en 7000 m² quedó de manifiesto que en ningún caso se puede relacionar el parcelario actual con el de época romana, que en sí mismo muestra una evolución muy compleja a lo largo de los siglos. Para otras zonas de la ciudad la información arqueológica es muy escasa y parcial y se revela la complejidad de la transformación de la estructura urbana que en general nunca ha podido ser establecida[14].

En cuanto a la cronología, ya no es suficiente hablar de "las murallas romanas". Por paralelos con otros yacimientos cercanos como *Italica* (Izquierdo 2021), podemos suponer que a mediados del siglo II a.C., cuando se consolidó la inmigración itálica en el Bajo Guadalquivir, *Hispalis* pudo amurallarse de nuevo, si es que lo estuvo antes, como sería lógico. En este sentido, parece que la paleotopografía pudiera servir para delimitar un área urbana previa al establecimiento del Imperio. A día de hoy, mientras que el estudio de la evolución de la llanura aluvial se sustenta por una creciente cantidad de datos estratigráficos, las elevaciones de la terraza fluvial sobre la que se originó el asentamiento permanecen mal definidas espacialmente. No obstante, la proximidad del río al talud occidental de la misma restringe el área ocupacional respecto a los siglos posteriores en los que la llanura aluvial fue ocupada a medida que el cauce se desplazaba lateralmente hacia el oeste (Borja 2021).

Sin duda, todos los investigadores consideran la *deductio* de la colonia augustea como el momento adecuado para la erección de un nuevo recinto (Caballos 2017). Esta cerca es la que pudo ser reformada a lo largo de los siglos siguientes o incluso ampliada (Jiménez y Pérez 2015: 101-05)[15], hasta su expolio generalizado a partir de los siglos XI y XII. En este punto, con los nuevos datos aquí presentados, añadimos como mínimo una fase más, al menos parcial, fechada a mediados del siglo III d.C.

En la actualidad, la exigencia científica debe ser implacable y no permite desde nuestro punto de vista elaborar hipótesis sobre suposiciones teóricas o datos de dudosa interpretación. Sólo se ha conseguido generar una reconstrucción sin base empírica que se ha repetido indefinidamente consolidándose como paradigma de la arqueología de Sevilla. Valga como ejemplo el caso de Zaragoza, que plasma de manera muy clara las dificultades de la investigación de murallas romanas (Valladares 2017).

La ubicación de Sevilla desde su origen en un ámbito tan dinámico como la llanura aluvial ha de tener su reflejo en la propia configuración urbana y en consecuencia en el trazado de las murallas. El estado actual del conocimiento de la evolución urbana de Sevilla está en parte condicionado por los estudios geoarqueológicos relativos a la dinámica fluvial. En cualquier caso, se pone de manifiesto que es necesaria una sectorización del yacimiento a nivel geomorfológico, ya que las numerosas intervenciones realizadas en la mitad occidental del casco urbano contrastan con el registro de la zona central que se asentaría sobre la terraza cuaternaria.. Lo mismo sucede con los sectores norte y sur en los que la influencia del río explica la expansión urbana del primero frente a la contracción que se muestra en el segundo (García Vargas 2021).

Para finalizar, queremos analizar dos hallazgos identificados como restos de la muralla romana, en cuyas excavaciones hemos participado directamente. El primero ya es conocido, sin embargo recogemos aquí una revisión crítica de su interpretación. El segundo es el detonante de este trabajo ya que plasma todas las carencias señaladas, pero también aspectos que no habían sido considerados anteriormente (Figura 24.2 Punto 6).

Plaza de la Encarnación (Figuras 24.3-24.4)

Las excavaciones realizadas en los niveles más profundos de la plaza de La Encarnación (2003-09) pusieron al descubierto un amplio sector de la ciudad romana limitado al norte por un gran *decumanus*, existiendo dos callejones ciegos que penetraban de sur a norte para acceder al interior de la gran manzana. En el extremo y límite norte de la parcela excavada se halló una potente estructura maciza, con medidas de 6 x 4.10 m de sus laterales registrados, realizada con sillares de piedra de alcor, bien trabados (Figura 24.4). La estructura estaba seccionada por la cimentación de la obra sin poder controlarla en mayor medida. De planta en V en relación con la traza norte sur del viario existe una alineación más amplia con esa diagonal que se ha mantenido desde el s. XI hasta 1810, gracias a una calle registrada en la excavación (Amores 2024: fig. 5). Esa alineación diagonal explica que se trata de

---

[14]   Un ejemplo de la capacidad predictiva de la investigación arqueológica es el caso de Écija, donde ha sido posible establecer el diseño urbano básico de la colonia augustea, que no se corresponde con el actual (García-Dils 2012).

[15]   Proponen que los supuestos restos de muralla podrían señalar dos recintos, el de la fundación colonial y otro más extenso, del siglo II d.C.

¿MURALLA?

VIARIO

0   5   10   15   20m

Figura 24.3. Plano de la fase II (mediados del s. I d.C.) de las excavaciones en el solar de la Encarnación.

Figura 24.4. Restos de la estructura de sillares descubierta en el solar de la Encarnación.

una estructura lineal y no de un hito aislado, aparte de que no se abren *kardines* hacia el norte desde el extenso *decumanus* registrado. Otros indicadores indirectos, usados en otros ejemplos citados, son la abundancia de elementos funerarios del s. I al VII d.C. reutilizados en las construcciones y la presencia de elementos dispersos de una iglesia tardoantigua (inscripción monumental conmemorativa y el *loculus*, depósito de reliquias) que corroboran un ambiente funerario y sagrado muy próximo extramuros. La excavación no documentó el arranque de la estructura y ha sido fechada por las estratigrafías generales, coincidentes en el proceso de urbanización y alguna realizada a 1 m de distancia, en un momento de mediados del s. I d.C. Hasta ahora se ha publicado como evidencia de muralla asumida en las últimas propuestas gráficas del recinto urbano altoimperial (González Acuña 2011; Beltrán y Rodríguez 2014; Jiménez y Pérez 2015) al que se le amputaría parte de su extremo norte triangular, vigente en las versiones de Collantes de Terán (1977), Blanco (1993) y Campos (1997) (Figura 24.2). No obstante, desde la proximidad que da la responsabilidad en dicha excavación, pero fieles al rigor que queremos mostrar, mantenemos cierta duda abierta en su identificación como muralla y ello es debido a la complicada geometría de encuentro con la retícula viaria, que condiciona su trazado, y a no haber documentado una porción más amplia de la estructura monumental. Hemos barajado incluso la opción de que se tratase de la base de un gran mausoleo de época de Augusto desmontado progresivamente

cuando la ciudad avanzó hasta este ámbito[16], aunque también hemos expuesto sus dificultades.

Plaza de San Francisco (Figuras 24.5-24.6)

En el año 2021 una intervención arqueológica en un solar con fachada a la plaza de San Francisco y a la calle Álvarez Quintero ha documentado, en orientación norte-sur, un tramo de 9.5 m de una estructura lineal de sillares y *opus caementicium* identificable con los restos de una muralla de mediados del siglo III d.C., fecha corroborada por asociaciones estratigráficas fiables (Figuras 24.5 y 24.6). Aunque tradicionalmente el recorrido de la muralla se situaba entre las calles Álvarez Quintero y Francos, también se había propuesto el recorrido de la muralla altoimperial por el centro de la manzana en base a la diferencia de cotas entre ambas fachadas (Corzo 1997).

La importancia de la nueva excavación no solo radica en el descubrimiento específico del muro defensivo tardío, sino que destaca por registrar una secuencia estratigráfica completamente diferente a ambos lados de la muralla (Jiménez 2022). Al interior, sobre vertidos de materiales constructivos de índole doméstica

---

[16] En unas estructuras del s. II-III d.C. de la propia excavación se encontraron elementos arquitectónicos apilastrados esculpidos sobre sillares de considerable tamaño (capitel corintio y fuste acanalado) y escultóricos (parte superior de togados menores del natural) que debieron formar parte de un gran mausoleo próximo (González Acuña 2011: fig. XI.3).

Figura 24.5. Restos de la muralla descubierta en la Plaza de Francisco, 11.

Figura 24.6. Restos de la muralla descubierta en la Plaza de Francisco, 11.

coetáneos del muro, se formaliza una calle y un contexto de ocupación que se mantiene hasta el siglo VI, no volviendo a ser ocupado hasta el siglo XI. Al exterior, sobre los sedimentos antropizados de la llanura, se genera igualmente un espacio abierto transitable de al menos 8 m de anchura, identificado como *pomerium*, delimitado al oeste por otras estructuras. Esta zona extramuros aparece cubierta por sedimentos aluviales sobre los que se instalará un cementerio musulmán hacia el siglo XI. El tramo de muralla presenta una cimentación de sillares irregulares, encima se dispone una franja de ladrillos de 95 cm que marca el inicio del alzado, el cual está definido por una base de sillares que sobresale 1.5 m del alzado propiamente dicho y cuya anchura sería de 3.5 m. La estructura comenzó a ser expoliada en el siglo XI quedando definitivamente saqueada y enterrada en el siglo XII. Desde la calle Álvarez Quintero la muralla aparece a 5.60 m de profundidad y desde la plaza de San Francisco a 2.10 m.

Este descubrimiento es del mayor interés por tratarse de un elemento tardío, algo inesperado; asimismo implica un avance del área intramuros en detrimento de la llanura aluvial durante un periodo de supuesta crisis y, finalmente, se documentan niveles de paso a un lado y otro de la muralla. No consideramos el prolongar la alineación descubierta hacia el norte o hacia el sur[17].

Desde un punto de vista estrictamente arqueológico se pone de manifiesto la complejidad y las variables que deben darse para poder alcanzar restos identificables de la cerca. La evolución urbana de la ciudad en relación con el río es una de esas variables y cualquier hipótesis al respecto requiere un soporte de evidencias claras. Así mismo, se demuestra que no es posible hablar de una única muralla, ni siquiera de que este nuevo tramo indique una nueva cerca completa.

En un entorno tan dinámico como en el que *Hispalis* se situaba, y con una dimensión portuaria de envergadura, la muralla o murallas no es la ciudad, esté donde esté. Lo urbano la desbordó y también se contrajo en determinadas zonas. Mientras aparecen o no sus diferentes formalizaciones en el tiempo... *keep calm and keep on digging.*

Bibliografía

Amores Carredano, F. 2020. El proyecto arqueológico de la Encarnación (Sevilla): del conflicto urbano al reto patrimonial e institucional, en P. Mateos y F. Palma (eds) *La Arqueología Urbana en las ciudades de la Hispania romana: Proyectos integrales de investigación, conservación y difusión*: 85-112. Mérida: Consorcio ciudad monumental histórico-artística y arqueológica de Mérida.

Amores Carredano, F. 2024. Dos mil años en la Encarnación: cinco modelos urbanos en el centro histórico de Sevilla, en A. Collantes de Terán (ed.) *Sevilla: fragmentos de ciudad*: 13-42. Sevilla: Real Academia de Buenas Letras.

Beltrán, J. y O. Rodríguez (eds) 2014. *Sevilla Arqueológica: la ciudad en época protohistórica, antigua y medieval*. Sevilla: Universidad de Sevilla.

Blanco Freijeiro, A. 1979. *Historia de Sevilla: la ciudad antigua (de la Prehistoria a los visigodos)*. Sevilla: Universidad de Sevilla.

Borja Barrera, F. 2021. Paisaje y Pasado. Sevilla: Medio natural y forma urbana, en J.M. Feria Toribio (ed.) *Sevilla: Historia de su forma urbana*: 25-39. Sevilla: Universidad de Sevilla.

Caballos Rufino, A. 2017. *Hispalis, de César a Augusto: la Colonia Romula y los orígenes institucionales de la Sevilla romana entre la República y el Imperio*. Sevilla: Universidad de Sevilla.

Campos Carrasco, J. 1993. La estructura urbana de la Colonia Iulia Romvla Hispalis en época imperial. *Anales de Arqueología Cordobesa* 4: 181-219.

Collantes de Terán Delorme, F. 1977. *Contribución al estudio de la topografía sevillana en la antigüedad y en la edad media*. Sevilla: Real academia de bellas artes de Santa Isabel de Hungría.

Corzo Sánchez, R. 1997. Sobre la topografía de Hispalis. *Boletín de la Real academia de bellas artes de Santa Isabel de Hungría* 25: 193-211.

García García, M.A. 2007. Aqua Hispalensis. Primer avance sobre la excavación de la cisterna romana de la Plaza de la Pescadería (Sevilla). *Romula* 6: 125-42.

García-Dils, S. 2012. Colonia Augusta Firma Astigi (Ecija, Sevilla), en J. Beltrán y O. Rodríguez (eds) *Hispaniae urbes: Investigaciones arqueológicas en ciudades históricas*: 723-62. Sevilla: Universidad de Sevilla.

García Vargas, E. 2021. La ciudad subyacente. La Sevilla más antigua, en J. Feria Toribio, G. Acosta Bono y F. Olmedo Granados (eds) *Sevilla: Historia de su forma urbana*: 43-65. Sevilla: Universidad de Sevilla.

González Acuña, D. 2011. *Forma Vrbis Hispalensis: El urbanismo de la ciudad romana de Hispalis a través de los testimonios arqueológicos*. Sevilla: Universidad de Sevilla. Focus-Abengoa.

Izquierdo de Montes, R. 2021. El flanco norte del Cerro de San Antonio: análisis arqueológico de la ocupación, en J. Beltrán y J.L. Escacena (eds) *Itálica: Investigaciones arqueológicas en la Vetus Urbs*: 125-54. Sevilla: Universidad de Sevilla.

Jiménez Maqueda, M. y P. Pérez Quesada 2015. El pomerium invisible. A propósito del trazado de los

---

[17] En 2014, en la Campana se documentaron restos de un muro de sillares y *opus caementicium* rehecho en el siglo X. Lo interpretamos, según el contexto paleogeográfico, como estructura relacionada con las obras de adecuación de la orilla (Jiménez *et al.* 2014). Comparado con los restos encontrados en la plaza de San Francisco, se evidencia una gran similitud entre ambos hallazgos, no obstante, la información estratigráfica del primero es mínima.

recintos amurallados de la Colonia Romula Hispalis. *Romula* 14: 53-125.

Jiménez Martín, A. 2002. Síntesis a modo de epílogo, en A. Jiménez Martin (ed.) *Magna Hispalensisi*, I: *Recuperación de la aljama almohade*: 473-81. Sevilla: Cabildo Metropolitano.

Jiménez Sancho, A. 2020. Actividad arqueológica preventiva para el soterramiento de contenedores en el distrito casco antiguo de Sevilla. Anuario Arqueológico de Andalucía 2014: 1-34. Sevilla. Junta de Andalucía. http://hdl.handle.net/20.500.11947/21447

Jiménez Sancho, A. 2021. El sector oriental del tell de Itálica: margas azules, terrazas y calles, en J. Beltrán y J.L. Escacena (eds) *Itálica: Investigaciones arqueológicas en la Vetus Urbs*: 51-68. Sevilla: Universidad de Sevilla.

Jiménez Sancho, A. 2022. El río y la muralla remueven la historia de Sevilla. *Andalucía en la Historia*, Octubre: 42-47.

Jiménez Sancho, A., F. Borja Barrera y P. Oliva Muñoz 2014. La orilla de Sevilla desde época altoimperial al periodo califal, en J. Beltrán y O. Rodríguez (eds) *Sevilla Arqueológica: La ciudad en época protohistórica, antigua y medieval*: 304-05. Sevilla. Universidad de Sevilla.

Jiménez Sancho, A., E. García Vargas, F.J. García Fernández y E. Ferrer Albelda 2006. Aportación al estudio de la Sevilla prerromana y romano-republicana. Repertorios cerámicos y secuencia edilicia en la estratigrafía de la calle Abades 41-43. *Spal* 15: 281-312.

Rodríguez Temiño, I. 1991. Algunas cuestiones sobre el urbanismo de Hispalis en época republicana. *Habis* 22: 157-75.

Tabales Rodríguez, M.A. 2001. Algunas aportaciones arqueológicas para el conocimiento urbano de Hispalis. *Habis* 32: 387-423.

Thouvenot, R. 1940. *Essai sur la province romaine de Bétique*. Paris: De Boccard.

Valencia Rodríguez, R. 1988. Sevilla musulmana hasta la caída del Califato. Contribución a su estudio. Tesis doctoral inédita, Universidad Complutense.

Valladares Lafuente, C. 2017. Las murallas de Caesaraugusta como paradigma de los amurallamientos de la Antigüedad Tardía en Hispania, en *Actas II Jornadas Doctorales en Ciencias de la Antigüedad*: 99-117. Zaragoza: Universidad de Zaragoza.

25. Nueva imagen arqueológica de la Itálica de Adriano[1]

José Manuel Rodríguez Hidalgo

En el año 1991, hace ahora treinta años, desde el Conjunto Arqueológico de Itálica se diseñó y ejecutó un proyecto de investigación que, partiendo de la objetividad arqueológica, pudiese delimitar el perímetro de esa Itálica proyectada por el emperador Adriano y evaluar su estado de conservación, para una posterior delimitación de la "Zona arqueológica de Itálica", como Bien de Interés Cultural (116 Has.). Por Real Orden de su Majestad, don Alfonso XIII, de 13 de diciembre de 1912, Itálica ya contaba con la categoría jurídica de Monumento Nacional, aunque se trataba de una declaración literal en la que se reconocía el interés histórico y arqueológico de la antigua ciudad romana, pero no se definían sus límites físicos. Por ello, dadas las expectativas urbanísticas que en aquellos momentos tenía el pueblo de Santiponce, en cuyo término municipal se ubica la ciudad romana de Itálica, se hacía totalmente necesario contar con una delimitación precisa donde se definiese la protección urbanística del suelo que ocupaba la antigua Itálica. Obviamente, como arqueólogos nuestra curiosidad iba mucho más allá de la necesidad de proteger jurídicamente un bien con incuestionables valores, conocidos y reconocidos a lo largo de los siglos; pues Itálica atesora, también, una dilatada y abundante historiografía y bibliografía desde el siglo XVI.

Conocí a Simon Keay en 1987, en los comienzos de ese año se celebraron en la ciudad de Málaga las II Jornadas de Arqueología en Andalucía. Buen conocedor de *Hispania romana*, en especial de la *Tarraconense*, decidió acercarse a la *Baetica*, una decisión en la que sin duda influyó el profesor José Remesal, de la Universidad de Barcelona, natural de Lora del Río (Sevilla), la antigua *Axati*. Por aquel entonces Simon Keay buscaba un yacimiento, una ciudad romana en la que poder desarrollar y dirigir su propio proyecto de investigación donde poner en práctica la metodología que estaba ensayando, muy apropiada y útil para grandes superficies, ya que, al menos inicialmente, no era necesario excavar para obtener información precisa y objetiva. El método consistía en compaginar la prospección superficial intensiva y la geofísica.

Sin duda, ya tenía madurada la idea, aunque no tanto la forma de ponerla en marcha y de ejecutarla. Le faltaba la experiencia administrativa, cómo montar el proyecto para obtener el permiso de la administración competente, en este caso de la Consejería de Cultura de la Junta de Andalucía. Nos presentamos y recuerdo que durante el tiempo que duraron las Jornadas mantuvimos largas y amistosas conversaciones, básicamente de arqueología y en mi calidad de responsable de la gestión administrativa de la arqueología en la provincia de Sevilla le ayudé a elegir el yacimiento *más idóneo* para sus intereses y le facilité todo cuanto estaba en mis manos para que pudiera poner en marcha su proyecto de investigación sistemática, en el que también estaban involucrados el referido J. Remesal y John Creighton, de la *Universidad de Reading*.

Entre otras posibles, la ciudad elegida fue Celti, perteneciente al actual municipio sevillano de Peñaflor. Un municipio Flavio, al igual que otros tantos, situado a orillas de la margen derecha del río Baetis, entre Corduba e Hispalis, como también la citada ciudad de Axati (Lora del Río), Arva y Canama (ambas en Alcolea de Río), Naeva (Cantillana) e Ilipa Magna (Alcalá del Río). Ciudades romanas, todas ellas asentadas sobre enclaves protohistóricos habitados desde el siglo VIII, a. C., que se abrían hacia la gran vía de comunicación que fue el Baetis, por donde daban salida hacia la Metrópolis sus productos agrícolas, especialmente el aceite, envasado en ánforas de las que S. Keay era un gran conocedor, al igual que lo es el profesor J. Remesal.

*E*n calidad de inspector de las actividades arqueológicas en *Celti*, pude conocer en detalle y valorar el diseño metodológico empleado en la parte más monumental de esa ciudad romana, propiedad de la Administración. Por aquel entonces, S. Keay ya era conocedor de la

[1] El pasado 26 de mayo de 2021, dentro del *V Curso del Foro Permanente, Itálica en-clave de Patrimonio Mundial*, organizado por el Consejo Asesor de la Candidatura, Itálica Patrimonio Mundial, en el Paraninfo de la Universidad de Sevilla, pronuncié una conferencia con el mismo título que este artículo; es decir: "Nueva Imagen arqueológica de la Itálica de Adriano (en homenaje a Simon Keay)". Durante la organización de ese V Curso, que abarca otras siete conferencias, desde el Consejo Asesor entendimos que, dado que se cumplían 30 años de la realización de las prospecciones que realizamos en el Conjunto Arqueológico de Itálica, sería oportuno recodarlas. Así mismo, yo quería rendirle mi homenaje más personal a Simon, que unos meses antes se había jubilado de sus tareas docentes en la Universidad de Southampton. Jamás pude pensar en tan luctuoso desenlace y lo que inicialmente se concibió como un momento de júbilo se transformó en un muy triste homenaje póstumo.
Dado el carácter efímero y coyuntural que poseen las conferencias, he querido perpetuar aquí la esencia de lo entonces pronunciado, que se sustenta, ante todo, en la larga y sincera amistad que compartía con el homenajeado y también el compromiso con Itálica, que tanto nos unía en lo profesional y en lo emocional.

Figura 25.1. Clasificando cerámica, abril 1991, Simon Keay, Ana Romo y Sonia Fernández
(fotografía José Manuel Rodríguez Hidalgo).

necesidad de ampliar la protección administrativa de Itálica y por ello, a lo largo de la segunda mitad del año 1990, le comenté la posibilidad de ejecutar en Itálica un proyecto parecido al que se estaba realizando en *Celti*. Ya habíamos cimentando una sólida amistad, lo que nos permitió afrontar sin fisuras un proyecto realmente ambicioso en una ciudad tan emblemática como es Itálica. Contábamos con la financiación y el beneplácito de las autoridades políticas de la Consejería de Cultura, en especial con el apoyo incondicional de Antonio Pozanco León, Delegado Provincial en Sevilla.

Los excepcionales resultados del proyecto pensado para Itálica superaron todas las expectativas, pues permitieron obtener una imagen general muy explícita de la Itálica de Adriano, así como conocer su proceso de construcción y de transformación hasta la antigüedad tardía. La geofísica, responsabilidad de David Jordan, con el empleo de técnicas de resistividad, magnetometría y geo-radar, nos mostró imágenes de enorme calidad y nitidez, que dejaban poco espacio a la subjetividad y a la duda. La clasificación y estudio de los abundantes materiales arqueológicos recogidos en superficie permitieron fechar los procesos constructivos y, por ejemplo, el estudio de los mármoles, aportado por Isabel Rodá, permitió reconocer la procedencia de la enorme diversidad de los mármoles empleados en las

construcciones, tanto públicas como privadas (Figura 25.1).

Grosso modo, podemos afirmar que se cumplieron y superaron con creces los planes inicialmente marcados, pues pudimos delimitar la ciudad, que era el objetivo de partida. También quedaron colmadas nuestra curiosidad y nuestras expectativas más ambiciosas, algo que desde entonces ha concitado, a su vez, un mayor interés por excavar y exhumar lo mucho y variado que aún subyace bajo el subsuelo de las más de 34 Has., sobre las que se desarrollaron, en algo más de dos semanas, las referidas prospecciones. Como consecuencia de todo ello se localizó el circuito de murallas que delimitaba a la ampliación adrianea, se identificó una muralla tardía, toda la trama urbana, el trazado de las calles, así como nuevos edificios públicos, de enormes dimensiones y también enormes edificaciones privadas de carácter palaciego, como las ya excavadas desde finales del siglo XIX (Figura 25.2).

Además, el resultado de las prospecciones tuvo una repercusión directa e inmediata sobre el yacimiento, ya que conociendo el trazado de las calles, las mismas se reprodujeron en la superficie, lo que sumado a las calles ya excavadas permitió proyectar y reproducir toda la urdimbre de los viarios. Es decir, se urbanizó,

LEYENDA: CONTORNO BIC

DELIMITACIÓN DEL BIC "ZONA ARQUEOLÓGICA DE ITÁLICA"
AUTOR: JOSÉ MANUEL RODRÍGUEZ HIDALGO
ESCALA 1:5.000

Figura 25.2. Delimitación del Bien de Interés Cultural, "Zona Arqueológica de Itálica" (José Manuel Rodríguez Hidalgo).

no para construir, cómo habría hecho el Emperador, sino para excavar, permitiendo a su vez que el visitante obtuviera una percepción física y directa sobre la escala urbana de la ampliación proyectada por Adriano (Estos últimos párrafos son una muy breve síntesis de esos trabajos efectuados en Itálica en abril de 1991. Para una información más detallada consultar Rodríguez Hidalgo 1997; Rodríguez Hidalgo *et al.* 1999).

Ahora, pasados los años, cuando Itálica aspira a ser reconocida por UNESCO como Patrimonio Mundial, es su urbanismo, arquetipo de ciudad adrianea, el "Valor Universal Excepcional" (V.U.E.) que resalta su singularidad. Esta afirmación es, sin duda, otra de las consecuencias directas de los resultados obtenidos entonces. Sin ellos, Itálica no hubiese tenido argumentos sólidos con los que postularse con firmeza y solidez como candidata al reconocimiento que otorga UNESCO.

Fue en 2016, bajo el patrocinio de CIVISUR, cuando un grupo de amigos y conocidos, de profesiones diversas (arqueólogos, historiadores, escritores, literatos, gestores, arquitectos, geógrafos, políticos, etc.), todos ellos conscientes de los múltiples valores que posee

Itálica, nos embarcamos en la aventura de conseguir el reconocimiento de Itálica como Patrimonio Mundial de UNESCO. Se partía de la conmemoración de una efeméride, la del año 117, cuando muere el *Optimus Princeps*, Trajano, el más ilustre de los italicences y le sucede Adriano, su hijo adoptivo, el gran valedor y creador de la *Colonia Aelia Augusta Italicensium (C.A.A.I.)*.

Las efemérides siempre son excusas fáciles para obtener algún tipo de rédito, por ello la Universidad de Sevilla y la Universidad Pablo de Olavide, ambas, también involucradas en el compromiso de conseguir el reconocimiento de UNESCO, al igual que la Universidad Internacional de Andalucía, supieron estar a la altura y reafirmar la transcendencia histórica de estos emperadores hispanos. El profesor Juan Manuel Cortés Copete, Catedrático de Historia Antigua de la Universidad Pablo de Olavide, desde su Universidad fue el promotor y comisario de una Exposición montada en el Museo Arqueológico de Sevilla denominada *Adriano-Metamorfosis*, **que tuvo su continuidad en una serie de programas de difusión en televisión. Por su parte, e**n la Universidad de Sevilla, el profesor Antonio Caballos Rufino, también Catedrático de Historia Antigua, conmemoró ese 1900º aniversario, con un congreso del máximo nivel: "De Trajano a Adriano. *Roma matura, Roma mutans*", avalado por la presencia de los mayores especialistas de ese momento histórico en que Trajano y Adriano, que tuvieron su patria en Itálica, llegaron a lo más alto como emperadores de Roma. Como diría el profesor Caballos, "Nunca, ni antes ni después a lo largo de la historia, unos personajes oriundos de *Hispania* han llegado a ser, como lo fueron ellos, dueños de los destinos del mundo".

En ese dilatado proceso de búsqueda de argumentos con los que armar la candidatura de Itálica a Patrimonio Mundial de UNESCO, así como de afirmar y reafirmar aquellos otros muchos que son incuestionables en lo histórico y lo arqueológico, S. Keay tuvo también un papel activo y solidario, como siempre lo era en todo aquello que se relacionaba con Itálica y lo que ello implicaba. El 22 de marzo de 2018, dentro del II *Curso del Foro Permanente, Itálica en-clave de Patrimonio Mundial*, organizado por el Consejo Asesor de la Candidatura, Itálica Patrimonio Mundial, S. Keay pronunció una brillante conferencia titulada: "Itálica en el contexto de las ciudades de época de Trajano y Adriano en el Mediterráneo occidental", que concluyó expresando de forma explícita su apoyo a la Candidatura de Itálica y al reconocimiento por parte de UNESCO[2].

Su conferencia, al igual que la de otros muchos especialistas, más de setenta en los cinco cursos desarrollados, ha servido y están sirviendo para actualizar de manera sintética y ordenada el conocimiento sobre Itálica, Adriano y lo adrianeo en el contexto del Imperio, para reflejar en el Formulario de UNESCO ese Valor Universal Excepcional (V.U.E.) que como redactores reconocemos en la Itálica de Adriano.

Lo que la arqueología fue esbozando con lentitud, y no poca dificultad secular, fue resuelto con rapidez y solvencia por la geofísica. Cómo apuntamos con anterioridad, teníamos ante nuestros ojos la imagen completa de la nueva Itálica, la *Nova Urbs* como la definió A. García y Bellido en contraposición a la ya existente, la *Vetus Urbs*. Al igual que hizo en otras ciudades del Imperio, Adriano en Itálica "regaló" nuevas edificaciones, pero aquí fue más allá, su acción fue más completa y su proyecto fue mucho más ambicioso, ya que construyó una ciudad nueva y, además, la dotó de un nuevo estatuto político, el de Colonia (*Colonia Aelia Augusta Italicensium*).

En palabras del profesor J.M. Cortés Copete, "...Itálica fue, por lo tanto, un campo de experimentación urbanística, artística y política para Adriano. Representa, pues, el giro, que suponía convertir a las ciudades de las provincias en beneficiarias naturales del Imperio que asumió su primera forma total en el diseño de Itálica". "Una metamorfosis, que se hace muy explícita en el libro 69 de Casio Dion, en el que cita sólo nueve ciudades de entre todas las del Imperio: Roma, Antioquía, Alejandría, Hadrianúteras, Antinoopolis y Claudiópolis, Jerusalén/Elia Capitolina, Atenas e Itálica, la única ciudad que aparece como la patria del emperador. No es necesario señalar que las ciudades relacionadas destacan por su importancia natural en el Imperio o por su especial relación con Adriano, quien las aupó a los primeros puestos entre las ciudades del Imperio. Casio Dion supo resumir magistralmente la transformación política —reflejada en los honores— y física —los dones magníficos— de la ciudad. Una metamorfosis total cuyo autor fue el emperador Adriano y que empezó a gestarse después de su estancia en *Hispania* (invierno del año 122, primeros meses del 123)"[3] (Figura 25.3).

A día de hoy, la dicotomía argumentada con criterios didácticos en su momento por A. García y Bellido (1960), que nos hablaba de dos ciudades diferenciadas por fundamentos urbanísticos y cronológicos, no se sostiene y aunque entonces supo percibir e intuir diferencias notables no tuvo en consideración otros datos objetivos, que ya entones se conocían y que al menos cuestionaban su propuesta. No consideró, por ejemplo, la abundante cantidad de epígrafes y esculturas adrianeas, que desde mediados del siglo XVIII hasta 1940, salieron precisamente en esa *vetus urbs* y más concretamente del denominado Cerro de San Antonio, en cuya ladera oriental se recuesta el Teatro, que aunque se empezó a excavar en 1971, su existencia ya era conocida entonces, ya parte de su graderío era visible en el corral de alguna casa.

Junto a la planificación urbanística *ex novo*, la investigación arqueológica más reciente nos ha confirmado, de manera incuestionable, que el proyecto adrianeo incidió de una manera directa y rotunda en la parte monumental de la Itálica pre adrianea, en concreto sobre la terraza superior del Teatro, donde se construyó un complejo monumental superpuesto a otro de Augusto, que es de donde proceden la mayoría de las esculturas que definen el programa iconográfico de Adriano y se exhiben en el Museo Arqueológico de Sevilla.

El veintiocho de enero de 2008, en el transcurso de una intervención arqueológica propiciada por el Conjunto

---

[2] La iniciativa emprendida por CIVISUR – la Unión Cívica del Sur de España - y capitaneada por Concha Cobreros Vime, al frente de un Consejo Asesor de la Candidatura de Itálica Patrimonio Mundial de UNESCO, está orientado a conseguir que Itálica entre en la Lista Definitiva donde se reconocen sus valores excepcionales. https://italicapatrimoniomundial.com/civisur/

[3] Fragmentos de texto redactado por Juna Manuel Cortés Copete para el Formulario de la candidatura de Itálica a Patrimonio Mundial, en el que se defiende el V.U.E., por el que entendemos que Itálica es merecedora de formar parte de la lista de UNESCO.

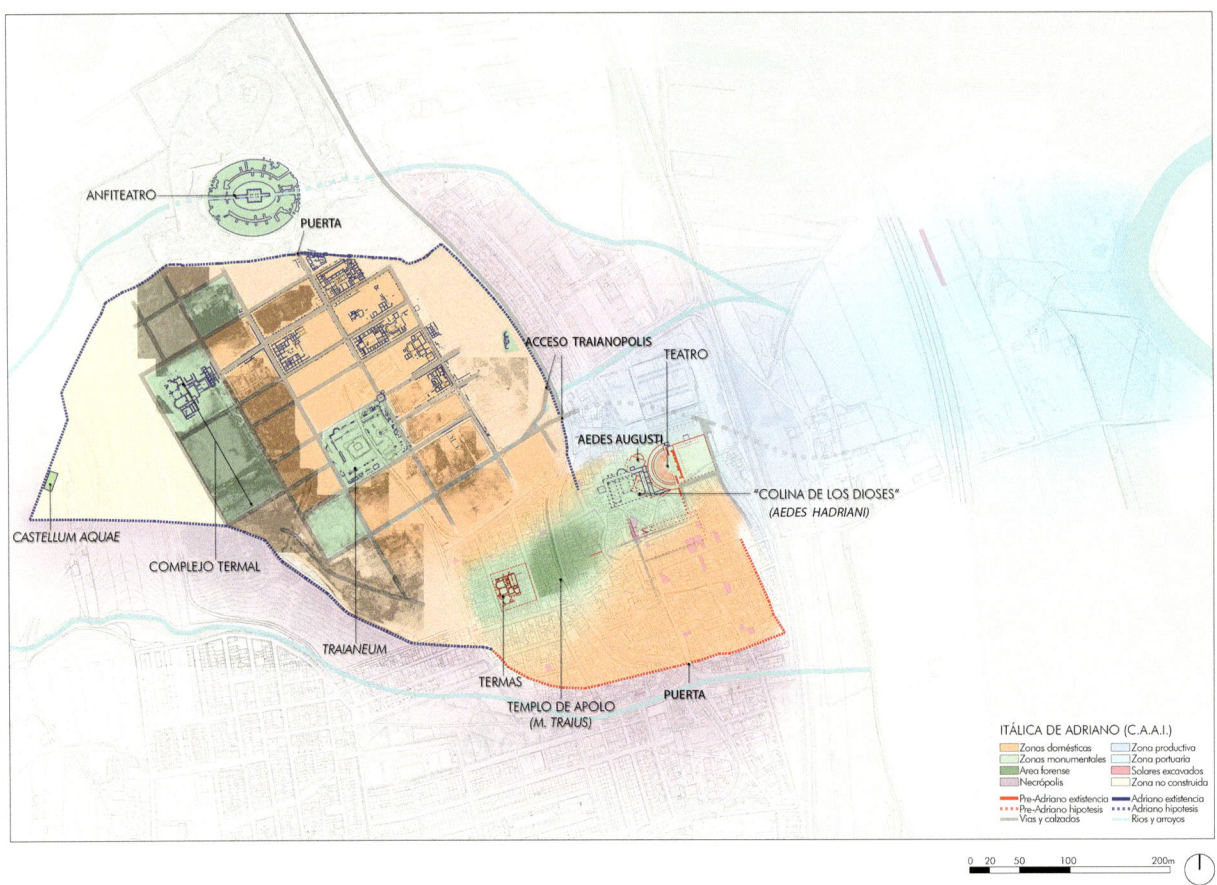

Figura 25.3. Itálica adrianea (José Manuel Rodríguez Hidalgo y Álvaro Jiménez Sancho. Elaboración técnica Miguel Ángel Pérez López y Margarita de Alba Romero).

Arqueológico de Itálica, bajo la dirección técnica de Oliva Rodríguez Gutiérrez y Álvaro Jiménez Sancho, se produjo el hallazgo de una nueva pieza escultórica de cronología adrianea, la cabeza de una joven divinidad con diadema (otra Venus u otra Diana). Por fin, después de muchos años, a unos treinta metros de donde en noviembre de 1940 se produjo el hallazgo casual de la Afrodita Anadyomene y a unos sesenta de donde en 1900 apareció Diana Cazadora, el suelo itálico, el subsuelo de Santiponce, ofrecía una nueva escultura, que a diferencia de las otras fue fruto de una excavación programada. Se excavaba en el solar que en su día ocupó el inmueble número 11, de la calle Siete Revueltas, adquirido años atrás por la Administración, para ampliar la superficie del "mirador del teatro romano", desde donde, entre potentes cimentaciones romanas de distinta cronología, es fácil la contemplación integra del monumento de carácter lúdico[4].

Itálica, Colina de Dioses es el título que dimos a la exposición que se organizó en el Museo Fernando Marmolejo de Santiponce para la presentación pública de esta joven diosa diademada. Con anterioridad a este último hallazgo, y aún sigue denominándose así, la por nosotros denominada "Colina de los dioses" es el "Cerro de San Antonio", así llamado por un San Antonio cobijado, desde un momento incierto del siglo XIX, en una pequeña hornacina labrada en el muro epónimo. De esta Colina es de donde desde el año 1753, comenzaron a extraerse una serie de epígrafes y esculturas de divinidades, que llegaron a formar parte de la colección arqueológica que, por iniciativa Real de S.M. Carlos III, atesoró Francisco de Bruna y Ahumada en el Real Alcázar de Sevilla. Aunque atribuidas a excavaciones

---

[4] No fue una intervención arqueológica única y aislada. Se estaba redactando el Plan Director del Conjunto Arqueológico, coordinado por su directora, Sandra Rodríguez de Guzmán Sánchez, y se hacía necesario ahondar en el conocimiento e investigar sobre la colina que se extiende por la parte alta del Teatro, donde ya habíamos destacado el interés y la trascendencia de esta zona del yacimiento, virgen en

excavaciones, no así de hallazgos. En 2009 se efectuó una intervención arqueológica puntual en distintas áreas del Teatro, y también en el inmueble núm. 19 de la calle La Feria, sobre la ladera norte de la colina, lo que sin duda amplió sustancialmente el conocimiento. Al mismo tiempo, con anterioridad y posterioridad a estas intervenciones, se desarrolló un amplio programa de sondeos y perforaciones de apoyo al conocimiento geoarqueológico de Itálica, centrado en el Teatro, su entorno y toda la mitad oriental del núcleo antiguo de Santiponce y de la *Vetus Urbs*, cuyos resultados analizados por Fco. Borja constituyen un sustento objetivo para nuestra hipótesis de trabajo.

de Bruna, en realidad esos hallazgos fueron fruto de los trabajos de los monjes jerónimos, en especial de Fray Fernando de Zevallos, quien identificó este sitio como *El Palacio* (Rodriguez Hidalgo 2009; 2018; Rodriguez Hidalgo y Jiménez Sancho 2015).

"La nueva imagen arqueológica de la Itálica de Adriano", con la que nos adherimos al merecido homenaje a nuestro querido amigo S. Keay, presenta de manera muy sintética la imagen de la obra de Adriano sobre la terraza monumental de Teatro. Las limitaciones que plantea la presente edición no permiten aportar todo cuanto el tema demanda. Soy consciente de ello, pero aun así, al igual que en las numerosas conversaciones telefónicas o emails nos poníamos al corriente de nuestras últimas investigaciones, quiero desde aquí hacerle partícipe de la novedad que supone la interpretación de las potentes estructuras arquitectónicas que de época adrianea son visibles sobre la terraza del Teatro. Obviamente, S. Keay conocía de forma directa esas enormes estructuras adrianeas, las había visitado en varias ocasiones y lamento muy sinceramente que no pueda expresar su opinión al respecto, seguro que sus comentarios habrían sido muy enriquecedores.

Apuntamos con anterioridad el revulsivo que está suponiendo la elaboración de la ingente y variada documentación que se está preparando para la solicitud de la candidatura de Itálica a Patrimonio Mundial de UNESCO. En estos últimos años se está hablando sobre Itálica y también se está investigando mucho, reconsiderando viejas cuestiones. Estamos afianzando y actualizando el conocimiento que sobre ella tenemos. En esta línea la profesora Pilar León acaba de publicar un libro (León 2021) y los profesores José Beltrán y José Luis Escacena han coordinado la edición de una monografía centrada en la *vetus* [5] (Beltrán y Escacena coords).

En esta última publicación es donde tiene un mayor desarrollo la síntesis que aquí aportamos (Rodriguez Hidalgo 2021). En ella, conscientes de la diversidad de artículos que se incluyen, consideramos oportuno aportar una planimetría y documentación gráfica homogénea de conjunto, válida para todos, que permita una visión global de Itálica en sus tres realidades urbanísticas: la pre-adrianéa, la adrianéa y la post-adrianéa. Así mismo, analizamos en detalle y nos centramos en la denominada "Colina de los dioses", para presentar y representar su evolución y su transformación urbanística, desde época de Augusto hasta época de Adriano.

Será precisamente en esa "Colina de los dioses", en la terraza existente sobre el Teatro, donde el Emperador Adriano dejó su impronta constructiva más personal. Allí ejecutó un gran complejo edilicio amortizando edificaciones augusteas en conexión abierta con los límites septentrionales del Foro y creando una galería abierta hacia el Este, para acceder al *Aedes Augusti* y conectar mediante unas gradas con el Teatro, permitiendo además la contemplación del *Baetis* y de la llanura aluvial, con vistas a *Hispalis* (Sevilla), *Carmo* (Carmona) e *Ilippa Magna* (Alcalá de Río). Así mismo, con una galería igualmente abierta hacia el norte para mantener una conexión visual directa e inmediata con la nueva ampliación urbanística, la "Trainapolis", presidida por el *Traianeum.*

Precisamente, de esas construcciones augusteas y del *Aedes Augusti*, trata en esa publicación Álvaro Jiménez (Jimenez Sancho 2021), que participó siendo alumno de la Universidad de Sevilla en las campañas de *Celti* y también en las de Itálica, y del mismo modo que lo adrianéo se relaciona con lo augusteo, la planimetría que presentamos es el resultado de un análisis conjunto, donde se han evaluado y relacionado restos que habían sido excavados hace décadas. Todo ello imposible de describir con palabras y de exponer sin la planimetría y los 3D elaborados por Margarita de Alba Romero, quien ha sabido usar con maestría las herramientas necesarias para presentar este conjunto imperial.

Sin duda, la situación preminente le ha inferido a este sector nororiental de Itálica pre- adrianea un carácter preferente respecto al resto de la ciudad y su entorno. Aquí, la comprensión de la relación topográfica ha supuesto un auténtico reto, pues se trata de una parte de Santiponce asentada de antiguo sobre unos restos romanos muy desdibujados por los expolios y ocupada por múltiples inmuebles de pequeñas dimensiones, que se adosan unos a otros, adaptándose a una topografía irregular, con un urbanismo de calles tortuosas. El auténtico reto ha sido justificar la falta de registro arqueológico que se producía en no pocas de las intervenciones realizadas en la zona, especialmente en las zanjas abiertas en los ejes de muchas de las calles de este sector del pueblo para la sustitución y renovación de las redes de suministro y evacuación de aguas.

El programa de sondeos y perforaciones mecánicas se convirtió en una herramienta muy útil, ya que permitió la localización de la tierra virgen y con ella la estratificación de los sedimentos, aunque la clave para la compresión del proceso constructivo la facilitó las intervenciónes arqueológicas realizadas por A. Jiménez en los inmuebles números 15 y 17-19 de la calle Real de Santiponce donde se localizó e identificó un potente muro que corría paralelo a la calle y que sirvió en su día para la contención de un complejo

---

[5] Beltrán, J. y J.L. Escacena (coords) *ITÁLICA: Investigaciones arqueológicas en la vetus urbs.* Sevilla: Editorial Universidad de Sevilla, 2021.

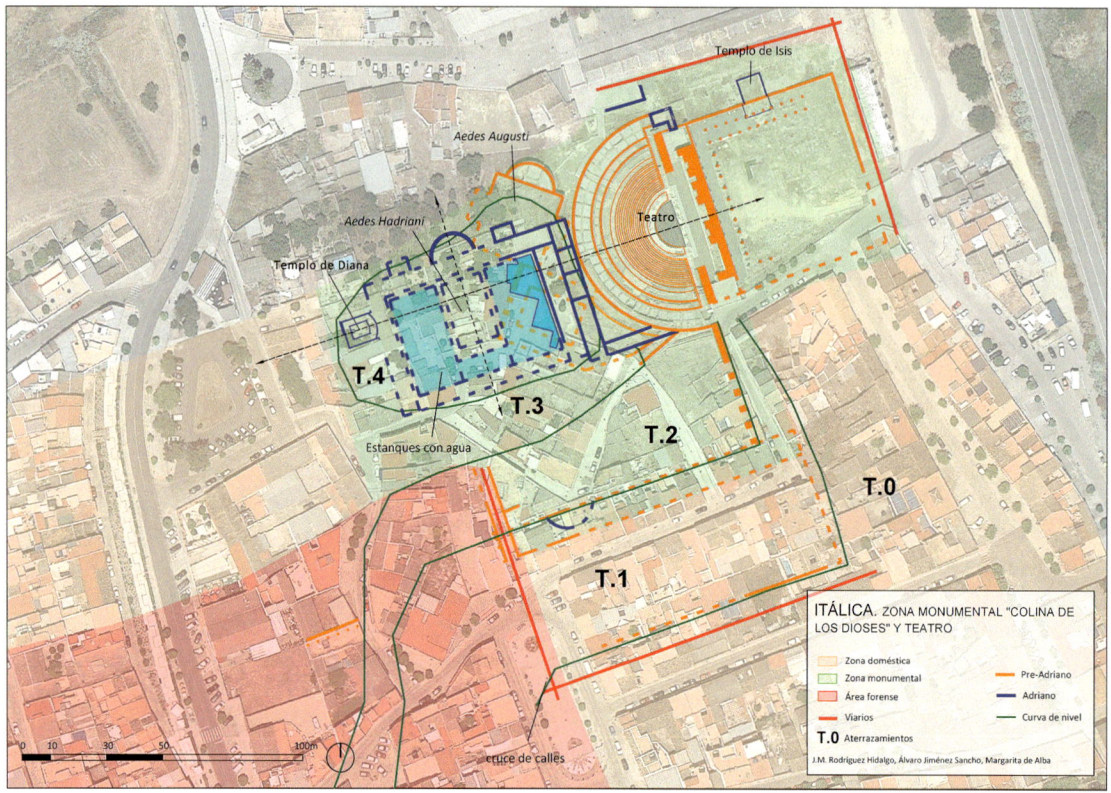

Figura 25.4. Italica. Zona Monumental, la "Colina de los dioses". Análisis topográfico, las terrazas (J.M.R.H, Á.J.S y M.A.R.).

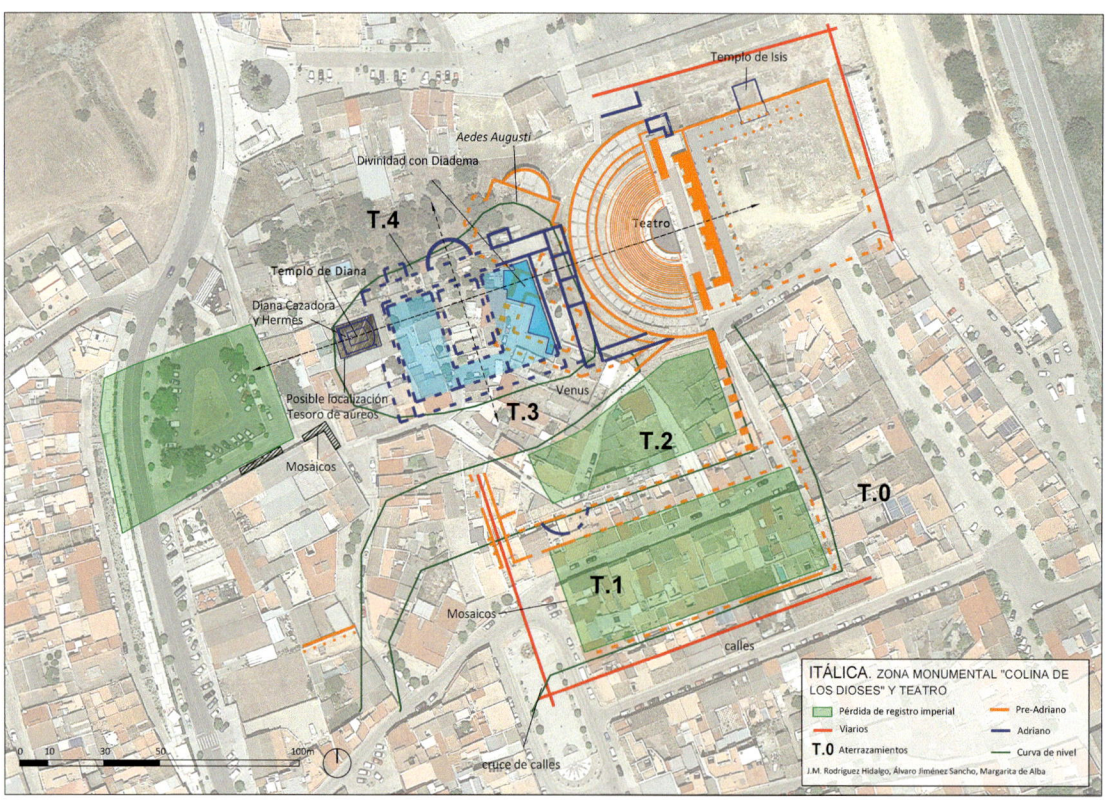

Figura 25.5. Italica. Zona Monumental, la "Colina de los dioses". Información arqueológica (J.M.R.H, Á.J.S y M.A.R.).

edilicio a base de terrazas, de más de 15.750 m², que tenía el arranque de su segunda terraza en otro muro de similar funcionalidad en el calle Clavel, número 1 (Jimenez Sancho 2021b). Se trata pues de un complejo constructivo de época augustea a base de terrazas que remataban en una cuarta terraza donde, como se ha referido, A. Jiménez analizó y relacionó una serie de estructuras de cronología augustea, que ha identificado como integrantes de un *Aedes Augusti*; es decir, un santuario de culto al Emperador Augusto.

Sobre esa cuarta terraza, de más de cinco mil m², a unos 16 metros de altura sobre la cota base de la terraza primera, amortizando parte de la obra de Augusto, será donde Adriano proyectó, según nuestra opinión, su obra más personal en Itálica. Un complejo edilicio donde el agua tenía, cómo es habitual en su obra, una presencia muy destacada. Ocupando la cota más alta de la ciudad, a una altura similar a la del *Traianeum*, se abría hacia el sur, sobre la zona forense. Desgraciadamente, aún no tenemos datos ciertos del cierre de ese complejo hacia el lado sur, que constituiría el acceso principal desde el Foro, ni tampoco de esa tercera terraza, que permitiría la conexión hacia esa plaza rodeada de galerías abiertas, con grandes estanques que circundarían a una edificación central, no localizada, aunque sí la exedra norte, de planta semicircular, que marca el eje del complejo, flanqueada a su vez por dos exedras cuadrangulares, de menores dimensiones. Unas formas marcadas por la simetría, semejantes, pues, a las *Traianeum* y Palestra del Complejo Termal. Como se ha

dicho, las galerías oriental y norte estarían abiertas al paisaje, mientras que en la occidental se adosaría un templo a Diana, sin que sea descartable la existencia de otros templos de pequeñas dimensiones o capillas en ese mismo flanco occidental, que estaría en contacto con una zona de la ciudad destinada a uso doméstico (Figuras 25.4 y 25.5).

Ese templo de Diana fue excavado en agosto de 1901, después que en noviembre del año anterior, de manera fortuita, en el corral de Casimiro Arrivas Martín (actual calle Velázquez, número 3, de Santiponce), al hacer un hoyo para plantar árboles, se encontrara otra escultura completa de Diana Cazadora, ya que en 1781 había aparecido el torso de una Ártemis. Fruto de la excavación se recogieron cinco capiteles, cuatro basas una columna completa, doce fragmentos de fustes y la pierna izquierda de una escultura de Mercurio, la correspondiente al *Hermes Dionysóphoros* aparecido en 1782. Una vez concluida la excavación, Francisco Aurelio Álvarez Millán, arquitecto de la Diputación Provincial, realizó el levantamiento planimétrico del espacio donde se encontraba la escultura. Interpretado como "Capilla", con criterio arqueológico la planta del edificio se grabó posteriormente en una placa de mármol, que se fijó en la parte frontal del pedestal sobre el que se colocó la Diana Cazadora, permaneciendo en la actualidad en los almacenes del Museo.

Sin duda, somos conscientes que hemos afianzado los primeros pasos y que se abren nuevos retos. Las

Figura 25.6. La zona monumental del Teatro y *Aedes Augusti* (Á.J.S y M.A.R).

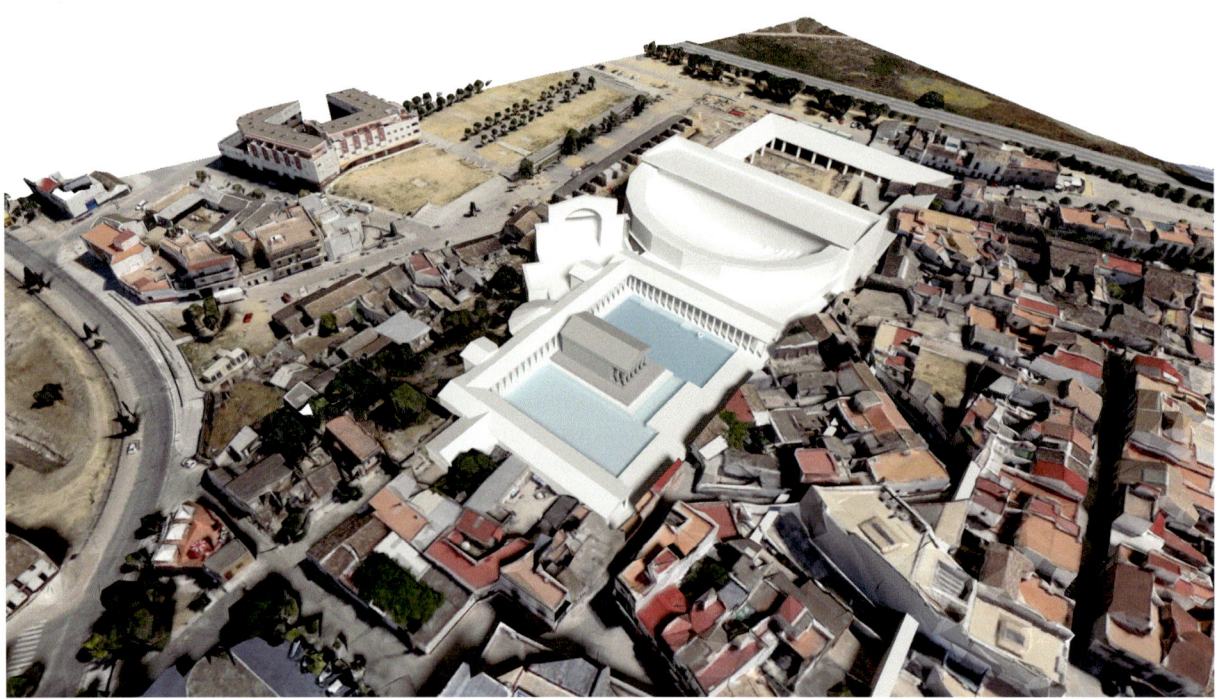

Figura 25.7. El complejo monumental desde el Suroeste: Teatro, *Aedes Augusti* (pervivencia) y *Aedes Adriani* (J.M.R.H, Á.J.S y M.A.R.).

Figura 25.8. El complejo monumental desde el Noroeste. En primer término la entrada principal bífida a la ampliación adrianea, la muralla y puertas estarían bajo la carretera (J.M.R.H, Á.J.S y M.A.R.).

futuras intervenciones arqueológicas deberán prestar especial interés en documentar y fechar esos expolios que, de forma sistemática y desde época islámica, han esquilmado los niveles de uso de las referidas terrazas, al igual que de casi toda la Itálica que subyace bajo el pueblo de Santiponce. Se ha de seguir investigando sobre la totalidad de hallazgos antiguos depositados en el Museo Arqueológico de Sevilla, no sólo las grandes esculturas. Junto a ellas, en los fondos del Museo se atesoran multitud de fragmentos escultóricos y también arquitectónicos procedentes de excavaciones y hallazgos antiguos, que precisan estudios. En esta línea de revisiones, el pasado año la profesora F. Chaves Tristán publicó un interesante artículo sobre el hallazgo de un tesorillo presumiblemente perteneciente a ese referido templo de Diana (Chaves Tristán 2021). Hay que proyectar sondeos auscultatorios y excavar en aquellos lugares concretos donde podamos corroborar algunas de las hipótesis presentadas y también reexcavar y recuperar el templo de Diana, para comprender así la verdadera dimensión de este complejo edilicio que interpretamos como un *Aedes Hadriani* en el que pervive parte del *Aedes Augusti* (Figuras 25.6-25.8). Finalmente, entendemos que urge redactar un Plan Especial de Protección de este sector noreste de Santiponce, desde el que gestionar sus incuestionables valores patrimoniales en relación con el desarrollo local.

Bibliografía

Beltrán, J. y J.L. Escacena (eds) 2021. *ITÁLICA: Investigaciones arqueológicas en la vetus urbs.* Sevilla: Editorial Universidad de Sevilla.

Chaves Tristán, Fca. 2020. El tesoro de áureos hallado en Itálica. *Habis* 51: 161-91.

García Y Bellido, A. 1960. *Colonia Aelia Augusta Italica.* Madrid: Instituto español de arqueologia.

Jimenez Sancho, A. 2021a. Acerca del gran ábside junto al teatro de Itálica: ¿*Aedes Augusti*?, en J. Beltrán y J.L. Escacena (eds). *ITÁLICA: Investigaciones arqueológicas en la vetus urbs.* En prensa, Sevilla.

Jimenez Sancho, A. 2021b. El sector oriental del tell de Itálica: margas azules, terrazas y calles, en J. Beltrán y J.L. Escacena (eds) *ITÁLICA: Investigaciones arqueológicas en la vetus urbs.* En prensa, Sevilla.

León, P. 2021. *ITALICA: la ciudad de Trajano y Adriano* (SPAL. Monografías Arqueología 35). Sevilla: Editorial Universidad de Sevilla.

Rodríguez Hidalgo, J.M. 1997. La nueva imagen de la Itálica de Adriano, en A. Caballos y P. León (eds) *ITALICA MMCC*: 87-113. Sevilla: Consejería de cultura.

Rodriguez Hidalgo, J.M. 2009. El Palacio de Itálica. Colina de los Dioses, en *Itálica: Colina de dioses.* Exposición, Museo Municipal Fernando Marmolejo. Santiponce: 15-39. Sevilla: Consejería de cultura.

Rodriguez Hidalgo, J.M. 2018. Itálica, entre Zevallos y Bruna, en J. Beltrán, P. León y E. Vila (eds y coordinadores científicos) *Francisco de Bruna (1719-1807) y su colección de antigüedades en el Real Alcázar de Sevilla*: 211-44. Sevilla: Universidad de Sevilla.

Rodriguez Hidalgo, J.M. 2021. Hitos del urbanismo romano de la *vetus urbs* en época de los emperadores Augusto y Adriano. Planimetría y documentación gráfica, en J. Beltrán y J.L. Escacena (eds) *ITÁLICA: Investigaciones arqueológicas en la vetus urbs.* En prensa, Sevilla.

Rodriguez Hidalgo, J.M. y A. Jiménez Sancho 2015. Itálica, la Colina de los Dioses. De Augusto a Adriano, en J. García Sánchez, I. Mañas Romero y F. Salcedo Garcés (eds) *Navigare necesse est: Estudios en homenaje a José María Luzón Nogué*: 231-42. Madrid: Universidad Complutense de Madrid.

Rodríguez Hidalgo, J.M., S.J. Keay, D. Jordan y J. Creighton 1999. La Itálica de Adriano. Resultado de las prospecciones arqueológicas de 1991 y 1993. *Archivo Español de Arqueología* 72.179-80: 73-97.

26. Nueva mirada a la imagen de *Italica*

Pilar León

El acontecimiento más relevante en la arqueología contemporánea de *Italica* va unido al nombre de Simon Keay. Como buen conocedor de la problemática del yacimiento y de sus posibilidades comprendió la oportunidad que suponía la introducción de las nuevas técnicas de prospección geomagnética en un yacimiento con las características de *Italica*. La estrecha colaboración de Simon Keay con José Manuel Rodríguez Hidalgo desde tiempos anteriores facilitó la puesta en marcha de un proyecto de investigación arqueológica desarrollado a comienzos de los años 90, entre 1991 y 1993. El equipo de la Universidad de Southampton, con amplia experiencia en esta actividad pionera, combinó técnicas de prospección sistemática superficial con técnicas geofísicas de resistividad, magnetometría y radar terrestre, a lo que se unió la realización de un vuelo fotogramétrico digitalizado. Los resultados fueron sorprendentes y espectaculares y la publicación inicial marcó un hito en la historia de las investigaciones arqueológicas en *Italica* (Rodríguez Hidalgo 1997).

Fue un trabajo de equipo, pero el referente fue Simon Keay, porque a los conocimientos técnicos propios de la nueva metodología unía la visión histórica, territorial y paisajística imprescindible para el análisis de la nueva evidencia arqueológica. La fisionomía de la *Nova Urbs* cambió radicalmente, se conocieron nuevos edificios, se vio más clara la red viaria, todo lo cual se había conseguido sin necesidad de excavación. Las expectativas creadas fueron grandes, porque las imágenes obtenidas del subsuelo planteaban nuevas cuestiones y, en consecuencia, incitaban a los arqueólogos a proseguir la búsqueda de respuestas y el planteamiento de nuevas hipótesis. La nueva metodología se revelaba como un instrumento de trabajo sumamente útil, que facilitaba y acortaba el proceso de investigación, por más que requiriera corroboración en aquellos aspectos puntuales que se estimaran convenientes.

Las campañas 1991-93 en *Italica* representaron un revulsivo metodológico sin precedentes, que pronto encontraría eco en otros yacimientos de la Península Ibérica. El vínculo de Simon Keay con la arqueología española, y más concretamente con la de *Italica*, quedó así consolidado, ha proseguido a lo largo de los años y ha convertido a Simon Keay en una de las voces más autorizadas en temas arqueológicos hispanos a nivel nacional e internacional.

Aquella primera imagen de la *Italica* subyacente abrió nuevas perspectivas a la hora de reflexionar sobre cuestiones candentes relacionadas con la topografía, el urbanismo y la imagen de la ciudad, no sólo en el área de la ampliación adrianea, sino también en lo concerniente a la fusión de ésta con la entidad urbana precedente. Los aspectos estructurales, funcionales y ornamentales de la *Colonia Aelia Augusta Italicensium* entraban en una nueva dimensión, cuya valoración debía hacerse con criterio renovado y acorde con la configuración de gran ciudad, que *Italica* revalidaba a partir de los descubrimientos de las mencionadas campañas de prospección geofísica.

Los estudios de los últimos años sobre el urbanismo, la arquitectura y los proyectos ornamentales han dejado de manifiesto la necesidad de plantear una revisión y una renovación de la imagen de *Italica*. La valoración de la importancia que adquiere en ella la fachada E. es cuestión prioritaria y merece que se le preste atención. Por regla general, cuando se habla de una imagen renovada de *Italica* se pone el foco sobre la *Nova Urbs*, o sea, sobre la ampliación de la ciudad por el norte acometida en época de Adriano. Sin embargo, si se atiende a la evidencia histórica y arqueológica, *Italica* parece haber sido una ciudad predispuesta siempre a cambiar de imagen, a renovarla paulatinamente al menos. Que el hito culminante de ese proceso evolutivo fue la transformación operada en época adrianea está fuera de duda, pues la metamorfosis urbanística y monumental de entonces fue de tal envergadura, que superó con mucho los cambios acaecidos previamente. No por ello se debe pasar sobre éstos últimos sin apreciarlos debidamente, ya que hoy sabemos hasta qué punto fueron decisivos (León 2018; 2020; 2020b; 2021). Basta recordar que algunos de ellos se han convertido en problemas arduos, pendientes de solución en la arqueología italicense, para comprender la utilidad de volver sobre ellos con otra visión.

El primero bien puede ser el binomio de los cerros de San Antonio y Los Palacios (Santiponce, Sevilla), esencial para la imagen de *Italica* desde los tiempos más remotos. Uno al E., otro al O., ambos relacionados con

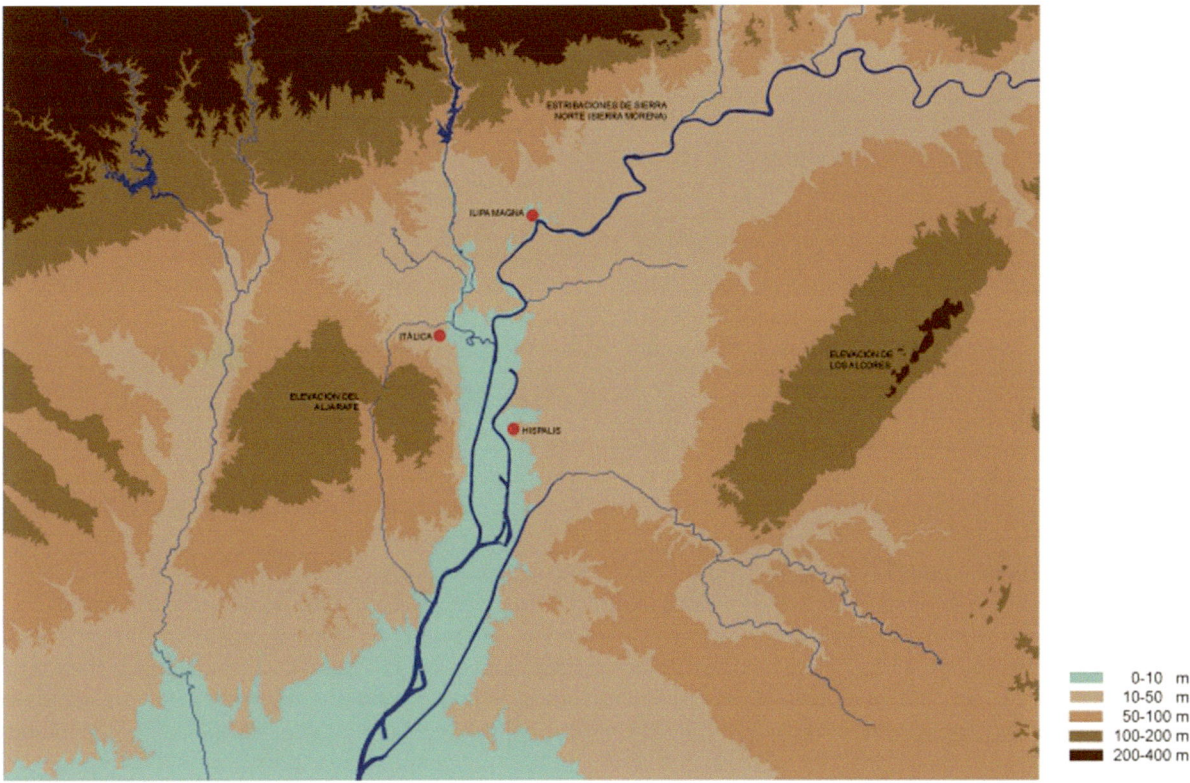

Figura 26.1. Relación Italica-río Baetis (Alarcón y Montero-Fernández 2017).

una de las cuestiones más acuciantes de la ciudad -el foro-, algunas de cuyas incógnitas han sido despejadas por José Beltrán (Beltrán 2012). Problemas no menos relevantes y pendientes de solución son los centrados en torno al *Baetis*, al puerto y al acceso a la ciudad desde la zona baja de la fachada E., interrogantes que se mantienen abiertas. Todas ellas necesitan esclarecimiento y suponen una exigencia improrrogable para la investigación.

Pruebas claras de la atención que merece la cuestión del diálogo entre *Italica* y el *Baetis* son hechos tan contundentes como la posición del recinto de culto imperial, el *Traianeum*; o bien la organización del itinerario cultual, cívico y monumental; o bien el funcionamiento del puerto, cuyo papel fundamental ha sido señalado por José Beltrán en relación con el comercio del mármol, que sin ser el único, en *Italica* fue siempre muy activo (Beltrán 2013: 244-45. 248). Piénsese, por ejemplo, en las exigencias que requirió el acarreo de material constructivo pesado -especialmente cantidades ingentes de mármol, que sólo pudieron llegar por el *Baetis*- y piénsese en la organización y desarrollo del proceso constructivo -instalaciones, talleres, grúas- y se comprenderá de inmediato la importancia que adquieren factores como el río y el itinerario E-O en la ejecución de aquella obra magna. Punto crucial en esta reflexión fue la propuesta de Álvaro Jiménez (Jiménez y Borja 2015), que efectivamente defendía la llegada

de los materiales constructivos por el río, el traslado hacia el interior por la Cañada Honda en dirección E-O y la ubicación del puerto de obras al final de la Cañada Honda, junto al emplazamiento monumental.

Las cuestiones aquí apuntadas hacen ver que la renovación de la imagen de *Italica* pasa por el esclarecimiento de aspectos constitutivos, a los que no se ha prestado atención suficiente. Entre ellos hay uno, que se presenta como un reto y que consiste en lanzar una mirada retrospectiva más lejana, determinante en la configuración de la imagen de la ciudad. Es un reto inquietante, porque introduce un elemento nuevo, habitualmente disociado de *Italica*: el mar. Las circunstancias que enlazan a *Italica* con el mar son una realidad geológica imperante en la morfología del territorio que circunda a *Italica* y cuyo eje vertebrador mutó de mar a río, o mejor, a un vasto escenario de marismas, meandros, lagunas, cauces fluviales menores confluyentes en el *Baetis*. La proximidad de *Italica* al *Baetis* (Figura 26.1) es factor crucial, para sopesar la importancia del diálogo entre la ciudad y el río, pues al discurrir éste por el flanco oriental de aquélla, la fachada E. de la ciudad se veía potenciada. Antes de desarrollar esta hipótesis, conviene examinar aportaciones previas, en las que se encuentra el punto de partida.

En los que podríamos llamar albores de la imagen de *Italica*, un mapa de la Bética del siglo II d.C. debido a

Ptolomeo y reproducido por un manuscrito coloreado, merece atención. Como hizo constar José Manuel Rodríguez Hidalgo (Rodríguez Hidalgo 2012: 14-15, fig. 1), los límites de la provincia Bética con la Tarraconense y con la Lusitania están señalados, como también la línea de costa y los mares que la bordean. Dentro del territorio bético el eje vertebrador es el río *Baetis*, en torno al que se concentra una gran cantidad de ciudades, entre las cuales se reconocen de E. a O. los nombres de Corduba, Carmona, Hispalis, Italica, Nabrissa y ya más abajo una bifurcación de bocas del río, con las que se representa la zona de marisma, que precede a la desembocadura. De forma escueta y con las irregularidades explicables en la cartografía de la época es importante ver a *Italica* situada entre las poblaciones que jalonan el cauce bajo del *Baetis*.

Datos y elementos geográficos para considerar en la formación de la nueva imagen de *Italica* se encuentran en una serie de vistas e imágenes de siglos pasados seleccionadas por José Mª Luzón. La más antigua es el dibujo muy conocido de Anton van den Wyngaerde, fechado en 1567 (Luzón 1999: 26-27). Existen descripciones literarias precedentes, como las de Andrea Navagero y Luis de Peraza (León 1993: 30-31), pero es el dibujo de van den Wyngaerde el primero que ofrece una imagen de las ruinas, es decir, de lo que se identificaba en ellas -el Anfiteatro- y de los elementos paisajísticos vecinos. Así el Monasterio de San Isidoro del Campo aparece en el ángulo inferior izquierdo, mientras en el lado opuesto se consignan referencias de gran importancia, a los efectos que aquí nos interesan, entre los que destaca el río Guadalquivir, antiguo Betis, apenas marcado con una línea a la ligera, pero claramente consignado. De 1585 es la conocida vista de Sevilla de Ambrosius Brambilla, en la que se observan correctamente ubicadas al norte las ruinas del Anfiteatro de *Italica* y el Monasterio de San Isidoro del Campo, las dos referencias iconográficas más potentes para la identificación de *Italica* (Luzón 1999: 20. 27-28). De esta representación deriva la placa, probablemente de hueso o marfil, incrustada en una bargueño italiano de hacia 1590, en la que se reproducen con claridad, pese al tamaño reducido, el Anfiteatro, La Algaba, y el meandro del río afrontados *Italica* (Luzón 1999: 28-29).

Idéntico interés ostenta una curiosa vista del cauce del bajo Guadalquivir, obra de Diego Cuelvis de hacia 1600, que abarca el territorio comprendido entre *Italica* y la desembocadura del Guadalquivir en Sanlúcar de Barrameda (Cádiz) (Luzón 1999: 21. 28). Esta imagen es interesante por doble motivo; en primer lugar, por la presencia de *Italica*, mencionada como "Sevilla la Vieja", y reconocible por el Anfiteatro y por el Monasterio de San Isidoro del Campo; en segundo lugar, por la configuración geográfica peculiar que adquiere el Guadalquivir al final de su cauce, debida a la presencia de afluentes, brazos secundarios, meandros, islas de la

marisma y desembocadura. Todo lo cual constituye una unidad geográfica y paisajística bien definida, en la que queda incluida *Italica*.

Sin ser las únicas, las vistas aquí comentadas son significativas y merecedoras de comentario a causa de dos razones principales; la primera de ellas es porque se llevan a cabo por el tiempo en que se está formando la imagen literaria de *Italica* entre los siglos XVI-XVII, gracias a las descripciones, poemas y escritos de los humanistas del Renacimiento y del Barroco (Beltrán *et al.* 2018: 340-42; León 1993: 31-37). La segunda razón es porque ya por entonces los autores de esas vistas se percatan de la importancia de un rasgo geográfico insuficientemente valorado con posterioridad. Se trata de la pertenencia de *Italica* al escenario hidrológico natural, por el que discurre el cauce del bajo Guadalquivir entre Alcalá del Río (Sevilla), la antigua *Ilipa Magna*, y Sanlúcar de Barrameda (Cádiz). La red intrincada de afluentes, cauces menores, islas, marismas, crea un panorama singular, en el que el protagonismo recae sobre la corriente marina y fluvial, que dejó en esos lugares y en las poblaciones asentadas en ellos una herencia marítima perdurable.

Todavía en el plano topográfico de 1811, levantado durante la ocupación francesa, se aprecia con toda claridad la situación de las ruinas de *Italica* en medio de una fértil campiña de olivares y de una orografía suave, que pone de manifiesto la proximidad y la correlación de *Itálica* con el cauce del Guadalquivir (Rodríguez Hidalgo 2012: 19-20, fig. 5).

En relación con *Italica* y en sentido arqueológico es obligado señalar, que el icono por excelencia en todas esas representaciones gráficas y el reproducido con más frecuencia, por ser el más potente, es el Anfiteatro, pictograma por el que se identifica a *Italica*.

Hito crucial en la configuración de la imagen de *Italica* y en la visión que se tendrá de ella en adelante es el Plano General de Demetrio de los Ríos, fechado en 1865. Conocemos bien sus pormenores arqueológicos e historiográficos (Luzón 2012; Fernández 1998: 25-28), que conviene recordar por el interés que adquieren respecto al tema aquí planteado. Ese plano es versión reducida y simplificada de la versión original de 1862 dada a conocer por Demetrio de los Ríos como Plano Topográfico de las Ruinas de *Italica* y entregada a la Comisión de Monumentos. La versión de 1862 era de mayor formato, más cuidada y detallada, a pesar de lo cual quedó relegada por la versión de 1865, que por ser menor resultaba más manejable y disponible como grabado, de ahí que haya sido la utilizada preferentemente por los investigadores.

Es fundamental, sin embargo, dirigir la mirada al plano original, a la versión de 1862, para constatar el cambio que representa en la iconografía de *Italica* (Luzón 2012: fig. 1). Distanciado desde tiempo atrás el Guadalquivir de la ciudad, en el plano de Demetrio de los Ríos no queda rastro del río. Las ruinas se esparcen entre colinas y algunas alcanzan el caserío del vecino Santiponce (Sevilla); olivares y tierras de labor rodean el sitio arqueológico. Es una *Italica* de tierra adentro, disociada del medio acuático, de la corriente fluvial. Tan sólo el Arroyo del Cernícalo está vagamente indicado al sur de Santiponce, mientras los de la Cañada Honda al norte y el próximo al Anfiteatro aún más al norte apenas si son reconocibles. El contrapunto a esta situación lo ponen unos segmentos de muros marcados con el número XIV en el ángulo exterior NE de Santiponce y la llanura limítrofe marcada con el número XXVIII (Luzón 2012: fig. 3). Los segmentos de muro son designados por Demetrio de los Ríos "muros y otras construcciones del antiguo muelle"; la llanura es designada "terreno bajo y pantanoso por donde iba antes el río que bañaba los muros de Itálica" (Fernández 1998: 27-28). Resulta así que, aunque omitido el río en las dos versiones del plano de Demetrio de los Ríos, en la de 1862 se intuye su presencia en las ruinas. Sobre la importancia y sobre la valoración que la investigación actual hace de estos datos, volveremos.

Si relevancia adquiere este cambio para la configuración de la imagen de *Italica*, no es menor la que adquiere el punto de vista u orientación adoptada para su plano por Demetrio de los Ríos. La ciudad es avistada desde el sur o desde el suroeste, si se prefiere; la carretera de Extremadura recorre el flanco oriental de las ruinas y secciona el solar de Santiponce, situado a Levante. El trazado de la muralla se da completo y en él se señalan puertas y torres, así como el *castellum aquae* contiguo al ángulo pronunciado de la muralla por el oeste. La orientación S-N imprime carácter en la imagen de *Italica* y perdura hasta el presente, por más que sea perturbadora respecto a la fachada de la ciudad durante la Antigüedad. Cuando se considera esta alteración y se piensa en la preparación y formación de Demetrio de los Ríos como arquitecto y topógrafo, la distorsión debe ser atribuida con probabilidad a dos factores entrelazados; en primer lugar está la posición al sur respecto a *Italica* del Monasterio de San Isidoro del Campo, punto de referencia ancestral para el yacimiento, como ya se ha visto; en segundo lugar y motivo más funcional, es la llegada del visitante a las ruinas -a *Italica*- desde Sevilla, o sea, desde el sur. A favor de esta explicación hay un argumento proveniente de la abundante información historiográfica de los siglos XVIII-XIX. Se trata de la descripción de *Italica* debida a Francisco Pérez Bayer, la única que sigue un criterio ordenado e intenta eludir los inconvenientes de una toponimia farragosa e insegura. La descripción de Pérez Bayer sigue un recorrido de orientación cardinal, que se inicia en el monasterio de San Isidoro del Campo, penetra en el

campo de ruinas y avanza hacia el Anfiteatro, situado en el extremo septentrional de la ciudad (León 1993: 42-43). Como habrá ocasión de ver, la imagen S-N de *Italica* se ha mantenido a lo largo de siglos y en posición aún más vertical y axial permanecerá preponderante hasta el presente.

La versión de 1862 del Plano Topográfico de las Ruinas de *Italica* de Demetrio de los Ríos sirvió de base al plano elaborado en 1902 por Pelayo Quintero, para ilustrar los lugares de hallazgo de mosaicos. Tal vez para entonces la memoria de un puerto o muelle en la vieja *Italica* se había debilitado, pues los muros que Demetrio de los Ríos señalaba como restos del antiguo muelle en el ángulo NE de Santiponce, Pelayo Quintero los interpreta como "muralla antigua" (Quintero 1902; Beltrán 2008: 53, fig. 5). Sin embargo la proximidad del Guadalquivir, el antiguo *Baetis*, y las condiciones de navegabilidad a la altura de *Italica* han hecho pensar a los investigadores en la existencia de un puerto, cuya localización ha sido y es un reto de primera magnitud para la arqueología de *Italica* (García y Bellido 1960: 118), además de ser un factor relevante en la configuración de la fachada E. de la ciudad.

El plano de Pelayo Quintero introduce dos aportaciones curiosas, una de carácter hidrológico y otra de carácter topográfico. En relación con el aspecto hidrológico hay que resaltar, que los arroyos o corrientes de agua locales, el del Cernícalo, el de la cañada Honda y el del Anfiteatro, constan con mayor claridad en este plano, de suerte que se puede suponer la importancia del manto acuático, que bañaba a *Italica* por el flanco oriental. Aunque hoy es difícil de percibir a causa de las alteraciones del terreno, tanto el arroyo del Cernícalo como el de la Cañada Honda actuaban de defensa respecto a los cerros o cabezos de la vieja *Italica*. En relación con el aspecto topográfico hay que advertir además en el plano de P. Quintero la presencia de curvas de nivel trazadas de manera simple y elemental, pero útiles para reconocer e identificar las alturas o elevaciones del terreno tanto de la ampliación adrianea como de la vieja *Italica* (Santiponce). Concretamente respecto a ésta última tenemos aquí un punto de partida para saber, que en el solar de *Italica* se articulaban varios cerros o promontorios y que entre ellos se formaba una hondonada o ensenada. Dos de ellos son los bien conocidos cerros de San Antonio al E. y de Los Palacios al O., a los que se suma un tercero menos pronunciado al S. Entre los cerros de San Antonio y de Los Palacios se produce una hondonada o espacio llano y rehundido, que es fundamental en la configuración geológica de *Italica* y en su imagen, pues corresponde a la zona en la que se suele ubicar el foro.

En un curioso ensayo de carácter didáctico elaborado en el año 2000 se ofrece una perspectiva general de la

Figura 26.2. Vista ideal de Italica (Fernández *et al.* 2000).

Figura 26.3. Vista paramétrica de Italica (Alarcón y Montero Fernández 2017).

gran *Italica* adrianea desde la fachada de Levante y en ella una vista del puerto (Fernández *et al.* 2000: 13-14). La ciudad afronta el río, como es lógico en una ciudad fluvial e incluso cuando se adopta la orientación N-S desde detrás del Anfiteatro, se advierte el desarrollo de la fachada E. por la presencia del puerto (Fernández *et al.* 2000: 18). Aun cuando se trata de vistas o reconstrucciones ideales, resulta evidente cómo el factor río condiciona y determina la imagen de *Italica* (Figura 26.2).

Ahora bien, el protagonismo de los flujos hídricos, cuestión clave para conocer el desarrollo urbanístico y la imagen de *Italica*, sólo ha recibido atención en tiempos recientes. En el año 2012 se produce

un cambio de signo sumamente positivo para la investigación, cuyas consecuencias resultan decisivas. Las excavaciones arqueológicas llevadas a cabo en el Cerro de San Antonio y en sus aledaños, especialmente en la zona del Teatro, demostraban la importancia de los flujos hídricos en todo el solar sobre el que se asentará *Italica*. Esta observación puso de manifiesto la conveniencia de plantear una indagación específica sobre el origen y naturaleza de dichos flujos, que se centró en la zona mencionada del Teatro, pero que se pudo hacer extensiva a la *Vetus Urbs*. De hecho, resultó posible conocer y documentar el dinamismo, la presencia continuada y a gran escala del agua en *Italica* tanto en tiempos prehistóricos como históricos. Solamente los cambios geológicos sobrevenidos con

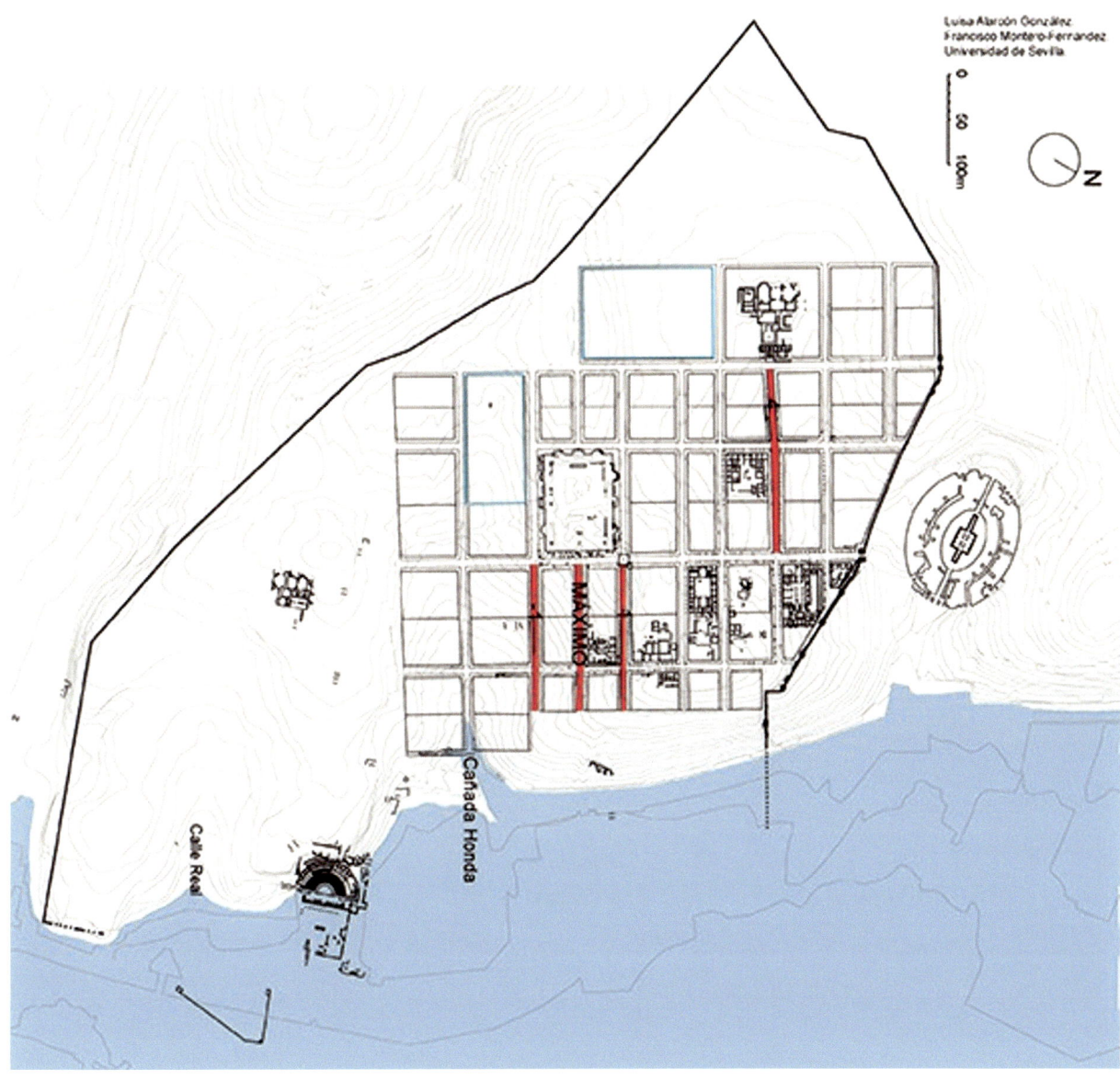

Figura 26.4. Vías principales con orientación E.-O.

los siglos modificaron la forma de manifestarse la presencia del agua, que de ser expansiva pasó a verse reducida a inundaciones, a concentraciones temporales y a corrientes residuales. No obstante lo cual, el hecho de que estas nuevas manifestaciones se mostraran activas y pertinaces, habla claramente de la vitalidad de los flujos hídricos en el lugar (Borja *et al.* 2012; Jiménez y Borja 2015). En los últimos años se han producido nuevas aportaciones al conocimiento de los flujos hídricos en *Italica* y a la relación entre ella y el *Baetis*, así como aproximaciones a la actividad portuaria y por tanto a la localización del puerto, situación que lleva a revalorizar la fachada E. de la ciudad (Jiménez y Borja 2015: 91-92).

Alcanzado este punto, la investigación experimenta un avance considerable en la progresión hacia la nueva

imagen de *Italica* gracias a un trabajo de Luisa Alarcón y Francisco Montero-Fernández, dado a conocer en 2017. A partir de un planteamiento innovador, del que se desprenden conclusiones de máxima repercusión a efectos de imagen urbana, la realización de un nuevo análisis espacial y topográfico lleva, en primer lugar, a mostrar desnudo el solar de *Italica*, de modo que la configuración natural del terreno, sus peculiaridades topográficas, saltan a la vista con plena claridad. Asimismo la orientación del modelo urbano al E. aporta un cambio sustancial en la imagen urbana, pues ese margen geográfico se muestra abierto y despejado, en diálogo con el río y con las poblaciones de su extensa campiña; se puede decir que no hay mejor alternativa para la fachada principal de la ciudad (Alarcón y Montero-Fernández 2017: 251-54, fig. 1-2). Los dos tells o grandes terrazas, sobre las que se asentará *Italica* -la

Figura 26.5. Italica-Santiponce, Sevilla (CAI).

preadrianea en la terraza sur, la ampliación adrianea en la terraza norte- y las colinas o promontorios existentes en cada una de ellas ofrecen una imagen nítida, alterada progresivamente a causa del intenso proceso constructivo y del proceso natural de evolución geológica (Figura 26.3).

En segundo lugar, L. Alarcón y F.J. Montero-Fernández ponen especial énfasis en mostrar la relación estrecha entre *Italica* y la red hidrológica del Guadalquivir, que afecta a todo el entorno de la ciudad y que condiciona la situación de ésta en el valle (Alarcón, Montero-Fernández 2017: 254-55, fig. 3). Tanto es así, que dicha relación incide sobre la definición de la fachada urbana y sobre la ubicación del puerto tanto en el momento de instalación del asentamiento romano, esto es, en época republicana, como en el momento posterior de plena época imperial (Alarcón y Montero-Fernández 2017: fig. 4). De hecho las indicaciones antes mencionadas en el plano de Pelayo Quintero a propósito de la existencia

del puerto son tomadas por L. Alarcón y F. Montero-Fernández como indicios de su localización geográfica (Alarcón y Montero-Fernández 2017: 263-64, fig. 8) y, por tanto, elementos decisivos en la configuración de la imagen de *Italica* y en la valoración que se debe hacer de la fachada E. de la ciudad. La mejor prueba del valor de esta propuesta es la respuesta que se halla en la organización del viario urbano y más concretamente en el diseño del itinerario monumental (Figura 26.4) que desde la zona baja de la ciudad, es decir, desde el flanco oriental, se dirige a los accesos de edificios monumentales como las Termas Mayores y el *Traianeum* (Alarcón y Montero-Fernández 2017: 265, fig. 10; León 2021).

En tercer lugar es cuestión clave en el trabajo de L. Alarcón y F.J. Montero-Fernández la inmersión de *Italica* en el territorio y en el paisaje del bajo Guadalquivir (Alarcón y Montero-Fernández 2017: 255-57, fig. 5), con las consecuencias que ello supone en el establecimiento de diálogo entre la ciudad y el río, consecuencias que llevan a potenciar la fachada E.

Las consideraciones precedentes ayudan a comprender que la imagen tradicional de *Italica* ha estado marcada y condicionada por una visión historiográfica orientada en dirección N-S (Figura 26.5), que no tiene que ser necesariamente la de época antigua. Aunque al visitante hoy se le transmita la misma visión que imperaba en el siglo XIX, la investigación arqueológica gana terreno progresivamente y avanza hacia la configuración de una imagen más real y acorde con una situación geológica y topográfica, de la que todavía hoy resulta posible percatarse.

Bibliografía

Alarcón, L. y F.J. Montero-Fernández 2017. The Urbanism of Italica and the Traianeum. *Civiltà Romana* 4: 251-70.

Beltrán, J. 2008. Esculturas de Itálica aparecidas en siglo XVIII. *Spal* 17: 47-59.

Beltrán, J. 2012. El foro de Itálica, in F. Amores y J. Beltrán (eds) *Italica 1912-2012: Centenario de la declaración como Monumento Nacional*: 123-29. Granada: Fundación itálica de estudios clásicos.

Beltrán, J. 2013. Mármoles en la Bética durante el reinado de Adriano. El protagonismo de *Itálica*, in R. Hidalgo y P. León (eds) *Roma, Tibur, Baetica: Investigaciones adrianeas*: 225-50. Sevilla: Universidad de Sevilla.

Beltrán, J., P. León y E. Vila (eds) 2018. *Francisco de Bruna (1719-1807) y su colección de antigüedades en el Real Alcázar de Sevilla*. Sevilla: Universidad de Sevilla.

Borja, F., C. Borja y A. Borja y Lama 2012. Registro sedimentario y flujos. *Italica* 2: 77-98.

Fernández, F. (ed.) 1998. *Las excavaciones de Italica y don Demetrio de los Ríos a través de sus escritos*. Córdoba: Cajasur Publicaciones.

Fernández, J.J., J.L. Ravé y P.J. Respaldiza 2000. *Dibujos. F. Salado, Italica. Cuaderno del Profesorado*. Sevilla: Junta de Andalucía. Consejería de Educación y Ciencia. Consejería de Cultura. Gabinete Pedagógico de Bellas Arte.

García y Bellido, A 1960. *Colonia Aelia Augusta Italica*. Madrid: Consejo superior de investigaciones científicas.

Jiménez, A. y F. Borja 2015. El Teatro de Itálica y su entorno. Evolución del paisaje urbano entre el siglo II a.C. y el cambio de Era, in J. López Vilar (ed.) *Tarraco Biennal 2*: 87-93. Tarragona: Fundación Privada Mútua Catalana.

León, P. 1993. Las ruinas de Itálica. Una estampa arqueológica de prestigio, in F. Gascó y J. Beltrán (eds) *La Antigüedad como argumento: historiografía de arqueología e historia antigua en Andalucía*: 29-61. Sevilla: Consejería de cultura.

León, P. 2018. Itálica: de la madurez trajanea a la mutación adrianea, in A. Caballos Rufino (ed.) *De Trajano a Adriano: Roma matura, Roma mutans*: 729-65. Sevilla: Universidad de Sevilla.

León, P. 2020a. Italica, génesis y desarrollo del proyecto adrianeo, in R. Hidalgo, G.E. Cinque, A. Pizzo y A. Viscogliosi (eds) *Adventus Adriani*: 219-35. Roma: L'Erma di Bretschneider.

León, P. 2020b. Nuevas consideraciones sobre el Traianeum de Italica, in R. Hidalgo, G.E. Cinque, A. Pizzo y A. Viscogliosi (eds) *Adventus Adriani*: 237-48. Roma: L'Erma di Bretschneider.

León, P. 2021. *Italica: La ciudad de Trajano y Adriano*. Sevilla: Universidad de Sevilla.

Luzón, J.M 1999. *Sevilla la Vieja: un paseo histórico por las ruinas de Itálica*. Sevilla: Fundación Focus-Abengoa.

Luzón, J.M 2012. Plano topográfico de Itálica, in F. Amores y J. Beltrán (eds) *Itálica 1912-2012: Centenario de la Declaración como Monumento Nacional*: 117-22. Sevilla: Fundación itálica de estudios clásicos.

Quintero, P. 1902. *Principales mosaicos encontrados en Itálica: manuscrito de la Real Academia de la Historia*. Madrid.

Rodríguez Hidalgo, J.M. 1997. La nueva imagen de la Itálica de Adriano, in A. Caballos y P. León (eds) *Italica MMCC: actas de las jornadas del 2200 aniversario de la fundación de Itálica*: 89-113. Sevilla: Consejería de cultura.

Rodríguez Hidalgo, J.M. 2012. Hitos de una historia gráfica del descubrimiento de Italica. *Italica* 2: 13-27.

27. The Territory of *Italica* (Seville): An Ancient Mining Landscape

Pablo Garrido González

Years ago, a paper was published (Garrido *et al.* 2012) that attempted to delve deeper into the essential role of *Italica* in the Campo de Gerena area (north-west of Seville), based on the partial revision of a previous doctoral thesis (Garrido 2011). The aim was to expand that first study and to focus on a crucial aspect that had been relegated, not because of its lack of importance, but because the subject of that first thesis had focused mainly on the Guadiamar Valley and the Aznalcóllar mining basin. Fortunately, these first two works were largely complemented by the projects *The Guadiamar Landscapes. Historical Reconstruction and Archaeological Valorisation (2010-2015)* and *Smart Architectural and Archaeological Heritage Project (SMARCH)* (Tejedor *et al.* 2020), which made it possible to check and improve the previous data by applying some experimental systems supported by GIS and a transversal interpretation of ancient landscapes.

Recovering now this same discourse, we can review all the documentation generated from the perspective of the central role of *Italica*, for which we will use two types of approach: the most recent archaeological data, analysed from the perspective of Landscape Archaeology, in the immediate context of the city in the northern Aljarafe Plateau, the Aznalcóllar mining basin, and Campo de Gerena, which were subjected to an analysis of locational variables (a brief summary of which is presented here); and others compiled from projects in more distant areas, which confirm the historical role of the colony beyond its immediate surroundings, towards the middle Gudiamar Valley and the middle and lower course of the River Guadalquivir.

1. The Second Iron Age (5th-2nd Centuries BC)

According to Amores *et al.* (2014), during the Second Iron Age, after the peak of the Orientalizing period, in the lower Guadalquivir region there was a general phenomenon of concentration in larger nuclei that resulted in a significant decrease in the number of settlements (Figure 27.1); the total extinction of any metallurgical evidence attributable to this period south of the Aznalcóllar mining basin is also relevant. However, the settlement in the immediate surroundings of the Aznalcóllar mines did not suffer such a notable retraction and clearly spread towards the Campo de Gerena (Figures 27.1-27.2), in the immediate vicinity of the future site of *Italica*. Based on all this, it has recently been postulated (Amores *et al.* 2014) that the Aznalcóllar mines may have continued to be active at this time, but that in any case the exploitation must have been controlled by a power outside the valley and the metallurgical production evacuated by an alternative route to the Guadiamar Valley.

Although there were important settlements in the Aljarafe and Guadalquivir Valley at this time, before the foundation of *Italica* the densest settlement was found in the southern foothills of Sierra Morena, along the axis formed by the headwaters of the Guadiamar Valley, Gerena, Castrejón, and as far as Alcalá del Río, the ancient *Ilipa* (Figure 27.1).

In the locational analyses carried out in 2011 and 2012, the prominent roles of Gerena and the ancient *oppidum* of Higueras stood out above all (Figures 27.1-27.2). We do not know the exact importance of Gerena in this period, while that of Higueras seems much more certain: a fortified settlement, about 5ha in extension and surrounded by a belt of smaller settlements, with substantial evidence of metallurgical activity. Therefore, shortly before the arrival of the Romans, Higueras had formed an important agglomeration at the western end of the Campo de Gerena region.

Everything suggests that Higueras was a crucial settlement for controlling the western end of the Gerena-*Ilipa* corridor and the routes from it and the sierras towards the Guadiamar Valley, at least between the 6th and 3rd centuries BC. Later on, coinciding with the Roman conquest, Gerena gradually displaced Higueras as the central settlement in this area.

A series of surveys in 2008-10 (Guisado *et al.* 2009) made it possible to locate or contrast the existence of other settlements which, without being central places like Gerena or Higueras, also played a very important role in the area (from west to east): La Viña, Toruñuelo C, Castrejón and Matahijas (Figures 27.1-27.2). None of them stood out in the analysis for their locational values (Garrido 2011), but their prolonged occupation and considerable size suggest that they functioned

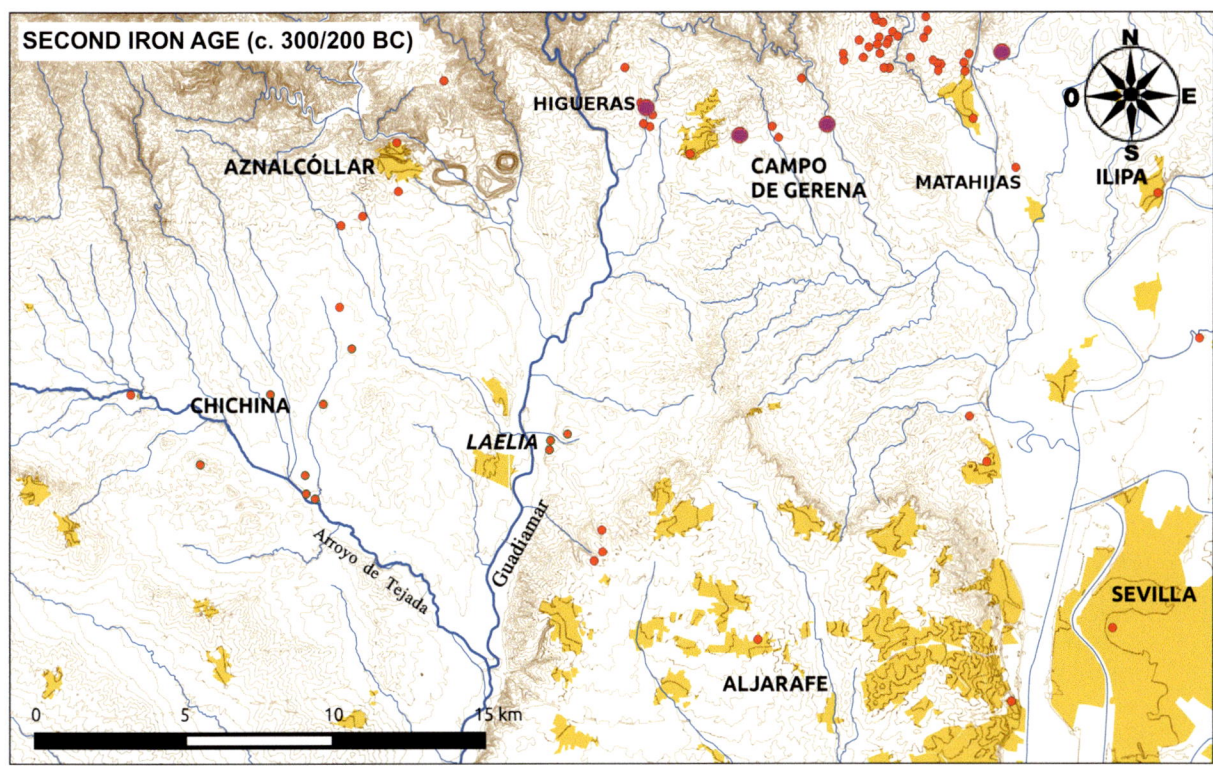

Figure 27.1. Second Iron Age settlement in the area under consideration; the larger circles correspond to fortified settlements (own elaboration based on data from The Guadiamar Landscapes project, 2010-14).

as local centres where a moderate-sized population resided. Among them, La Viña stands out, a one-hectare settlement with strong fortifications that controlled the access road to Gerena and Higueras from the east. The other settlements mentioned, however, do not show any evidence of fortifications, or evidence exists but could be later, as for example Castrejón, inhabited until the 15th century AD (Corzo 1998).

The last link in this chain was Matahijas, on the ford of the Rivera de Huelva, right at the junction of the east-west road from *Ilipa* to Gerena and the Vereda de Salteras (the later Roman road to Mérida), in a north-south direction (Figures 27.1-27.2). It was a settlement of about 14ha, which lasted until the 1200s, against the only Roman dating previously stated by some scholars (Ponsich 1974).

Thus most of archaeological evidence from the Second Iron Age in the whole area is concentrated between Higueras, on the Guadiamar Valley, and Matahijas at the ford over the Rivera de Huelva (Figures 27.1-27.2). Apart from these prominent *oppida* and other intermediate settlements, in the Campo de Gerena there was another category of smaller farmsteads, with modest surface materials. If the concentration of small settlements in the mid Campo de Gerena shown in Figures 27.1-27.2 is mostly based on one particular work (Camacho and Jiménez 2007), also

many other field data (Hunt 2003) confirm a certain expansion of dispersed habitat in this area between the 3rd-2nd centuries BC. Although it is true that the high agrological quality of the soils of the Campo de Gerena would support the hypothesis of an expansion of agriculture at this time, material evidence of the settlements makes it clear that the process must have begun very shortly before the arrival of the Romans, if it does not coincide with the very conquest. Thus, dispersion and expansion, certainly, but with all the caution due to the lateness of the process.

In contrast, in the extreme west of the Campo de Gerena, nothing supports the same process (Figures 27.1-27.2). Settlements of this period are few and of generally intermediate size; most are located around the Aznalcóllar mining basin. However, two prominent settlements closest to these mines, Cortijo del Negro and Vereda de la Carne, were already inhabited. Would this be an indication that the mines were active at this time? This is difficult to prove, as there is no clear archaeometallurgical evidence, except for both earlier and later periods (Hunt 2003). In any case, activity during the late Second Iron Age is highly probable (Domergue 1990), as suggested by the proliferation of mints in the area (Chaves and García 1994).

An overview of the main settlement axes (Figure 27.2) will probably allow us to understand the territorial

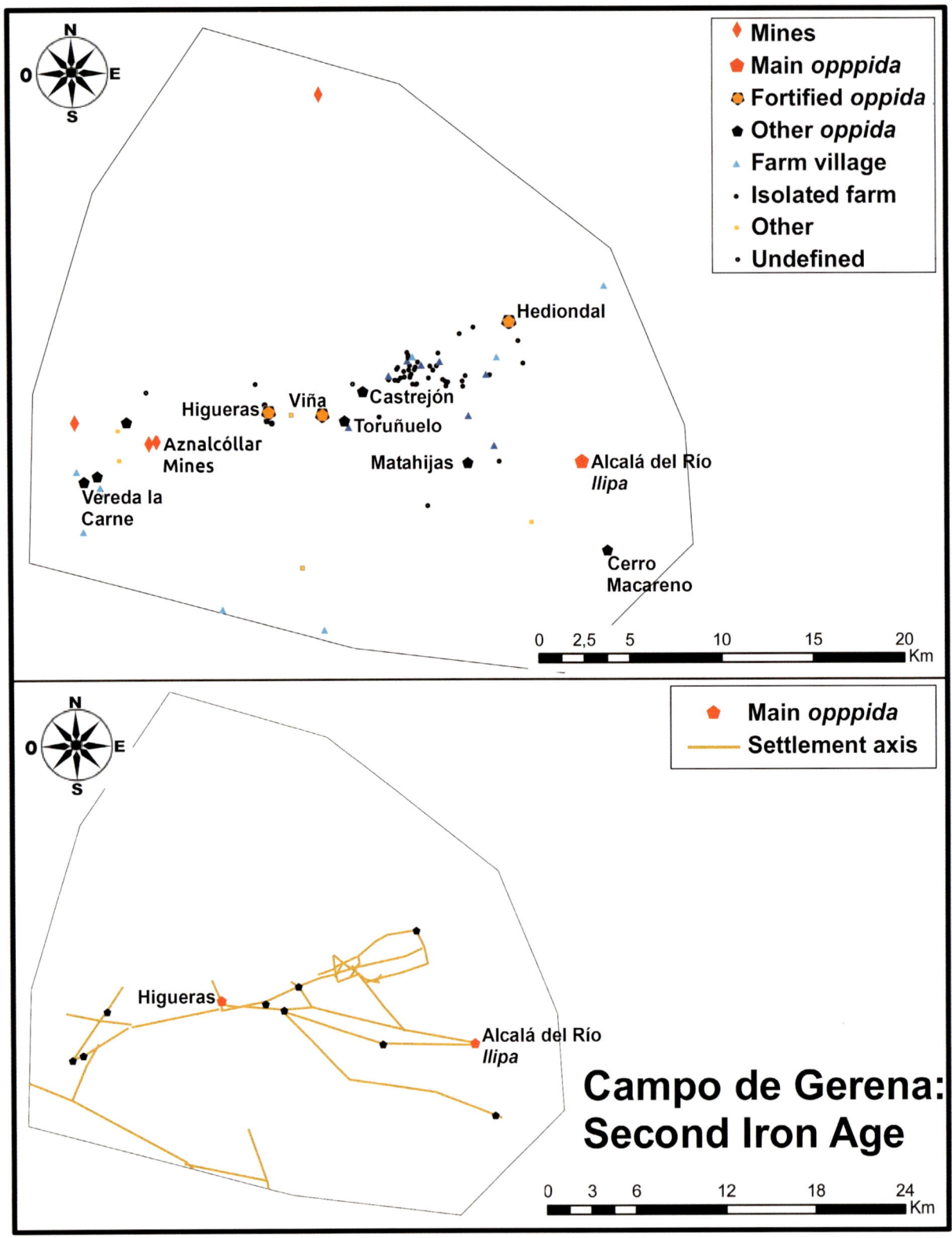

Figure 27.2. Campo de Gerena: Second Iron Age sites subjected to analysis of locational variables (reworked from Garrido *et al.* 2012: 152, fig. 1).

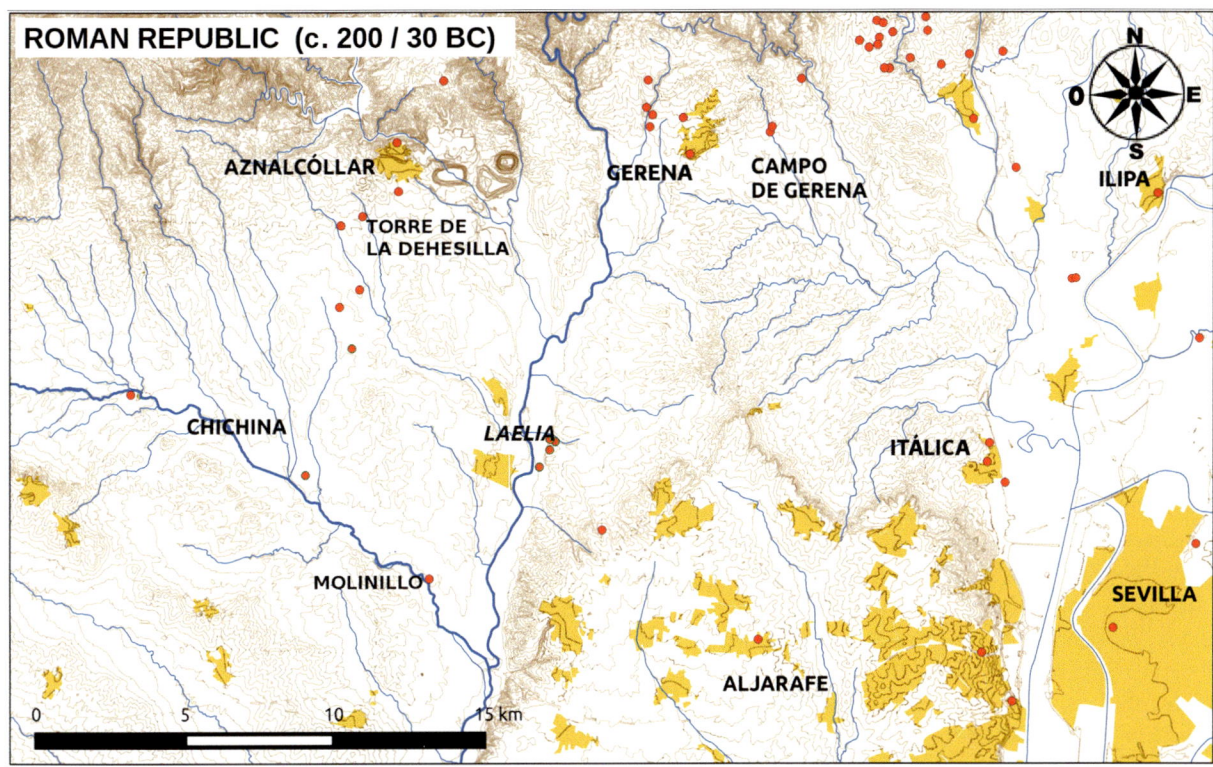

Figure 27.3. Roman Republican period settlement in the area considered in this work (own elaboration based on data from the project *The Guadiamar Landscapes*, 2010-14).

system of this period a little better. It is important to note that these axes confirm their transversality, i.e. that there is clear east-west communication between the Guadalquivir and the Guadiamar Valleys. On the other hand, the north-south axes are not so clearly reflected in the layout, except in specific cases.

In this horizontal communication, the Aznalcóllar mines-*Ilipa* axis stands out above them all, passing through the area controlled by Gerena and Higueras. But only Higueras, fortified, was occupied at this time with total certainty; was Higueras then the *Ilipa* outpost on the headwaters of the Guadiamar and the Aznalcóllar mining basin?

It is certainly difficult to know whether Higueras was in any way subordinate to *Ilipa*, but, regardless of this, the data from the Second Iron Age seem to support the traditional hypothesis that this important city in some way controlled access to the Aznalcóllar mines, as well as others located to the north along the Rivera de Huelva route. The metallurgical belt around Higueras mentioned above probably belonged to this period, and it is not at all unreasonable that it was related to a possible route to the east to get the metals to *Ilipa*, or some other point controlled by it (Velasco 2007). Be that as it may, if this hypothesis is true, the fundamental stopovers to vertebrate this route could have been

Higueras (fortified)-La Viña (fortified)-Toruñuelo C-Castrejón (fortified?)-Matahijas-*Ilipa* (Figures 27.1-27.2).

R. Corzo (1998) even suggests that Castrejón, in addition to strategically controlling the corridor towards the Rivera de Huelva Valley, was the site of important mining and metallurgical activity. Unfortunately, this information is very vague, and although mining evidence has been found at the site (Díaz-Zorita *et al.* 2017), it has so far been dated to prehistoric and Roman times, but it is difficult to pinpoint anything for the Second Iron Age. It is even possible that the metal was shipped to the strategic Matahijas, located at the mouth of the Rivera de Huelva on the River Guadalquivir, in an area most probably navigable, at least for shallow-draft barges.

2. The Roman Republican Period (2nd-1st Centuries BC)

Throughout the Campo de Gerena region archaeological data from this period reflect a slight but generalised decline in the number of settlements, albeit relative and uneven (Figures 27.3-27.4). It has often been discussed whether this could be largely attributable to the poor archaeological traceability of surface materials from the Republican period, but also to the events that accompany any process of conquest and the resulting restructuring. The loss of settlement, grouped or dispersed, is evident in the Sierra Morena and Campo de Gerena, but in contrast it increases noticeably in the Guadalquivir Valley, especially between *Ilipa* and the mouth of the *Baetis* (Figure 27.3). In the Aznalcóllar mining basin there is also evidence of the extinction of some Turdetanian settlements, although most of them tend to survive (Garrido 2011). However, the Republican period is a long one, and from all that has been said so far, the most significant changes, even if not too many, took place quite late, during the early 1st century BC.

After the Second Punic War, the most notable and immediate fact is the emergence of *Italica*, regardless of the controversial pre-existence of a Turdetanian settlement and its exact nature (Luzón 1973). The military purpose of this enclave is undeniable, a fact also well supported by the locational analysis carried out in 2011 and 2012 (Garrido 2011; Garrido *et al.* 2012). In that analysis it had emerged how *Italica* and Gerena each controlled one end of the corridor, and how they even projected their influence towards Sierra Morena and the northern part of the Guadiamar Valley. We have just postulated that this corridor had previously been controlled by *Ilipa*, but the (re)foundation of *Italica* must have brought profound changes to the area, some of which can be seen in the archaeological record.

Based on the works cited above (Garrido 2011; Garrido *et al.* 2012) we postulate that *Italica* was not only a strategic point to defend the Guadalquivir Valley from Lusitanian raids, or any other potential aggression, but that it was located in that place with another primary and fundamental objective: to control the natural access to the Guadiamar Valley and, with it, to the Aznalcóllar mining basin. This surely does not mean that the mines were immediately put into operation by the Romans. In our opinion, at least until Roman rule was consolidated in these lands to the west of *Italica*, it was more a matter of control than management or appropriation, and therefore more linked to a military than an administrative strategy.

It certainly seems no chance that the emergence of *Italica* coincides with the restructuring of the settlement of the Sierra skirts and Campo de Gerena, the most perceptible of the whole region under consideration (Figures 27.3-27.4). While Higueras and other fortified settlements disappeared or began to show clear signs of depopulation, Gerena and its immediate surroundings underwent the opposite process. Therefore, in our opinion, the potentiation of *Italica* can, and indeed must, be interpreted as a direct military intervention by the Roman state to secure this strategic space. Not only did it completely condition *Ilipa*'s access to this region, but it also meant the empowerment of Gerena

as opposed to the ancient settlement of Higueras, whose abandonment or depopulation seems to have been relatively rapid after a small Roman fort was erected very close to the northern wall of the *oppidum* (Garrido 2011).

On the other hand, the archaeological data from the immediate surroundings of Aznalcóllar, beyond some occasional disappearances, reveal an apparent continuity of structures with respect to the preceding stage, with the sole exception of two *ex novo* settlements that provide more or less important metallurgical evidence in the first half of the 1st century BC. Further archaeological data from recent years (Amores *et al.* 2014) allow us to postulate that, in fact, the Roman conquest did not immediately introduce significant changes in the mining environment of Aznalcóllar, not until the acquisitions were secured, already in the transition from the 2nd to the 1st century BC. Therefore Rome probably decided to militarily control access to the Guadiamar Valley by means of its two bridgeheads (Gerena and *Italica*), while it allowed or ceded to other indigenous *oppida* in the area to continue exploiting the Sierra de Tejada-Aznalcóllar mineralisation. In other words, the new masters may have been Roman, but the productive system remained essentially in local hands (Chaves 2000); only after the definitive pacification of the region would the direct entry of Roman mining interests become visible, with the first *ex novo* settlements dedicated to metallurgy.

How is all this reflected in settlement axes? Figures 27.3-27.4 show a notable loss of the transversality that we referred to for the Second Iron Age, where we highlighted the existing east-west communication between the Guadalquivir Valley and the headwaters of the Guadiamar Valley, through the Gerena-Alcalá del Río corridor. Although at first glance it might seem that there is not such an obvious disappearance of these east-west axes (Figure 27.4), it should be noted:

- First, these axes were plotted after a *Kernel* surface density tool to avoid visual bias; then they were weighted with optimal routes linked to metallurgy (Figure 27.5), and finally, as discussed in detail elsewhere (Amores *et al.* 2014), they were linked only to those sites that do not deviate more than 50m from previously plotted areas of influence, after considering a series of cartographic corrections.
- Second, it is not so much the evident extinction of the direct axes between *Ilipa* and Higueras, an absolutely relevant fact, as the clear displacement of the weight of gravity towards Gerena and the Aznalcóllar mining basin, which we attribute to the potentiation of *Italica* and the resulting restructuring (Figures 27.3-27.4). This

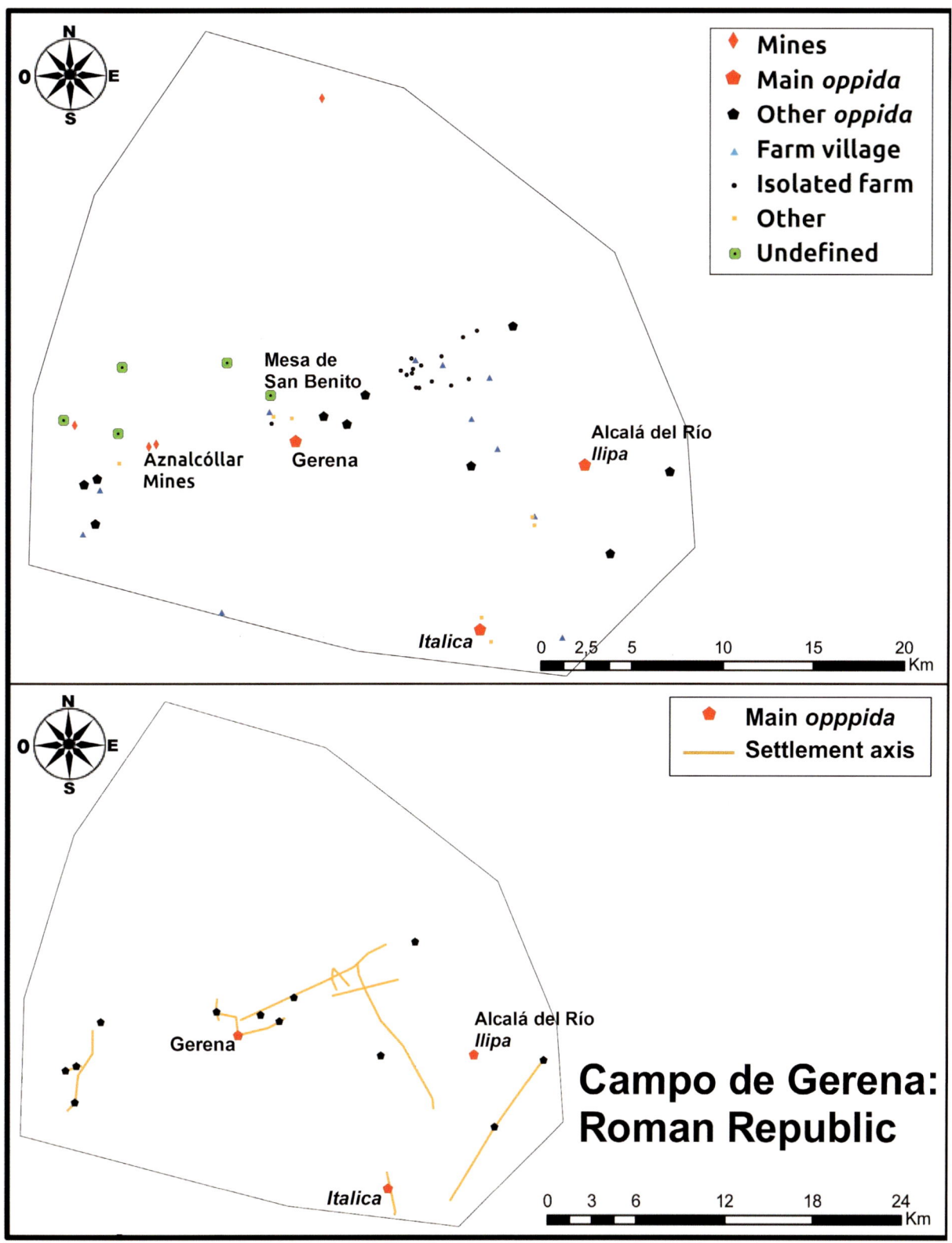

Figure 27.4. Campo de Gerena: sites from the Roman Republican period subjected to analysis of locational variables (reworked from Garrido *et al.* 2012: 53, fig. 2).

Main least cost pathways

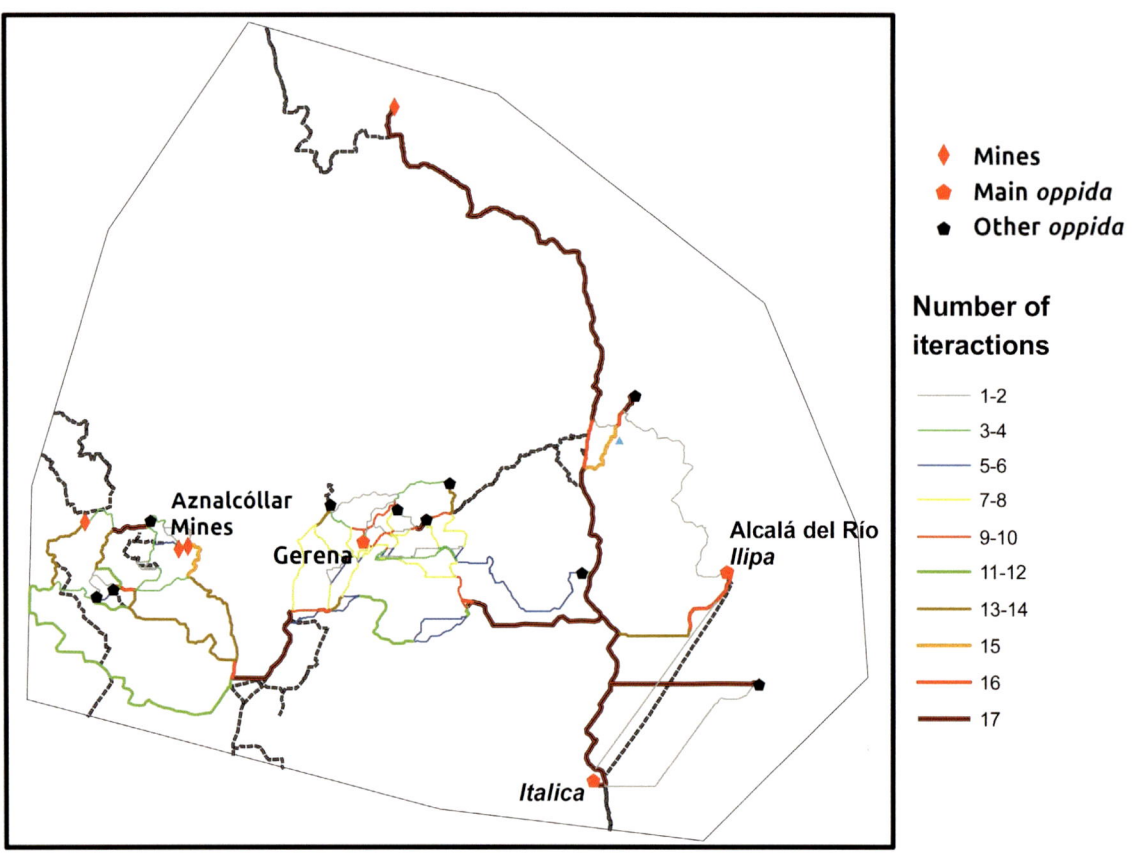

Figure 27.5. Main least-cost paths related to mining-metallurgical activity in the area considered (reworked from Garrido et al. 2012: 154, fig. 3).

does not necessary mean a punishment for *Ilipa*, since we know that it did not lose importance and continued to mint until the 1st century BC (Chaves 2007). But Rome's interest and the right of the victor prevailed; moreover, the least-cost paths that run through the Gerena-Alcalá del Río area for this period are not among those with highest iterations (Figure 27.5). They would still be relevant roads, but surely their direct relationship with mining was already very weak. In the meantime, the north-south routes were clearly consolidated, and *Italica* – not *Ilipa* – was on one of the main routes which, after forking a little further north, headed towards Gerena (Figure 27.5); even Matahijas seems to be on the fringes of this new scheme, although its strategic position would undoubtedly guarantee its existence for centuries to come. Thus, it cannot be ruled out that *Ilipa* retained some access to the Aznalcóllar mining basin, but we believe it is undeniable that from now on it had to do so under the military supervision of Rome, through *Italica*, Gerena, and other military establishments.

Furthermore, the aforementioned loss of transversality is opposed, albeit still weakly, by the incipient formation of north-south routes which, at least in some areas of the Guadalquivir Valley, coincide with Roman roads proposed by F. Sillières (1990). Undoubtedly, the dismantling of the previous road axes reflects the alternatives that Rome preferred to develop, linking the strategic centres for the new state.

On the other hand, if we consider that, from the first half of the 1st century BC at the latest, the reactivation of the Aznalcóllar mines seems unquestionable (Hunt *et al.* 2018), we must assume that the routes to evacuate the mining production must have begun to be developed. If then settlement axes, as well as least-cost paths, confirm the loss of that transversality of the previous phase (Figures 27.1-27.5), we cannot know where the metal began to be shipped at this time – although if the theory of Chaves and García (2004) is correct, we can already guess the Guadiamar option, which will be consolidated under Augustus (Amores *et al.* 2014) – but what seems certain is that it was no longer through the Gerena-*Ilipa* corridor, nor were *Hispalis* or other cities of the middle and lower Guadalquivir involved. Not yet.

In summary, with the Roman conquest (Figures 27.3-27.4), although the changes were slow at first, we can observe in the Guadiamar Valley the progressive creation of *ex novo* settlements from the Republican period and the metallurgical reactivation of the city of *Laelia* (Olivares, Seville), which even minted coins between the 2nd and 1st centuries BC (Chaves and García 2004), and whose full dedication to silver is already confirmed for the Augustan period onwards (31 BC-AD 14) (Garrido 2011). Analogous to what happened in the Second Iron Age, the field data do not allow us to affirm at this stage that *Italica* was directly responsible for this change in trend, but we can affirm that, coinciding precisely with its (re)foundation (*c.* 206 BC), the previous situation would cease: the metallurgical exploitations in the Guadiamar Valley are reactivated and a series of changes are gradually introduced that will be fully visible towards the change of Era. In other words, after the emergence of *Italica*, a series of changes took place, gradual at first, then very rapid, which prepared the ground for the exceptional situation of the 1st-2nd centuries AD, which transcends the chronological scope we have set for this analysis.

Whether or not this process was led directly by *Italica* or its Roman citizens is not yet clear, although we know, for example, that the fortunes of Trajan's (AD 98-117) family (the *Ulpii*) – and of other great Italican families, came largely from mining (Caballos 1990; Chic 2008).

3. Towards a Definition of the Ancient Territory of *Italica* during the Late Roman Republic

If we are right, we can try to define the political and economic role of the main cities in the area just before the reign of Augustus (*c.* 31 BC):

- *Hispalis* (modern Seville) consolidates as main harbour, although its real boom would come later. It seems to be more concentrated in its immediate surroundings, although we do not know to what extent it was already projecting its influence towards the Aljarafe Plateau and to the south. In any case, its progressive growth in importance, a fact undoubtedly favoured by Rome, necessarily had to modify the traditional role of *Ilipa* and *Karmo*.
- *Ilipa* continued to play a prominent role and to control the resources of its area, including some mines to the north, though always within the space that Rome would tolerate. The only thing that seems certain, in our opinion, is that it lost effective control of the Campo de Gerena to *Italica*. This idea clashes in part with the theory that the pre-eminence of its mint in the territories between the Guadalquivir and the Guadiana (Chaves 2007; Velasco 2007) in the 2nd-

1st centuries BC is a perpetuation of its political and economic control (García *et al.* 2008). These same authors insist that other testimonies (lead teapots, Neopunic legends...) support the probable existence of a kind of consortium led by *Ilipa* to exploit the mines and forests in the area, one proof of which would be an 'A' in the Republican coins from several mints.

According to that first hypothesis, the strong military control in the area – by means of republican forts such as Mesa S. Benito (Garrido 2011), Castillejo, or Valpajoso (Pérez 2006) (Figure 27.3) – would only have been intended to consolidate and pacify these territories after the Lusitanian Wars and to protect and maintain the mining infrastructures. In our opinion, this is indeed its primary objective, of course, but we believe that the evident military control also speaks of the Roman state's direct interest in these territories, and although *Ilipa* was able to maintain a certain role in the systems of mining production and extraction, it could only do so completely subordinated to Rome, and that, therefore, the potentiation of *Italica* was decisive in this change of situation.

The fortunes of *Italica* seem to be closely linked to those of Gerena, since together they control both ends of the natural route between the mining headwaters of the Guadiamar Valley and access to the Guadalquivir basin, just where the Rivera de Huelva confluence occurs. It seems quite likely that the latter was in some way subordinate to the former, which makes it plausible that *Italica* controlled, at least in this period, all the territory between the Rivera de Huelva and the Aznalcóllar mining basin, including the northern half of the Aljarafe Plateau and the southern slopes of the Sierra Morena. This fits with the only truly appreciable territorial changes in the Campo de Gerena-Aljarafe region in the 2nd-1st centuries BC, and leaves *Italica* benefiting most from the new situation.

In order to reinforce the hypothesis that the potentiation of *Italica* would be directly related to access to the Aznalcóllar mining basin, through the Campo de Gerena (Figures 27.3-27.4), and at the same time to configure a closer approximation to the ancient territory of the city, it is necessary to take into account some additional aspects. In the locational analyses by Garrido (2011), other variables were included, of which a small selection will be presented here in a very summarised form:

1. *Accessibility* to and from different settlements, weighted by *isochrones*, determined, in the case of *Italica*, that it had high accessibility over medium and long distances, but very low accessibility over short distances, something that could be related to its military character and notable relative altitude, as confirmed by its

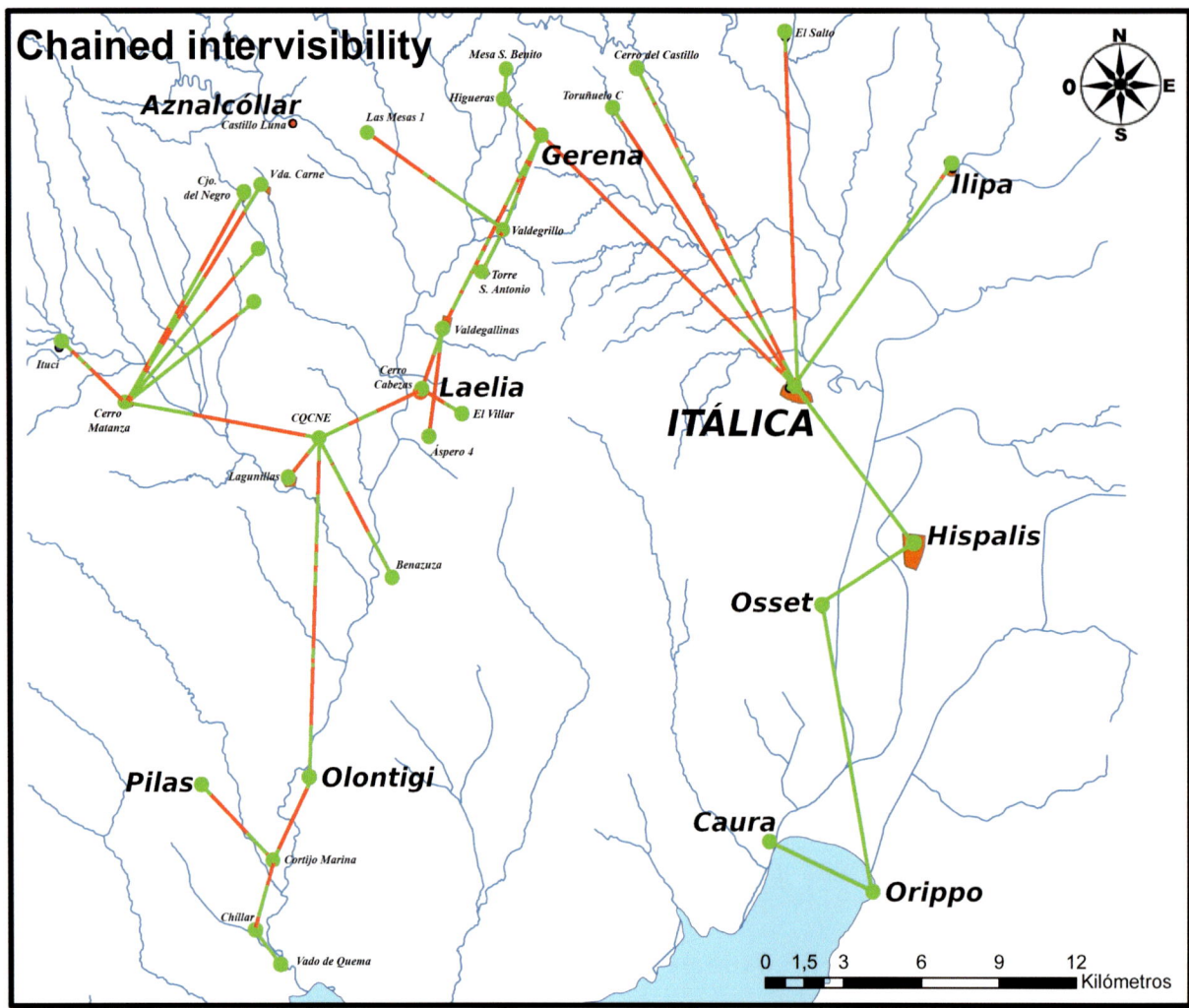

Figure 27.6. Chained intervisibility between main settlements in the area considered (reworked from Garrido 2011: 803, fig. 42).

strategic position on an escarpment above the river corridor of the Guadalquivir and the Rivera de Huelva. The values obtained for this variable reflect a central location in a very flat territory, but in just the right place to be defensible and to control the position from fairly distant distances.

2. *Chained intervisibility*. To arrive at the result shown in Figure 27.6, the first step was to take the most locally representative *nuclei* of the different areas studied, together with others which, even if they were not notable for their high visibility values, it seemed appropriate to integrate: towns and settlements larger than 8/9ha, fundamentally. The second step consisted of checking whether there was a direct and bidirectional connection (*intervisibility*) between two settlements. In principle, the nearest site is taken, and if such a connection is not bidirectional, then the next nearest site is taken, and so on until a site is found that establishes

such a bidirectional relationship with the first one. Normally this relationship is between neighbouring sites, but in specific areas such a connection may occur with sites reasonably further away. As distances are extended, the likelihood increases that particular settlements accumulate these intervisibility relationships, i.e. that they become the necessary links to ensure that others are connected to a chain from different sources, and not only from immediate neighbouring areas (Figure 27.6).

The result of this procedure showed that *Italica* has the highest values of chained intervisibility in the region considered, and that it also emerged as an almost unique and essential link between the settlements of the Aznalcóllar mining basin, the southern foothills of the Sierra Morena, the Campo de Gerena, and the Seville plain (Figure 27.6). The most interesting aspect of this result is that the second most important key to ensure

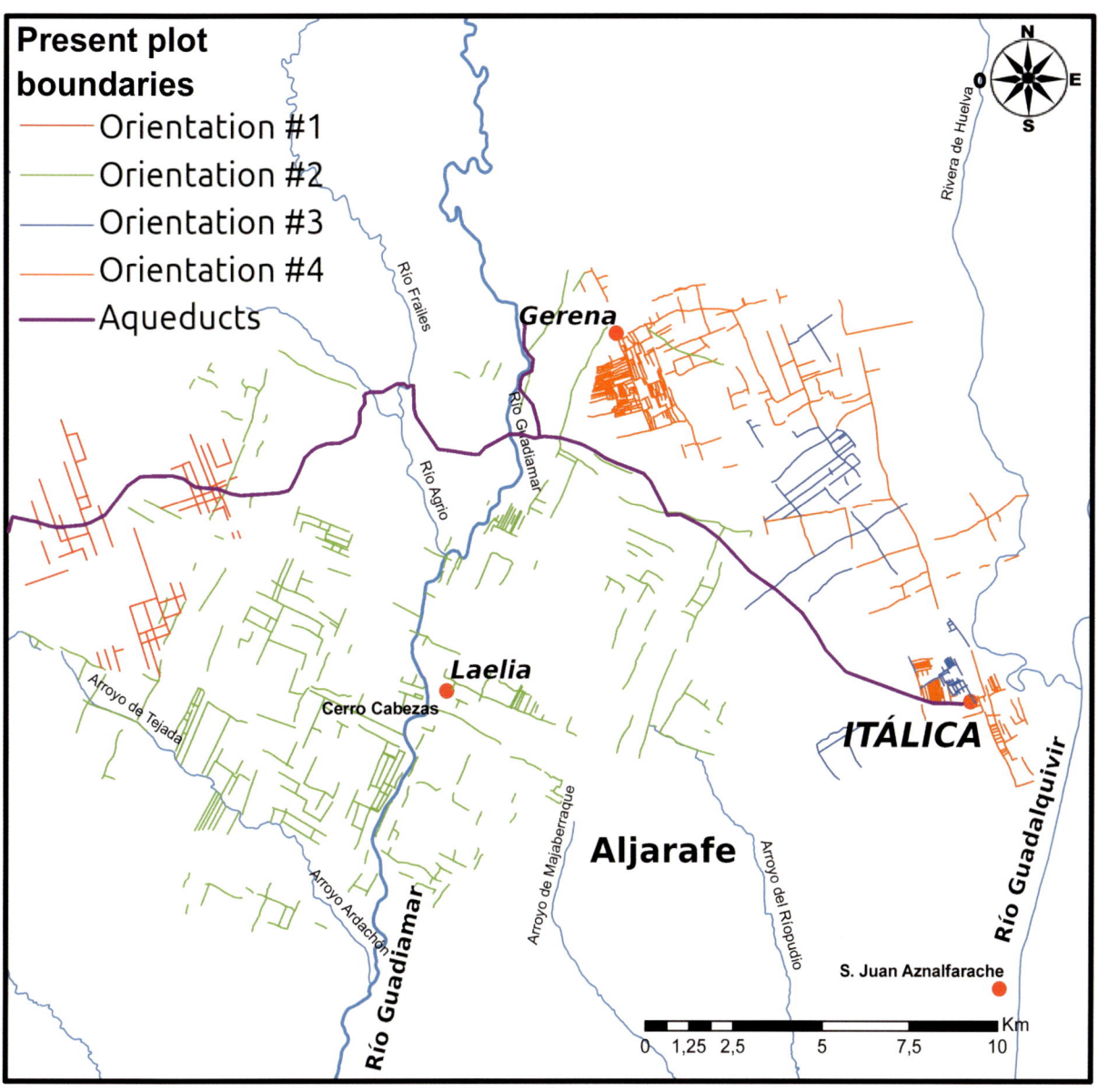

Figure 27.7. Orientation of present plots and Roman aqueducts of Italica (reworked from Garrido 2011: 825, fig. 64).

this link was Gerena, a necessary link in the chain for several first-order settlements between the Aznalcóllar mining basin and the Guadalquivir River corridor.

In other words, the fundamental role of *Italica* in the chained intervisibility variable would not be possible without the Gerena link; if *Italica* played a determining role in the mining headwaters of Aznalcóllar and the rich agricultural fields of the area, it had to do so in some way through Gerena.

3. *Plots.* The tracing of this variable is nothing new; this tool can be used to search for traces of ancient cadastres (Ariño *et al.* 2004), not necessarily a centuriation (Corzo 1982). Figure

27.7 shows the main and dominant orientations of plot boundaries today. Without entering the discussion of the effectiveness of these orientations to extrapolate them to ancient times, from a broader perspective, which includes the resilience of certain trends (Amores *et al.* 2014), their validity as an extra variable cannot be denied. Especially because the comparison of these orientations with recent works yet to be published (Garrido in press), confirm the high correlation existing in the middle Guadiamar Valley between Roman settlements and the plot axes shown in Figure 27.7. If so, we have yet another indication that clearly points to the projection of the city of *Italica* towards the Campo de Gerena and Aznalcóllar mining basin,

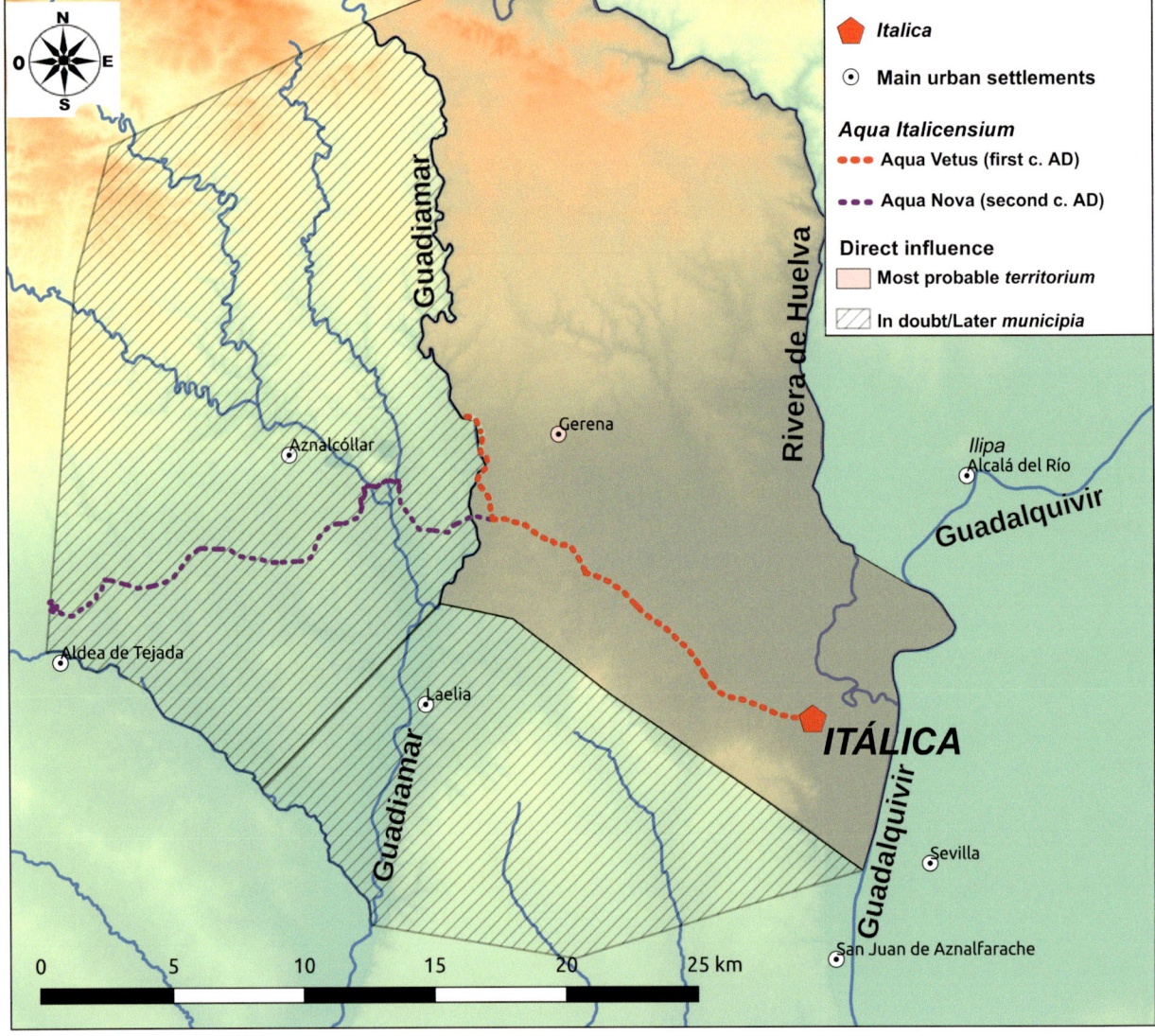

Figure 27.8. Possible territorium of ancient Italica and branches of its aqueduct.

probably another trace towards the definition of the ancient territory of the city.

4. *Aqueducts.* They constitute a palpable example of the spatial influence of *Italica* beyond the mining network and its possible *territorium* (Figure 27.7), even at an advanced imperial stage. They run for dozens of kilometres (Canto 1979), and recently considerable progress has been made in specifying the layout of their two branches, especially in the Aznalcóllar and Gerena sectors (Guisado *et al.* 2009; Hunt *et al.* 2018).

In short, these last four aspects not only reinforce the line of work we have been defending, but also add more evidence to trace the ancient territory of *Italica*, regardless of whether or not Gerena reached a municipal status from the Flavian period onwards (last third of the 1st century AD), although its dependence – at least in certain aspects – had to be maintained, as

other data testify, as in the case of the link between the Paleochristian basilica of Gerena and the Italian bishopric during Late Antiquity (Fernández *et al.* 1987).

Conclusions

We have undertaken a synthesis based on the most recent data that can bring us closer to the historical reality of the ancient territory of *Italica*. From previous archaeological evidence and thanks to research projects in recent years, this territory is now much better known and it has been possible to demonstrate the enormous projection of the ancient Roman city in areas relatively distant from its most immediate area, such as the middle valley of the Guadiamar and the mining basin of Aznalcóllar (Figures 27.7-27.8).

The evolution of this *territorium* over time is quite another matter, as it is clear that it could not have been constant over so many centuries (3rd century BC to 7th century AD). To begin with, although we believe that the (re)foundation of *Italica* is in direct connection with Roman interests in the Aznalcóllar mines, it has been clearly established (Garrido 2011; Amores *et al.* 2014) that the administrative restructuring of Augustus (31 BC-AD 14) involved radical changes in this area, especially because of the more than likely passage of the Aznalcóllar mines into state hands (although *Italica* may have retained others further north) and the colonial deductions of *Hispalis*, whose rise as main city of the whole area is indisputable. The municipal promotion of *Italica* under the first emperor probably also entailed a first drastic restructuring of its territory, which does not necessarily mean that it came out badly.

But new changes were to take place from the Flavian period, from the last third of the 1st century AD onwards. We know that a new and important restructuring of mining in southern Spain took place when most of the efforts to mine silver were redirected towards copper (García 2010), which also led to a readjustment of the territories previously assigned to the state mines and the promotion of new *municipia*, which could either occupy part of the previous mining *saltus* (Chic 2008) or were created from old *peregrinae* or dependent cities, necessarily redefining the limits of the Roman colonies and municipalities in the immediate vicinity.

The last significant change, of course, came with the colonial development of *Italica* by Hadrian (AD 117-38). However, although the urban scope of this operation does not deserve to be commented on here due to its obviousness, it is not so obvious at the territorial level, since there is still reasonable doubt that a centuriation (Corzo 1982) of the Italic territory was undertaken at such a late date and in an area that was already densely populated at that time. For this reason, in Figure 27.8, where we have tried to hypothesise the extent of the ancient territory of *Italica*, we have marked all those areas which either never belonged to *Italica* or which could pass into other hands over the centuries, but which, in any case, must have formed part of its orbit of direct influence, which was always decreasing in line with the rise of the other great surrounding city, Seville, especially from the Julio-Claudian period onwards.

Bibliography

Amores, F., E. García, P. Garrido, M.A. Hunt, J. Vázquez and J. Rodríguez 2014. Los paisajes del Guadiamar: la minería y la metalurgia en el extremo oriental del Cinturón Ibérico de Piritas. *Cuadernos de prehistoria y arqueología de la Universidad de Granada* 24: 203-37.

Ariño, E., J.M. Gurt and J.M. Palet 2004. *El pasado presente: arqueología de los paisajes en la Hispania Romana*. Barcelona: Universitat de Barcelona-Universidad de Salamanca.

Caballos Rufino, A. 1990. *Los senadores hispanorromanos y la romanización de Hispania (siglos I-III)*. Ecija: Gráficas Sol.

Camacho, J.A. and A.M. Jiménez 2007. Memoria de las prospecciones arqueológicas en Guillena. Unpublished report, Delegación territorial de cultura en Sevilla.

Canto, A. 1979. Aquae Italicenses: El acueducto romano de Itálica. *Madrider Mitteilungen* 20: 282-337.

Chaves, F. 2000. Moneda, territorio y administración. Hispania Ulterior: de los inicios de la conquista al final del siglo II a.C., in *Moneda i administració del territori*: 9-35. Barcelona: Museu nacional d'art de Catalunya.

Chaves, F. 2007. Una aproximación a la ceca de Ilipa, in E. Ferrer, A. Fernández and J.L. Escacena (eds) *Ilipa Antiqua: de la Prehistoria a la época romana; actas del I Congreso de Historia de Alcalá del Río*: 211-26. Alcalá del Río: Ayto. Alcalá del Río-Departmento de prehistoria y arqueología, Universidad de Sevilla.

Chaves, F. and E. García 1994. Gadir y el comercio atlántico a través de las cecas occidentales de la Ulterior, in J. Campos, J.A. Pérez and F. Gómez (eds) *Arqueología en el entorno del bajo Guadiana*: 375-92. Huelva: Universidad de Huelva.

Chic, G. 2008. Los saltus y las explotaciones mineras. *Boletín Arkeolan* 15: 143-63.

Corzo, R. 1982. Organización del territorio y evolución urbana en Itálica. *Archivo Español de Arqueología* 121: 301-19.

Corzo, R. 1998. *El Esparragal y su entorno*. Seville: Ed. Cortijo del Esparragal.

Díaz-Zorita, M., M. Hunt, J. Vázquez and P. Garrido 2017. Memoria de la actividad arqueológica puntual prospección arqueominera de la Sierra Norte de Sevilla. Unpublished report, Delegación territorial de cultura en Sevilla.

Domergue, C. 1990. *Les mines de la Péninsule Ibérique dans l'antiquité romaine*. Rome: École française de Rome.

Fernández, F., J. Alonso and M.G. Lasso de la Vega 1987. La basílica y necrópolis paleocristianas de Gerena (Sevilla). *Noticiario arqueológico hispánico* 29: 103-99.

García, E. 2010. El Guadiamar romano. Un sol reflejado en el río, in F. Amores (ed.) *De la Tierra al Sol: Historia de los paisajes del Guadiamar*: 121-31. Seville: Focus-Abengoa.

García, E., E. Ferrer and F.J. García 2008. La romanización del Bajo Guadalquivir: ciudad, territorio y economía (siglos II-I BC). *Mainake* 30: 247-70.

Garrido, P. 2011. La ocupación romana del Guadiamar y la conexión minera. Unpublished PhD dissertation, Universidad de Sevilla.

Garrido, P. (in press). Los Paisajes del Guadiamar, in F. Amores and E. García (eds) *Los paisajes del Guadiamar*. Seville: Universidad de Sevilla.

Garrido, P., F. Guisado and M.E. Costa 2012. Itálica y las minas. De la hegemonía ilipense al municipium augusteo (ss. III-I a.C.). Itálica. *Revista de arqueología clásica de Andalucía 2*: 147-62.

Guisado, F., P. Garrido and M.E. Costa 2009. Memoria de la prospección arqueológica en el ámbito comarcal vinculado a la Vía de la Plata. Términos municipales de Guillena y El Garrobo. Unpublished report, Delegación territorial de cultura en Sevilla.

Hunt, M.A. 2003. Intervención arqueológica en el Coto Minero de Aznalcóllar (Sevilla): El yacimiento calcolítico de Los Páramos y la necrópolis de cistas de Las Mesas. *III Anuario Arqueológico de Andalucía 2: Actividades de Urgencia 2000*: 1196-1202.

Hunt, M.A., J. Vázquez and P. Garrido 2018. Memoria preliminar de la actividad arqueológica preventiva prospección arqueológica superficial y sondeos en el área de afección del Proyecto de Mina Los Frailes, en Aznalcóllar (Sevilla). Unpublished report, Delegación territorial de cultura en Sevilla.

Luzón, J.M. 1973. Excavaciones en Itálica. Estratigrafía en el Pajar de Artillo (Campaña de 1970) (Archivo español de arqueología 78). Madrid: Comisaría general de excavaciones arqueológicas.

Pérez, J.A. 2006. *La huella de Roma*. Huelva: Delegación de Cultura-Diputación de Huelva.

Ponsich, M. 1974. *Implantation rurale antique sur le Bas-Guadalquivir*, I. Madrid: Publications de la Casa de Velázquez.

Sillières, P. 1990. *Les voies de communication de l'Hispanie meridionale*. Paris: Publications du Centre Pierre Paris.

Tejedor, A., M. López and R. Merino (eds) 2020. *Innovación para la gestión y integrada del Patrimonio, el paisaje y el turismo*. Seville: Universidad de Sevilla-Universidad de Valladolid.

Velasco, M.C. 2007. Aproximación al estudio de las téseras monetiformes de Ilipa Magna, in E. Ferrer, A. Fernández and J.L. Escacena (eds) *Ilipa antiqua: de la prehistoria a la época romana; actas del I Congreso de historia de Alcalá del Río*: 361-66. Alcalá del Río: Ayto. Alcalá del Río-Dpto. de prehistoria y arqueología Universidad de Sevilla.

28. Roman Sculptures from *Celti*
(Peñaflor, Province of Seville, Spain)

José Beltrán Fortes and María Luisa Loza Azuaga

We would like to pay tribute to the memory of our admired colleague and friend, Simon J. Keay, with this study on Roman sculptures discovered in *Celti* (Peñaflor), a site where he had carried out an important archaeological intervention towards the end of the 20th century. Professor Simon Keay's link with archaeological research in the province of Seville was an important section of his brilliant academic career; in turn, it became an important chapter in the development of the history of Roman archaeology in this area of the Roman province of *Baetica*. Thus, after having engaged in archaeological research of Cataluña during the 1980s, S. Keay turned his attention to this sector of the province of Seville, probably guided by José Remesal, Professor

of Ancient History at the University of Barcelona and a native of Seville. Together with José Remesal and John Creighton, he co-directed a systematic archaeological project in *Celti*, a Roman city located at the current town of Peñaflor (Figure 28.1). Archaeological surveys and excavations were conducted between 1987 and 1992, the results published in a monograph edition, first in English (Keay *et al.* 2000) and later in Spanish, within the series 'Arqueología. Monografías' of the Ministry of Culture of the Junta de Andalucía (Keay *et al.* 2001b; cf. the review in Beltrán 2003). Jointly with Fernando Amores, he carried out another study worth highlighting; in this case, on local imitations of Italic Terra Sigillata (TS) they called 'Peñaflor type', which

Figure 28.1. Aerial photo of the site of *Celti*, next to Peñaflor, from Keay *et al.* 2001: 17, fig. 1.4. No. 1: Former railway ('RENFE'). No. 3: 'El Calvario'. No. 7: 'El Higuerón' (cyclopean construction, possible Roman port).

are currently included among the early TS productions in the Iberian Peninsula (Amores and Keay 1999).

Coinciding with the termination of this project, between 1991 and 1993, an exceptional archaeological project was carried out in *Italica* (Santiponce), under joint direction with the former head of the Archaeological Complex, José Manuel Rodríguez Hidalgo. The intervention consisted of a geophysical survey covering all of the area known as *Nova Vrbs*, which provided spectacular results. For example, a great palaestra adjoined to the Hadrianic baths – the so-called 'Termas Mayores' – was identified, also a new walled enclosure dated between the end of the 3rd and beginning of the 4th century AD (cf. Hidalgo-Prieto *et al.* 2023: 4th-5th centuries AD), as well as some exceptionally clear *domus* plans, such as the so-called 'House of David', located next to the thermal complex (Rodríguez-Hidalgo *et al.* 1999; Rodríguez-Hidalgo 1997). Recently this study has been highlighted as being an important example of pioneering archaeological methodology in Andalusia (León 2021: 104). As a result of his interest in the Roman archaeology of Seville, S. Keay issued various studies in the 1990s on the 'Romanisation' process of this territory (Keay 1992; 1996; 1997), which soon culminated in the organisation and edition of the collective work *The Archaeology of Early Roman Baetica*, providing interesting historical-archaeological analyses for the time period (Keay 1998). His dedication to Sevillian archaeology during the early 21st century (for example, Keay 2000; 2003; Keay *et al.* 2001a) brought about a new project on 'Urban Connectivity in Southern Spain in the Iberian and Roman Era', which was funded by the Arts and Humanities Research Council of Great Britain, focusing on the middle and lower Guadalquivir territories (Keay and Earl 2006; 2007; Keay 2015). All of this testifies to the relevance that historical-archaeological studies on the western area of *Baetica* – and, more specifically, of the current province of Seville – had to Professor Keay's career during the decades between the 20th-21st centuries.

1. Lion Funerary Sculpture (Figure 28.2)

The name *Celti* is of Tartessian-Turdetan origin, and, like many other cities of *Baetica*, it was most likely promoted to a Latin municipality under the Flavians. Pliny the Elder (*NH* 3.11) cites its location within the *Conventus Hispalensis*, appearing also in the Antonine Itinerary (414.5) as *Celtici* and, in Late Antiquity, in the Anonymous Cosmography of Ravenna (315.2) as *Celtum* (Correa 2016: 274-75). In the 17th century, some scholars had already identified the place with Peñaflor and, although some authors have maintained different proposals, the epigraphic record confirms this location (*CILA Sevilla*: 139-40). All different sectors of the ancient city are known by individual names. The excavation

conducted by S. Keay, J. Creighton, and J. Remesal focused on a sector known as 'La Viña' – next to the so-called 'Pared Blanca' – where possibly the town's *forum* was discovered (Figure 28.3). Part of the *forum* square and the porticos were excavated, as well as a building located to one of the sides and identified as an *aedes Augusti*. The excavated area corresponds with the monumentalisation project of the urban centre undertaken between the mid-1st century AD and its end: 'Previous structures were demolished and a large new complex was built just below the highest point of the site, facing south by the Guadalquivir River [...] in the centre of a new layout of orthogonal streets that contrasted with the alignment of other presumably earlier streets' (Keay *et al.* 2001b: 247).

Suggestions have also been made concerning the existence of a theatre and an amphitheatre (López 2004; 2014) (Figure 28.3, 7-8); most likely, the theatre was located west of the *forum*, as the discovery of the statues analysed below seems to indicate (cf. Loza and Beltrán 2017: 75-76). *Forum* and theatre were spatially related public buildings, following a well-documented layout in Hispano-Roman theatres (Jiménez 1994). Archaeological records also include several *columbaria* belonging to the town's eastern necropolis ('El Cortinal de las Cruces'), and various burials in the northern sector (Figure 28.3, 6). However, the western necropolis generates greater interest, especially the site known as 'El Camello' (Figure 28.3, 5), where 'a carved stone lion dated to the Roman Republic period and currently preserved in the Museu Arqueològic of Barcelona' was recovered (Keay *et al.* 2001b: 21, fig. 1.9).

This type of zoomorphic funerary sculpture was quite common to areas of southern *Hispania* from at least the late Republican period. In the upper Guadalquivir as well as in other areas of *Hispania Ulterior* they are directly related to Iberian traditions, whereas in the middle and lower Guadalquivir they derive from Roman influence and models originating in the Italian Peninsula (cf. Pérez 1999; Aranegui 2004). In effect, these large zoomorphic sculptures were not a part of the ancient Turdetanian culture prior to the arrival of Rome in the 2nd-1st centuries BC (cf. for example, Beltrán 2014). Thus, these leonine monuments, which are usually made with local stones, such as calcarenites or limestones, then stuccoed and painted, are dated between the 2nd-1st centuries BC to the 1st century AD. Originally they would have stood in pairs crowning funerary monuments 'a dado' – according to the Italian term – as seen in the *Stronnii monumentum* of the *Porta Nocera* necropolis in Pompeii (cf. Beltrán 2002: 233-41).

The lion of Peñaflor was presumably holding his right front paw on another animal's head, perhaps a ram's head, but now, fractured; the pose has an ancestral

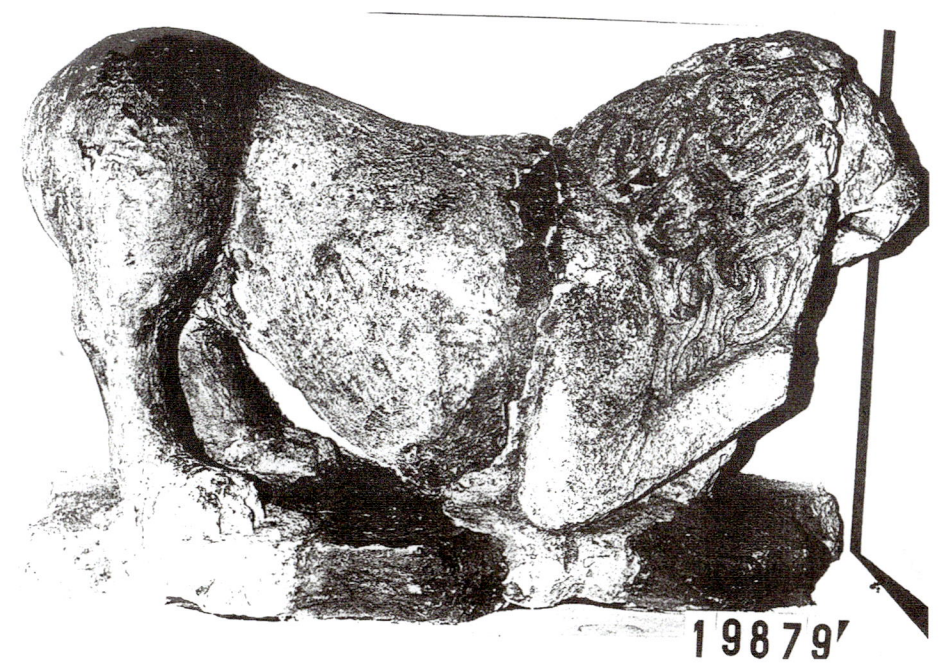

Figure 28.2. Funerary lion sculpture from *Celti*. Archaeological Museum of Barcelona (inv. no. 19879) (from Keay *et al.* 2001b: 22, fig. 1.9).

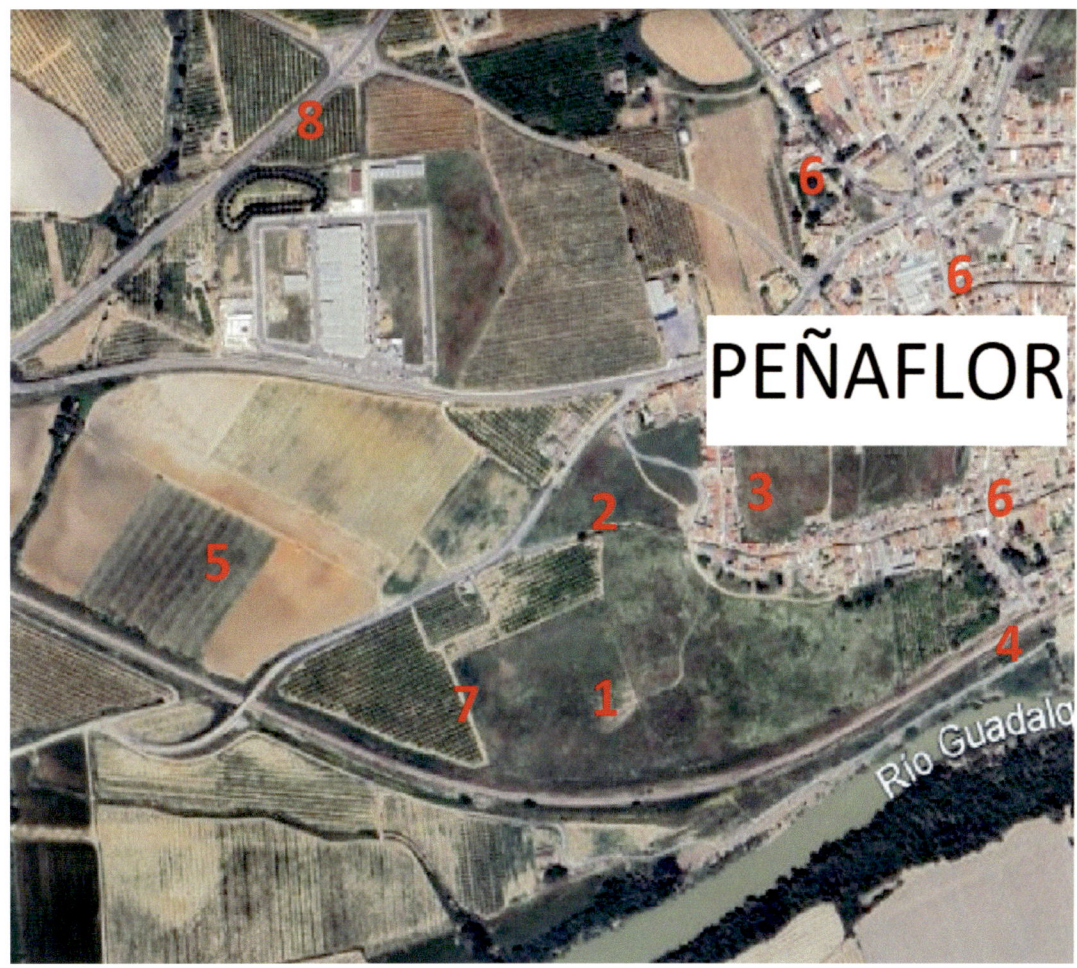

Figure 28.3. Aerial photo (from Google Maps) of the archaeological site of *Celti* and the town of Peñaflor. No. 1: 'La Viña' (archaeological excavation site of S. Keay, J. Creighton, and J. Remesal). No. 2: 'Pared Blanca'. No. 3: 'El Calvario'. No. 4: 'El Higuerón'. No. 5: Western Necropolis ('El Camello'). No. 6: Eastern and Northern Necropolis ('El Cortinal de las Cruces'). No. 7: Possible site of the Roman theatre. No. 8: Possible site of the Roman amphitheatre.

apotropaic meaning associated with the protection of the deceased's soul. The examples known demonstrate that in the lower Guadalquivir and areas of the middle Guadalquivir – up to Alcolea del Río (Seville) – funerary lions were specifically associated with animal heads, usually rams; further north this same sculpture type coexists with another form in which the lion is represented with a human head, following a model that originates from Iberian traditions (Pérez 1999; Beltrán and Loza 2005). The only examples of this variant located further south were found in the urban necropolis of *Canama* and *Arva*, located within the municipality of Alcolea del Río (Beltrán 2006).

In the case of the lion of *Celti*, besides the loss of the right front area, the upper body also has a longitudinal fracture, resulting in two large fragments that have been joined together. Its formal and stylistic features are realistic and naturalistic, depicted with its hindquarter raised and with an outstanding rendition of a long mane arranged in a disorderly manner. All this leads us to suggest that it was manufactured during the 1st century AD, most probably in the Julio-Claudian period; also, it would have been produced in a local workshop or in this area of *Baetica*. In fact, with its naturalistic appearance and the manner in which the animal is represented, it resembles one of the lion statues from *Arva*, although here the left front paw rests on a young man's chest (Beltrán 2006). This sculpture type, dated between the Roman Republican period and the 1st century AD, is mainly found in the southern part of the current province of Seville (Beltrán 2000) and, especially, in the central-north area of Cádiz, where a notable number from the Roman cities of *Carissa Aurelia* (Bornos-Espera) and *Cappa* (Espera) stand out (Beltrán and Loza 2020: 105-07).

2. Two Honorific Female Statues (Figures 28.4-28.5)

In their book on *Celti*, S. Keay, J. Creighton, and J. Remesal also refer to the discovery of 'two female marble statues [...] (now privately owned, at nº 2 Guzmán el Bueno street in Seville)', adding that 'C. Fernandez Chicarro reports that they were unearthed at Pared Blanca as a result of the railway works in 1865' (Keay *et al.* 2001b: 21, fig. 1.8); however, they were actually found in 1842 (Ramírez 1844). Both female marble statues are depicted completely robed and, although their state of conservation is good, the portrait heads and upper limbs are missing, which were, in this case, made of separate pieces. The first reference to statues appeared in the *Semanario Pintoresco Español* where Luis María Ramírez y las Casas-Deza claims they were discovered in 1842 'together near the surface on the outskirts of the town, and on the same road leading to Seville' (Ramírez 1844: 372). The drawing of the two sculptures that illustrates that text leaves no room for doubt that they correspond

to the two statues preserved today. Thirty-five years after their discovery, in 1877, Elías García Tuñón y Quirós wrote that they had been found in the amphitheatre and claimed they represented Minerva and Mercury (García 1877). Towards the end of the century, in George E. Bonsor's description of the excavations he carried out in Peñaflor, there is a mention of the two female sculptures standing in the courtyard of the house of Antonio Coba, at the time mayor of Peñaflor (Bonsor 1989 [1931]: 34-39; cf. Maier 1999). In 1916 they were photographed flanking the entrance of the courtyard, the photo appearing in a brief anonymous article published by *Betica. Revista Ilustrada* (Anonymous 1916); in this case, the statues were said to have been found in the theatre and were representations of muses. The same photograph appears in S. Keay, J. Creighton, and J. Remesal's aforementioned book on Peñaflor (2001: 21, fig. 1.8). The statues have been with the Coba family since then, although they were transferred to Seville to be part of the exhibit held in the Fine Arts Pavilion, current site of the Archaeological Museum, within the framework of the Ibero-American Exposition of 1929 (San Martín 2014). Lastly, in 2010 they were taken to Palma del Río, a town in the province of Córdoba, where we were able to study them in 2014; the first statue was in the Portocarrero Palace and the second in the 'Hotel Monasterio de San Francisco', although currently we are not sure about their location.

The first statue measures 1.62 × 0.60 × 0.34m and, as said, it lacks all of the separately attached pieces: the portrait head, right forearm and hand, left hand, as well as the tip of the left foot (Figure 28.4). By visual examination it seems to be made with Luni marble, possibly a *bardiglio* variety; and is depicted resting its weight on the right leg, while slightly bending the other. Fully dressed in a tunic, stole, and mantle, only the remaining foot is fitted with a closed shoe or *calceolus*. The mantle is arranged in a singular manner, presenting a wide *balteus* covering the left shoulder and wrapping around the torso horizontally just below the breasts; below, the lower part of the tunic is arranged in an array of folds. The statue is a variant of the Greek Artemisia type in which a curved *balteus* drapes over the lower abdomen; it closely resembles the Artemis-Delphi or Moschine variant (Loza and Beltrán 2017: 82-86; 2018: 627-31). Among the Hispano-Roman productions it shares certain formal similarities with a female statue from *Colonia Patricia*, kept in the Archaeological Museum of Córdoba collection (Baena 2009: 262, fig. 356), which coincides in the right-leg pose and in the placement and straight arrangement of the *balteus*.

The second statue (Figure 28.5) measures 1.59 × 0.60 × 0.33m and, likewise, is missing the portrait head, forearm, and right hand and left hand; it also appears to be made with Luni *bardiglio* marble, while the pose

Figure 28.4. Female statue from *Celti* (no. 1). Palma del Río, private collection (photo: M.L. Loza).

Figure 28.5. Female statue from *Celti* (no. 2). Palma del Río, private collection (photo: M.L. Loza).

is slightly different, the body weight resting on the left leg as it bends towards the right. Both arms are directed forward in a well-known offering gesture. Also, in this case, the mantle is arranged differently, where besides the *balteus* that drapes over the upper abdomen and wraps around the left forearm, there is another *balteus* that falls from the left shoulder to the right hip. It is a combination of the Artemisia type mentioned above and a *Koré/Persephone* model that dates back to the 4th-century BC circle of Praxiteles. The representation of a double *balteus* is a unique iconographic motif, linking

it to statues with similar offering gestures or poses from the Italian Peninsula (cf. Loza and Beltrán 2017: 86-90; 2018: 631-34). Hence, we can mention the *capite velato* statue of *Lucus Feroniae* (Capena), dated firstly to late Augustan era (Moretti 1982-84: 87-89) and now to Trajan's period (Cristilli 2020), which would justify the presence of a large mantle around the right arm; or, also, the bronze *capite velato* statue of *Herculanum* in the Museum of Naples (inv. no. 5609) and dated to the mid-1st century AD (Boschung 2002: 120, no. 42.6, lam. 94, 1; Cesarano 2015: 78, 97-98); or, finally, the statue of Livia as Ceres in the basilica of *Velleia,* dated to Caligula's reign (Saletti 1968: 33ss., no. 4, lams. 11-14, erroneously given as Drusilla; Boschung 2002: 25, no. 2.6, lams. 16, 1, 18, 1-3), and seemingly the closest formal parallel, although somewhat different in style. In *Hispania*, there are two female *Koré* type statues from *Augusta Emerita* (Mérida) that share some formal similarities, although in both the *balteus* appears just slightly hinted over the abdomen, while a large series of folds drape from the left shoulder across the chest. The statue found in the colonial *forum* is possibly a representation of Livia (Nogales 1996: 126-27, lam. V; Garriguet 2001: 7-8, no. 11, lam. IV, 3) and dated to the second quarter of the 1st century AD, while the one unearthed in the provincial *forum* is dated to Claudius and Nero's times (Garriguet 2001: 12, no. 18, lam. VI, 1).

The material and workmanship in both *Celti* statues are very similar, but slightly different in iconography and style. The first statue dates to the Tiberian-Caligulan period, whereas the second dates to Claudius and Nero's times. Even though both were made with Italic marble, they had been manufactured in the same native workshop, located in *Celti* or at another settlement nearby, which would have been operating at least during the Julio-Claudian period. We must not leave out that during this period several sculpture workshops were functioning in different Baetican cities, until all production was presumably interrupted during the Flavian dynasty, at least in the case of preserved Roman portraits (León 2001). On the other hand, the fact that the statues appeared together and both can be dated to the Julio-Claudian period indicates that they were part of a common statuary programme,

either an imperial project or of the *Celti* oligarchy. We have also suggested that they could have been part of the ornamentation of the probable theatre of *Celti*, since both were found in an area that contained a great number of ashlars, corresponding possibly to the seating (Loza and Beltrán 2017: 94-96). In addition, Emil Hübner in his commentary on the inscription *CIL* II 2328 indicates that next to the two statues was discovered a 'fragmentum tabulae marmoreae ingentis, epistylii puto aedifici alicuuius sive sacri sive publici' (a fragment of a huge marble slab; I think the architrave of some building whether sacred or public); although only two letters were legible, [---] *E R* [---], it was associated with a public building, perhaps the theatre. Finally, it must be said that honorary statuary programmes are well known in Roman theatres, including those of *Hispania* (Fuchs 1987), although logically in the case in study it remains only a hypothesis until verified.

3. Statue of Silenus (Figure 28.6)

Perhaps this hypothesis above can be reinforced by another of *Celti*'s Roman statues: in this case, a statue-fountain of an elderly Silenus represented asleep with his head resting on a wineskin from which water poured. This sculptural type usually appears in fountain decorations on the *frons pulpiti* of Roman theatres (Loza 1994). Luis María Ramírez de las Casas-Deza also refers to this piece and adds an illustration of it (Ramírez 1844: 373; cf. Reinach 1910: 61, fig. 1); therefore, there is no doubt that it is the same sculpture preserved in the Romero de Torres Museum of Córdoba. As stated in an 1844 publication, the sculpture had been purchased in 1835 and moved to the Cordoban town of Hornachuelos,

Figure 28.6. Silenus statue from *Celti*. Córdoba, Romero de Torres Museum (photo: A. Vallejo).

later entering the Romero de Torres collection (Loza 1994: 275-78, no. 25, figs 6-7; Loza and Beltrán 2017: 80-82).

Indeed, many *frontes pulpiti* in Roman theatres were decorated with statue-fountains of sleeping Silenus (Fuchs 1987: 71-72, 109-10, 146-47, examples of *Caere*, *Falerii*, Arles, and Vienne), a fashion that also became popular in *Hispania*. Examples from the province of *Lusitania* can be found in the theatres of *Olisipo* (Lisbon), *Metellinum* (Medellín), and *Augusta Emerita* (Mérida), and in *Baetica* at the theatre of *Baelo Claudia* (Bolonia, Tarifa), as well as a probable fragmented piece from Baena, although without archaeological context (Loza 1994). Most of these pieces are dated to late Julio-Claudian times; surely this Silenus statue from *Celti*, manufactured most likely during the period of Claudius/Nero, was probably used to ornament the town's theatre.

4. Statue Head of Mars (Figure 28.7)

Lastly, it has been possible to ascribe another sculpture, currently in the Archaeological Museum of Córdoba collection, and formerly thought to be from *Colonia Patricia*, to *Celti* based on newly found documents, as described by D. Ojeda (2018: 200-02). The statue piece corresponds with a head, possibly from a free-standing statue, originally considered a representation of the god Vulcan (Blanco 1975; 1982-83), however, it in fact depicts Mars. According to D. Ojeda, what had been interpreted as the *pileus* is an attachment to enable a metal Corinthian helmet to be fixed to the head. This was done with a metal spike that was introduced into a circular hole in the upper part of the head. It corresponds to a statue of *Mars Ultor*, bearded and dated to the 1st century AD: in the opinion of A. Blanco (1975; 1982-83) the style suggests a Claudian-period dating. Blanco also suggests it was part of a cult statue (cf. Rodríguez-Oliva 2009: 76, fig. 63). Again, we must keep in mind that already in the 1st century AD various cities of Roman *Hispania* had copies of the statues found in the *Forum* of Augustus in Rome (León 2020).

A similar statue head of Mars was discovered in a nearby geographical area, the aforementioned Roman city of *Arva* (Alcolea del Río) (Figure 28.8). It is characterised by the same manner in which the helmet was added as a separate piece, surely a metal piece, attached by a metal spike inserted in a small hole opened in the upper part of the head. This piece, unearthed in *Arva* during an excavation carried out by Arthur Engel in 1890, is currently found in the archaeological section of the University of Seville's Heritage Collection (cf. http://www.patrimonioartistico.us.es). It had been donated to the former Ateneo y Sociedad de Excursiones de Sevilla Museum and later entered the former Archaeological

Figure 28.7. Statue head of Mars. Córdoba, Museo Arqueológico Provincial (from Rodríguez-Oliva 1999: 76, fig. 63).

Museum of the Faculty of Philosophy and Letters, University of Seville (Beltrán and Loza 2021; cf. Beltrán and Henares 2012: 115-16, 163; on the collections of these institutions: Henares 2020).

The Mars statue head completes this study on sculptures from *Celti*, a modest collection, but highly interesting due to their connection with the analysis of the function of sculpture within Hispano-Roman society. It covers various genres: funerary (lion statue), honorific (female statues), ornamental (Silenus statue), and religious (Mars head), and as a collection it is dated within the Julio-Claudian period, that is, before this community had achieved the administrative category of *municipium*; the same process is recorded in other cities of the province *Baetica* (for example, León and Rodríguez Oliva 1993). This course combined the incorporation of statuary according to Roman models and fashions with the development of urban monumentalisation, as an expression of commitment to the *Domus Augusta* and likewise, as a political and socioeconomic phenomenon of self-representation of the oligarchies within the framework of the flourishing Roman province *Baetica*.

Figure 28.8. Map of Roman *Baetica*, western part; in the rectangle, the Roman cities of *Celti* (Peñaflor) and *Arva* (Alcolea del Río).

5. Bibliography

Amores Carredano, F. and S. Keay 1999. Producciones tipo Peñaflor, in M. Roca and M.I. Fernández (eds) *Terra Sigillata Hispanica: Centros de fabricación y producciones altoimperiales*: 235-52. Málaga: Universidad de Málaga.

Anonymous 1916. Pueblos andaluces: Peñaflor. *Betica: Revista Ilustrada* 15-30 May: 57-58.

Aranegui Gascó, C. 2004. Leones funerarios de época iberorromana: la serie asociada a cabezas humanas, in *IV Reunión sobre Escultura Romana en Hispania*: 213-27. Madrid: Ministerio de Cultura.

Baena del Alcázar, L. 2009. Estatuas togadas y femeninas vestidas, in P. León (ed.), *Arte Romano de la Bética: Escultura*: 235-74. Seville: Fundación Focus-Abengoa.

Beltrán Fortes, J. 2000. Leones de piedra romanos de Las Cabezas de San Juan: a propósito de un nuevo ejemplar identificado. *Spal* 9: 435-50.

Beltrán Fortes, J. 2002. La arquitectura funeraria en la *Hispania* meridional durante los siglos II a.C.-I d.C., in D. Vaquerizo and J.F. Murillo (eds) *Espacios y usos funerarios en el Occidente Romano*, I: 233-58. Córdoba: Universidad de Córdoba.

Beltrán Fortes, J. 2003. Review of: Keay, S., J. Creighton and J. Remesal Rodríguez 2001. *Celti (Peñaflor): La arqueología de una ciudad hispanorromana en la Bética: Prospecciones y excavaciones 1987-1992. Habis* 34.

Beltrán Fortes, J. 2006. Esculturas romanas de *Arva* (Alcolea del Río, Sevilla), conservadas en el Museo Arqueológico de Córdoba, in D. Vaquerizo and J. Murillo (eds) *El concepto de lo provincial en el mundo* antiguo: *Homenaje a la Profesora Pilar León*, II: 249-58. Córdoba: Universidad de Córdoba.

Beltrán Fortes, J. 2014. Identidades cívicas en época romana republicana y altoimperial (ss. II a.C.-I d.C.) en la *Hispania* meridional, en los antiguos territorios de la Turdetania y la Oretania: algunas consideraciones sobre la escultura funeraria como tema de análisis, in T. Tortosa (ed.) *Diálogo de identidades: bajo el prisma de las manifestaciones religiosas en el ámbito mediterráneo (s. III a.C.-s. I d.C.)*: 251-74. Mérida: Consejo superior de investigaciones científicas.

Beltrán Fortes, J. and M.T. Henares Guerra 2012. El Museo Arqueológico de la Facultad de Filosofía y Letras de Sevilla, in J. Beltrán, M.T. Henares and R. Huarte, *Un Museo en la Universidad: colecciones arqueológicas de la Universidad de Sevilla (siglos XIX y XX)*: 89-129. Seville: Universidad de Sevilla.

Beltrán Fortes, J. and M.L. Loza Azuaga 2005. El 'oso de Porcuna'. Una escultura funeraria excepcional de la Hispania romana. *Romula* 4: 163-76.

Beltrán Fortes, J. and M.L. Loza Azuaga 2020. *Provincia de Cádiz (Hispania Vlterior Baetica)* (CSIR-España 1.8). Cádiz: Universidad de Cádiz.

Beltrán Fortes, J. and M.L. Loza Azuaga 2021. Una cabeza romana de Marte en la colección arqueológica de la Universidad de Sevilla. *Habis* 52: 137-47.

Blanco Freijeiro, A. 1975. Ein Kopf des Vulkan in Córdoba. *Madrider Mitteilungen* 16: 263-66.

Blanco Freijeiro, A. 1982-83. Cabeza de Vulcano en el Museo de Córdoba. *Corduba Archaeologica* 13, 25-33.

Bonsor, J. 1989 [1931]. *Expedición arqueológica a lo largo del Guadalquivir. 1889-1901*. Écija: Gráficas Sol (original edition, New York, 1931).

Boschung, D. 2002. *Gens Augusta: Untersuchungen zu Aufstellung, Wirkung und Bedeutung der Statuengruppen des julisch-claudischen Kaiserhauses*. Mainz am Rhein: Von Zabern.

Cesarano, M. 2015. *In honorem Domus Divinae: Introduzione allo studio dei cicli statuari giulio-claudii a Roma e in Occidente*. Rome: Edizioni Quasar.

CILA Sevilla = González Fernández, J. 1991. *Corpus de Inscripciones Latinas de Andalucía: Sevilla*, II.1. Seville: Consejería de Cultura y Medio Ambiente de la Junta de Andalucía.

Correa Rodríguez, J.A. 2016. *Toponimia antigua de Andalucía*. Seville: Editorial Universidad de Sevilla.

Cristilli A. 2019. Per una risistemazione dell'arredo dell'*Aedes Genii Coloniae* a *Lucus Feroniae*: la statua nel tipo Offerente e il togato inv. 91421, in J.M. Noguera and L. Ruiz (eds) *Escultura Romana en Hispania*, IX: 33-44. Yecla-Murcia: Ayuntamiento de Yecla-Universidad de Murcia.

Fuchs, M. 1987. *Untersuchungen zur Ausstattung römischer Theater in Italien und den Westprovinzen des Imperium Romanum*. Mainz am Rhein: Von Zabern.

García Tuñón y Quirós, E. 1877. Ms., Real Academia de la Historia, CAJ/9/7958/13(1).

Garriguet Mata, J.A. 2001. *La imagen del poder imperial en Hispania: tipos estatuarios*. Murcia: Tabularium.

Henares Guerra, M.T. 2020. *Historia de cuatro museos: los museos arqueológicos de la Universidad, el Ateneo y Sociedad de Excursiones de Sevilla y la Sociedad Española de Historia Natural, en la Sevilla de finales del siglo XIX*. Seville: Editorial Universidad de Sevilla.

Hidalgo-Prieto, R., I. Carrasco, M.T. Velázquez, F. Hermann, U. Kiesow and F. Teichner 2023. Comparing geophysical prospection data with archaeological excavation at the later wall of Roman *Italica* (Santiponce, Sevilla). *Mediterranean Archaeology and Archaeometry* 23.1: 267-82.

Jiménez Salvador, J.L. 1994. Teatro y monumentalización urbana en Hispania. *Braçal* 10: 53-74.

Keay, S. 1992. The Romanization of Turdetania, *Oxford Journal of Archaeology* 11.2: 275-315.

Keay, S. 1996. La romanización en el Sur y Levante de España hasta época de Augusto, in J.M. Blázquez and J. Alvar (eds) *La romanización en Occidente*: 147-77. Madrid: Actas.

Keay, S. 1997. Early Roman Italica and the Romanization of Western Baetica, in A. Caballos and P. León (eds) *Italica MMCC: Actas de las Jornadas del 2200 aniversario de la fundación de Italica*: 21-47. Seville: Junta de Andalucía.

Keay, S. (ed.) 1998. *The Archaeology of Early Roman Baetica*. Portsmouth (RI): Journal of Roman Archaeology.

Keay, S. 2000. Ceramic chronology and Roman rural settlement in the lower Guadalquivir Valley during the Augustan period, in R. Francovich and H. Patterson (eds) *Extracting meaning from ploughsoil assemblages* (The Archaeology of Mediterranean Landscapes 5): 163-73. Oxford: Oxbow.

Keay, S. 2003. Recent archaeological work in Roman Iberia (1990-2002). *Journal of Roman Studies* 90: 146-211.

Keay, S. 2015. Understanding inter-settlement visibility in Iron Age and Roman southern Spain with exponential random graph models for visibility networks. *Journal of Archaeological Method & Theory* 22.1: 58-143.

Keay, S. and G. Earl 2006. Inscriptions and social networks in western Baetica, in A. Sartori and A. Valvo (eds) *Hiberia-Italia, Italia-Hiberia: convegno internazionale di Epigrafia e Storia Antica; Gargnano-Brescia (28-30 Aprile)*: 269-91. Milan: Cisalpino.

Keay, S. and G. Earl 2007. Structuring of the provincial landscape. The towns in central and western *Baetica* in their geographical context, in G. Cruz, P. Le Roux and P. Moret (eds) *La invención de una Geografía de la Península Ibérica*, II: *La época imperial*: 305-58. Málaga: Servicio de publicaciones del Centro de Ediciones de la Diputación de Málaga.

Keay, S., J. Creighton and J. Remesal 2000. *Celti: The Archaeology of a Hispano-Roman Town in Baetica; Survey and Excavations 1987-1992*. Oxford: Oxbow.

Keay, S., J. Creighton and J. Remesal Rodríguez 2001b. *Celti (Peñaflor): La arqueología de una ciudad hispanorromana en la Bética; prospecciones y excavaciones 1987-1992*. Seville: Junta de Andalucía.

Keay, S., D. Wheatley and S. Poppy 2001a. The territory of Carmona during the Turdetanian and Roman periods: some preliminary notes about visibility and urban location, in A. Caballos (ed.), *Carmona Romana*: 397-412. Carmona: Ayuntamiento de Carmona-Universidad de Sevilla.

León, P. 2001. *Retratos romanos de la Bética*. Seville: Fundación El Monte.

León, P. 2020. Le copie ispaniche dei cicli mitologici del Foro di Augusto, in C. Capaldi (ed.) *Augusto e la Campania: da Ottaviano a Divo Augusto 14-2014 d.C.; atti del convegno internazionale Napoli 14 e 15 maggio 2015*: 483-95. Naples: Naus Editora.

León, P. 2021. *Italica: La ciudad de Trajano y Adriano*. Seville: Editorial Universidad de Sevilla.

León, P. and P. Rodríguez Oliva 1993. La ciudad hispanorromana en Andalucía, in M. Bendala (ed.), *La ciudad hispanorromana*: 12-53. Madrid: Ministerio de Cultura.

López Muñoz, J.F. 2004. Identificación de las estructuras arqueológicas del posible anfiteatro del municipio romano de Celti. *Arte, arqueología e historia* 11: 61-65.

López Muñoz, J.F. 2014. Apuntes sobre la posible existencia de un teatro en el municipio romano de Celti. *Arte, historia y arqueología* 21: 155-60.

Loza Azuaga, M.L. 1994. El agua en los teatros hispanorromanos: elementos escultóricos. *Habis* 25: 263-83.

Loza Azuaga, M.L. and J. Beltrán Fortes 2017. Esculturas romanas de la ciudad de *Celti* (Peñaflor, Sevilla): ¿la decoración del teatro? *Archivo Hispalense* 100: 73-96.

Loza Azuaga, M.L. and J. Beltrán Fortes 2018. Dos estatuas femeninas de *Celti* (Peñaflor), in C. Márquez and D. Ojeda (ed.) *Escultura Romana en Hispania*, VIII: 625-48. Córdoba: UCOPress.

Maier Allende, J. 1999. *Jorge Bonsor (1855-1930): un académico correspondiente de la Real Academia de la Historia y la arqueología española*. Madrid: Real Academia de la Historia.

Moretti Sgubini, A.M. 1982-1984. Statue e ritratti onorari da Lucus Feroniae. *Atti della Pontificia accademia romana di archeologia: rendiconti* 55-56: 71-109.

Nogales Basarrate, T. 1996. Programas iconográficos del foro del Mérida, en *II Reunión sobre escultura romana en Hispania: actas*: 115-34. Tarragona: Museo Nacional Arqueológico de Tarragona.

Ojeda Nogales, D. 2018. Anstückungen an kaiserzeitlichen Idealskulpturen. Zu drei aus der Baetica stammenden Statuen des Mars. *Archäologischer Anzeiger* 2: 193-208.

Pérez López, I. 1999: *Leones romanos en Hispania*. Madrid: Fundación de Estudios Clásicos-Fundación Focus-Abengoa.

Ramírez y Las Casas-Deza, L.M. 1844. Arqueología. Descubrimientos en Peñaflor. *Semanario Pintoresco Español* 47: 371-73.

Reinach, S. 1910. *Répertoire de la statuaire grecque et romaine*, IV. Paris: Leroux.

Rodríguez-Hidalgo, J.M. 1997. La nueva imagen de la *Italica* de Adriano, in A. Caballos and P. León (eds) *Italica MMCC: Actas de las jornadas del 2200 aniversario de la fundación de Italica*: 87-114. Seville: Junta de Andalucía.

Rodríguez-Hidalgo, J.M., S. Keay, D. Jordan, J. Creighton and I. Rodà 1999. La Itálica de Adriano. Resultado de las prospecciones arqueológicas de 1991 y 1993. *Archivo Español de Arqueología* 72: 73-97.

Rodríguez-Oliva, P. 2009. La escultura ideal, in P. León (ed.) *Arte romano de la Bética: escultura*: 41-152. Seville: Fundación Focus-Abengoa.

Saletti, C. 1968. *Il ciclo statuario della Basilica di Velleia*. Milan: Ceschina.

San Martín Montilla, C. 2014. Informe sobre 'busto romano femenino'. Expediente de exportación demandado por Christies Ibérica S.L. Museo Arqueológico de Sevilla, unpublished report.

29. Simon Keay e l'avventura del Comitato Scientifico del Parco archeologico di Ostia antica

Mariarosaria Barbera

Fra le tante attività svolte da Simon nella sua densa vita di studioso in Italia, voglio qui ricordare l'incarico di componente del Comitato Scientifico del Parco Archeologico di Ostia antica. La cd. "Riforma Franceschini", che a partire dal 2014 ha radicalmente trasformato l'assetto del Ministero oggi della Cultura (già per i Beni Culturali nelle varie declinazioni), ha infatti individuato un certo numero di Istituti autonomi - Musei e Parchi Archeologici, questi ultimi dotati anche di un territorio di competenza - presso i quali insediare un organo collegiale destinato, negli intenti, a supportare il Direttore nei programmi e nelle attività scientifiche dell'Istituto. Il nome di Simon fu votato all'unanimità dal Consiglio Superiore del Ministero, a cui spettava indicare un componente per ognuno dei Comitati istituiti: ciò in considerazione di un curriculum impeccabile, che per di più parlava la lingua specifica di Ostia e *Portus*, i luoghi che costituivano fisicamente il territorio di riferimento del Parco (Figura 29.1).

Il Comitato scientifico di Ostia antica, nominato effettivamente nel dicembre 2017 (D.M. Rep. 550) alcuni mesi dopo il mio arrivo alla direzione del Parco - e che ho avuto l'onore di presiedere fino al giugno 2020 - includeva altri tre colleghi di indubbio spessore scientifico, Carlo Pavolini, Rita Turchetti e Fausto Zevi.

Ci mettemmo all'opera già nel gennaio 2018 e mi piace ricordare che, nel vasto mondo degli Istituti autonomi del Ministero per i Beni Culturali, il nostro Comitato si è distinto per qualità ed efficacia della sua azione, nonché

per l'armonia dei rapporti interni e con i colleghi del Parco. Se molto ha giovato la conoscenza reciproca, accompagnata dalla condivisione di interessi scientifici e delle modalità di approccio alla disciplina archeologica e alle problematiche del territorio, i componenti sono stati interlocutori attenti in sommo grado a ogni idea, proposta e progetto, lanciati nell'ambito delle numerose attività scientifiche messe in campo.

Tutti i progetti sono stati analizzati e discussi, e con essi anche i problemi del Parco: tra i primi, il Piano strategico per il triennio 2018-20, appena elaborato e pubblicato sul nuovo sito web, che subito si è dovuto confrontare con le caratteristiche "olistiche" del nuovo Istituto autonomo. Tra i problemi, rimane attuale la perenne scarsità di risorse umane, strumentali ed economiche, tara endemica degli Uffici ministeriali, insieme con la rigidità normativa del contesto gestionale generale, che il preteso Istituto autonomo non aveva mezzi e facoltà né per trasformare, né per scalfire.

Fin dall'insediamento del Comitato, si condivise la proposta di varare un programma di conferenze pubbliche, al quale Simon e altri vollero partecipare personalmente, svolgendo argomenti di loro scelta coerenti con le finalità individuate. L'iniziativa prese poi la forma del Ciclo di Conversazioni sull'archeologia pubblica e la legalità, dal titolo "Vediamoci a Ostia Antica", che si è svolto fra marzo 2018 e giugno 2020 con un totale di 30 conferenze a tema: dieci nel primo anno, dodici nel secondo e ben otto nel solo primo

Figura 29.1. Portus, veduta dei Casali Torlonia.

semestre del 2020, quando il lockdown determinato dalla pandemia da COVID-19 ha portato il Parco ad infittire le attività on line.

Nelle conversazioni/conferenze sono stati trattati molti argomenti, sia di natura più squisitamente storico-archeologica, relativi ad aspetti e territori estesi ben oltre i confini del Parco, sia incentrati intorno al tema della legalità, in base al convincimento che un ufficio dello Stato deve improntare la sua attività e il comportamento *erga omnes* a valori di etica pubblica. L'esigenza si avvertiva tanto più forte, considerando le caratteristiche del territorio ostiense, oggetto di campagne mediatiche e azioni di ordine pubblico che hanno portato allo scoperto la presenza della criminalità organizzata e della mafia romana. Voglio ricordare che la convinta partecipazione degli amici del Comitato è stata fondamentale per la buona riuscita dell'iniziativa.

L'inizio del Ciclo fu timido, anche perché il Parco era reduce da una serie di pesanti scossoni organizzativi dovuti al decennio di variazioni dell'assetto disposte dal Ministero, tanto che l'Istituto finalmente "reso autonomo" scontava sconcertanti pendenze economico-amministrative. Le continue fluttuazioni ne avevano compresso la capacità di rimanere da protagonista sul palcoscenico scientifico, che pure aveva calcato per decenni; contestualmente, cominciava a profilarsi l'avvio di quella attività di comunicazione che, negli ultimi anni, ha incrementato l'interesse per le attività del Parco da parte del pubblico e delle forze politiche e culturali.

La stessa formula del Ciclo, dal titolo completo "Vediamoci a Ostia antica. Conversazioni di archeologia pubblica e legalità", molto ben condotto grazie a preziose collaborazioni[1], ha svolto un'importante azione di comunicazione dinamica verso un pubblico vario e con le comunità locali (nelle modalità della partecipazione in presenza e on line), potenziando l'attività complessiva di tutela e valorizzazione (Figura 29.2). Naturalmente il Ciclo non si sarebbe tenuto senza la generosa disponibilità dei tanti relatori, studiosi di alto profilo, importanti protagonisti della società civile, eccellenti funzionari e collaboratori del Parco e di altri Istituti, che hanno condiviso con il pubblico contenuti di grande interesse e novità: i loro nomi sono indicati di seguito.

La conferenza di avvio, nel marzo 2018, fu dedicata alla "Evoluzione paleoambientale del suolo di Ostia antica": Paola Germoni, Alessandra Ghelli e Carlo Rosa raccontarono le trasformazioni dell'assetto del litorale durante l'Impero, incluse le ipotesi sulla zona di Tor Boacciana, sul letto fluviale ecc., presentando la ricostruzione del paesaggio antico[2]. Inevitabile e sotteso alle tesi esposte, era il costante riferimento all'importante lavoro compiuto con l'Università di Southampton da Simon Keay, che per primo aveva ipotizzato l'esistenza della via d'acqua naturale di collegamento fra i porti imperiali di Ostia e di *Portus* e identificato la laguna in cui navigarono i relitti ritrovati nel 2011.

Portus fu oggetto anche di una seconda conferenza, tenuta nel settembre dello stesso anno, dal titolo accattivante "Portus, il porto degli imperatori". In questa Cinzia Morelli, Simon Keay e Renato Sebastiani condivisero con il pubblico i risultati delle ricerche sui moli, sull'isola-faro, sul Palazzo Imperiale e i cd. *Navalia*, senza trascurare le indagini nel Trastevere Ostiense, concludendo con la presentazione del progetto preliminare di riapertura del Museo delle Navi di Fiumicino[3].

L'intreccio di temi più specificamente archeologici con quelli di attualità politica e sociale proseguì, incastonando il racconto "Una formidabile occasione di conoscenza, gli scavi nei cantieri della Metro C", svolto da Rossella Rea e Simona Morretta, tra le conversazioni sulla "Cittadinanza europea e diritti civili" a cura di Louis Godart[4] e la discussione sul rapporto fra "Cultura e legalità, idee per Ostia", sviluppato dal Commissario di governo per Ostia, Domenico Vulpiani e dal colonnello Pasqualino Toscani, comandante del Gruppo Interforze dei Carabinieri che aveva da poco decapitato il purtroppo noto clan Spada[5],

[1] L'organizzazione del Ciclo è stata efficacemente supportata da Cristiano Brughitta, che ha svolto durante il mio mandato un'intensa e utilissima attività di Ufficio Stampa. Gli aspetti tecnici e la regia di tutte le conferenze, inclusa la loro diffusione sul web (VIMEO), si devono alla capacità di Bruno Fruttini. Referenti dell'operazione per il Parco sono stati: per il rapporto con i social Marina Lo Blundo, per la logistica Alberto Tulli. Preciso che il presente testo si riferisce al triennio 2017-20.

[2] Paola Germoni, allora funzionario del Parco e Alessandra Ghelli, del Segretariato Regionale della Calabria in part time a Ostia, sono autrici di importanti contributi sul tema. Carlo Rosa, geologo dell'Istituto Italiano di Paleontologia Umana, era uno storico ed esperto collaboratore del Parco.

[3] Cinzia Morelli è un funzionario archeologo del Parco; Renato Sebastiani, allora incardinato nella Soprintendenza Speciale ABAP di Roma, collaborava con il Parco per il Museo delle Navi di Fiumicino: entrambi hanno studiato l'area archeologica di Porto, a prosecuzione del lavoro di Lidia Paroli e Angelo Pellegrino. Per un contrattempo, Simon non poté partecipare fisicamente all'evento, ma il suo intervento venne letto da Sebastiani.

[4] Rossella Rea e Simona Morretta, funzionarie della Soprintendenza Speciale per i Beni Archeologici di Roma, hanno seguito i lavori della Metropolitana, maturando una grande esperienza anche in materia di archeologia preventiva; la prima ha concluso la sua attività come direttore del Colosseo, la seconda presta tuttora servizio presso la Soprintendenza. Louis Godart, accademico belga naturalizzato italiano e professore universitario di Micenologia, è stato Consigliere per la Conservazione del Patrimonio Artistico di due Presidenti della Repubblica Italiana (Ciampi e Napolitano); all'attività scientifica unisce da sempre una grande passione civile.

[5] Il Prefetto Vulpiani era dall'agosto 2015 Commissario Prefettizio per l'amministrazione straordinaria del X Municipio di Roma Capitale, sciolto per infiltrazione mafiosa. Il Colonnello Toscani ha

Figura 29.2. Locandina del Ciclo Ostia 2018.

Il tema delle infiltrazioni criminali nel tessuto del litorale fu ulteriormente approfondito grazie alla testimonianza diretta di Federica Angeli, giornalista d'assalto le cui instancabili denunce la costringono tuttora a vivere sotto scorta (è suo il libro "A mano disarmata") e di Gianpiero Cioffredi, Presidente dell'Osservatorio per la Sicurezza e la Legalità della Regione Lazio, che ha illustrato il Terzo Rapporto Mafie nel Lazio[6].

Nelle discussioni con il Comitato Scientifico, era stata rappresentata la necessità per il Parco di uscire dai confini della comunicazione specialistica tradizionale, aprendosi ai nativi digitali: a questa finalità si rispose (anche) con la conferenza a tre voci "Archeosocial. Comunicare l'archeologia ai tempi dei social media", tenuta dalle archeologhe e blogger Astrid D'Eredità, Antonia Falcone e Marina Lo Blundo[7].

L'intreccio di argomenti programmato per l'autunno vide alternarsi alla già citata conversazione settembrina su Portus: il vibrante intervento di Christian Greco "Biografia degli oggetti, il dialogo fra Egittologia e Scienza" che travolse i presenti con lo sbendaggio virtuale della mummia di Kha; i bagliori della città romana che Carlo Pavolini fece risplendere nella sala illustrando "Ostia tardo antica. Il lusso in tempo

---

comandato il gruppo Carabinieri di Roma Ostia dal 2017 al settembre 2020, quando ha assunto l'incarico di Comandante provinciale dei Carabinieri di Parma

[6] Dal libro "A mano disarmata" è stato tratto nel 2019 il film omonimo; la giornalista è stata insignita dal Presidente della Repubblica Sergio Mattarella del titolo di Ufficiale dell'Ordine al merito della Repubblica Italiana, per il suo impegno nella lotta alle mafie. Del nutrito CV di Cioffredi, consultabile sulla pagina web della Regione Lazio, segnalo che nel 1991 ha fondato l'Associazione nazionale di volontariato antirazzista "Nero e Non Solo", promuovendo durante la sua presidenza un patto di collaborazione con il sindacato di Polizia sul tema della legalità ed integrazione.

[7] D'Eredità e Falcone sono le autrici del libro "Archeosocial. L'archeologia riscrive il web. Esperienze, strategie e nuove pratiche"; Marina Lo Blundo è funzionaria presso il Parco di Ostia, dove si occupa fra l'altro dei rapporti con il mondo dei social.

di crisi"[8] e, a conclusione del primo ciclo, il tema dal multiforme aspetto del rapporto fra "Uomo e natura. I paesaggi del litorale romano", che puntò l'attenzione sulla vocazione e le trasformazioni del territorio, nel dialogo fra l'economista Alessandro Leon, l'architetto Luca Bragalli e la giornalista Anna Longo[9].

Preso l'abbrivio e sperimentata la formula, nel 2019 i temi archeologici e civili continuarono a intrecciarsi con sempre maggior successo, testimoniato dal crescente affollamento fisico dei partecipanti e dalle visualizzazioni di followers soddisfatti e perfino entusiasti. L'occasione per sfatare il mito sempiterno della "razza" fu ben còlta dal paleoantropologo Giorgio Manzi nel suo intervento "Made in Africa, il lungo cammino dell'evoluzione umana"[10]. L'incontro "Ostia un anno dopo, prospettive del patto fra cultura e legalità" pose nuovamente al centro della discussione il tema civile delle infiltrazioni mafiose nella zona del litorale, presentato dalle magistrate Tiziana Coccoluto e Alessandra Tudino[11]. Mi piace ricordare che, con un gradito fuori programma, il Ciclo di conferenze si arricchì con la presentazione fuori programma del bel libro "Il padrino dell'Antimafia. Una cronaca italiana sul potere infetto", in cui il giornalista Attilio Bolzoni ha rimesso sulla scena il rapporto perverso della criminalità mafiosa tra la Sicilia e "il continente"[12].

Il Ciclo ostiense ha ripetutamente puntato lo sguardo al cuore del mondo romano, il Mediterraneo (Mare Nostrum), come crocevia di traffici e commerci che mettevano in comunicazione luoghi, popoli e idee: dal tema della "Archeologia subacquea. La storia di Roma riemerge dal Mediterraneo" a cura di Roberto Petriaggi, riallacciatosi magnificamente alle precedenti conferenze sulle funzioni di Portus così care a Simon; all'integrazione delle province, anche le più lontane, trattata da Sergio Rinaldi Tufi nell'incontro "Souvenir dall'Impero. Ostia racconta le province romane"[13]. La trasformazione e diffusione capillare del culto di Iside, di cui alla conferenza "Dal Nilo al Tevere. Il culto di Iside in Egitto e a Ostia", sono state delineate da Christian Greco e dalla scrivente in un intervento che si è esteso nel tempo e nello spazio, dall'Egitto dei faraoni all'intero Mediterraneo romano[14].

Gli elementi caratterizzanti del territorio di prossimità sono stati tracciati in altre seguitissime conversazioni, come quella sul "Vicus Augustanus, l'archeologia del territorio laurentino", in cui Paolo Liverani ha dipanato davanti a un pubblico attento le trasformazioni dei luoghi connessi con il ritorno di Enea da Troia, fino alle soglie del Medioevo[15]. Il complesso sistema idraulico di Ostia antica, tuttora parzialmente in uso e oggetto di recenti lavori di rifunzionalizzazione a cura del Parco, è stato presentato nella conferenza "Le forme dell'acqua" a cura di due studiose militanti, l'architetto Elettra Santucci e l'archeologa Silvia Calvigioni. Ancora rivolta a Ostia è la conversazione di Marcello Turci, "Strutture sepolte fuori Porta Marina. Indagini tecnologiche e nuove ipotesi", che ha illustrato le prospettive attuali di ricerca con tecniche non invasive sul vasto complesso pubblico (ca 15.000 mq) appena percepibile oltre la porta di Ostia antica verso il mare[16].

Il rapporto tra ricerca, disseminazione delle conoscenze e presentazione al pubblico è stato declinato da due big dell'archeologia, Fausto Zevi e Salvatore Settis. Zevi, "padre nobile" dell'archeologia ostiense, con l'intervento "Il Museo Ostiense e le sue collezioni: vecchi e nuovi allestimenti", ha affascinato il pubblico intrecciando storia dell'arte e museografia e fornendo anche una base preziosa per l'elaborazione progettuale del rinnovato Museo ostiense, in via di realizzazione con i fondi CIPE[17].

---

[8] Christian Greco, dopo una lunga esperienza in Olanda, è oggi Direttore del rinnovato Museo Egizio di Torino, nonché docente di Egittologia all'Università di Torino. Carlo Pavolini, componente del Comitato Scientifico del Parco, ha diviso la sua ricca vita professionale da funzionario tra le Soprintendenze (Ostia e poi quella Speciale di Roma), da docente presso l'Università della Tuscia.

[9] Alessandro Leon: economista, Presidente del CLES (Centro ricerche e studi sui problemi di Lavoro, Economia e Sviluppo), componente del Consiglio di Amministrazione del Parco; Luca Bragalli: Commissario della Riserva naturale statale del Litorale; Anna Longo: giornalista culturale RAI e vicepresidente locale di Italia Nostra.

[10] Giorgio Manzi è docente ordinario di Paleoantropologia all'Università La Sapienza di Roma e divulgatore scientifico; fra le tante esperienze è stato anche curatore di museo.

[11] Tiziana Coccoluto dai Tribunali di Latina e Roma era approdata al Ministero per i Beni Culturali come Capo di Gabinetto; Alessandra Tudino, giudice a Cassino e Roma "ha messo il primo mattone per smantellare la filiera criminale" di Ostia. Con loro voglio ricordare la compianta Simonetta D'Alessandro: è sua l'autorizzazione ai 32 arresti destinati a minare il ruolo del clan Spada di Ostia.

[12] Bolzoni, storica firma del quotidiano "La Repubblica", è autore di varie opere sulla mafia, singolarmente e insieme con Giuseppe D'Avanzo; dal 1° gennaio 2021 è passato a "Domani".

[13] Roberto Petriaggi, funzionario MiBACT ed eccellente archeologo subacqueo, ha svolto anche attività di docenza universitaria, partic. presso Roma Tre; dirige la rivista "Archaeologia Maritima Mediterranea". Sergio Rinaldi Tufi, storico docente in varie Università di Archeologia delle province romane e Archeologia classica, poi Direttore di Dipartimento a Urbino, è attentissimo agli aspetti della divulgazione scientifica, collaborando abitualmente con quotidiani e riviste di attualità.

[14] Per Greco v. nota 8; il CV della scrivente è disponibile in rete sul sito del Ministero della Cultura (sezione Dirigenti in quiescenza) e sul sito della Fondazione Scuola del Patrimonio.

[15] Paolo Liverani, già titolare di importanti incarichi presso i Musei Vaticani, è oggi docente ordinario di Topografia all'Università di Firenze e Presidente della Consulta Universitaria di Topografia.

[16] Elettra Santucci, architetto, è esperta di sistemi idraulici del mondo romano e attiva collaboratrice del Parco in vari importanti lavori; di questi sistemi Silvia Calvigioni, archeologa e PhD presso l'Università di Roma Tre, ha studiato gli aspetti archeologici. Marcello Turci, archeologo già specializzato in Archeologia classica, è ricercatore post-doc all'Università di Aix-Marseille, Centre Camille Jullian ed ha elaborato interessanti teorie e progetti relativi all'area ostiense di Porta Marina.

[17] La vita professionale di Fausto Zevi, componente del Comitato Scientifico del Parco, è maturata fra gli incarichi di Soprintendente a Ostia, Napoli, Roma e di docente universitario, da ultimo alla Sapienza di Roma. Tralasciando gli ulteriori titoli (Accademia dei Lincei,

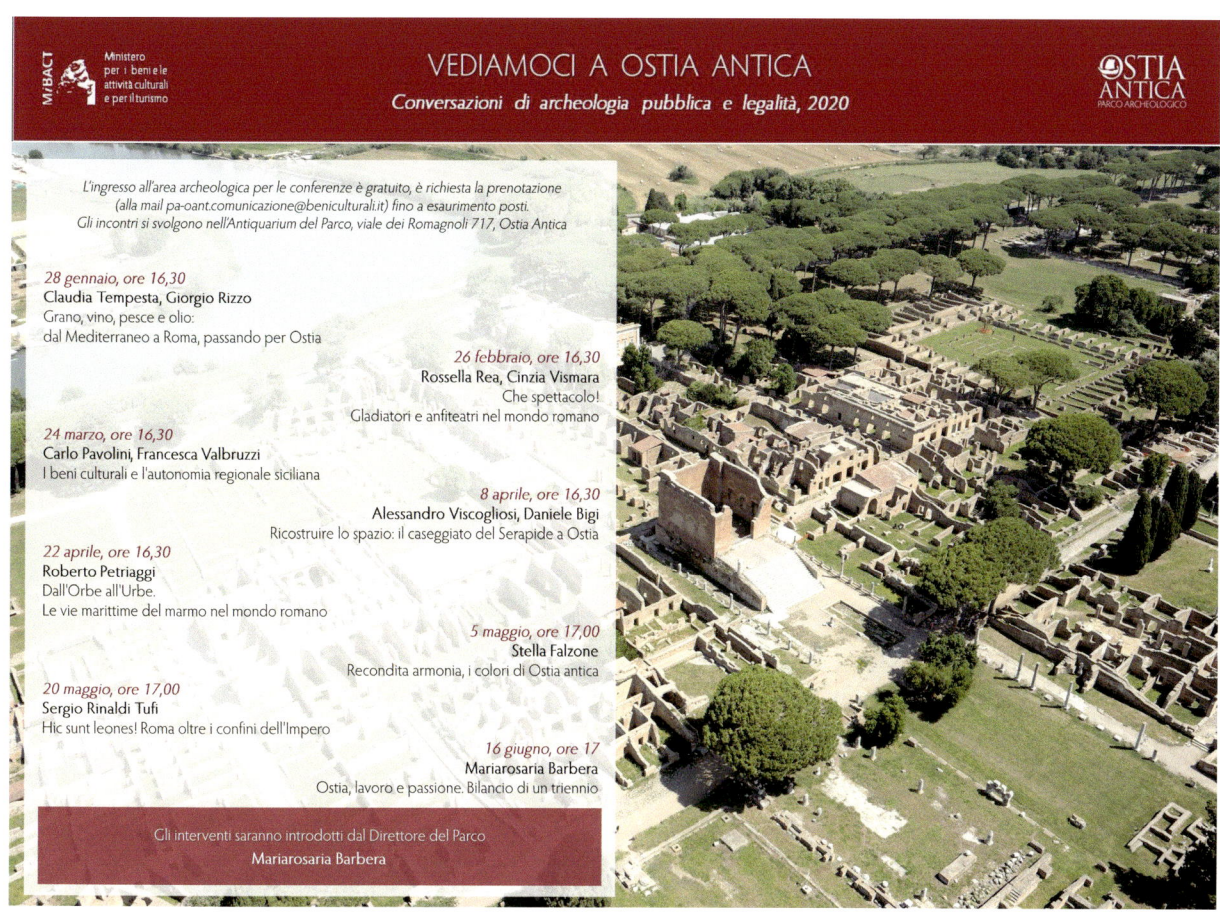

Figura 29.3. Locandina del Ciclo Ostia 2020.

A sua volta, Settis ha affascinato gli astanti col tema "Mostrare l'arte classica. Ricerca, narrazione, allestimento" dove, prendendo le mosse dalla sua bella mostra milanese "Serial Classic", ha posto l'accento sul forte filo narrativo che deve partire dalla ricerca specialistica, per produrre forme di allestimento coerenti con questa finalità.[18]

Naturalmente anche nella stagione 2020 del Ciclo, benché limitata al primo semestre, il Comitato Scientifico ha condiviso la formula sperimentata alternando, per il passato, il binario del "particolare" di Ostia antica con quello più generale del contesto del mondo romano; per il presente, i temi dell'attualità della ricerca e del quadro normativo politico in cui conoscenza, tutela e valorizzazione si muovono (Figura 29.3).

Tra le conferenze del primo "filone", quella di inaugurazione dell'anno trattava di "Grano, vino, olio e pesce. Dal Mediterraneo a Roma passando per Ostia": in essa Claudia Tempesta e Giorgio Rizzo hanno illustrato l'immensa rete organizzativa che consentì per secoli di sfamare la più grande capitale del mondo antico[19]. La funzione di consenso popolare verso il potere, legato alla rete degli approvvigionamenti, si coglie anche nel capillare sistema degli spettacoli anfiteatrali, offerti gratuitamente fino alle contrarie disposizioni cristiane, come illustrato da Rossella Rea e Cinzia Vismara nella Conferenza "Che spettacolo! Gladiatori e anfiteatri nel mondo romano"[20].

Ancora una volta, il tema di una globalizzazione ante litteram è stato trattato nella densa conversazione "Dall'orbe all'Urbe. Le vie marittime del marmo nel

---

Istituto Archeologico Germanico, British School ecc.) è considerato da molti il più profondo e attento conoscitore del territorio e delle tematiche ostiensi.

[18] Del densissimo CV di Salvatore Settis, archeologo e storico dell'arte di fama internazionale, mi limito a citare gli incarichi di docenza universitaria, la direzione della Normale di Pisa e del Getty Center di Los Angeles e la Presidenza del Consiglio Scientifico del Louvre; la sua sterminata produzione scientifica è attenta ai risvolti sociali e civili della gestione del patrimonio culturale del Paese, anche in contrasto con le scelte della politica.

[19] Claudia Tempesta è un funzionario archeologo del Parco, con pregresse esperienze presso il MiBAC; Giorgio Rizzo, archeologo classico, è specializzato in studi di ceramologia romana che abbracciano il bacino del Mediterraneo.
[20] Di Rossella Rea si è detto alla nota 2; Cinzia Vismara è stata docente di Archeologia delle Province Romane presso l'Università di Cassino e direttore di vari scavi in Italia e all'estero; dal 2014 è l'anima della rivista "Antiquités africaines". Entrambe sono esperte riconosciute del mondo degli anfiteatri e della gladiatura.

Figura 29.4. La sala del Parco durante una conferenza.

mondo romano" col ritorno di Roberto Petriaggi, che ha fatto sfilare la serie infinita di traffici, imbarcazioni e porti del Mare Nostrum per l'approvvigionamento di un materiale di lusso. Le regioni più lontane del mondo romano hanno trovato adeguato spazio di illustrazione nell'intervento "Hic sunt leones. Roma oltre i confini dell'Impero", dove Sergio Rinaldi Tufi si è spinto dall'Atlantico all'Eufrate e al Nilo, oltre i deserti africani, i vasti territori asiatici e gli oltre 10.000 chilometri di limes[21].

Le tematiche architettoniche legate all'urbanistica intensiva di Ostia, che vide la massima densità abitativa nel II secolo d.C., sono state tratteggiate da Alessandro Viscogliosi e Gabriele Bigi nella presentazione de "Il Caseggiato del Serapide. Un gioiello dell'architettura adrianea" che, sorprendentemente, anticipa per certi aspetti il modello del Palazzo rinascimentale all'italiana. E sempre su Ostia è puntato il coloratissimo contributo di Stella Falzone dal titolo "operistico" "Recondita armonia. I colori di Ostia antica", che ha anche evidenziato come in questa città multietnica, vero laboratorio di diversità, la decorazione ad affresco connotasse accanto alle residenze di lusso anche *insulae* e case della classe media[22].

Al di fuori della sequenza cronologica fin qui seguita, voglio ricordare le due conferenze più "politiche" del semestre 2020 che, come tutte quelle tenute a partire da marzo, si sono svolte on line e non dal vivo, per le disposizioni anti-COVID 19.

L'appassionato intervento di Francesca Valbruzzi ha dato corpo all'appuntamento "I Beni Culturali e l'autonomia regionale siciliana", in canto e controcanto con Carlo Pavolini, nella presentazione del volume "Utopia e impostura. Tutela e uso sociale dei beni culturali in Sicilia al tempo dell'Autonomia", della Valbruzzi medesima e di Paolo Russo[23]. La descrizione dei passaggi che portarono la gestione del patrimonio culturale in Sicilia prima all'autonomia, poi a un uso spesso distorto, dovuto a politiche culturali prive di spessore e non di rado improntate al clientelismo, si conclude tuttavia con una speranza da coltivare, anche in un rapporto più stretto fra l'isola e il "continente".

La conclusione del triennio del Ciclo nel giugno 2020 ha coinciso con quella del mio incarico di direttore del Parco (Figura 29.4). Si è quindi còlta l'occasione per

---

[21] Per Petriaggi e Rinaldi Tufi rimando alla nota 10.

[22] Alessandro Viscogliosi, architetto e raffinato studioso dell'architettura antica, è docente alla Facoltà di Architettura "Valle Giulia" della Sapienza, nonché Direttore della Scuola di Specializzazione. A Gabriele Bigi, allievo poi dottorato di Viscogliosi, si deve un approfondito e innovativo studio sul Caseggiato del

Serapide. Stella Falzone, storica collaboratrice della Soprintendenza Ostiense nelle sue varie denominazioni ed esperta di pittura romana, già ricercatrice presso l'Accademia Austriaca delle Scienze, dirige oggi il Museo Archeologico di Taranto (MarTa).

[23] Francesca Valbruzzi, funzionario archeologo della Regione Siciliana, ha dedicato la sua vita professionale alla tutela del territorio, soprattutto di Enna e dei Nebrodi; affianca all'attività scientifica una passione civile e politica espressa in varie pubblicazioni. Su Pavolini si veda nota 8.

Figura 29.5. Museo di Ostia, sala V simulazione (Balletti e Sabatini).

condividere con il pubblico a casa una veloce cavalcata tra il lavoro svolto, i problemi affrontati, i risultati raggiunti, nella consapevolezza della lunga strada ancora da percorrere. La conversazione "Ostia, lavoro e passione. Bilancio di un triennio", svolta il 16 giugno del 2020, ha sintetizzato brevemente questo quadro: dai lavori di manutenzione e di restauro alla didattica, alla comunicazione, alle conferenze, alle ricerche, ai rapporti con gli Istituti di cultura e con le Università italiane e straniere. Un particolare accento è stato posto sui progetti di valorizzazione, realizzati e in fase di sviluppo, sui Grandi Progetti Strategici e CIPE. Non meno significativo è il conferimento del Marchio del Patrimonio Europeo (Cultural Heritage Label) al Parco di Ostia, nel marzo 2020, dalla Commissione Europea per l'Innovazione, la Ricerca, la Cultura, l'Educazione e la Gioventù, in ragione del percorso culturale e sociale compiuto nel triennio a servizio del patrimonio e delle comunità. Tutte le conferenze del Ciclo "Vediamoci a Ostia antica" sono reperibili sulla pagina web del Parco <https://www.ostiaantica.beniculturali.it>.

L'avventura del Parco e del suo Comitato ha riguardato infine il riallestimento di due Musei: di Ostia e delle Navi di Fiumicino, entrambi crucci costanti dell'Istituto perché inadeguati alle esigenze attuali di fruizione e di sicurezza. Queste ultime hanno fatto da detonatore per l'elaborazione di ipotesi di trasformazione radicale sia dei contenuti, sia del racconto al pubblico dell'intero sistema Ostia-*Portus*-Isola Sacra e dell'allestimento dei materiali. Lunghe e approfondite discussioni in seno al

Comitato hanno segnato le varie fasi della progettazione di entrambi i Musei, scandita da confronti progressivi che hanno confermato e migliorato l'impianto generale proposto.

Per il Museo delle Navi, rimando ad altri contributi in questa e altra sede[24]: la sua chiusura dal 2002 è stata vissuta con particolare dispiacere da Simon, che ha voluto arricchire personalmente e continuamente il progetto del nuovo allestimento, curato per la parte archeologica da Renato Sebastiani, con la fattiva collaborazione di Giulia Boetto. Per ragioni tecnico-amministrative e di tempi di esecuzione legati ai finanziamenti, l'esposizione rimane nell'hangar costruito parecchi decenni fa per contenere i relitti. Eppure, un contenitore così anonimo, dalle linee oggi impensabili e inadatte per un museo di nuova concezione, è stato analizzato e "trattato" sul piano scientifico e della comunicazione in modo da assicurare lo svolgimento di un racconto complesso, ben "giocato" nel rapporto tra gli oggetti fisici e la dimensione virtuale, oggi indispensabile in ogni allestimento che voglia parlare ai diversi "pubblici" dei nostri Musei. Contestualmente, si è dotata l'area di Porto di una nuova

---

[24] Da ultimo, C. Collettini, M.T. Donzelli e R. Sebastiani, Dal museo al museo, 1979-2016: v. <https://cirili.hypotheses.org/315>; <https://ia601509.us.archive.org/31/items/MuseoNavi/Museo_Navi.pdf>; R. Sebastiani, C. Collettini, S. Borghini e G. Boetto, I relitti e il museo delle navi di Fiumicino, in G. Boetto e B. Davidde Petriaggi (eds) *De l'épave au musée: étude, conservation, restauration et exposition des navires antiques en Italie et en Europe, Convegno Internazionale Studi Roma EFR, 7-8 marzo 2018*

Figura 29.6. Mostra di Fiumicino in peparazione.

Figura 29.7. Mostra di Tampere, pubblicità in strada.

Figura 29.8. Mostra di Tampere, ricostruzione del bacino di Portus.

biglietteria, collocata alla fine di un percorso d'ingresso che informa e prepara il visitatore alla scoperta dei luoghi.

Quanto al Museo Ostiense, il cui progetto esecutivo è stato consegnato nell'estate 2020, ne sono state fornite anticipazioni sia nella conversazione on line di fine mandato, sia nella conferenza "Ostian Museum reloaded: il progetto del nuovo allestimento", tenuta alla British School il 27 gennaio 2021, ambedue reperibili in rete. L'impostazione progettuale ha ripensato l'esposizione in tutte le componenti, dall'ordinamento e tipologia dei materiali in un percorso più attento al collegamento del Museo con il territorio ostiense, alle innovative scelte architettoniche e impiantistiche, alle modalità di comunicazione e tecnologie relative, per consentire una effettiva interazione col pubblico (Figura 29.5). Il progetto di restauro dei materiali selezionati ha accompagnato, in ogni fase, il lavoro sull'edificio.

Il gruppo di archeologi, architetti, ingegneri e restauratori che hanno lavorato con entusiasmo, integrando contributi e saperi delle diverse professionalità[25] ha pubblicato il progetto nel Bollettino

di Archeologia (Supplemento XII, 2021/4) dal titolo "Il rinnovato Museo Ostiense: progetto del nuovo museo archeologico di Ostia antica", a cura di chi scrive e di Paola Olivanti. Il Museo rinnovato è stato riaperto nel luglio 2024 dall'attuale Direttore del Parco, Alessandro D'Alessio.

Nella certezza che altri, con maggior competenza, tratteranno in questa sede dei risultati del grande lavoro compiuto da Simon e dalla sua équipe a *Portus* (Portus Project, Portus Limen), voglio ricordare che proprio a questo scopo fu rinnovata nel 2019 una specifica convenzione, con cui la progettualità e le interrelazioni scientifiche venivano ampliate fino a comprendere in un unico grande contesto, ruotante intorno al Parco, l'Università di Southampton, la British School at Rome, l'Ecole Française e l'Università di Huelva.

Per Simon l'approccio all'archeologia non si è mai limitato al livello accademico, come confermano due episodi *a latere* della sua inesauribile attività scientifica. Il primo è la collaborazione al fumetto "Tiberio e la perla del Mare", un'operazione che ha avvicinato

---

[25] Progetto scientifico: Paola Germoni (coordinamento), Stella Falzone, Cristina Genovese, Filippo Marini Recchia, Paola Olivanti, Claudia Valeri. Progetto tecnico: Valeria Casella (coordinamento), Monica Cola, Carolina De Camillis, Riccardo Fibbi, Valentina Iannilli, Fabio Maizza, Federica Pierdominici, Lucio Verrecchia;

progetto dell'allestimento Balletti e Sabbatini architetti. Progetto di restauro: Antonella Docci, Tiziana Sorgoni con Kristian Schneider. Comunicazione multimediale: Filippo Marini Recchia. Del Procedimento la scrivente è stata Responsabile Unico, con la costante collaborazione di Romina Cianciaruso, fino alla consegna degli atti al direttore subentrato D'Alessio.

alla storia di *Portus* migliaia di scolari e studenti, non soltanto di Fiumicino: qualità del disegno e vivacità della storia si sono unite all'uso di elementi storico-archeologici attentamente sorvegliato da lui e da Renato Sebastiani. L'altro episodio ha visto Simon coordinarsi pazientemente con gli staff di Ostia e Sky Arte per le riprese di un bel documentario a più voci su Ostia e *Portus*, dal titolo "Destinazione Ostia, sulle sponde della storia", andato in onda dopo lunga gestazione nel gennaio 2020.

L'archeologia pubblica, infatti, è stata sempre nel DNA di questo eccellente studioso, che si è trovato in perfetta sintonia con la visione del Parco e dell'intero Comitato scientifico. Fra le iniziative condivise, vanno inoltre ricordate anche altre attività di cui il Parco di Ostia è stato protagonista. Penso alle mostre a rotazione nell'aeroporto di Fiumicino: quella del 2019, che tanto piacque a Simon, fu dedicata alle "Immagini del tempo" (Figura 29.6). Infine, va citata la grande mostra organizzata a Tampere dagli amici finlandesi, in stretta collaborazione col Parco, nel cui catalogo spiccano i suoi aggiornatissimi contributi su *Portus* e Isola Sacra[26] (Figure 29.7-29.8).

Oggi *Portus* è un polo di studi e ricerche internazionali, al centro di accordi di valorizzazione e di progetti di ricerche: fra questi cito almeno FosPhora, che risponde allo scopo di mettere in relazione il sistema Ostia-*Portus* con l'odierna Fos-sur-Mer, alla foce del Rodano, sede di un importante complesso industriale portuale che è parte del bacino ovest del Gran porto marittimo di Marsiglia.

Delle ricerche e degli studi sul porto laziale, Simon è stato sicuramente un "padre nobile": il ricordo più bello che ho di lui è quando, mentre si dialogava negli incontri del Comitato, il suo sguardo color del mare si accendeva vivacissimo appena si toccavano le attività e i tanti progetti comuni che riguardavano l'amata *Portus*.

---

[26] A. Karivieri (ed.) *Life and Death in a Multicultural Harbour City: Ostia Antica from the Republic through Late Antiquity*, Roma: Institutum Romanum Finlandiae, 2020: 41-54.

30. The Roman Villa at Matrice:
Geophysical Survey and Archaeological Excavation

Elena Pomar

The methodology adopted for the research project at Matrice follows an approach implemented by Simon Keay many years ago as part of the Roman Towns Project, which he directed together with Martin Millett. The Roman Towns Project used geophysical and topographical surveys to investigate the landscape around the Tiber Valley and study a variety of Roman urban contexts. The project dedicated specific attention to the methodological aspect, with a focus on geophysical prospection, demonstrating the importance of integrating different techniques (Keay *et al.* 2004; Johnson *et al.* 2004).

I would like to present the following in acknowledgement of the value of Simon's work in this field, as well as his faith in the extensive use of non-invasive survey methods to support and complement traditional excavation.

Historical and Archaeological Context

Matrice is located in central Italy, in the upper Biferno Valley, which was part of ancient Samnium. The area was occupied by the Samnite group of the Pentrians, whose main settlement was in *Bovianum* (modern Bojano), along with a major religious centre at Pietrabbondante. The Samnites fought against the expansion of Rome until their political and military independence was eliminated in the 1st century BC, following the Social War. Although Strabo (5.4.11) describes the military campaign of Sulla in 82-81 BC as a terrible devastation, archaeological evidence demonstrates that the reality was probably less dramatic and long-lasting. After the Social War, Roman law spread across the Italian Peninsula and the Samnites were absorbed into the Roman state, acquiring citizenship (Barker 1995; Buonocore 2002: 29-45). In the following period, Caesar started an intervention of reorganisation in the territory, later continued by Augustus, and towns such as *Saepinum*, *Bovianum*, and *Faegifulae* grew and became *municipia* (Letta 2021). The rural landscape was occupied by villas and farmsteads, albeit fewer in number than the previous period (Barker 1995: 217-26; Patterson 2004). Samnium remained part of Roman Italy until the rise of the Ostrogothic kingdom in the 5th century AD.

The term 'villa' is generally used to refer to the large late republican-early imperial building at Matrice and it will be adopted in this text as well. The term 'villa', however, is used with diverse meanings by ancient and modern authors and this complicates consistent use of terminology and interpretation (cf. Rothe 2018). The building at Matrice fits the general definition of a Roman *villa rustica*: a farm estate in the countryside engaged, above all, in agricultural production. However, the site at Matrice does not share all the elements of the *villae rusticae* known elsewhere in central Italy (Marzano 2007: 102-24). The latter – generally comprising a *pars urbana*, *pars rustica*, and *pars fructuaria* – held a social significance that does not appear at Matrice. Rather, this villa displays aspects peculiar to its specific geographical context.

The archaeological site is located at the edge of the southern Biferno watershed, about 10km north-east of Campobasso, in the region of Molise. The Roman villa lies *c.* 200m north of the medieval church of Santa Maria della Strada (Figure 30.1), by whose name it is also known in the literature. The site, *c.* 812m above sea level, overlooked the valley and was sited in a strategic position connected to ancient routes. The villa is positioned along the *tratturo* Cotile-Centocelle, a transhumance route which links the inland to the coast eastward. Moreover, the existence of a road joining the two cities of Bovianum and Larinum is attested in the Tabula Peutingeriana, dated to the 4th century AD (De Benedittis 2010: 63-66). The relationship of this area to traffic routes is also emphasised by the toponym of the nearby church 'della Strada', documented since the 12th century. Although the allusion to a road is explicit in the church title, it is not yet known to which road the reference was made: to the nearby *tratturo*, the *via Frentana Apula*, or if it was instead a general appellative (Gianandrea 2018: 434; Jaminson 1938: 34).

The Archaeological Site at Santa Maria della Strada, Matrice

Over the several occupational phases at Matrice the structures made partial reuse of earlier walls and followed the same general north-east-south-west alignment.

Figure 30.1. The archaeological site at Matrice, to the left, crossed by the modern asphalt road SP140, with the church of Santa Maria della Strada in the background (looking south, photo Stephen Kay).

The first occupation of the site is dated by scattered materials to the late Bronze Age (and C[14] analysis of some samples date indicate 850 BC ±60); however, the first stone structure belongs to a late Samnite building, *c.* 200 BC (Lloyd 1991b: 262). The building had a square plan (*c.* 18 × 18m) with large roughly trimmed limestone blocks and was presumably a farmstead (Figure 30.2). Farmsteads in the hinterland of Samnium are known and typically dated using black glazed pottery production, from the late 4th to the 1st centuries BC (Lloyd 1991a). These were familiar units often found along transhumance routes and involved in a mix of subsistence economic activities (Di Niro and Petrone 1993). The Samnite building at Matrice can be compared with that of Pesco Morelli at Cercemaggiore, 12km south-east of Campobasso, dated to the 3rd century BC. The building at Cercemaggiore has an almost square plan of 19 × 17m and the outer walls were built with similar polygonal blocks (Barker 1995: 195-96; Ceccarelli *et al.* 2017: 167-69). The excavation at Cercemaggiore discovered working and storage installations suggestive of a farmstead (Di Niro and Petrone 1993: 17). Similarities with the Matrice structure strongly suggests that they belong to the same structural typology.

A significant enlargement of the structure occurred in the late 2nd-1st centuries BC, followed by a substantial renovation at the beginning of the Imperial period during the rule of Tiberius or Claudius (Figure 30.2). At this time the site fell within the territory of *Faegifulae*, the nearest large Roman settlement, located a few kilometres to the west in the modern Comune of Montagano. The building was devoted to production activities, displaying aspects of a rural villa or large working farmhouse, and was 60m long occupying a space of *c.* 2500m[2] articulated into two wings and joined by a corridor facing a central open courtyard (Barker 1995: 224-26; Lloyd *et al.* 1984). The north wing was dedicated to working activities, indicated by a series of rooms with sunken *dolia defossa* and low rectangular masonry platforms (Lloyd 1984: 2-3). Although it is not possible to precisely identify the function of these installations, *cocciopesto* on exposed surfaces indicates that large quantities of liquid were involved (Lloyd 1984: 3). The palaeobotanical remains collected, which include grape pips, might suggest wine production (Lloyd 1981: 6). However, the scale of this production must have been smaller than sometimes hypothesised, and there is no clear evidence at present for use of a *torcularium* (cf. Ceccarelli *et al.* 2017: 291-92). It remains possible that wine was made simply by treading grapes on the waterproofed floors or using simple pressing devices that no longer survive archaeologically. The presence of mortar floors, tile hearths, and two large *dolia*, in the southern wing suggest that this area of the villa was also devoted to production activities (Lloyd *et al.* 1982: 7-8). Palaeobotanical analysis indicated a spread of agricultural production, including cereals, legumes, vines, and fruit. Archaeozoological remains

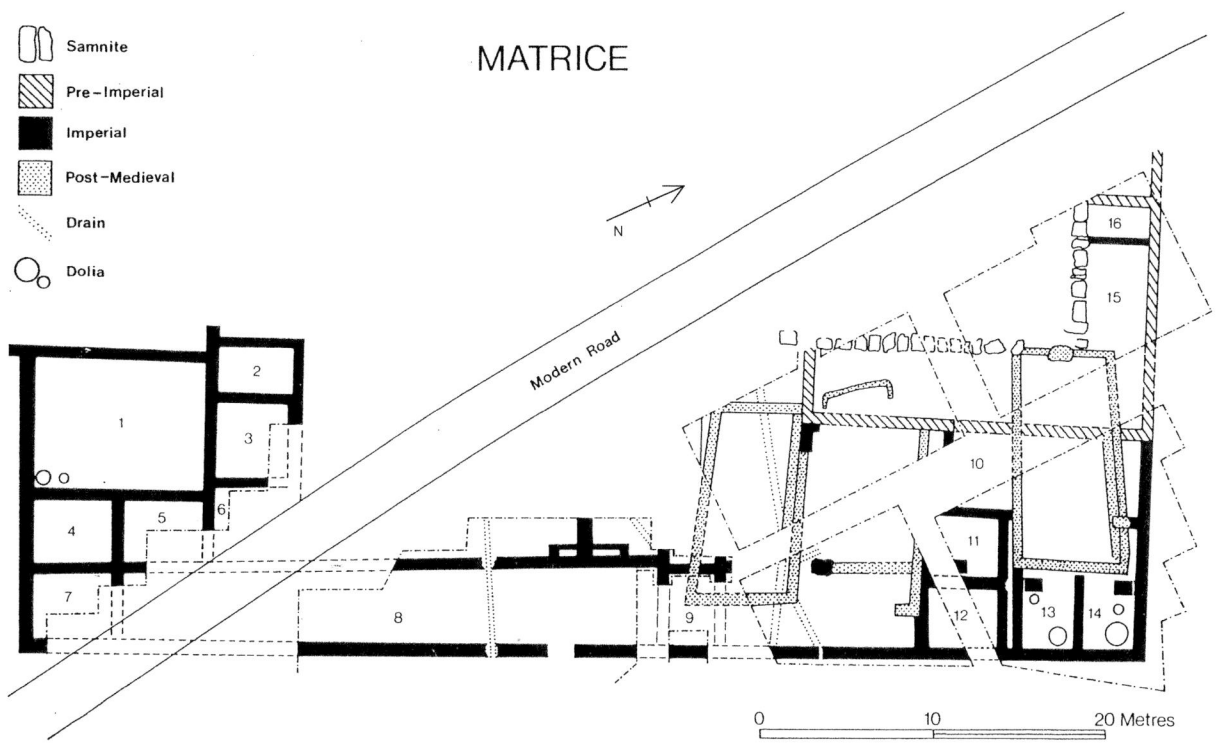

Figure 30.2. The archaeological site of Santa Maria della Strada at Matrice (after Barker 2001, fig. 85).

indicated the presence of pig and sheep/goat (Lloyd 1991b: 262; Lloyd *et al.* 1983; Lloyd *et al.* 1982: 9-11; Lloyd 1981).

The only traces of modest decoration were found in a few rooms on the eastern side of the road, including large mosaic *tesserae* embedded in a mortar floor and small fragments of coloured wall-plaster. Unfortunately, those rooms were disturbed by a series of pits and later construction layers (Lloyd *et al.* 1982: 8; Lloyd 1981: 1). Nevertheless, a proper *pars urbana*, normally expected in a Roman *villa rustica*, is missing at Matrice. The lack of high-quality architectural decoration, mosaics, and frescoes has suggested that the owner did not live there but in the nearby town. The estate may have been under the management and control of a *vilicus* (Roberts 1988: 33-59). However, categorising the structure within a specific type of building is challenging. It seems likely that the villa of Matrice portrays a unique type of building that strongly reflects the specific geographical and cultural context in which it is situated. Imported pottery and amphorae from Puglia, Campania, and North Africa were found as well as fine, non-local tableware – indicators of the villa's setting within commercial networks of exchange.

Despite a period of decline in the 2nd and 3rd centuries AD, artefacts and coins suggest occupation at least up to the 5th-early 6th centuries AD. The burial of an infant in a drain deposit, dated to AD 550, may mark a significant moment within the history of the site's abandonment (Lloyd 1984). It remained unoccupied until the 1600s when an agrarian building – probably a barn – was constructed over the ancient ruins (Lloyd 1984: 2).

Previous Archaeological Research

The first important survey of this area of Samnium was conducted over *c.* 400km[2] by Graeme Barker, between 1974 and 1978. The Biferno Valley Survey located several rural settlements and identified different patterns of land occupation (Barker 1995; 2001). In the upper valley, 26 sites dated to the Imperial period were identified, including the villa at Matrice. The number of sites is smaller than the previous Samnite period and the building at Matrice stood out as one of the few known in the area where the density of habitation decreased in the Roman period.

The archaeological site at Matrice is crossed by a modern asphalt road (SP140) (Figure 30.1). The structure was first discovered and came to the attention of the Soprintendenza per le Antichità del Molise, during the construction of SP140 in the 1970s. During the Biferno Valley Survey it was provisionally identified by Graeme Barker and John Lloyd as a Roman *villa rustica*. Given the interest of John Lloyd in investigating a small to medium-sized farmstead and in consideration of the visible remains, which suggested a good state of preservation, the site was chosen for excavation. The structures, in fact, seemed to be only partially damaged by the road construction and offered a suitable case study (Lloyd 1981). Between 1980 and 1984, a joint team from the Universities of Sheffield and Aberdeen led by John Lloyd in collaboration with the local authority of the Soprintendenza, undertook several seasons of excavation (Lloyd *et al.* 1984). Whilst large parts of the site were exposed, the complete layout of the villa remained unclear due to the presence of the road and the superimposed post-medieval building. The premature death of John Lloyd in 1999 led to an interruption of the research and publication of the excavation, which was reported only as preliminary notes.

Renewed Research by the British School at Rome, Ashmolean Museum of Oxford University, and King's College London

A new phase of research, funded by the Society for the Promotion of Roman Studies, started in 2017 as a joint study directed by Stephen Kay (British School at Rome), Paul Roberts (Ashmolean Museum of Oxford University), and Dominic Rathbone (King's College London). The aim of the project is to complete the study of the villa, continuing the work of John Lloyd, and better understand the role of the site within the Roman rural landscape of Molise, as well as bring the site to publication.

The first stage of fieldwork aimed to identify features that might assist in ascribing, with more certainty, the typology of the site. As described above, the building at Matrice lacks some elements typical of central Italian Roman *villae rusticae* (Marzano 2007). A season of geophysical prospection was carried out to: a) complete the plan of the villa; b) assess whether it extended towards the west (on the opposite side of the road SP140); and c) verify the extent of the structure to the north, south, and east (Pomar 2024). This would be followed by two seasons of excavation to verify the results of the geophysics and to collect precise stratigraphic and chronological information (Kay *et al.* 2019; Kay *et al.* 2023).

Geophysical Survey[1]

Geophysical prospection was used to investigate the accessible areas around the villa with the aim of defining the limits of the site and locating further structures. The survey combined two techniques: magnetometry and Ground-Penetrating Radar (GPR). Where possible, the latter was preferred for its higher

data resolution and to provide information concerning depth. Magnetometry was used in an area of 0.5ha to the west of the road, which was mostly unsuitable for GPR due to the rough terrain and sloping topography.

On its north-eastern side, the villa is surrounded by a dense wooded area and GPR prospection was carried out between the trees where access allowed. A strip of the SP140 road was also surveyed with the purpose of documenting buried walls that linked the two areas of the building. Finally, GPR survey was completed where possible on areas close to the excavation trenches from the 1980s.

The magnetometry survey used a Bartington fluxgate gradiometer along parallel traverses at an interval of 0.5m with readings collected every 0.25m. The GPR survey used a GSSI SIR-3000 instrument coupled with a 400MHz antenna with a traverse interval of 0.25m. The latter survey was split over several different areas, due to varying topography and ground surfaces, which required different instrument settings.

Survey Results

West of the road, the magnetometry survey did not show an extension of the site to the south of the excavated structures or to the west of the southern wing. However, a positive magnetic anomaly, measuring *c.* 9.5 × 5.5m and oriented north-west-south-west, was recorded in the central area of the survey (*M1* in Figure 30.3). This strong positive value indicated the presence of highly magnetic material, for example fired objects, such as tiles or bricks. This technique is particularly sensitive to this type of material, which has a thermoremanent magnetisation resulting from a production process where the clay is subject to high temperatures (Aspinall *et al.* 2008: 21-22). The anomaly's regular, almost-rectangular geometry and alignment with the excavated structures indicated that it was a feature of archaeological interest. The strength of the signal and dimensions of the anomaly, however, suggested an accumulation of magnetic material rather than a large, solid structure. The interpretation of this feature (*M1*) remained unclear and required further investigation. To the north of *M1* other scattered magnetic anomalies were located (*M2* in Figure 30.3). While they potentially indicated the continuation of the villa to the west of the road, and were, thus, of potential archaeological interest, their interpretation remained uncertain. The GPR survey grid that overlapped the area surveyed by magnetometry, just south of *M1*, did not record any significant features (Figure 30.4).

The GPR survey outside the northern, eastern, and southern perimeter of the villa aimed to determine whether any structures continued into the wooded

[1] The geophysical survey, undertaken by the BSR in 2017, was led by Stephen Kay with Elena Pomar and Gabriella Carpentiero.

Figure 30.3. Magnetic map of the gradiometer survey carried out west of the modern road SP140, with the anomalies *M1* and *M2* indicated (by author).

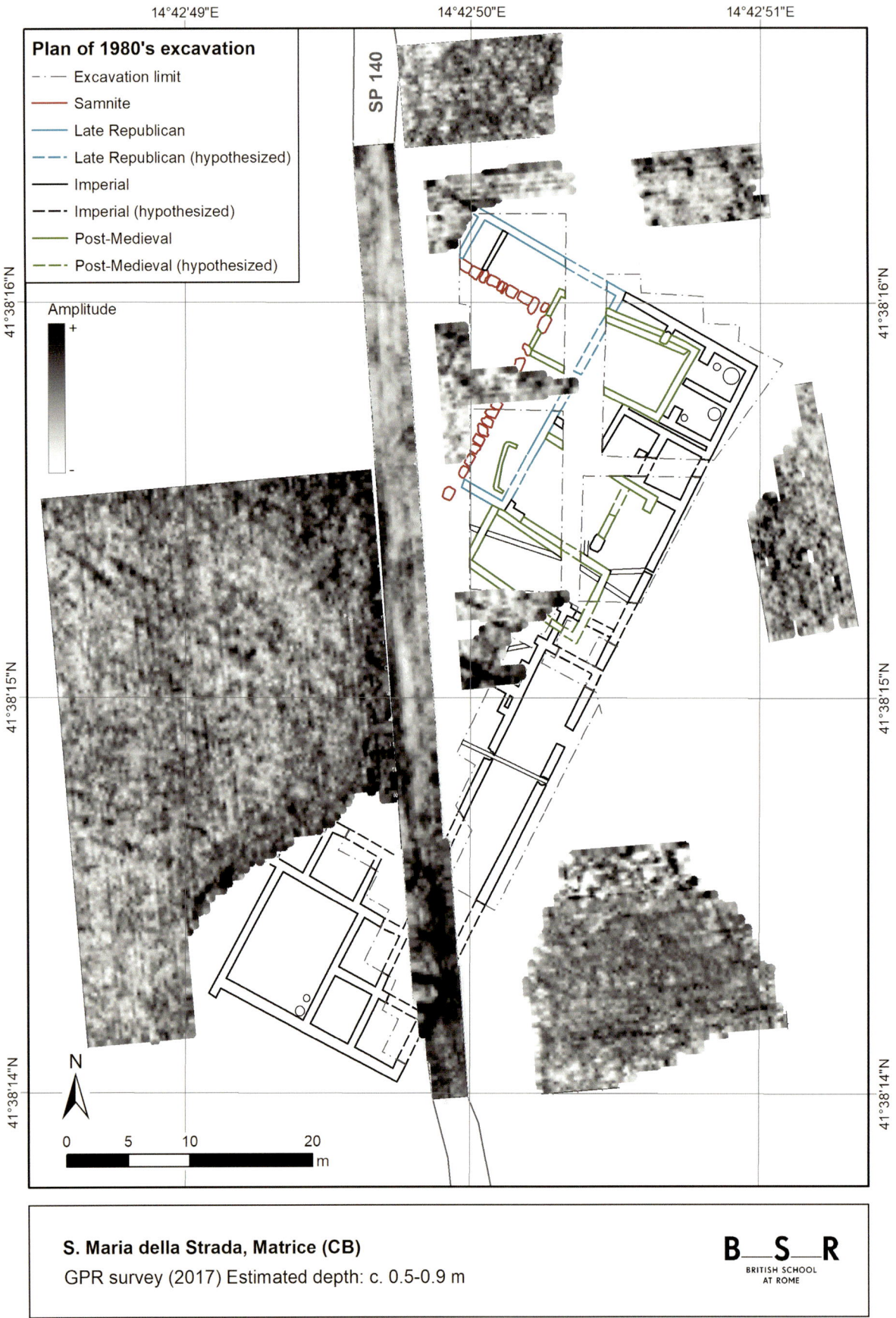

Figure 30.4. Amplitude time-slice of the GPR survey at an estimated depth of *c.* 0.5-0.9m (by author).

area and whether the previous excavation correctly interpreted the southern wall as an external wall. The results indicated that the villa does not appear to extend further east and south.

The most significant GPR data was collected along the modern asphalt road and in areas closer to the 1980s trenches (Figures 30.4 and 30.5). A series of walls buried under the road were located on the southern wing of the villa (*G1* in Figure 30.5). These recorded features display a distribution slightly different from the hypothesised plan and, therefore, allowed adjustments to be made. Further to the north, the absence of structures recorded by the GPR, both along and to the west of the road, supports the hypothesised presence of a courtyard in the central section of the building.

The GPR survey adjacent to the 1980s trenches provided further detail regarding the plan of the building and located a series of structural features. The alignment of some of these with the known trajectory of excavated walls has permitted a hypothesis to be made as to the phasing of the features (Figures 30.5 and 30.6). The northernmost GPR grid within the excavation area recorded a continuation of the northern wall, while the central grid recorded a series of walls, including one belonging perhaps to the Samnite phase. The southernmost grid appears to be an area with a complex stratigraphic archaeological sequence in the first 3m below ground level. Several archaeological features were located here, including a high amplitude reflector of circular shape at a depth of *c*. 1m (*G2* in Figure 30.6). This feature was interpreted as a possible well, due to its shape and its continuation at deeper levels.

2018 Excavation Season

Following the geophysical survey some areas required further investigation. In 2018, five areas (see Figure 30.7) were selected for excavation to: a) analyse the stratigraphic sequence of target areas highlighted by the GPR survey (Areas 1, 2, and 5); b) inspect the rectangular magnetic anomaly *M1* (Area 3); and c) investigate the potential western continuation of the northern wall across the modern road (Area 4) (Kay *et al.* 2019).

The large magnetic anomaly *M1* led to a concerted excavation effort in Area 3 during the 2018 season. Just below the topsoil a series of walls delimiting a rectangular space (*c*. 7 × 3.5m) were found. Two sondages at the eastern and western ends of the rectangular structure were dug, reaching a floor surface preserved 1.42m below, and this uncovered a cistern filled with heterogenous collapsed material (Figure 30.8). The material indicated that it was disused by the 3rd century AD. The cistern structure was built of tiles

and stones, lined with red *cocciopesto*, and a tiled roof (the remains of which were found in the collapsed layer above the floor). On the eastern side, the cistern lies against a thick foundation wall cutting across a drain, which was only partially exposed along the trench limit. Originally the drain, running north-west-south-east, probably joined the villa, but it seems that it was damaged by modern road construction, since it was not located by the GPR survey along SP140. The discovery of this cistern improves our understanding of the water supply to the villa.

The excavation in Area 1 revealed structures belonging to three different phases: republican, imperial, and late antique. The architecture and alignment of the excavated structures generally confirmed the prior interpretation of the geophysical survey; however, the high amplitude reflector (*G2* in Figure 30.6), which was initially interpreted as a possible well, was shown to be multiple superimposed walls of subsequent phases (Figure 30.9). These included a late republican wall, partially demolished and substituted by a new structure in the imperial phase, and a late antique drain.

In Area 2, seven large roughly trimmed limestone blocks of the 2nd century BC were exposed in alignment with the limestone wall already excavated. This confirmed the geophysical interpretation of the feature identified as a possible Samnite wall. The wall seems to indicate a division of the internal space of the building, like Cercemaggiore where a series of rooms surround a central courtyard.

The geophysical interpretation was confirmed in Area 5, where a segment of the villa's northern limit wall was excavated. Excavations here also exposed an occupation layer of the 5th century AD.

On the opposite side of the modern road, the excavation in Area 4 uncovered a structure heavily disturbed by deep ploughing and the construction of the road.

Further Works

After a brief hiatus, due to the COVID pandemic, the project carried out further geophysical prospection in 2022 to explore the area surrounding the church of Santa Maria della Strada. The survey aimed to verify possible links between the archaeological site and the area of the medieval church. The GPR survey was carried out to assess any pre-existing occupation of the area. The results showed a series of structural features on the same alignment as the church and are likely related to its initial phase as a monastery. The new data collected are currently subject to analysis and archival comparison and will help to better understand the earlier phases of the church's history. However,

Figure 30.5. Interpretation of the GPR survey results at an estimated depth of *c*. 0.5-0.9m (by author).

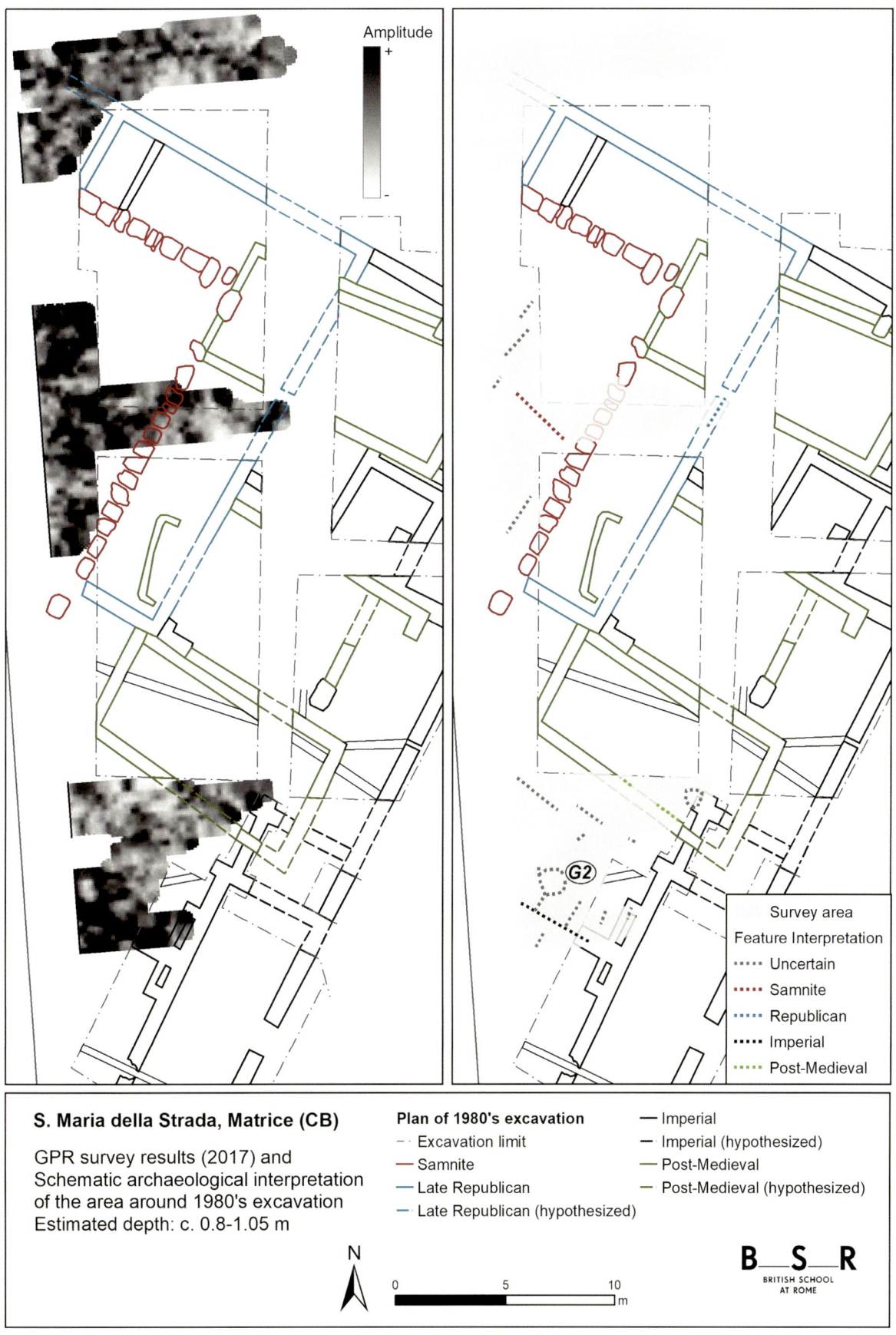

Figure 30.6 Interpretation of the GPR survey results at an estimated depth of *c.* 0.8-1.05m, with the anomaly *G1* indicated (by author).

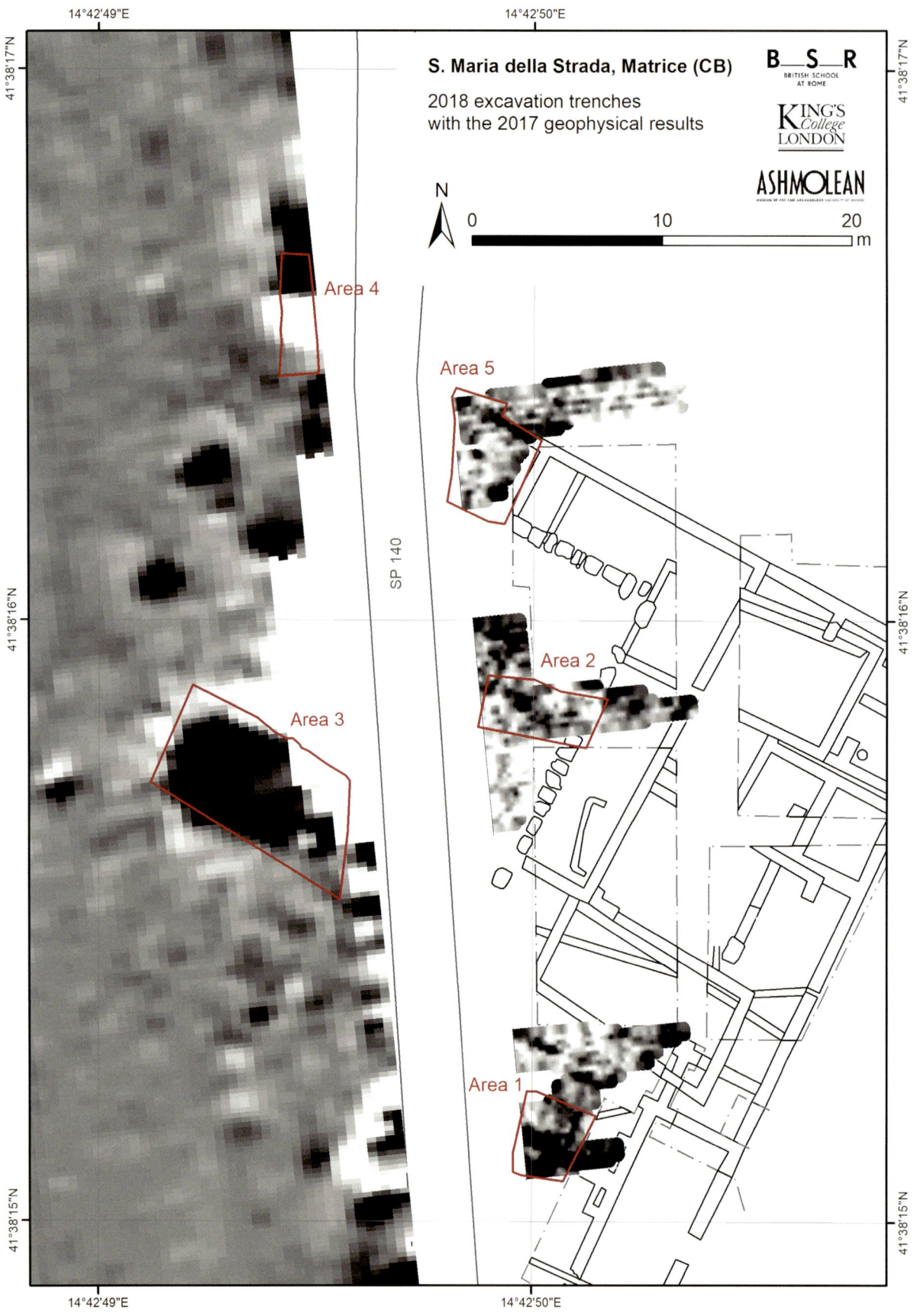

Figure 30.7. Location of the trenches excavated in 2018 in relation to the 2017 geophysics results (by author).

Figure 30.8. 3D photogrammetric model of the cistern excavated in Area 3 (by author).

the results do not seem to show evidence related to a potential previous Roman occupation.

In 2023 a new season of target excavation was carried out to further collect stratigraphic data and explore the initial phase of the site (Kay *et al.* 2023). The results of 2023 season are not discussed in this paper, whose focus was the comparison and integration between non-invasive survey and archaeological excavation. All the data that have been collected since the beginning of the project in 2017 will be included in the final publication of the site together with the revisited data from the 1980s excavations.

Discussion

From a methodological perspective, the Matrice archaeological project made strategic use of geophysical survey before excavation to identify and target areas of interest. Non-invasive geophysical prospection was also the only possible way to investigate below the modern asphalt road and, thus, record buried walls to complete the plan of the villa's southern wing. Survey in the areas around the villa helped to ascertain the extent of the site. An absence of features recorded by the GPR in these peripheral areas indicates the site's probable limit and a lack of other structures in the immediate vicinity of the villa.

Whilst the use of geophysical techniques provided important support to the excavation, the latter also helped to verify the geophysical interpretation. The magnetic anomaly *M1* was initially thought to be an accumulation of archaeological material, but excavation revealed a Roman cistern with the strong magnetic signal caused by collapsed roof tiles filling the structure (Area 3). Similarly, the feature *G2*, detected by the GPR survey, was initially interpreted as a well; however, excavation uncovered a much more complex stratigraphic situation, which would have been impossible to interpret with only the geophysical data. The discovery of the cistern showed for the first time how the occupants of the villa collected and stored water. Moreover the dimensions and capacity of the cistern suggest that the water stored was insufficient for agricultural irrigation (Pomar 2024). Therefore it is likely that the agricultural products cultivated did not require intensive irrigation, an hypothesis compatible with viticulture.

The archaeological site at Santa Maria della Strada, Matrice, is one of many that were enlarged around the mid-1st century AD with the use of new building techniques, such as *opus reticulatum*, and acquired new importance in the rural landscape (Witcher 2020). The development of the villa might be framed in the reorganisation of Samnium, after the Social War, begun by Julius Caesar, whose intervention is attested with certainty at *Bovianum* (Letta 2021). These recent investigations at Matrice have, however, confirmed the absence of some distinctive elements of the Roman *villa rustica* considering its definition as an elite villa in a

Figure 30.9. Excavation in Area 1 (photo Stephen Kay).

rural context that was involved in agricultural activities but also in the practice of *otium* (Marzano 2007: 83-87). These villas developed close to urban centres, and many are known in the countryside surrounding Rome itself. The structure at Matrice does not seem to share the luxurious decoration, infrastructure, and architecture of other *villae rusticae* – though the degree of luxurious 'elite' varies widely – nor their socio-cultural significance and, thus, does not achieve the same status of 'villa'. The dimensions of the building during the Imperial period, the presence of specialised installations and imported material show, on the other hand, an organisation more complex than that expected in rural houses and farmsteads engaged in subsistence economy. The scale of production at Matrice increased in relation to the new organisation of the territory, as also noted at other sites of the Samnium (Fratianni 2017: 274-76). However, the latter can be more easily associated with the Roman villas, often displaying baths and rich decorations (Iasiello 2007: 155-73; Fratianni 2017: 281-88). The villa at Matrice can be framed within the general evolution of rural sites of the region, proportional to its small scale and marginal situation.

An additional aspect to consider is the proximity of the site to communication and transport routes. It was clearly embedded within networks of exchange and interregional connectivity is reflected in the ceramic material, highlighting access to goods from North Africa, Puglia, and Campania (Roberts 1988). The importance of this strategic position has been stressed previously, although there is still not enough evidence to conclusively support the identification of the building as a *mansio* (cf. Lloyd *et al.* 1984: 219).

Considering this evidence, the Roman site at Matrice possesses various characteristics that do not clearly place it within a rigid structural or settlement category. The villa exhibits peculiarities derived from its local context. A member of the elite of *Faegifulae* might not experience the same prosperity as the elite class of a large city – such a phenomenon could be reflected in the modesty and small dimensions of this rural estate. While humble, within their geographical and chronological context, the owner of the villa must have been of local importance. It is also clear that at Matrice agricultural and practical production was prioritised over social needs and the desire to display opulence.

Conclusion

The site of Matrice offers a unique case study to observe the development of a rural site over the *longue durée*. The long story of the site is likely to be the result of the tight connection of the area with communication routes. In particular the importance of the transhumance routes, *tratturi*, have been fundamental for the economy of the Apennine central Italy from antiquity to the modern era. Reflections here are not conclusive and a comprehensive study by the project team is in progress. This includes environmental and archaeozoological analysis, the classification of pottery, and the study of other materials and small finds. The final stage of this project, prior to publication, will involve the integration of the more recent information with the considerable quantity of data generated during the project under John Lloyd.

Acknowledgements

I would like to take this opportunity to share my gratitude towards Simon, who was strongly supportive of my work at the British School at Rome. As Chair of the archaeology department, he encouraged my participation in many different projects, including that at Matrice.

I would like to thank the directors of the project, Dominic Rathbone, Paul Roberts, and Stephen Kay, for involving me in such interesting research. I also would like to thank my colleague Emlyn Dodd (previous Assistant Director at the BSR) for his stimulating comments on the text.

The geophysical surveys and excavation were conducted with the support and permission of the Soprintendenza Archeologia, Belle arti e Paesaggio del Molise and the Comune di Matrice. The geophysical prospection was funded by a grant from the Society for the Promotion of Roman Studies and the excavation by King's College London, the Ashmolean Museum Oxford University, and the British School at Rome.

Bibliography

Aspinall, A., C. Gaffney and A. Schmidt 2008. *Magnetometry for Archaeologists.* Plymouth (RI): AltaMira Press.

Barker, G. 1995. *A Mediterranean Valley: Landscape Archaeology and Annales History in the Biferno Valley.* Leicester: Leicester University Press.

Barker, G. 2001. *La Valle del Biferno: Archeologia del territorio e storia annalistica.* Campobasso: Istituto regionale per gli studi storici del Molise 'V. Cuoco' Premio 'E.T. Salamon'.

Buonocore, M. 2002. *L'Abruzzo e il Molise in età romana tra storia ed epigrafia.* L'Aquila: Edizioni libreria Colacchi.

Ceccarelli, A. and G. Fratianni 2017. *Molise* (Archeologia delle regioni d'Italia). Rome: Bradypus.

Di Niro, A. and P. Petrone 1993. Insediamenti di epoca sannitica nel territorio circostante la Valle del Torrente Tappino (Campobasso, Molise). *Papers of the British School at Rome* 61: 7-50.

Gianandrea, M. 2018. Il complesso di Santa Maria della Strada presso Matrice nel Medioevo, in F. Marazzi (ed.) *Molise medievale cristiano: edilizia religiosa e territorio (secoli IV-XIII)*: 433-45. Cerro al Volturano: Volturnia Edizioni.

Iasiello, I.M. 2007. *Samnium. Assetti e trasformazioni di una provincia dell'Italia tardoantica*, Bari, Edipuglia.

Kay, S., P. Roberts and D. Rathbone 2019. The Samnite and Roman settlement at Santa Maria della Strada (comune di Matrice, provincia di Campobasso, Regione Molise). *Papers of the British School at Rome* 87: 341-45.

Kay, S., D. Rathbone and P. Roberts 2023. The 2022 excavations at the Samninte and Roman settlement at Santa Maria della Strada, Matrice (provincia di Campobasso, regione Molise). *Papers of the British School at Rome* 91: 342-45.

Keay, S., M. Millet, S. Poppy, J. Robinson, J. Tylor and N. Terrenato 2004. New approaches to Roman urbanism in the Tiber Valley, in H. Patterson (ed.) *Bridging the Tiber: Approaches to Regional Archaeology in the Middle Tiber Valley* (Archaeological Monograph of the British School at Rome 13): 223-36. Rome: The British School at Rome.

Jaminson, E. 1938. Notes on Santa Maria della Strada at Matrice, its history and sculpture. *Papers of the British School at Rome* 14: 32-97.

Johnson, P., S. Keay and M. Millet 2004. Lesser urban sites in the Tiber Valley: Baccanae, Forum Cassii and Castellum Amerinum. *Papers of the British School at Rome* 72: 69-99.

Letta, C. 2021. La municipalizzazione tardiva del Sannio, in T.D. Stek (ed.) *The State of the Samnites* (Papers of the Royal Netherlands Institute in Rome 69): 65-78. London: Edizioni Quasar.

Lloyd, J.A. 1981. The Roman Villa at Matrice. A preliminary report on the 1981 excavations. Unpublished excavation report.

Lloyd, J.A. 1984. Excavations at the villa rustica near Matrice, Italy, 1984. Unpublished excavation report.

Lloyd, J.A. 1991a. Farming the highlands: Samnium and Arcadia in the Hellenistic and early Roman Imperial periods, in G. Baker G. and J. Lloyd (eds) *Roman Landscape: Archaeological Survey in the Mediterranean Region* (Archaeological Monographs of the British School at Rome 2): 180-93. London: The British School at Rome.

Lloyd, J.A 1991b. The Roman Villa at Santa Maria della Strada, Matrice, in S. Capini and A. Di Niro (eds) *Samnium: archeologia del Molise*: 261-62. Rome: Quasar.

Lloyd, J.A. and D. Rathbone 1984. La villa romana a Matrice. *Conoscenze* 1: 216-19.

Lloyd, J.A. and D. Rathbone 1983. Excavation at the Matrice Roman villa, Italy, 1983. Unpublished excavation report.

Lloyd, J.A., D. Rathbone and A. Upson 1982. The Roman villa at Matrice. A report on the third season of excavation. Unpublished excavation report.

Marzano, A. 2007. *Roman Villas in Central Italy: A Social and Economic History*. Leiden: Brill.

Patterson, J.R. 2004. Samnium under the Roman Empire, in H. Jones (ed.) *Samnium: Settlement and Cultural Change*: 51-68. Providence: Brown University.

Pomar, E. 2024. La villa romana di Matrice tra geofisica e scavo. *Archeologia e calcolatori* 35.1: 329-48.

Roberts, P. 1988. Pottery and settlement in the province of Molise during the Roman Imperial period. Unpublished PhD thesis, University of Cambridge.

Rothe, U. 2018. The Roman villa: definitions and variations, in A. Marzano and G.P.R. Métraux (eds) *The Roman Villa in the Mediterranean Basin: Late Republic to Late Antiquity*: 42-62. Cambridge: Cambridge University Press.

Witcher, R. 2020. The early and mid-imperial landscapes of the middle Tiber Valley (c. 50 BC – AD 250), in H. Patterson, R. Witcher and H. Di Giuseppe (eds) *The Changing Landscapes of Rome's Northern Hinterland: The British School at Rome's Tiber Valley Project*: 117-207. Oxford: Archaeopress.

31. *Septempeda:*
Integrating Non-invasive Surveys, Legacy Data, and New Stratigraphic Evidence in the Mapping of a Roman Townscape in *Picenum*

Frank Vermeulen and Devi Taelman

Introduction

Urbanism, as an instrument of colonial policy for Rome, but also as an engine for the self-development and organisation of integrated socio-economic territories, reveals itself quite distinctly in central Adriatic Italy. In this predominantly hilly region south of the Po Plain, and between the Apennines and the Adriatic coast, mainly coinciding with the early Imperial Region V (*Picenum*) and parts of Region VI (*Umbria et ager Gallicus*), with one of the highest concentrations of towns in the whole Roman Empire, urbanism played an enormous role in stimulating change and adaptation (Silani 2017; Vermeulen 2017). Frantic documentation by hundreds of local researchers between the 18th century and the beginning of the new millennium has created a wealth of data about the Roman towns of central Adriatic Italy, and particularly in the modern region of Marche (Luni 2003). Many observations in towns with continuity – and this is still the majority of towns in this region – are, however, very partial and limited, and the full scientific information required is documented only in certain favourable conditions. The difficult and rather sparse excavations in current town centres over a long period have created a problematic bias towards monumental architecture, public buildings of the Imperial period, but provided much less information about the oldest phases and early evolution of Roman towns, the precise extent of the urban centres, and crucial aspects of urbanism such as street networks, functional zoning, and the nature of domestic architecture. More progress in crucial knowledge acquisition about regional urbanism has been made in the past two decades, thanks to a landscape archaeology approach to the phenomenon of towns and their effect on the hinterland. This evolution was much spurred by the activity of British archaeologists working in the Tyrrhenian part of central Italy, and the role played by Simon Keay in this new dynamic was no doubt pivotal. In the 1990s there was a realisation in Roman archaeology in the Mediterranean that the same techniques which had markedly changed the study of the wider landscape might also revolutionise our understanding of urban sites. This was greatly enacted in the Italian Peninsula by landmark projects such as the study of *Falerii Novi* (Keay *et al.* 2000) and later of *Portus* (Keay *et al.* 2005; Keay 2012), as well as by the general refinement of geophysical techniques and aerial photography that could be used for the fine-grained analysis required to bring out the details of an urban layout (Guaitoli 2003; Johnson and Millett 2013; Vermeulen 2011). The consequence of these developments, including the widespread use of GIS in archaeology, has been an upsurge in the non-destructive survey of urban sites, in central Adriatic Italy as elsewhere in the peninsula (e.g. Christie and Augenti 2012; Corsi *et al.* 2013; Vermeulen 2013; Vermeulen *et al.* 2012). Large and complex urban sites, which had previously been studied with a piecemeal approach largely directed by the monument-based interests of earlier scholars, were now increasingly being 'scanned' using survey techniques to cost-effectively generate plans of partial, or, in some cases, complete townscapes. This has also led to a revolution in how archaeologists approach urban sites, with survey techniques being used increasingly to collect more data about the extent, the internal organisation, and even the chronology of the towns. It has also led to investigations of the full range of urban sites available, and not just those in a good state of preservation, or where the financial means or the right administrative or scientific context were available for excavation. Greenfield sites were especially suited to such a holistic approach, where the ancient population had partly or often completely abandoned their original urban area to move elsewhere.

Today, better and more reliable information about urban site size and layout, and sometimes even early town development, can be found in a series of deserted towns in the central Adriatic region, where almost 50% of the Roman town sites were partly or totally abandoned or displaced after the Roman Imperial period. The strategy of extensive non-invasive survey was introduced here from 2002 onwards by a Ghent

University team directed by one of this article's authors (FV), in particular in the town sites of *Potentia, Ricina, Trea*, and *Septempeda* in northern *Picenum* (Vermeulen *et al.* 2017). The approach has since then been applied by several teams working in recent years on abandoned Roman towns and their hinterlands in the region (e.g. *Suasa, Ostra, Sentinum, Forum Sempronii, Tifernum Mataurense*), which before 2000 were known only via a few excavated 'windows' in their sometimes ill-defined town areas. A whole series of these partially or fully abandoned Roman towns are now being uncovered via intensive total surveys, integrated into apposite excavations in carefully selected areas. Such well-integrated strategies mean that it is now not only possible to obtain good information about their size, general internal organisation, and functions during their heydays, but sometimes also to gain a better understanding of the early phases of town formation, and of certain changes and sometimes radical shifts in the urban development of these centres. In this way it is now within reach to derive a realistic hierarchy of town sites in the region, based on better estimations of size and associated population numbers, and more meaningful observations are also likely regarding the degree of urbanisation, the interrelationship between urban centres in the region, urban networks, and the integration or complementarity of towns with each other within the wider regional context.

In what follows we wish to focus attention on the strategy and main results obtained in one of the four towns studied by the Ghent team of archaeologists, *Septempeda*. Not only is this a town where the non-invasive field operations were very successful, contributing in a major way to the understanding of the ancient topography, but it is also here that the most recent fieldwork operations (summer 2021) were undertaken, providing some fascinating first-hand results.

Septempeda, a Small Town on the Road from Rome to Ancona

The site of *Septempeda*, near San Severino Marche (Macerata, Marche), can best be defined as the location of an Imperial Roman urban centre, possibly preceded by a mid- to late Republican village, situated along a *diverticulum* of the *via Flaminia* that links the consular road from Nocera Umbra through the valley of the River Potenza to Ancona and the Adriatic coast (Figure 31.1). The Roman site was abandoned in early medieval times, and was replaced by a fortified hilltop site near the current town centre of San Severino, some two kilometres south-west of *Septempeda*. The ancient Roman site is located directly north of the River Potenza, on a relatively flat to slightly sloping river terrace formed during the Pleistocene, but the former town

area also encloses a small hill stretching immediately north of this terrace. Today arable land prevails, and the small rural *pieve* church and a few modern houses are the only constructions in the now legally protected archaeological park, whose limits coincide more or less with the abandoned Roman town area.

Fieldwork by several actors during the 20th century led to the excavation of an Imperial Roman bath complex in *Septempeda*, of small parts of at least two early Imperial *domus* with mosaics, some stretches of town streets, and several elements of the city wall, including two monumental gates with towers in the south-western and eastern sides of the wall circuit (Landolfi 2003; Landolfi and Perna 2004). The main extramural remains of Imperial times discovered in that period include small groups of Roman burials located near the main outgoing road west and east of the city centre and parts of a large pottery workshop outside the presumed western gate. All these testimonies point to a certain urban floruit during the early Imperial period partly hiding an older past. The very limited data on the origin of the city suggests that the core of this urban settlement was a roadside agglomeration, still called *oppidum* in the *Liber Coloniarum* (Blume *et al.* 1848: 253). Probably soon after establishment, when Roman and Latin colonists settled here in the late 3rd or early 2nd century BC, the place received the status of *praefectura* to control the surrounding area. It became a *municipium* only around the mid-1st century BC (Paci 1998; Sisani 2006). This rise in status was preceded by the erection of a monumental city wall, in the *opus quadratum* technique, with local sandstone blocks, incorporating the habitation nucleus near the river and the adjoining small hill (a possible *arx*) into an enclosed irregular area of approximately 15ha. The still ill-understood old settlement core along the east-west oriented *via Flaminia per Picenum Anconam* certainly comprised a late Republican artisanal unit that produced black gloss ceramics, while certain reused architectonic decoration fragments found in the later bath complex suggest the existence of a late Republican sacral building nearby, maybe to be identified with the temple for the goddess Feronia (CIL 5711, Landolfi 2003: 58-59). It is not yet clear when exactly the city wall construction can be dated, but suggestions have been made of a date connected with events a few years after the Social War, such as an intervention by Sulla who settled the veterans of war operations in *Picenum* in their region of origin shortly after 90 BC (e.g. at *Auximum*), and this is currently the most likely option (Perna 2012: 386-87). That one of the gates belonging to this wall, in the south-west of the city, was built over a series of 2nd- to early 1st-century BC graves, demonstrates the spatial expansion of the settlement by the beginning of the last century BC. It looks as if a former burial area was by this time incorporated into the now larger settlement with urban features.

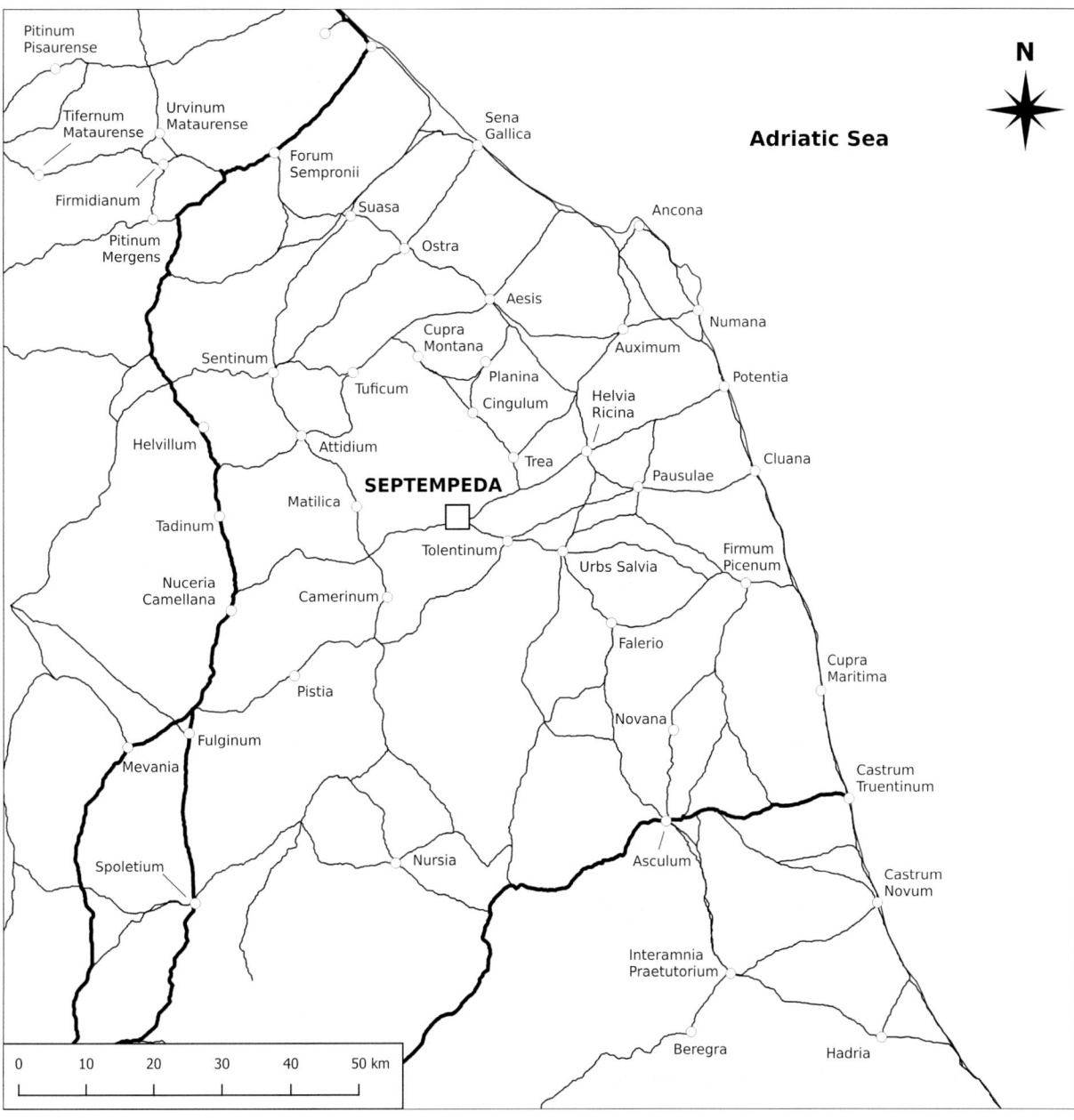

Figure 31.1. Main road network and towns in central Adriatic Italy during the early Imperial period (D. Taelman).

So while the 20th-century excavations and the study of antiquarian collections of sculpture and epigraphy from the territory of *Septempeda* (Landolfi 2003; Marengo 1996) revealed essential but very fragmented information about the ancient town, most of the urban topography remained obscure. This was not helped by the almost silent ancient written sources about the city, or by the fact that no above-ground traces of its architecture remain visible today. Since 2004, however, the site has been the object of more systematic archaeological investigations, using a battery of techniques currently employed for urban surveys on greenfield sites in the Mediterranean. On the one hand,

a series of non-invasive prospections allowed the team of Ghent University to get a firm grip on the internal organisation of the urban topography of this Roman town (Vermeulen *et al.* 2017: 126-27). The main field operations of the Belgian archaeologists so far include monitoring with oblique and low-altitude aerial photography, geophysical prospection of the whole city site using magnetic, georadar, and earth resistance methods, artefact surveys, and the study of the high-resolution satellite imagery and LiDAR data. On the other hand, a whole series of limited stratigraphic excavations and trial trenches, dug under the supervision of the Soprintendenza Archeologia Belle

Arti e Paesaggio of the Marche region, and a focused augering campaign by the Ghent team, allowed some of the older excavation and remote sensing evidence to be verified in recent years, and the discovery of a whole series of new structures pertaining to the city defences and to several intra- and extramural areas. Both approaches, the non-invasive and the invasive, and the most relevant new information on urbanism and architecture resulting from them, are briefly presented here.

Non-invasive Survey Strategy

It was a major aim of the Ghent University 'Potenza Valley Survey project' (Vermeulen et al. 2017) that started in 2000, and of which the study of Septempeda is a part, to supplement existing but 'static' remote sensing material, such as vertical aerial photographs and satellite images, with new images taken from the air, with a more direct archaeological impact. This new material, closely integrated with information from intensive fieldwork in the Potenza river valley, was obtained from a systematic programme of low-altitude aerial photography conducted along the entire, approximately 80-km-long valley. Although the site of Septempeda had long since been located and identified, these aerial photography flights did not for a long time procure the expected crop- or soil marks of its buried remains. This changed dramatically in September 2004 when flights showed a whole series of distinct crop marks in fields of alfalfa herbs covering large parts of the intramural areas, allowing us to reveal many elements of the urban street network (Figure 31.2), of the architecture in housing sectors, and of the location of the forum. More intensive monitoring from the air in the following years, and an especially successful flight in July 2007, procured a mass of new topographic information about the eastern edge of the city. Here, a previously unknown south-eastern gate was revealed and, next to the now clearly visible outgoing road, a monumental complex with porticoes was discovered, initially interpreted as a possible sanctuary. Monitoring the whole city area by way of classic aerial photography in subsequent seasons and years could not procure extra elements of the ancient town, although some near infrared imagery taken in April 2007 over the eastern area from a so-called 'helikite' delivered excellent details of the south-eastern gate and the nearby city wall (Verhoeven et al. 2009). A few extra structures of the ancient city were discovered during the continuing campaigns of traditional aeroplane reconnaissance until 2014, but these did not reveal important additional aspects of the town's topography. Only very recently, in July 2021, when the stressed crops of alfalfa again gave away many of the underlying buried archaeological structures during a prolonged period of drought, has a palimpsest of new elements of the town's housing sectors (Figure 31.6) and street system been revealed.

Following the excellent results of the aerial reconnaissance work, a multi-method geophysical research strategy was conceptualised from 2010 onwards (Figure 31.3). Due to time and funding constraints, the focus was initially on the central and eastern areas of the city, including the extramural zone where the newly discovered complex with porticoes was located. In September 2010, collaboration with a team from the University of Ljubljana allowed an examination of this particular area using magnetometry and earth resistance prospection (Vermeulen et al. 2017: 86-88). The techniques were deployed over roughly the same area, covering just over 4ha, using a caesium gradiometer and twin probe resistance meter. A Geoscan Research RM15 and PA5 probe array were used for earth resistance mapping on a regular grid of 1 by 1m, with separation between mobile probes of 0.5m. Twin pole array gives a good depth of investigation: under favourable conditions of ground humidity, the effective depth at which signals are detected is 1.0m at 0.5m separation between mobile probes. Using a Geometrics G-858 caesium gradiometer (0.05nT resolution), measurements were taken at a 0.2s acquisition time, which gives a sample interval of about 13cm along profiles laid out at 0.5m intervals. A second geophysical campaign was organised in July 2021 in collaboration with a team from the Berlin-based company Eastern Atlas. Magnetometer prospection now covered most of the remaining accessible parts of the site (and its immediate extramural surroundings), bringing the total surface covered in the 2021 campaign near to 10ha (Figure 31.4). The surveys were conducted using two mobile LEA MAX systems mounted on flexible carts, one with four Sensys gradiometer probes and one with ten Förster FEREX CON 650 probes, equally mounted at 0.5m distance, and with a 0.05m sampling interval. A differential GPS and a survey wheel were used to position the survey data.

Two additional geophysical techniques were tested in order to obtain more detailed information for specific structures detected or suggested by the previous techniques, namely a large rectangular structure belonging to the large square with porticoes east of the urban area, the immediate surroundings of the excavated bathhouse in the city centre, and the western gate and its adjoining features on the other side of the city. The Ghent team proceeded in July 2013 with a georadar survey on the eastern site, using 500MHz antennas, however, no structures were detected with this technique. As also observed during GPR prospection on other sites in the region, this could be attributed to the conductive properties of the soil, which had a high clay content, which could attenuate the radar waves to a large extent, even in dry circumstances. On the western edge and in the centre of town, a series of deep 2D vertical sections were made by the Berlin team, making resistivity measurements along profiles of 40

Figure 31.2. Aerial photograph taken of *Septempeda* taken from a drone in July 2021, showing crop marks of streets and building structures visible in alfalfa vegetation (photo M. Aballe)

Figure 31.3. Geophysical prospection coverage at the site of Septempeda, with the proposed location of the Roman wall circuit indicated (ill. D. Taelman).

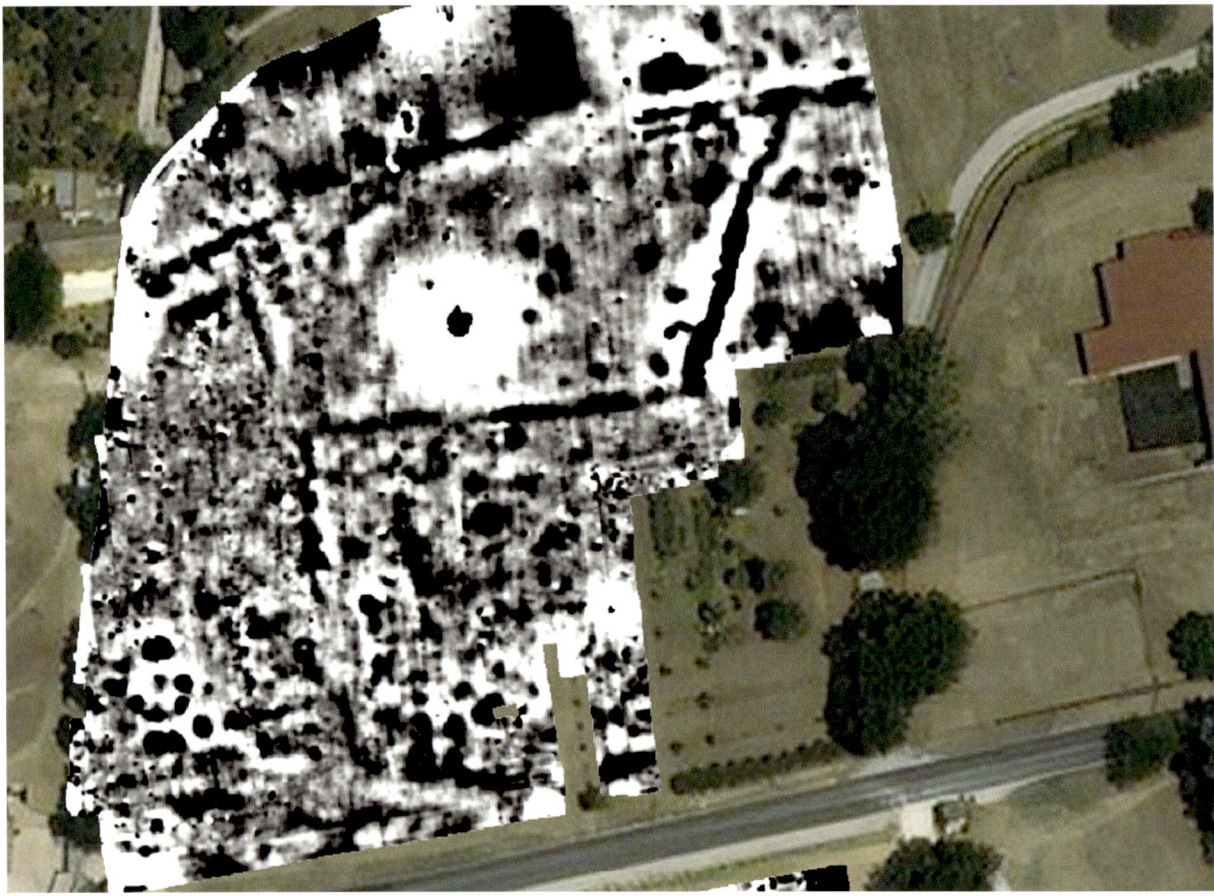

Figure 31.4. Magnetometer results from 2021 in the western part of the city area, overlaid on a vertical aerial photograph. Well visible are several city streets, the western gate and many other archaeological features (ill. Eastern Atlas)

and 59m length with an electrode distance of between 0.5 and 1.0m using the 4Point*light* resistivity meter. The positioning and depth measurement of the city wall and additional anomalies related to a tower along the wall, and some probable lime kilns located near the gate, were the satisfactory results of this spatially smaller exercise.

Recent Invasive Archaeological Operations

Between 2004 and 2018, and thus simultaneously with the phase of survey operations, a whole series of small-scale stratigraphic excavations and trial trenches were conducted on the urban site under supervision of the Soprintendenza Archeologia Belle Arti e Paesaggio. These opportunities for subsoil verification were offered by the development-led archaeology resulting from and financed by interventions to enhance the modern infrastructure of the municipality of San Severino. They comprise: the building of a roundabout immediately west of the site, the construction of an underground aqueduct crossing the whole ancient urban area from west to east along the modern road that follows the line of its *decumanus maximus*, and the implementation of some works near modern houses in

the western and southern part of the site (Figure 31.5). Although the locations of most of these interventions were not the result of deliberate archaeological choices, the outcome of these well-documented excavations allowed us to compare stratigraphic data with the results from remote sensing operations. They allowed us to verify some of the older excavations and to discover a whole series of new structures pertaining to the city defences, and to structures and architecture in several intra- and extramural areas. They added very valuable information about the dating, depth, and character of the presumed archaeology, confirmed or changed many hypotheses, and also provided a good sample for the study of the material culture of this city. In total, approximately 1,250 m² was excavated in this opportunistic manner.

More planned, but much less invasive in nature, was a hand-augering campaign organised by the Ghent archaeological team in July 2021. The aims of the augering survey were to improve our understanding of the near-surface geology, the geomorphological situation, and the evolution history of the site, to verify the nature of particular features detected by geophysical and aerial survey, to determine the depth

Figure 31.5. View of the 2015 rescue excavation of one of the Roman towers along the southern stretch of the city wall circuit (ill. Soprintendenza Archeologia Belle Arti e Paesaggio of the Marche region)

and character of archaeological deposits and to detect and date the earliest Republican phases of the town, and if possible to obtain samples for environmental analysis. The augering focused on two sectors: a north-south transect almost fully crossing the urban area in its central part (ten augerings) and the western intramural sector of the city (24 augerings), where a whole series of crop marks remarkably revealed structures such as roads, housing floors, and the west gate at the time of

this campaign. Eijkelkamp hand auger equipment was used for the survey, equipped with different auger types (Edelman auger, stony soil auger, spiral auger, soft soil auger, stone catcher, and riverside auger) depending on the dominant sediment texture. Augerings were stopped when natural soil was reached (generally not deeper than 2.5m). At several locations, the augering was obstructed at a very low depth (40-55cm), due to a layer of building materials or rubble, or at the depth

Figure 31.6. View of crop marks indicating rectangular building structures in the western part of the city area (ill. D. Taelman).

of sturdy structures found '*in situ*', such as the ancient road deck, building walls/foundations, or an intact floor.

Fieldwork Results

The results of the remote sensing operations with wider spatial impact (aerial photography, magnetometer, and earth resistance prospection) in particular, have allowed the mapping, in recent years, of many elements of the basic urban plan of *Septempeda*. Presumably this map predominantly illustrates the shape of the city in the phase in which it flourished the most, the early Imperial period, even if several elements (city wall, forum, etc.) were planned here earlier, surviving necessary adaptations and changes throughout the centuries (Figures 31.7, 31.8). Although the quality and resolution of the new data from the town's infrastructure cannot attain the completeness and fascinating details reached recently by the full GPR prospection of an urban site dear to Simon Keay, namely *Falerii Novi* (Verdonck *et al.* 2020), a great deal of progress has been made in understanding what this small city must have looked like. At *Septempeda*, the resulting survey data can now

be clearly linked to stratigraphic observations from the recent small-scale excavations and augerings, and from the legacy data incorporating less well-documented but still important excavated structures (e.g. bathhouse, two gates). We will summarise here the most significant results from this integration of data.

The monumental city wall, built in *opus quadratum* and measuring on average slightly more than 2m in width, is approximately 1.5km long. The many observations of its underground remains, using almost all the field approaches mentioned above, combined with observations in the field and LiDAR imagery of height differences in the terrain surface (especially along its northern trace), allow us to specify its irregular pentagonal circuit. It incorporated almost the whole habitation nucleus near the river and an adjoining small hill to create an extra element for defence and visual control. Stratigraphic excavations near the east gate in 2018 showed that the wall was flanked on its inner side by an earthen bank (*agger*) 9 to 10m wide, probably bordered on the town side by a small wall or ditch. Bank and ditch were confirmed by remote sensing in several areas of the circuit, respectively by aerial photography

Figure 31.7. Provisional map of the major features detected within the urban area of *Septempeda* (ill. F. Vermeulen/D. Taelman).

in the east part of the wall circuit and deep earth resistance prospection near the west gate. The wall had at least five monumental entrance gates (east, south-east, north, west, and south-west), two of which – the south-eastern and western gates – were detected only by remote sensing, and one – the northern gate – which remains somewhat hypothetically positioned on the map. Apart from the towers connected with the gates – the western, south-western, and eastern gate each with two towers, the south-eastern gate with only one – a series of isolated towers was also found (Figure 31.5), creating a defensible wall circuit with strong points at more or less regular inter-distances varying between 50 and 90m. Most of the towers are round, with a diameter of some 7.5m, but near the south-eastern gate a rectangular tower was constructed, indicating maybe a later date and addition to the defensive system. The two gates connected with the main central east-west street of the city were no doubt the most important, as they ultimately connected *Septempeda* with Rome (western gate) and Ancona (eastern gate). The excavated south-western gate, which possibly gave access to a necropolis and maybe to a crossing (bridge?) over the River Potenza, was also equally impressive. All four discovered gates are of the so-called courtyard

type, with an inner courtyard with the axis of the court extending perpendicularly inward from the line of the wall. Outwards, the three main courtyard gates were half closed by an additional stretch of wall joining two flanking towers, thus creating a very defendable semicircular or piriform concave outer space. This type of gate was developed in the Hellenistic East and was introduced in Italy in a series of late Republican cities built by Rome, in particular during the reign of Sulla (Perna 2012).

The often spectacular and very detailed aerial and geophysical imagery of traces interpretable as buried streets allow us to map large parts of the town's Roman street system (Figures 31.4, 31.6). This survey data can be linked to stratigraphic observations of the streets in a few places, both inside and outside the wall circuit, such as via small-scale excavations near the existing *pieve* church, the baths, and immediately west of the town area, and via a few augerings following up on the remote sensing evidence. These observations show that, at least during the early Empire, most streets were paved, and that they had an average width of no more than 4m. The street system of a Roman town is partly conditioned by the need for connections with its

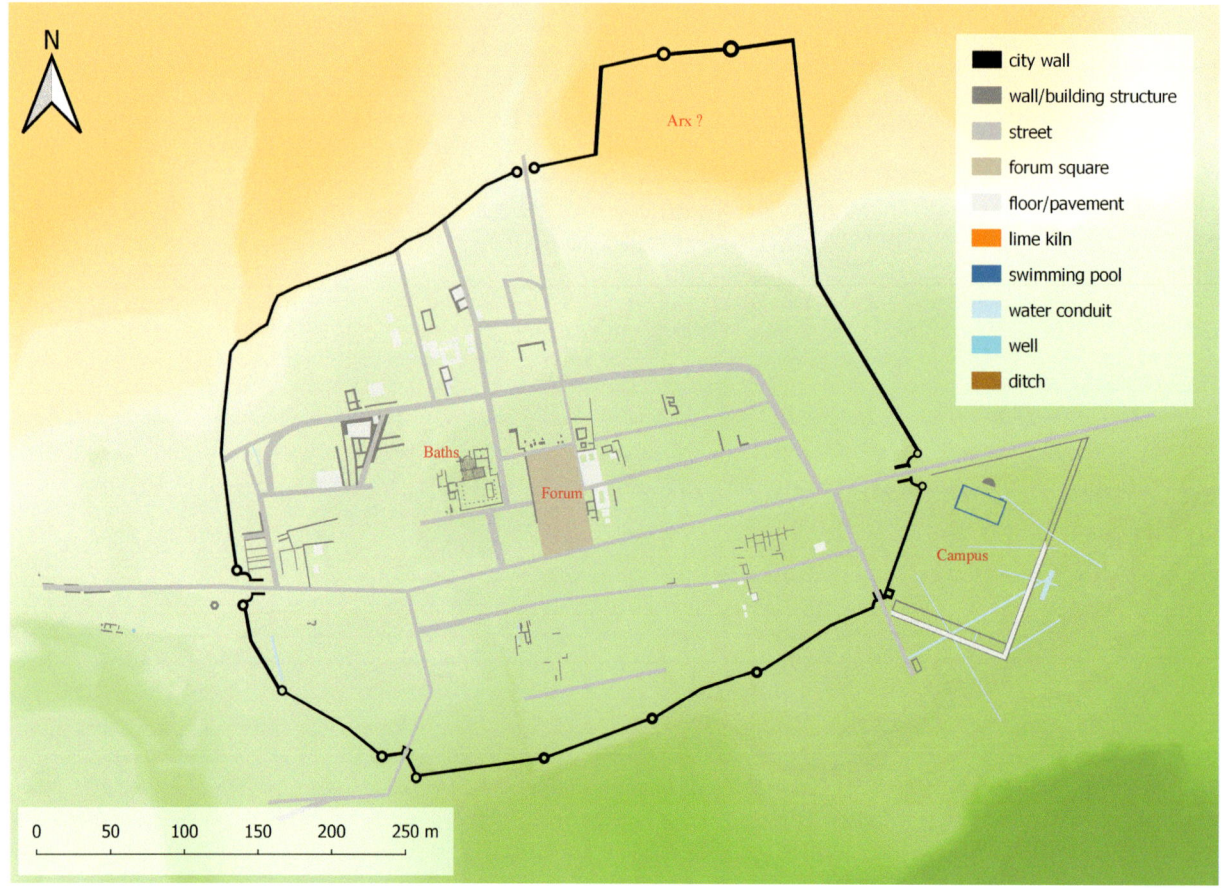

Figure 31.8. Provisional map of the major features detected within the urban area of *Septempeda*, with proposed functional interpretations (ill. F. Vermeulen/D. Taelman).

territory, and with the world beyond its borders, and partly by the urbanistic planning of the city centre itself. In *Septempeda* the east-west oriented *diverticulum* linking the *via Flaminia* at *Nuceria* (Nocera Umbra) with the Adriatic coast became the conditioning factor, as it was from the street village around this *decumanus maximus* that the urban reality emerged, and that access was given to far away Rome and Ancona (and their related coastal areas) and to other towns in or near the Potenza Valley, such as *Camerinum, Matilica, Trea, Ricina,* and *Potentia.* Other internal city streets were connected to the three remaining gates, giving access to the agricultural areas north of the city, to cemeteries, and to the valley floor and the presumed river crossing in the south, beyond which other nearby towns, such as *Tolentinum* and *Urbs Salvia* could be reached. Although the city planning does not seem to have involved a very strict orthogonal street system, and the network of observed and assumed streets might have grown rather gradually, there was surely an intention to create a series of axes parallel to the central road, and a few perpendicular connections to ensure easy access all around. This evolution must be seen in association with the demographic bloom of the settlement whose living quarters perhaps only slowly filled the intramural space once the town wall was built.

To convey the idea of a Roman town, a forum was developed in the very centre of the settlement, along the main east-west street. The insertion of such a public centre, probably in the late Republican roadside settlement of *Septempeda* (Vermeulen 2024) can, together with the completion of the wall circuit, be seen as crucial for the urbanism effort during the 1st century BC. It demonstrates the adaptation of Italic population centres to the new standards of the Roman way of life and surely promoted the acculturation of the local population. It is probably here that cults for the gods Feronia and Jupiter, both attested by inscriptions (Marengo 1996), and later for the emperor, must have concentrated their activity. But it was also a marketplace, well connected to the road system, and the focus for the whole surrounding territory, as well as the place for the legal, political, and cultural matters of the community. The precise location of the forum of *Septempeda* was only discovered in 2009. Thanks to the integration of aerial photography with geophysical prospection, it was possible to map a rectangular square of roughly 60 by 30m, positioned with its longitudinal axis perpendicular to, and immediately north of the main *decumanus*. The square was at some point in time surrounded by a series of public buildings and monuments, such as a possible basilica to the north, the (excavated) bath complex to the west, and perhaps several temples and *tabernae* to the east. The southern limit was formed by the central east-west street and maybe by a series of rich *domus* that, according to some limited excavation evidence, were concentrated in this sector of town. Although there is still a lack of precise chronological information about the different buildings surrounding the forum square, it can be presumed on the basis of parallels in the region that the period between the last decades of the 1st century BC and the 2nd century AD were the main phases of transformation and the monumentalisation of this city centre. More detailed chronology is only available for the bathhouse, which was probably built in the early 1st century AD, and may have been in use until the early 5th century AD.

The character and evolution of housing in Roman *Septempeda* is still difficult to trace, as no fully excavated houses are known so far. Thanks to discoveries during explorations in the 1920s and 1970s in an area south-west of the forum, where four mosaic floors and the remains of painted stucco were found and minimally documented, and more recently due to the integration of aerial photography, geophysics, and focused augering, it is now possible to map parts of houses in almost all intramural sectors of the city. Very provisional data indicates that the richer and larger ones, belonging to the *domus* type that emulates Hellenistic and central Tyrrhenian residences, are mostly to be found near the central area, especially near the forum and along the main *decumanus*. They are characterised by their elongated rectangular shape, a certain symmetry, the presence of an *atrium* surrounded by rooms at the centre, and often one or more *peristilia* towards the back. Excavation and augering evidence suggest the use of solid building materials, and sometimes more luxurious mosaic floor decorations in several houses. Of course, smaller houses, or combinations of simple housing with typical economic urban infrastructure (e.g. shops, workshops) must also have been present, but these are more difficult to identify among the ephemeral evidence of crop marks. Along some streets and around the forum a few *tabernae* are certainly suggested by the remote sensing evidence, and near the western gate a large construction with parallel elongated rooms might even suggest the presence of a *horreum* for food storage.

The archaeological excavations have further demonstrated that certain extramural parts of *Septempeda* were the subject of urban expansion during the first decades of the Imperial period. While there is still no theatre or amphitheatre, which are typical dominant urban landmarks, among the discoveries, the monumental precinct found via aerial photography east of the eastern gate and city wall can now definitely be identified as the first archaeologically attested *campus* in central Adriatic Italy (Vermeulen *et al.* forthcoming). Its discovery during a reconnaissance flight in 2004 was later confirmed by the geophysical prospections of 2010, and in 2019 by the partial excavation, in the framework of the construction of a modern aqueduct, of its main central structure: a large swimming pool approximately 30m long and 15m wide. This *natatio* was located centrally in an open courtyard (of approximately 12,000m^2) bordered by the city wall, two porticoes, and the outgoing main urban street leading to the coast. The sports complex was, according to a first evaluation of the finds, built in the 1st century AD. The original meaning of the word *campus* is that of a free and flat space, used as a multifunctional public area with a civic purpose: the physical training and armed exercises by the young citizens of a community take place here. This physical training, in particular arms drill, horse riding, and swimming, but also gymnastics and other sports, was supposed to complete their intellectual training (Borlenghi 2011). The *campus* is also one of the main public spaces intended for the community, where each person has the opportunity to take care of their body, to devote themselves to exercises, to walk and to socialise in the shade of trees or under sheltering porticoes. In a relatively small town like *Septempeda* the presence of such a complex might also have replaced the need for a more monumental, but also more expensive, amphitheatre building. The mapping and identification of this particular complex, including its water distribution and evacuation system, is a fine example of the need to integrate a series of approaches to arrive at an acceptable mapping result and interpretation. Here, more than anywhere else in the city, the data from aerial photographs, magnetometry, earth resistance survey, augering, artefact survey, and finally some excavations demonstrated the complementarity of archaeological methods. It is noteworthy that the use of legacy data also led to knowledge acquisition, by combining aerial photography and some recovered archive data. We noted a dark linear cropmark on the aerial photos taken during the first successful flight over the site, of approximately 1m wide starting near the now excavated north-western corner of the *natatio* and crossing the field until its limit in a south-eastern direction. This trace can now be connected with a chance discovery from April 1989, during construction works for a new house on the plot immediately east of this terrain. A well-constructed Roman sewer was found, which drained the water from the now identified swimming pool to the south-east until it probably discharged into or near the Potenza River. No datable finds were recovered during the inspection works, but the quality of the sewer structure, with a roof made of *tegulae* placed 'a capuccina' and two side walls of mortar mixed with clay and river pebbles, agrees well with the early Imperial construction date of the *natatio*.

Conclusion

The example of *Septempeda* clearly illustrates the importance of using integrated non-invasive archaeological strategies to study the topography and urbanism of (partly) abandoned Roman towns. At the same time, the GIS-based processing of now adequately positioned and analysed stratigraphic data from old and recent excavations and augering observations was necessary in order to propose reliable interpretative mapping and to obtain crucial indications of the urban chronology. This is equally true for the many still understudied ancient urban sites in Italy and beyond that, because limited modern excavations and non-existent survey approaches still await decent mapping and wider understanding.

The small city of *Septempeda* can now more reasonably be situated within the evolution and Romanisation of this part of Italy. The main transformation from street village to urban reality probably involved a number of steps during the course of the 1st century BC and the first decades of the 1st century AD. When the monumental city wall was built and new members of the community, from *Latium* and the Adriatic region itself, started pouring in, the crucial components of the urban fabric were given their final shape. It is possible that the major civic and public amenities around the forum were projected and erected in the decades after the rise to the status of *municipium*, during the second half of the 1st century AD and the reign of Augustus. Possibly the expansion beyond the walls was in full operation only in the later part of Julio-Claudian times, or even under the Flavians. The socio-culturally important *campus* must then have been added to the public infrastructure of this city, neatly squeezed as it is, on a large extramural plot between two outgoing roads. The cemeteries and a series of extramural workshops may also have only fully extended beyond the walls during the early Imperial period, giving this town its full maturity, and its maximum archaeological visibility to this day.

Acknowledgements

This research was organised by Ghent University, Department of Archaeology, and predominantly funded by the Fund for Scientific Research – Flanders and Belgian Science Policy. We are grateful for support from the Soprintendenza Archeologia Belle Arti e Paesaggio of the Marche region, in particular from the responsible archaeologist for this area Dr Tommaso Casci Ceccacci. For the geophysical prospection the Ghent team was assisted by teams from Eastern Atlas (dir. Dr Burkhart Ullrich) and Ljubljana University (dir. Prof. Božidar Slapšak). Finally, the authors thank all other staff members and students of the Potenza Valley Survey team participating in the fieldwork, the services of the municipality of San Severino Marche, and the landowners and users of several plots on the site of *Septempeda*.

Bibliography

Blume, F., K. Lachmann and K. Rudorff (eds) 1848. *Gromatici veteres: Die Schriften der römischen Feldmesser*. Berlin: Reimer.

Borlenghi, A. 2011. *Il campus: organizzazione e funzione di uno spazio pubblico in età romana; le testimonianze in Italia e nelle province occidentali*. Rome: Quasar.

Corsi, C., B. Slapsak and F. Vermeulen (eds) 2013. *Good Practice in Archaeological Diagnostics: Non-invasive Survey of Complex Archaeological Sites* (Natural Science in Archaeology 69). Cham: Springer.

Christie, N. and A. Augenti (eds) 2012. *Urbes extinctae: Archaeologies of Abandoned Classical Towns*. Farnham: Ashgate.

Guaitoli, M. 2003. *Lo sguardo di Icaro: le collezioni dell'Aerofototeca Nazionale per la conoscenza del territorio*. Rome: Campisano Editore.

Johnson, P. And Millett, M. 2013, *Archaeological Survey and the City*. Oxford; Oxbow.

Keay, S. (ed.) 2012. *Rome, Portus and the Mediterranean* (Archaeological Monographs of the British School at Rome 21). London: The British School at Rome.

Keay, S., M. Millett, L. Paroli and K. Strutt (eds) 2005. *Portus: An Archaeological Survey of the Port of Imperial Rome* (Archaeological Monograph 15). London: The British School at Rome.

Keay, S., M. Millett, S. Poppy, J. Robinson, J. Taylor and N. Terrenato 2000. Falerii Novi: A New Survey of the Walled Area. *Papers of the British School at Rome* 68: 1-93.

Landolfi, M. 2003. *Il Museo Civico Archeologico di San Severino Marche*. San Severino Marche: Città di San Severino Marche.

Landolfi, M. and R. Perna 2004. Septempeda, in G. Paci, G.M. Fabrini and R. Perna (eds) *Beni Archeologici della Provincia di Macerata*: 89-91. Pescara: Carsa.

Luni, M. (ed.) 2003. *Archeologia nelle Marche: dalla preistoria all'età tardoantica*. Florence: Mondadori.

Marengo, S.M. 1996. *Septempeda* (Supplementa Italica, n.s. 13): 193-228. Rome: Quasar.

Paci, G. 1998. Dalla prefettura al municipio nell'agro Gallico e Piceno, in *Los orígenes de la ciudad en el Noroeste Hispánico: actas del congreso internacional (Lugo, 15-18 de Mayo 1996)*: 55-64. Lugo: Deputación de Lugo.

Perna, R. 2012. Nascita e sviluppo della forma urbana in età romana: alcuni casi nelle città delle Regiones V e VI, in G. De Marinis, G.M. Fabrini, G. Paci, R. Perna and M. Silvestrini (eds) *I processi formativi ed evolutivi della città in area adriatica* (British Archaeological Reports, International Series 2419): 375-99. Oxford: Archaeopress.

Silani, M. 2017. *Città e territorio: la formazione della città romana nell'Ager Gallicus*. Bologna: Bononia University Press.

Sisani, S. 2006. *Umbria, Marche: guide archeologiche Laterza*. Rome: Laterza.

Verdonck, L., A. Launaro, F. Vermeulen and M. Millett 2020. Ground-penetrating radar survey at Falerii Novi: a new approach to the study of Roman cities. *Antiquity* 94: 705-23.

Verhoeven, G., J. Loenders, F. Vermeulen and R. Docter 2009. Helikite aerial photography – a versatile means of unmanned, radio controlled, low-altitude aerial archaeology. *Archaeological Prospection* 16: 125-38.

Vermeulen, F. 2011. Reviewing 10 years of aerial photography in the valley of the River Potenza (Le Marche). *Archeologia aerea* 4-5: 259-64.

Vermeulen, F. 2013. Interdisciplinary non-invasive survey approaches to ancient towns: some applications and visualisations from the Roman West, in J. Poblome (ed.) *Exempli Gratia: Sagalassos, Marc Waelkens and Interdisciplinary Archaeology*: 165-82. Leuven: Leuven University Press.

Vermeulen, F. 2017. *From the Mountains to the Sea: The Roman Colonisation and Urbanisation of Central Adriatic Italy* (Babesch Supplements 30). Leuven: Peeters.

Vermeulen, F. 2024. Septempeda: integrated approaches for revealing a 'small town' in Picenum, in A. Launaro (ed.) *Roman Urbanism in Italy: Recent Discoveries and New Directions*: 138-50, plates 9.1-9.2. Oxford: Oxbow.

Vermeulen, F., G.J. Burgers, S. Keay and C. Corsi (eds) 2012. *Urban Landscape Survey in Italy and the Mediterranean*. Oxford: Oxbow.

Vermeulen, F., T.Casci Ceccacci andG. Cilla (2020), Scoperta di un campus extra-murale nella città romana di Septempeda (Picenum), Archeologia Aerea 14: 33-47.

Vermeulen, F., D. Van Limbergen, P. Monsieur and D. Taelman (eds) 2017. *The Potenza Valley Survey (Marche, Italy): Settlement Dynamics and Changing Material Culture in an Adriatic Valley between Iron Age and Late Antiquity* (Academia Belgica. Studia Archaeologica 1). Rome: Fondazione Dià Cultura.

32. Comercialización del broccatello de Dertosa en Álava/Araba[1]

Isabel Rodà, Miguel Loza, Javier Niso y Anna Gutiérrez Garcia-M.

Cuando estábamos acumulando material para confeccionar este trabajo, lo hacíamos con la ilusión de poder ofrecer a Simon Keay un trabajo que le gustara tratando un tema al que había dedicado su atención en los últimos tiempos: la cuestión de las redes comerciales por vía acuática. También, su última conferencia en Barcelona (noviembre de 2019) abordó directamente el tema del mármol: "Making Rome a city of marble: reconsidering the organization of marble import, storage and distribution at Portus" (Keay 2022). Él, desde Portus, había hecho crecer un amplio proyecto sobre los puertos marítimos mediterráneos para cuyo desarrollo mereció ser el director de un importante ERC Advanced Grant. Un puerto esencial para el comercio de un preciado material lapídeo fue el de *Dertosa*, actual Tortosa, que capitalizó la exportación del preciado broccatello o jaspe de la Cinta por diferentes puntos de Hispania y del Mediterráneo occidental, pero también a través de la gran vía fluvial que fue el *Hiberus*, hoy el río Ebro. No imaginamos nunca que Simon no llegaría a ver editado el volumen que, con todo nuestro pesar, ahora es póstumo. Sean estas líneas un sentido homenaje a quien fue no sólo un gran arqueólogo sino una persona con unas enormes cualidades por las que fue querido y admirado, además de ser profesor y amigo desde sus primeros trabajos en la Tarraconense; siempre estará en nuestros pensamientos y corazones.

El broccatello

Este *marmor* fue el más apreciado de entre los polícromos explotados en la península Ibérica en época romana.

No se trata de un mármol geológicamente hablando, sino que es una caliza con aspecto de lumaquela, formada por restos malacológicos varios, con una amplia gama de coloraciones, desde los amarillos más intensos hasta los colores rojizos y violetas que los italiano denominaron como "broccatello" porque evoca un brocado de oro sobre un fondo púrpura. En Cataluña se le da también el nombre de "jaspi/jaspe de la Cinta" porque con placas de este material se recubrió la capilla de la Virgen de la Cinta en la Catedral de Tortosa. Es un material lapídeo muy compacto que permite un pulido de gran calidad (Àlvarez *et al.* 2009b: 74-79).

Las canteras se encuentran cerca de la ciudad de Tortosa, el *municipium* romano de *Dertosa*; las más conocidas son las llamadas "Pedrera dels Valencians" y "Pedrera de la Cinta" por ser ésta última la que proporcionó el material para las placas de revestimiento de la capilla antes mencionada (Gutiérrez Garcia-M. 2009: 229-45; 2020: 23-25). Sin embargo, existen muchos otros puntos de extracción en sus alrededores, testigos de la intensa explotación, y algunos de los cuales han sido identificados muy recientemente (Gutiérrez Garcia-M. y Muñoz 2022: 461-63). Por lo que a sus usos se refiere, lo más habitual son placas de revestimiento arquitectónico, cornisas y otros elementos usados en la arquitectura (fustes de columna y más raramente capiteles tardíos). También se empleó como soporte epigráfico; en cambio por sus características físicas no es un material dúctil para ser utilizado en la manufactura de esculturas.

La exportación de este material tuvo un gran radio de difusión por amplias zonas de la península Ibérica, en especial el Levante y los valles del Guadalquivir y el Ebro. También llegó a muchos puntos del Mediterráneo occidental, como Narbona en el sur de Francia, Útica en Túnez, hasta Ostia y Roma (además de las obras citadas en las dos notas anteriores, con bibliografía sobre el tema, v., Àlvarez *et al.* 2011; Falcone y Lazzarini 1998: 87-97; Mayer y Rodà 1999: 43-52; Lazzarini 2004: 118, fig. 24; AA.VV. 2009; Gutiérrez Garcia-M. 2014; 2021; Rodà y Alcubierre 2020).

Gracias a las excavaciones llevadas a cabo en el foro de *Segobriga* (Cuenca), y en concreto de la curia, se pudo demostrar que la explotación del broccatello se inició en época augustea (Àlvarez et al. 2009a). En época altoimperial fue ampliamente usado y exportado, continuando su auge en la Antigüedad tardía, como demuestra su uso masivo en algunas *domus* y villas

[1] Trabajo realizado dentro del proyecto de investigación, falta inicio de "*Sulcato marmore ferro (SULMARE)*. Canteras, talleres, artesanos y comitentes de las producciones artísticas en piedra en la Hispania Tarraconensis" (PID2019-106967GB-I00). Queremos expresar nuestro profundo agradecimiento a la actual directora del Museo de Arqueología de Álava/Arabako Arkeologia Museoa. BIBAT, Jaione Aguirre García y a Raúl Sánchez Rincón, técnico del mismo museo por su inestimable ayuda durante la realización de este estudio. También hacemos extensivo nuestro agradecimiento a quien estaba en 2014 al frente del Museo, Javier Fernández Bordegarai, actualmente Jefe del Servicio de Museos de Arqueología, y a la técnica, Elisa García Retes, en servicio hasta su jubilación en 2020; realmente ambos nos facilitaron el acceso a todo el material que pudimos consultar con toda comodidad en 2014.

remodeladas y monumentalizadas en esta época (Rodà y Alcubierre 2020).

El broccatello en Álava/Araba

La vía navegable del Ebro fue el gran camino para la penetración hacia el interior de este llamativo material lapídeo; los puntos de dispersión quedaron ya cartografíados de modo somero pero bien ilustrativo por L. Lazzarini (2004: fig. 24) y se han ido completando en los últimos años; ejemplo de ello es la identificación del significativo empleo de broccatello en las termas suburbanas de *Pompelo*, hoy Pamplona (García-Entero *et al.* 2024). En la gran capital conventual que fue *Caesar Augusta*, Zaragoza, se empleó abundantemente en el enlosado de la *orchestra* del teatro (Lapuente et al. 2006); piezas tan emblemáticas como el pilar de la Virgen y

el sarcófago de santa Engracia fueron elaborados en broccatello.

Para entender el mensaje simbólico de este material lapídeo, baste mencionar que para el sepulcro más venerado no se recurrió a sarcófagos esculturados importados de los talleres de Roma, sino a un sarcófago de paredes lisas pero, eso sí, de los vistosos colores que proporcionaba el broccatello; las recientes excavaciones lo han puesto de manifiesto (Mostalac 2014: 12-14 y 56-61).

De todas maneras, sorprende la gran cantidad inesperada de piezas para decoración arquitectónica que llegaron a dos yacimientos alaveses:

Iruña-*Veleia* y Arkaia-*Suestatium* (Figuras 32.1 y 32.2). Lo pudimos comprobar en una estancia de investigación en

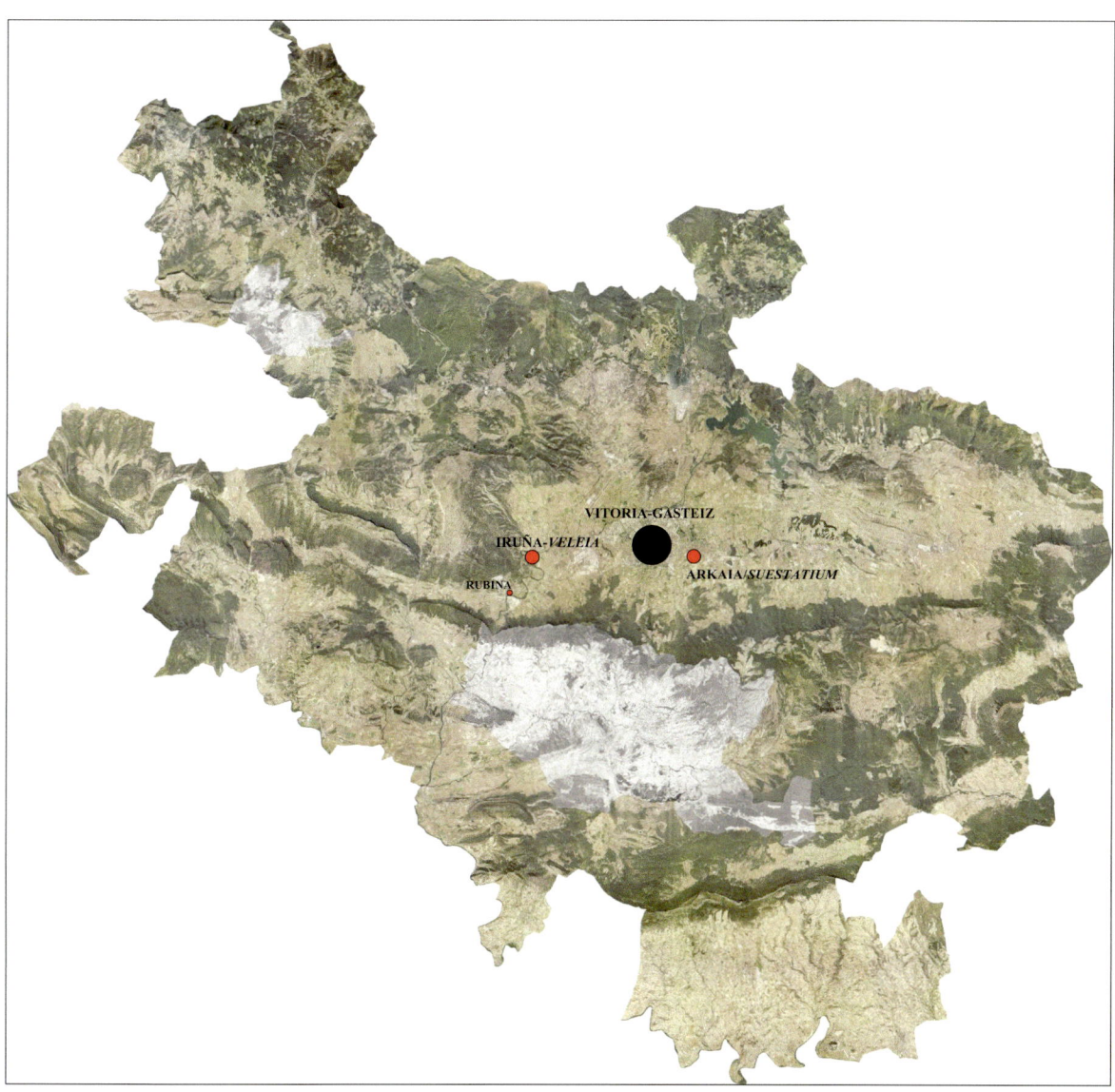

Figura 32.1. Ubicación en la provincia de Álava de los yacimientos con presencia de broccatello (autor: Iterbide S.C.).

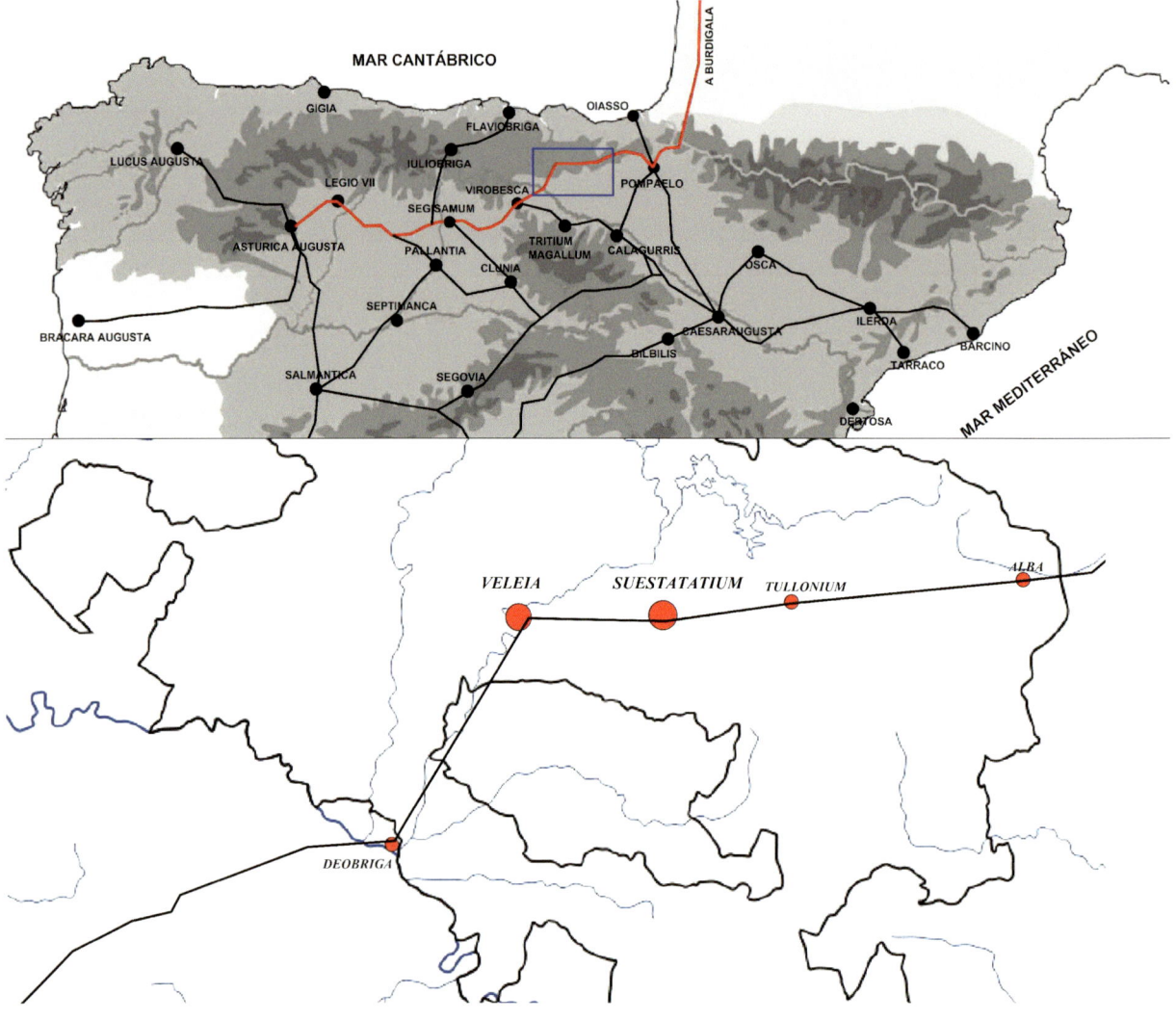

Figura 32.2. Ubicación de las *mansiones* de *Veleia* y *Suestatium* en el *Iter XXXIV* (autor: Iterbide S.C.).

el Museo de Arqueología de Álava en septiembre de 2014 en la cual pudimos consultar principalmente materiales de Iruña, gracias a las facilidades que pusieron a nuestra disposición los técnicos del Museo (v. nota 1); también se han ido incorporando los hallazgos realizados en las sucesivas campañas de excavación, según detallaremos. Podemos adelantar que los hallazgos en estos dos enclaves superan, y en gran número, los hallazgos de placas y elementos moldurados de pequeño formato procedentes de las zonas más próximas a *Dertosa;* nos referimos a la propia capital provincial, *Tarraco,* y también a la colonia de *Barcino* (AA.VV. 2009; Rodà y Alcubierre 2020), aunque aquí contamos con pedestales paralelepipédicos inscritos, columnas y capiteles.

Iruña, antigua *Veleia*

El yacimiento de Iruña se encuentra a escasos kilómetros al oeste de la ciudad de Vitoria-Gasteiz, dentro del territorio de la actual localidad de Trespuentes (Iruña de Oca, Álava).

Este yacimiento es conocido desde antiguo, siendo un icono y una referencia indispensable para la arqueología alavesa desde tiempos remotos. Consecuencia de ello es la gran proliferación de actuaciones arqueológicas que desde el siglo XIX se han venido desarrollando en él y las cuantiosas publicaciones que sobre el mismo han ido apareciendo.

A día de hoy nadie pone en duda que Iruña corresponde a la antigua *mansio* de *Veleia* mencionada por distintas fuentes clásicas. Gracias a la *Notitia Dignitatum* sabemos que, en época tardorromana, se instaló aquí la *Cohors I Gallica* (*Pars occidentalis* XLII, 32). En este sentido cabe recordar que, recientemente, se documentó una pequeña ara votiva dedicada por un esclavo de la propia ciudad a la diosa *Mater* en la que aparece por primera vez mencionada la *res publica Veleian(orum).* Este epígrafe (Núñez *et al.* 2012) vino a disipar las pocas dudas que podían existir al respecto. Asimismo, el descubrimiento de un nuevo fragmento de inscripción en el año 2014, mencionaba parte del *cursus honorum* de

354

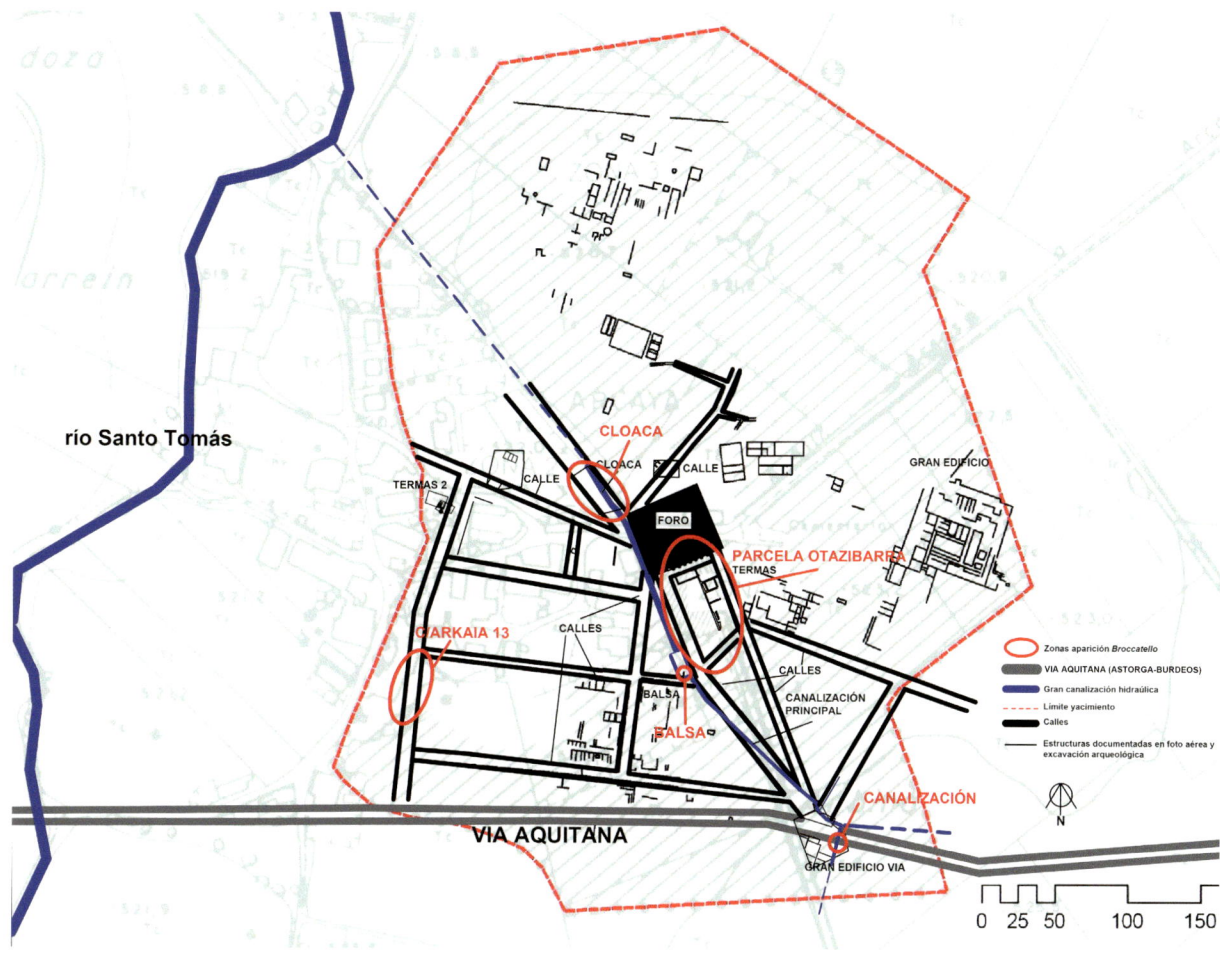

Figura 32.3. Plano de la ciudad amurallada de Iruña-*Veleia* en el que se indican los puntos donde se han producido hallazgos de piezas de broccatello (autor: Iterbide S.C. a partir del plano original elaborado por Lurmen S.L.).

un ciudadano romano, en concreto una magistratura y un sacerdocio local (Ciprés *et al.* 2015), permitió avanzar en el conocimiento sobre el estatuto jurídico-político de esta antigua *civitas* caristia, sin duda la mayor urbe romana de la actual Comunidad Autónoma Vasca.

Los importantes restos arqueológicos demuestran de manera bien patente la preeminencia de esta ciudad en su entorno más inmediato. La estatuaria, representada en la famosa dama de Iruña, los grandes capiteles corintios o los enormes tambores de columna de casi un metro de diámetro constituyen ejemplos preclaros de la monumentalidad de algunos de sus edificios públicos más representativos, todavía hoy no bien identificados. Asimismo, sus imponentes murallas tardías, símbolo del lugar, indican la importancia de este enclave en fechas más avanzadas (Filloy y Gil 2000: 129-36).

Debido a todo lo que hemos dicho en síntesis, no sorprende que sea en este yacimiento donde se haya documentado la mayor colección de broccatello de todo Álava, con más de mil quinientos fragmentos. Muchos

son los puntos en los que se han recogido fragmentos de este tipo de *marmor*, tanto en las distintas prospecciones efectuadas a lo largo de los años como en las distintas excavaciones llevadas a cabo[2], pero fue en un área concreta donde se documentó el mayor volumen de evidencias (Figura 32.3).

Se trata del sector 2 de las excavaciones dirigidas por Eliseo Gil entre 1994 y 2005 y que se superponían al sector H de las ejecutadas en los años 50 del siglo pasado por Gratiniano Nieto. El arqueólogo Eliseo Gil destacaba "la impresionante cantidad de elementos en mármol (aplacados, cornisas, molduras, restos de epígrafes en capital cuadrada, lápidas, tambor de columna, etc.), provenientes de los edificios altoimperiales ya abandonados" (Gil 1995: 90) y que este mismo autor

---

[2] El número de fragmentos en estos sectores no es suficiente para poder pensar en que esos hallazgos pertenecieran al programa decorativo de las construcciones en cuyo entorno se recogieron. Parece, aunque esta afirmación tampoco se puede asegurar, que estas evidencias formarían parte de distintas acumulaciones de vertederos y escombros que se acumularon en el sitio.

no dudó en calificarlos como "edificio público nº 2" sin entrar en más detalles. Por lo tanto, podemos afirmar que en ese sector, en lo que para ellos debió ser un edificio público, pero del cual no se llegó a especificar su funcionalidad, se usó en gran cantidad el broccatello para enriquecer su programa decorativo.

Además, cabe mencionar la presencia en el denominado sector I por G. Nieto, a escasos metros al norte del H, de una sala con un "pavimento formado por grandes placas de mármol rosado con vetas blancas: las placas están muy fragmentadas por la presión de la tierra y de las raíces: cubrían una habitación de 5.35 × 2.85 m de la que pudieron reconocerse los muros hechos con lajas y argamasa de 0.60 m de espesor. Se comprobó en el del oeste que estuvieron recubiertos con placas de mármol de la misma calidad que las del piso, las cuales estaban unidas al muro por una capa de 3 cm de espesor. Se encontraron también abundantes fragmentos de moldura de mármol que seguramente serían del remate del zócalo" (Nieto 1958: 81-82)[3]. Con la información disponible es imposible asegurar si estos mármoles corresponderían al broccatello ya que perfectamente pudiera tratarse de caliza de Ereño (Vizcaya/Bizkaia), reiteradamente constatada en *Veleia,* pero en cualquier caso conviene tener presente este antiguo hallazgo. Aunque fue un material con poca irradiación más allá de un ámbito local, es importante aumentar los testimonios del uso en época romana del *marmor* explotado en las canteras de Ereño (Àlvarez *et al.* 2009: 50-53; Damas Mollá *et al.* 2022) y que en época contemporánea fue conocido como "rojo Bilbao", emblemático en los edificios de los años 70 del siglo XX. En los trabajos de investigación de 2014, pudimos reconocer gruesas *crustae* de Ereño entre los materiales de las excavaciones de 1975 de J.C. Elorza (testigo C6-C-9) y entre los de las prospecciones de 1988 de J.M. Tarriño, según las fechas anotadas en las cajas que los contenían. Como la caliza de Ereño presenta igualmente tonos rojizos y fósiles, no es extraño que, cuando todavía no se había desarrollado el interés en Hispania por la determinación de los materiales lapídeos, se prestaran a confusión las piezas de broccatello con las de Ereño, aunque no deja de sorprender que, por lo que hasta ahora sabemos[4], las importaciones de *Dertosa* superan, y en mucho, el uso de los materiales locales del País Vasco.

Lo mismo ocurre con una serie de epígrafes en mármol, publicados por Juan Carlos Elorza y hoy lamentablemente perdidos, cuya descripción "mármol rosa veteado de blanco, mármol sonrosado, mármol rojo y blanco" (Elorza 1967: 146-59) también pudiera sugerir que, al menos, alguno de ellos fuera realizado en broccatello. A este respecto, recientes revisiones de todo el material marmóreo del yacimiento han permitido identificar un buen número de inscripciones, siempre en forma de placa. La mayoría de los fragmentos procedían del sector 2 (excavaciones de 1994-95): algunos eran de ciertas dimensiones mientras que otros eran minúsculos, sin poder restituir un epígrafe completo, realizado todo ello en broccatello que no hacen sino que constatar el papel que este material tuvo en el momento de llevar a cabo el programa no solo decorativo sino también epigráfico. Apuntamos las placas recientemente publicadas por la profesora Pilar Ciprés[5] en un trabajo sobre las inscripciones romanas de Iruña-*Veleia* (Ciprés 2022). Son las que van desde el nº 54 al nº 78, es decir, son 25 fragmentos que tal y como dice la autora no se pueden ni asegurar ni descartar que en algunos casos formaran parte de un mismo epígrafe.

En 2014 pudimos consultar gran número de cajas, conteniendo principalmente material de este yacimiento. La mayoría correspondía a *crustae* lisas, con alguna placa de decoración parietal y cornisas molduradas (Figura 32.4). Los primeros fragmentos de placas recogidos e inventariados correspondían a las excavaciones de G Nieto de 1950-51 (sector A, torre cuadrada de la muralla), una de ellas epigráfica, sólo con un fragmento de E o F al final de línea (finca de Emeterio Ibáñez).

En las excavaciones de J.C. Elorza de 1975 apareció en el cuadro 1, nivel 4, un fragmento de cornisa moldurada. En 1989, en los trabajos de limpieza del sector H de G. Nieto, tres fragmentos de placas (núms IR/89 109, 123, 126) y en 2003, otros tres en el sector B durante una prospección. En 1988, en trabajos de prospección, J.M. Tarriño recogió 8 fragmentos de *crustae* y en 1990 aparecieron otros 5 durante la operación de limpieza del sector Elorza, recogidos asimismo por J.M. Tarriño (núms IR/90 502 a 504, 506, 510). En 1998, el Dr. T. Caseras entregó al museo una cornisa moldurada hallada en fecha antigua.

Fueron las excavaciones de E. Gil en los sectores 2, 3 (continuación de las excavaciones de J.C. Elorza), 5 y 12 donde apareció un mayor número de fragmentos de broccatello, en especial en el 2 que reservamos para el final (Figura 32.3).

---

[3] Es posible que esta sala fuera la misma que la localizada por la Comisión de Monumentos de Álava años antes y descrita "como un piso embaldosado de mármoles jaspeados oscuros y rojos-claros" (Comisión de Monumentos Históricos y Artísticos de Álava 1867: 28).

[4] A este respecto, podemos avanzar que en los últimos 10 años se ha estado trabajando fuera del recinto amurallado de Iruña-*Veleia* (sector 22) en excavaciones, dirigidas por el profesor de la UPV/EHU, Julio Núñez Marcén. En una habitación de este sector se documentó un programa decorativo que incluía caliza de Ereño; (Ortiz de Urbina et al. 2023: 93-94).
Zócalo inferior de mármol rojo de Ereño con una moldura superior del mismo material.

[5] A quien queremos agradecer la información que nos avanzó dentro de su estudio de los fragmentos de placa con restos de inscripción del yacimiento de Iruña.

Figura 32.4. Conjunto de fragmentos broccatello documentados en Iruña-*Veleia*. **1.** Fragmento de moldura recuperado en el sector 12, en el recinto 3 de la campaña del año 2005 (inv. 11984). **2.** Fragmento de placa con casetón decorativo recuperado en la UE 2025 del sector 2 en el año 1995. **3.** Fragmento de placa moldurada a modo de una placa acanalada, recuperado en el sector 12, en el recinto 3 del año 2005 (inv. 12552) (autor: Iterbide S.C.).

Del sector 3, proceden dos pequeños fragmentos de placa (UE 3037 B) de los trabajos del año 2003. En 2004 (UE 3025) otros tres; otro, en la limpieza de la rampa de los barracones y un segundo en el seguimiento de la zanja de la luz. En 2005 se halló un fragmento de cornisa moldurada (inv. 11375) y también en la UE 3023, un pequeño fragmento de *crusta*.

En el sector 5, en 1996, se halló también un pequeño fragmento de placa (inv. 7709). En 1997 (UE 5001 B), otro más. En 1998, se encontró otro con marcas de la banda de serrado (inv. 3174) y un fragmento de cornisa (inv. 3506). En trabajos diversos de 2002 se recogieron otros tres (inv. 4934, 1081, 5550). En la UE 5001 (cubierta vegetal) se localizaron en 2004, dos pequeños fragmentos de placa.

En el sector 12 se hallaron en 2005 una cornisa moldurada (inv. 11984) y una placa con acanaladuras convexas (inv. 12552) (Figura 32.4, 1 y 3).

Llegamos al sector 2. Durante las excavaciones de 1994 y 1995 se halló una cantidad ingente de fragmentos de elementos manufacturados en broccatello, en especial en el cuadro 35 (UE entre 1001 a 2113); constituyen un dato significativo para pensar que este punto correspondería a una zona pública de *Veleia*. Están todavía sin inventariar y entre las piezas se cuentan cornisas, placas molduradas, placas con inscripción y sobre todo placas de revestimiento o *crustae* lisas, algunas de las cuales son fragmentos minúsculos. No hay fragmentos de gran tamaño, máximo de 20 cm. de altura y los más tienen menos de 10 cm. Todo este material se almacena en cuatro cajas núms. 17 a 20; la 17 con 45 fragmentos (35 de ellos minúsculos), la 18 con 38 con bastantes placas molduradas, la 19 con 91 y la 20, con 43. Además hay otras 18 cajas con un total de 1383 fragmentos mayoritariamente de placas lisas de diferentes tamaños y un grosor que oscila entre 4-1 cm.

De momento, pues en este sector 2 se han localizado 1600 fragmentos de elementos arquitectónicos elaborados en broccatello, mayormente placas de revestimiento, aunque ninguno de ellos de grandes dimensiones y, por el momento, no se han localizado fustes o capiteles de columnas. De todas maneras, es impresionante la cantidad de broccatello en el casco urbano de *Veleia*, en contraste, por ejemplo, con el empleo mucho menos abundante de la caliza fosilífera local de Ereño, como hemos comentado más arriba.

Arcaya/Arkaia, antigua *Suestatium*

El yacimiento de Arcaya se sitúa en la localidad alavesa del mismo nombre, perteneciente al Ayuntamiento de Vitoria-Gasteiz. Se encuentra situado al este de la propia ciudad, a una distancia de 5 km, desde su centro geográfico.

Este yacimiento es conocido desde antiguo y ya en el siglo XVIII el ilustre historiador alavés Lorenzo Prestamero hablaba de la presencia de "muchos cascos de mármoles rotos y *barros Saguntinos*" en su superficie (González de Echavarri 1900: 307). Sin embargo, no fue hasta finales de los 70 cuando comenzaron las primeras actuaciones arqueológicas con la excavación, por parte de Ramón Loza, de unas termas romanas monumentales en la parcela de Otazibarra. En esos primeros momentos el complejo termal era un oasis en el desierto; así, el mismo director de la excavación, entre otras posibilidades, sugería que los restos documentados pudieran corresponder a los de una "villa agrícola al estilo de las navarras" (Loza Lengaran 1984).

Desde entonces, y gracias a las numerosas intervenciones arqueológicas efectuadas en los últimos años, se ha podido avanzar en el conocimiento el yacimiento, lo que ha permitido tener una idea bastante nítida de lo que Arcaya fue en la antigüedad.

Su génesis como una aldea caristia de cierta entidad y su transformación en una pequeña ciudad romana en época de los emperadores Julio-Claudios, posiblemente coincidiendo en el tiempo con la construcción de la Iter XXXIV. En época Flavia o con los primeros Antoninos, repitiendo el esquema de un buen número ciudades Hispanas, la urbe experimenta una fuerte monumentalización alcanzando su mayor extensión y construyéndose las principales infraestructuras públicas. Pocos años después de alcanzar su plenitud, hacia la segunda mitad del siglo II d.C., empieza su decadencia con el abandono de buena parte de su infraestructura pública. La urbe, no obstante, sobrevive a esta crisis adaptándose a esta nueva situación y continuando su existencia hasta la actualidad.

Por todo ello, en los últimos años nadie duda en relacionar Arcaya con la *Suestatium* mencionada en las fuentes clásicas, fundamentalmente en el *Itinerario de Antonino*, el "Anónimo de Rávena" y *Ptolomeo* (Loza Lengaran *et al.* 2014a: 450-51).

Suestatium aparece como una de las *mansiones* situada en el trazado de la vía XXXIV desde Hispania a Aquitania, a su paso por Álava, que unía las actuales poblaciones de Astorga y Burdeos, concretamente entre *Veleia* y *Tullonium* (Figura 32.2). Este itinerario también está atestiguado arqueológicamente por la aparición de la calzada al sur del yacimiento (Sáenz de Urturi 1996: 21-22)[6] y el hallazgo en el cercano lugar de Errekaleor

(Vitoria-Gasteiz) de un miliario del emperador Póstumo (Lostal Pros 1992, pp. 132-133, nùm128; CIL XVII/1, 201).

Sobre su entidad jurídico-política no se tiene ninguna referencia, ni literaria, ni epigráfica. Sin embargo, recientemente se ha propuesto que, debido a la ya mencionada entidad del yacimiento y a la referencia epigráfica de la *origo Suestatiensis* de algunos individuos hallados fuera del área de influencia de *Suestatium,* pudiera ser una *civitas peregrina*, al menos, hasta la concesión del *ius Latii* a todos los habitantes de *Hispania* sobre el 73/74 d.C. (Loza y Niso 2014a: 452-53 ; Andreu Pintado y Romero Novella 2022).

Por el momento, la información sobre el urbanismo de la ciudad romana es bastante parcial, ya que está muy condicionada a los puntos del mismo en los que se ha podido actuar. Esta parcialidad se ha podido paliar de algún modo con el análisis de distintas fotografías de áreas históricas que han permitido disponer de una visión más global. Gracias a ello se ha podido construir un primer boceto del urbanismo de el ciudad en la que se aprecian sectores muy bien ordenados y regulares y otros más irregulares y anárquicos que parecen ser resultado de esos primeros testimonios caristios que se perpetuaron en el tiempo y que condicionaron la futura trama urbana de la urbe.

La parcela de Otazibarra sería el área pública principal de esta *civitas* (Figura 32.5). Este complejo edilicio se empezaría a construir en los años centrales del siglo I d.C. y, con importantes reformas en época Flavia y Antonina, llegaría hasta finales del siglo II d.C., cuando todas las grandes construcciones parecen abandonarse.

En esta manzana ha sido donde se han detectado las estructuras murarias de mayores dimensiones con mejor fábrica, los pavimentos de más calidad, los elementos arquitectónicos de mayor porte (molduras, basas, fustes y capiteles correspondientes como mínimo a dos tipos de columnas) y los principales restos epigráficos y escultóricos. Es en esta zona donde ha aparecido también la mayor concentración de elementos labrados en broccatello, más de un centenar de fragmentos (Figura 32.6). Es por ello por lo que pensamos que es el único lugar en el que se puede asegurar su empleo dentro del programa decorativo general del complejo[7]. Resulta complicado establecer con exactitud en qué dependencias se ubicaba debido a que nunca se ha encontrado *in situ*, pero es evidente su papel protagonista en la ornamentación de una o más salas.

---

[6] Desde el año 2024 se está llevando a cabo una excavación arqueológica que ha descubierto un tramo de unos 20 m de calzada con un gran edificio asociado

[7] Los fragmentos recuperados en otros puntos del yacimiento no formaban parte de la decoración del lugar donde se encontraron sino que eran aportes traídos de otros sitios como basura. En este sentido destacan los más de 50 fragmentos del broccatello que aparecieron en el relleno de colmatación de la cloaca principal de la ciudad.

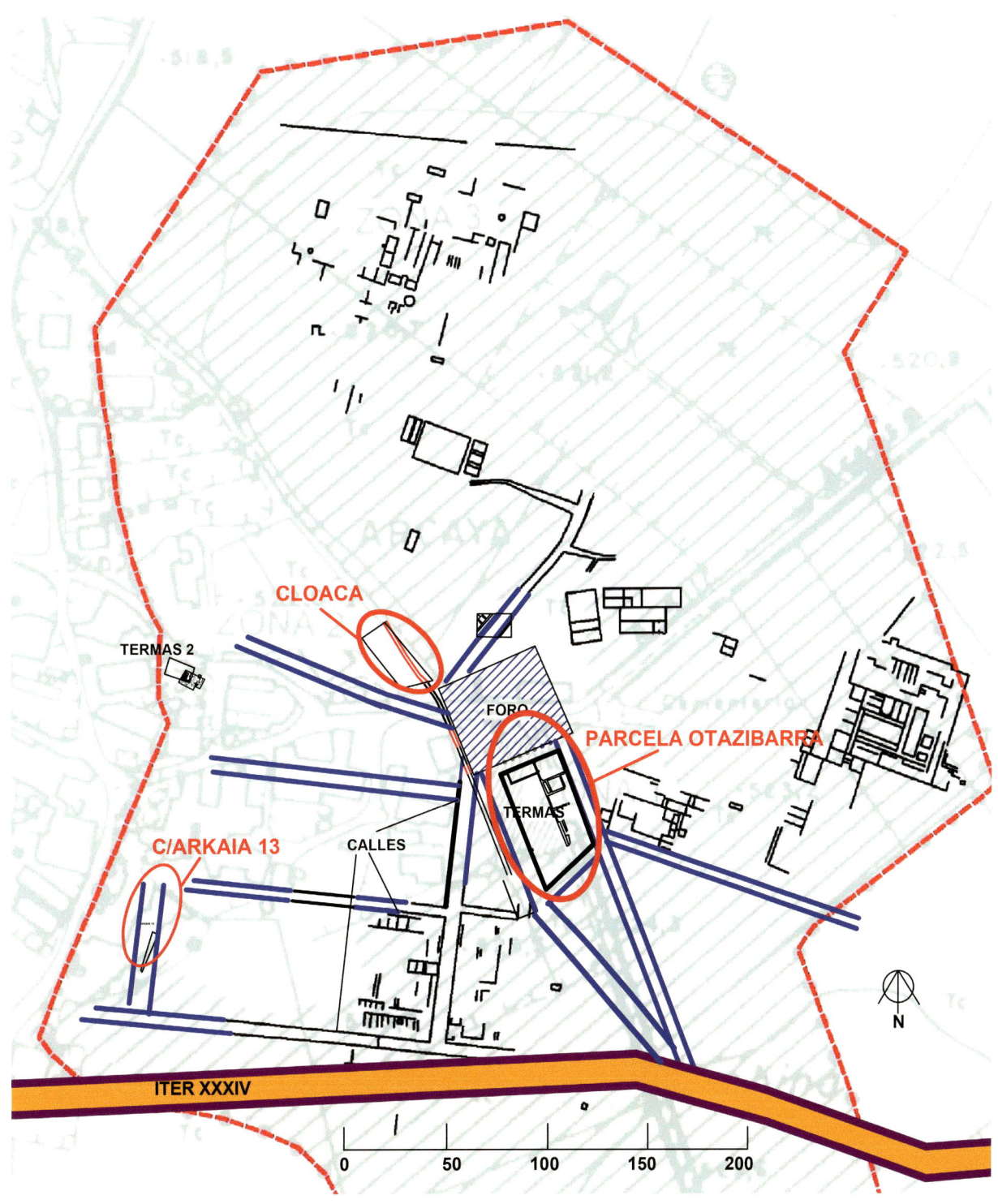

Figura 32.5. Plano de la ciudad de Arkaia-*Suestatium* en el que se indican los puntos donde se han producido los hallazgos de las piezas de broccatello (autor: Iterbide S.C. a partir del plano original elaborado por Arkikus S.L.).

La mayoría de las piezas recuperadas se trataba de fragmentos de placas lisas o *crustae* de revestimiento, pero junto a ellos también aparecían algunas piezas de especial interés. De la excavaciones antiguas destacamos una inscripción fragmentaria de broccatello, hallada en las excavaciones de 1979-80 en Otazibarra (Figura 32.7, 1) ya publicada (Sáenz

de Buruaga 1988: 539-41; *HEp* 3, 1993, 17; Loza y Niso 2014b; 375-77), actualmente expuesta en el Museo de Arqueología de Álava[8]. También sobresale un fragmento

---

[8] Además de este fragmento de inscripción, en los últimos años han aprecido tres nuevos fragmentos. Apenas conservan texto pero ponen de manifiesto el uso de este material para la realización de placas epigráficas

Figura 32.6. Conjunto de piezas de distinta tipología y tamaños, recuperado este mismo año de 2021 en la parcela de Otazibarra (autor: Iterbide S.C.).

de placa de revestimiento con acanadaluras convexas, hallado en el año 2007 (ARC.07.33.10) (Figura 32.7, 5) (Muñoz Ojeda 2014: 382-83). Un hallazgo ligeramente anterior (2006) lo constituye una placa moldurada fragmentaria de revestimiento parietal, localizada en el solar de Arkaia n°13 en la UE 1016 fechada en el siglo IV (ARC-IV.06.1016 181) (Figura 32.7, 4). Podríamos añadir un fragmento de cornisa moldurada documentada por por P. Saénz de Urturi durante una prospección del año 1996-97. De las últimas excavaciones en la parcela de Otazibarra (2020-24) queremos recoger varios fragmentos hallados en la campaña de 2021. Por un lado, dos fragmentos de cornisa moldurada localizadas en el abandono de la plaza del foro (Figura 32.7, 3), y por otro un fragmento de placa con decoración incisa con motivo floral (posible flor de lis)[9], en la UE 5 o relleno de abandono, datado a finales del siglo II d.C., de la zona de foro (Figura 32.7, 2).

En las intervenciones arqueológicas llevadas a cabo entre los años 2023 y 2024 han aparecido nuevos fragmentos de placas. Tres de ellos, en el relleno de amortización UE 535 del ensanchamiento a modo de aliviadero del gran sistema hidráulico documentado en los últimos años. Este depósito se data a finales del

siglo II o inicios del III d.C. Se trata de dos fragmentos de placas lisas y otro, una placa estrecha con acanaladuras. Otro fragmento de placa lisa se ha recogido al sur del yacimiento, en uno de los canales que atraviesa la calzada, y que desemboca en la gran canalización. Su relleno de abandono se data en el siglo III d.C.

Por último, hay que subrayar la aparición en prospección superficial de un fragmento de basa de broccatello hallazgo único hasta la fecha en Álava (Figura 32.8). Se trata de una pieza de 41 cm de diámetro y una altura de unos 15 cm. Aunque está muy deteriorada por el paso del tiempo y por una más que posible reutilización, lo que complica su lectura, uno de sus laterales es plano por lo que es posible que se adosara a alguna pared a modo de semicolumna. Un ejemplo similar de columna en broccatello se localizó en la Plaça del Rei de Barcelona (Rodà y Alcubierre 2020).

A modo de resumen, en toda Arkaia contabilizamos más de 150 fragmentos del broccatello. La gran mayoría de los fragmentos se recogieron en la parcela de Otazibarra, el área pública principal de la ciudad, aunque también se documentó una buena colección de más de 100 ejemplares en la amortización de la cloaca.

En su mayoría corresponden a fragmentos de *crustae* o placas lisas, pero también se recogieron cornisas, placas

---

[9] Había tres fragmentos más de pequeñas placas con motivos florales en estos rellenos de abandono, lo cual pudiera sugerir que alguna pared estuviese decorada con este tipo de ornamentación.

Figura 32.7. Fragmentos de broccatello documentados en Arkaia-*Suestatium*. **1.** Fragmento de inscripción localizado en la parcela de Otazibarra en 1979 y sin un contexto determinado (*HEp* 3, 1993, 17). **2.** Fragmento de placa con decoración tallada con motivo floral, asimismo de la parcela de Otazibarra (2021). **3.** Fragmento de pequeña cornisa moldurada recuperado también en 2021 en la parcela de Otazibarra **4.** Fragmento de placa moldurada (ARC-IV/06. 1016 181). **5.** Fragmento de placa acanalada, localizado también en la parcela de Otazibarra en el año 2007 (ARC.07.33.10) (autor: Iterbide S.C.).

molduradas, placas decoradas, una basa de columna y varios fragmentos de inscripción.

Conclusiones

Aunque ya se conocían desde hace tiempo elementos manufacturados en broccatello en Álava, hasta las recientes excavaciones en Arkaia y la revisión de los materiales depositados en el Museo de Arqueología de Álava/Arabako Arkeologia Museoa. BIBAT, no hemos podido hacernos una idea del impacto real del material lapídeo explotado en las canteras de *Dertosa,* hoy Tortosa. Remontando el Ebro, el broccatello se comercializó en grandes cantidades para ornamentar las ciudades de *Veleia*-Iruña y *Suestatium*-Arkaia, en especial sus espacios públicos.

Por lo que hasta ahora sabemos, llegaron sólo piezas pequeñas, seguramente ya cortadas en origen; en la mayoría de los casos se trata de placas lisas o *crustae* de revestimiento, de pequeñas cornisas molduradas y placas molduradas de revestimiento parietal. También se usó el broccatello como soporte para inscripciones, siempre en forma de placas. Sobresalen los más de 25 fragmentos de placa documentados en Iruña-*Veleia* y recientemente publicados (Ciprés 2022) que se suma al ya conocido de Arkaia-*Suestatium* (Sáenz de Buruaga 1988: 539-51; *HEp* 3, 1993, 17: Loza y Niso 2014b: 375-77). A estos se les podía añadir alguno de los epígrafes publicados por Juan Carlos Elorza (Elorza 1967: 146-59) hoy en día desaparecidos pero que por sus características perfectamente pudieran corresponder a este material.

Además, ya hemos mencionado la aparición de un fragmento de basa de semicolumna que indica la utilización de esta material en elementos arquitectónicos de mayor entidad.

Figura 32.8. Basa de semicolumna elaborada en broccatello documentada en prospección en Arkaia-*Suestaium* (fotografías y dibujo, autor: Iterbide S.C.).

También hemos podido comprobar a lo largo del estudio, la presencia tanto en Iruña como en Arkaia de placas elaboradas en la roja caliza de Ereño, también fosilífera como el broccatello. Por ahora, hay mucha más caliza de Tortosa que de Ereño, siendo en consecuencia más abundante la piedra lejana que la de proximidad, quizás porque el comercio fluvial estaba perfectamente normalizado o porque todavía no se han publicado los últimos resultados de las campañas en Iruña. Así, los hallazgos que hemos presentado no sólo tienen un papel en la definición más precisa del espacio geográfico por el que circuló el brocatello, sino que también parecen alinearse con la propuesta planteada sobre la posible competencia en la comercialización y uso de ciertas rocas hispanas de tonalidades similares a partir del caso del Espejón[10] y el broccatello, cuya distribución pudo tener el valle del Ebro como frontera (García-Entero 2020: 147-75).

Respecto a la cronología, se ha podido constatar el uso de broccatello en época altoimperial (siglos I-II), siendo necesario comprobar si en la antigüedad tardía los hallazgos corresponden a un uso primario o bien a un aporte en estratos de relleno del siglo IV.

Con todo ello ha quedado bien patente la fluidez comercial que articulaba el Ebro, desde su desembocadura, controlada por *Dertosa*, hasta las tierras alavesas en sus dos yacimientos señeros, *Veleia* y *Suestatium*.

Bibliografía

AA.VV. 2009. *Tarraco, pedra a pedra.* Tarragona: Museu nacional arqueològic de Tarragona.

Àlvarez, A., Cebrián, R. y I. Rodà 2009a. El mármol de Almadén de la Plata y los marmora importados del foro de Segobriga, en T. Nogales y J. Beltrán (eds) *Marmora Hispana: explotación y uso de los materiales pétreos en la Hispania Romana*: 101-120. Roma: L'Erma di Bretschneider.

Àlvarez, A., A. Domènech, P. Lapuente, A. Pitarch y H. Royo 2009b. *Marbles and Stones of Hispania/Marbres*

---

[10] Nos referimos a las calizas y el conglomerado del área extractiva de Espejón (Soria), cuyas variedades de color amarillo y violáceo fueron las más utilizadas en época romana en el interior peninsular y a cuyo estudio se ha venido dedicando una serie de proyectos de investigación de gran relevancia (García-Entero 2020: con bibliografía sobre el tema).

i pedres d'Hispània/Mármoles y piedras de Hispania. Tarragona: Institut català d'arqueologia clàssica.

Àlvarez, A., A. Gutiérrez Garcia-M. y I. Rodà 2011. Las rocas ornamentales en las provincias del Imperio: el caso del broccatello y la piedra de Santa Tecla, en S. Camporeale, A. Pizzo, E. Dessales (eds) *Atti del Workshop I cantieri edili dell'Italia e delle province romane (Certosa di Ponigniano 2008)* (Anejos de *AEspA* 57): 539-54. Mérida: Archivo español de arqueología.

Andreu Pintado, J y L. Romero Novella 2022. Santa Criz de Eslava y los *parvua oppida Vasconum*. Novedades sobre la vida urbana en territorio vascón, en P. Mateos, M.H. Olcina Domènech, A. Pizzo y T.G. Schattner (coords.) *Small Towns, una realidad urbana en la Hispania romana*, vol. 1: 195-204. Mérida: Instituto de arqueología de Mérida.

CIL XVII/1= Schmidt, M.F. y C. Campedelli (eds.) 2015. Milliariae provinciae Hispaniae Citerioris. Berlin - Boston: De Gruyter. Ciprés, P. 2022. *Las inscripciones romanas de Iruña-Veleia, Memoria Iruña-Veleia (2010-2020)*. Vitoria-Gasteiz: Diputación foral de Álava.

Ciprés, P., J. Gorrochategui y J. Núñez 2015. Nuevo fragmento de inscripción procedente de Veleia (Iruña de Oca, Álava) con posible expresión de un magistrado local. *Veleia* 32: 217-29.

Comisión de Monumentos Históricos y Artísticos de Álava 1867. *Monumentos: provincia de Alava; sesion extraordinaria que para su reorganizacion celebró la Comision de monumentos históricos y artísticos bajo la presidencia del Señor Gobernador de la provincia*. Vitoria: Imprenta de los hijos de Mantedi.

Damas Mollá, L., A. Aranburu, F. García-Gamilla, J.Á. Uriarte, A. Zabaleta, A. Bodego y I. Antiguedad 2022. Cantera Gorria and Red Ereño: Natural and Cultural Geoheritage (Basque Country, Spain). *Geoheritage* 14.2: 76.

Elorza, J.C. 1967. Ensayo topográfico de epigrafía romana alavesa. *Estudios de arqueología Alavesa* 2: 119-86.

Falcone, R. y L. Lazzarini 1998. Note storico scientifiche sul broccatello di Spagna, en P. Pensabene (ed.) *Marmi antichi*, II: *Cave e tecnica di lavorazione: provenienza e distribuzione*: 87-97. Roma: L'Erma di Bretschneider.

Filloy, I. y E. Gil 2000. *La romanización en Álava: catálogo de la exposicion permanente sobre Álava en época romana del Museo de Arqueología de Álava*. Vitoria-Gasteiz: Diputación foral de Álava.

García-Entero, V. 2020. Poniendo el *marmor Cluniensis* en el mapa de *Hispania*. El uso de la principal roca ornamental de color de procedencia ibérica en el interior peninsular en época romana, en V. García-Entero, S. Vidal Álvarez, A. Gutiérrez Garcia-M. y R. Aranda González (eds) *Paisajes e historias en torno a la piedra. La ocupación y explotación del territorio de la cantería y las estrategias de distribución, consumo y reutilización de los materiales lapídeos desde la Antigüedad* (Monografías de prehistoria y arqueología UNED 1): 117-90. Madrid: Universidad nacional de educación a distancia.

García-Entero, V., M. García-Barberena Unzu, M. Peréx Agorreta, A. Gutiérrez Garcia-M., y M. Unzu Urmeneta 2024. El color de *Pompelo*. Primera aproximación al estudio del *marmor* empleado en la ciudad romana. El área del Foro, en J. Martínez Sarasate, J. Andreu Pintado y M. Peréx Agorreta (eds) *Del registro arqueológico al Museo: el camino de la Historia; estudios en homenaje a Mercedes Unzu Urmeneta*, 219-50. Pamplona: Eunsa.

Gil, E. 1995. Ciudad romana de Iruña/Veleia (Iruña de Oca). *Arkeoikuska* 94: 89-93.

González de Echavarri, V. 1900. *Alaveses ilustres*, I. Vitoria-Gasteiz: Diputación foral de Álava.

Gutiérrez Garcia-M., A. 2009. *Roman Quarries in the Northeast of Hispania (Modern Catalonia)* (Documenta 10). Tarragona: Institut català d'arqueologia clàssica.

Gutiérrez Garcia-M., A. 2014. Nuevos datos sobre la presencia del *broccatello di Spagna* en Roma, en J.M. Álvarez, T. Nogales y I. Rodà (eds) *Actas del XVIII Congreso internacional de arqueología clásica: centro y periferia en el mundo clásico (Mérida 2013)*, II: 321-29. Mérida: Museo nacional de arte romano.

Gutiérrez Garcia-M., A. 2020. Canteras y materiales. Panorama actual y reflexiones sobre los modelos y mecanismos de explotación y abastecimeinto en zonas costeras o costero-fluviales del NE hispano, en M.S. Vinci, A. Ottati y D Gorostidi (eds) *La cava e il monumento*, 15-30. Roma: Edizioni Quasar.

Gutiérrez Garcia-M., A. 2021. El color del lujo y el lujo del color: contexto y avances en el estudio del *broccatello*, en M. Cisneros (ed.) *Color, lujo y moda en la época romana: Piedras preciosas y ornamentales y sus imitaciones* (Anejos de *AEspA* 93): 105-24. Madrid: Archivo español de arqueología.

Gutiérrez Garcia-M., A. y J.H. Muñoz 2022. Broccatello... de Tortosa? Darreres novetats entorn l'explotació del jaspi de la Cinta, dels romans al segle XVIII, en D. Gorostidi y A. Gutiérrez Garcia-M. (eds) *Tituli-Imagines-Marmora: materia y prestigio en mármol* (Anejos de AEspA 95): 457-67. Madrid: Archivo Español de Arqueología.

HEp = Hispania Epigraphica, Universidad Complutense de Madrid.

Keay, S.J. 2022. Making Rome a City of Marble. Reconsidering the Organization of Marble Import, Storage and Distribution at Portus, en D. Gorostidi y A. Gutiérrez Garcia-M. (eds) *Tituli-Imagines-Marmora: materia y prestigio en mármol* (Anejos de AEspA 95): 543-560. Madrid: Archivo Español de Arqueología.

Lapuente, M.P., Turi, B. y Ph. Blanc 2006. Marbles and coloured stones from the Theatre of Caesaraugusta (Hispania). Preliminary study, en Y. Maniatis (ed) ASMOSIA VII. Proceedings of the 7th International Conference (Thassos 15-20 September, 2003), Bulletin de

Correspondance Hellénique, 51: 509-521. Atenas: École française d'Athènes.

Lazzarini, L. 2004. *Pietre e marmi antichi: natura, caratterizzazione, origine, storia d'uso, diffusione, collezionismo.* Milano: CEDAM.

Lostal Pros, J. 1992. Los miliarios de la provincia Tarraconense. Zaragoza: Institución Fernando el Católico.

Loza Lengaran, R. 1984. *Arcaya, un asentamiento romano en Vitoria-Gasteiz.* Vitoria-Gasteiz: Diputación foral de Álava.

Loza, M. y J. Niso 2014a. Evolución, identificación y entidad político-jurídica de Arcaya/*Suestatium*, en R. Loza Lengaran, M. Loza Uriarte y J. Niso Lorenzo (eds) *Las termas romanas de Arcaya/Suestatium: memoria de las intervenciones arqueológicas en Otazibarra (1976-1982):* 449-53. Vitoria-Gasteiz: Diputación foral de Álava.

Loza, M. y J. Niso 2014b. Inscripciones romanas de Arcaya, en *Las termas romanas de Arcaya/Suestatium: memoria de las intervenciones arqueológicas en Otazibarra (1976-1982),* en R. Loza Lengaran, M. Loza Uriarte y J. Niso Lorenzo (eds) *Las termas romanas de Arcaya/Suestatium: memoria de las intervenciones arqueológicas en Otazibarra (1976-1982):* 374-79. Vitoria-Gasteiz: Diputación foral de Álava.

Mayer, M. y I. Rodà 1999. El broccatello de Tortosa: testimonios arqueológicos. *Pallas 50: Mélanges C. Domergue 2:* 43-52.

Mostalac, A. 2014. Testimonios arqueológicos sobre el criatianismo en la diócesis de Zaragoza (siglos I al VII), en D. Buesa (ed.) *Diócesis de Zaragoza: ocho momentos de su historia* (Papeles del Mudiz 3): 9-91. Zaragoza: Museo Diocesano.

Muñoz Ojeda, J. 2014. Estudio de la decoración arquitectónica y su soporte de las termas de Arcaya, en R. Loza Lengaran, M. Loza Uriarte y J. Niso Lorenzo (eds) *Las termas romanas de Arcaya/Suestatium: memoria de las intervenciones arqueológicas en Otazibarra (1976-1982):* 380-89. Vitoria-Gasteiz: Diputación foral de Álava.

Nieto, G. 1958. *Oppidum de Iruña (Álava): memoria de las excavaciones.* Vitoria: Consejo de Cultura de la Diputación foral de Álava.

Núñez, J., D. Martínez, P. Ciprés y J. Gorrochategui 2012. Nueva ara dedicada a *Mater Dea* procedente de *Veleia* (Iruña de Oca, Álava). *Veleia* 29: 441-51.

Ortiz de Urbina, C., Martínez, A. y López, B. 2023. *Iruña-Veleia. Guía arqueológica.* Vitoria-Gasteiz: Diputación Foral de Álava.

Rodà, I. y D. Alcubierre 2020. El "broccatello" o jaspi de la Cinta a *Barcino,* en X. Aquilué, J. Beltrán de Heredia, À Caixal, J. Fierro y H. Kirchner (eds) *Estudis sobre ceràmica i arqueologia de l'arquitectura: homenatge al Dr. Alberto López Mullor:* 445-53 Barcelona: Institut d'estudis catalans.

Sáenz de Buruaga, A. 1988. Nuevas inscripciones de época romana en Álava. *Estudios de Arquelogía Alavesa* 16: 531-56.

Sáenz de Urturi, P. 1996. Excavaciones en Arcaya: Otazibarra (ARC-2) y Arzua (ARC-3) (Vitoria-Gasteiz). *Arkeoikuska* 95: 267-92.

33. Landscapes of Change.
A Reflection on Working on Simon's Projects

Kristian Strutt

Having worked with Simon Keay for over 20 years, this paper represents a reminiscence of sorts, grounded in the brilliant research of Simon, and being mindful of the outstanding work and efforts of dozens of colleagues and friends who were involved in Simon's work. It hopefully also serves to emphasise the achievements of Simon's research and scholarship, as well as the pastoral support and guidance that he gave to so many of his students and colleagues.

I first met Simon just before graduating from the MA programme in Archaeological Survey at Durham University in 1998. The programme was convened by Martin Millett and, having completed the assessed work, Martin asked if I would like to join the survey team about to undertake the first season of work at Portus. As a result, I found myself staying in the city of Fiumicino, together with Julia Robinson and Stephen Kay (graduates of Durham University), Doug Murphy, Tim Sly (University of Southampton), Frances Condron, Letizia Ceccarelli, and others. Simon was a considerate and engaging individual, supportive of the team members and, together with Martin, directed the following seasons of survey work at Portus.

Over the following six years a team of individuals were involved in topographic and geophysical surveys conducted within the main site and the surrounding landscape at Portus. First Stephen Kay, then myself, then Paul Johnson all undertook fieldwork here while working as Camerone Assistants at the British School at Rome. Throughout this time Sophie Hay worked with the team, and by 2004 we were both based at the University of Southampton, and continuing the geophysical survey at Portus, completing work to the east of the main site in the substantial area of the Claudian Canal (Keay *et al.* 2005). It was Simon's vision that, together with Martin, drove the project forwards, and led to the continued application of these integrated methods on sites in the Mediterranean (Figure 33.1). From a personal perspective, the support of Simon and Martin provided scope and opportunities that were beyond the wildest dreams of a student from the North-East of England. In terms of work and research opportunities, but also in terms of lived experience. Working for two years at the British School at Rome, under the direction

Figure 33.1. Simon Keay and Martin Millett at Portus in 2001 (photo: K. Strutt).

of Helen Patterson, provided the opportunity to survey on diverse sites, both within the Roman Towns in the Middle and Lower Tiber Valley project (see Hay and Kay in this volume; Carlucci *et al.* 2007; Johnson *et al.* 2004; Keay *et al.* 2006), but also elsewhere, first at San Vincenzo al Volturno (Marazzi and Strutt 2001), then at Vagnari, near Gravina in Puglia (Strutt *et al.* 2012).

The project work of Simon meant that, over the following years, a team of colleagues became involved in survey projects across sites in Italy, Spain, and elsewhere. Working at the University of Southampton also meant

Figure 33.2. Simon with members of the survey team at Vignale, Civita Castellana in 2000 (photo: K. Strutt).

conducting fieldwork at sites in the UK, leading to geophysical surveys at Bitterne Manor (Roman Clausentum) and sites in Hampshire (Hay and Strutt 2003). Throughout this work Simon was supportive, happy to provide advice and engage in discussions on methodology and approaches to fieldwork. However, his area of interest was always the Mediterranean, leading to fieldwork conducting geophysical surveys in Italy and then Spain (Amores Carredano *et al.* 2010; Prevosti *et al.* 2010; Wheatley *et al.* 2012), and spending significant amounts of time at Portus and its environs.

The Geophysical Surveys at Portus

The geophysical surveys at Portus took the established methodology that had been so successful at Falerii Novi (Keay *et al.* 2000) and the small town sites along the Tiber Valley (Carlucci *et al.* 2007; Johnson *et al.* 2004; Keay *et al.* 2006) and applied it on a larger scale across the landscape of Rome's imperial port. The project commenced in 1998 with survey of the archaeological park and the private estate that encompassed the Trajanic Harbour at the site. With other sites fluxgate gradiometry (a form of magnetometer survey) had been used to brilliant effect, and the use of this method continued to provide excellent results at Portus (Keay *et al.* 2008). The team incorporated a topographic survey team (directed by Tim Sly) and two magnetometer teams (directed by Julia Robinson). Gradiometer survey utilised the Geoscan Research FM36 fluxgate gradiometers, an instrument that was used at the site continually until 2008 and that, with its compact dimensions, was ideal for surveying through the vegetation and woodland of the Archaeological Park (Keay *et al.* 2005).

As the project extended the survey area, seasons in 1999 focused on the extensive open fields to the south,

with a survey of the Claudian Harbour basin and mole conducted by Stephen Kay and Letizia Ceccarelli (Keay *et al.* 2005). For the large-scale summer and autumn seasons this provided the opportunity to integrate fieldwalking into the survey methodology. Simon directed the surface collection and recording of the materials, and the results of this provided data on the material culture across the area, complementing the gradiometer survey (Keay *et al.* 2005: 173).

In 2000 and 2001 magnetometry was conducted over the so-called Imperial Palace area of the archaeological park and around the 4th-century basilica and *Foro Olitorio* with a team including Stephen Kay, Shawn Graham, and Dominic Holland in 2000, and Paul Johnson in 2001, together with Italian and US archaeologists, and students from the University of Southampton. The magnetometry was also extended across the fields adjacent to the Tiber in these seasons. In 2004 and 2006 the survey extended to the land to the east of the Trajanic Harbour immediately to the south of the Fiumicino to Rome railway line. Survey mapped the course of the Claudian Canal and variations in the sediment of the floodplain, together with several other archaeological features (Keay *et al.* 2005: 137).

The geophysical survey and fieldwalking in the areas to the east and south of the Trajanic Harbour were enhanced by the use of air photographic images taken in 2001 by the *Soprintendenza per I Beni Archeologici di Ostia*. These rather fortuitous photographs showed the arable land in the vicinity of the Tiber River at a point when differential growth in vegetation highlighted the presence of structures and features, not all of which were visible in the magnetometry (Keay *et al.* 2005: 139). The air photos were rectified by Paul Johnson and the interpretation was incorporated into the survey data, augmenting the result of the geophysics. The collaborative nature of the project as envisaged by Simon facilitated an integrated methodology that explored potential weaknesses in the collected data, and presented opportunities to compare other datasets in mapping the port complex.

Results of the survey, published in 2005, with further survey conducted in 2006, exposed the scale of the port infrastructure, canal system, and the layout of the complex overall. The volume compared the existing plans and knowledge of the site to the new material from the integrated field approach, addressing the choice of such a site in the Claudian period, and the extension of the complex, and its function in the broader network of trade for imperial Rome (Keay *et al.* 2005). It also hinted at projects to come in terms of Simon's interests in deepening research into the Imperial Palace area of the Archaeological Park and interpreting the broader landscape and links to the site of Ostia.

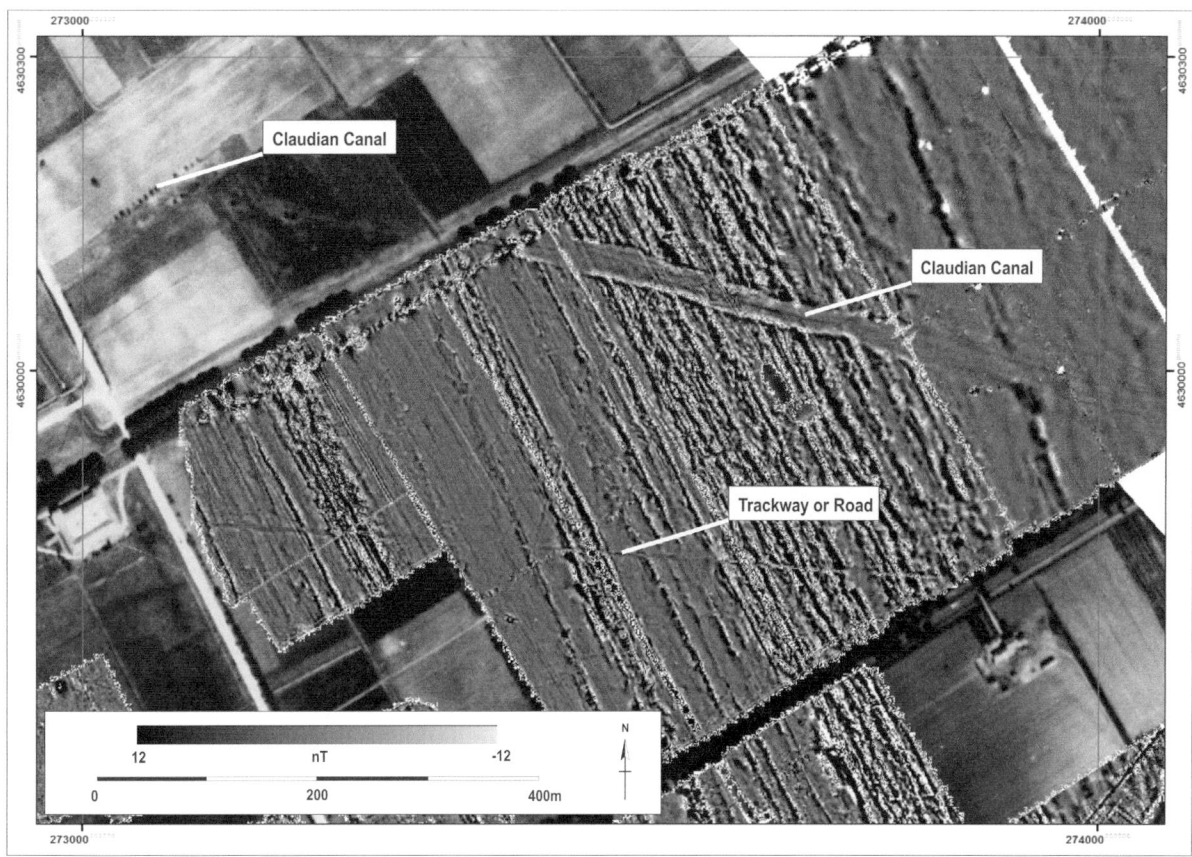

Figure 33.3. Geophysical survey results for the Claudian Canal (Keay *et al.* 2014a).

In the spring and summer of 2005 as part of continued survey work in the area, I worked with Cinzia Filippone on some geophysical survey at Ostia Antica and also conducted a survey of the area of the Baths of Matidia in the Isola Sacra. This work was completed in the summer of 2005 with Helen Woodhouse and students from the University of Southampton and presaged the start of the Portus Project directed by Simon in 2007. The strategy devised by Simon would deepen the investigation of the site of Portus, while also extending the survey across the area between Portus and Ostia.

Further Geophysics at Portus

The area of the Archaeological Park at Portus became the focal point of Simon's research from 2007. Taking the results of the geophysical and topographic surveys conducted in the previous years, he directed research investigating the nature and layout of the Imperial Palace area through intrusive methods but also continuing to apply non-intrusive survey such as Ground Penetrating Radar (GPR) and Electrical Resistivity Tomography. GPR and earth resistance survey were conducted at the Imperial Palace in 2007 with a team from the British School at Rome and the University of Southampton including Betta de Gaetano, Leonie Pett, Rose Ferraby, and Greg Tucker. This preliminary work demonstrated

the excellent results from earth resistance in general. Initial ERT profiles across the area demonstrated the excellent contrasts between the brick structures, paving, and the surrounding sediment. These were integrated with results from a borehole survey using a hand auger to assess the nature of the sediments. Further surveys led by Jessica Ogden provided an integrated high-resolution dataset that formed the core part of Jess's MSc dissertation and later analysis and publication (Keay *et al.* 2013; Ogden *et al.* 2009). The GPR survey was then followed by a more extensive ERT survey undertaken with Greg Tucker across the Imperial Palace area, and in the vicinity of the Severan magazines (Figure 33.4). Results of this survey were utilised for the continuing excavations in the Imperial Palace area.

The survey continued during the seasons of excavation conducted in the area from 2007 (see Bousquet et al; Hay and Kay this volume). While the focus was on this area of the Archaeological Park, however, work was already being carried out across the *Fossa Traiana* to the south.

Isola Sacra and the Tiber Delta

From 2008 to 2012, as part of the Portus Project, the area of the Isola Sacra was surveyed using fluxgate

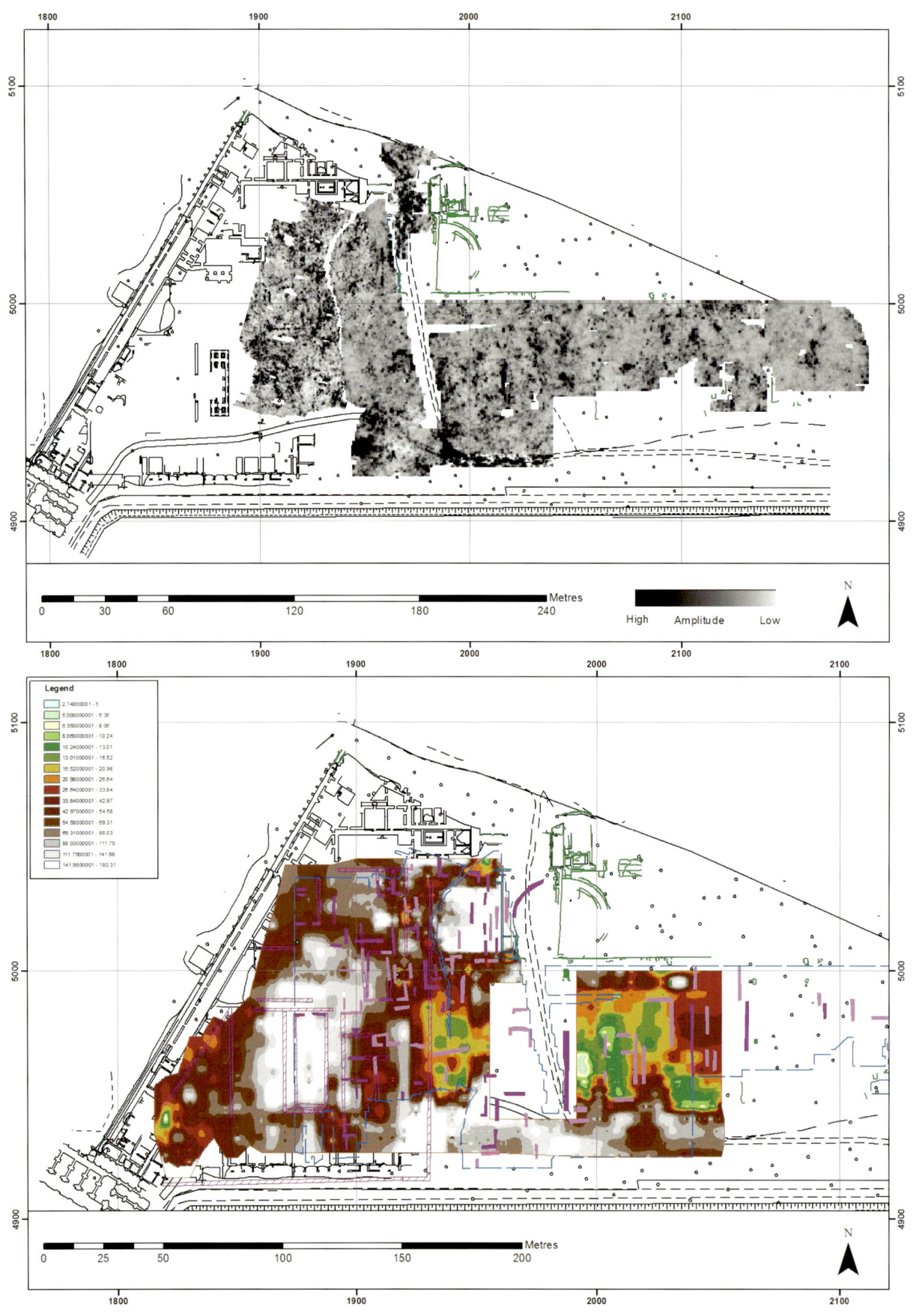

Figure 33.4. Results of the GPR and ERT surveys at the Imperial Palace (Keay *et al.* 2014b).

gradiometry, covering 100ha of a 150ha area from the Baths of Matidia to the River Tiber, bounded by the *Fossa Traiana*, the Tiber, and the ancient Roman coastline of the river delta (Keay *et al.* 2011; 2020). It is testament to Simon's intellect that, while this non-intrusive survey was being conducted, he was also directing the excavations within the archaeological park.

The survey of the Isola Sacra was conducted using twin sensor Bartington Instruments Grad 601-2 fluxgate gradiometers (Fig. 33.5) that suited the more open nature of the terrain with less constraining vegetation and obstacles, and allowed collection of higher-resolution data. Work included team members from the British School at Rome, University of Southampton, University of Cambridge, and, in 2011, a team from Eastern Atlas using a multi-sensor fluxgate gradiometer array. The practical logistics of the survey varied across the terrain, with some accessible areas covering a large area surveyed in the 2008 season, to areas where crops or small enclosed allotment areas limited the scope of survey. The administrative work for the latter meant gaining permission for access to over 100 different parcels of land, an endeavour completed by Roberta Cascino at the British School at Rome, and the *Soprintendenza Speciale per i Beni Archeologici di Ostia* and the *Soprintendenza per i Beni Archeologici di Roma*.

Results of the survey were integrated with existing maps and plans of the area, including a gazetteer of known excavated locations, and the plans from Calza's (1940) excavations at the Necropolis (Baldassare *et al.* 1996; 2019). The outcome was an interpretation of the area between Portus and Ostia that indicated a large complex linking the two sites. A massive canal was located running north-south across the Isola Sacra, with drainage channels indicating land divisions and possible land plots from the Roman period, their alignment at odds with the 20th-century *Bonifica* drainage channels in the landscape.

Survey results from the Portus survey (Keay *et al.* 2005) and the Isola Sacra (Keay *et al.* 2020) pointed to the dynamics between the establishing of a port at Ostia, and imperial port at Portus and the natural and anthropogenic human water courses and their effect on the erosion and deposition of sediment across the port complex and the Tiber Delta as a whole. Once again the evaluation of the nature of these interactions and the development of the prograding Tiber Delta was an important consideration for Simon in terms of interpreting the port landscape. The result was a collaboration with Jean-Philippe Goiran and Ferreol Salomon in survey of the geomorphology of the landscape, designed to complement the geophysical survey results and excavations (Salomon *et al.* 2017). This facilitated the creation of a sequence for the sediments and delta progradation suggesting, among

Figure 33.5. Fluxgate gradiometry being carried out close to the River Tiber (Photo: K. Strutt).

other things, the progressive shift of the Tiber river mouth southwards, and the building of the canal linking Portus and Ostia in the late 1st or early 2nd century AD and its abandonment in the early 3rd century (Keay *et al.* 2020: 139). The continued work of Jean-Philippe and Ferreol at Portus, the Isola Sacra, and Ostia provided a broader temporal and spatial view of the delta (Salomon *et al.* 2023) in terms of the coastal and river deposits, and the relationship between these and the archaeology.

Simon's collaboration with colleagues in archaeology also allowed the addressing of the broader landscape surrounding Portus. In addition to the continuing geophysical survey in the landscape, the project provided the opportunity to review the 20th-century air photographic evidence of the area. The archives at the *Istituto Centrale per il Catagolo e la Documentazione* (ICCD) permitted the air photographic archives to be consulted, providing images of high-altitude RAF photos that were already known (Bradford 1957) but also Italian Airforce photos that facilitated in the interpretation of archaeology across the Isola Sacra. In addition, the research involved a collaboration with Sarah Parçak on analysis of remote sensing satellite data, integrating satellite imagery, LiDAR, and air photographic data with the results of the geophysics (Keay *et al.* 2014a; 2014b) and indicating the continuation of the large Portus to Ostia canal on the Isola Sacra (Figure 33.6) where geophysical survey could not be conducted.

The dedication of Simon and his colleagues in the research of Portus and its landscape pushed forwards the knowledge of the area immensely over 20 years. From the known archaeological record, the non-intrusive survey and integration of other datasets mapped an extensive area of some 360ha. The results allowed interpretation of the phases of development

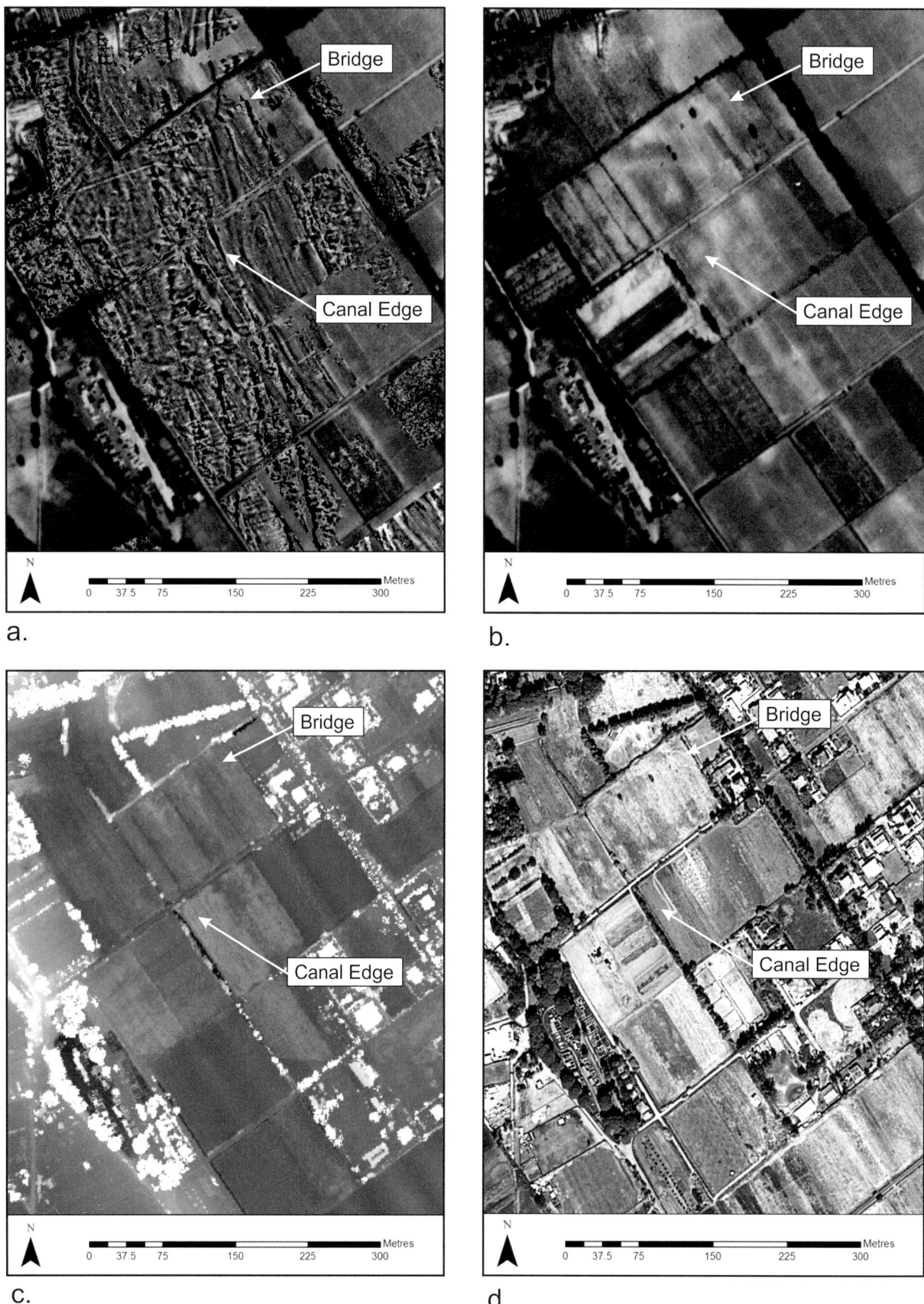

Figure 33.6. Composite images of the Isola Sacra showing results of magnetometry, air photos, LiDAR, and satellite imagery (Keay *et al.* 2014b).

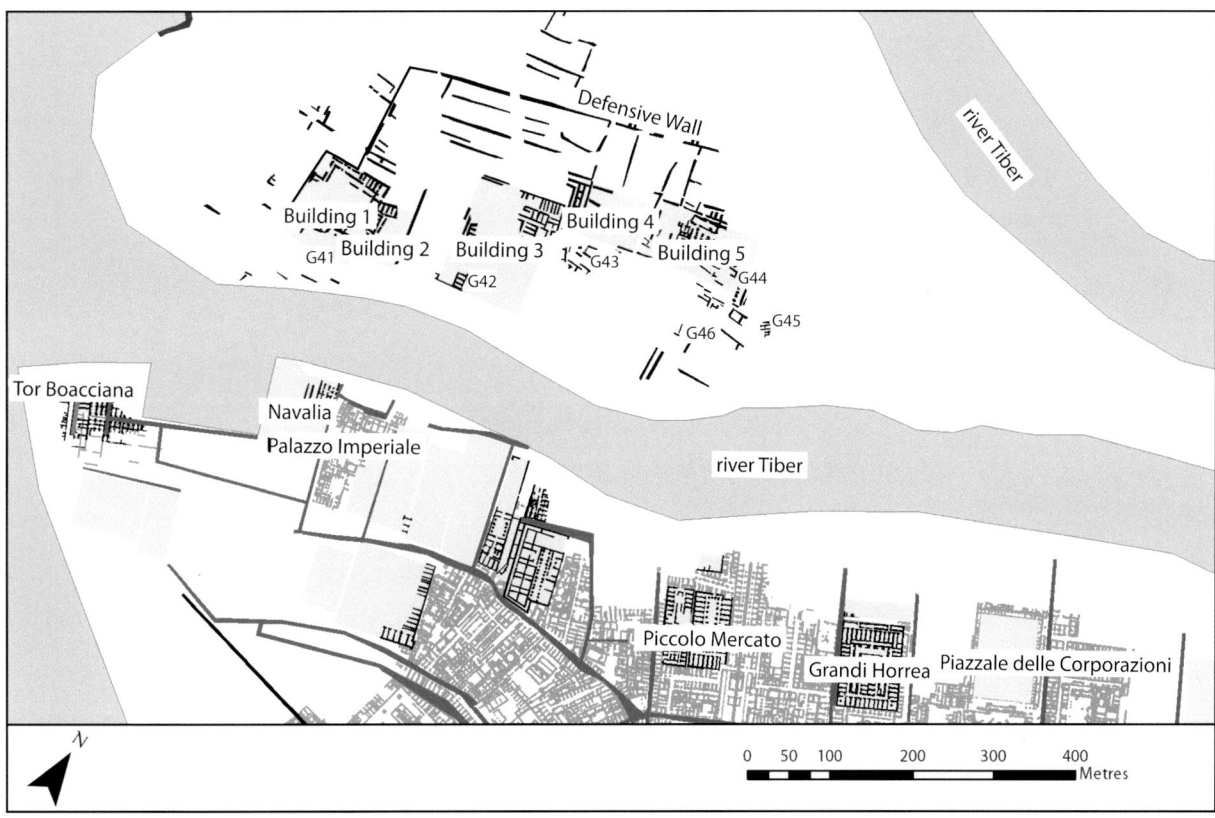

Figure 33.7. The southern part of the Isola Sacra, showing the location of structures (Keay *et al.* 2020).

and change in the area. This comprised the significant canal network in the delta associated with the port complex, the extent of construction to the north of the Tiber as part of the town of Ostia (Fig. 33.7), together with the continued line of the *via Flavia*, and an interpretation of the mouth of the Portus-Ostia canal. It also laid out the nature of the landscape between Portus and Ostia in terms of some of the more recent deposits in the delta, and their potential use as parcels of land, with a network of small drainage channels (Fig. 33.8). Together with the results of survey and excavation work at Ostia (Heinzelmann 2020) the corpus of data on the development and scale of the Tiber Delta is incredible.

The Portuslimen and Broader Mediterranean

From 2013 Simon followed up his work at Portus and Isola Sacra with a project exploring Roman ports throughout the Mediterranean, in the form of the Portuslimen Project. The research drew on Simon's extremely collegiate approach to project work, and involved collaborations with multiple institutions across the Mediterranean, studying the spatial layout of the sites and their environs, but also drawing on documentary research and a range of disciplinary skills. As a component of this, fieldwork including geophysical surveys and geoarchaeological borehole sampling were conducted at sites in Spain, Italy, Tunisia, France, and

Turkey (Bernal Casasola *et al.* 2017; Hay and Kay this volume). The seasons involved the British School at Rome, the University of Southampton, and colleagues from hosting institutions including the University of Cadiz, the *Deutsches Archäologisches Institut*, and the *Österreichisches Archäologisches Institut* among others.

The collaborative work in this immense project is reflected in the breadth of contributors in this volume, and the variety that can be seen in subject material, approaches, and interpretations. These include research on the port of Tarragona, Baelo Claudia, Narbonne (Lasheras, Bernal Casasola, Carayon this volume), also Ephesus, Utica, and Kane and Pitane (Hay and Kay this volume).

The analysis of data from this project, from results of fieldwork to collaborations with colleagues across the Mediterranean and beyond, provided an incredible environment for the development of ideas and theories embedded in strong archaeological evidence and processes, that contributed amazing amounts of knowledge to different port sites and their environs, and to the study of the connectivity of commerce and trade across the Mediterranean.

Over his career, Simon not only contributed to the study of the Roman Empire in the Mediterranean but steered

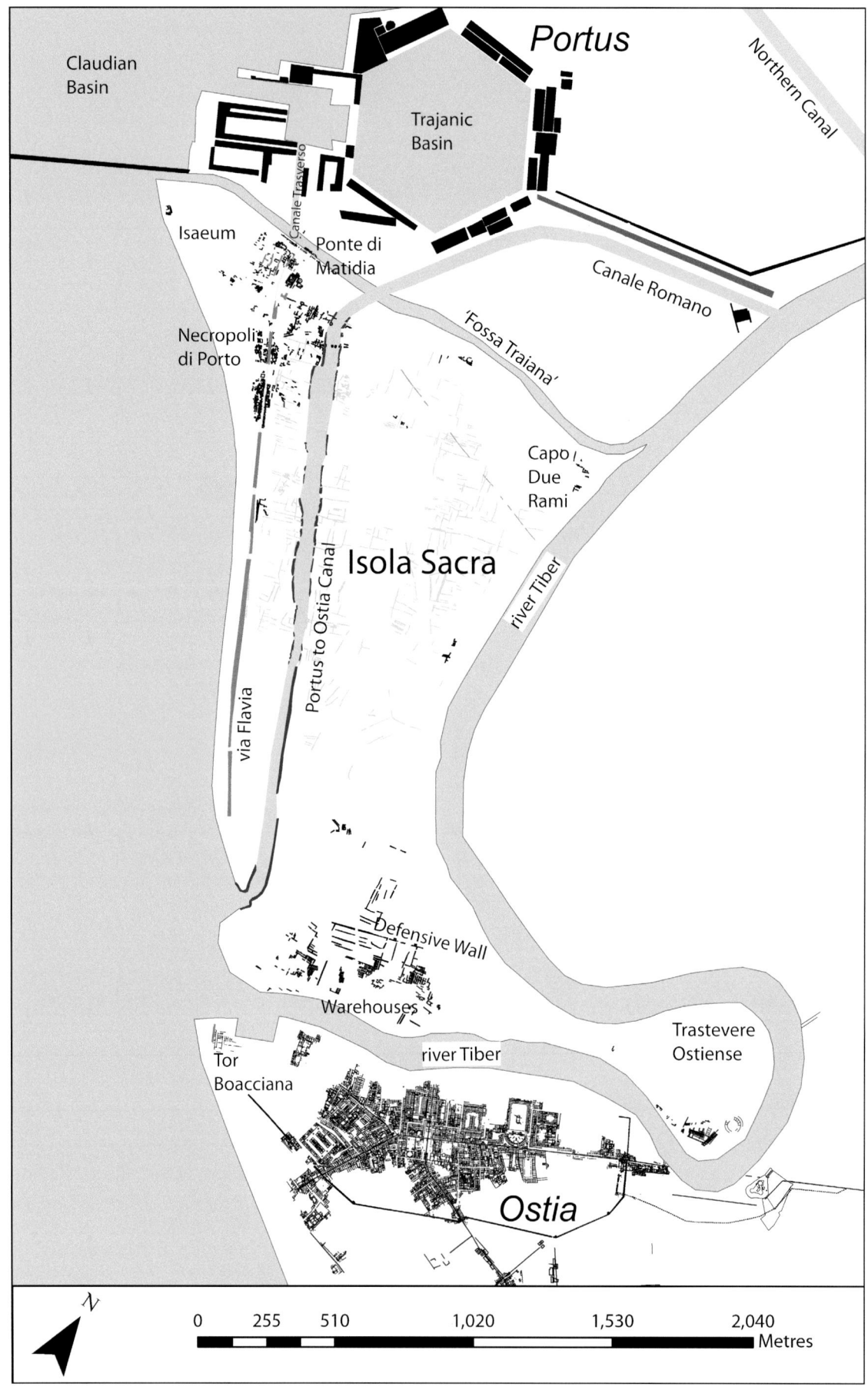

Figure 33.8. Portus, Ostia, and the Isola Sacra in the high Imperial period (Keay *et al.* 2020).

the direction and approach to different aspects of the discipline. From his PhD studies on Roman amphorae, to his initial projects in Spain, and on through his project work at Portus, he was always fascinated by the archaeology of landscapes and what they could tell us about the past. A brilliant colleague, he had a lasting effect on my own development in so many ways, but his rigour and supportive nature has helped so many scholars and field practitioners develop their own skills and interests. The experience of work on such a range of incredible projects, with engaging and interesting friends and colleagues, is indescribable, and something that will always stay with me, as will Simon's influence on my approach to archaeology overall.

References

Amores Carredano, F., E.L. Dominguez Berenjeno, P. Garrido González, S. Keay, M.C. Rodriguez-Bobada y Gil and K. Strutt 2010. El patrimonio arqueológico del valle del Guadiamar: registro y métodos de análisis e interpretación de las huellas del pasado en el paisaje histórico, in F. Amores Carredano (ed.) *De la Tierra al Sol. Historia de las paisajes del Guadiamar*. Seville: Focus Abengoa, 65-106.

Baldassarre, I., I. Bragantini, A.M. Dolciotti, C. Morselli and F. Taglietti 2019. Necropoli dell'Isola Sacra. Le ricerche 1968-1989. Ripercorrendo un'esperienza, in M. Cébeillac-Gervasoni, N. Laubry and F. Zevi (eds) *Ricerche su Ostia e il suo territorio*: 53-66. Rome: Publications de l'École française de Rome, <https://doi.org/10.4000/books.efr.3637>.

Baldassarre, I., I. Bragantini, C. Morselli and F. Taglietti 1996. *Necropoli di Porto: Isola Sacra* (Nuova serie itinerari dei musei, gallerie, scavi e monumenti d'Italia). Rome: Istituto poligrafico e zecca dello stato.

Bernal-Casasola, D., J. Ángel Expósito, J.J. Díaz, N. Carayon, K. Strutt, F. Salomon and S. Keay 2017. Baelo Claudia, Puerto pesquero, comercial y de viajeros. Nuevas perspectivas, in J.M. Campos Carrasco and J. Meléndez (eds) *Los Puertos Atlánticos Béticos y Lusitanos y su relación commercial con el Mediterráneo* (Hispania antigua. Serie arqueolgica 7): 309-44. Rome: L'Erma di Bretschneider.

Calza, G. 1940. *La necropoli del Porto di Roma nell'Isola Sacra*. Rome: Istituto poligrafico dello stato.

Carlucci, C., A.M. De Lucia Brolli, S. Keay, M. Millett and K.D. Strutt 2007. An archaeological survey of the Faliscan settlement at Vignale, Falerii Veteres (Province of Viterbo). *Papers of the British School at Rome* 75: 39-121.

Germoni, P., S. Keay, M. Millett and K. Strutt 2018. Ostia beyond the Tiber: recent archaeological discoveries in the Isola Sacra, in M. Cébeillac-Gervasoni, N. Laubry and F. Zevi, *Ricerche su Ostia e il suo territorio: atti del terzo seminario Ostiense (Roma, École française de Rome, 21-22 ottobre 2015)*. Rome: Publications de l'École

française de Rome, <https://doi.org/10.4000/books.efr.3734>.

Hay, S., S. Keay and M. Millett 2013. *Ocriculum (Otricoli): An Archaeological Survey* (Archaeological Monographs of the British School at Rome 22). London: British School at Rome.

Hay, S., M. Keay, M. Millett and K. Strutt 2006. Roman urban landscapes in Italy: an integrated approach, in S. Campana and M. Forte (eds) *From Space to Place: 2nd International Conference on Remote Sensing in Archaeology; Proceedings of the 2nd International Workshop, CNR, Rome, Italy, December 4-7, 2006*: 149-56. Oxford: Archaeopress.

Heinzelmann, M. 2020. *Ostia, I: Forma Urbis Ostiae: Untersuchungen zur Entwicklung der Hafenstadt Roms von der Zeit der Republik bis ins frühe Mittelalter* (Sonderschriften 25). Wiesbaden: Harrassowitz.

Johnson, P., S. Keay and M. Millett 2004. Lesser urban sites in the Tiber Valley: Baccanae, Forum Cassii and Castellum Amerinum. *Papers of the British School at Rome* 72: 69-99.

Kay, S., E. Pomar, S. Keay, K. Strutt, S. Chapkanski and J.-P. Goiran 2019. Integrating geophysical and geoarcheological surveys for the reconstruction of a Roman port infrastructure: the Claudian harbour at Portus, in J. Bonsall (ed.) *New Global Perspectives on Archaeological Prospection*: 99-103. Oxford: Archaeopress.

Keay, S., G. Earl, G. Beale, N. Davis, J. Ogden and K. Strutt 2013. Challenges of port landscapes. Integrating geophysics, open area excavation and computer graphic visualisation at Portus and the Isola Sacra, in P. Johnson and M. Millett (eds) *Archaeological Survey and the City* (University of Cambridge Museum of Classical Archaeology Monographs 2): 303-57. Oxford: Oxbow.

Keay, S., G. Earl, S. Hay, S. Kay, J. Ogden and K. Strutt 2009. The role of integrated geophysical survey methods in the assessment of archaeological landscapes: the case of Portus. *Archaeological Prospection* 16: 1-13.

Keay, S., M. Millett, L. Paroli and K. Strutt 2005. Portus. An archaeological survey of the port of Imperial Rome (Archaeological Monographs of the British School at Rome 15). London: British School at Rome.

Keay, S., M. Millett, J. Robinson, J. Taylor and N. Terrenato 2000. Falerii Novi: a new survey of the walled area. *Papers of the British School at Rome* 68: 1-94.

Keay, S., M. Millett and K. Strutt 2006. An archaeological survey of Capena (La Civitucola, Provincia di Roma). *Papers of the British School at Rome* 74: 73-118.

Keay, S.J., M. Millett and K. Strutt 2008. Recent archaeological survey at Portus, in R.L. Hohlfelder (ed.) *The Maritime World of Ancient Rome: Proceedings of 'The Maritime World of Ancient Rome' Conference Held at the American Academy in Rome 27-29 March 2003*: 97-104. Ann Arbor: University of Michigan.

Keay, S., M. Millett and K. Strutt 2014a. The canal system and Tiber delta at Portus. Assessing the nature of man-made waterways and their relationship with the natural environment. *Journal of Water History* 6.1: 11-30.

Keay, S., S. Parcak and K. Strutt 2014b. High Resolution space and ground-based remote sensing and implications for landscape archaeology: the case from Portus, Italy. *Journal of Archaeological Science* 52, 277-92.

Marazzi, F. and K. Strutt 2001. San Vincenzo al Volturno 1999-2000. Interventi di diagnostica preliminare sul campo, in S.P. Uggeri (ed.) *Scavi medievali in Italia: atti della seconda conferenza italiana di archeologia medievale*. Rome: Herder.

Ogden, J., S. Keay, G. Earl, K. Strutt and S. Kay 2010. Geophysical prospection at Portus: an evaluation of an integrated approach to interpreting subsurface archaeological features, in *Proceedings of the Computer Applications in Archaeology Conference, West Virginia, 2009*, 1-17, viewed 1 May 2025, <https://eprints.soton.ac.uk/341590/1/ogdenetal2009.pdf>.

Prevosti, M., K. Strutt and C. Carreras 2010. *Ager Tarraconensis* project (right side of river Francoli) (PAT): geophysical surveys to identify rural Roman settlements typologies, in C. Corsi and F. Vermeulen (eds) *Changing Landscapes: Proceedings of the International Colloquium on Landscape Archaeology, 15th and 16th May 2008*, held at Castelo de Vide, Portugal, 205-16. Bologna: Ante Quem.

Salomon, F., S. Keay, N. Carayon and J.-P. Goiran 2017. A 'palaeoenvironmental age-depth model' to interpret sedimentary sequences in harbour context (Portus, Italy). *Quaternaire* 28.2: 167-72.

Salomon, F., K.D. Strutt, D. Mladenovic, J.-P. Goiran and S. Keay 2023. Management of fluvio-coastal dynamics in the Tiber delta during the Roman period: using an integrated waterways system to cope with environmental challenges at Ostia and Portus. *Water History* 15.1: 1-19

Strutt, K., J. Hunt and A.M. Small 2012. Results of the geophysical survey at Vagnari in Puglia, 2000-2007, in A.M. Small (ed.) *Vagnari: Il villaggio, l'artigianato, la proprietà Imperiale: 73-86*. Bari: Edipuglia.

Wheatley, D., K.D. Strutt, L. Garcia Sanjuan, J. Peinado Cucarella and C. Mora Molina 2012. New evidence on the spatial organisation of the Valencina de la Concepción Copper Age settlement: geophysical survey between La Pastora and Montelirio. *Trabajos de Prehistoria* 69: 6579.